"INDEX TO AMERICA"
Life and Customs–
Nineteenth Century

by

Norma Olin Ireland

Scarecrow Press, Inc.
Metuchen, N.J., & London
1984

Library of Congress Cataloging in Publication Data
(Revised for vol. 3)

Ireland, Norma Olin, 1907-
  Index to America.

  Previous vol. published by F. W. Faxon, Westward,
Mass.
  Contents: v. 1. Seventeenth century -- v. 2.
Eighteenth century -- v. 3. 19th century.
    1.   United States--History--Indexes.   I. Title.
Z1236.I73   [E178]   016.973   76-7196
ISBN 0-87305-108-4 (v. 2)
ISBN 0-8108-1661-X (v. 3)

To my friend Mrs. Mabel Gray Turner, of Seattle, Washington, who has been a "real friend" for over 35 years, altho living at some distance. In recent years, she has given me three "happy Christmases," with the help of her family, while on visits here and in Seattle. We congratulate our friend for her great courage as a widow, commend her for her special love of animals, and honor her for a long, unselfish life, beloved by all who know her.

Born in Albia, Iowa, Mabel was the daughter of a physician, raised with four brothers, and was the granddaughter of the founder of Penn (Quaker) College. She graduated from Grinnell College, then did graduate work at Columbia University, specializing in (Broadway) playwriting. Hers was one of three prizewinners out of 600 scripts submitted in a Drake University contest. She was an English and dramatic teacher in Albia High School for five years, and a social service worker during the Depression. During the War she was director and supervisor of seven war projects for airplane workers (5,000 families, 25,000 people), in Wichita, Kansas. She has done some newspaper work, but her play and novel writing had to be put aside for her 18-year marriage to rancher Harold Turner of Pasadena, California. She willingly gave up her own career to devote her life to her husband's career, and we dedicate this book to her, whose life has always been one of great service.

ACKNOWLEDGMENTS

Again we thank the Fallbrook branch of the San Diego Library for help in securing interlibrary loans, through the main County Library and Sutro State library, covering libraries all over the state of California. To Deborah Gregson, librarian, and to Rose Castro, Addie Key, and Leona Ault, assistants, we give personal appreciation for their constant co-operation. To the Carlsbad and Oceanside Libraries, we include thanks not only for the use of their books but also for their telephone reference service.

It has been personally pleasurable to read, in some detail, about life in the 19th century because that was my parents' century. It brought back memories of the stories they used to tell about their early activities and family life. It was also interesting to read about the development of the West, especially California, my present home. We who live in the late 20th century think we have seen many marvels in our lifetime, but the 19th century had its marvels, too--many "firsts" in science and the arts! Their lives and work made possible the development of today's marvels. We are happy to capsule them in this Index, to accompany our work on the two previous centuries.

Norma Olin Ireland

PREFACE

This book is the third volume in the four-volume series Index to America: Life and Customs. The titles of the series are as follows:

> Vol. I--17th century (Faxon, 1978)
> Vol. II--18th century (Faxon, 1976)
> Vol. III--19th century (Scarecrow, 1984)
> Vol. IV--20th century to date (in progress)

Purpose and Scope

The purpose of this Index is to coordinate into one work references to many of the chief publications about the 19th century and its life and customs, concentrating on popular, recent books, but also including some older, readable volumes of historical value.

Since it is intended as a popular rather than scholarly compilation, we have not indexed many fine historical series and biographies or classical volumes to be found primarily in academic libraries. This work is designed to be used in both public and school libraries, including college and university libraries.

Users must remember that primarily this is an index to the life and customs of the times and not an index to historical events. Some material on specific historical events (e.g., Civil War) and on government and politics is, of course, included because such forces always influence the quality of life. A few biographies were indexed and those chosen (such as the lives of Mary Lincoln, Peggy Eaton, and "Stormy" Ben Butler) provide information which was difficult to find in more general sources, and include many events and personalities, some controversial. We have included a few popular sets, such as American Heritage New Illustrated History of U.S. and Life History of U.S., because of their appeal to

younger readers, and because of their fine illustrations. Likewise some history books and a few textbooks were chosen to illustrate the changes in American life and thought, as recounted in a succinct, popular manner. Foreign titles have not been indexed as, of course, this Index is intended primarily for use by American libraries; but some fine diaries and articles by foreign writers have been tapped for their pertinent comments on the 19th century.

We have indexed a representative selection of 161 books which can be found in major libraries. The number of books included is considerably larger for the 19th century than indexed in either Volume I or II. Altho all books indexed are suitable for use by young people, we have indicated by asterisk (*) those especially suitable for younger readers and cataloged as such in libraries (see List of Collections Analyzed).

In selecting books for inclusion in the Index, we did not use the recent age of books as a criterion, but rather chose books still available in libraries. Because most indexing was completed in early 1980, the 1970s were the most easily available. The percentage of books indexed, according to the date of publication, is as follows:

1970s--38%
1960s--29%
1950s--18%
1940s & 1930s--14+%

Please note that we have not indicated out-of-print books because many older books are still available in libraries and some of these titles are exceptionally good.

Arrangement and Subject Headings

This subject index is arranged alphabetically, word by word, in one alphabet--as have been all of our previous works. It contains over 4,950 different subject headings, not including subheadings or cross-references. We have, however, sometimes put entries under more than one subject to avoid the nuisance of too many cross-references.

People (who make events) are certainly a large part of any country's life and customs and therefore we have included the names of many personalities (including famous Indians) of the times. Some are writers whose views on subjects

and people are certainly apropos. A few 20th-century writers may be found. Our list of women is a large one and is
included as a separate Appendix (as in previous volumes), because of their omission in so many books published.

Subject headings for our Index (and other indexes of
this type) are not the same as found in the card catalog or
subject heading books (altho we have used some of both).
They are book index headings, based on both large and small
indexed subjects found to be similar in books about this century. Checking and double-checking almost 5000 different
headings, their subdivisions and cross-references, is a real
exercise in subject heading work! We have intentionally included some archaic terms of the period, with explanations
in parentheses or cross-references. We felt that these terms
reflected the spirit and atmosphere of the period. We have
tried to use the same subject headings as found in Volumes
I and II, with some changes--and of course many additions
and omissions.

In our indexing we have followed a combination of
methods: first; checking main subjects in chapters, page
by page; then scanning the book's Index for the inclusion of
special subjects emphasized, and for headings which seem
suitable for the general period or subject matter covered.
We never depend, however, solely on a book's index, as
many have mistakes. In those instances when we judge a
particular book's index to be reliable and when the book's
index lists many references and subheadings on a certain
subject, we sometimes use the notation "See index, p---"
after the book's title symbol.

(*--suitable for young people)

*ADELMAN--FAMOUS
    Adelman, Joseph. Famous women. New York: Ellis M.
    Lonow, 1926. 328p

ALDEN--PIONEER
    Alden, John R. Pioneer America. New York: Knopf, 1966. 309p

AMERICA 200
    America 200. The legacy of our lands. U. S. Department of
    Interior (Conservation yearbook 11) 1975-1976. 160p paper

American Heritage. The American Heritage history of the American people. See WEISBERGER--AMER.

American Heritage. American manners. See CABLE--AMERICAN

AMER. HER. --INDIANS
    American Heritage, ed. The American Heritage book of Indians.
    New York: American Heritage, 1961. 384p

*AMER. HER. --NEW (5)
    American Heritage new illustrated history of the United States.
    Vol. 5, Young America by Robert G. Athearn. New York:
    American Heritage; Fawcett, 1970. 448p, E149-E185p

*AMER. HER. --NEW (6)
    American Heritage new illustrated history of the United States.
    Vol. 6, The frontier by Robert G. Athearn. New York:
    American Heritage; Fawcett, c1963, 1971. 538p, E222p

*AMER. HER. --NEW (7)
    American Heritage new illustrated history of the United States.
    Vol. 7, War with Mexico by Robert C. Athearn. New York:
    American Heritage; Fawcett, c1963, 1971. p545-628, E225-
    E259p

*AMER. HER. --NEW (8)
    American Heritage new illustrated history of the United States.
    Vol. 8, The Civil war by Robert G. Athearn, New York:
    American Heritage, c1963, 1971. p635-718, E260-296p

*AMER. HER. --NEW (9)
  American Heritage new illustrated history of the United States.
  Vol. 9, Winning the West, by Robert G. Athearn. New York:
  American Heritage; Dell, c1963, 1971. p725-808

*AMER. HER. --NEW (10)
  American Heritage new illustrated history of the United States,
  Vol. 10, Age of steel, by Robert G. Athearn. New York:
  American Heritage; Dell, c1963, 1971. p814-899

*AMER. HER. --NEW (11)
  American Heritage new illustrated history of the United States,
  Vol. 11, The Gilded age, by Robert G. Athearn. New York:
  American Heritage; Fawcett, c1963, 1971. p905-988; E371-
  407

*AMER. HER. --NEW (12)
  American Heritage new illustrated history of the United States,
  Vol. 12, A World power, by Robert G. Athearn. New York:
  American Heritage; Fawcett, c1963, 1971. p994-1078; E410-
  444

*AMER. HER. --90's
  American Heritage, Ed. The nineties. New York: American
  Heritage, 1967. 144p

*AMERICA'S HIST.
  America's historylands. Touring our landmarks of liberty.
  Washington, D.C.: National Geographic Society, 1962. 576p

*ANDREWS--INDIAN LEADERS
  Andrews, Ralph W. Indian leaders who helped shape America.
  Seattle, Wash.: Seattle Publishing, n.d. 184p

*ANDREWS--INDIANS
  Andrews, Ralph W. Indians as the Westerners saw them. New
  York: Bonanza, 1963. 176p

ANDREWS--WOMEN
  Andrews, Matthew Page. The women of the South in war times.
  Baltimore: Norman, Remington, 1920. 466p

ANGLE--AMERICAN
  Angle, Paul McClelland, ed. The American reader. New York:
  Rand-McNally, 1958. 703p

ANGLE--BY
  Angle, Paul McClelland. By these words. Great documents of
  American liberty.... New York: Rand-McNally, 1954. 427p

BARTLETT--NEW
  Bartlett, Richard A. The new country. A social history of the
  American frontier, 1776-1890. New York: Oxford University
  Press, 1974. 487p

BILLINGTON--FAR
 Billington, Roy Allen. The far western frontier, 1830-1860. New
 York: Harper & Brothers, 1956. 324p

*BLUM--STAGE
 Blum, Daniel. Great stars of the American stage. A pictorial
 record. New York: Greenberg, 1952. 150 profiles; n. p.

*BLUM--THEATRE
 Blum, Daniel. A pictorial history of the American theatre. 100
 years, 1860-1960. Philadelphia: Chilton, c1950, 1960.

*BOARDMAN--CIVIL
 Boardman, Fon W. America and the Civil War era, 1850-1875.
 New York: Walck (David McKay Co.), 1976. 209p

*BOARDMAN--GILDED
 Boardman, Fon W. America and the gilded age: 1876-1900.
 New York: Walck, 1972. 202p

*BOARDMAN--JACKSON.
 Boardman, Fon W. America and the Jacksonian era, 1825-1850.
 New York: Walck, 1975. 212p

*BOARDMAN--VIRGINIA
 Boardman, Fon W. America and the Virginia dynasty, 1800-1825.
 New York: Walck, 1974. 218p

BODE--ANATOMY
 Bode, Carl. The anatomy of American popular culture, 1840-
 1861. Berkeley & Los Angeles: University of California
 Press, 1959. 292p

*BONTE--AMERICA
 Bonte, George Willard. America marches past. A pictorial re-
 view of America through the years. New York: Appleton-
 Century, 1936. 196p

BOORSTIN--AMERICANS
 Boorstin, Daniel J. The Americans. The national experience.
 New York: Random House (Vintage Books), 1965. 518p paper
 See also PORTRAITS--AMERICANS

BORDEN--PORTRAIT (1), (2)
 Borden, Morton and Otis L. Graham, Jr., with Roderick W.
 Nash and Richard E. Oglesby. Portrait of a nation. A history of the United States. Lexington, Mass.: Heath, 1973.
 v. 1--248p; v. 2--280p paper

BROOKS--FLOWER.
 Brooks, Van Wyck. The flowering of New England, 1815-1865.
 New and rev. ed. New York: Dutton, c1936, 1940. 550p

Brooks--Our. See OUR LITERARY

*BROWN--WESTERNERS
  Brown, Dee Alexander. The westerners. New York: Holt,
  Rinehart & Winston, 1974. 288p

BURNER--AMERICA (1)
  Burner, David and Robert D. Marcus. America through the
  looking glass; a historical reader in popular culture. Vol. 1.
  Englewood Cliffs, N.J.: Prentice-Hall, 1974. 350p

BUTTERFIELD--AMER.
  Butterfield, Roger. The American past. New York: Simon &
  Schuster, c1947. 476p

CABLE--AMERICAN
  Cable, Mary and Editors of American Heritage. American manners and morals. A picture history of how we behaved and
  misbehaved. New York: American Heritage, 1969. 399p

CARMAN--HISTORY (1)
  Carman, Harry J., Harold C. Syrett and Bernard W. Wishy.
  A history of the American people. 2nd ed. Vol. 1 - to 1877.
  New York: Knopf, c1952, 1961. 860p

CARMAN--HISTORY (2)
  Carman, Harry J., Harold C. Syrett and Bernard W. Wishy.
  A history of the American people. Vol. 2 - since 1865. New
  York: Knopf, 1961. 972p

CARSON--POLITE
  Carson--Gerald. The polite Americans. A wide-angle view of
  our more or less good manners over 300 years. New York:
  Morrow, 1966. 346p

CASE--EMPIRE
  Case, Robert Ormond. The empire builders. Garden City,
  N.Y.: Doubleday, 1947. 333p

CHASE--AMERICA'S
  Chase, Gilbert. America's music. From the Pilgrims to the
  present. New York: McGraw-Hill, 1955. 733p

COLLINS--STORY
  Collins, Alan C. The story of America in pictures, new rev. ed.
  Garden City, N.Y.: Doubleday, 1953. 480p

COMMAGER--HERITAGE
  Commager, Henry Steele and Allan Nevins. The heritage of
  America. rev. & enl. ed. Boston: Little, Brown, 1951.
  1227p

COOK--CITY
  Cook, Ann, Marilyn Gittell and Herb Mack. City life, 1865-
  1900. Views of urban America. New York: Praeger, 1973.
  292p

*COUNTRY--LINCOLN
  Country Beautiful, eds. Lincoln, his words and his world.
  (Disabled American Veterans). Waukesha, Wis.: Country
  Beautiful Foundation, Inc., 1965. 94p

DANNETT--NOBLE
  Dannett, Sylvia G. L. Noble women of the North. New York:
  Yoseloff, 1959. 419p

DAVIDSON--LIFE (2)
  Davidson, Marshall B. Life in America. Vol. 2. Boston:
  Houghton Mifflin, 1974. 503p

DAVIE--PROFILE
  Davie, Emily. Profile of America. An autobiography of the
  U.S.A. Foreword by Charles A. Lindbergh. New York:
  Crowell, 1954. 413p

DEVOTO--YEAR
  DeVoto, Bernard. The year of decision. 1846. Boston: Little,
  Brown, 1943. 524p

*DOLIN--GREAT
  Dolin, Arnold. (World famous) Great American heroines. New
  York: Hart, 1960. 191p paper

DOWDEY--EXPERIMENT
  Dowdey, Clifford. Experiment in rebellion. (The human story of
  the men who guided the Confederacy). Garden City, N.Y.:
  Doubleday, 1947. 455p

DOWNEY--OUR
  Downey, Fairfax. Our lusty forefathers. Being devious chron-
  icles of the fervors, fights, festivities, and failings of our
  American ancestors. New York: Scribner's, 1947. 359p

*DREPPARD--PIONEER
  Dreppard, Carl William. Pioneer America. It's first three
  centuries. New York: Doubleday, 1949. 311p

DRURY--MIDWEST
  Drury, John. Midwest heritage. New York: Wyn, 1948. 176p

*DULLES--HISTORY
  Dulles, Foster Rhea. A history of recreation. American learns
  to play. 2nd ed. New York: Appleton-Century-Crofts, c1940,
  1965. 446p paper

DULLES--UNITED
  Dulles, Foster Rhea. The United States since 1865. Ann Arbor: University of Michigan Press, 1959. 546p paper

*EARLE--TWO CENT. (2)
  Two centuries of costume in America 1620-1820. Rutland, Vt.:

Tuttle, 1971. Vol. 2 (Reprint of lat. ed. published by Macmillan)
Rutland, Vt. p391-824 paper

FURNAS--AMERICANS
Furnas, J. C. The Americans. A social history of the United
States, 1587-1914. New York: Putnam's, 1969. 1015p

GARRISON--LOST
Garrison, Webb. Lost pages from American history. Harrisburg,
Pa.: Stackpole, 1976. 192p

*GILBERT--TRAIL.
Gilbert, Bil and Editors of Time-Life Books. The trailblazers.
New York: Time-Life, 1973. 236p

GOWANS--IMAGES
Gowans, Alan. Images of American living. Four centuries of
architecture and furniture as cultural expression. Philadelphia:
Lippincott, 1964. 498p

GRIMSTED--MELODRAMA
Grimsted, David. Melodrama unveiled. American theater and
culture, 1800-1850. Chicago: University of Chicago Press,
1968. 285p

GRIMSTED--NOTIONS
Grimsted, David, ed. Notions of the Americans 1820-1860.
New York: Braziller, 1970. 347p

GURKO--LADIES
Gurko, Miriam. The ladies of Seneca Falls. The birth of the
Woman's Rights Movement. New York: Schocken, c1974,
1976. 328p

HANDLIN--THIS
Handlin, Oscar. This was America. True accounts of people
and places, manners and customs, as recorded by European
travelers to the Western shore in the ... nineteenth ... centuries. Cambridge, Mass.: Harvard University Press, 1949.
602p

*HARLOW--STORY
Harlow, Ralph Volney and Hermon M. Noyes. Story of America.
New York: Holt, Rinehart & Winston, c1937, 1961. 822p

HARRIS--LAND
Harris, Neil, ed. The land of contrasts, 1880-1901. New York:
Braziller, 1970. 365p

HART--POPULAR
Hart, James D. The popular book. A history of America's
literary taste. New York: Oxford University Press, 1950.
551p

HEATH--WOMEN (4)
    Heath, Monroe. Great American women. Great Americans at a glance, vol. IV. Menlo Park, Calif.: Pacific Coast, 1957. 32p paper

HEFFNER--DOC.
    Heffner, Richard D. A documentary history of the United States. New York: New American Library, c1952, 1954. 287p paper

*HILTON--WAY
    Hilton, Suzanne. The way it was--1876. Philadelphia: Westminster, 1975. 216p

HINE--AMERICAN
    Hine, Robert V. The American West, an interpretive history. Boston: Little, Brown, 1973. 371p

HOLLINGSWORTH--AMER.
    Hollingsworth, J. Rogers, ed. American expansion in the late nineteenth century, Colonial or anticolonialist? New York: Holt, Rinehart & Winston, 1968. 121p paper

HOLZMAN--STORMY
    Holzman, Robert S. Stormy Ben Butler. New York: Collier, c1954, 1961. 280p

*HOWARD--OUR
    Howard, John Tasker. Our American music. Three hundred years of it. New York: Crowell, 1946. 841p

HUNT--LIFE
    Hunt, Gaillard. Life in America one hundred years ago. New York: Harper & Brothers, 1914. 298p

HURD--TREASURY
    Hurd, Charles. A treasury of great American speeches. Our country's life in the words of its great men. New York: Hawthorn, 1959. 288p

*JOHNSON--PICTORIAL
    Johnson, Paul C. Pictorial history of California. New York: Bonanza, 1970. 224p

JONES--AGE
    Jones, Howard Mumford. The age of energy. Varieties of American experience, 1865-1915. New York: Viking, c1970, 1971. 545p

JONES--SHAPING
    Jones, Thomas C., comp. Shaping the spirit of America. Articles from Harper's and Century magazines recalling events and times that helped determine the present national image of the United States of America. Chicago, Ill.: Ferguson, 1964. 318p

*JORDAN--CIVIL
    Jordan, Robert Paul. The Civil war. Washington, D.C.: National Geographic Society, 1969. 216p

KANE--GONE
    Kane, Harnett T. Gone are the days. An illustrated history of the old South. New York: Bramhall, 1956. 344p

KELLER--AFFAIRS
    Keller, Morton. Affairs of state: public life in late nineteenth century America. Cambridge, Mass.: Harvard University Press, 1977. 631p

*KEYES--HOPE
    Keyes, Nelson Beecher and Edward Felix Gallagher. Hope of the nation. Dedicated to the restoration and expression of our American heritage. Gastonia, N.C.: Good Will, c1952. 403p

KRAUS--U.S.
    Kraus, Michael. The United States to 1865. Ann Arbor, Mich.: University of Michigan Press, 1959. 529p

*KRYTHE--SAMPLER
    Krythe, Haymie R. Sampler of American songs. New York: Harper & Row, 1969. 245p

*LANDMARKS--LIBERTY
    Landmarks of liberty, Profile series (Disabled American Veterans). Maplewood, N.J.: Hammond, 1970. 93p

*LANGDON--EVERYDAY (2)
    Langdon, William Chauncy. Everyday things in American life. Vol.2, 1776-1876. New York: Scribner's, c1941, 1969. 353p

LARKIN--ART
    Larkin, Oliver W. Art and life in America. New York: Rinehart, 1949. 547p

LEWIS--BIG
    Lewis, Oscar. The big four. The story of Huntington, Stanford, Hopkins, and Crocker, and of the building of the Central Pacific. New York: Knopf, 1938. 418p

LEWIS--IT
    Lewis, Lloyd. It takes all kinds. New York: Harcourt, Brace, c1928, 1947. 274p

*LIFE--AMERICA'S
    Life, Editors of. America's arts and skills. New York: Dutton, 1957. 172p

*LIFE--GROWING (3)
    Life history of the United States. "The growing years," by

Margaret L. Coit. (v. 3, 1789-1829). New York: Time-
Life, 1963. 176p

*LIFE--NEW (5)
Life history of the United States. "The Union sundered," by
T. Harry Williams. (v. 5, 1849-1865). New York: Time-
Life, 1963. 160p

*LIFE--REACHING (8)
Life history of the United States. "Reaching for Empire," by
Bernard A. Weisberger. (v. 8, 1890-1901). New York: Time-
Life, c1964, 1975. 176p

*LIFE--STEEL (7)
Life history of the United States. "Steel and steam," by Bernard
A. Weisberger. (v. 7, 1877-1890). New York: Time-Life,
c1964, 1975. 160p

*LIFE--SWEEP (4)
Life history of the United States. "The sweep westward," by
Margaret L. Coit. (v. 4, 1829-1849). New York: Time-Life,
1963. 160p

*LIFE--UNION
Life history of the United States. "The Union restored," by T.
Harry Williams & Editors. (v. 6, 1861-1876). New York:
Time-Life, c1963, 1974. Reprinted, 1975. 176p

LINTON--BICENTENNIAL
Linton, Calvin D. The Bicentennial almanac, 1776-1976: 200
years of America. New York: Nelson, 1975. 448p

LOWENS--MUSIC
Lowens, Irving. Music and musicians in early America. New
York: Norton, 1964. 328p

LYNES--DOMESTIC.
Lynes, Russell. The domesticated Americans. New York:
Harper & Row, c1957, 1963. 308p

LYNES--TASTE.
Lynes, Russell. The tastemakers. New York: Harper &
Brothers, c1949, 1954. 362p

*McCLINTON--ANTIQUES
McClinton, Katharine Morrison. Antiques of American childhood.
New York: Bramhall House, 1970. 351p

*MACKSEY--BOOK
Macksey, Joan. The book of women's achievements. New York:
Stein & Day, 1976. 288p

MARZIO--NATION
Marzio, Peter C., ed. A nation of nations. The people who

came to America as seen through the objects, prints, and photographs at the Smithsonian Institution. New York: Harper & Row, 1976. 671p paper

MAUROIS--ILLUS.
Maurois, André. An illustrated history of the United States. New York: Viking, 1969. 296p

*MELICK--WIVES
Melick, Arden Davis. Wives of the presidents. Maplewood, N.J.: Hammond, 1972. 93p

*MEREDITH--WORLD
Meredith, Roy. The world of Mathew Brady. Portraits of the Civil War period. Los Angeles: Brooks House, 1971. 240p

MIERS--AMERICAN
Miers, Earl Schenck, ed. The American story. The age of exploration to the age of the atom. Great Neck, N.Y.: Channel, 1956. 352p

*MORRIS--ENCY.
Morris, Richard B., ed. Encyclopedia of American history. New York: Harper & Brothers, 1953. 776p

MOTT--GOLDEN
Mott, Frank Luther. Golden multitudes. The story of best sellers in the United States. New York: Macmillan, 1947. 357p

MUMFORD--BROWN
Mumford, Lewis. The Brown decades. A study of the arts in America, 1865-1895. New York: Dover, 1959 (orig. ed. Harcourt Brace, 1931). 266p

MUSSEY--OLD
Mussey, Barrows. Old New England. New York: Wyn, 1946. 128p

NATION IN MOTION
A nation in motion. Historic American transportation sites. An informal compilation by the United States Department of Transportation. Washington, D.C.: Government Printing Office. August 1976. 133p paper

NEIDLE--AMERICA'S
Neidle, Cecyle S. America's immigrant women. Boston: G. K. Hall (Twayne Publications), 1975. 312p

*NOSTALGIA
Nostalgia. Our heritage in pictures and words. Nashville, Tenn.: Crusade Bible Publishers, 1975. 845p

NYE--CULTURAL
Nye, Russel Blaine. Cultural life of the new nation, 1776-1830. New York: Harper & Brothers, 1960. 324p

NYE--UNEMBAR.
 Nye, Russel B. The unembarrassed muse; the popular arts in
  America. New York: Dial, 1970. 497p

*OUR LITERARY
 Our literary heritage. A pictorial history of the writer in
  America. New York: Dutton, 1956. (Paddington Press,
  reprint). 246p

*PARTRIDGE--AS
 Partridge, Bellamy and Otto Bettmann. As we were. Family
  life in America, 1850-1900. New York: McGraw-Hill,
  Whittlesey House, 1946. 184p

PEACOCK--FAMOUS
 Peacock, Virginia Tatnall. Famous American belles of the nineteenth century. Philadelphia: Lippincott, c1900, 1901. 297p

PECK--NINETEENTH
 Peck & Snyder, 1886. Nineteenth century game and sporting
  goods. (American historical catalog collection). Princeton,
  N.J.: Pyne, 1971. n.p.

PHILLIPS--THAT
 Phillips, Leon. That Eaton woman. In defense of Peggy O'Neale
  Eaton. Barre, Mass.: Barre, 1974. 184p

*PORTRAITS--AMERICANS
 Portraits from The Americans: The Democratic experience ...
  based on Daniel J. Boorstin's book. New York: Random
  House, 1975. 160p
 See also BOORSTIN--AMERICANS

*PRATT--CIVIL
 Pratt, Fletcher. The Civil War. Garden City, N.Y.: Doubleday, 1955. 62p

RANDALL--MARY
 Randall, Ruth Painter. Mary Lincoln. Biography of a marriage.
  Boston: Little, Brown, 1953. (Dell, 1961). 280p paper

RANDEL--CENTENNIAL
 Randel, William Peirce Centennial; American life in 1876.
  Philadelphia: Chilton, 1969. 475p

*READER'S--STORY
 Reader's Digest of America. The story of America. Pleasant-
  ville, N.Y.: The Reader's Digest Association, 1975. 527p

RIDGE--AMERICA'S
 Ridge, Martin and Ray Allen Billington. America's frontier
  story: a documentary history of Western expansion. New
  York: Holt, Rinehart & Winston, 1969. 657p

*ROBERTSON--BOOK
  Robertson, Patrick. The book of firsts. New York: Bramhall
  House, 1974. 256p

*ROSS--HEROINES
  Ross, Nancy Wilson. Heroines of the early West. New York:
  Random House, c1944, 1960. 182p

*ROSS--TASTE
  Ross, Ishbel. Taste in America. New York: Crowell, 1967.
  343p

*ROSS--WESTWARD
  Ross, Nancy Wilson. Westward the women. New York: Knopf,
  1944. 199p

*SCHWARTZ--WHEN
  Schwartz, Alvin, ed. When I grew up long ago. Older people
  talk about the days when they were young. Philadelphia:
  Lippincott, 1978. 224p

SOCHEN--HERSTORY
  Sochen, June. Herstory. A woman's view of American history.
  New York: Alfred, 1974. 448p

TRACHTENBERG--DEMO.
  Trachtenberg, Alan, ed. Democratic vistas, 1860-1880. New
  York: Braziller, 1970. 368p

*TRAIN--STORY
  Train, Arthur, Jr. The story of everyday things. New York:
  Harper & Brothers, c1941. 428p

TREASURY AMER.
  A treasury of American heritage. A selection from the first
  five years of the Magazine of History. New York: Simon &
  Schuster, c1954, 1960. 400p

TROLLOPE--DOMESTIC
  Trollope, Frances. Domestic manners of the Americans. Edited
  by Donald Smalley. New York: Vintage, 1960. 454p paper

*TUNIS--FRONTIER
  Tunis, Edwin. Frontier living. Cleveland, Ohio: World, 1961.
  166p

*TUNIS--YOUNG
  Tunis, Edwin. The young United States, 1783-1830. A time of
  change and growth; a time of learning democracy; a time of
  new ways of living, thinking, and doing. New York: World,
  1969. 160p

*200 YEARS (1) (2)
  200 years. A bicentennial illustrated history of the United States.

Washington, D.C.: U.S. News and World Report, c1973, 1975. v. 1--351p; v. 2--356p

TYLER--FREEDOM'S
Tyler, Alice Felt. Freedom's ferment. Phases of American social history to 1860. Minneapolis, Minn.: University of Minnesota Press, 1944. 608p

*VANDERBILT--LIVING
Vanderbilt, Cornelius, Jr. The living past of America. A pictorial treasury of our historic houses and villages that have been preserved and restored. New York: Crown, 1955. 234p

*VAN WAGENEN--GOLDEN
Van Wagenen, Jared, Jr. The golden age of homespun. New York: Hill & Wang, 1953. 280p paper

VIEWPOINTS
Viewpoints. A selection of the pictorial collections of the Library of Congress. Washington, D.C.: Library of Congress, 1975. 223p

*WALKER--EVERY.
Walker, Robert H. Everyday life in the age of enterprise (1865-1900). New York: Putnam's, 1967. 256p

WALKER--REFORM
Walker, Robert H., ed. The reform spirit in America. A documentation of the pattern of reform in the American republic. New York: Putnam's, 1976. 682p

*WARREN--PICTORIAL
Warren, Ruth. A pictorial history of women in America. New York: Crown, 1975. 228p

WATKINS--GOLD
Watkins, T. H. Gold and silver in the West. The illustrated history of an American dream. Palo Alto, Calif.: American West, 1971. 287p

*WEISBERGER--AMER.
Weisberger, Bernard A. The American Heritage history of the American people. New York: American Heritage, c1970, 1971. 396p

WHITE--AMERICAN
White, John I. American vignettes. A collection of footnotes to history. Convent Station, N.J.: Travel Vision, 1976. 192p

*WHITNEY--AMERICAN
Whitney, David C. American presidents. Garden City, N.Y.: Doubleday, 1967. 372p

*WILSON--AMERICAN
   Wilson, Mitchell. American science and invention. A pictorial
   history. New York: Bonanza, 1960. 437p

*WILSON--EARLY
   Wilson, Everett B. Early America at work. A pictorial guide
   to our vanishing occupations. New York: A. S. Barnes,
   1963. 188p

*WILSON--FOLKWAYS
   Wilson, Everett B. America's vanishing folkways. New York:
   A. S. Barnes, 1965. 224p

*WILSON--VANISH.
   Wilson, Everett B. Vanishing Americana. New York: A. S.
   Barnes, 1961. 187p

*WOODWARD--WAY
   Woodward, W. E. The way our people lived. An intimate
   American history. New York: Dutton, 1944. 403p and
   illustrations.

WRIGHT--CULTURE
   Wright, Louis B. Culture on the moving frontier. New York:
   Harper & Brothers, 1955. 275p

*WRIGHT--EVERY.
   Wright, Louis B. Everyday life in the new nation 1787-1860.
   New York: Putnam's, 1972. 255p

YOUNG--WOMEN
   Young, Agatha. The women and the crisis. Women of the
   North in the Civil War. New York: McDowell, Obolensky,
   1959. 389p

A AND M COLLEGES
  Furnas--Americans p746-747
A & P
  Randel--Centennial p316-317
  Ross--Taste p61
ABBEY, EDWIN AUSTIN
  Larkin--Art p255
ABBOTT, EMMA
  Adelman--Famous p227
ABBOTT AND DOWNING CO.
  -Coaches
    Tunis--Frontier p140
ABEL, MRS. L.G.
  , on management of children
    Burner--America (1) p190-193
ABOLITIONISTS
  See also names of abolitionists
  Alden--Pioneer p225-230
  Amer. Her. New (6) p491-494,
    E188
  Boardman--Virginia p130-133
  Bode--Anatomy p27-28,185-
    186,196
  Carman--History (1) p502,530-
    535,595-596,601,604,640,719
  Commager--Heritage p483-501
  Furnas--Americans. See index
    p975
  Harlow--Story p255-258
  Heffner--Doc. p103-106
  Jordan--Civil p12-13,17-19,27,
    33,119
  Kraus--U.S. p445-448
  Life--New (5). See index p156
  Life--Sweep (4) p66-67,138
  Linton--Bicentennial. See index
    p438
  Reader's--Story p339-340
  -Congressional controversy 1837
    Morris--Ency. p179-180
  -Early, to 1831
    Tyler--Freedom's p481-484
  -Propaganda, 1835
    Morris--Ency. p175-176
  -Societies
    Tyler--Freedom's p483-484

-Versus war; views of Rufus
  Choate
    Hurd--Treasury p66-68
-Views of William Lloyd Garrison
  Alden--Pioneer p225-229
  200 Years (1) p298
-Women
  Andrews--Women. See index
    p459
  Macksey--Book p110-111
  Sochen--Herstory p130-134
, Yankee
  Butterfield--Amer. p96-97
ABOMINATIONS, TARIFF OF. See
TARIFF OF ABOMINATIONS
ABORTIONS
  Cable--American p228,231-232
"AB-SA-RA-KA"
  Andrews--Indians p65-75
ACADEMIES
  See also SEMINARIES
  Bartlett--New p392-393
  Boardman--Jackson. p135
  Dreppard--Pioneer p223
  Harlow--Story p251-252
  Hunt--Life p131-133
  Nye--Cultural p161-162
  Tunis--Young p130
  , and seminaries
    Furnas--Americans p540-541,
      740-745
  -Graniteville, S.C.
    Woodward--Way p354-358
  -Pennsylvania
    Wright--Culture p85-86
  -Service, 1876
    Hilton--Way p70
ACADEMY OF MUSIC
  Handlin--This p344-345
ACCESSORIES
  See also names of accessories
  -Children's printed kerchiefs
    McClinton--Antiques p329-335
  , Men's
    Wilson--Vanish. p116-119
  , Women's

1

Wilson--Vanish. p112-115
ACROBATS
Dulles--History p132-133
ACTORS AND ACTRESSES
See also THEATER
Boardman--Civil p165-166
Boardman--Gilded p149-151
Dulles--History p108-113
Furnas--Americans p566-568
Handlin--This p127, 375-376
Hunt--Life p88-89
Morris--Ency. p590-591
-1802, 1848
Viewpoints p163-164
-1890's
Amer. Her. --90's p98-105
, Attitudes toward
Grimsted--Melodrama p2, 26-
27, 85-87
, Child
Grimsted--Melodrama p103-
104
-Salaries
Grimsted--Melodrama p62-
63, 91-92, 97
, Stage
Grimsted--Melodrama p87-
91, 94-98, 240
-Views of Noah Ludlow
Angle--American p278-279
ACTOR'S FUND OF AMERICA
-1882
Blum--Theatre p31
ADAMS, ABIGAIL
, on new White House, 1800
Angle--American p137-139
ADAMS, ANDY
, on cattle drive, Texas
Commager--Heritage p853-
857
ADAMS, CHARLES FRANCIS
Harlow--Story p313-315, 347-348
Holzman--Stormy p94-95
Keller--Affairs. See index p607
Life--New (5) p50, 111-112
Morris--Ency. p209, 233, 240,
242, 250
Our literary p150, 152-153
Treasury Amer. p128-129
-Biography
Amer. Her. --New (7) pE225
Morris--Ency. p628
ADAMS, CHARLES FRANCIS, JR.
Randel--Centennial p169-170
-The Revere catastrophe
Trachtenberg--Demo. p210-226
226
ADAMS, GEORGE HENRY

, on land reform
Walker--Reform p83-87
ADAMS, HENRY BROOKS
Our literary p150-156
-Biography
Amer. Her. --New (11) pE373
Morris--Ency. p628-629
ADAMS, HERBERT BAXTER
Randel--Centennial p414-415
ADAMS, JOHN
Life--Growing. See index p172
-Cabinet
Life--Growing. p39-41
-Presidency
Reader's--Story p332
-Views of Edward Everett
Hurd--Treasury p53-55
ADAMS, JOHN QUINCY
Amer. Her. --New (5) p392-393,
E151
Boardman--Jackson. See index
p205
Boardman--Virginia. See index
p211
Borden--Portrait (1) p157, 159
Butterfield--Amer. p74-75
Carman--History (1) p411-417;
see also index pi
Kraus--U.S. p325, 329, 337, 339,
344, 433, 446-447
Life--Growing. See index p172
Life--Sweep (4). See index p156
Linton--Bicentennial. See index
p438
Maurois--Illus. p118-120
Morris--Ency. See index p737
Phillips--That p28-29, 41, 44-45, 67,
84, 90, 105
200 Years (1) p324-325; see also
index p345
, and society
Cable--American p85, 102, 137
-Biography
Morris--Ency. p629-630
Whitney--American p57-63
-Death
-Views of Philip Hone
Commager--Heritage p623-625
, on forefathers and posterity
Hurd--Treasury p42-44
-Presidency
Alden--Pioneer p180-182
Borden--Portrait (1) p159
Commager--Heritage p609-611
Harlow--Story p223-224
Reader's--Story p332
-Views of Martin Van Buren
Commager--Heritage p609-611
ADAMS, LOUISA

Melick--Wives p26-27
ADAMS, MAUDE
 Blum--Stage Profile 7
ADAMS, WILLIAM TAYLOR. See
OPTIC, OLIVER
ADAMS FAMILY
 Treasury Amer. p130-134
 -Papers, preservation by John
 Quincy Adams
  Treasury Amer. p128
ADAMS-ONIS TREATY
 Amer.Her.--New (5) pE151-152
 Boardman--Virginia p58-59
 Morris--Ency. p422
ADDAMS, JANE
 Boardman--Gilded p160-161
 Bonte--America p155
 Dolin--Great p154-161
 Heath--Women (4) p22
 Life--Reaching (8) p39
 Macksey--Book p117,126
 Warren--Pictorial p148
 -Biography
  Amer.Her.--New (11) pE373-
  374
  Morris--Ency. p630
 -Hull House. See HULL HOUSE
 ,on Bohemians in Chicago
  Cook--City p89-91
"ADDRESS OF THE SOUTHERN
DELEGATES," 1848
 Morris--Ency. p209-210
"ADENA" (home of Thomas Worth-
inton, Chillicothe, Ohio)
 Vanderbilt--Living p149
ADLER, FELIX
 Randel--Centennial p444-446
ADOEETE (BIG TREE) (Kiowa)
 Andrews--Indian leaders p141
ADOPTION
 Keller--Affairs p463-464
ADULT EDUCATION
 Harlow--Story p428
 Kraus--U.S. p376-377
 Reader's--Story p137
ADVENTISTS (SEVENTH-DAY AD-
VENTISTS)
 Boardman--Jackson. p133
 Boardman--Virginia p173
 Carman--History (1) p506-507
 Reader's--Story p102
 Wright--Every. p215
ADVENTURE
 Hilton--Way p91-95
ADVERTISING
 Boardman--Gilded, p166-167
 Bonte--America p135
 Furnas--Americans p557-559,
 629, 859, 903-904

Harris--Land p313-322
Walker--Every. p39,104-105,139,
 180-187,198
-1840's
 Lynes--Taste. p10-11
-1870's
 Viewpoints p114-115
-Agencies
 Handlin--This p356
,and press
 Handlin--This p357
,Early Views of Albert D. Lasker
 Angle--American p386-389
-Films, first, 1897
 Robertson--Book p64-65
-"Help wanted," 1822
 -Effect on West
  Brown--Westerners p57
-Ornaments and "elegancies"
 Dreppard--Pioneer p63-79
,Personal
 Handlin--This p198,253,255
,Post Civil war
 Partridge--As p88-89
,Prevalence of
 Handlin--This p242,351-352
-"Singing commercials," 1849
 Butterfield--Amer. p127
,Society figures
 Carson--Polite p212-213
AERIALISTS. See BALLOONS AND
BALLOONISTS
AERONAUTICS
 Garrison--Lost p112-116
 Wilson--American p342-343
 -Airplane landing, first, on war-
 ship deck
  Treasury Amer. p344-345
AFRICAN COMPANY (theatrical)
 Boardman--Virginia p147
AGASSIZ, ELIZABETH CABOT
 Adelman--Famous p236-237
AGASSIZ, LOUIS
 Amer.Her.--New (5) pE152
 Boardman--Jackson. p168
 Marzio--Nation p324-325
 Reader's--Story p307
 Wilson--American p98-99
"AGE OF ENTERPRISE"
 America's Hist. p517-541
 -Views of Allan Nevins
  Miers--American p239-244
"AGE OF INNOCENCE"
-1890's
 200 Years (2) p95
AGENCIES
,Administrative
 Borden--Portrait (2) p19-
 20

, Secular
    Wright--Culture p198-241
, Spiritual
    Wright--Culture p168-197
AGNOSTICISM
    Furnas--Americans p880-882
AGRICULTURAL MACHINERY.
    See FARM IMPLEMENTS
AGRICULTURE
    See also CATTLE; INDIANS--
      Agriculture; LIVESTOCK;
      SHARECROPPING; names of
      crops, etc.
    Boardman--Gilded. See index
      p197
    Boardman--Jackson. p88-92
    Boardman--Virginia p75, 77-80
    Carman--History p482-487, 582
    Furnas--Americans. See index
      p975
    Keller--Affairs p371-372, 384-
      390
    Kraus--U.S. p425-427, 456
    Life--New (5). See index p156
    Morris--Ency. p479-481
    -1820's
      Life--Sweep (4) p22-25
    -1825-1860
      Train--Story p174-176
    -1877-1890
      Life--Steel (7). See index
      p156
    -1890's
      Life--Reaching (8) p20, 61,
      85-86, 93, 149
    -Adversity and agitation
      Amer.Her.--New (10)
      p845-860
, and Industrial Revolution
    200 Years (2) p89, 91-92
, and labor
    Dulles--United p69-88
, and Populism
    Keller--Affairs p571-577
    -California missions
      Billington--Far p6-7
    -Commercial expansion
      Carman--History (1) p476
    -Commodities, production and
      prices, 1865-1899
      Carman--History (2) p221
    -Developments
      Wright--Every. p154-157
    -Discontent, 1884
      Morris--Ency. p257
    -Education
      Train--Story p276
      Tyler--Freedom p261
      -1876

    Randel--Centennial p419-
      420
    -Growth
      Bonte--America p99
      Morris--Ency. p481
    -Hudson's Bay Co.
      Billington--Far p156
    -Middlewest
      Harlow--Story p213-216
    -Mormons
      Billington--Far p200-203, 208
, Post Civil war
    Partridge--As p78-79
    -Regional specialization
      Morris--Ency. p480
    -South
      Collins--Story p153
      Morris--Ency. p480-481
      -Post Civil war
        Carman--History (1) p717-
        719
        Harlow--Story p357-358
        Life--Union (6) p120-121,
        128-130
    -Texas
      Billington--Far p135-136
    -Towns
      Bartlett--New p422-432
    -Views of Jesse Buel, 1840
      Burner--America (1) p292-295
    -West
      Boardman--Civil p93-100
      Borden--Portrait (2) p46-47
      Carman--History (1) p482-485
      Hine--American p156-176; see
      also index p359
      Marzio--Nation p142-159
      Reader's--Story p114
      -Labor
        Hine--American p158, 210,
        214, 219, 222

AGUE
    See also FEVER
    Trollope--Domestic p179-180
AGUINALSO, EMILIO
    -Biography
      Amer.Her.--New (12) p E410
AIR CONDITIONING
, First, to help President Gar-
    field
    Garrison--Lost p78-179
AIRPLANES. See AERONAUTICS
AKRON, OHIO
    Linton--Bicentennial p92
ALABAMA
    Carman--History (1) p359, 634,
      782
    Handlin--This p161-162, 203, 336,
      340-341, 351

Life--Growing (3) p121,126
Life--New (5) p89, 91, 95, 137
Life--Steel (7) p100-101, 103-
104, 108-109
, in Civil war
    Dowdey--Experiment p10, 14,
    48, 94, 181, 226, 228-229, 270-
    272, 307, 399
    Jordan--Civil p34, 205-206
-Selma
    Furnas--Americans p615-616
ALABAMA (ship)
    Dowdey--Experiment p211-213,
    217, 264, 326, 359, 402
    Jordan--Civil p166-167
    Life--Union (6) p40-41, 156
-Claims
    Harlow--Story p329-330
    Holzman--Stormy p186-187
    Morris--Ency. p280-281
"ALAMO"
    See also TRAVIS, WILLIAM
    BARR
    America's Hist. p386-391
    Butterfield--Amer. p98-99
    Collins--Story p199
    Hine--American p86-87, 97, 333
    Keyes--Hope p192-193
    Life--Sweep (4) p82, 96-98
    Linton--Bicentennial p108-110
    Ridge--America's p430-432
    Vanderbilt--Living p188
-Command of William Barret
Travis
    Angle--American p235-238
    Commager--Heritage p598-
    599
-"Runaway scrape," 1852
    Ridge--America's p432-433
-Views of Davy Crockett
    Commager--Heritage p592-
    598
ALASKA
    America's Hist. p542-545
    Linton--Bicentennial. See index
    p438
-Gold, discovery and mining
    Watkins--Gold p145-147, 156
-Life
    Watkins--Gold p144-146, 152
-Population
    Watkins--Gold p141, 143, 145,
    155-156
-Production
    Watkins--Gold p156
-Purchase, 1867
    See also SEWARD, WILLIAM
    Butterfield--Amer. p192-193
    Carman--History (2) p268-270

    Collins--Story p239
    Harlow--Story p330
    Keyes--Hope p257
    Morris--Ency. p280
    White--American p73-80
, Rush to
    Watkins--Gold p141-143, 147-
    149, 154-155
-Sitka, 1875
    Randel--Centennial p73-74
, Transportation to
    Watkins--Gold p141, 148-155
ALASKA COMMERCIAL COMPANY
    Amer. Her. --Indians p284
ALBANY, NEW YORK
    Furnas--Americans p457-458, 497
    Van Wagenen--Golden p23-25
ALBINE, SISTER
    Ross--Heroines p149-150, 153, 155
ALBUMS, AUTOGRAPH. See
AUTOGRAPH ALBUMS
ALCARAZ, RAMON
-Mexican view of the Mexican
war, 1850
    Ridge--America's p506-508
ALCOHOLISM
    See also LIQUOR; TEMPERANCE
    Cable--American p298
    Carson--Polite p86-87
    Dulles--History p67, 70, 90, 151,
    168, 170, 172, 178, 249
    Handlin--This p141, 177, 210, 396-
    397
    Hunt--Life p171-175
    Tyler--Freedom's p309-312
    Wilson--Folkways p152-154
-"The bottle and the pledge"
    Butterfield--Amer. p128-129
-Views of Frances Trollope
    Trollope--Domestic. See
    index. p. v
-Vocabulary
    Boorstin--Americans p286-287
ALCOTT, (AMOS) BRONSON
    See also "FRUITLANDS"
    Amer. Her. --New (6) p E188
    Boardman--Jackson. p125
    Brooks--Flower. See index
    p539
    Our literary p74-76
    Tyler--Freedom's. See index
    p590
ALCOTT, LOUISA MAY
    Adelman--Famous p216-217
    Boardman--Civil p157
    Heath--Women (4) p18
    Macksey--Book p188
    Morris--Ency. p579
    Our literary p75

Warren--Pictorial p128-129
Young--Women p17, 28, 34-35, 38,
  45, 67-68, 228-232, 300, 308, 311
-Biography
  Morris--Ency. p630-631
  Young--Women p365-366
ALCOTT, WILLIAM
  Bode--Anatomy p124-127, 152
ALCOTT FAMILY
  Our literary p74-76
ALDRICH, THOMAS BAILEY
  Dulles--United p110-111
ALEXANDER I
  Amer. Her. --New (5) pE152
ALEXANDRIA, VIRGINIA
  -Views of Frances Trollope
    Trollope--Domestic. See
    index p. i
ALGER, HORATIO, JR.
  Amer. Her. --90's p120-121
  Boardman--Gilded p134
  Cable--American p314-315
  Mott--Golden p158-159
  Nye--Unembar. p62-72
  Our literary p157
  Partridge--As p103
  Randel--Centennial p312-313, 359
  200 Years (2) p104-105
  -Biography
    Amer. Her. --New (11) p963,
    E374
  -Books
    Life--Steel (7) p134
ALGERIAN WAR
  Boardman--Virginia p50-51
ALLEGHENY MOUNTAINS
  , Journey over, by Frances
    Trollope
    Trollope--Domestic p192-201
ALLEN, HORATIO
  Train--Story p277-279
  Wilson--American p148-151
ALLEN, LEWIS F.
  Lynes--Taste. p26-27
ALLEN, SAMANTHA (Marietta
  Holley)
  Furnas--Americans p735-737,
  764, 800
ALLEN, VIOLA
  Blum--Stage Profile 19
ALLIANCES
  See also TREATIES
  , Farmers'
    Life--Reaching (8) p84
ALLIBONE, S. A.
  Bode--Anatomy p23, 114-115, 199
ALLOTMENT ACT, 1887
  Amer. Her. --Indians p408-409

ALLSTON, WASHINGTON
  Boardman--Virginia p153-154
  Brooks--Flower. p159-165; see
    also index p539
  Larkin--Art p142-143; see also
    index p515
  Nye--Cultural p286-288
ALMANACS
  Hilton--Way p34, 75-76, 152
ALMSHOUSES. See POOR RELIEF
ALOYSIA, SISTER
  Ross--Heroines p127-131, 134-
    135, 140, 142, 147-148, 152-153
  Ross--Westward p78-92
ALPHABET PLATES. See CHIL-
  DREN'S DISHES--Plates
ALSTON, THEODOSIA BURR. See
  BURR, THEODOSIA
"ALTA CALIFORNIA"
  Tunis--Frontier p124-129
ALTGELD, JOHN PETER
  Boardman--Gilded p78-79, 81
  Harlow--Story p408-410
  Life--Reaching (8) p88, 91, 103,
    106-107, 109
  -Cleveland controversy
    Angle--By p297-303
  -Pardon of anarchists
    Commager--Heritage p1001-
    1003
AMANA SOCIETY
  Boardman--Jackson. p127
  Life--Sweep (4) p64
  Tyler--Freedom p130-132
AMBRISTER, ROBERT. See
  ARBUTHNOT, ALEXANDER--
  Ambrister affair
AMENDMENTS. See CONSTITU-
  TION--Amendments
AMERICA
  , among the nations
    Trachtenberg--Demo. p83-100
  -Civilization, critics of
    Larkin--Art p259-262
  -Enterprise
    Trollope--Domestic See
    index p. vi
  , European attitude to
    Handlin--This p154, 169, 321-
    324
  , "for Americans"
    Burner--America (1) p173-175
  -Life
    Davidson--Life (2) p364-377
    -1850's
      Life--New (5) p9-17
    -1860-1862
      -Views of Lester Frank

Ward
  Burner--America (1)
  p230-234
-1893
  -Views of Charles Joseph
  Paul
    Handlin--This p370-383
-Maps
  Boorstin--Americans p225-228
, Victorian
  Gowans--Images p243-386
"AMERICA" (schooner)
  Collins--Story p160
AMERICAN ANTISLAVERY
SOCIETY
  See also ABOLITIONISTS
  Alden--Pioneer p228-229
  Boardman--Jackson. p114-115,
  118-119
  Gurko--Ladies p34, 37-38, 48-49,
  54, 67, 116-117, 197, 199, 232
  Tyler--Freedom's p493
  -Women
    Tyler--Freedom's p445-446
AMERICAN ART UNION
  Bode--Anatomy p60-79
  Cable--American p155
  Davidson--Life (2) p154-155
  Lynes--Taste. p14-18, 21
AMERICAN BAR ASSOCIATION
  Keller--Affairs. See index
  p607
AMERICAN BIBLE SOCIETY
  Bode--Anatomy p142-144
AMERICAN COLONIZATION
SOCIETY
  Alden--Pioneer p226
  Amer. Her. --New (6) p491-492,
  E188-189
  Boardman--Jackson. p114, 118
  Boardman--Virginia p131-132
  Boorstin--Americans p186
  Carman--History (1) p531
  Furnas--Americans p319-320
  Hunt--Life p236-238
  Tyler--Freedom's p476-481
AMERICAN ECONOMIC ASSOCIA-
TION, 1885
  Life--Reaching (8) p15
AMERICAN EQUAL RIGHTS
ASSOCIATION
  Furnas--Americans p641-642
  Gurko--Ladies p214-215, 223-224,
  231-233
  Keller--Affairs p607
AMERICAN EXPRESS COMPANY
  Randel--Centennial p162-163

AMERICAN FEDERATION OF LABOR
  Amer. Her. --New (10) p829-830
  Carman--History (2) p148-150;
  see also index p.i
  Harlow--Story p404-406
  Life--Steel (7) p84-85, 96
  Morris--Ency. p523
  Nostalgia p66-69
  -Foundations
    Dulles--United p81-82
  -Organization, 1886
    Collins--Story p260
  -Views of Samuel Gompers
    Angle--American p392-395
AMERICAN FUR COMPANY
  Bartlett--New p87, 258
  Billington--Far p56-60, 62-65, 82
  Boardman--Jackson p64
  Carman--History (1) p370-371, 378
  DeVoto--Year p18-19, 51-66, 115,
  141, 148, 360, 362-363
  Hine--American p47-49, 53, 289
  Tunis--Young p110-112, 117
AMERICAN GEOLOGICAL SOCIETY
  Nye--Cultural p91
AMERICAN HOME MISSIONARY
SOCIETY
  Wright--Culture p107-108, 140,
  145-146
AMERICAN INDIANS. See INDIANS;
names of tribes
AMERICAN LIBRARY ASSOCIATION
  -Founding
    Randel--Centennial p348, 425-
    426
AMERICAN MEDICAL ASSOCIATION
  Randel--Centennial p325-326
  -Founding
    Reader's--Story p296
AMERICAN MUSEUM (Barnum's)
  Burner--America (1) p255-265
  Dulles--History p122-125, 135, 219
AMERICAN PARTY
  Furnas--Americans p527-528
  Whitney--American p114, 116-117
AMERICAN PEACE SOCIETY
  Amer. Her. --New (6) p E189
  Tyler--Freedom's p404-413
AMERICAN PROTECTIVE ASSOCIA-
TION, 1887
  Amer. Her. --New (10) p887
  Cable--American p301
AMERICAN RAILWAY UNION
  Boardman--Gilded p80-81
  Furnas--Americans p710-711, 722
  Life--Reaching (8) p89-90
"AMERICAN RENAISSANCE"

Alden--Pioneer p202-217
AMERICAN REPUBLICAN PARTY
  Boardman--Jackson. p184-185
  Morris--Ency. p187
AMERICAN SUNDAY SCHOOL
UNION
  Tyler--Freedom's p259
  Wright--Culture p195
"AMERICAN SYSTEM" (of Henry
Clay)
  Boardman--Virginia p54-56
  Boorstin--Americans p20-21,
    26-27, 30-34
  Carman--History (1) p412-413,
    431, 444, 451
  Harlow--Story p186-187
  Keyes--Hope p204-205
  Life--Growing p147-148, 152, 155
  Linton--Bicentennial p78, 90
  Morris--Ency. p162-163
AMERICAN TEMPERANCE UNION
  Amer. Her. --New (6) p E189
  Furnas--Americans p289, 505-
    507
AMERICAN TOBACCO COMPANY
  Life--Steel (7) p105, 134-135
AMERICAN TRACT SOCIETY
  Bode--Anatomy p132-140
"AMERICAN WAY." See
AMERICA--Life
AMERICAN WOMAN SUFFRAGE
ASSOCIATION
  See also NATIONAL (AMERI-
    CAN) WOMAN'S SUFFRAGE
    ASSOCIATION
  Furnas--Americans p643-645
  Gurko--Ladies p233-237, 248, 263
  Warren--Pictorial p117
AMERICANISM. See PATRIOTISM
"AMERICANISMS." See QUOTA-
TIONS--"Americanisms"
AMERICANS
  , at home
    Lynes--Domestic. p277-291
  -Characteristics
    Amer. Her. --New (6) p496
    Bartlett--New p147-149
    Handlin--This p130-131, 173,
      175, 178, 258, 305, 323-324,
      355-356, 361-362, 370, 390-
      392
    Lynes--Domestic. p37, 96
  , and creed
    Life--New (5) p8-9, 53
  , and frontier
    Ridge--America's p2-24
  , by state
    Hunt--Life p35-36

-Coldness
  -Views of Frances Trollope
    Trollope--Domestic. See
      index p. iv
-Common sense
  Lynes--Domestic. p86
-Conscience
  Larkin--Art p261-265
-Gentility
  Lynes--Domestic. See
    index p302
-Influence on house
  Lynes--Domestic. p4, 277-291
-Middle states
  Hunt--Life p38
, Great
  -"Views of each other"
    200 Years (1) p310-311
AMES, FISHER
  Walker--Reform p34-35
AMES, MARY C.
  Adelman--Famous p201
AMES, OAKES
  Butterfield--Amer. p204
AMESBURY, MASSACHUSETTS
  Vanderbilt--Living p16
AMISTAD CASE
  Amer. Her. --New (5) p E152-153
  Morris--Ency. p184
AMUSEMENT PARKS
  See also TROLLEYS--Carnivals
    Cable--American p298, 330-331
    Dulles--History p98, 163-164,
      166, 222-223
AMUSEMENTS
  See also HOLIDAYS; PARTIES;
    SPORTS AND GAMES; names of
    amusements
  Boardman--Gilded p168-170
  Boardman--Virginia p186-189
  Cable--American p110, 296, 298,
    355-356
  Carson--Polite p196-198
  Dulles--United p98-100
  Harris--Land p159-190
  Partridge--As p149-178
  Ross--Taste p80-81
  -1876
    Randel--Centennial p17, 51, 67-
      68
  -Late 19th century
    Borden--Portrait (2) p59-63
  -Cities
    Harlow--Story p435-437
  -Illustrations
    Grimsted--Notions p197-203
  -Middlewest
    Drury--Midwest p80-81, 84-86

-New England
  Dulles--History p44-50, 101-
  102, 183-184
-New York City
  Tunis--Young p119-121
, Outdoor
  Life--New (5) p58, 60-61,
  64-65
-Views of Frances Trollope
  Trollope--Domestic. See
  index p.i
ANAGRAMS
, First
  McClinton--Antiques p227
ANARCHISTS
  See also names of anarchists
  Furnas--Americans p711, 714-
  716, 829, 838
  Harlow--Story p408
ANDERSON, ROBERT
  Dannett--Noble p29, 32-33, 40,
  42-44
  Kraus--U.S. p485-486
  -Biography
    Amer.Her. --New p E225
  , on "Mill of the King" (Mexico
  City, 1847)
    Angle--American p246-248
ANDERSONVILLE (GEORGIA)
PRISON
  Amer.Her. --New (8) p E262
  Andrews--Women p218-220,
  402-403
  Boardman--Civil p60
  Life--Union (6) p74-75, 130
  Randel--Centennial p242, 244-
  245
  -Views of Eliza Frances
  Andrews
    Commager--Heritage p719-
    721
ANDREW JOHN A.
  Holzman--Stormy p40-42, 44,
  67-68, 145
ANDREWS, ELIZA FRANCIS
  , on Andersonville prison, 1863
    Commager--Heritage p719-
    721
  , on "Burnt country"
    Commager--Heritage p776-
    778
  , on disintegration of Confeder-
  ate army
    Commager--Heritage p721-
    725
ANDREWS, SIDNEY
  , on war-torn South, 1865
    Commager--Heritage p800-808

ANDREWS, STEPHEN A.
  Furnas--Americans p643-645
ANDREWS RAID ("Great locomotive
chase")
  Meredith--World p134-139
ANESTHESIA
  Boardman--Jackson. p170-171
  Morris--Ency. p542-543
  Reader's--Story p295
  Train--Story p291
  Wilson--American p104-107
  -Discovery, by Dr. William Nor-
  ton
    Commager--Heritage p394-399
    Davie--Profile p202-203
  -First surgery, 1842
    Robertson--Book p18
ANGELINE, PRINCESS (Indian)
  Ross--Westward p107-108
ANGLE, PAUL M.
  -Cities of the Middle border
    Treasury Amer. p256-263
  , on Emancipation proclamation
    Miers--American p188-192
"ANGLO-SAXONISM"
  Furnas--Americans p610-613
  Reader's--Story p329-330
ANIMAL HUSBANDRY. See LIVE-
STOCK; names of animals
ANIMALS
  See also LIVESTOCK; names of
  animals
  -City streets
    Furnas--Americans p455-457
  , Wild
    Jones--Age p318-320
    Randel--Centennial p44, 48-49,
    124, 129
ANNAPOLIS (U.S. Naval Academy)
  Randel--Centennial p272-273
ANTARCTICA
  -Discovery
    Garrison--Lost p62-64
  -"Palmer's Land"
    Garrison--Lost p64
ANTHONY, SUSAN BROWNELL
  Adelman--Famous p170-171
  Boardman--Civil p190
  Butterfield--Amer. p216
  Dolin--Great p111-119
  Furnas--Americans. See index
  p976
  Gurko--Ladies. See index p321
  Harlow--Story p254-255
  Heath--Women (4) p13
  Macksey--Book p86
  Reader's--Story p432
  Ross--Heroines p168-169

Sochen--Herstory p85, 131, 134-
135, 170, 174-175, 181, 232
Tyler--Freedom's p431; see also
index p591
Warren--Pictorial p99-100, 102,
113-120, 122, 131, 135, 159
-Biography
Morris--Ency. p631
, on women as citizens
Hurd--Treasury p101-102
, on women's right to suffrage,
1873
Davie--Profile p121-123
-Women's Rights movement
Tyler--Freedom's p459-460
ANTHONY (A. & H.T.) COMPANY
(ANSCO)
Wilson--American p380
ANTHONY FAMILY
Gurko--Ladies. See index p321
ANTI-CATHOLICISM
Boardman--Jackson. p183-184
Borden--Portrait (1) p194-196
Furnas--Americans p523-528, 729
Weisberger--Amer. p247
-Immigration and Nativisim
Tyler--Freedom's p374-377
-Immorality motif
Tyler--Freedom's p371-374
, Inception of
Tyler--Freedom's p363-365
-Literature, 1830's
Tyler--Freedom's p365
-Propaganda, after 1840
Tyler--Freedom's p382-385
-Riots
Tyler--Freedom's p380-381
-School issue
Tyler--Freedom's p378-380
-Societies and denominations
Tyler--Freedom's p369-371
ANTI-COLONIALISM
Hollingsworth--Amer. p96-98
ANTIETAM BATTLE
Collins--Story p219
Harlow--Story p317-318
Jordan--Civil p104-107, 112, 117
Life--New (5) p104, 118
Life--Union (6) p56-57, 96-97
Maurois--Illus. p150-151, 157
Meredith--World p144-147
Morris--Ency. p237-238
Pratt--Civil p30
-200 Years p22-23, 25
-Doubleday's troops crossing
Potomac
Keyes--Hope p230-231, 233
, Role of tobacco in

Garrison--Lost p38-47
ANTI-IMPERIALISTS
Hollingsworth--Amer. p89-95
ANTI-MASONIC PARTY
Boardman--Jackson. p21
Butterfield--Amer. p94
Carman--History (1) p422-423
Furnas--Americans p523
Life--Sweep (4) p9
Linton--Bicentennial. See index
p438
Morris--Ency. p170-171
Tyler--Freedom's p351-358
-National convention, first
Harlow--Story p232
ANTI-MONOPOLY PARTY
Holzman--Story p217-218
ANTIN, MARY
, and Immigrants p919-922
"ANTI-NEBRASKANS"
See also REPUBLICANS
Butterfield--Amer. p145
, and Stephen A. Douglas
Butterfield--Amer. p144-145
ANTIOCH COLLEGE
Drury--Midwest p105-108
Furnas--Americans p541-542, 745
ANTIQUES
, Collecting of
Furnas--Americans p598-602
ANTIRENT WAR, 1839-1846
Morris--Ency. p192
ANTI-SEMITISM
Furnas--Americans p705-710, 820
ANTISLAVERY MOVEMENT
See also ABOLITIONISTS; AMER-
ICAN ANTISLAVERY SOCIETY
Boardman--Civil p1-4, 15-16, 152-
153, 187-189
Gurko--Ladies. See index p372
Keyes--Hope p248
Kraus--U.S. p387, 445-453
Life--New (5). See index p156
Life--Sweep (4) p156
Linton--Bicentennial. See index
p438
-Organization
Tyler--Freedom's p491-493
-Societies
Boardman--Jackson. p114
-Women
Tyler--Freedom's p443-448
Warren--Pictorial p83-90,
99, 103-104
, Black
Warren--Pictorial p85-
88
-Writers

Brooks--Flower. p388-403
ANTITRUST ACT
  Butterfield--Amer. p254-255
APACHE INDIANS
  See also CHIRACAHUA APACHE
  INDIANS; JICARILLA APACHE
  INDIANS
  Amer. Her. --Indians. See index
  p419
  Billington--Far p13, 28, 249-251,
  285
  Boardman--Civil p106-107
  Boardman--Gilded p95-96
  Boardman--Jackson. p73-74
  Brown--Westerners p82, 87, 149,
  205, 207, 261
  DeVoto--Year p244, 268, 324, 327,
  350, 352, 369, 371, 376-377, 381,
  391, 393, 398-400, 402, 404
  Watkins--Gold p127-132, 134
  , as captured prostitutes and
  slaves
    Amer. Her. --Indians p384-385
  -Campaign for extermination
    Amer. Her. --Indians p385
APARTMENT HOUSES
  Furnas--Americans p624-625
  Lynes--Domestic. p105-108
  Marzio--Nation p486, 496
  -"Dakota" (N.Y. City)
    Cook--City p121-123
    Furnas--Americans p615, 624-
    625
  , First (1869)
    Marzio--Nation p486
APOLLO ASSOCIATION
  See also AMERICAN ART UNION
  Cable--American p155
  Lynes--Taste. p14
APPALACHIAN GOLDFIELDS. See
  GEORGIA--Appalachian goldfields
APPALACHIAN MOUNTAINS
  , Migration over
    Alden--Pioneer p157-173
APPARATUS
  , Mathematical and philosophical
    Dreppard--Pioneer p95-96
APPAREL. See CLOTHING AND
  DRESS; names of apparel
"APPEAL OF THE INDEPENDENT
  DEMOCRATS, " 1854
  Angle--By p193-198
APPENDECTOMY
  , First, 1887 (Philadelphia)
    Robertson--Book p18
APPLEBY, JOHN F.
  Train--Story p330

APPLEGATE, JESSE
  , on Oregon "Great emigration"
    Commager--Heritage p521-530
  -"The Westward march, 1846"
    Ridge--America's p456-459
APPLESEED, JOHNNY (JOHN
  CHAPMAN)
  Amer. Her. --New (6) p E197
  America's Hist. p272
  Boardman--Virginia p199
  Reader's--Story p172
APPLETON, NATHAN
  Boardman--Virginia p69-70
APPOMATTOX, VIRGINIA
  Davie--Profile p281-286
  Dulles--United p3-4
  Harlow--Story p322
  Jordan--Civil p90, 200-201, 203,
  205
  Kraus--U.S. p511-515
  Landmarks--Liberty p10-11
  Life--Union (6) p89-92
  Morris--Ency. p245
  Vanderbilt--Living p111
APPRENTICES
  Handlin--This p142, 258-259
  Wright--Every. p196-197
ARAPAHO INDIANS
  Andrews--Indian leaders. See
  index p183
  Andrews--Indians. See index
  p175
  Brown--Westerners p82, 98-99,
  191, 195, 198, 201, 233, 236, 244,
  246
  De Voto--Year p60, 63, 153, 167,
  177, 196, 244, 260-262, 294, 296,
  485
ARBOR DAY
  Hilton--Way p180-181
ARBUTHNOT, ALEXANDER
  -Ambrister affair
    Amer. Her. --New (5) p E153
ARCHAEOLOGY
  Boardman--Jackson. p169
ARCHERY
  Life--Steel (7) p147
  -Supplies
    Peck--Nineteenth n. p.
ARCHES
  , Largest (St. Louis, Mo.)
    Reader's--Story p498
ARCHITECTURE
  See also BUILDINGS; HOMES;
  HOUSES; names of famous
  houses, etc.
  Boardman--Civil p169-173

Boardman--Gilded p141-145
Boardman--Jackson. p162-163
Boardman--Virginia p157-161
Carman--History (2) p380-383
Cook--City p95-135
Furnas--Americans. See index
   p976
Harlow--Story p249-250
Kraus--U.S. p382-383
Larkin--Art p92-98, 282-291
Lynes--Domestic. p76-84
Lynes--Taste. See index p348
Morris--Ency. p602-603, 607-608
Mumford--Brown p107-181
Nye--Cultural p271-274
Ross--Taste p10-29
Walker--Every. p15-16, 75, 121-
   122, 128, 201, 211, 223-224
-1876
   Randel--Centennial. See
      index p466
-1890's
   Life--Reaching (8) p34-35,
      96-97, 100-101
, and environment
   -Views of Barre Ferree
      Cook--City p98-100
, and genteel tradition
   Jones--Age p253-254
-"Beaux-artiness"
   Furnas--Americans p764-
      766, 770-774
-Bungalows
   Furnas--Americans p782-783
   Lynes--Domestic. p108-109
-Churches. See CHURCHES--
   Architecture
-Classic to Gothic (1820-1860)
   Grimsted--Notions p38-44
-Colleges and universities
   Larkin--Art p95
-Columns and porticoes
   Furnas--Americans p267-
      269, 272-274
-"Crockets and finials"
   Larkin--Art p167-177
-Cupolas
   Wilson--Vanish. p84
, Early Victorian
   Gowans--Images p291-292,
      297
-Egyptian revival
   Reader's--Story p237
-"False front"
   Larkin--Art p243-249
-Firms
   Gowans--Images. See index
      p494
-French Renaissance

   Furnas--Americans p613-614
-French 2nd empire
   Larkin--Art p243-244, 246
-Functionalism
   Furnas--Americans p767-770
-Germanophile
   Furnas--Americans p614-615
-"Gingerbread age"
   Walker--Every. p12, 16
-Gothic revival
   Boardman--Jackson. p162-164
   Bode--Anatomy p45-47
   Furnas--Americans p418-420
   Life--America's p82-85
   Reader's--Story p236
   Ross--Taste p17-22, 26, 29
   Train--Story p266-267
   -"Neo-Gothic renaissance,"
      1886
         Life--Steel (7) p138-139
-Greek revival
   Boardman--Jackson. p162-163
   Boardman--Virginia p157-160
   Bode--Anatomy p40-41, 44-45
   Langdon--Everyday (2) p235-
      237
   Life--America's p71
   Lynes--Domestic. p88-96
   Reader's--Story p234, 236
   Ross--Taste p13-16
   Vanderbilt--Living p169
   , and women
      Lynes--Domestic. p94-95
-High Victorian
   Gowans--Images p356
-Illustrations (1820-1860)
   Grimsted--Notions p38-44
-Italianate
   Bode--Anatomy p47-49
   Furnas--Americans p422-425
   Lynes--Taste. p28-29, 31, 35-
      36, 54, 98, 163
   Reader's--Story p237
, Late Victorian academic
   Gowans--Images p382, 384
-Mining towns
   Life--America's p110-111
-Mission (Southwest provincial)
   Furnas--Americans p372
-Newport "cottages"
   Furnas--Americans p772-774
, Octagonal
   Furnas--Americans p438-440
   Ross--Taste p12, 23-24
   White--American p37-40
, of Thomas Jefferson
   See also "MONTICELLO"
   Treasury Amer. p135
, Picturesque

Lynes--Domestic. p96-100
-Post Civil war
    Harlow--Story p432-434
, Quaint and artistic
    Lynes--Domestic. p100-103
-Queen Anne
    Furnas--Americans p616-620,
    623
    Lynes--Taste. p97, 108-112,
    114, 129, 147
    Ross--Taste p22
, Romanesque
    Reader's--Story p237
-Romantic period
    Jones--Age p218
, Rural
    Lynes--Taste. p23-29, 31-
    33, 36
-South
    Larkin--Art p163-165
-Swiss chalet
    Furnas--Americans p420-422
-Tudor
    Life--America's p142
, Victorian
    See also ARCHITECTURE--
    Early Victorian; High Vic-
    torian
    Life--Steel (7) p139, 148-151
    Reader's--Story p23
-Views of Frances Trollope
    Trollope--Domestic. See
    index p. i
-Villas and cottages
    Larkin--Art p172-175
-"Widow's walk"
ARGONAUTS
    America's Hist. p309
    Tunis--Frontier p131-132
"ARGONAUTS OF'49"
    Boorstin--Americans p68
ARIKARA (ARICARA) INDIANS
    Boardman--Virginia p119
    Brown--Westerners p43, 58
    DeVoto--Year p52-53, 60, 485
    Gilbert--Trail p27, 61, 72
-Fight with William H. Ashley
    Ridge--America's p382-386
ARISTOCRACY
    See also "FOUR HUNDRED";
    SOCIETY
    Handlin--This p145-146, 198,
    245, 319, 390
, of wealth
    Lynes--Taste. p144, 166
-South
    Alden--Pioneer p192, 194-195
    Kraus--U.S. p401-403

ARITHMETIC
-1876
    Hilton--Way p63, 65-66
, Elizur Wright's
    Portraits--Americans p70
ARIZONA
    Billington--Far p4, 13, 282-285
ARKANSAS
    Carman--History (1) p373, 634,
    782
-1870's
    Randel--Centennial p110-111
-Reconstruction graft
    Life--Union (6) p135-136
-Wheel works, 1867
    Nation in motion p78
"ARLINGTON HISTORICAL SHRINE"
(Birmingham, Ala.)
    Vanderbilt--Living p141
"ARLINGTON HOUSE" (Lee mansion
national monument, Arlington, Va.)
    Vanderbilt--Living p98
ARMORY SQUARE HOSPITAL
    Dannett--Noble p302, 315, 328, 343,
    371
ARMOUR, PHILIP DANFORTH
    Boardman--Gilded p48
    Portraits--Americans p115
ARMSTRONG, SAMUEL C.
    Furnas--Americans p850-851
ARMY. See CONFEDERACY--
    Army; U.S. --Army
"ARMY ENGINEERS"
    Bartlett--New p246-247, 271, 287
    Randel--Centennial p262, 268-269
ARMY NURSING CORPS
    Young--Women p98-99, 193, 228,
    286
ARMY OF THE WEST
-1840's
    DeVoto--Year. See index
    p513
ARMY POSTS AND FORTS
    See also names of posts and
    forts
-1874-1876
    Randel--Centennial p48, 73-75,
    127-129, 132, 211, 270
ARNOLD, PHILIP
    Garrison--Lost p168-171
AROOSTOOK INDIANS & WAR
    Amer. Her. --New (6) p189 (facing)
    Boardman--Jackson. p30-31
    Morris--Ency. p181
ART
    See also ARTISTS: CRAFTS AND
    CRAFTSMANSHIP; DRAWING;
    ILLUSTRATIONS; IMPRESSION-

ISM; PAINTERS AND PAINTING:
SCULPTURE; etc.
Alden--Pioneer p170, 192
Boardman--Civil p159-162
Boardman--Gilded p135-140
Boardman--Jackson. p152-155
Boardman--Virginia p151-157
Carman--History (2) p374-378
Handlin--This p145-146, 198,
245, 319, 390
Lynes--Taste. See index p348-
349
Life--Steel (7) p142-145
-1876
See also ARTISTS--Women
Hilton--Way p65, 114
-1890's
Amer. Her. --90's p64-79
Jones--Age p16-17
-"Artistic craze"
Lynes--Taste. p111, 115-117,
147, 165, 190
-Books and Reading, illustrated
(1870's-1880's)
Larkin--Art p253-254
-Calligraphic drawing
McClinton--Antiques p87-89
-Centennial
Hilton--Way p181-183
-Collections
Ross--Taste p46
-Criticism
-Beginnings
Larkin--Art p115
, Burlesque of
Trachtenberg--Demo. p313-
319
, Development of
Larkin--Art p153
-Dealers
Lynes--Taste. p13-14, 18,
45-48, 64
-Decoration
Lynes--Taste. See index p352
Walker--Ency. p17-18, 20-21,
24-25, 170, 216, 224
-Design
See also INDEX OF AMERI-
CAN DESIGN; ART--Orna-
ment
-Greek revival patterns
Life--America's p74-75
-Etchings
Viewpoints p200-201, 204-205
-Exhibitions
See also ART--Galleries;
ART MUSEUMS
Larkin--Art p115

Lynes--Taste. See index
(under Exhibitions of art)
p353
-"Fenway Court"
Amer. Her. --New (11) p978-
988
-Galleries
Lynes--Taste. See index
(under Galleries) p353-354
-Lotteries
Lynes--Taste. p16-18
-Cosmopolitan Art Association
Bode--Anatomy p100-102
, Nudity in
Furnas--Americans p572
-Ornament
Gowans--Images p307-308,
334-342
, People's
Larkin--Art p224-231
Lyne's--Taste. p156-159, 162
, Power of
Harris--Land p271-288
, Realism in
Harris--Land p279-288
-Romanticism
Nye--Cultural p292-294
-School courses, 1876
Hilton--Way p65
-Training
See also ART SCHOOLS AND
SOCIETIES
Jones--Age p246-247
-Views of Frances Trollope
Trollope--Domestic. See
index p. i-ii
-West
See also REMINGTON, FRED-
ERIC
Hines--American p181, 250,
260-262, 267, 283-299
-Whalers'
Life--America's p93
-Women
Furnas--Americans. See
index p1014
ART INSTITUTE OF CHICAGO
Lynes--Taste. p149-150, 161
ART MUSEUMS
Larkin--Art p113-114, 251
"ART NOUVEAU"
Boardman--Gilded p139-140
Furnas--Americans p912-913
ART SCHOOLS AND SOCIETIES
Lynes--Taste. p148-153, 155, 162
Nye--Cultural p288-289
ART UNIONS
Larkin--Art p151-153

Lynes--Taste.p14-18, 21, 38,
48, 117, 151
ARTHUR, CHESTER ALAN
Boardman--Gilded p20-22
Butterfield--Amer. p232-233
Carman--History (2) p184, 228,
232-236
Harlow--Story p449, 452-455, 456
Life--Steel (7) p13-14, 17, 26, 45, 72
Linton--Bicentennial p220-225,
225 (facing)
Morris--Ency. p255-257
200 Years (2) p91, 314, 316-317
-Biography
Morris--Ency. p631-632
Whitney--American p179-184
-"The emergence of governmental
Indian policy"
Ridge--America's p587-588
-Presidency
Dulles--United p134-135
Reader's--Story p334
ARTHUR, ELLEN
Melick--Wives p49
ARTHUR, TIMOTHY SHAY
Amer. Her. --New (6) p E189-190
Bode--Anatomy p120-124
ARTILLERY. See GUNS
ARTISTS
See also PAINTERS AND PAINT-
ING
Amer. Her. --New (11) p972-973
Boardman--Virginia p151-156
Lynes--Taste. p18, 40, 45, 114
-"Ash Can School"
-Views of James Thomas Flex-
ner
Miers--American p279-283
-New England
Mussey--Old p126-127
-Views of Oliver W. Larkin
Miers--American p162-166
, Western
Boardman--Virginia p102
Gilbert--Trail. p6-13
-Women
Macksey--Book p207
Warren--Pictorial p154-157
ASH HOPPERS
Tunis--Frontier p80
"ASH LAWN" (Monroe's home,
Charlottesville, Va.)
Vanderbilt--Living p108
ASHBY, TURNER
Amer. Her. --New (8) p E262
Furnas--Americans p410-411
ASHERIES
Van Wagenen--Golden p165-167

"ASHLAND" (Clay's home, Lexing-
ton, Ky.)
Vanderbilt--Living p116-117
ASHLEY, WILLIAM HENRY
Amer. Her. --New (6) p E189-190
Bartlett--New p86, 256-257
Boardman--Virginia p109-110
Brown--Westerners p57-61
Gilbert--Trail. p60-61, 64, 77, 96
Hine--American p50-54, 57
Tunis--Frontier p112
-Expeditions
Reader's--Story p166-169
-"Fight with the Arikara, " 1823,
by James Clyman
Ridge--America's p382-386
ASSEOLA (POWELL) (Seminole
Indian). See OSCEOLA
ASSINIBOINE INDIANS
Brown--Westerners p58, 77
ASSOCIATED PRESS
Harlow--Story p430
"ASSOCIATIONISTS"
Alden--Pioneer p224
Carman--History (1) p529
ASSOCIATIONS
Handlin--This p177-178, 220, 230-
231, 265-269, 359
-Development
Jones--Age p166-168
-Science and technology
Jones--Age p169-170
-Social sciences
Jones--Age p169
, Voluntary
Keller--Affairs p7-13, 517-518
ASTOR, CAROLINE SCHERMERHORN
(Mrs. William Backhouse, Jr.)
Cable--American p274-276, 279
Life--Reaching (8) p44, 46, 52
ASTOR, JOHN JACOB
Amer. Her. --New (6) p514, E190
Bartlett--New p256, 258, 408
Boardman--Jackson. p64, 80
Carman--History (1) p369-371,
556
Gilbert--Trail. p53, 58, 61
Hine--American p47, 52, 73
Morris--Ency. p187, 505, 632
Reader's--Story p164, 166
Tunis--Frontier p110-111
-Fort, on Columbia river, 1803
Case--Empire p15-25
ASTOR PLACE RIOT, 1849
Boardman--Jackson. p156-157
Morris--Ency. p591
ASTORIA, OREGON
Bartlett--New p89-91, 102, 258, 408

Brown--Westerners p52, 56
"ASTORIANS" (fur traders)
DeVoto--Year p57, 65, 170, 174,
485
ASTRONOMY AND ASTRONOMERS
See also names of astronomers
Boardman--Jackson. p168-169
Morris--Ency. p531-532
Wilson--American p272-277
-Observatories
Boardman--Jackson. p167
Reader's--Story p309-310
-Women
Warren--Pictorial p74
Wilson--America p276
ASTROPHYSICS
, of George Ellery Hale
Wilson--American p352-353
ATCHISON, DAVID R.
Life--New (5) p68-69, 75
ATCHISON, TOPEKA & SANTA
FE RAILROAD
Boardman--Civil p140
Life--Steel (7) p30-32
ATHERTON, GERTRUDE
Furnas--Americans p371-372
ATHLETIC CLUB, GERMAN.
See "TURNVEREINE"
ATHLETICS
See also SPORTS AND GAMES;
etc.
-Rules, 1876
Hilton--Way p101, 103, 109-
110
, School, 1876
Hilton--Way p58-59
ATLANTA, GEORGIA
Carman--History (1) p668, 698,
711
, in Civil War
Burner--America (1) p324-
326
Collins--Story p216
Dowdey--Experiment p355-
363
Jordan--Civil. See index
p212
Life--Union (6) p69, 83-84,
86-89, 103
ATLANTIC AND PACIFIC TEA
COMPANY. See A & P
ATLANTIC CABLE
Collins--Story p162
Commager--Heritage p941-947
Keyes--Hope p268-269
Wilson--American p172-177
ATLANTIC CITY, NEW JERSEY
-1876

Randel--Centennial p322-323
ATLANTIC MONTHLY
Our literary p92-93
Randel--Centennial p98, 349-350
ATTICS
Partridge--As p16-17
AUDUBON, JOHN JAMES
Amer. Her. --New (5) p E153
Boardman--Virginia p156, 177-178
Larkin--Art p110-111. See also
index p516
Morris--Ency. p530, 601
Reader's-Story p307, 380
Wilson--American p96-97
-Biography
Morris--Ency. p632-633
AUGUSTA, GEORGIA
, 1807
Woodward--Way p160-197
AURORA SETTLEMENT (Oregon)
Life--Sweep (4) p63-64
Tyler--Freedom p127-128
AUSTIN, BASIL
Watkins--Gold p151-152, 156
AUSTIN, MOSES
Amer. Her. --New (6) p E190
Boardman--Virginia p103
Keyes--Hope p241
Life--Sweep (4) p81-82
AUSTIN, STEPHEN FULLER
Amer. Her. --New (6) p E190-191
Bartlett--New p97-99
Billington--Far p16-21, 117, 119,
123-124, 126, 133
Boardman--Virginia p103
Harlow--Story p265
Hine--American p81-86, 126, 337
Keyes--Hope p241
Kraus--U.S. p419-420
Life--Sweep (4) p81-82, 94
Morris--Ency. p176, 422
Tunis--Frontier p98
-Biography
Morris--Ency. p632-633
-"Causes of the Texan Revolu-
tion" 1835
Ridge--America's p426-429
-"Cultural conflict in Texas, "
1833
Ridge--America's p423-426
-"Stephen F. Austin advertises
for settlers, " 1823
Ridge--America's p414-416
AUSTRIA
-Immigrants
Life--Reaching (8) p60-63, 69
AUTHORS
See also names and types of

authors
Alden--Pioneer p170-172, 212-216
-1890's
    Amer. Her. --90's p81, 85-87
, Antislavery
    Hart--Popular p110-116
-Best sellers--Women
    Sochen--Herstory p142-145
-California
    Wright--Culture p156-158
-Crusaders
    Mott--Golden p165-171
, "Ghetto"
    Our literary p182-183
-Middlewest pioneer and farm
life
    Boardman--Gilded p128-129
-New England
    Boardman--Gilded p129
    -Views of William Dean
    Howells, 1865-1880
        Angle--American p423-427
-Realists, 1890's
    Amer. Her. --90's p85-86
-Reformers
    Amer. Her. --90's p86-87
-South
    Boardman--Gilded p129-130
-West
    Wright--Culture p120-122
-Women
    See also AUTHORS--Best
    sellers--Women
    Macksey--Book p184-186, 188
    Our literary p174-175
    Sochen--Herstory p142-146,
    223-227
    Tyler--Freedom's p435-440
    Warren--Pictorial p68-70, 128-
    130
AUTOBIOGRAPHY. See BIOGRAPHY
"THE AUTOCRAT." See HOLMES,
OLIVER WENDELL
AUTOGRAPH ALBUMS
, Children's
    McClinton--Antiques p125-134
AUTOMOBILES
    See also DURYEA BROTHERS;
    FORD, HENRY
    Boardman--Gilded p69-70
    Carson--Polite p232
    Hilton--Way p110
    Life--America's p138
    Marzio--Nation p551
    Morris--Ency. p538
    Portraits--Americans p37-40
    Reader's--Story p268
    Walker--Every. p57-58, 113

, First, 1892
    Ross--Taste p274
    -Duryea Bros., Springfield,
    Mass., 1895
        Nation in motion p80
        Wilson--American p324-325
-Ford-Selden patent squabble
    White--American p127-134
"Motor buggies"
    Reader's--Story p202
-Patents, first
    Garrison--Lost p53-57
-Races and racing
    White--American p135-139
    -Views of Frank Duryea, 1895
        Angle--American p417-418
-"Road engines," 1895
    Portraits--Americans p37
-Tires, pneumatic
    Boardman--Gilded p70
AVARY, MYRTA LOCKETT
, on hardships of planters, 1865
    Commager--Heritage p308-811
AVIATION. See AERONAUTICS
"AWAKENING, GREAT." See
"GREAK AWAKENING" (2)
AXES.
    See also BROADAXES
    Bartlett--New p176-177
    Van Wagenen--Golden p27-29, 46

                    B

BABCOCK, ORVILLE E.
    Amer. Her. --New (8) p E262-263
    Butterfield--Amer. p205
BABIES
    See also CHILD-BEARING;
    CHILDREN; CHRISTENINGS
    Cable--American p178
    Partridge--As p18
    -Shows, first (Springfield, O.,
    1854)
        Robertson--Book p21
BABY CARRIAGES
    McClinton--Antiques p153-155
BACHE, ALEXANDER DALLAS
    Boardman--Jackson. p169
"BACK GALLERIES" (Back porches)
    Lynes--Domestic. p102
BACK YARDS
    Walker--Every. p221-222
BADEAU, ADAM
    Young--Women p332-334
BADGES AND ORNAMENTS
-1880's
    Peck--Nineteenth n. p.

BAEKELAND (BAKELAND), LEO
HENDRIK
  Reader's--Story p270
  Wilson--American p380-382
BAGBY, GEORGE WILLIAM
  -"The old Virginia gentleman"
    Trachtenberg--Demo. p126-135
BAGGAGE
  Wilson--Folkways p142-144
BAGLEY, LUCY
  Warren--Pictorial p94-95
BAGLEY, SARAH
  Macksey--Book p164
  Reader's--Story p436
BAGOT, CHARLES, SIR
  Amer. Her. --New (5) p E153
BAKELAND, LEO HENDRIK. See
  BAEKELAND, LEO HENDRIK
BAKER, BENJAMIN FRANKLIN
  Howard--Our p147-148
BAKER, (EDWARD) LEWIS
  , and Mary Lincoln
    Randall--Mary p472-474
BALATKA, HANS
  Howard--Our p272-273
"BALD-KNOBBERS" (Vigilantes)
  Keller--Affairs p487-488
BALDWIN, LELAND D.
  -"Gilded age"
    Miers--American p215-219
BALDWIN, MATHIAS W.
  Boardman--Jackson. p97
BALDWIN HOTEL (San Francisco,
Ca.)
  Jones--Age p130
BALLET
  Dulles--History p100, 116-117
  Grimsted--Melodrama p26, 107-
  110, 237, 254, 258-261
BALLOONS AND BALLOONISTS
  Dreppard--Pioneer p99, 306
  Life--New (5) p58-59
  Ross--Taste p89
  -1876
    Hilton--Way p149
  -"Atlantic"--distance record,
  1859
    Garrison--Lost p25-29
  -Civil war
    Meredith--World p110-113
    Wilson--American p184-187
BALLOTS. See SUFFRAGE
BALLOU, ADIN, REV.
  Tyler--Freedom p166-171, 413-
  414
BALLS (for games)
  Dulles--United p92
BALLS AND BALLROOMS. See

DANCES AND DANCING
BALTIMORE, MARYLAND
  Davidson--Life (2) p112
  Handlin--This p117, 127, 195, 299
  Holzman--Stormy p38, 44-50, 141
  Hunt--Life. See index p289
  Wright--Every. p124-125
  -Views of Frances Trollope
    Trollope--Domestic. See
    index p. ii
BALTIMORE AND OHIO CANAL
  Carman--History (1) p465, 467
BALTIMORE AND OHIO RAILROAD
  Alden--Pioneer p204
  Bartlett--New p314, 318, 322-324
  Boardman--Jackson. p95
  Carman--History (1) p467-469
  Langdon--Everyday (2) p118, 334,
  343-345, 347
  Life--Growing p164-165
  Nostalgia p13-15
  Tunis--Frontier p95-96
  Wright--Every. p90-91
BANCROFT, GEORGE
  Amer. Her. --New (6) p E191
  Boardman--Jackson. p146-147
  Boorstin--Americans p369-373
  Brooks--Flower. p126-134; see
  also index p539
  Kraus--U. S. p330, 350, 372-373
  Morris--Ency. p190, 519, 569-570
  Our literary p50-51
  -Biography
    Morris--Ency. p633
BANCROFT, HUBERT HOWE
  Boardman--Civil p153-154
  Watkins--Gold p85-86, 224
  Wright--Culture p163
BAND SAWS
  Life--Steel (7) p30
BANDITS
  -California, 1850's
    Johnson--Pictorial p122-123
  , in "dime novels"
    Our literary p128-129
  , Mexican
    Hine--American p212-213
  , Social
    Hine--American p310-311
  -West
    Hine--American p212-213,
    310-311
BANDS
  Boardman--Gilded p172
  Walker--Every. p164, 166
BANDSTANDS
  , Village
    Wilson--Vanish. p154

BANGOR, MAINE
  Mussey--Old p31
BANJOS (BONJAS)
  Chase--America's p262-263, 440
BANK OF CALIFORNIA
  Watkins--Gold p79-80, 258
BANK OF THE UNITED STATES
  Boardman--Virginia p73-76
  Borden--Portrait (1) p166-169
  Kraus--U.S. p330, 343, 361-364
  Life--Sweep (4). See index
    p156
  Linton--Bicentennial. See
    index p438
  Tunis--Frontier p85-86
  Whitney--American p34, 46, 76-
    78, 80, 97
  -Charter renewal debate, 1811
    Morris--Ency. p139
  -Second
    Alden--Pioneer p175-177,
      184-188
    Amer. Her. --New (5) p401-
      402, E179
    Boardman--Jackson. p17-20,
      22-23
    Carman--History (1) p367,
      401-402, 436-443
    Collins--Story p178
    Harlow--Story p188
    Morris--Ency. p154-155, 505
    Tunis--Frontier p86
    , and Andrew Jackson
      Butterfield--Amer. p90-91
      Harlow--Story p231
      Heffner--Doc. p87-93
      Walker--Reform p64-70
    -Removal of deposits, 1833
      Morris--Ency. p174-175
BANKHEAD, MINERVA
  , and Eaton affair
    Phillips--That p86-87, 123,
      136
BANKRUPTCY
  Federal acts
  -1800 (first)
    Morris--Ency. p130
  -1841
    Morris--Ency. p184
  -1867
    Keller--Affairs p172, 184, 421
  -1898
    Keller--Affairs p421-422
    Morris--Ency. p265
BANKS, LOUIS A.
  -"The Hall of Fame"
    Harris--Land p305-312

BANKS, NATHANIEL PRENTISS
  Amer. Her. --New (8) p E263
BANKS, TOY
  Amer. Her. --New (5) p402
  McClinton--Antiques p272-276
  Peck--Nineteenth n. p.
BANKS AND BANKING
  See also BANK OF THE UNITED
    STATES; NATIONAL BANK ACT
    OF 1863; NATIONAL BANKING
    SYSTEM
  Boardman--Jackson. p17-20
  Boardman--Virginia p73-76
  Carman--History (2) p107-109
  Handlin--This p123, 135-136, 157,
    206-207, 209, 367
  Morris--Ency. p504-506
  -1890's
    Life--Reaching (8) p84, 86-88
  -"Bank war," 1832
    Amer. Her. --New (5) p400-402
  -"Cheap money"
    Harlow--Story p449-452, 463-
      465, 468-469, 471-475
  -West
    Carman--History (1) p366-367
  -"Wildcat banking"
    Harlow--Story p234
BANNOCK INDIANS
  Bartlett--New p110-111
  Gilbert--Trail. p101
BANVARD, JOHN
  Boorstin--Americans p237-238
BAPTISM
  -Georgia, 1899
    Schwartz--When p139
BAPTISTS
  Bartlett--New p140, 375-379
  Boardman--Jackson. p132-133
  Boardman--Virginia p167-168, 171-
    172
  Davidson--Life (2) p340-341
  Hine--American p227, 236, 244-245
  Nye--Cultural p230
  Wright--Culture. See index p259
  Wright--Every. p206-207, 210
BARATTA, EUMONE
  Bode--Anatomy p100-101
BARBARY PIRATES
  -War against, by Thomas Jeffer-
    son
    Wright--Every. p49-50
BARBARY WARS
  Boardman--Virginia p50-51
  Harlow--Story p171, 173
  Reader's--Story p442
BARBECUES

-Washington, D.C., 1800's
Wright--Every. p66-67
BARBED WIRE (fences)
Amer. Her. --New (9) p770-772
Bartlett--New p220-221
Carman--History (2) p200-201
Dulles--United p47-48
Furnas--Americans p687-688
Life--Steel (7) p57
Reader's--Story p114
Tunis--Frontier p159-160
Wilson--American p234-235
-1867, First, Kent., O.
Robertson--Book p22
-1873-1876
Randel--Centennial p140-141
-1876
Hilton--Way p158
BARBER, JEDEDIAH
Boardman--Virginia p190
BARBER, JOHN WARNER
Mussey--Old p126-127
BARBER POLES
Wilson--Vanish. p145
BARGES AND PACKET BOATS
Langdon--Everyday (2) p96-97
BARING, ALEXANDER
-Biography
Amer. Her. --New (7) p E225-226
BARKER, EUGENE C.
-"Moving toward independence"
Ridge--America's p429-430
BARKER, JAMES NELSON
Morris--Ency. p590
BARLOW, ARABELLA
Young--Women p276-278, 327
BARLOW, JOEL
Boardman--Virginia p139-140
, and "Columbiad"
Hunt--Life p142-143
BARLOW, SAMUEL K.
Case--Empire p139-146
BARLOW TRAIL
Case--Empire p137-146
BARN ("BRAN") DANCES. See
DANCES AND DANCING
BARNARD, CHARLOTTE ALINGTON
Howard--Our p646
BARNARD, FREDERICK A. P.
Boardman--Civil p182-183
BARNARD, HENRY
Amer. Her. --New (6) p E191-192
Furnas--Americans p545-546
Harlow--Story p252
-Biography
Morris--Ency. p633

"BARNBURNERS" (political)
Morris--Ency. p192
BARNES, JANE
Ross--Westward p122-123
BARNS
Treasury Amer. p365
Van Wagenen--Golden p239
-Old Northwest
Tunis--Frontier p76-77
"BARNSTORMERS" (daredevils)
White--American p41-47
Wilson--Early p117-118
BARNUM, PHINEAS TAYLOR
See also "IRANISTAN" (home)
Amer. Her. --New (6) p E192
Amer. Her. --New (11) p940
Boardman--Civil p198
Boardman--Jackson p176-177
Burner--America (1) p254-265
Cable--American p123
Dulles--History p122-125, 138-139
Furnas--Americans. See index
p977
Mussey--Old p122-123
Our literary p102, 105-107
Partridge--As p164
Randel--Centennial p327-328
Reader's--Story p464-466
Wright--Every. p231-234
-Biography
Morris--Ency. p633-634
BARNUM'S AMERICAN MUSEUM.
See AMERICAN MUSEUM
BARR, AMELIA EDITH
Adelman--Famous p255-256
BARRETT, O. O.
Holzman--Stormy p225-226
BARRIE, JAMES M.
-Popularity in America
Mott--Golden p191-192
BARRISTERS. See LAW AND
LAWYERS
BARROWS, KATHERINE ISABEL
Adelman--Famous p246
BARRY, WILLIAM T.
Amer. Her. --New (5) p E153-154
, and Eaton affair
Phillips--That p16, 59, 87-88,
90, 95, 108, 112
BARRY, MRS. WILLIAM T.
, and Eaton affair
Phillips--That p59-60, 62, 74,
86, 108, 136
BARRYMORE FAMILY
Boardman--Gilded p150
BARTLETT, AMY, pseud. See
WARNER, ANNA BARTLETT

BARTON, CLARA
  Adelman--Famous p197-198
  Boardman--Civil p72
  Dannett--Noble p208-209,306,309
  Dolin--Great p126-131
  Harlow--Story p323
  Heath--Women (4) p15
  Macksey--Book p123-124
  Meredith--World p174
  Warren--Pictorial p108-109
  Young--Women. See index p385
  -Biography
    Morris--Ency. p634
    Young--Women p366
BARTRAM, WILLIAM
  Nye--Cultural p90
BASEBALL; KNICKERBOCKER
  BASEBALL CLUB
  See also DOUBLEDAY, ABNER
  Amer. Her. --New (11) p939-940
  Boardman--Civil p201-202
  Boardman--Gilded p173-174
  Boardman--Jackson. p178-179
  Cable--American p266-267, 296,
    298
  Davidson--Life (2) p57-62
  Dulles--History p185-191
  Harlow--Story p437
  Jones--Age p344
  Life--New (5) p58-61
  Life--Reaching (8) p37-38
  Life--Steel (7) p146-147
  Marzio--Nation p461-462
  Partridge--As p155-156
  Reader's--Story p483-485
  Walker--Every. p153-157
  Woodward--Way p249
  Wright--Every. p241-242
  -1871-1876
    Randel--Centennial p319-320
  -1875-1899
    -Views of Albert G. Spalding
      Angle--American p411-413
  -1876
    Hilton--Way p101-104
  -1880's
    -Equipment
      Peck--Nineteenth n. p.
  -1890's
    Dulles--History p223-226,
      240, 263-264
  -First "diamond," 1839
    Train--Story p290
  -Hall of Fame & Museum,
    Cooperstown, N.Y.
    Vanderbilt--Living p53
  -Negroes as players

  Marzio--Nation p462
  -Organization, 1839
    Ross--Taste p95
  , Professional
    Dulles--United p100
  -World Series, first, 1883
    Harlow--Story p437
BASEMENTS. See CELLARS
BASKETBALL
  Boardman--Gilded p175
  Jones--Age p344
  Reader's--Story p489-490
BASKETS
  Van Wagenen--Golden p212-214
BASS, SAM
  Reader's--Story p172
BASTARDS. See ILLEGITIMACY
"BAT" (Indian). See "ROMAN
  NOSE" (Cheyenne Indian)
BATCHELDER, GEORGE A.
  -"Propaganda for immigrants:
    the Dakota territory"
    Ridge--America's p619-621
BATEAUX (flatboats)
  Bartlett--New p309-310
  Langdon--Everyday (2) p92
  Tunis--Frontier p67
BATEMAN, KATE
  Adelman--Famous p252-253
BATES, EDWARD
  -Biography
    Amer. Her. --New (7) p E226
BATES, ISSACHAR
  Tyler--Freedom's p145-146
BATHROOMS
  Cable--American p225, 236-237,
    248-249
  Lynes--Domestic. p218-227; see
    also index p298
  Ross--Taste p126, 128-130
  Walker--Every. p222-223
  -Plumbing
    Partridge--As p133
BATHS AND BATHING
  Hilton--Way p14-16, 105-107
  Ross--Taste p185-186, 188
  , Beach
    Davidson--Life (2) p9
    Life--Reaching (8) p55
    Partridge--As p169
    Ross--Taste p90
    Wilson--Folkways p24-26
    -Women
      Dulles--History p152,
        201-202
  , Health cults
    Furnas--Americans p441-443

-Home
    Cable--American p248-249
    Wilson--Folkways p27-31
    , Frequency of
        Lynes--Domestic. p223
        Wilson--Vanish. p51
-Machines, 1890's
    Ross--Taste p185-186
-New York City, free rain of
1894
    Cook--City p141
-Salt-water, 1876
    Hilton--Way p121-122, 139-140
-Types
    Lynes--Domestic. p219-220
BATHTUBS
    Hilton--Way p14-15
    Langdon--Everyday (2) p232-233
    Ross--Taste p126
    Woodward--Way p232, 289
    -"Battle of Horseshoe Bend," by
    Andrew Jackson, 1814
        Ridge--America's p270-273
"BATTLE HYMN OF THE REPUB-
LIC." See SONGS
"BATTLE OF THE BEAUTIFUL
VIEW," 1847
    Angle--American p241-243
"BATTLE OF THE LITTLE BIG
HORN," 1876
    Randel--Centennial p129-134
"BATTLE OF THE WILDERNESS"
    -Attack at Spottsylvania
        Collins--Story p225
        Morris--Ency. p242
        200 Years (2) p34-35, 40-41
BATTLEDORE AND SHUTTLE-
COCK (game)
    McClinton--Antiques p78-79,
    203-204
BAUMANN, JOHN
    "The round-up, 1887"
        Ridge--America's p606-608
BAWMEIER, JOSEPH MICHAEL.
See BIMELER, JOSEPH MICHAEL
BAYARD, TRYPHENA CADY
    Gurko--Ladies p64-66, 149, 203
BAYARD-CHAMBERLAIN TREATY,
1888
    Morris--Ency. p283
BAYER, ADELE PARMENTIER
    Neidle--America's p75-76
BAZAAR, TROLLOPE
    Trollope--Domestic. See index
    p. ii
BEACH, AMY MARCY (MRS. H. H. A.)
    Howard--Our p319-323

BEADLE, ERASTUS
    Treasury Amer. p368
    -Books published
        Hart--Popular p153-156
BEADLE, JOHN H.
    -"The Hell on Wheels" of the
    Union Pacific, 1873
        Ridge--America's p565-567
BEALE, EDWARD F., LIEUTENANT
    Randel--Centennial p144-145
    Watkins--Gold p27-28
BEALE, HOWARD K.
    , on Andrew Jackson and the rad-
    icals
        Miers--American p205-212
BEAN, ROY, JUDGE
    Reader's--Story p172
    -Court, Langtry, Texas
        Vanderbilt--Living p189
BEANS
    Van Wagenen--Golden p87-88
    , Baked (first, in New England,
    1829)
        Robertson--Book p21
BEAR FLAG REVOLT. See
CALIFORNIA--Bear Flag Revolt
BEARD, GEORGE M.
    -"Causes of American nervous-
    ness"
        Trachtenburg--Demo. p238-247
BEARDS AND MUSTACHES
    Carson--Polite p131-137
    Peck--Nineteenth n. p.
    Ross--Taste p239, 241, 243
    Train--Story p272, 328
    -1870's
        Woodward--Way p287
BEAUJOUR, FELIX DE
    , on America
        Hunt--Life p30
BEAUMONT, WILLIAM, DR.
    Wilson--American p102-103
    -Biography
        Morris--Ency. p634
    -Digestive research
        White--American p24-25
BEAUREGARD, PIERRE GUSTAVE
TOUTANT DE, GENERAL
    Dowdey--Experiment. See index
    p443
    Life--New (5) p98-99
    Life--Union (6) p13, 32-33, 36-39,
    86, 137
    200 Years (2) p12-13, 21, 45
    Young--Women p108, 111, 132-133,
    136, 303
    -Biography

Amer. Her. --New (7) p E226
BEAUTY AIDS. See COSMETICS
BEAVER, HERBERT, (MR. & MRS.)
Case--Empire p64-69
BEAVERS
See also FUR TRADE; HUNTING
AND TRAPPING
Bartlett--New p254-255, 259-260
Gilbert--Trail. p46-47, 53-57, 62,
69, 155
-Skins
Brown--Westerners p45, 51-52,
56-62
-Traps and trapping
Reader's--Story p165
Tunis--Frontier p113
BECKWORTH, JAMES P. ("JIM")
Amer. Her. --New (6) p E192
Gilbert--Trail.p68, 80
Reader's--Story p168
BEDS AND BEDDING
Lynes--Domestic. p204-217;
see also index p298
Ross--Taste p105-106
, Canopy
Wilson--Vanish. p44
-Mattresses, materials of
Lynes--Domestic. p207-208
-Steps
Wilson--Vanish. p45
, Trundle
Wilson--Vanish. p45
"BEE HIVE HOUSE" (Salt Lake
City, Utah)
Vanderbilt--Living p194-195
BEECHER, CATHERINE ESTHER
Adelman--Famous p129-130
Boardman--Virginia p165-167
Furnas--Americans. See index
p978
Lynes--Domestic. p59-64; see
also index p298
Macksey--Book p15
Portraits--Americans p61-62
Sochen--Herstory p141
Tyler--Freedom's p251-254;
see also index p591
Warren--Pictorial p71-72
-Kitchen organization plans
Marzio--Nation p491
, on Religion and national security
Hurd--Treasury p96-98
-Victorian code
Cable--American p137, 149, 151
BEECHER, HENRY WARD, REV.
Boardman--Civil p187
Butterfield--Amer. p240

Cable--American p153, 176, 234,
246, 321
Gurko--Ladies p233, 248-249
Life--Reaching (8) p10-13
Randel--Centennial p173, 434, 439-
440, 446, 461 fn11
-"The advance of a century, " 1876
Trachtenberg--Demo. p67-82
-Biography
Amer. Her. --New (7) p E226-
227
Amer. Her. --New (11) p914-917
Morris--Ency. p634-635
, on religious and national liberty
Hurd--Treasury p96-98
-Slave auction
Burner--America (1) p275-277
BEECHER, LYMAN, REV;
Boardman--Virginia p167
Boorstin--Americans p318, 320
BEEF. See MEAT PACKING INDUS-
TRY
BEER
Handlin--This p168, 263-264, 385-
387, 389
Marzio--Nation p598-599
, and Germans
Cable--American p313
Weisberger--Amer. p142-143
BEES (insects)
Van Wagenen--Golden p174-179
BEES (social functions)
See also types of Bees
Wilson--Folkways p96-98
BEGGARS
, Child (New York City, 1875)
Cook--City p219-220
BEHAN, ADA
Adelman--Famous p251
BELASCO, DAVID
Boardman--Gilded p148-149
-Theatrical productions
Blum--Theatre p39, 51
BELKNAP, WILLIAM WORTH
Amer. Her. --New (8) p E263
Boardman--Civil p105-106
Butterfield--Amer. p204
Randel--Centennial p207-214
-Impeachment
Collins--Story p246
Morris--Ency. p252
BELL, ALEXANDER GRAHAM
See also TELEPHONE
America's Hist. p556-557
Boardman--Gilded p71
Hilton--Way p173-174
Life--Steel (7) p38, 42-43

Marzio--Nation p610-611
Morris--Ency. p537
Portraits--Americans p33
Randel--Centennial p178-179, 186
Reader's--Story p271
White--American p104-105
Wilson--American p278-285
-Biography
    Morris--Ency. p635
BELL, JOHN
    Boardman--Civil p25
    Life--New (5) p92-94
BELL, SHERMAN
    Watkins--Gold p218-219
BELL, TOM HODGES
    Tunis--Frontier p137-138
BELL, WILLIAM A.
    -"The symphony of track-
        laying," 1869
        Ridge--America's p564-565
BELLA COOLA INDIANS
    Gilbert--Trail. p25
BELLAMY, EDWARD
    Boardman--Gilded p114-115
    Borden--Portrait (2) p29
    Brown--Mumford p47-49
    Furnas--Americans p715, 724-728,
        730, 749
    Life--Reaching (8) p91-92
    Mott--Golden p168-170
    Our literary p163
    Randel--Centennial p458-459
    -Biography
        Amer. Her. --New (11) p E374-
            375
    -"Looking backward"
        Hart--Popular p169-172
    -"With the eyes shut"
        Harris--Land p46-62
"BELLE CREOLE" (ship)
    Keyes--Hope p384, 386
"BELLONA." See EATON, PEGGY
O'NEALE TIMBERLAKE
BELLOWS, HENRY W., DR.
    Young--Women p5, 67, 73, 75-80,
        108-109, 351
"BELLOWS TOYS." See "PIP
SQUEAK OR BELLOWS" TOYS
BELLS
    , and horns, as early communica-
        tion
        Wilson--Folkways p188-194
BELMONT, AUGUST
    Amer. Her. --90's p62-63
BELMONT, PERRY
    Randel--Centennial p135-136
BELOW, ERNST
    -Views on America, 1894

Handlin--This p383-389
BELTER, JOHN HENRY
    Reader's--Story p224-225
BEMAN, SOLON S.
    Portraits--Americans p96
BENEVOLENT ENTERPRISES. See
CHARITIES; POOR RELIEF; etc.
BENJAMIN, I. J.
    -Views on America, 1855
        Handlin--This p270-285
BENJAMIN, JUDAH PHILIP
    Amer. Her. --New (8) p E263-264
    Dowdey--Experiment. See index
        p443-444
    Life--New (5) p133-134, 137
    Portraits--Americans p31
BENNETT, EMERSON
    Boardman--Jackson p150-151
BENNETT, JAMES GORDON
    Boardman--Jackson. p183
    Morris--Ency. p583
    Walker--Every. p128-129
    -Biography
        Amer. Her. --New (7) p E227
        Amer. Her. --New (11) p E375
        Morris--Ency. p635-636
BENTON, JESSIE. See FREMONT,
JESSIE BENTON
BENTON, THOMAS HART
    Amer. Her. --New (5) p E154
    Boardman--Jackson. p55-56
    Butterfield--Amer. p93, 133
    Carman--History (1) p366, 425,
        427, 430, 441, 556, 562, 571
    DeVoto--Year. See index p513
    Gilbert--Trail. p155, 157-159,
        170, 172
    Kraus--U. S. p344, 348, 357-358,
        363-364, 367
    Life--Growing p146, 151-152
    Life--New (5) p35, 39
    Life--Sweep (4) p14-15; see also
        index p156
    Morris--Ency. See index p740
    -"The demand for all Oregon,"
        1846
        Ridge--America's p497-498
"BENTON" (ship)
    Young--Women p257-258
BERGMANN, CARL
    Howard--Our p214
"BERIAH SELLER" LINIMENT
    Life--Steel (7) p37
BERING SEA
    -Dispute, 1892
        Morris--Ency. p284-285
BERLIN CONFERENCE (on Samoa,
1889). See SAMOA, AMERICAN

BERLINER, EMILE
 Portraits--Americans p36
BERMUDA HUNDRED, VIRGINIA
 Holzman--Stormy p120-122
BERNHARDT, SARAH
 Blum--Stage profile 3
 Boardman--Gilded p150-151
BERRIEN, JOHN M.
 Phillips--That. See index p177
"BERRY HILL" (Virginia, 1830)
 Ross--Taste p11
BESSEMER, HENRY
 , and "Bessemer process"
  Life--Steel (7) p32-33
  Train--Story p285-286
BESSEMER STEEL INDUSTRY
 Langdon--Everyday (2) p300-301
 Morris--Ency. p496-497
"BEST SELLERS"
 Keyes--Hope p219
 -1801-1899
  Mott--Golden p317-324
 -1803-1860
  Sochen--Herstory p143
 -1816-1860
  Morris--Ency. p565-566
 -1862-1899
  Morris--Ency. p571
 -1890's
  Lynes--Domestic. p239
 , by women
  Warren--Pictorial p128-129
BETHEL SETTLEMENT (Missouri)
 Tyler--Freedom p125-128
BETHUNE, LOUISE
 Macksey--Book p166
BETHUNE, LOUISE BLANCHARD
 Reader's--Story p436
BEVERAGES
 See also names of beverages
 Wilson--Folkways p152-155
 , Iced
  Furnas--Americans p457-459
BEVERIDGE, ALBERT J.
 Butterfield--Amer. p287
BEVERLY HOSPITAL (Philadel-
 phia, Pa.)
 Dannett--Noble p304-306
BIBLE
 Bode--Anatomy p141-145
 Hine--American p228-229, 241,
  255, 324
 Wright--Culture. See index
  p260
 -Reading, in public schools
  Keller--Affairs p139-140, 484
 -Sales and influence
  Bode--Anatomy p140-142

BIBLE SOCIETIES
 See also names of Bible societies
 Tyler--Freedom's p32
BIBLE SOCIETY OF THE CONFED-
 ERATE STATES
 Carman--History (1) p655
BICKERDYKE, MARY ANN
 ("MOTHER")
 Dannett--Noble p231-232, 317, 388,
  390, 393
 Macksey--Book p149
 Warren--Pictorial p108-109
 Young--Women. See index p385
 -Biography
  Young--Women p367
BICYCLING
 See also "SCORCHERS"
 Boardman--Gilded p69-70
 Cable--American p268-269, 277-
  278, 323
 Davidson--Life (2) p64-67
 Dulles--History p194-196
 Furnas--Americans p809-812
 Life--Reaching (8) p44, 49-51, 56
 Partridge--As p153
 Peck--Nineteenth n. p.
 Ross--Taste p89-90, 92-93
 Train--Story p327, 344-345
 Walker--Every. p56, 183-184
 -1876
  Hilton--Way p95-97
 -1890
  Amer. Her. --90's p11
 , Big-wheeled
  Wilson--Vanish. p185
 -"Columbia" type, 1880
  Woodward--Way p329-330
 -Girls
  Harris--Land p270
 -Pedespeed and decemtuple
  Life--Steel (7) p31
 -Velocipedes, 1880's
  Peck--Nineteenth n. p.
 -Women
  Dulles--History p266-267
BIDDLE, NICHOLAS
 Amer. Her. --New (5) p400-401,
  E154
 Boardman--Jackson. p18-20
 Boardman--Virginia p73-74
 Carman--History (1) p437-439,
  442
 Kraus--U. S. p361-362, 364, 368
 Life--Sweep (4) p36, 38-41
 Morris--Ency. p155, 173-174, 505
 200 Years (1) p230, 232-234
 -Biography
  Morris--Ency. p636

BIDWELL, JOHN
 -Bidwell-Bartleson migration to
 California, 1842
  Ridge--America's p477-482
 -"The first emigrant train to
 California"
  Jones--Shaping p112-136
 -"Life in California before gold
 discovery"
  Jones--Shaping p91-111
BIERCE, AMBROSE GWINETT
 -Biography
  Amer. Her. --New (12)
  p E410-411
BIERSTADT, ALBERT
 Amer. Her. --New (6) p E192-193
 Hine--American p293-294, 296,
 298, 330
 Reader's--Story p380
BIG BETHEL, VIRGINIA
 Holzman--Stormy p58-59
"BIG FOUR" (railroad magnates)
 See also CROCKER, CHARLES;
 HOPKINS, MARK; HUNTING-
 TON, COLLIS P.; STANFORD,
 LELAND
 Brown--Westerners p171, 176-177
 Johnson--Pictorial p134
 -Views of John L. Davie
  Lewis--Big p370-376, 379-384
"BIG TREE" (Indian). See
 ADOEETE (Indian)
BIGELOW, ALBERT
 , on Samuel Clemens
  Angle--American p429-431
BIGELOW, ELLEN
 -Trip on Great Lakes, 1835
  Angle--American p196-199
BIGELOW, HENRY W.
 Brown--Westerners p118-119, 132
BIGELOW PAPERS. See LOWELL,
 JAMES RUSSELL
BIGOTRY. See INTOLERANCE
BILLIARD ROOMS
 Lynes--Domestic. p244
BILLINGS, WILLIAM
 Chase--America's p139-145
BILLINGTON, RAY A.
 , on disappearance of frontier
  Miers--American p253-258
"BILLY THE KID" (William H.
 Bonney)
 Lewis--It p101-119
 Randel--Centennial p145-146
 Reader's--Story p172
"BILTMORE HOUSE" (Vanderbilt
 home, Asheville, S.C.)
 Lynes--Taste. p121-122, 131, 144,

211
 Vanderbilt--Living p128-129
BIMELER (BAUMELER), Joseph
 Michael
 Tyler--Freedom's p129-130
BIMETALLISM
 Keller--Affairs p193-195, 381
 Life--Reaching (8) p86-88, 106
BINDING AND CRADLING
 Tunis--Frontier p78
BINGHAM, GEORGE CALEB
 Amer. Her. --New (5) p E154-155
 Boardman--Jackson. p154
 Bode--Anatomy p64, 73-75
 Hine--American p292
 Larkin--Art p218-220; see also
 index p517
 Life--New (5) p18-29
 -Paintings of Western politics
  Butterfield--Amer. p118-121
BINGHAM, JOHN ARMOR
 Meredith--World p228-230, 232-
 233
BIOGRAPHY (literature)
 Mott--Golden p96-97
 -Autobiography
  Mott--Golden p96-97
BIRCH, JIM
 Tunis--Frontier p135, 137, 139
BIRD, ROBERT MONTGOMERY, DR.
 Boardman--Jackson. p158-159
 -"The Gladiator"
  Bode--Anatomy p6-7, 13-16
"BIRD WOMAN" (Indian). See
 SACAJAWEA (Indian)
BIRDS AND FOWL
 See also names of types
 Bartlett--New p248-252
 -Destruction of species
  Bartlett--New p248-252
 -Imported pests
  Bartlett--New p248
 -New York state
  Van Wagenen--Golden p97
 , Toy
  McClinton--Antiques. See
  index p345
BIRKBECK, MORRIS
 Boardman--Jackson. p61
 -"Englishmen settle the Illinois
 prairie," 1818
  Ridge--America's p280-281
 -"A frontiersman settles in
 Illinois," 1843
  Davie--Profile p146
 -"The great migration of 1816"
  Ridge--America's p274-276
 , on Westward journey

Commager--Heritage p259-261
BIRNEY, JAMES GILLESPIE
Amer. Her. --New (6) p E193
Boardman--Jackson. p33-34, 37-
38, 117-118
Carman--History (1) p530-532,
596, 784
BIRTH CONTROL
-Views of Robert Dale Owen
Cable--American p194-195,
225-228
BIRTHDAYS
Schwartz--When p119-120
BISHOP, ABRAHAM
, on Republicanism
Walker--Reform p36-45
BISHOP, NATHANIEL
Randel--Centennial p41-45
BISHOP, W. H.
-"Story-paper literature"
Trachtenberg--Demo. p286-
298
BISHOP HILL COLONY (Illinois)
Tyler--Freedom's p132-138
BISON. See BUFFALOES
BISSELL, GEORGE H.
Portraits--Americans p4, 6-7
"BITTERS"
Furnas--Americans p904-905
BLACK, ALEXANDER
-Moving pictures
Wilson--American p296-297
"BLACK BALL" PACKETS
Reader's--Story p176-177
"BLACK CODES" (Negro laws)
Boardman--Civil p78-79
Boardman--Virginia p125-126
Carman--History (1) p726-728
Furnas--Americans p520, 750-
751
Keller--Affairs p63, 203-204,
208
Life--Union (6) p113-114
Morris--Ency. p247
Reader's--Story p131
"BLACK FRIDAY" (Sept. 24, 1869)
Harlow--Story p346
Morris--Ency. p250
"BLACK HAWK" (Kiowa-Apache;
Sauk and Fox Indians)
Amer. Her. --Indian p202, 210, 247
Andrews--Indian leaders p74-77,
145
Boardman--Jackson. p71
Life--Sweep (4) p43
Reader's--Story p85
BLACK HAWK WAR
Amer. Her. --Indians p202, 210, 247

Amer. Her. --New (6) p E193
Bonte--America p103
Carman--History (1) p376-377
Ridge--America's p286-289
Tunis--Frontier p99
-Battle of Bad Axe
Collins--Story p197
BLACK HILLS (South Dakota)
See also "HOLY WILDERNESS"
, Capital in
Watkins--Gold p109
-Gold discoveries
Watkins--Gold p107-108, 112-
113
-Life
Watkins--Gold p114-115
-Population
Watkins--Gold p114
"BLACK KETTLE" (Cheyenne
Indian)
Amer. Her. --Indians p345
Andrews--Indian leaders p118-
120, 124-125, 150
Boardman--Civil p107-108
Brown--Westerners p195-196,
198, 201, 236
"BLACK PARLIAMENT," 1873
-Views of James S. Pike
Angle--American p346-349
"BLACK PENNY," 1869
Collins--Story p241
BLACKENSTOE, VIRGINIA. See
REID, VIRGINIA
BLACKFOOT INDIANS
Amer. Her. --Indians p262-263,
339-340, 349, 355
Andrews--Indians p73, 82, 128,
147, 166
Billington--Far p49, 53-56, 59-60,
63
Boardman--Jackson. p64, 74-75
Brown--Westerners p50, 55-56,
77, 93
DeVoto--Year p54, 60, 63, 244,
294, 296, 485, 493
Gilbert--Trail. p33, 49, 56, 60, 72,
95, 134-135, 150-151
, and George Catlin
Gilbert--Trail. p142-151
, and John Colter
Reader's--Story p164
BLACKS. See NEGROES; SLAVES
AND SLAVERY
BLACKSMITHS
Wilson--Vanish. p148
, Country town (village smithies)
Partridge--As p34
-Pennsylvania, 1840's

Nation in motion p81
BLACKWELL, ANTOINETTE BROWN
    Boardman--Civil p188
    Gurko--Ladies p131-134, 139, 159,
        161, 165, 192-193, 196, 204
    Tyler--Freedom's p433
BLACKWELL, ELIZABETH, DR.
    Adelman--Famous p219-220
    Dannett--Noble p54-57, 59, 373
    Dolin--Great p120-125
    Heath--Women (4) p14
    Macksey--Book p68
    Neidle--America's p189-201
    Reader's--Story p295, 436
    Sochen--Herstory p104-106
    Tyler--Freedom's p432-433,
        437, 451, 453
    Warren--Pictorial p77-79, 104
    Young--Women p9, 20, 72-76
    -Biography
        Young--Women p367-368
BLACKWELL, EMILY
    Neidle--America's p189, 191,
        193, 196, 198-200
    Tyler--Freedom's p432-433
BLACKWELL, MRS. HENRY,
    See STONE, LUCY
BLACKWELL FAMILY
    Gurko--Ladies. See index p322
BLAINE, JAMES GILLESPIE
    Boardman--Gilded p20-21, 23-
        24, 34-36
    Butterfield--Amer. p236-237
    Carman--History (2). See
        index p. iii
    Dulles--United p127, 131, 135-
        137, 140
    Harlow--Story p456-457
    Holzman--Stormy p217-219
    Keller--Affairs. See index
        p609
    Life--Steel (7) p12-16, 26-27
    Linton--Bicentennial p213, 219-
        221, 225, 230, 233
    Morris--Ency. p252, 255, 257,
        282-284
    Randel--Centennial p217-220,
        242-245
    -Biography
        Morris--Ency. p636
    -Latin-American policy, 1889
        Morris--Ency. p283-284
    -Tribute to James A. Garfield
        Hurd--Treasury p112-113
    -Views on, by Robert G. Inger-
        soll
        Hurd--Treasury p126-129

BLAIR, FRANCIS P.
    Amer. Her. --New (5) p E155
BLAIR, MONTGOMERY
    Holzman--Stormy p60-61
BLAKE, LILLIE DEVEREAUX
    Adelman--Famous p205
BLANCHARD, THOMAS
    Reader's--Story p258
BLAND, JAMES A.
    Howard--Our p643-644
    , and "Carry me back to old
        Virginny"
        Kryther--Sampler p158-176
BLAND, RICHARD PARKS ("Silver
    Dick")
    Life--Reaching (8) p88, 106
"BLAND-ALLISON" ACT, 1878
    Boardman--Gilded p19-20
    Dulles--United p73-74
    Harlow--Story p451-452, 462-464
    Morris--Ency. p254
BLASPHEMY. See PROFANITY
BLATT, JOSEPHINE
    Macksey--Book p258
BLAVATSKY, HELENA PETROVNA
    Neidle--America's p67-70
BLENNERHASSET, HARMAN
    , and Aaron Burr
        Commager--Heritage p218-229
BLIND
    Hilton--Way p88
    Hunt--Life p199
    -Education
        Boorstin--Americans p45
        Tyler--Freedom's p296-298
BLINN, HOLBROOK
    Blum--Stage Profile 65
BLISS, PHILIP PAUL
    Lewis--It p123-141
BLIZZARDS. See SNOW
BLOCKS, CHILDREN'S
    McClinton--Antiques p243-248
BLOOD, JAMES
    Furnas--Americans p643-645
BLOOD TRANSFUSIONS
    Hilton--Way p81-82
BLOOMER, AMELIA JENKS
    Amer. Her. --New (6) p493,
        p E193
    Furnas--Americans p493
    Gurko--Ladies p119-120, 142, 144-
        147, 150-153, 157-158, 162, 171
    Life--Sweep (4) p65
    Macksey--Book p266
    Ross--Taste p174, 177
    White--American p43-45
BLOOMERS

Furnas--Americans p492-494
Ross--Taste p173-174
Tyler--Freedom's p441-442
BLUE-LAWS. See SABBATARIAN-
ISM
BLUE RIDGE MOUNTAINS
Boardman--Virginia p93
BLY, NELLIE, pseud. (ELIZA-
BETH COCHRANE)
Amer. Her. --90's p10
Boardman--Gilded p177-178
Life--Reaching (8) p37
Macksey--Book p190
Portraits--Americans p52-53
White--American p121-123
-Biography
Amer. Her. --New (11) p E377
B'NAI B'RITH
Boardman--Civil p186-187
BOARD GAMES
McClinton--Antiques p225-242
BOARDING HOUSES
Cable--American p108, 188-189
Lynes--Domestic. p39-49
Ross--Taste p301
, in country
Partridge--As p173-177
-Views of Frances Trollope
Trollope--Domestic. See
index p. ii
-Women
Lynes--Domestic. p42-43,
45-47
BOARDS OF CHARITY
Keller--Affairs p124-125
BOARDS OF TRADE
Keller--Affairs p414-416, 422
BOAS, FRANZ
Portraits--Americans p77
-Biography
Morris--Ency. p636-637
-Statistical questionnaire
Portraits--Americans p77
BOASTFULNESS. See BRAGGARTS
BOAT RACING
Boardman--Jackson. p179
Randel--Centennial p203, 320-321
BOATS AND BOATING
See also CANAL BOATS; FLAT-
BOATS; SHIPS AND SHIPPING;
etc.
Dulles--History p58, 75, 357
Hilton--Way p104
Lynes--Taste. p89-94, 125-126
-Boatmen
Wilson--Early p141-143
-Boat-yards

Furnas--Americans p296-297
BODIE MINES
Watkins--Gold p163-164
BODMER, CARL (KARL)
Amer. Her. --New (5) p E155
Boardman--Jackson. p153-154
Gilbert--Trail. p12-13, 131-135
Hine--American p286
BOGARDUS, JAMES
Boardman--Jackson. p165
Portraits--Americans p43
BOISE CITY, IDAHO
Watkins--Gold p87-89
BOISSEVAIN, CHARLES
, on America, 1880
Handlin--This p333-343
BOK, EDWARD
Carman--History (2) p373-374
Harlow--Story p430
Lynes--Taste. p172, 175-178, 221
BOLIVAR, SIMON
, and first American League of
Nations
Harlow--Story p223-224
BOLLES, ALBERT S.
Randel--Centennial p175-176, 192,
345, 379
BOLTON, SARAH T.
Furnas--Americans p554-555
"BONANZA" FARMS AND TOWNS
Furnas--Americans p685-686
Hine--American p164-165, 167, 214
Wilson--American p239
BONAPARTE, JOSEPH
, on life in America
White--American p22-23
BOND, CARRIE JACOBS
Bonte--America p119
BOND, WILLIAM C.
Boardman--Jackson. p167
BONNER, ROBERT
Bode--Anatomy p257-258
Furnas--Americans p559-560
BONNETS. See HATS AND HAT-
TERS
BONNEVILLE, BENJAMIN E.,
CAPTAIN
Boardman--Jackson. p64-65
Commager--Heritage p508-511
Gilbert--Trail. p94-95
BONNEY, WILLIAM (BORNEY).
See "BILLY THE KID"
BONUS BILL, 1817
-Veto
Morris--Ency. p155
"BOODLING" (political favors)
-Chicago, Ill., 1894

Cook--City p208-212
BOOK COLLECTING
-Children's books
McClinton--Antiques p102-115
BOOK PUBLISHING. See PUB-
LISHERS AND PUBLISHING
"BOOKMAN" (periodical)
Mott--Golden p204-206
BOOKS AND READING
See also ART--Books and read-
ing; BEST SELLERS; CHIL-
DREN'S BOOKS AND READ-
ING; DIME NOVELS; LIBRAR-
IES; LITERATURE; POETS
AND POETRY; TEXTBOOKS
Bode--Anatomy. See index p286
Walker--Every. p24, 167-169
Wright--Every. p237-239
-1880's-1890's
Dulles--United p106-107
-"Cheap book" libraries, 1873-
1893
Mott--Golden p151-155, 191
-Chronology of books most
widely read, 1800-1899
Hart--Popular p304-310
-Civil war
Hart--Popular p151-153
-Detective story, first, 1841
Robertson--Book p48
-Dried flowers, 1876
Hilton--Way p46
-Economics
Life--Reaching (8) p91-92
-Family reading
Mott--Golden p102-103
-Gift books
Hart--Popular p88-89
, Home influence of
Hart--Popular p85-105
-House building
Lynes--Domestic. p76-81
-"How-to" manuals
Cable--American p150-151
, Increase of
Bode--Anatomy p109-110
-Kentucky
Wright--Culture p67-71, 75
-Medicine, for women
Warren--Pictorial p126-127
, of social inquiry, 1880's-
1890's
Hart--Popular p167-179
, Phonographed
Harris--Land p46-62
-Public taste
Hunt--Life p147
-Romances

Hart--Popular p79-80, 202-204
-"Puritanian"
Hart--Popular p192-194
, Rural reading
Hunt--Life p104-105
-Sports and games, 1880's
Peck--Nineteenth, n. p.
-Subscription books
Hart--Popular p151-153
-Travel books
Bode--Anatomy p222-235, 252,
254, 271
Jones--Age p263-264
-Post Civil war
Jones--Age p264-278
-Value, manufactured, 1840-1860
Bode--Anatomy p116
-West, popularity in
Wright--Culture p208-209
, Women's
Warren--Pictorial p128-130
BOOKSHOPS AND BOOKSELLERS
Bode--Anatomy p110-112
Furnas--Americans p734-736
"BOOMERS"
Dulles--United p50-51
BOONE, DANIEL
Amer. Her. --New (6) p E194
Hine--American p66-68, 243, 274,
292, 322, 325
"BOOSTERS"
See also COLLEGES AND UNI-
VERSITIES
Bartlett--New p430-431
Boorstin--Americans p49, 113-168
, in literature
Boorstin--Americans p343
, in talk
Boorstin--Americans p296-298
, of nation
Boorstin--Americans p389
BOOTH, EDWIN THOMAS
Boardman--Civil p166
Meredith--World p36-41
Viewpoints p168
Walker--Every. p158-159
-Biography
Amer. Her. --New (4) p E375-
376
Morris--Ency. p637
BOOTH, EVANGELINE
Neidle--America's p79-84
BOOTH, JOHN WILKES
Amer. Her. --New (8) p E264
Butterfield--Amer. p180
Harlow--Story p329
Jones--Shaping p205-208
Life--New (5) p62-63, 79, 108

Life--Union (6) p109-110
Meredith--World p218-224
-Accomplices
   Butterfield--Amer. p182-183
BOOTH, JUNIUS BRUTUS
Meredith--World p37-38, 40
BOOTH, MARY LOUISE
Adelman--Famous p200-201
Macksey--Book p265
BOOTH FAMILY
Boardman--Jackson. p157
Boardman--Virginia p145-146
Life--New (5) p62-63
Marzio--Nation p412-413
BOOTS AND SHOES. See SHOES
BORDEN, GAIL
Boardman--Civil p148
Portraits--Americans p112-113
BORDEN, LIZZIE ANDREW
Boardman--Gilded p176-177
Harris--Land p191, 203-214
BORDER DISPUTES AND SETTLE-
MENTS
Life--Sweep (4) p86-87, 89-91,
101-104, 113
"BORDER RUFFIANS" (Kansas,
1856)
Boardman--Civil p15
Morris--Ency. p220
BOSSISM. See POLITICS--
Bossism
BOSTON, MASSACHUSETTS
Brooks--Flower. p1-20
Davidson--Life (2) p110-111
Furnas--Americans. See index
   p979
Handlin--This. See index p579
Hunt--Life. See index p289
Life--Sweep (4) p10-11, 26, 30-
31, 60-61
Mussey--Old p27, 38-45, 124-125
Wright--Every. p122-124
-1833
   Cable--American p103
, as port, 1830-1840
   Life--Growing p42-43
-Common
   Ross--Taste p147-148, 153
-Music Hall
   Furnas--Americans p659-661
-Population, location of, 1850
   Cook--City p57
-Society
   Cable--American p280
   Hunt--Life p70-71
-Temple School
   Tyler--Freedom's p246-248
-Theater. See THEATER--

Boston
-Trinity Church. See TRINITY
CHURCH--Boston
-West
   Brooks--Flower. p374-387
"BOSTON GROUP" (women reform-
ers)
Gurko--Ladies p225-228, 232-235,
246, 282
BOSTON MANUFACTURING COM-
PANY
Wilson--American p88-89
BOSTON MERCHANTS' EXCHANGE
Mussey--Old p105
BOSTON PUBLIC LIBRARY
Larkin--Art p299-300
-Board of directors, 1894
   Amer. Her. --90's p50-51
BOSTON WEEKLY MAGAZINE
Grimsted--Melodrama p37-38, 41-
42, 96-97
BOTANY AND BOTANISTS
Boardman--Jackson. p168-169
Reader's--Story p307
-1818-1860
   Morris--Ency. p531
BOTTA, ANNE CHARLOTTE LYNCH
Adelman--Famous p178
BOTUME, ELIZABETH HYDE
Young--Women p304-305
-Biography
   Young--Women p368
BOUCHERVILLE, THOMAS VER-
CHERES DE
, on Detroit surrender, 1812
   Angle--American p178-179
BOUCICAULT, DION
Marzio--Nation p412-413
Morris--Ency. p591
BOUDINOT, ELIAS
Boardman--Virginia p173-174
BOUNTIES
-Civil war
   Carman--History (1) p647-648
BOURGET, CHARLES JOSEPH PAUL
, on America, 1893
   Handlin--This p370-383
, on football, 1895
   Davie--Profile p388
BOWDITCH, NATHANIEL
Boardman--Virginia p91
Nye--Cultural p85
Our literary p46
, as navigator
   Wilson--American p46-47
, on meteorites, 1807
   Wilson--American p46
BOWEL, ABEL
Mussey--Old p127

BOWERY THEATRE (N. Y. City)
Dulles--History p103, 105, 213-214
BOWIE, JAMES
America's Hist. p389
-Biography
Amer. Her. --New (7) p E227-228
"BOWLEG BILL"
Reader's--Story p172
BOWLES, SAMUEL
-"San Francisco, city of entrepreneurs"
Cook--City p29-32
BOWLING
Dulles--History p150-156, 220
Partridge--As p152
BOXING
Boardman--Civil p201
Boardman--Gilded p174-175
Boardman--Jackson. p179
Davidson--Life (2) p33
Downey--Our p303-315
Dulles--History p144-147, 171-172, 226-228, 352-353
Dulles--United p100
Handlin--This p102-103, 326, 373-375
Hilton--Way p109
Jones--Age p344-345
Life--Hunt p181
Life--New (5) p60
Life--Reaching (8) p37-38
Reader's--Story p487-488
Walker--Every. p151-153, 244-245
-Sullivan vs. Corbett, 1892
Angle--American p414-417
BOYCOTTS
Keller--Affairs p405-406
BOYD, BELLE
Warren--Pictorial p110
BOYNTON, PAUL, CAPTAIN
Hilton--Way p108-109
BRACE, CHARLES LORING
Cable--American p293-294, 296
BRADBURY, JOHN
Gilbert--Trail. p126-127
-"The Ohio constitution and backwoods democracy," 1819
Ridge--America's p248-251
BRADBURY, WILLIAM BATCH-ELDER
Chase--America's p162
Howard--Our p144-146
BRADLEY, JOSEPH P.
Amer. Her. --New (8) p E264-265

BRADSTREET, JOHN M.
Portraits--Americans p12
BRADWELL, MYRA
Macksey--Book p125
Sochen--Herstory p103-104
BRADY, JAMES BUCHANAN ("DIAMOND JIM")
Amer. Her. --New (11) p E376
Amer. Her. --90's p97-98, 122, 124-125
Jones--Age p121
BRADY, MATHEW B.
Amer. Her. --New (8) p E265
Meredith--World p2-7, 239-240
BRAGG, BRAXTON, General
Amer. Her. --New (8) p E265-266
Boardman--Civil p48-49
Jordan--Civil p118, 122, 138, 140-141, 143, 181
Life--Union (6) p13, 18, 39, 60-61, 63, 81-84
Young--Women p234-235, 237-239, 243, 312
, in Kentucky, 1862
Pratt--Civil p30, 32
BRAGGARTS
-Views of Frances Trollope
Trollope--Domestic. See index under Boastfulness p. ii
"BRAHMINS"
Alden--Pioneer p212-214
BRAMAH, JOSEPH
Amer. Her. --New (5) p E155
BRANCH, JOHN
, and Eaton affair
Phillips--That p59, 75, 84, 89, 91, 95-96, 105, 113, 117, 127, 129
BRANCH, MRS. JOHN
, and Eaton affair
Phillips--That p59, 67, 74, 84, 91, 98
BRANDING IRONS
Tunis--Frontier p146
-"The wild freedom of the mountain men"
Treasury Amer. p156-161
"BRANKS" (punishment)
Wilson--Folkways p220-221
BRANNAN, SAMUEL ("SAM")
Amer. Her. --New (6) p E194
BRAYTON, GEORGE
-Patent for first engine to use petroleum as fuel
Wilson--American p322
"BREAD RIOT" (Richmond, Va.)
Dowdey--Experiment p272-273
BREADS AND BISCUITS

Van Wagenen--Golden p66-69
, Baking of
  Wilson--Vanish. p103
-Dough troughs
  Tunis--Frontier p80
-Old Northwest
  Tunis--Frontier p80
"THE BREAKERS" (Cornelius
Vanderbilt palace, Newport, R. I.)
  Life--Steel (7) p148-151
  Vanderbilt--Living p26
BREAKFASTS
  Furnas--Americans p900-901
  Langdon--Everyday p186-187
  Partridge--As p127
  Walker--Every. p225-226
-1830's
  Train--Story p274
-First cereal, 1893
  Robertson--Book p27
BRECKENRIDGE, JOHN CABELL
  Boardman--Civil p24-25
  Carman--History (1) p629, 632-
  633, 725, 785, 787, 791
  Dowdey--Experiment p122-123,
  349, 356, 390-391, 403-404, 414-
  428
  Kraus--U. S. p478-479
  Life--New (5) p90, 92-94
-Biography
  Amer. Her. --New (7) p E228
BREEN, PATRICK
, on Donner party, 1846
  Angle--American p229-231
-"The tragedy of the Donner
party, " 1847
  Ridge--America's p484-486
"BREEZEWAYS"
, Log-cabin
  Lynes--Domestic. p27
BREMER, FREDRIKA
, on America, 1849
  Handlin--This p219-231
"BRENTANO'S LITERARY EMPORI-
UM" (N. Y. City, 1870)
  Ross--Taste p44
BREWERIES. See DISTILLERIES
AND BREWERIES
BRICKS
  Van Wagenen--Golden p204, 206-
  209
-"Milwaukee cream"
  Drury--Midwest p69
BRIDGER, JAMES ("JIM")
  Amer. Her. --New (6) p E194-195
  Billington--Far p44, 54-55, 57-60,
  103-104, 199
  Boardman--Virginia p108

Brown--Westerners. See index
  p285
Gilbert--Trail. p47, 61, 64, 72, 82,
  214, 217
Hine--American p52-53
Reader's--Story p172
Ross--Heroines p60-61, 77
Tunis--Frontier p113, 117-118,
  120, 123
-Meeting with Mormons
  DeVoto--Year p447-448
BRIDGES
See also names of bridges
  Boardman--Civil p144-145
  Boardman--Gilded p144-145
  Boardman--Virginia p89-91
  Davidson--Life (2) p206
  Handlin--This p156, 161
  Van Wagenen--Golden p146-153
-Builders
  Langdon--Everyday p60, 62
  Marzio--Nation p192-195
-California, 1856-1892
  Nation in motion p58
-Connecticut, 1898
  Nation in motion p59
, Covered
  Train--Story p333
  Wilson--Vanish. p166-167
-District of Columbia, 1853
  Nation in motion p59
-Georgia, 1886-1895
  Nation in motion p60-61
-Illinois, 1895
  Nation in motion p61
-Indiana, 1840
  Nation in motion p61-62
-Iowa, 1857
  Nation in motion p62
-Maryland, 1819-1840
  Nation in motion p62-63
-Massachusetts, 1840-1886
  Nation in motion p63
-Michigan, 1867-1887
  Nation in motion p64-65
-Missouri, 1862-1871
  Nation in motion p65
-New Hampshire, 1852
  Nation in motion p65-66
-New Jersey, 1870-1885
  Nation in motion p66
-New York, 1867
  Nation in motion p66
-Niagara
  Marzio--Nation p195
-North Carolina, 1891
  Nation in motion p66
-Ohio, 1870-1877

Nation in motion p67
-Oklahoma, 1888, 19th century
   Nation in motion p67
-Pennsylvania, 1807-1889
   Nation in motion p69-70
-Puerto Rico, 1854
   Nation in motion p71
, Railroad
   -Alabama, 1869-1872
     Nation in motion p91
   -Arizona, 1890
     Nation in motion p91
   -Arkansas, 1873
     Nation in motion p92
   -Florida, 1890's
     Nation in motion p92
   -New Mexico, 1898
     Nation in motion p93
   -New York, 1888
     Nation in motion p93
   -North Carolina, 1840's-1857
     Nation in motion p93-94
   -Oklahoma, 1889-1890
     Nation in motion p94-95
   -Oregon, 1880
     Nation in motion p95
   -Pennsylvania, 1882
     Nation in motion p95
   -Rhode Island, 1837
     Nation in motion p96
   -Tennessee, 1892
     Nation in motion p96
   -Utah, 1884
     Nation in motion p96
-Rhode Island, 1870-1895
   Nation in motion p71
-Vermont, 1852
   Nation in motion p71-72
-Virginia, 1810-1898
   Nation in motion p72-73
-West Virginia, 1815,c1890,1893
   Nation in motion p74
BRISBANE, ALBERT
  Boardman--Jackson. p123
BRISTOW, BENJAMIN
  Randel--Centennial p202-207, 220
BRISTOW, GEORGE FREDERICK
  Chase--America's p326-330
  Howard--Our p247-252
BROADAXES
  Tunis--Frontier p74-75
"BROADHORNS." See FLATBOATS
BROADSIDES
  -Poetry
    Nye--Unembar. p85-90, 113-
    114
  -Songs
    Grimsted--Notions p139-160

BRODIE, STEVE
  , and Brooklyn bridge
    White--American p115-117
"BROOK FARM"
  Alden--Pioneer p224
  Amer. Her. --New (6) p E195
  Boardman--Jackson.p124
  Borden--Portrait (1) p182-183
  Brooks--Flower. p228-251
  Carman--History (1) p529, 537, 540
  Furnas--Americans p500-501
  Harlow--Story p259
  Life--Sweep (4) p61-62
  Our literary p72-73
  Tyler--Freedom's p175-184
  -Goals
    200 Years (1) p299
  -Life
    -Views of Amy L. Reed
      Angle--American p268-271
    -Views of George William Cur-
    tis
      Tyler--Freedom's p182-183
BROOKLYN BRIDGE
  Boardman--Gilded p144-145
  Harlow--Story p434
  Keyes--Hope p275-276, 384-386
  Larkin--Art p283-284
  Marzio--Nation p195
  Mumford--Brown p97, 99-100, 102-
  103
  Viewpoints p116-117
  , and Augustus Roebling
    Life--Steel (7) p35, 44-45
  , and Steve Brodie
    White--American p115-117
  -Opening, 1883
    Collins--Story p256
BROOKLYN COLLEGIATE INSTI-
TUTE FOR YOUNG LADIES
  -Views of Frances Trollope
    Trollope--Domestic p340-342
BROOKS, JAMES
  Butterfield--Amer. p205
BROOKS, PHILLIPS
  Boardman--Civil p187-188
  -Biography
    Amer. Her. --New (11) p E376
    Morris--Ency. p638
BROOKS, PRESTON SMITH
  Butterfield--Amer. p147
  Furnas--Americans p530-531
  -Beating of Sen. Sumner
    See also SUMNER--BROOKS
    CONTROVERSY
    Harlow--Story p295
    Morris--Ency. p221
  -Biography

Amer. Her. --New p E228
BROTHELS. See PROSTITUTION
"BROTHERHOOD OF THE UNION"
Bode--Anatomy p167-168
Boorstin--Americans p381
BROUGHER, WILSE
Watkins--Gold p167-168
BROWN, ANTOINETTE. See
BLACKWELL, ANTOINETTE
BROWN
BROWN, "GRANDMOTHER." See
BROWN, MARIA D.
BROWN, HENRY COLLINS
, on life in New York City,
1890's
Angle--American p408-413
BROWN, HENRY KIRKE
Morris--Ency. p601
BROWN, J. ROSS
Watkins--Gold p72, 74-77, 130-
132, 163-224
-The Comstock Lode, 1861
Ridge--America's p538-541
BROWN, JOHN
America's Hist. p411, 413-415
Boardman--Civil p22-23
Davie--Profile p113-114
Keyes--Hope p248-249
Kraus--U.S. p453, 475-476
Reader's--Story p172
200 Years (1) p264, 277, 282-283,
285, 287-288
Young--Women p27-28, 31, 35, 38,
68, 300-302
-Biography
Amer. Her. --New (7) p E228-
229
-Execution
Collins--Story p207
Davie--Profile p114-117
-Views of David Hunter
Strother
Angle--American p299-301
-Harper's Ferry
Amer. Her. --New (7) p E241
America's Hist. p410-415
Andrews--Women p209-210
Angle--By p199-201
Borden--Portrait (1) p225-227
Butterfield--Amer. p154-155
Carman--History (1) p615-
616, 626-627
Collins--Story p207
Commager--Heritage p500-
501
Harlow--Story p297-298
Jordan--Civil p12, 16-17, 33,
104, 107

Keller--Affairs. See index
p617-618
Life--New (5) p69, 77-81, 86-87
Morris--Ency. p225
200 Years (1) p282-283, 285,
287-288
Tyler--Freedom's p541-542
Young--Women p29-30, 208-
210, 271, 300
-"Last speech," 1859
Angle--By p201-202
, on innocence and trial
Hurd--Treasury p84-86
BROWN, MARIA D. ("GRAND-
MOTHER")
, On Ohio life
Burner--America (1) p227-230
Commager--Heritage p279-289
BROWN, MOSES
Amer. Her. --New (5) p E155-
E156
Boardman--Virginia p69
BROWN, TABITHA
Case--Empire p191-202
"BROWN DECADES"
Mumford--Brown. See index
p259
BROWN UNIVERSITY
-Curriculum, 1833
Train--Story p289
BROWN VS. MARYLAND
Amer. Her. --New (5) p373, E156
BROWNE, CHARLES FARRAR.
See "WARD, ARTEMUS," pseud.
BROWNELL, KATHY
Amer. Her. --New (8) p E266
Young--Women p95, 111, 114-115,
118-125, 308
-Biography
Young--Women p368-369
BROWNING, ORVILLE
Life--New (5) p56
BROWNLOW, WILLIAM G.
Hart--Popular p114-116
Mott--Golden p165-167
BROWNSON, ORESTES A.
Amer. Her. --New (6) p E195
Brooks--Flower. p246-249, 268,
293
Our literary p73
Tyler--Freedom's p63-65; see
also index p592
, and Catholicism
Tyler--Freedom's p384-385
BRUCE, CATTON
, on Robert E. Lee
Miers--American p202-205
BRUNEL, MARC (BAMBARD, SIR)

Amer. Her. --New (5) p E156
BRUNEL, MARY BLACKMAR, DR.
Dannett--Noble p343-344
BRYAN, THOMAS JEFFERSON
Lynes--Taste. p42-44, 48, 56, 64
BRYAN, WILLIAM JENNINGS
Amer. Her. --New (10) p860
Amer. Her. --90's p132-138
Boardman--Gilded p181-184
Carman--History (2) p21, 225,
262-264, 289, 296
Collins--Story p275
Dulles--United p148-150
Harlow--Story p473-475
Keller--Affairs. See index
p610
Life--Reaching (8). See index
p172
Linton--Bicentennial. See index
p439
Morris--Ency. See index p741
200 Years (2) p92-94
Whitney--American p196, 211,
213, 221
-Biography
Amer. Her. --New (10) p890-
898
Morris--Ency. p638-639
-Campaign, 1896
Commager--Heritage p1032-
1036
-"Cross of Gold" (speech, 1896)
Butterfield--Amer. p270-271
Commager--Heritage p1028-
1032
Dulles--United p150-151
Harlow--Story p473
Heffner--Doc. p187-193
Hurd--Treasury p120-123
-Opinions
Butterfield--Amer. p272-273
-Views of Emma F. Goldman
Miers--American p229-234
-Views of Eric F. Goldman
Miers--Americans p229-234
-Views of G. W. Stevens
Angle--American p458-461
BRYANT, DAN
, and minstrels
Chase--America's p260, 268,
272-273, 275
BRYANT, EDWIN
DeVoto--Year. See index p514
BRYANT, WILLIAM CULLEN
Amer. Her. --New (6) p E195-196
Boardman--Jackson. p140
Boardman--Virginia p138-139
Morris--Ency. p566-567, 582

Nye--Unembar. p105-106
Our literary p36-40
Randel--Centennial p215-216, 360-
361, 363
Reader's--Story p410
-Biography
Morris--Ency. p639
BRYCE, JAMES
Bartlett--New p430-431
-"The American commonwealth:
Why great men are not chosen
presidents" (1890)
Amer. Her. --90's p81-82
-"Function of state governments"
(1896)
Davie--Profile p66
BUCHANAN, JAMES
Amer. Her. --New (7) p558
Boardman--Civil p16-17, 19-21
Borden--Portrait (1). See index
p238
Butterfield--Amer. p149
Carman--History (1). See index
p. iv
DeVoto--Year. See index p514
Harlow--Story p295-296, 300-302
Kraus--U. S. See index p. ii
Life--New (5). See index p156
Morris--Ency. See index p741
200 Years (1) p259, 281, 288, 342-
343
, and Eaton affair
Phillips--That p103, 157, 162,
170
, Biography
Amer. Her. --New (7) p E229-
230
Morris--Ency. p639-640
Whitney--American p127-132
-Cabinet
Carman--History (1). See
index p. iv
-Kansas problem
Treasury Amer. p216-223
-Presidency
Linton--Bicentennial p149-157
Reader's--Story p333
BUCHIGNANI, ANTONIO
, and Peggy Eaton
Phillips--That p161-162, 164-
166
BUCK, DUDLEY
Chase--America's p334-335
Howard--Our p592-595
"BUCKAROOS." See COWBOYS
"BUCKET SHOPS" (investment
gambling)
Keller--Affairs p415

BUCKETS
, Sap
 Van Wagenen--Golden p107-
 108
BUCKLES
, Children's shoe and knee
 McClinton--Antiques p63
BUCKLIN, SOPHRONIA E.
 Dannett--Noble p67, 95, 99, 168,
 234, 253-254, 282, 348, 376
BUCKNER, SIMON BOLIVAR
 Amer. Her. --New (8) p E266
BUCKWHEAT
 -New York state
 Van Wagenen--Golden p69-71
BUEL, DAVID, JR.
, on extension of suffrage
 Walker--Reform p54-55
, on N. Y. Constitutional conven-
 tion
 Walker--Reform p55-61
BUEL, JAMES W.
, on accidents in slums, N. Y.
 city, 1891
 Cook--City p243
, on agriculture, 1840
 Burner--America (1) p292-
 295
, on fortune tellers
 Cook--City p266
BUEL, JESSE
 Boardman--Jackson. p92
BUELL, DON CARLOS, GENERAL
 Amer. Her. --New (8) p E266-267
 Life--Union (6) p12-13, 35-38,
 60-61
 Young--Women p158-161, 164-165
BUENA VISTA BATTLE, 1847
 Colling--Story p200
 Life--Sweep (4) p104, 107-108,
 122-123
 Morris--Ency. p204
, Zachary Taylor at
 Amer. Her. --New (7) p570-
 571
"BUFFALO BILL." See CODY,
WILLIAM F.
BUFFALOES
 Andrews--Indian leaders p116
 Bartlett--New p110, 253, 256,
 260-262, 331
 Billington--Far p30-31, 51-52,
 102
 Boardman--Gilded p84-85, 94
 Boardman--Jackson. p72-73
 Brown--Westerners. See
 index p285
 Davidson--Life (2) p50-51

 Hine--American. See index p360
 Jones--Shaping p123-125
 Reader's--Story p170
 Tunis--Frontier p119-120, 144
 200 Years (2) p61, 67
 Van Wagenen--Golden p96-97
 -1840's
 DeVoto--Year. See index
 p514
 -Burning of, 1813
 Morris--Ency. p147
 -Extermination, 1893, by Hamlin
 Russell
 Ridge--America's p581-583
 -Hunters and hunting
 Andrews--Indians p159-165
 Treasury Amer. p292-297
 200 Years (1) p302
, for Russian Grand Duke, 1872
 White--American p92-98
 -"How they killed the buffalo, "
 by Wayne Gard
 Treasury Amer. p292-297
, Indian
 Amer. Her. --New (6) p500-
 501
 -"My last buffalo hunt, " 1861
 Andrews--Indians p159-165
, on Fremont expedition, 1843
 Davie--Profile p146-149
BUGBEE, M.
, on fire departments
 Cook--City p151-154
BUGGIES
 Train--Story p332
, Gasoline
 Train--Story p333-334
, Horses and
 Wilson--Vanish. p32
, Texas
 Drury--Midwest p90-91
BUGLE CALLS ("TAPS")
 Garrison--Lost p98-100
 Jordan--Civil p5, 184
BUILDERS AND BUILDING
 See also ARCHITECTURE;
 HOUSES; types of building ma-
 terials; names of buildings
 Boardman--Civil p172-173
 Furnas--Americans. See index
 (under Public buildings) p1004
 Larkin--Art. p154-158, 287-290,
 243-245
, High
 -Views of A. L. A. Himmel-
 wright, 1883
 Cook--City p100-101
 -Largest in world (Centennial)

Randel--Centennial p293
-Materials
  Boardman--Jackson. p165
, "on vanishing landscape"
  Treasury Amer. p364
-Skyscrapers, 1891, 1892, 1899
  Reader's--Story p241
-Wages
  Bode--Anatomy p39-40
BULFINCH, CHARLES
Harlow--Story p250
BULL, OLE BORNEMAN
Chase--America's p181-182
Howard--Our p200-202
Meredith--World p42-47
-Tour of America
  Bode--Anatomy p31-32
BULL RUN BATTLES
Amer. Her. --New (8) p636
Carman--History (1) p659, 661-662
Dannett--Noble p105-106, 109-110, 113, 121, 128, 132, 199, 205-206
Jordan--Civil. See index p212
Kraus--U.S. p487-491
Meredith--World p87-89
Morris--Ency. p232-237
Pratt--Civil p12-14
Viewpoints p76-77
Young--Women p117-126, 197-198
, and Stonewall Jackson
  Collins--Story p211
-Views of John G. Nicolay
  Angle--American p315-316
-Views of William Howard Russell
  Commager--Heritage p738-746
BULLBOATS
Tunis--Frontier p109-110
, Indian
  Marzio--Nation p162
"BULLWHACKERS"
Andrews--Indians p168
Billington--Far p274-276
BUNAU-VARILLA, PHILIPPE
-Biography
  Amer. Her. --New (12) p E411-412
BUNNELL, L. H.
-"Discovery and naming of Yosemite," 1851
  Davie--Profile p158-159
BUNNER, HENRY C.
Our literary p183
BUNYAN, PAUL
Reader's--Story p172

BURBANK, LUTHER
America's--Hist. p559
Boardman--Gilded p123
Reader's--Story p116
BURCHARD, SAMUEL
Butterfield--Amer. p241
BUREAU OF FREEDMEN, REFUGEES, AND ABANDONED LANDS
Keller--Affairs p13, 208-209, 219, 223
BURIALS
See also CEMETERIES; DEATHS; FUNERALS
Schwartz--When p180
, Premature
  Cable--American p175
BURK, MARTHA CANNARY. See "CALAMITY JANE"
BURLEND, REBECCA
Neidle--America's p97-98
BURLESQUE
See also DRAMA--Farce
Dulles--History p100, 117, 123, 217, 306-307
Grimsted--Melodrama p105, 237-240
Walker--Every. p164
-1840's
  Boardman--Jackson. p177-178
-1870's
  Blum--Theatre p20
-1890's
  Dulles--United p99
BURLINGAME, ANSON
Furnas--Americans p530-531
BURLINGAME TREATY (with China, 1868)
Hine--American p217
BURNETT, FRANCES ELIZA HODGSON
Adelman--Famous p270-271
Furnas--Americans p608-610
BURNETT, PETER H.
-"The 1843 migration; organizing the caravan"
  Ridge--America's p454-455
-"Propaganda for Oregon,"
Edward H. Lenox
  Ridge--America's p453-454
BURNHAM, DANIEL
-Biography
  Amer. Her. --New (12) p E412-413
BURNS, ANTHONY
-Fugitive slave case
  Commager--Heritage p494-499
BURNS, ROBERT
-Eulogy by Ralph Waldo Emerson

Hurd--Treasury p87-89
BURNSIDE, AMBROSE E., GEN-
ERAL
Jordan--Civil p107-109, 115, 120,
141, 191, 196
Life--Union (6) p12, 57-59, 96-97
Young--Women p50, 95, 125, 192,
210, 216-219, 234, 246, 308
BURR, AARON
Boardman--Virginia p13-14, 27-
32
Butterfield--Amer. p33, 42-43,
45
Carman--History (1) p311, 324,
327-329
Garrison--Lost p109-111
Harlow--Story p164-165, 171
Kraus--U. S. p307-308
Life--Growing. p41; see also
index p172
Wright--Every. p50-51
-Address to Army
Collins--Story p171
-at Blennerhasset Island
Commager--Heritage p218-
221
-Biography
Morris--Ency. p640
-Duel with Hamilton, 1804
Alden--Pioneer p150-151
Angle--American p143-144
Collins--Story p170
Life--Growing (3) p81-82, 85
Morris--Ency. p133
-Trial
Morris--Ency. p135
-Views of Washington Irving
Angle--American p144-146
BURR, THEODOSIA (THEODOSIA
BURR ALSTON)
Boardman--Virginia p31-32
Peacock--Famous p18-38
BURRITT, ELIHU
Boardman--Jackson. p131
Kraus--U. S. p388
Tyler--Freedom p346, 419-422
BURROUGHS, JOHN
, on Walt Whitman
Angle--American p428-429
BUSHNELL, HORACE
Boardman--Jackson. p134
Randel--Centennial p457-458
-"Our obligations to the dead"
Trachtenburg--Demo. p36-50
BUSINESS
See also COMMERCE; CRAFTS
AND CRAFTSMANSHIP: SHOPS
AND SHOPKEEPERS: TRADE;

types of business
Handlin--This p128, 141, 194, 239,
244, 262, 273, 279, 349
Life--Sweep (4) p8, 10, 20, 36-37,
47
-1850-1875
Boardman--Civil p133-137
-1876
Randel--Centennial. See index
p466
-1877-1890
Life--Steel (7). See index
p156
-1890's
Life--Reaching (8). See index
p172
, and culture
Lynes--Taste. p20, 42, 62-63
, and politics
Life--Union (6) p150-151
Wilson--American p220-221
, and Spanish-American war
Hollingsworth--Amer. p51-58
-Contributions to "big business"
Harlow--Story p397-398
, Post Civil war
Harlow--Story p381-398
Partridge--As p90-91
-Procedures
Wilson--Folkways p156-181
-Regulation, private and public
Carman--History (2) p84-129
Harlow--Story p396-397
, Sanctified
Hart--Population p160-161
BUSINESS CYCLES
Morris--Ency. p508-510
Reader's--Story p285
BUSINESS DEPRESSIONS
See also PANIC OF
Boardman--Civil p135-136
Boardman--Virginia p75-77
Whitney--American. See index
p362
-1802-1897
Morris--Ency. p508
-1873
Hine--American p164, 170, 217,
253, 258
-1893
Boardman--Gilded p55-56, 66,
88
Hine--American p189, 258
Reader's--Story p285
BUSINESSMEN
, as American institution
Boorstin--Americans p115-123
, Versatility of

Boorstin--Americans p14-15,
17-18, 26, 117-118, 123
-West
Hine--American. See index
p360
BUTCHER SHOPS
Wilson--Vanish. p134
BUTCHERING
-Use of products, 1876
Hilton--Way p159-160
BUTLER, ANDREW PICKENS
-Biography
Amer. Her. --New (7) p E230
BUTLER, BENJAMIN FRANKLIN
("BEAST")
Amer. Her. --New (8) p E267
Boardman--Civil p44-45
Butterfield--Amer. p224
Dowdey--Experiment p444
Holzman--Stormy. See index
p272
Keller--Affairs. See index
p610
BUTLER, JAMES
Watkins--Gold p167-168
BUTLER, NICHOLAS MURRAY
-Biography
Morris--Ency. p640
BUTLER, SARAH HILDRETH
Holzman--Stormy. See index
p273
BUTLER, THOMAS
-"Pigtail" controversy
White--American p17-19
BUTLER FAMILY
Holzman--Stormy. See index
p272-273
BUTTE, MONTANA
Bartlett--New p263, 266
BUTTE MINES, MONTANA
Watkins--Gold p92-93
BUTTER
Handlin--This p110, 114-115, 117
-Sculpture
Furnas--Americans p636-637
BUTTERFIELD, DANIEL
Garrison--Lost p98-100
BUTTERFIELD, JAMES AUSTIN
Howard--Our p645-646
BUTTERFIELD, JOHN
Brown--Westerners p143-152
Hine--American p140-143
Tunis--Frontier p139-141
-The Adams papers--"Whatever
you write, preserve"
Treasury Amer. p124-134
BUTTERFIELD OVERLAND STAGE
COMPANY

Billington--Far p279-285, 290-292
Harlow--Story p363-364
Johnson--Pictorial p136
-"Oxbow route"
Bartlett--New p302
-Views of Waterman L. Ormsby
Ridge--America's p555-558
BUTTONS
Dreppard--Pioneer p298
McClinton--Antiques p69-74; see
also index p346
-Manufacture
Marzio--Nation p224, 228
BYRD FAMILY
-Manors, Westover, Va.
Life--New (5) p148-149

C

C.S.A. See CONFEDERACY--
Treasury notes (C.S.A.)
CABET, ETIENNE
Boardman--Jackson. p124
Tyler--Freedom's p220-223
CABINETMAKERS
See also FURNITURE
Van Wagenen--Golden p113-114
-Nativity
Marzio--Nation p213-214
-Wages
Marzio--Nation p218
CABINETS, PRESIDENTIAL. See
names of presidents, subdivision
Cabinet
CABLE, GEORGE WASHINGTON
Amer. Her. --New (11) p968-970
Harlow--Story p431
Our literary p140-141
-Biography
Amer. Her. --New (11) p E376-
377
CABLES
See also ATLANTIC CABLE
Marzio--Nation p612-615
Train--Story p284-285
Walker--Every. p52
CABRINI, FRANCESCA (MOTHER)
Neidle--America's p72-74
CADY, ELIZABETH. See STAN-
TON, ELIZABETH CADY
CAHAN, ABRAHAM
Our literary p183
CAIRO, ILLINOIS
Drury--Midwest p133-134
, in Civil war
Young--Women p89-104
"CALAMITY JANE" (Mary or Martha

Jane Cannary)
  Hine--American p268,274-275
  Randel--Centennial p147-148
  Reader's--Story p172
  Warren--Pictorial p96
"CALASHES" (Hoods)
  Ross--Taste p210
CALDWELL, WILLIAM
  Chase--America's p194
CALHOUN, JOHN CALDWELL
  Amer.Her.--New (5) p394,396, E156-157
  Amer.Her.--New (7) p552-554
  Boardman--Jackson. See index p206
  Boardman--Virginia p53-56
  Borden--Portrait (1) p162
  Butterfield--Amer. p67,86-87, 92,134-135
  Carman--History (1). See index p.iv
  Harlow--Story. See index p805
  Kraus--U.S. See index p.ii
  Life--Growing (3). See index p172
  Life--New (5) p16,31-32,35-37
  Life--Sweep (4). See index p156
  Linton--Bicentennial. See index p439
  Meredith--World p18-23
  Morris--Ency. p742
  Reader's--Story p67
  200 Years (1) p225-230; see also index p345
  -"American system." See "AMERICAN SYSTEM"
  , and Andrew Jackson
      Morris--Ency. p169
  , and Eaton affair
      Phillips--That p24,27-29,37, 50,54,57,74,75,81-82,84-86, 89,92,95,107-108,111,128-131
  , and nullification
      -Views of Charles M. Wiltse
          Miers--American p174-178
  -Biography
      Morris--Every. p641
  -"Fort Hill" (home, Clemens, S.C.)
      Vanderbilt--Living p131
  -"Indian removal: the government policy," 1825
      Ridge--America's p281-283
  , "On slavery question," 1850
      Heffner--Doc. p111-121
  , on union preservation

      Hurd--Treasury p64-66
  -Resolutions, 1847
      Morris--Ency. p202-203
CALHOUN, MRS. JOHN
  , and Eaton affair
      Phillips--That p57,59,62,74-75,85-86,91-92,97-98,107,154
CALIFORNIA
  See also MISSIONS AND MISSIONARIES--California
  Alden--Pioneer p238-241,243, 245,248-249,251
  Amer.Her.--New (6) p522-524
  Billington--Far. See index p314
  Boardman--Jackson. See index p206
  Boorstin--Americans p79,84-85, 151,273
  Brown--Westerners. See index p285
  Carman--History (1) p565-566; see also index p.iv
  Furnas--Americans. See index p980
  Gilbert--Trail. See index p234
  Handlin--This p153,303,315,333, 366
  Hine--American. See index p360-361
  Kraus--U.S. p429-431,433
  Life--New (5) p10,32-35,38-39, 68
  Life--Steel (7) p31,51-52,59,129
  Life--Sweep (4). See index p156
  Tunis--Frontier p124-129,142
  -1830's
      Ridge--America's p462-467
  -1830-1850
  - Johnson--Pictorial p61-91
  -1840's
      See also CALIFORNIA--Gold rush; etc.
      Life--Sweep p130-136
  -1848
      Train--Story p312
  -1850-1870
      Johnson--Pictorial p114-131
  -1876
      Randel--Centennial p38,119-121,264,323-324
  , Acquisition of
      DeVoto--Year p6,13-15
  -Advertised by Hastings
      DeVoto--Year p43-47,49-50, 53,55-56,60,113-144,165
  -American designs on, by James K. Polk, 1845

Ridge--America's p498-501
-American personnel and senti-
ment
  DeVoto--Year p65, 109-110,
  113, 117-118, 122-124
-Amusements, early
  Gilbert--Trail. p117
, and American expansionism
  DeVoto--Year p6, 8-10, 14,
  16-19
  Ridge--America's p462-486,
  498-501
, and Clay Compromise
  Collins--Story p185
-"Bear flag revolt"
  Billington--Far p165-167
  Collins--Story p201
  DeVoto--Year p218-225, 228,
  288, 313, 349-351
  Harlow--Story p271-272
  Morris--Ency. p200
  -Views of Simon Ide
    Ridge--America's p501-503
, before gold discovery
  Jones--Shaping p91-111
, British designs on, 1847
  Ridge--America's p487-490
, by Isthmus of Panama, 1849
  -Views of Bayard Taylor
    Angle--American p250-253
-Camps and camping, 1850-
1870's
  Johnson--Pictorial p162
-Capitols (5)
  Johnson--Pictorial p124-125
-Chinese labor, opposition to
  Life--Steel (7) p74-75, 78-79
, Conquest of
  DeVoto--Year p27-29, 39-40,
  187, 194-197, 229-230, 255-
  256, 271-276
  Morris--Ency. p199-201
-Constitution
  -1849, "Free soil"
    Butterfield--Amer. p131
  -1879
    Keller--Affairs p113-114
-Customhouses and contraband
  Johnson--Pictorial p68-69
-Divided sentiments
  DeVoto--Year p71-72, 124-
  125, 143, 145, 147-148, 164
-Early settlements
  Harlow--Story p270-271
-Early settlers, names of
  Jones--Shaping p102-103
-Feudal fiefdoms
  Johnson--Pictorial p64-65

-Frontier, Methodists on
  Wright--Culture p136-137
-Gold, discovery of, 1849
  See also Marshall, James
  Amer. Her. --New (6) p469-473
  Brown--Westerners p120, 130
  Case--Empire p203-215
  Dulles--United p35
  Commager--Heritage p551-554
  Davie--Profile p151-152
  Garrison--Lost p68-71
  Hilton--Way p91-93
  Johnson--Pictorial p93
  Kraus--U.S. p435-437
  Linton--Bicentennial p132
  Morris--Ency. p207
  Reader's--Story p77
  Ridge--America's p530-531
  Watkins--Gold p26-27
  -Sutter's Mill and Sutter's
  Fort (Sacramento)
    Vanderbilt--Living p201
  -Views of James Marshall
    Davie--Profile p151-152
  -Views of John Augustus Sutter
    Angle--American p248-250
-Gold mines and mining
  Colling--Story p158
  Reader's--Story p78-79
  -Europeans in mines
    Johnson--Pictorial p94, 99
  -Production
    Hine--American p113
    Watkins--Gold p27, 40
  -Social conditions and life
    Billington--Far p235-238
    Commager--Heritage p559-
    562
  -Views of Walter Colton
    Commager--Heritage p555-
    559
  Ridge--America's p531-532
-Gold rush
  Amer. Her. --New (6) p469-485,
  E203-204
  Amer. Her. --New (9) p730
  Billington--Far p218-242
  Boardman--Jackson. p57-58
  Brown--Westerners p117-132,
  171
  Butterfield--Amer. p130-131
  Carman--History (1) p573-577
  Commager--Heritage p551-582
  Davie--Profile p150
  Furnas--Americans p373-377,
  699-700, 780
  Harlow--Story p277, 284-285,
  360

Hine--American p96, 188, 198
Johnson--Pictorial p92-113
Keyes--Hope p242-243
Life--Sweep (4) p140-151; see
    also index (under Gold Rush)
    p157
Ridge--America's p531-532
Train--Story p282, 306, 311,
    313, 316
Tunis--Frontier p131-135
Watkins--Gold p27-29, 35-39
-Commercial heritage
    Johnson--Pictorial p112-
    113
-"Four young men," 1840's
    Woodward--Way p244-277
-Negroes
    Johnson--Pictorial p93
-Overland parties, wagon
trains
    Johnson--Pictorial p96-97
    Woodward--Way p260-272
-Propaganda reaches East,
1848
    Ridge--America's p532-533
-Sea voyages
    Johnson--Pictorial p98-99
-Towns
    Johnson--Pictorial p102
-Washington state song
    Burner--America (1) p234-
    235
, Women in
    Warren--Pictorial p95-96
-"Great boom" (1880-1899)
Johnson--Pictorial p151-169
-Hotels. See HOTELS--
California
-Immigrants
    , Early
    Jones--Shaping p97, 112-136
    Reader's--Story p78-80
    Ridge--America's p477-484
    -Professional men
        Wright--Culture p135-136
    -Runaway sailors
        Jones--Shaping p101-102
-Indians. See INDIANS--
California
, Kearny's arrival in
    DeVoto--Year p356-359, 372
, Land travel to
    See also Gold Rush--Overland
    parties, wagon trains
    Watkins--Gold p28, 32-35
-Life
    Watkins--Gold p25, 35-40, 45
-"Life in California ... in the

1830's, by Guadalupe Vallejo
    Ridge--America's p462-467
, Mexican, social conditions
    Billington--Far p4-13
-Monterey
    Tunis--Frontier p126, 128-129,
    131
-Mormon battalion
    DeVoto--Year p372-375, 377,
    400-440, 455-464, 475-480, 494-
    495, 509-511
-Mormons
    DeVoto--Year p86-89, 105, 194,
    272-275, 353-355, 386, 411, 448,
    453-455, 457
-Oranges (1870's-1880's)
    Johnson--Pictorial p168-169
-Parks, state
    Johnson--Pictorial p130-131
-Population (1848-1860)
    Watkins--Gold p40
-Ports
    Johnson--Pictorial p135, 146,
    148-149
, Prewar American relations with
    DeVoto--Year p17-21
-"Prospects"
    Keyes--Hope p228-229
-Ranchos and rancheros
    Johnson--Pictorial p61-63, 67
    Ridge--America's p462-467
-Republic
    See also CALIFORNIA--"Bear
    flag revolt"
    DeVoto--Year p220-225, 255,
    272, 306
-Resorts
    Johnson--Pictorial p158-159
-Road ("Trail of the moldering
ox")
    Life--Sweep (4) p144-145
-San Joaquin valley
    Billington--Far p42-43, 62, 77,
    93-94
-Santa Barbara
    -Early settlers, 1845
        Jones--Shaping p103
, Sea travel to
    See also CALIFORNIA--Gold
    Rush--Sea voyages
    Watkins--Gold p28-29, 28n, 32
-Silver mines and mining
    Commager--Heritage p578-582
, Spanish
    Alden--Pioneer p238-239
    DeVoto--Year p6, 13-14
-Statehood
    Alden--Pioneer p248-249

Harlow--Story p285-287
-Theater. See THEATER--
California
-University
Randel--Centennial p417-418
-Views of Richard Henry Dana, Jr.
(1836-1837)
Commager--Heritage p516-
521
-Wagon trains, First, 1849
Davie--Profile p152-155
-Wealth
Wright--Culture p164-167
-Women, scarcity of
Life--Sweep (4) p137
-"Yankee take-over"
Johnson--Pictorial p76-91
CALIFORNIA ARGONAUTS
Amer.Her.--New (6) p E196
"CALIFORNIA TRAIL"
DeVoto--Year p165-166, 177-181
Watkins--Gold p32-34
"CALIFORNIOS"
Tunis--Frontier p125-128
CALL, MARY KIRKMAN
, and Eaton affair
Phillips--That p137-139
CALL, RICHARD K.
, and Eaton affair
Phillips--That p 1-44, 70, 73,
137-138, 141
"CALLING CARDS"
Cable--American p216, 218
CALLIOPES
Viewpoints p168-169
CALVINISTS
See also HUGUENOTS
Furnas--Americans p324-326
CAMBRIDGE, MASSACHUSETTS
Brooks--Flower. p303-322
-1850's
Brooks--Flower. p443-459
CAMEAHWAIT (Indian)
Ross--Heroines p43-44
CAMEL CORPS
-California
Johnson--Pictorial p138
CAMERON, J. DONALD
Life--Steel (7) p11, 14
Randel--Centennial p135
CAMERON, SIMON
Holzman--Stormy p55-56
Life--Steel (7) p11
-Biography
Amer.Her.--New (7) p E230
CAMP, WALTER CHAUNCEY
Reader's--Story p486-487
-"College sports"

Harris--Land p335-339
-"The moral factors in foot-
ball"
Harris--Land p339-343
CAMP MEETINGS
See also EVANGELISM
Boardman--Virginia p169-170
Cable--American p138-139
Chase--America's p207-231
Davidson--Life (2) p22-23
Furnas--Americans p327-329
Partridge--As p43
Tyler--Freedom's p35-42
Wright--Every. p216-219
, First, 1800 (Kentucky)
Chase--America's p207
, Frontier, religious fervor of
Downey--Our p217
Dulles--History p80-83
-West
Hine--American p222-225, 228,
235, 324, 328
CAMPBELL, ALEXANDER
Bartlett--New p378-379, 382
Boardman--Virginia p171-172
Hine--American p227-228, 235,
244-341
CAMPBELL, JOHN L.
Randel--Centennial p283-284
CAMPBELL, JOHN N.
, and Eaton affair
Phillips--That p76-84, 129,
137-139
CAMPBELL, THOMAS
Boardman--Virginia p171-172
CAMPBELLITES. See DISCIPLES
OF CHRIST
CAMPS
, Summer, for children
Harlow--Story p435-436
CANADA AND CANADIANS
200 Years (1) p182-185, 187-190,
195
-American invasion, 1812
Ridge--America's p267-268
-Capture of Fort George
Collins--Story p186
-Montreal, attempt to take, 1813
Morris--Ency. p146
CANADIAN RECIPROCITY TREATY,
1854
Morris--Ency. p217
CANAL BOATS AND BARGES
Bartlett--New p314-316
Cable--American p99-100
Furnas--Americans p289-292, 354
Marzio--Nation p176-177
Woodward--Way p222-225

Wright--Every. p85-89
CANALS
  See also names of canals
  Amer.Her. --New (5) p420-421,
    E157
  American's Hist. p274
  Bartlett--New p311-317
  Boardman--Jackson p94-95
  Boardman--Virginia p89
  Carman--History (1) p463-467,
    469
  Davidson--Life (2) p214-223
  Furnas--Americans. See index
    p980
  Handlin--This p153, 155-156, 158,
    160, 233, 244
  Harlow--Story p198-200
  Keyes--Hope p235-236
  Marzio--Nation p176-177
  Tunis--Young p143-146
  200 Years (1) p202-203
  Wilson--American p76-77
  Wilson--Vanish. p170-171
  -Georgia
    Nation in motion p13-14
  -Indiana, 1839, 1853
    Nation in motion p14-15
  -Kentucky, 1830
    Nation in motion p15
  -Locks, 1830's
    Tunis--Frontier p89, 92
  -Maine, 1846
    Nation in motion p15
  -Maryland, 1817
    Nation in motion p16
  -Michigan, 1869
    Nation in motion p16
  -Minnesota, 1871
    Nation in motion p16
  -North Carolina, 1825
    Nation in motion p17
  -Pennsylvania, 1840's
    Nation in motion p18
  -South Carolina, 1880, c1825
    Nation in motion p18
  , to tidewater
    Morris--Ency. p424
  -Views of Frances Trollope
    Trollope--Domestic. See
      index p.iii
  -Virginia, 1802, 1804, 1827,
    1828, 1843, c1850, 1856,
    1860
    Nation in motion p19-20
  -West Virginia, 1874
    Nation in motion p20
  , Western
    Morris--Ency. p424-426

  -Wisconsin, 1856, 1882
    Nation in motion p21
CANBY, HENRY SEIDEL
  , on colleges and universities,
    1898 p432-435
CANDLES AND CANDLE-MAKING
  Wilson--Folkways p132-134
  -Molds
    Wilson--Vanish. p43
  -Substitutes for, 1860's
    Andrews--Women p23-24
CANDY
  -Pulling
    Partridge--As p13
CANE-RIDGE, KENTUCKY
  Furnas--Americans p327-329
CANNING, GEORGE
  Amer.Her. --New (5) p E157
  Kraus--U.S. p317, 338-339
CANNING, JOSEPH GURNEY
  Amer.Her. --New (12) p E413
CANNON. See GUNS
CANS AND CANNING
  Furnas--Americans p690-692
  Hilton--Way p20-21
  Woodward--Way p259-260
  -Industry
    Boardman--Civil p123-124
    Ross--Taste p63
  -Mason jars
    Furnas--Americans p691-692
CANYON DESERT, NEVADA
  Viewpoints p112
CAPELLINI, GIOVANNI
  -Views on America, 1863
    Handlin--This p285-291
CAPITAL. See FINANCE
CAPITAL PUNISHMENT
  Keller--Affairs p126, 493, 498-499
  -Views of Frances Trollope
    Trollope--Domestic p163-166,
      285
CAPITALISM
  See also INDUSTRIALISTS
  Life--Steel (7) p36-37, 74, 78-79,
    85
  -West
    Hine--American. See index
      p361
CAPITOL. See WASHINGTON, D.C.
"CAPTAIN JACK" (Indian) (Kint-
  puash)
  Boardman--Civil p109
CARAVANS
  , of emigrants
    Boorstin--Americans p54-56,
      58
  , of fur trade

Boorstin--Americans p59-60
CARD-PLAYING
  Dulles--History p70, 150, 158,
  176, 252, 373
  Hunt--Life p181-182
  -1880's
    Peck--Nineteenth n. p.
  -Games, 1876
    Hilton--Way p43-44
"CARDIFF GIANT"
  White--American p81-83
CAREY ACT, 1894
  Morris--Ency. p440
CAREY SISTERS. See CARY
"CARLISTS"
  Phillips--That p144-145, 150
CARMER, CARL
  -"The lordly Hudson"
    Treasury Amer. p173-191
  -Views on Erie Canal
    Miers--American p126-131
CARNEGIE, ANDREW
  See also LIBRARIES
  Amer. Her. --New (10) p866-867
  Amer. Her. --New (11) p962
  Boardman--Gilded p43-44, 161-
  162
  Butterfield--Amer. p314
  Carman--History (2) p103-104
  Dulles--United p57-58
  Harlow--Story p382-384
  Life--Reaching (8) p9, 10, 15,
  61, 67, 138, 150
  Life--Steel (7) p33-34, 36-37,
  96, 130-132
  Morris--Ency. p497, 579
  Portraits--Americans p135
  Reader's--Story p283
  200 Years (2) p72, 81-82, 87, 89
  -Autobiography
    Commager--Heritage p947-954
  -Biography
    Amer. Her. --New (12) p E413
    Morris--Ency. p641-642
  -"The Gospel of Wealth"
    Amer. Her. --90's p84-86
    Davie--Profile p259
  , on charities
    Cook--City p217
    Heffner--Doc. p158-165
  -on first oil boom, Pennsyl-
  vania, 1862
    Angle--American p376-378
CAROLINAS
  See also NORTH CAROLINA;
  SOUTH CAROLINA
  , Civil war in
    Andrews--Women p221-229

"CAROLINE AFFAIR" (ship), 1836
  Boardman--Jackson. p30-31
  Carman--History (1) p453-454
  Linton--Bicentennial p113-114
  Morris--Ency. p180-181
CARPENTER, FRANK B.
  -"How Lincoln was nominated"
    Jones--Shaping p168-175
CARPENTERS
  Van Wagenen--Golden p106
"CARPET-BAGGERS"
  Boardman--Civil p81-82
  Bonte--America p133
  Carman--History (1) p734, 737-
  738
  Collins--Story p235
  Furnas--Americans p411-412, 751-
  752
  Handlin--This p339-340
  Harlow--Story p342-344
  Holzman--Stormy p178-179
  Life--Union (6) p118-133-135
CARPET BEATERS
  Wilson--Vanish. p98
CARPET SWEEPERS
  , First, 1876
    Hilton--Way p24
    Robertson--Book p33
"CARPETBAGS"
  Train--Story p340
CARPETS
  Dreppard--Pioneer p70
  Lynes--Taste. p9, 30, 99
CARR, PETER
  -Thomas Jefferson letter on edu-
  cation, 1817
    Davie--Profile p313-315
CARRIAGES
  See also COACHES; types of
  carriages
  Davidson--Life (2) p52-53
  Wilson--Vanish. p30
  -1876
    Hilton--Way p131-136
  -Houses
    Wilson--Vanish. p110-111
  , in Currier & Ives prints
    Life--Reaching (8) p24-25
  -Makers
    Wilson--Early p137-138
  -Omnibus
    Davidson--Life (2) p138
  -Views of Frances Trollope
    Trollope--Domestic p272, 302-
    304, 352-353
"CARRINGTON HOUSE" (Providence,
  R.I.)
  Vanderbilt--Living p28

CARROLL, ANNA ELLA
  Macksey--Book p55
  Tyler--Freedom's p440
  Young--Women p143-147
  -Biography
    Young--Women p369
CARROLL, JAMES P.
  Chase--America's p192-193
CARSE, MATILDA BRADLEY
  Neidle--America's p45-46
CARSON, CHRISTOPHER ("KIT")
  Amer. Her. --New (6) p E196
  Boardman--Jackson. p64-65
  DeVoto--Year. See index p514
  Gilbert--Trail. p69, 80, 83, 85,
    160-161, 166-167, 170, 214, 216-
    217
  Life--Sweep. (4) p135
  Reader's--Story p171
CARSON, J. H.
  -"Social life, California gold-
    mining"
    Commager--Heritage p559-
    562
CARTER, CAROLINE LOUISE DUD-
  LEY (MRS. LESLIE CARTER)
  Blum--Stage. profile 11
CARTOONS AND CARICATURES
  See also NAST, THOMAS
  Marzio--Nation p279
  Walker--Every. p36, 144, 171-174
  , Newspaper
    , First, 1814 (Wash. D.C.)
  , Political
    Butterfield--Amer. p290-311
    Life--Steel (7) p18-27
    Marzio--Nation p408-409
CARTS
  -California
    Jones--Shaping p98-99
  -New Mexico
    -Medieval type
      Marzio--Nation p165
CARTWRIGHT, ALEXANDER JOY
  Reader's--Story p483-484
CARTWRIGHT, PETER
  Boardman--Jackson. p134
  Boardman--Virginia p168-169
  Boorstin--Americans p318-319
  Hine--American p223
  Ross--Taste p38
CARVER, GEORGE WASHINGTON
  America's Hist. p558
  Boardman--Gilded p101
  Reader's--Story p116
  -Biography
    Morris--Ency. p642
CARY, ALICE

Adelman--Famous p176-177
Nye--Unembar. p107-108
CARY, ANNIE LOUISE
  Adelman--Famous p263
CARY, CONSTANCE
  Dowdey--Experiment p234-236,
    238, 272, 317
CARY, HETTIE (HETTY)
  Andrews--Women p67-69
  Dowdey--Experiment p234-235, 238
CARY, JENNIE
  Andrews--Women p67-68
  Dowdey--Experiment p234-235
CARY, MARY ANN SHADD
  Warren--Pictorial p85-86
CARY, PHOEBE
  Adelman--Famous p177
  Nye--Unembar. p107-108
CASH REGISTERS
  Portraits--Americans p73-74
  , First, 1879 (Dayton, Ohio)
    Robertson--Book p33
  -Patterson's Model 3, 1884
    Portraits--Americans p73
CASKETS. See COFFINS
CASS, LEWIS
  Boardman--Jackson. p192-193
  Boardman--Virginia p40-41
  Life--Sweep (4) p136, 138-139
CASS, LEWIS, GOVERNOR
  , and Henry R. Schoolcraft
    , on upper Missouri, 1820
      Angle--American p166-170
  -Biography
    Amer. Her. --New (7) p E230
CASSAT, MARY DUDLEY
  Heath--Women (4) p20
  Macksey--Book p206
  Portraits--Americans p147-148,
    150
  Reader's--Story p384
  Warren--Pictorial p154, 159
"CAST IRON" HOUSE, AND PALACE
  , Bogardus's 1849
    Portraits--Americans p43
  -Stewart's, 1876 (New York)
    Hilton--Way p171
    Portraits--Americans p41
"CASTLE GARDEN" (Immigration
  station, Manhattan)
  Keyes--Hope p387, 389
  Marzio--Nation p131-134
CATHERINE, SISTER
  Ross--Heroines p149-150
CATHOLICISM
  See also ANTI-CATHOLICISM;
  JESUITS; MISSIONS AND MIS-
  SIONARIES

Bartlett--New p156, 368, 372
Boardman--Civil p185
Boardman--Jackson. p133, 183-
184
Boardman--Virginia p171
Carman--History (1) p506, 509-
514, 556
Carman--History (2) p289, 360,
362-363
Davidson--Life (2) p342-343,
350, 373
Furnas--Americans p364-369,
382, 639, 698, 749
Handlin--This p148-149, 188,
248, 254, 259, 298, 358, 390-391
Hunt--Life p122
Keller--Affairs p135, 137-142,
484-485, 570
Kraus--U.S. p399
Randel--Centennial p435, 439,
441, 446-447
Reader's--Story p98-99
Tyler--Freedom's p360-363
Weisberger--Amer. p162, 165-
167, 170-171
, and Orestes Brownson
Tyler--Freedom's p384-385
-Control of church property
Tyler--Freedom's p377-378
, in literature
Mott--Golden p174-175, 245-
246
, Opposition to
Alden--Pioneer p253
-Persecution
Reader's--Story p326-327
-Propaganda press and debates
Tyler--Freedom's p367-369
-School funds, distribution of
Tyler--Freedom's p378-379
-Views of Frances Trollope
Trollope--Domestic. See
index (under Roman Catholic
church) p. xiv
-West
Hine--American. See index
p361
CATLIN, GEORGE
See also BLACKFOOT INDIANS
Amer. Her. --New (6) p E196-197
Boardman--Jackson. p153
Boorstin--Americans p240
Brown--Westerners p70-87
Gilbert--Trail. See index p234
Hine--American p285-287, 299,
343
Reader's--Story p380
-Collection of Indian paintings

Downey--Our p269-278
-"Indian creed"
Sochen--Herstory p192-193
, on navigation difficulties
Wright--Every. p83-84
CATON SISTERS
Peacock--Famous p61, 88
CATT, CARRIE L. CHAPMAN
Bonte--American p155
Heath--Women (4) p21
Macksey--Book p87
Reader's--Story p434
CATTARAUGUS COUNTY, NEW
YORK
Van Wagenen--Golden. See index
p271
-Census, 1835-1845
Van Wagenen--Golden p7-12, 18
CATTLE
See also "COW HUNTS"; LIVE-
STOCK
Bartlett--New p192-193, 209-210,
224-234, 416-417
Boardman--Gilded p86-88
Brown--Westerners p203-213, 247,
263, 265, 268
Furnas--Americans p683-688
Handlin--This p115, 117-118, 121,
162
Harlow--Story p367-369
Life--Steel (7) p55-57. See also
index p156
200 Years (2) p68-69
-1873-1876
Randel--Centennial p140-144
, Beef
Furnas--Americans p683-688
-Brands
Life--Steel (7) p56-57
Train--Story p300
-California
Johnson--Pictorial p66-67
, Devon
Van Wagenen--Golden p40
-Economy
Borden--Portrait (2) p45-46
-Hide and tallow trade
Ridge--America's p467-470
-Investment in range, 1885
Ridge--America's p608-610
-"Kingdoms"
Amer. Her. --New (9) p763-767
America's Hist. p502-507
Dulles--United p43-46
Hine--American p134-135
Morris--Ency. p431
-"Long drives"
Amer. Her. --New (9) p751-753,

760-763
Angle--American p358-363
Bartlett--New p229
Ridge--America's p592-595,
  597-599
Tunis--Frontier p157-158
200 Years (2) p69
, and sodbusters
  Tunis--Frontier p154-160
-"The beginning of the long
  drive," 1866
  Ridge--America's p592-595
-Texas
  Commager--Heritage p853-
  857
-Longhorns
  Tunis--Frontier p145-146
-Milking
  Wilson--Vanish. p64
-Open range
  Ridge--America's p602-604
, End of
  Ridge--America's p610-612
-vs. homesteaders
  Wilson--American p235
-Round-up, 1887
  Amer. Her. --New (9) p744
  Ridge--America's p606-608
-"Rustlers"
  Hine--American p307-308
-Stampedes
  Reader's--Story p119
-Texas
  See also CATTLE--"Long
  drives"--Texas
  Hine--American p125-126,128,
  132-133,135
  -Stations, 1860's
  Nation in motion p82-83
-Trails
  Hine--American. See index
  p361
-West
  Carman--History (2) p191-200
  Hine--American. See index
  p361
  Train--Story p292-293
-Wyoming
  Hine--American p126,128,
  135,218,270,307-308
CATTLEMEN
  See also COWBOYS; ILIFF,
  JOHN H.
  Walker--Every. p93-94
, and homesteaders
  Amer. Her. --New (9) p758-
  790
-Tools

Life--America's p120-121
CATTLEMEN'S ASSOCIATION
-Organization, 1884
  Ridge--America's p604-608
CATTON, BRUCE
"Hayfoot, strawfoot"!
  Treasury Amer. p242-247
, on Ulysses S. Grant, contrast
  with
  Miers--American p202-205
-"We were there, waiting"
  Treasury Amer. p224-226
CAYUGA INDIANS
  Andrews--Indian leaders p13,28,
  36-37
-National traditions
  Marzio--Nation p18
CAYUSE INDIANS
  Boardman--Jackson. p69-70
  Case--Empire p231-242
  Ross--Heroines p65-67, 79-80, 82-
  86, 88-89
, and Oregon missions
  Amer. Her. --Indians p310-311,
  327
CELESTIALS. See CHINESE--
Immigrants
CELIBACY
  Handlin--This p165-166
"CELLAR DIGGERS"
  Walker--Reform p84-87
CELLARS
  Lynes--Domestic. p98,127
CEMENT
, Portland
  Train--Story p319
CEMETERIES
  Cable--American p174-176
CENSUS--U.S.
  Boorstin--Americans p425-426
  Keller--Affairs p102-103,373,384
  -1800-1890
  Davie--Profile p169
  -1890
  Amer. Her. --90's p127-128
  -Machines
  Portraits--Americans p65-68
, Negroes in
  Boorstin--Americans p180,184
CENTENNIAL COMMISSION, 1872-
1876
  Randel--Centennial p284-286,300,
  303,400
CENTENNIAL EXPOSITION OF 1876
(Philadelphia, Pa.)
  America 200 p66
  Boardman--Gilded p3-4
  Butterfield--Amer. p214-215

Collins--Story p249
Furnas--Americans. See index
 p980
Jones--Age p139-143
Keyes--Hope p260
Langdon--Everyday (2) p370-382
Larkin--Art p240-242
Life--Union (6) p158,164-167
Lynes--Taste. p97,112-117,128
Partridge--As p113-119
Randel--Centennial p283-306;
 see also index p467
Reader's--Story p250
Trachtenberg--Demo. p83-100
Wilson--American p216-221
, before opening
 Hilton--Way p178-179,181,183
-Highlights for young people
 Hilton--Way p190-196
, Influences on
 Hilton--Way. See index p212
-Jerome park
 Randel--Centennial p28, 79-80,
 320
-Machinery Hall
 Wilson--American p244-245
-Opening
 Hilton--Way p184-186
CENTRAL AMERICA
, U.S. expansion in
 Life--New (5) p53-54
CENTRAL ART ASSOCIATION
(Chicago, Ill.)
 Lynes--Taste. p151-153,155-156
CENTRAL OVERLAND CALIFORNIA
AND PIKE'S PEAK EXPRESS CO.
 Brown--Westerners p151-152,
 158,164
CENTRAL OVERLAND ROAD
 200 Years (2) p59
CENTRAL PACIFIC RAILROAD
 See also SOUTHERN PACIFIC
 RAILROAD
 Boardman--Civil p141-143
 Brown--Westerners p168,170-
 172,176-177,184-186
 Furnas--Americans p349-350,
 375,699,796-797
 Harlow--Story p366-367
 Hine--American p144-148,153,
 215
 Johnson--Pictorial p134-135
 Keller--Affairs p165,387-388
 Lewis--Big. See index p. i
 Randel--Centennial p117-118,164
 Ridge--America's p567-570
 Tunis--Frontier p142-143
CENTRAL TRADE COUNCILS. See

"CITY CENTRALS"
CERAMICS. See POTTERY AND
 POTTERS
CEREAL FARMING
 See also names of cereals
 , Dry
 Furnas--Americans p900-901
CEREMONIES. See types of cere-
 monies
CERVERA, PASCUAL
 -Biography
 Amer.Her.--New (12) p E414
CHADWICK, GEORGE W.
 Howard--Our p306-310
CHAIN STORES
 Boardman--Civil p133
 Boardman--Gilded p54
 Portraits--Americans p46-48
 Walker--Every. p124-125
 , First, 1879
 Robertson--Book p114
CHAIRS
 Ross--Taste p110
 , Children's
 McClinton--Antiques p149-153
 -High chairs
 McClinton--Antiques p147-
 148
 , Rocking
 Wilson--Vanish. p95-96
CHALKWARE
 Dreppard--Pioneer p58-59, 68
CHAMPION HILL, MISSISSIPPI
 -Battle
 Jordan--Civil p9,11,84,127,
 129,211
CHANCELLORSVILLE, VIRGINIA
 -Battle
 Collins--Story p221
 Dannett--Noble p234-235,239-
 240,246
 Dowdey--Experiment p275,
 280-281,284
 Jordan--Civil p117-122
 Pratt--Civil p37-39
CHANDLER, ZACHARIAH
 Amer.Her.--New (8) p E267-268
 Life--Steel (7) p11-12
CHANGING, EDWARD TYREL
 Brooks--Flower. p34,43-45,54,
 73,103,111-113,165,308
CHANNING, WILLIAM ELLERY
(1780-1842)
 Brooks--Flower. See index
 p540
 Morris--Ency. p552,567
 Our literary p47
 Tyler--Freedom's p402-404; see

also index p593
-Biography
Morris--Ency. p642-643
CHANNING, WILLIAM ELLERY
(1818-1901)
Brooks--Flower. See index
p541
CHANNING, WILLIAM HENRY
Brooks--Flower. p130, 249-251,
428, 460
Our literary p73
CHAPERONAGE
Cable--American p212, 223, 285
Carson--Polite p226-228
Ross--Taste p292, 294
Wilson--Early p110-112
-Etiquette
Cable--American p167
CHAPIN, HENRY D.
, on crowding of schools and
disease, 1895
Cook--City p225-226
CHAPLINE, HORACE, DR.
-"Mansion House" (Wheeling,
W. Va.)
Vanderbilt--Living p114
CHAPMAN, JOHN. See
APPLESEED, JOHNNY
CHAPPEL, ALONZO
Amer. Her. --New (5) p E157
CHAPULTEPEC
-Battle
Amer. Her. --New (7) p576-
577
CHARACTER
-"Self-made" man
Carson--Polite p84
CHARBONNEAU (Indian)
Ross--Heroines p37-41
CHARCOAL
, Making of
Van Wagenen--Golden p161-
164
CHARITIES
See also BOARDS OF CHARITY,
etc.
Boardman--Gilded p161-162
-Associations
Hunt--Life p197
-Public, principles of
Tyler--Freedom's p299
-Views of Andrew Carnegie, 1889
Cook--City p217
-Views of C. M. Robinson, 1899
Cook--City p229-231
-Views of Jane Addams, 1899
Cook--City p231-235
CHARIVARI

Walker--Ency. p38
CHARLESTON, SOUTH CAROLINA
Davidson--Life (2) p116
Furnas--Americans. See index
p981
Handlin--This p117, 120-121, 160,
200-201
Life--Sweep (4) p17-19
Vanderbilt--Living p132-135
, in Civil war
Dowdey--Experiment. See
index p444
Jordan--Civil. See index p212
Life--Union (6) p47, 83, 119,
124-125, 127
CHASE, KATE. See SPRAGUE,
KATE CHASE
CHASE, OWEN
, and shipwreck
Wright--Every. p171-172
CHASE, SALMON PORTLAND
Boardman--Civil p30-31, 64-65
Boardman--Virginia p19-20
Carman--History (1). See index
p. v
Garrison--Lost p109-111
Keller--Affairs. See index p611
Life--New (5) p32, 35-36, 92, 113-
114, 120-121
Life--Sweep (4) p139
Morris--Ency. See index p743
-Biography
Amer. Her. --New (7) p E230-
231
Morris--Ency. p643
, on Lincoln's cabinet
Commager--Heritage p661-664
CHASE, WILLIAM M.
Larkin--Art p301-302; see also
index p520
"CHASSEUR" AND "ST. LAW-
RENCE" (privateers)
Collins--Story p191
CHATILLON, HENRY
Brown--Westerners p91-96, 192
CHATTANOOGA, TENNESSEE
, in Civil war
Dowdey--Experiment p228-229,
251, 311, 313, 352
Jordan--Civil p92, 122, 140-143
Life--Union (6) p16, 60-61, 63,
81-83, 100-101
Morris--Ency. p242
Pratt--Civil p45-46
CHAUTAUQUA (LYCEUMS)
Cable--American p154, 202-203
Dulles--History p258, 260
Dulles--United p105-106

Harlow--Story p428
Jones--Age p197-200
Lynes--Taste. p153-155
Reader's--Story p468
Ross--Taste p36,38
-South Dakota
  Commager--Heritage p932-938
-Views of Guy MacLaren
  Commager--Heritage p932-938
"CHEAP (BOOK) LIBRARIES." See
BOOKS AND READING--"Cheap
(Book) Libraries"
CHEEVER, HENRY T.
, on whalers and whaling, 1850
  Angle--American p217-219
CHEMISTRY AND CHEMISTS
Morris--Ency. p530,532
, in inventions
  Reader's--Story p270
, Industrial
  Wilson--American p384-385
CHEROKEE INDIANS
Amer.Her. --New (5) p157-158,
397-398
Andrews--Indian Leaders p78,
86-93
Boardman--Jackson. p69-70
Boardman--Virginia p116-117
Carman--History (1) p364-365
Watkins--Gold p21-22, 49, 51
-Alphabet, by Sequoia
  Amer.Her. --Indians p220-221
  Reader's--Story p130
-Culture and legal system
  Amer-Her. --Indians p230
-"Trail of tears"
  Amer.Her. --Indians p234-235
  200 Years (1) p231,233
  Watkins--Gold p21
"CHEROKEE STRIP" (Oklahoma)
Tunis--Frontier p161
-Homesteading rush
  -Views of Seth K. Humphrey
    Angle--American p371-375
"CHESAPEAKE" (ship)
Borden--Portrait (1) p139-140
Harlow--Story p173-174
Jones--Shaping p72-76
Morris--Ency. p135-136,145
200 Years (1) p179,190
CHESAPEAKE AND OHIO CANAL
American's Hist. p274-275, 278-
283
Wright--Every. p86
CHESS
Meredith--World p60-65
-"Automaton" player (wooden
mannequin)

White--American p35-36
CHESTER HOSPITAL
, in Civil war
  Andrews--Women p45-47
CHESTNUT, MARY BOYKIN MILLER
Dowdey--Experiment. See index
p444
Warren--Pictorial p112-113
, on Fort Sumter attack, 1861
  Commager--Heritage p729-733
CHESTNUT TREES
Bartlett--New p248
CHEVALIER, MICHEL
Reader's--Story p500
, on United States, 1835
  Reader's--Story p504
CHEVES, LANGDON
Amer.Her. --New (6) p E197
Boardman--Virginia p73
CHEW, MISS. See MASON, JANE
"CHEWING TOBACCO ERA." See
TOBACCO--"Chewing Tobacco Era"
CHEYENNE, WYOMING
-1873
  Cable--American p233
CHEYENNE INDIANS
Amer.Her. --Indians. See index
p419
Andrews--Indian leaders. See
index p183
Andrews--Indians. See index
p175
Boardman--Civil p107-108
Brown--Westerners p37, 59, 78,
168, 175, 180, 191, 195, 198, 201,
233, 236, 240, 243, 246, 269
DeVoto--Year p153, 249, 260, 296,
481, 502
Hine--American p194-196; see
also index p361
Jones--Shaping p122-123
Watkins--Gold p110-111
CHICAGO, ILLINOIS
See also MEAT PACKING INDUS-
TRY
American 200 p65-69
Bartlett--New p240, 407-409, 443
Cable--American p286-287
Collins--Story p152
Davidson--Life (2) p120-122
Drury--Midwest p28-54
Furnas--Americans. See index
p981
Handlin--This. p205, 285, 302-304,
354, 401-402, 404-405
Life--Reaching (8). See index
p172
Life--Steel (7). See index p156

-1840-1890's
  Woodward--Way p278-318
-1870's
  Woodward--Way p278-318
-1871
  Harlow--Story p426
-1876
  Randel--Centennial. See
  index p467
-1890's
  Amer. Her. --90's p12-29
-1893
  Harris--Land p344-362
-1899
  Cable--American p345
-"Bohemians"
  -Views of Jane Addams
    Cook--City p89-91
-"The Derby"
  Amer. Her. --90's p28-29
-"Fabulous Chicago," poem by
  Emmett Dedmore, 1868
    Cook--City p149-150
-Fire, 1871
  Collins--Story p242
  Cook--City p154
  Drury--Midwest p38-40
  Life--Reaching (8) p30-31
  -Fires and fire protection
    Woodward--Way p311-316
  -"Mrs. O'Leary and cow"
    myth
    Woodward--Way p315
  -Views of Horace White
    Commager--Heritage p878-
    885
-"If Christ came to Chicago, "
  by William Stead, 1894
    Cook--City p62-64
-La Salle street
  Drury--Midwest p52
-Life, 1876
  Cook--City p258-259
  Jones--Age p179
-Palmer House
  Jones--Age p130-131
-Politics
  -Views of Julian Ralph, 1892
    Cook--City p185
-Railroads
  -Views of Julian Ralph
    Cook--City p45, 47
-Slums
  -Views of Agnes Sinclair
    Holbrook
    Cook--City p130-131
-Streets, 1892
  Cook--City p61

-Suburbs, 1873
  Cook--City p54-56
-Sweatshops
  -Views of Florence Kelly
    Cook--City p252-253
  -Views of Joseph Kirkland
    Angle--American p399-400
  -Views of Rudyard Kipling
    Cook--City p37-39
  -Views of John S. Wright, 1868
    Cook--City p44-45
"CHICAGO COMMONS" (settlement
house)
  Cook--City p235-238
CHICAGO PHILHARMONIC SOCIETY
  Howard--Our p270-271
CHICAGO WORLD'S EXPOSITION,
1893. See COLUMBIAN EXPOSI-
TION
CHICKAMAUGA, TENNESSEE
  -Battle
    Jordan--Civil p138-142
    Life--Union (6) p81-83, 100
    Morris--Ency. p242
CHICKASAW INDIANS
  Amer. Her. --Indians. See index
  p419
  Boardman--Jackson. p69
"CHIEF CLERK CAPERS" (C.S.A.).
See CONFEDERACY--Treasury
notes (C.S.A.)
CHIEF JOSEPH. See JOSEPH (Nez
Perce Indian)
CHILD, LYDIA MARIA
  Adelman--Famous p176
  Macksey--Book p184
CHILD LABOR
  Boardman--Jackson. p87-88
  Carman--History (1) p494-496
  Furnas--Americans p749, 839,
  842-845
  Life--Reaching (8) p74, 76-77
  Wilson--Early p98-102
  -Sweatshops
    200 Years (2) p83
  -Views of John Spargo
    Commager--Heritage p954-958
CHILDBEARING
  Lynes--Domestic. p69, 204
  Schwartz--When p21
  Walker--Every. p39-40
  , on wagon trains
    Ross--Heroines p11
CHILDREN AND CHILDHOOD
  See also BABIES; CHILDBEAR-
  ING; CHILDREN'S BOOKS AND
  READING; CLOTHING AND
  DRESS, Children's; TOYS; etc.

Handlin--This. See index p580
McClinton--Antiques p15-21
Partridge--As p134-135
-1800
   Boardman--Virginia p184
-Discipline
   See also SCHOOLS--Discipline
   Furnas--Americans p537-539,
   591-592
-Duties
   Bartlett--New p362
-"Fresh air excursions" (1880)
   Cook--City p280-282
-Games
   Partridge--As p18
-Illustrations
   Grimsted--Notions p231-237
-Life
   McClinton--Antiques p15-21
, Management of
   -Views of Mrs. L. G. Abell
     Burner--America (1) p190-
     193
   -Views of Frances Trollope
     Trollope--Domestic. See
     index p. iii
   -Views of Frederick Marryat
     Burner--America (1) p193-196
-Welfare
   Boardman--Civil p191
   Cook--City p279
CHILDREN'S AID SOCIETY (New
York, 1875)
   Cable--American p294
CHILDREN's BOOKS AND READ-
ING
   See also FAIRY TALES
   Boardman--Civil p156-157
   Boardman--Gilded p134
   Dreppard--Pioneer p134
   Dulles--United p107
   Furnas--Americans p552-553,
   608-610
   McClinton--Antiques p75-134;
   see also index (under Books)
   p345
   Mott--Golden p97-103, 155-165
-1876
   Hilton--Way p36-41
-Amusements
   McClinton--Antiques p102-134
, Boys'
   Hilton--Way p39-40
, Cloth
   McClinton--Antiques p334-335
, Coloring
   McClinton--Antiques p93, 95-
   96

, Girls'
   Hilton--Way p36-39
-Riddles
   McClinton--Antiques p116-122
-Stories and Poetry
   McClinton--Antiques p102-115
CHILDREN'S CLOTHES. See
  CLOTHING AND DRESS, Children's
CHILDREN'S DISHES
   McClinton--Antiques p166-183
-Plates
   McClinton--Antiques p179-183
CHILDREN'S GAMES
   -"Kissing games"
     Schwartz--When p117
CHILDREN'S LIBRARY
, First (Salisbury, Conn., 1803)
   Robertson--Book p34
CHILDREN's MAGAZINES
   McClinton--Antiques p105, 112
CHILDREN'S NEEDLEWORK
   See also DOLLS--Clothes
   McClinton--Antiques p198-201
-Berlin work patterns
   McClinton--Antiques p194-195
-Pen wipers
   McClinton--Antiques p196, 198
-Pictures
   McClinton--Antiques p190-192
-Pincushion dolls
   McClinton--Antiques p197-199
-Sewing
   McClinton--Antiques p196-201
-Sewing dolls
   McClinton--Antiques p198
CHILDREN'S TOYS. See TOYS
CHILE
, and Central America incidents
   Keyes--Hope p280
, Controversy with, 1891
   Morris--Ency. p284
CHILKAT INDIANS
   Amer. Her.--Indians p278-281
CHILKOOT PASS, ALASKA
   Watkins--Gold p150-151
CHIMNEY SWEEPS
   Schwartz--When p54-55
   Wilson--Early p27
CHINA
   -"Open door" policy, 1899
     Dulles--United p173-174
   -Trade
     Life--Growing (3) p42, 46-47,
     80
     Wright--Every. p164-165
     -Cargoes of luxuries
       Reader's--Story p180
CHINESE

Reader's--Story p330
Weisberger--Amer. See index p390
-Arts and crafts
  Marzio--Nation p254-258
, Discrimination against
  Watkins--Gold p235-236, 238, 243
  -Views of Franklin Miller
    Cook--City p86-87
-Exclusion, 1868-1882
  See also CHINESE EXCLU-
  SION ACT, 1882
  Morris--Ency. p448
-Immigrants
  Bartlett--New p165-170, 328, 330, 413, 439
  Butterfield--Amer. p228-229
  Furnas--Americans p699-701
  Keller--Affairs p156-158, 397, 443-445
  Life--Reaching (8) p62-63, 66
  Life--Steel (7) p30, 75-76, 78-79
, Riots against--West, 1880
  Collins--Story p253
-San Francisco, Ca.
  -Views of Rudyard Kipling
    Cook--City p87-89
-Treaty, 1880
  Morris--Ency. p281-282
-West
  Hine--American p121, 149, 214-220
CHINESE EXCLUSION ACT OF 1882
  Boardman--Gilded p103
  Life--Reading (8) p66
  Weisberger--Amer. p217-221
CHINOOK INDIANS
  Gilbert--Trail. p32
CHIPPEWA
  -Battle
    Collins--Story p187
CHIRICAHUA APACHE INDIANS
  Amer. Her. --Indians p129, 385, 388, 398-399
CHISHOLM, WILLIAM WALLACE
  Randel--Centennial p255-256
"CHISHOLM TRAIL" (Texas)
  Train--Story p331
  White--American p88-91
CHITTEE YOHOLO (Seminole Indian)
  Andrews--Indian leaders p72
CHITTENDEN, L. E.
  , on Lincoln's pardon of a sentinel

Commager--Heritage p653-659
CHIVALRY
  Furnas--Americans p409-411
CHIVINGTON MASSACRE, 1864
  -Lieut. James Conner, with Lieut. Cramer
    Ridge--America's p572-574
CHOATE, JOSEPH HODGES
  , on lawyers
    Hurd--Treasury p109-110
CHOATE, RUFUS
  , on abolitionism vs. war
    Hurd--Treasury p66-68
CHOCTAW INDIANS
  Amer. Her. --Indians. See index p419-420
  Andrews--Indian leaders. See index p183
  Boardman--Jackson. p69
CHOLERA
  -Epidemics
    Cable--Americans p291-292
CHOPIN, KATE O'FLAHERTY
  Sochen--Herstory p223-224
CHORAL SOCIETIES
  Morris--Ency. p614-615
CHORES
  , Boys', 1876
    Hilton--Way p35
  , Children's
    Wilson--Folkways p83-85
  , Girls'
    Hilton--Way p35
CHOUTEAU FAMILY (traders)
  Boardman--Virginia. See index p212
CHRISTENINGS
  -Materials
    McClinton--Antiques p32-38, 62
CHRISTIAN COMMISSION
  Carman--History (1) p655
  Dannett--Noble p54, 97, 102, 173, 244, 251, 263, 273, 286-287, 305, 341, 394
  Young--Women p19, 225, 249, 264, 286, 319, 326
CHRISTIAN LABOR UNION, 1871-1876
  Randel--Centennial p447-449
CHRISTIAN SCIENCE
  Reader's--Story p102
  -1875-1892
    Morris--Ency. p553
CHRISTIAN SOCIALISM (Social gospel)
  Boardman--Gilded p158
CHRISTIANITY. See RELIGION
CHRISTMAS

Cable--American p163, 320
Mussey--Old p94
Partridge--As p27-29
Walker--Every. p35-36
-1875-1876
　Randel--Centennial p67-68,
　　73-74, 76, 409
-1876
　Hilton--Way p201-204
, in cartoons
　Marzio--Nation p408-409
-Middlewest
　Drury--Midwest p87
-New Orleans, La., 1890
　Schwartz--When p132-133
-New York City
　Tunis--Young p120-121
-"Pennsylvania Dutch"
　Ross--Taste p81-82
-Richmond, Va., 1864
　Andrews--Women p393-394
CHRISTMAS TREES
, First
　Ross--Taste p81
, First electrically-lighted, 1882
(N.Y. City)
　Robertson--Book p37
-Ornaments
　Dreppard--Pioneer p128
CHROMOLITHOGRAPHS
　Furnas--Americans p628-629
CHRONOLOGY (dates)
-1800-1829
　Life--Growing (3) p168-169
-1800-1899
　Linton--Bicentennial p57-255
-1818-1860
　200 Years (1) p213
-1829-1849
　Life--Sweep (4) p152-153
-1835
　-Views of Michel Chevalier
　　Reader's--Story p504
-1840's
　Butterfield--Amer. p124-125
　Tyler--Freedom's p377-382
-1849-1865
　Life--New (5) p151-152
-1861-1876
　Life--Union (6) p168-169
-1861-1894
　200 Years (2) p9
-1877-1890
　Life--Steel (7) p152-153
-1890
　Amer. Her. --90's p6-11,
　　127-129
-1890's

, Boyhood in
　Amer. Her. --90's p90-96
, in photographs
　Amer. Her. --90's p36-59
-View from abroad
　Amer. Her. --90's p80-90
-1899
　-Prophecy for future
　　Amer. Her. --90's p142-143
-"Firsts"
　Robertson--Book p219-232
CHUCK WAGONS
　Reader's--Story p119
　Tunis--Frontier p152, 158
CHURCH, FREDERICK EDWIN
　Larkin--Art p210-211; see also
　index p520
CHURCH OF LATTER DAY SAINTS.
See MORMONS
CHURCHES
　See also RELIGION; names of
　churches, denominations
　Handlin--This. See index p580-
　581
　Keller--Affairs p43, 136-142, 507-
　509, 519
　Schwartz--When p139
　Walker--Every. p33, 78, 109, 147-
　148, 235
-1870's
　Randel--Centennial p436-460;
　　see also index p467
-1876
　Hilton--Way p49-50
-Amusements
　Dulles--History p88-90, 204-
　　209, 249-251
, and slavery
　Morris--Ency. p552
, and social life
　Carson--Polite p87, 90-91
-Architecture
　Ross--Taste p25-29
-Campgrounds
　Furnas--Americans p329-331
, Country
　Collins--Story p284
　Partridge--As p41-42
-Design
　Viewpoints p144
-Gothic revival
　Larkin--Art p171-172
-Greek revival
　Larkin--Art p158-159
, of negroes
　Boorstin--Americans p196-199
-Women, status in
　Carson--Polite p91

Gurko--Ladies. See index
    (under Religion) p325-326
CHURCHILL, JEANNETTE (JEN-
NIE) JEROME, LADY RANDOLPH
    Peacock--Famous p239-256
CHURNS
    , Butter
        Wilson--Vanish. p54
CIDER AND CIDER-MAKING
    Wilson--Vanish. p65
"CIGAR STORE INDIANS"
    Train--Story p335
    Wilson--Vanish. p144
    Woodward--Way p292
CIGARETTES
    , and women
        Furnas--Americans p894-895
        Life--Steel (7) p103
CIGARS
    Handlin--This p187, 336, 386-387
CINCINNATI, OHIO
    Boardman--Virginia p197
    Drury--Midwest p123-129
    Furnas--Americans. See index
    p981
    Handlin--This p111, 241, 262, 304
    Treasury Amer. p260, 262
    Weisberger--Amer. p160-161
    Woodward--Way p225-243
    -1876
        Randel--Centennial p2, 55-56,
        105, 312
    -Development
        Wright--Culture p93-95
    -Germans
        Weisberger--Amer. p126,
        130, 132, 134-135, 138-143,
        160-161
    -Irish
        Weisberger--Amer. p160-161
    -Photographs, 1840's
        Life--Sweep p74-75
    -Sanitation
        Cook--City p143
    -Views of Frances Trollope
        Trollope--Domestic. See
        index p.iii, iv
CIRCUIT RIDERS
    Bartlett--New p368-370, 372
    Boardman--Virginia p168-169
    Case--Empire p257-268
    Chase--America's p207, 209, 223
    Commager--Heritage p269-272
    Hine--American p222-224, 227-
    228, 244, 323-324, 328
CIRCUS
    Boardman--Civil p198
    Boardman--Gilded p168-169

Boardman--Jackson. p177
Boardman--Virginia p188
Dulles--History p131-135, 282-286
Furnas--Americans p562-563
Marzio--Nation p424, 426
Nye--Unembar. p189-190
Reader's--Story p466-467
200 Years (2) p102-103
Walker--Every. p86-88
-1876
    Hilton--Way p196-197
-Barnum and Bailey
    Dulles--United p102
-Clowns, 1856
    Viewpoints p166-167
-Parades
    Wilson--Vanish. p164
CISTERNS. See WELLS
CITIES
    See also TOWNS; names of cities
    Amer. Her. --New (11) p930-957
    Boardman--Gilded p68-69, 105-110
    Boardman--Jackson. p180-182
    Boardman--Virginia p193-199
    Handlin--This p139, 153, 295-297,
    390
    Life--Reaching (8) p40-43; see
    also index p172
    -1800
        Alden--Pioneer p160
    -1850-1875
        Boardman--Civil p111-114
    -"City and country," by Henry
    George (1898)
        Cook--City p6
    -Entertainment
        Life--New (5) p58, 60, 62-63
    -Fads and fancies
        Life--Sweep (4) p26-27; see
        also index p156
    -Government
        Boardman--Gilded p109-110
        , and social life
            Nye--Cultural p125-128
        , Good
            -Views of Herbert Welsh,
            1894
                Cook--City p205-206
    -Growth
        Commager--Heritage p877-915
        Davidson--Life (2) p126-177
        Dulles--United p89-90
        Lynes--Taste. p163-164
        Walker--Every. p108, 113, 126-
        127, 138
    -1895
        Cook--City p17-18
    -1899

Cook--City p18-19
-"Why the city grows," by
Josiah Strong
    Cook--City p15-17
-Hazards
    Cook--City p136-176
-Improvement
    -Views of C. M. Robinson,
    1899
        Cook--City p103-106
-Life
    Borden--Portrait (2) p22-23
    Harlow--Story p416-437
    Life--Reaching (8) p32-43;
    see also index p172
    Wright--Every. p135-136
    -1876
        Hilton--Way p161-175
    -1890
        Cook--City p240-241
, Lure of
    Partridge--As p93-178
-"Mannahatta," by Walt Whit-
man
    Cook--City p4-5
-Midwest
    Treasury Amer. p242-247
-Migration from farms, 1895
    Cook--City p8-9
, of the lakes
    Drury--Midwest p55-69
-Planning
    Cable--American p101
    Gowans--Images p312-313,
    378-379
    Walker--Every. p121-122, 138
-Population
    Hunt--Life p22
    -1880-1890
        Cook--City p22
    -North
        Alden--Pioneer p205
-Problems
    Boardman--Gilded p106-107
    -1893
        Cook--City p115-117
-Recreation, influence on growth
    Dulles--History p84-85, 136-
    138, 204, 211-213
-Reform, 1890's
    Borden--Portrait (2) p75-76
    Dulles--United p96-98
-Streets
    -Life and business
        Partridge--As p95-111
-Summer heat, 1898
    Cook--City p166-167
-"The tendency of men to live in

cities," by F.J. Kingsbury, 1895
    Cook--City p11-13
-Versus country--views of Blacks
    Cook--City p7
-Vice
    Life--Reaching (8) p42-43
CITIZENSHIP--U.S.
-Naturalization, easy
    Marzio--Nation p300
, Requirements for
    Davie--Profile p75-76
CITRUS INDUSTRY
    Furnas--Americans p776-778,
    781, 786
"CITY CENTRALS" (Central trade
councils)
    Morris--Ency. p519
CITY LIFE. See CITIES--Life
"CITY OF MEMPHIS" (ship)
    Young--Women p149-151, 170, 257
CIVIL RIGHTS
    Keller--Affairs p142-153, 202-204
    Life--Union (6) p113-116, 134,
    136-137
CIVIL RIGHTS ACTS
-1866
    Amer. Her.--New (8) p E268
    Keller--Affairs p64-66, 143-
    144, 148, 219
    Morris--Ency. p247
-1873
    Morris--Ency. p251
-1875
    Keller--Affairs p146-148, 151,
    444, 448
    Reader's--Story p341
CIVIL SERVICE
    See also "PENDLETON ACT,"
    1883
    Harlow--Story p448-449, 452-455,
    458, 482
    Keyes--Hope p276-277
    Whitney--American p162, 170-171,
    178, 182-183, 190
-Policy, 1825
    Morris--Ency. p164
-Reform
    Boardman--Gilded p21-22, 24
    Life--Steel (7) p11, 13-14, 17
    -1881-1893
        Collins--Story p257
    -Views of Rutherford B. Hayes
        Harlow--Story p448-449
CIVIL SERVICE ACT, 1883
    Boardman--Civil p88-89
    Dulles--United p134
    Keyes--Hope p276
    Linton--Bicentennial p223

CIVIL SERVICE COMMISSION. See
 CIVIL SERVICE ACT
CIVIL WAR
 See also CONFEDERACY; LIN-
 COLN, ABRAHAM; RECON-
 STRUCTION; SOLDIERS--Civil
 war; names of cities, generals,
 etc.
 Alden--Pioneer p261-287
 America's Hist. p424-467
 Angle--American p308-342
 Butterfield--Amer. p168-171
 Carman--History (1) p646-699;
 see also index p. v
 Davidson--Life (2) p384-391
 Davie--Profile p274-288
 Furnas--American. See index
 p981
 Handlin--This p154, 277-278,
 286-289, 339, 386
 Keyes--Hope p251-254
 Kraus--U.S. p486-515
 Life--New (5). See index p156
 Life--Union (6). See index
 p172-173
 Linton--Bicentennial. See index
 p439
 Maurois--Illus. p145-147
 Morris--Ency. p228-245
 Partridge--As p51-67
 Reader's--Story p141-157
 Sochen--Herstory p155-166
 200 Years (2). See index p352
 Whitney--American. See index
 p360
 -Aims
  Morris--Ency. p232
 -Ambulances
  Young--Women p129-130
 , and England
  Kraus--U.S. p491-492
 , and Europe
  Kraus--U.S. p498-499
  Morris--Ency. p233
 , and France
  Life--New (5) p139-141
 , and telegraph
  Wilson--American p180-183
  -Codes. See TELEGRAPH
  CODES, SECRET--Civil
  war
 -Blockade
  America's Hist. p439
  Dowdey--Experiment p158,
  202, 243, 256, 267-269, 292,
  364-367, 400
  Jordan--Civil. See index
  p212

 Life--New (5) p115, 141, 147-
 148
 Life--Union (6) p19, 33-34, 40,
 46-48, 83
 Morris--Ency. p233
 Pratt--Civil p14-15
 -Runners
  Jordan--Civil p48, 54-55, 67,
  69, 183
 -Border states
  Morris--Ency. p230-231
 -Camps
  See also ANDERSONVILLE
  (Military prison, Ga.)
  Amer. Her.--New (8) p670
  Young--Women p82-88
  -Health and sanitation
  Young--Women p82-84
 -Causes
  Alden--Pioneer p217, 256-257
  Andrews--Women p6
 -Cavalry
  Lewis--It p47-66
 -Chickamauga battle
  Morris--Ency. p242
 -Chronology
  -1820-1860 (pre-war)
  Jordan--Civil p9-39
  -1860-1861 (beginning)
  Bonte--America p122
  Jordan--Civil p41-71
  Pratt--Civil p11-35
  -1861-1865
  Reader's--Story p147
  -1862-1863
  Jordan--Civil p73-109, 111-
  145
  -1863
  Bonte--America p127
  Pratt--Civil p37-46
  -1864
  Jordan--Civil p147-179
  -1864-1865
  Bonte--America p129
  Pratt--Civil p49-62
  -1865
  Jordan--Civil p181-211
 -Cold Harbor battle
  Morris--Ency. p243
 -Committee on the Conduct of
 War
  Holzman--Stormy p154-160
 -Draft (conscription)
  Dowdey--Experiment p164-
  166, 182, 374-376
  Marzio--Nation p327-328
  -Laws
  Life--Union (6) p8-10

-Riots
  Amer. Her. --New (8)
  p E270-271
  Furnas--Americans p521,
  701-702
  -New York City, N. Y.
    -Views of Anna Dickin-
    son
      Commager--Heritage
      p696-702
-East
  America's Hist. p434-438
  Morris--Ency. p236
-Economic conditions
  Carman--History (1) p685-692
  Harlow--Story p323-326
-Food
  Meredith--World p155
-Generals
  See also names of generals
  Treasury Amer. p230-239
-Guns. See GUNS--Civil war
-Industrialization
  Jones--Age p102-103
-Legacy
  Carman--History (1) p702-752
  Carman--History (2) p3-53
-Losses
  Morris--Ency. p245
-Medicines
  Andrews--Women p49n, 61,
  117, 133
-Milk, Scarcity of
  Andrews--Women p23
-Nashville battle
  Morris--Ency. p243-244
-Naval battles
  Amer. Her. --New (8) p685-
  695
  Bonte--America p124-125
  Jordan--Civil p55, 78-79, 83,
  94-95, 151, 165-167, 182-183;
  See also index (under Union
  --Navy) p215
  -Ironclads
    Jordan--Civil p67, 73, 78-
    79, 83, 94
    Pratt--Civil p15-16
-Negroes
  Amer. Her. --New (8)
  p E287-288
  Jordan--Civil p67, 112-113,
  120, 148-149, 162-163, 184-
  185, 191, 196
  Life--Union (6) p10, 18
-North
  Burner--America (1) p327-
  335

-Opium, use in
  Garrison--Lost p65-67
-Opposing forces
  Morris--Ency. p231
-Palmetto battery, Charleston,
  S. C., 1863
  Viewpoints p82
-Peace
  Dowdey--Experiment p299, 341,
  354, 359-360, 382-387, 394
-Peace commissioners, Confed-
erate
  Dowdey--Experiment p387, 388-
  389
-Peninsular campaign, 1862
  Life--Union (6) p19, 54-55, 71,
  94-95
, Post-war
  See also RECONSTRUCTION
  Dulles--United p3-19
  Partridge--As p69-91
  -Diplomatic victories
    Harlow--Story p329-330
-Prisons and prisoners
  Andrews--Women. See index
  p463
-Racketeering
  Partridge--As p62
-Raids, by Jubal Early
  Morris--Ency. p243
-Rationing
  See also CIVIL WAR--Food
  Partridge--As p61
-Recollections, by Cornelia
Branch Stone
  Andrews--Women p420-424
-Recruitment
  See also CIVIL WAR--Draft
  Boardman--Civil p70-71
  Commager--Heritage p675-677
  Morris--Ency. p231-232
  -Bounties
    Furnas--Americans p694-695
  -Views of Edward Dicey
    Commager--Heritage p675-
    677
-Regiments
  Dowdey--Experiment. See
  index p452
  -Massachusetts
    Jordan--Civil p34-37, 112-
    113, 184-185
-Relief work
  Carman--History (1) p654-655
-Results
  Alden--Pioneer p285-287
-Sacking of Confederate home
  Commager--Heritage p689-695

-Scarcity (Richmond, Va.)
  -Views of J. B. Jones
    Commager--Heritage p705-
    710
-"Seven Days" battles (around
Richmond, 1862)
  Dowdey--Experiment p202-
  203, 240, 244, 260, 347
  Jordan--Civil p97-98, 100-101
  Morris--Ency. p237
  Pratt--Civil p20-21
-Seven Pines (Fair Oaks) battle
  Morris--Ency. p236-237
-Slogans
  Dowdey--Experiment p316
-Soldiers
  See also CONFEDERACY;
  CIVIL WAR--Union army
  Meredith--World p158-163
  Treasury Amer. p242-247
  , Dead, Union
    , Obligations to
      Trachtenberg--Demo.
      p35-50
  , Returning
    -Clothing and dress
      Partridge--As p85
-Songs. See SONGS--Civil war
-South
  Carman--History (1) p689-692
  Harlow--Story p305-339
  Kane--Gone p298-333
  -Yeomen
    -Views of Bell Irvin Wiley
      Miers--American p197-
      201
-Spies
  Dowdey--Experiment p2, 173-
  174, 211, 334-335
-Stone river, or Murfreesboro
battle, 1862
  Viewpoints p79
-Strategy
  Morris--Ency. p232
-Submarines. See SUBMARINES
--Civil war
-Surrender of Lee, Appomattox,
1865. See LEE, ROBERT E.--
Surrender at Appomattox, 1865
-Taxes
  Dowdey--Experiment p54,
  209, 263, 364-465
-Technology and warfare
  Reader's--Story p150
-Torpedoes. See TORPEDOES
--Civil war
-Union army
  Jordan--Civil. See index

(under Union army) p215
, of the Ohio
  Jordan--Civil p81
, of the Potomac
  Jordan--Civil. See index
  p212
, of the Tennessee
  Jordan--Civil p122
-Victory
  Amer. Her. --New (8) p667-684
  Harlow--Story p305-330
-War savings bonds
  Partridge--As p57
-Washington, D.C. See WASH-
INGTON, D.C. --Civil war
-West
  American's Hist. p448-457
  Morris--Ency. p235
  Tunis--Frontier p142-145
-Women
  Boardman--Civil p190
  Gurko--Ladies p116, 199, 208-
  212, 214, 224, 260
  Jordan--Civil p45, 86-87, 90,
  96, 110-111, 191
  Reader's--Story p431
  Warren--Pictorial p103-114
  , as workers
    Partridge--As p53-55, 58-
    59
  -North
    Life--New (5) p121-122,
    124-125
  , on battlefields
    Warren--Pictorial p107, 109
CLAFLIN, TENNESSEE. See
COOK, TENNESSEE CLAFLIN
CLAFLIN FAMILY
  Furnas--Americans p643-646
CLAIM ASSOCIATIONS (land regis-
tration clubs)
  Tunis--Frontier p101
  , and law
    Boorstin--Americans p74-80
  , Frontier, 1839
    Ridge--America's p408-410
  -Operation, 1843
    Ridge--America's p410-413
CLAIM SHACKS. See HOMESTEAD-
ERS
CLAPPE, LOUISE AMELIA KNAPP
SMITH ("DAME SHIRLEY")
  -"Mining techniques," 1851-1852
    Ridge--America's p533-535
  , on gold mining as "Nature's
  great lottery")
    Angle--American p255-258
CLARK, ALVIN G.

-Telescopes
  Reader's--Story p310
CLARK, CHAMP
  Harlow--Story p506-507
CLARK, WILLIAM
  See also LEWIS AND CLARK
    EXPEDITION
  Boardman--Virginia p98-101
  Brown--Westerners. See index
    p285
  Gilbert--Trail. See index p234
  Life--Growing (3) p69, 79-82, 86,
    88-89
  Life--Steel (7) p54, 130
  Morris--Ency. p133
  -Biography
    Morris--Ency. p687 (under
      Lewis, Meriwether)
  , on reaching the Pacific, 1805
    Angle--American p163-164
CLASSES
  See also ARISTOCRACY: SER-
    VANTS: SOCIETY; etc.
  Cable--American p209-210
  Furnas--Americans p314-315,
    451, 922-924
  -Consciousness
    -Views of Frances Trollope
      p154-155
  -"Leveling up"
    Furnas--Americans p921-925
  -New York City
    Partridge--As p98
  -"Poor whites"
    Furnas--Americans p407, 469
  -South
    Alden--Pioneer p195-197
    Kraus--U.S. p403-406
  -West
    Hine--American. See index
      p361
CLATSOP INDIANS
  Gilbert--Trail. p32
CLAY, CASSIUS MARCELLUS
  Boardman--Jackson. p116
  -Memoirs and writings (1848-
    1886)
    Grimsted--Notions p286-296
CLAY, HENRY
  Amer. Her. --New (5) p392,
    395; p E158
  Amer. Her. --New (7) p552-553,
    626
  Boardman--Civil p2
  Boardman--Jackson. See index
    p206
  Borden--Portrait (1). See
    index p239

Butterfield--Amer. p68-69, 93,
  132-133, 140
Carman--History (1) p410-413;
  see also index p. v
Harlow--Story. See index p506
Kraus--U.S. See index p. ii
Life--Growing (3). See index
  p172
Life--New (5) p34-35, 37-38
Life--Sweep (4). See index p156
Morris--Ency. See index p743
Reader's--Story p67
200 Years (1). See index p346
Whitney--American. See index
  p361
, and Eaton affair
  Phillips--That p12, 24, 29, 37,
    41, 44-46, 49-50, 65, 86, 90
, and "Force bill"
  Collins--Story p179
-Biography
  Morris--Ency. p643-644
, on compromise of 1850
  Hurd--Treasury p68-70
, on New England weather
  Hurd--Treasury p105-106
, on working together, 1832
  Reader's--Story p504
-Resignation from Senate, 1842
  Morris--Ency. p187
-Speech for war, 1811
  Ridge--America's p264-267
-Van Buren letters
  Morris--Ency. p189-190
CLAY, JOHN
  -"End of the open range: The
    winter of 1886-1887"
    Ridge--America's p610-612
CLAY COMPROMISE TARIFF. See
  COMPROMISE OF 1833
CLAYTON, WILLIAM
  -"The pioneer band reaches
    Utah," 1847
    Ridge--America's p512-515
CLAYTON-BULWER TREATY
  Amer. Her. --New (6) p E197-198
  Amer. Her. --New (12) p1025
  Carman--History (1) p574-575
  Morris--Ency. p213-214
CLEANING
  , Spring
    Walker--Every. p34
CLEANLINESS
  See also BATHS AND BATHING
  Cable--American p248-249
CLEATHER, ALICE LEIGHTON
  Neidle--America's p70
CLEAVER, JOSEPH, JR.

, on life in colleges and univer-
sities, 1850's
Burner--America (1) p204-213
CLEMENS, SAMUEL LANGHORNE
(MARK TWAIN)
Amer. Her.--New (11) p964-967,
970, E401-402 (under Mark
Twain)
Boardman--Civil p150
Boardman--Gilded p124-127
Bode--Anatomy p45, 52-55, 152
Carman--History (2) p338-340
Drury--Midwest p10, 15-16
Dulles--United p112-114
Furnas--Americans. See index
(under Twain, Mark) p1011
Harlow--Story p432-433
Hart--Popular p146-150
Hilton--Way p49-50, 126-127
Jones--Age p69, 229, 342, 352
Jones--Shaping p235-238
Life--Reaching (8) p114-125
Life--Steel (7) p22, 37-38, 53,
104-105
Meredith--World p70-75
Morris--Ency. p572-573
Mott--Golden p155-157
Our literary p142-149
Randel--Centennial. See index
p467
Reader's--Story p414-415
Walker--Every. p54-55, 167-
169, 196
, as a pilot
Commager--Heritage p329-
339
-Biography
Morris--Ency. p644
-Boyhood home (Hannibal, Mo.)
Vanderbilt--Living p173
-"The joys of overland coaching,
1872"
Ridge--America's p558-561
, on New England weather
Hurd--Treasury p105-106
, on parlor "whatnots" p52-55
Bode--Anatomy p52-55
, on Pony Express
Commager--Heritage p546-548
Davie--Profile p162-164
-"The Pony Express: meeting a
rider on the plains, 1872"
Ridge--America's p561-562
, on Virginia City
Commager--Heritage p715-719
-Publishing aid to Ulysses S.
Grant
White--American p111-114

-"Study," a literary shrine (El-
mira, N.Y.)
Vanderbilt--Living p51
-Temper saved life
Garrison--Lost p89-93
-"An unbiased criticism"
Trachtenberg--Demo. p314-319
-Views of Albert Bigelow
Angle--American p429-431
CLERGYMEN
See also names of clergymen
Cable--American p246-247
Handlin--This p119, 135, 148-150,
164, 253, 261, 358-359
Wilson--Early p103-104
, and wealth
Amer. Her.--New (11) p914-
918
-Etiquette
Cable--American p84
, Protestant
Boardman--Civil p187-188
-Views of Frances Trollope
Trollope--Domestic. See
index (under Clergy) p. iv
"CLERMONT" (steamboat)
Collins--Story p148
Wilson--American p68-69
Wright--Every. p81
CLEVELAND, FRANCES FOLSOM
Life--Steel (7) p17
Melick--Wives p50-51
CLEVELAND, GROVER
Boardman--Gilded. See index
p198
Bonte--America p140, 144
Butterfield--Amer. p238-239,
242-244
Carman--History (2). See index
p. v
Harlow--Story p456-459
Holzman--Stormy p214-219
Keller--Affairs. See index p611
Life--Reaching (8) p82-84; see
also index p172
Life--Steel (7) p16-18, 26, 45, 56
Maurois--Illus. p207-208, 210,
215, 217
Morris--Ency. See index p743
Treasury Amer. p338-343
200 Years (2) p89, 91-92, 318-319
, and foreign markets
Hollingsworth--Amer. p41-50
, and reform
Harlow--Story p455-459
-Biography
Morris--Ency. p644
Whitney--American p185-197

-Controversy with Altgeld, 1894
  Angle--By p297-300
-Marriage
  Butterfield--Amer. p242
, on veterans' pensions
  Harlow--Story p259-960
-Presidency
  Amer. Her. --New (10) p879
  Dulles--United p137-138, 140-
  142
    Linton--Bicentennial. See
    index p440
  Reader's--Story p334
-Scandals
  Garrison--Lost p49-52
-Venezuelan policy
  Hollingsworth--Amer. p29-50
CLEVELAND, OHIO
  Boardman--Virginia p197-198
  Drury--Midwest p55-61
  Treasury Amer. p262-263
CLIMATE. See WEATHER
CLINTON, DE WITT
  Amer. Her. --New (5) p E159
  Boardman--Virginia p37, 89, 195
  Harlow--Story p199, 250
  Morris--Ency. p142, 422, 556
, and Eaton affair
  Phillips--That p18-20
-Biography
  Morris--Ency. p644-645
CLINTON, GEORGE
  Boardman--Virginia p23-24
CLINTON DITCH. See ERIE
CANAL
CLIPPER SHIPS
  Amer. Her. --New (7) p600-601
  Boardman--Jackson. p82-83
  Carman--History (1) p474-475
  Furnas--Americans p305, 359-
  360
  Harlow--Story p198
  Reader's--Story p177-179
  Train--Story p282-283
  200 Years (1) p210-211
  Wilson--American p156-161
-"Clippermen" (sailors)
  Wilson--Early p77-78
-Log of the "Flying Cloud,"
  1851
  Davie--Profile p159, 162
-Speed records
  Reader's--Story p179
, to Orient
  Amer. Her. --New (7) p602-
  603
-Western travel
  Amer. Her. --New (7) p604-

  605
CLOCKS AND CLOCKMAKERS
  Dreppard--Pioneer p7, 79
  Trachtenberg--Demo. p240-241
, "Grandfather"
  Wilson--Vanish. p87
-Toys. See TOYS, Clockwork
, Wooden
  Van Wagenen--Golden p156
CLOTH. See FABRICS
CLOTH BOOKS. See CHILDREN'S
BOOKS AND READING, Cloth
CLOTH DOLLS. See DOLLS, Cloth
CLOTH TOYS. See TOYS, Cloth
CLOTHING AND DRESS
  See also ACCESSORIES; FASHION
  Boardman--Virginia p185-186
  Furnas--Americans p435, 493,
  667-668, 810, 815
  Handlin--This. See index p581
  Hilton--Way. See index p212
  Langdon--Everyday (2) p266-273
  Schwartz--When p46-47
  Train--Story p170-173, 324-329
  Walker--Every. p31, 37, 150-
  151, 184-186
-1854
  Viewpoints p106
-1876
  Randel--Centennial. See in-
  dex p468 (under Fashion and
  dress)
-1896
  Ross--Taste p185
-Anglophilia
  Furnas--Americans p607, 609-
  610
-Bathing girls, 1890's
  Ross--Taste p181, 185
-Bloomers
  Gurko--Ladies p141-145, 147-
  154, 157-158, 176, 206
  Ross--Heroines p17-18
  White--American p43-45
, Boys'
  McClinton--Antiques p53-59, 69
  -Trousers
    Earle--Two cent. (2) p778-
    780
, Bridal
  Earle--Two cent. (2) p638-644
  Ross--Taste p194, 196, 200
-Bustles and hoopskirts
  Furnas--Americans p667-668
  Partridge--As p140-142
  Train--Story p325-327
  Woodward--Way p287
, Children's

See also CLOTHING AND
　DRESS, Boys'; ... Girls'
Cable--American p148-149,
　179
McClinton--Antiques p53-63
Ross--Taste p201
-Civil war
　-Soldiers, returning
　　Partridge--As p85
-Cloaks
　Ross--Taste p173
, Color of, 1876
　Hilton--Way p27
-Corsets
　Cable--American p106, 234-
　235, 262-263
-Cowboys
　Furnas--Americans p684-685
　Train--Story p295
　Tunis--Frontier p149-150
　-Bandannas
　　Tunis--Frontier p149-150
　-Chaps
　　Tunis--Frontier p149-150
　-Levis
　　Tunis--Frontier p149-150
-Cowhands, western
　Tunis--Frontier p149-150
-Crinolines
　Ross--Taste p175, 178
-Empire
　Earle--Two cent. (2) p783-
　793
, Flannel
　Furnas--Americans p432-433,
　438
, Gamblers'
　Train--Story p310
, Girls'
　Schwartz--When p48
　Wilson--Folkways p45
　-Pantaloons (pantalets)
　　Earle--Two cent. (2)
　　p776-778
-Jeans
　, First, 1850 (San Francisco,
　Ca.)
　　Robertson--Book p89
-Levis
　See also CLOTHING AND
　DRESS--Cowboys--Levis
　Furnas--Americans p899-900
-Magazines
　Furnas--Americans p559-560
, Men's
　Boardman--Virginia p185-186
　Carson--Polite p85
　Hunt--Life p63

Partridge--As p147
Train--Story p273
Tunis--Young p101-102
Wilson--Folkways p44-49
-Coats ("Prince Albert")
　Woodward--Way p287
-Suits
　Woodward--Way p296-298
, Miners'
　Train--Story p308-310
-Mittens
　Ross--Taste p217
-Mountain men
　Tunis--Frontier p113
-Mourning
　Ross--Taste p184
-Muffs
　Ross--Taste p217
-Old Northwest
　Tunis--Frontier p81-82
-Overalls
　Furnas--Americans p898-899
-Overland mail drivers
　Furnas--Americans p280
-Pantaloons and gaiters
　See also CLOTHING AND
　DRESS, Girls'--Pantaloons
　　Earle--Two cent. (2) p769
, Paper costume, 1867
　Ross--Taste p185
-Patterns
　Furnas--Americans p668
　Hilton--Way p115
　Lynes--Taste. p75-79
-Petticoats (1890's)
　Ross--Taste p214
, Ready-made
　Furnas--Americans p669-671
-Reform
　Ross--Taste p211
-Riding habits
　Earle--Two cent. (2) p625-628
-Shawls
　Ross--Taste p221
-Sizes
　Ross--Taste p62
-Social calls
　Ross--Taste p184
-"Spencers"
　Earle--Two cent. (2) p799-802
-Sports
　Furnas--Americans p810, 898-
　899
　-1880's
　　Peck--Nineteenth. n. p.
　-1896
　　Ross--Taste p180-181
-Underwear

Furnas--Americans p432-433, 896-898
, Unhealthy
Cable--American p106
, Victorian
Amer. Her. --New (11) p934-957
-Views of Frances Trollope
Trollope--Domestic. See index (under Dress) p. v
-West
Gilbert--Trail. p62-63
Train--Story p295-303, 308-310
-Widows and widowers
Cable--American p176
-Women's
Boardman--Civil p193
Boardman--Virginia p185
Cable--American p215-216, 234-235
Handlin--This p108, 127-128, 183, 261
Hilton--Way p114-122
Hunt--Life p61, facing 64
Tunis--Young p103-104
Wilson--Folkways p36-43
-Trousers
Earle--Two cent. (2) p773-778
-Work clothes
Furnas--Americans p898-900
, Yachting, 1894
Ross--Taste p180
CLOTHING INDUSTRY (Garment trade)
Furnas--Americans p669-671, 708
-Jews and Italians
Marzio--Nation p362-363
CLUBS AND SOCIETIES
See also ASSOCIATIONS; names of clubs; special subjects
Handlin--This p179-180, 194, 360, 394-395, 397
Ross--Taste p47, 50-51
Walker--Every. p110-111, 120, 140-149
, Children's, 1876
Hilton--Way p47
, City
Carson--Polite p242-244
, Men's
Cable--American p219-220
Life--Reaching (8) p56
Walker--Every. p146-147
, Social
Dulles--History p63-64

, Women's
Boardman--Jackson. p188
Drury--Midwest p90
Dulles--History p256-257
Dulles--United p103
Furnas--Americans p890-893
Life--Reaching (8) p39
Walker--Every. p142-143
Warren--Pictorial p137-138
CLYMAN, JAMES
Amer. Her. --New (6) p E198
DeVoto--Year. See index p514
-"William H. Ashley's fight with the Arikara," 1823
Ridge--America's p382-386
CLYMER, HEISTER
Randel--Centennial p128, 210-212, 234
COACHES
See also STAGECOACHES; "TALLYHOS"
-California
Tunis--Frontier p137-138
, for overland mail
See also POSTAL SERVICE
Tunis--Frontier p139-140
-Last, Deadwood, S.D.
Viewpoints p45
-Old Northwest
Tunis--Frontier p72-73
, Private
Wilson--Early p134-135
-Travel
Cable--American p277, 328-329
COACHING (parade)
Life--Steel (7) p147
Partridge--As p158
COACHING CLUBS
-1876
Randel--Centennial p78-79, 321-322
COAHULA-TEXAS COLONIZATION ACT, 1825
Empresario system
Ridge--America's p416-419
COAL
Furnas--Americans p427-432
Handlin--This p113, 158-159, 295, 333, 364
Langdon--Everyday (2) p280-298
Van Wagenen--Golden p157-158
-Bins
Wilson--Vanish. p109
-Strikes
Life--Steel (7) p79, 86, 88-89
COBB, HOWELL
Life--New (5) p32-33

, and secession movement
    Young--Women p37
    -Biography
        Amer. Her. --New (7) p E231
COBBLERS. See HOMEMAKERS
COBURN, JOE
    Meredith--World p46
COCA-COLA
    Marzio--Nation p565
    -First, 1886
        Boardman--Gilded p180
        Reader's--Story p124
COCHISE (Indian)
    Boardman--Civil p107
    Reader's--Story p85
COCHRAN, THOMAS C.
    , on New England factories
        Miers--American p121-126
COCHRANE, ELIZABETH. See
    BLY, NELLY
COCKFIGHTING
    Dulles--History p50, 52, 57-58,
    65, 75, 138, 159, 172
COCKRELL, FRANCIS MARION
    Butterfield--Amer. p262
COCKTAILS
    , First, 1806
        Robertson--Book p40
        Ross--Taste p59
CODY, WILLIAM F. ("BUFFALO
    BILL")
    Boardman--Civil p198
    Brown--Westerners p159, 166,
    168, 197, 255-256
    Hine--American p141, 201, 268,
    274-279, 322
    Marzio--Nation p425
    Maurois--Illus. p191, 193
    Reader's--Story p172, 466
    -Biography
        Amer. Her. --New (11) p E377-
        378
    -Buffalo hunt for Russian Grand
    Duke
        White--American p92-98
    -Wild West company and shows
        Amer. Her. --New (11) p940-
        941
        Amer. Her. --90's p122-123
        Dulles--History p216-217
COFFEE, JOHN
    , and Eaton affair
        Phillips--That p27, 67, 101-
        102, 121, 132
COFFEE
    -Mills
        Wilson--Vanish. p102
    , Substitutes for

Andrews--Women p22
COFFEEHOUSES
    Wilson--Early p57-58
COFFIN, C. C.
    -"Bonanza farming in Minnesota,"
    1880
        Ridge--America's p630-631
COFFIN, LEVI
    Life--New (5) p82-83
    , and Underground railroad
        Boardman--Jackson. p121
        Commager--Heritage p489-493
COFFINS
    Cable--American p174-175
    Schwartz--When p177-178
COHENS VS. VIRGINIA
    Amer. Her. --New (5) p371, E159
COINAGE ACT, 1873
    Harlow--Story p451
    Morris--Ency. p251
COINS. See CURRENCY
COIN'S FINANCIAL SCHOOL
    Harlow--Story p471-472
COLD HARBOR, VIRGINIA
    -Lee's victory, 1864
        -Views of Theodore Lyman
            Angle--American p331-333
COLE, ARTHUR C.
    , on Daniel Webster and northern
    industrialism
        Miers--American p169-173
COLE, THOMAS
    Boardman--Jackson. p152-153
    Bode--Anatomy p69-71
    Larkin--Art p200-204; see also
    index p520
    Reader's--Story p377
COLFAX, SCHUYLER
    Amer. Her. --New (8) p E268
    Butterfield--Amer. p205
    -Exposé of Credit Mobilier
        Morris--Ency. p250-251
COLLECTIVE BARGAINING
    Harlow--Story p402
COLLECTORS AND COLLECTING
    See also types of collections
    Hilton--Way p44-46
    Lynes--Taste. See index p351
COLLEGES AND UNIVERSITIES
    See also A and M COLLEGES;
    ARCHITECTURE--Colleges;
    MEDICAL SCHOOLS; SPORTS
    AND GAMES; names of colleges
    and universities
    Bartlett--New p394-397
    Boardman--Civil p180-184
    Boardman--Jackson. p136-137
    Boardman--Virginia p164

Borden--Portrait (2) p55-56
Carman--History (1) p516-517,
523, 688
Dulles--United p118-120
Furnas--Americans p541-542,
740-747
Handlin--This p142-143, 179, 271,
276, 281
Harlow--Story p252-253, 427-428
Life--Reaching (8) p13-14
Tunis--Young p131-133
Tyler--Freedom's p254-259
Walker--Every. p103, 117-121,
166
-1860's-1870's
Carman--History (2) p367-
369
-1870-1899
Amer. Her. --New (11) p942-
943
-Before Civil War
Wright--Culture p179
, "Booster"
Boorstin--Americans p152-161
-California
Johnson--Pictorial p164-165
Wright--Culture p144-153
-Curriculum
See also COLLEGES AND
UNIVERSITIES--Technical
subjects
Nye--Cultural p189-194
, Denominational
Boorstin--Americans p153-160
Hunt--Life p127-128
Nye--Cultural p179
Tyler--Freedom's p255-257
Wright--Culture p103, 106-
110, 144-153
-Discipline, relaxed
Cable--American p166
-Faculty
Nye--Cultural p183-184
-Finance
Nye--Cultural p181-182
, for negroes
Boardman--Civil p182
-Graduates
-Men, 1870
Cable--American p166
, Number of, 1815
Hunt--Life p129
-Women, 1870
Cable--American p166-167
-Indiana
Wright--Culture p106-107
-Land-grant
Furnas--Americans p746-747,

752-753
Hine--American p246
-Life
See also COLLEGES AND
UNIVERSITIES--Students
Cable--American p164-166, 319
-1850's
-Views of Joseph Cleaver,
Jr.
Burner--America (1)
p204-213
, Methodist
Wright--Culture p143-145
-Ohio
Wright--Culture p104-105
-Post Civil war
Mumford--Brown p39-42
-Professional schools
Hunt--Life p129-131
Train--Story p342-343
-Riots and unrest
Cable--American p165-166
-South, 1870's
Randel--Centennial p421-424
, State
Davidson--Life (2) p362-363
Morris--Ency. p557
Nye--Cultural p179-180
Tyler--Freedom's p258-259
-Students
Nye--Cultural p185-187
Walker--Every. p118-120
Wright--Every. p200-201
-Women
Boardman--Gilded p155
Boardman--Jackson. p137
Hine--American p248-249
-Technical subjects
Our literary p156-157
-Views of Henry Seidel Canby,
1898
Angle--American p432-435
-West
Hine--American p243-247, 249-
250, 333
, Women's
Boardman--Civil p181-182
Life--Reaching (8) p39
Warren--Pictorial p128
, First (Oberlin, O., 1833)
Robertson--Book p208
COLLIER, WILLIAM
Blum--Stage   Profile 44
COLLINS, PERRY McDONOUGH
-Overland telegraph
White--American p63-67
COLORADO
See also DENVER, COLORADO

Billington--Far p259-268, 285-287
Carman--History (1) p783
-1870's
　　Randel--Centennial p115-116,
　　263-264
-Creede
　　Watkins--Gold p97-98, 234, 253
-Cripple Creek
　　Watkins--Gold p98-100
-Gold discoveries
　　See also COLORADO--Rockies
　　(and names of areas)
　　Dulles--United p35-36
　　Ridge--America's p542-544
　　Watkins--Gold p49-60
-Mines and mining
　-Social conditions (life)
　　　Billington--Far p266-268
-Rockies
　, Gold rush to
　　　Watkins--Gold p47-57, 59,
　　　63, 65, 96
　　-Life
　　　Watkins--Gold p60, 96-97,
　　　100
　, Travel to
　　　Watkins--Gold p53-55, 93-
　　　94
COLPORTAGE (religious society)
　Bode--Anatomy p134-135
COLT, SAMUEL
　Amer. Her. --New (5) p E159
　Lynes--Taste. p98-99
　, and guns
　　Marzio--Nation p520-529
COLTER, JOHN
　Brown--Westerners p52-56
　Gilbert--Trail. p53-56, 60, 126
　Hine--American p49-50
　Reader's--Story p163-164
　, and Blackfoot Indians
　　Reader's--Story p164
COLTON, DAVID DOUTY,
GENERAL
　Lewis--Big p283-320
COLTON, WALTER
　, on Monterey gold fever
　　Commager--Heritage p555-
　　559
　-"Spread of the gold fever in
　　California, " 1850
　　Ridge--America's p531-532
COLUMBIA, SOUTH CAROLINA
　, Burning of
　　Andrews--Women p257-277
COLUMBIA FUR COMPANY
　Carman--History (1) p371-372
COLUMBIA RIVER AND VALLEY

Boardman--Jackson. p50-52
Hine--American p46-47, 73, 76-77,
　88-96, 179
-Gorge ("Bridge of the Gods
　Legend")
　Case--Empire p323-333
COLUMBIA (CALIFORNIA) STATE
PARK
　Vanderbilt--Living p207
COLUMBIAN EXPOSITION, CHI-
CAGO, 1893
　See also CHICAGO, ILLINOIS,
　as fair city
　America 200 p70
　Boardman--Gilded p142-144, 179-
　180
　Butterfield--Amer. p260-261
　Cable--American p286
　Furnas--Americans. See index
　p981
　Harris--Land p291-303
　Jones--Age p144, 250-251, 253-
　258, 279-280
　Larkin--Art p290, 310-317
　Lynes--Taste. p142-144, 147, 163,
　212, 250
　, Women in
　　Warren--Pictorial p159
COLUMBUS, OHIO
　Drury--Midwest p105
COLUMNISTS. See JOURNALISTS--
Columnists
COMANCHE INDIANS
　Amer. Her. --Indians. See index
　p420
　Andrews--Indian leaders. See
　index p183
　Billington--Far p28, 36-38, 137,
　285
　Boardman--Civil p106-107
　Boardman--Jackson. p73-74
　Brown--Westerners p69, 81-83,
　103, 195-196, 201, 204, 206-208,
　210-211, 236
　DeVoto--Year p71, 153, 243-245,
　258, 260, 263, 269, 392, 401, 484,
　495, 502
COMBE, GEORGE
　Furnas--Americans p445-447, 455
COMIC STRIPS
　Dulles--United p199
　Furnas--Americans p867-868
　Marzio--Nation p600-601
　Reader's--Story p365
　Walker--Every. p174, 195
COMMERCE
　See also EXPORTS AND IM-
　PORTS; INDUSTRY: SHIPS

AND SHIPPING: TRADE AND
TRADING; names of cities
  Boardman--Jackson. p77-78
  Kraus--U.S. p391
  Morris--Ency. p488-489
  -Neutral rights, 1806
    Morris--Ency. p134
  -South
    Kraus--U.S. p409-410
"COMMON MAN"
  , Rise of
    Harlow--Story p224-227
"COMMONWEALTH VS. HUNT, "
1842
  Angle--By p184-190
  Harlow--Story p210, 403
COMMUNICATION
  See also CABLES; POSTAL
    SERVICE; TELEGRAPH;
    TELEPHONE; TRANSPORTA-
    TION: TRAVEL AND TRAV-
    ELERS
  Boardman--Civil p145-146
  Boardman--Jackson. p99-101
  Harris--Land p45-70
  Walker--Every. p51-54, 139
  Wilson--Folkways p188-193
COMMUNISM
  See also names of settlements;
    UTOPIAS
  -Early organizations
    Tyler--Freedom's p108-139
  -Projects and enterprises
    Carman--History (1) p529-
    530
  Furnas--Americans. See index
  p982
  -Societies
    Life--Sweep (4) p59, 61-64
COMMUNITARIAN MOVEMENT
  Burner--America (1) p287-291
COMMUNITIES
  See also specific names
  Furnas--Americans. See index
  p982
  , of travelers
    Boorstin--Americans p49,
    51-56, 68
COMMUNITY LIFE. See names
of places, subdivision Life
COMMUNITY OF TRUE INSPIRA-
TION. See AMANA SOCIETY
COMPOSERS
  See also names of composers
  Furnas--Americans p584-585,
  589-590, 664-665
  Howard--Our p295-296, 298,
  361-365

  -American vs. European
    Chase--America's p327-345
  -Boston, Mass.
    Howard--Our p306-323
  , Foreign, in America
    Morris--Ency. p614, 616-617
  , of songs
    Bonte--America p119
COMPROMISE OF 1820
  Boardman--Civil p14-15
COMPROMISE OF 1833
  Amer. Her. --New (5) p E159
  Carman--History (1) p433-434
COMPROMISE OF 1850
  See also CLAY, HENRY
  Alden--Pioneer p247-250, 257
  Amer. Her. --New (7) p E231-232;
  626
  Boardman--Civil p1-4
  Boardman--Jackson. p194-198
  Bonte--America p110
  Borden--Portrait (1) p216-217
  Butterfield--Amer. p132-133
  Carman--History (1) p600-607
  Harlow--Story p287-288
  Hurd--Treasury p68-70
  Kraus--U.S. p438-439, 445
  Life--New (5) p36-39, 49-54, 57
  Linton--Bicentennial p136, 141,
  143-144, 149
  Morris--Ency. p210-213
  , and California
    Collins--Story p185
COMPROMISE OF 1877
  Boardman--Gilded p10-11
  Carman--History (1) p750
  Carman--History (2) p46-53
  -Congressional debate
    Life--Sweep (4) p56-57
COMPUTERS
  , First, for data processing, 1889
    Robertson--Book p44
COMSTOCK, ANTHONY
  Randel--Centennial p312-314
COMSTOCK, HENRY T. P.
  See also "COMSTOCK LODE"
    (Nevada)
  Kraus--U.S. p469-470
  Watkins--Gold p66, 69-70, 73
"COMSTOCK LODE" (Nevada, 1859-
1861)
  Amer. Her. --New p730-733
  Billington--Far p251-259
  Boardman--Civil p101-102
  Collins--Story p280
  Commager--Heritage p578-582
  Ridge--America's p538-541
  Tunis--Frontier p135-136

Watkins--Gold. See index p284
-Views of Dan DeQuille
    Commager--Heritage p578-582
CONCERTS
    See also BANDS
    Dulles--History p126-127, 237-238
    Handlin--This p187-188, 190-193,
    196, 201-202
    -Life
        Howard--Our p150-158
    , Sacred
        Handlin--This p263-264
CONCORD, MASSACHUSETTS
    Brooks--Flower. p268-285
"CONCORD COACHES"
    See also OVERLAND COMPA-
    NIES
    Bartlett--New p300-301
    Billington--Far p280-281
    Hilton--Way p134
    Reader's--Story p193
    Tunis--Frontier p140-141
    200 Years (2) p61
"CONCORD GROUP" (literature)
    Reader's--Story p410-411
CONCRETE
    -Construction
        Gowans--Images p393-394,
        396
    -Oldest building (Milton, Wisc.)
        Vanderbilt--Living p168
CONESTOGA WAGONS
    Amer. Her. --New (5) p431-432;
    E159-160
    Bartlett--New p291-295, 300
    Boardman--Virginia p87-88
    Davidson--Life (2) p211
    Langdon--Everyday (2) p73-74
    Marzio--Nation p174-175
    Tunis--Frontier p71-72, 103-104
    200 Years (2) p60-61
CONFEDERACY (Confederate States
of America)
    Alden--Pioneer p260-287
    Amer. Her. --New (7) p616;
    p E232
    Boardman--Civil p29, 32-34,
    38, 59, 65
    Harlow--Story. See index
    p806-807
    Jordan--Civil. See index p212
    Keyes--Hope p250
    Life--New (5). See index p156
    Life--Union (6). See index
    p173
    Linton--Bicentennial. See index
    p440
    200 Years (2) p11-53

, and Britain
    Dowdey--Experiment. See
    index p446
    Morris--Ency. p240-241
, and Europe
    Jordan--Civil p53, 80, 104, 112,
    117-118, 135
-Army
    Dowdey--Experiment. See
    index p445
    Jordan--Civil. See index
    p212
    Life--New (5) p126, 135-138,
    142, 144-145, 147, 150-151
    Life--Union (6). See index
    p173
    , Disintegration of
        -Views of Eliza Frances
        Andrews
            Commager--Heritage
            p721-725
    , of N. Virginia (Lee's)
        Dowdey--Experiment. See
        index p443
        Jordan--Civil. See index
        p212
    , of Tennessee
        Jordan--Civil p190
-Cabinet
    -Views of J.B. Jones
        Commager--Heritage p678-
        680
-Commissioners
    Dowdey--Experiment p19-20,
    56, 102-103, 130-140, 209
-Congress
    Dowdey--Experiment p92, 148,
    152, 393
    Life--New (5) p133-136
    -Land survey and sales
        Bartlett--New p72-73
-Conscription
    Life--Union (6) p8-9
-Constitution
    Carman--History (1) p634-635
    Dowdey--Experiment p11-12,
    21, 165
    Morris--Ency. p228-229
-Diplomacy
    Dowdey--Experiment p291
-Flags
    Dowdey--Experiment p1, 10,
    22-23
    , Battle
        Morris--Ency. p280
-Forts, Clearing of, 1862
    Pratt--Civil p24-26
-Great seal

Dowdey--Experiment p255, 366,
429
-Landmarks
America's Hist. p420-421
-Last days
Morris--Ency. p244
-Military life
Amer. Her.--New (8) p668
-Money. See CONFEDERACY--
Treasury; MONEY--Confederacy
-Navy
Dowdey--Experiment p70-71,
124-125, 161
Life--Union (6). See index
p173
-Negroes (soldiers)
Jordan--Civil p151
-Purchasing agents
Dowdey--Experiment p170-
171
-State department (Richmond,
Va.)
Dowdey--Experiment p43, 56,
134, 148-149, 168, 173, 205
-Substitutes and makeshifts
Dowdey--Experiment p243,
308, 327, 384, 433
-Treasury
Commager--Heritage p711-
714
Dowdey--Experiment p43, 50,
52, 153, 209, 402, 405, 412,
421, 424-425, 429-430
-Treasury notes (C.S.A.)
Dowdey--Experiment p54, 92-
93, 209, 365
-War department
Dowdey--Experiment p79
-"West Point"
Jones--Shaping p179-189
"CONFIDENCE MEN" (Fraud)
Cable--American p260-261
CONFISCATION ACT, 1862
Life--New (5) p117
CONGO CONFERENCE, 1885
Morris--Ency. p282
CONGREGATIONALISTS
Bartlett--New p122, 375-377, 394
Boardman--Virginia p167, 169,
172, 177
Hine--American p90, 226-227,
244
Hunt--Life p122-123
Wright--Culture p96, 98, 107-
108; see also index p262
CONGRESS--U.S.
See also CONGRESSMEN
Hine--American p61, 64, 86, 95-96,

144, 153, 161-162, 246, 249
Life--Sweep (4). See index p156
-1830-1860
Billington--Far. See index
p315
Morris--Ency. p210
-1849-1864
Life--New (5). See index p156
-1876
Randel--Centennial. See index
p467
-1877-1890
Life--Steel (7). See index
p156
-1889-1890 ("Billion dollar")
Butterfield--Amer. p254
-1890's
Life--Reaching (8). See index
p172
, and President Johnson
Dulles--United p20-21
-Corruption and graft, 1865-1872
Butterfield--Amer. p204-205
-Radicals, 1866
Butterfield--Amer. p187
-Votes, South vs. North
Life--Sweep (4) p14
CONGRESSIONAL PEACE COMMIS-
SION, 1867
Ridge--America's p574-576
CONGRESSMEN
-Life
-Views of Manasseh Cutler,
1801
Angle--American p140-143
CONJURERS
Wilson--Early p122-124
CONKLING, ROSCOE
Butterfield--Amer. p223
Keller--Affairs. See index p612
Life--Steel (7) p12-15, 78
CONNECTICUT
Carman--History (1) p782
Hunt--Life. See index p290
-Life
-Views of Samuel Goodrich
Commager--Heritage p355-
359
-Norwich
, Boyhood in 1890's by Gerard
E. Jensen
Amer. Her.--90's p90-96
-Waterbury
-Button industry
McClinton--Antiques p69-70
"CONNECTICUT WITS" (Hartford
wits)
Boardman--Virginia p139-140

CONNER, JAMES
-"The Chivington massacre, "
  with Lieut. Cramer
    Ridge--America's p572-574
CONNER, WILLIAM
  Tunis--Young p135-140, 147
"CONSCIENCE WHIGS"
  Life--Sweep (4) p136
CONSERVATION
  See also BUFFALO; ENVIRON-
    MENT; NATURAL RESOURCES;
    WATER
  Bartlett--New p245
  Boardman--Gilded p162-163
  Jones--Age p92, 173-174, 307-
    310, 317-326
  Keller--Affairs p393-394
  Mumford--Brown p77-80
  -1876
    Randel--Centennial p274-275
  -1894
    Morris--Ency. p264
  , as national issue
    Jones--Age p321-324
  -Views of Alexis De Tocqueville
    Reader's--Story p502
  -Views of Capt. Frederick
    Marryat
    Reader's--Story p502
  -Views of Daniel Webster
    Reader's--Story p502
  -Views of Henry David Thoreau
    Reader's--Story p502
  -West
    Hine--American p58, 68, 154,
      164, 177-189, 325, 331-332
CONSERVATIVES
  , Post Civil war
    Dulles--United p26
    Keller--Affairs p49-52
"CONSTITUTION" (ship) ("Old
Ironsides")
  Jones--Shaping p62-66, 68-71
  Treasury Amer. p162-167
  Wright--Every. p38
  , and "Guerriere"
    Commager--Heritage p235-
      238
    Collins--Story p190
    -Views of Isaac Hull, 1812
      Angle--American p182-185
CONSTITUTION--U. S.
  Whitman--American p8, 42, 44-
    47, 52, 128, 132, 154
  -Amendments
    -12th-15th
      Keyes--Hope p394-395
      Morris--Ency. p458-460

Reader's--Story p157
-12th (1804)
  Amer. Her. --New (5) p E183
  Harlow--Story p125-126
    (text)
  Life--Growing p41
  Morris--Ency. p131
-13th (1865)
  Amer. Her. --New (8) p E293
  Carman--History (1) p697-
    698, 712, 726
  Gurko--Ladies p210-212
  Harlow--Story p126 (text);
    p318, 335
  Linton--Bicentennial p180,
    186, 190, 435
  Morris--Ency. p246
-14th (1868)
  Amer. Her. --New (8) p E275
  Borden--Portrait (2) p7-8
  Carman--History (1) p728-
    729, 739
  Dulles--United p16-17
  Gurko--Ladies p212-213,
    242-244, 249-250, 253, 255,
    259, 279
  Harlow--Story p339-340
  Harlow--Story p126-128
    (text)
  Keller--Affairs. See index
    p615-616
  Keyes--Hope p257
  Life--Union (6) p114-116,
    156
  Linton--Bicentennial. See
    index p441
  Morris--Ency. p247
  -Illegal voting
    Warren--Pictorial p118-
      120
-15th (1870)
  Amer. Her. --New (8)
    p E273-274
  Carman--History (1) p739,
    764-779
  Harlow--Story p128 (text)
  Morris--Ency. p248
  Warren--Pictorial p115-116
-16th (1895)
  Gurko--Ladies p227, 232-233
  Harlow--Story p128
-"Compact theory"
  Harlow--Story p229-231
-Views of Daniel Webster
  Davie--Profile p70-71
-Views of John Marshall, 1801-
1835
  Commager--Heritage p226-229

-Views of Lord Macaulay
    Davie--Profile p72-73
CONSTITUTIONAL CONVENTIONS
    Keller--Affairs p111-112, 200-
    201, 319-320
CONSTITUTIONAL UNION PARTY,
    1860
    Harlow--Story p299-300
CONTINENTAL DIVIDE
    Tunis--Frontier p112-113
CONTINENTALISM
    Hollingsworth--Amer. p18-24
CONTRACT LABOR
    Marzio--Nation p208
    Morris--Ency. p448
    -Laws
        Life--Steel (7) p74-75
CONTRACT LABOR ACT, 1885
    Morris--Ency. p448-449
CONVENTION OF 1818
    Amer. Her. --New (5) p E160
    Bartlett--New p39, 55-56
    Carman--History (1) p386
    Harlow--Story p190
    Morris--Ency. p157
CONVERSATION
    -Dinner party
        Lynes--Domestic. p195, 197
    , Parlor
        Lynes--Domestic. p145-147,
        149
    , Table
        Lynes--Domestic. p184-185
    -Views of Frances Trollope
        Trollope--Domestic. See
        index p. iv
CONVERTERS
    Train--Story p339
CONVICTS
    See also PRISONS AND
        PRISONERS
    -Labor
        Life--Steel (7) p75, 77, 82,
        103-104, 106
    -Lease system
        Keller--Affairs p236-237,
        495-496
CONWELL, RUSSELL
    -"Acres of diamonds"
        Hart--Popular p161-162
    -Biography
        Amer. Her. --New (11)
        p962-963; E378
COOK, JAMES H.
    , on cowboys' "long drive, "
        1870
        Angle--American p358-363
COOK, TENNESSEE CLAFLIN

("TENNIS C. ")
    Furnas--American p643-646, 648
    Gurko--Ladies p243-244
    Macksey--Book p166
COOKBOOKS
    Lynes--Domestic. p64
    Warren--Pictorial p125-126
    , and foreign recipes
        Marzio--Nation p581-585
    -"Best sellers"
        Lynes--Domestic. p285
COOKE, JAY
    Amer. Her. --New (8) p E268-269
    Carman--History (2) p11, 89, 94,
    108
    Morris--Ency. p251, 431, 506
    -Biography
        Morris--Ency. p645-646
    -Company
        Collins--Story p244
COOKE, JOHN ESTEN
    Boardman--Civil p155
COOKE, PHILIP ST. GEORGE
    DeVoto--Year. See index p514-
    515
COOKERY
    See also FOOD
    Cable--American p211, 282
    Furnas--Americans p426-427,
    461-462
    Hunt--Life p215-227
    Langdon--Everyday (2) p189-203
    -1876
        Hilton--Way p20-21
    , Cowboy
        Train--Story
    -Middlewest
        Drury--Midwest p86
    -Negroes
        Hunt--Life p218-219
    -Pies
        Furnas--Americans p460-461
        Schwartz--When p44
    -Schools
        Partridge--As p127
    -Stoves
        Furnas--Americans p426-427
        Marzio--Nation p493
        Ross--Taste p122
        Wilson--Vanish. p40
    -Utensils
        Dreppard--Pioneer p31-36
    -Views of Frances Trollope
        Trollope--Domestic. See
        index p. iv
COOKSTOVES
    Tunis--Young p111
    -1876

Hilton--Way p20-21
COOLEY, THOMAS McINTYRE
-Biography
Morris--Ency. p646
COOLIDGE, CLARISSA BALDWIN
Ross--Taste p169
"COON-SKINNERS"
-Presidential election, 1844
Butterfield--Amer. p111
COOPER, GEORGE
Howard--Our p645
COOPER, JAMES FENIMORE
See also COOPERSTOWN,
NEW YORK
Amer. Her. --New (6) p E198
Boardman--Jackson. p144-145
Boardman--Virginia p138
Brooks--Flower. p65, 113, 160,
163, 413-415, 420, 451, 473
Carman--History (1) p541, 543-
545
Davidson--Life (2) p370-372
Harlow--Story p243
Hart--Popular p80-82
Life--Sweep. (4) p60
Maurois--Illus. p126
Morris--Ency. p192, 566
Mott--Golden p73-76
Our literary p16-19
Reader's--Story p410
-Biography
Morris--Ency. p646-647
COOPER, PETER
Amer. Her. --New (5) p386-387;
E160
Boardman--Jackson. p80-81
Butterfield--Amer. p225
Life--New (5) p10
Morris--Ency. p252, 536-537, 556
Treasury Amer. p310-319
Tunis--Young p117, 147
-Biography
Morris--Ency. p647
COOPER, SAMUEL
Dowdey--Experiment p85, 91,
117, 190, 237, 361, 402, 415, 423
COOPER, WILLIAM
Van Wagenen--Golden p92-99
COOPER UNION FOR THE AD-
VANCEMENT OF SCIENCE AND
ART
-Foundation building, N.Y. City
Vanderbilt--Living p38
COOPERS
Van Wagenen--Golden p106-110
COOPERSTOWN, NEW YORK
America's Hist. p296-298
Vanderbilt--Living p52-53

COPPER AND COPPERSMITHS
See also MONTANA
Langdon--Everyday (2) p277-280
Life--Steel (7) p54-55
Watkins--Gold p92-93, 136
"COPPERHEADS" (Peace Demo-
crats)
See also WOOD, FERNANDO
Boardman--Civil p71-72
Butterfield--Amer. p174-175
Carman--History (1) p649, 691
Dowdey--Experiment p95, 250, 371
Harlow--Story p327
Life--New (5) p115-116, 119
COPPIN, FANNY MARION JACK-
SON
Reader's--Story p436
COPYRIGHT
Keller--Affairs p420-421
Randel--Centennial p346-347
, and piracy
Bode--Anatomy p153-154
Furnas--Americans p321-322,
552
CORBETT, "GENTLEMAN JIM"
Walker--Every. p152-153, 165
CORBETT, THOMAS P.
Lewis--It p254-274
CORBIN, JOHN
-"How the other half laughs"
Harris--Land p160-179
"CORDWAINERS" (shoemakers)
Furnas--Americans p451-452
-Boston, Mass., 1842
Angle--By p181-190
CORLISS, GEORGE HENRY
Furnas--Americans p635-637
CORLISS STEAM ENGINE
Collins--Story p250
Jones--Age p142-143, and frontis-
piece
CORN
Bartlett--New p195-196
Van Wagenen--Golden p72-75;
see also index p273
-1839-1849
Boardman--Jackson. p89
-Old Northwest
Tunis--Frontier p77
-Shellers
Wilson--Vanish. p73
-Shocks
Wilson--Vanish. p72
, Sweet--Origin
Van Wagenen--Golden p74
CORN-HUSKINGS. See HUSKING
BEES
CORNELIA, SISTER

Ross--Heroines p134-135, 148
CORNELL, EZRA
  Boardman--Civil p145
  Boardman--Jackson. p99-100
CORNELL, KATE LYON
  Ross--Taste p169
CORNELL UNIVERSITY
  Randel--Centennial. See index
    p467
CORNING, JAMES L.
  Reader's--Story p295
CORNISH
  -Immigrants
    Bartlett--New p163-164
"CORNPLANTER" (Indian)
  Boardman--Virginia p120
CORPORATIONS
  See also HOLDING COMPA-
    NIES; POOLS, TRUSTS; names
    of corporations
  Keller--Affairs. See index
    p612
  -Advantages
    Harlow--Story p389-390
  -Charters
    Keller--Affairs p173-174,
      184-185, 432
  -Development
    Furnas--Americans p651-652
    Jones--Age p159-160
  -West
    Hine--American. See index
      p362
"CORPS OF DISCOVERY"
  Gilbert--Trail. p24-33; see also
    index p234
CORRECTIONAL INSTITUTIONS
  See also names and types of
    correctional institutions
    Tyler--Freedom's p286-291
CORRESPONDENCE. See LET-
  TERS AND LETTER-WRITING
CORRESPONDENCE COURSES
  Lynes--Taste. p153
CORRUPTION
  -Business
    Carman--History (1) p705
  -Government
    Boardman--Civil p88-91,
      115-116
    Carman--History (1) p707-
      710, 735-737, 744
    Harlow--Story p421-423
  , Political
    Linton--Bicentennial p202, 204
    Whitney--American p163, 168,
      180
  -Post civil war

Life--Union (6) p135-136, 155
CORTINAS, JUAN
  Hine--American p213-214
CORYDON, INDIANA
  Drury--Midwest p131-132
COSMETICS
  Lynes--Domestic. p211-212
  Ross--Taste p225-226
    -1876
      Hilton--Way p22-23
    -Views of Frances Trollope
      Trollope--Domestic p299-300
COSMOPOLITAN ART ASSOCIATION
  Bode--Anatomy p60-61, 80-88,
    100-103
COST OF LIVING. See STANDARD
  OF LIVING
COSTUME. See CLOTHING AND
  DRESS
COTTAGES. See HOUSES--Cottages
COTTON
  See also COTTONSEED OIL; re-
    lated subjects
  Amer. Her. --New (5) p E160-161
  Bartlett--New p207-208
  Boardman--Jackson. p88-89, 104-
    105
  Boardman--Virginia p77-78
  Boorstin--American p173-175
  Furnas--American p394-395
  Handlin--This p110, 119-122, 126,
    133, 153, 160-161, 166, 203, 333,
    336-337, 351
  Kane--Gone p169-182
  Kraus--U.S. p399-400
  Langdon--Everyday (2) p255-261
  Life--Growing (3) p125, 134, 136,
    138-139
  Life--Steel (7) p100-101, 114, 122-
    123
  Life--Sweep (4) p11-12, 37, 42, 46
  Life--Union (6) p121, 128-130
  Tunis--Frontier p80, 88
  Wright--Every. p146-147
  -Civil war
    Boardman--Civil p65-66
    Dowdey--Experiment. See
      index p445
    -Burning
      Views of Sarah Morgan
        Dawson
          Commager--Heritage
            p687-689
  -Inventions
    See also COTTON GIN
    Marzio--Nation p197-202
  -New Orleans market
    Life--Steel (7) p122-123

-Production
  -1811
    Life--America's p78
  -1859, 1879, 1899, by state
    Carman--History (2) p213
  -1880's
    Carman--History (2) p80-
    82
-South
  Amer. Her. --New (7) p582-586
  America's Hist. p402-403
  Harlow--Story p210-213
  Keyes--Hope p245-246
  200 Years (1) p222
COTTON GIN
  Commager--Heritage p445-446
  Furnas--Americans p302-303
COTTON MILLS
  Harlow--Story p206-207
  , First
    Life--Growing (3) p50
  -Graniteville, S.C., 1880's
    Woodward--Way p319-358
  -Lowell, Mass.
    Wright--Every. p132-134
COTTONSEED OIL
  Langdon--Everyday (2) p262
  Life--Steel (7) p104-105, 134
COUNTING HOUSES
  Tunis--Young p88-89
COUNTRY CLUBS
  Boardman--Gilded p170
  Carson--Polite p244-245
  Dulles--History p241
  Furnas--Americans p815-816
  Harris--Land p134-146
  Walker--Every. p145-146
  -"Evolution of the country club, "
    by Caspar W. Whitney
    Harris--Land p134-146
  , First, 1880's
    Cable--American p277
COUNTRY FAIRS. See FAIRS,
  Country
COUNTRY LIFE
  See also FARMERS AND FARM-
    ING
  America's Hist. p292-303
  Hunt--Life p103-104
  Partridge--As p7-49
  Treasury Amer. p264-273
  -1876
    Hilton--Way p151-161
  , in Currier & Ives prints
    Life--Reaching (8) p20-21
  -Middlewest
    Drury--Midwest p86-87
COUNTRY STORES

See also GENERAL STORES
  America's Hist. p298-299
  Boardman--Virginia p190
  Collins--Story p281
  Partridge--As p31
  Ross--Taste p61
  Walker--Ency. p78-80, 109-111
  -Bulk goods
    Wilson--Vanish. p140
  -Commodities
    Van Wagenen--Golden p9-10
  -New England, 1898
    Ross--Taste p66
COUNTY FAIRS. See FAIRS,
  County
COUNTY SEATS
  , and "county seat wars"
    Boorstin--Americans p164-167
"COURTING STICKS"
  Ross--Taste p282
COURTS
  Handlin--This p148-149
  Keller--Affairs. See index p613
  , Juvenile
    , First, 1899, Chicago
      Robertson--Book p90
COURTSHIP
  Schwartz--When p19-20
  Walker--Ency. p32-33, 37, 130,
    241-242
  , and marriage
    Wilson--Folkways p15-23
  -Etiquette
    Cable--American p167-169
"COUSIN JACKS AND JENNIES."
  See CORNISH--Immigrants
COVERED BRIDGES
  Tunis--Everyday (2) p57-63
  Tunis--Young p77
  Van Wagenen--Golden p148-151
COVERED WAGONS
  See also CONESTOGA WAGONS
    Keyes--Hope p383-385
    Life--America's p98-99
    Schwartz--When p18
    -Description
      Ross--Heroines p19
"COW HANDS." See COWBOYS
"COW TOWNS"
  Amer. Her. --New (9) p754-755,
    760-763
  Dulles--History p168-181
  Ridge--America's p595-597, 599-
    601
    -Abilene, Texas--"First of the
    cow towns, " by Joseph G.
    McCoy
      Ridge--America's p595-597,

599-601
COWBOY MUSIC
See also SONGS
Dulles--History p176, 180
Dulles--United p45-46
Hine--American p130-131
Howard--Our p636-637
Walker--Every. p95
White--American p88-91
COWBOYS
See also CLOTHING AND
DRESS--Cowboys
Bartlett--New p228-229, 233-234
Boardman--Gilded p87
Cable--American p303
Collins--Story p286
Jones--Shaping p226-227
Life--Steel (7) p50, 55-57, 59-71
Reader's--Story p117-119
Walker--Every. p94-95
-Amusements
Dulles--History p174-181
Train--Story p303-305
-Characteristics
Dulles--United p45-46
-Cooks and cookery
Train--Story p293-295
-Equipment
See also COWBOYS--Saddles
and equipment
Amer. Her. --New (9) p746-
747
, "Father of" (Charles Goodnight)
Brown--Westerners p203-213
, First--"Vaqueros" (in Califor-
nia)
Amer. Her. --New (9) p742-743
Gilbert--Trail. p114-115
Johnson--Pictorial p66, 69-71
Tunis--Frontier p127, 150
-Food
Train--Story p293-294
-Homes
Train--Story p293-294
, in "dime novels"
Our literary p128-129
, "in town"
Amer. Her. --New (9) p756-
757
-Indian conflict
Life--Steel (7) p55, 62-63
-Injuries and ailments
Train--Story p303
-Life on range
Amer. Her. --New (9) p741-
758
-Negroes
200 Years (2) p69

, on the trail
Amer. Her. --New (9) p746-747
-Saddles and equipment
Tunis--Frontier p150-151
-Story-telling
Train--Story p304-305
-Texas
Tunis--Frontier p146-147
-versus farmers
Hine--American p132-133
-West
Furnas--Americans p683-687
Harlow--Story p368
Hine--American p125-138; see
also index p362
Tunis--Frontier p145, 148-152,
159
, Work of
Amer. Her. --New (9) p948-949
COWLEY, MALCOLM
-"The Hawthornes in paradise"
Treasury Amer. p300-309
"COWPUNCHERS" (COWPOKES)
See COWBOYS
COWS. See CATTLE
COX, SAMUEL SULLIVAN ("SUN-
SET")
Randel--Centennial p243-245
COXEY, JACOB S.
Boardman--Gilded p81-82
Life--Reaching (8) p88-89
200 Years (2) p90
-"Coxey's army (unemployed
march, 1894)
Butterfield--Amer. p264-265
Collins--Story p272
Harlow--Story p467-469
Life--Reaching (8) p88-89
Linton--Bicentennial p240-241
Morris--Ency. p263-264
Reader's--Story p345
CRABTREE, CHARLOTTE
Adelman--Famous p270
CRABTREE, SAMUEL
-"American letter"
Commager--Heritage p261-262
CRADLES
McClinton--Antiques p139-142
Wilson--Vanish. p49
, Christening
McClinton--Antiques p33-36
, Grain
Van Wagenen--Golden p225-229
-Makers
Van Wagenen--Golden p115-
116
CRAFTS AND CRAFTSMANSHIP
See also names of articles and

types
Wilson--Folkways p86-88
, and trades, technologies
    Marzio--Nation p208-244
-Decline (1825-1860)
    Train--Story p263-291
, Household
    Van Wagenen--Golden p249-
    256
, Pioneer
    Van Wagenen--Golden p6,
    8-9
, Women's
    Cable--American p118-119
CRANBERRIES
    Mussey--Old p90
CRANCH, CHRISTOPHER
    Brooks--Flower. p249-250,
    268, 271, 277
    Our literary p73
CRANDALL, JESSE
-Blocks and children's games
    McClinton--Antiques p243,
    248
CRANDALL, PRUDENCE
    Boardman--Jackson. p112
    Furnas--Americans p518-519
    Macksey--Book p68
    Reader's--Story p131
    Warren--Pictorial p74
CRANE, STEPHEN
    Amer. Her. --New (11) p E378-
    379
    Boardman--Gilded p128
    Dulles--United p116-117
    Morris--Ency. p574
    Our literary p184-185
-Biography
    Morris--Ency. p648
, on blizzards
    Cook--City p160-166
"CRANKS AND QUACKS"
    Furnas--Americans. See
    index p982
-California
    Jones--Shaping p103-104
CRAVEN, JOHN H.
, and Eaton affair
    Phillips--That p32, 77
-"Causes for migration,
    Southern soil exhaustion, "
    1833
    Ridge--America's p295-297
CRAWFORD, F. MARION
-"The novel: what it is, " 1893
    Amer. Her. --90's p83-84
CRAWFORD, JACK, Captain
    Randel--Centennial p132-133

CRAWFORD, SAMUEL WYLIE
, on South Carolina secession,
    1861
    Angle--American p308-311
CRAWFORD, THOMAS
    Larkin--Art p183-184; see also
    index p521
    Morris--Ency. p601
CRAWFORD, WILLIAM H.
    Amer. Her. --New (5) p E161
    Boardman--Jackson. p4-5
    Carman--History (1) p409-410,
    784, 787-788
    Hunt--Life p270-272
    Kraus--U.S. p341-342
, and Eaton affair
    Phillips--That p28-29, 44, 49-
    50, 107
"CRAZY HORSE" (Indian)
    Amer. Her. --Indians p347-348,
    366, 368-369
    Amer. Her. --New (9) p796
    Andrews--Indian leaders p150-152,
    154
    Boardman--Gilded p94-95
    Brown--Westerners p97, 194, 237,
    244, 246, 249, 260
    Hine--American p198-200, 204
    Reader's--Story p85
CREDIT AND CREDITORS
    Handlin--This p350, 354-355
CREDIT AND FINANCE CORPORA-
TION
    Brown--Westerners p176-177
CREDIT MOBILIER
    Bartlett--New p328-331
    Brown--Westerners p174-176
    Butterfield--Amer. p204-205
    Carman--History (1) p744-745
    Carman--History (2) p45-46
    Harlow--Story p345-346
    Life--Union (6) p153-154
    Morris--Ency. p250-251
CREEK INDIANS
    See also CREEK WAR
    Amer. Her. --Indians. See index
    p420
    Andrews--Indian leaders. See
    index p183
    Boardman--Jackson. p69
    Boardman--Virginia p117
    Carman--History (1) p364, 422
CREEK WAR
    Amer. Her. --Indians p219-221,
    232-233
    Morris--Ency. p148
CREELMAN, JAMES
-"Familiar glimpses of yellow

journalism"
  Harris--Land p62-70
CREIGHTON, EDWARD
  Brown--Westerners p162, 164-
  165
CREOLE CASE, 1842
  Boardman--Jackson. p109-110
  Morris--Ency. p185
CREOLE INDIANS
  Life--Steel (7) p116-117
  -Songs and dances
    Chase--America's p309-314
CRICKET (game)
  Furnas--Americans p657-658
CRIME AND CRIMINALS
  See also CONVICTS; HANG-
    INGS; LAW--Enforcement;
    PRISONS AND PRISONERS;
    PUNISHMENT
  Boardman--Gilded p176-177
  Davidson--Life (2) p151
  Hunt--Life p157-160, 166-168
  Keller--Affairs p125-126, 236-
    237, 491-496
  Life--Sweep (4). See index
    p156
  -1876
    Hilton--Way p106
    Randel--Centennial. See
      index p467
  , and police
    Cable--American p319
  , and punishment
    Wilson--Folkways p201-217
  -Cities
    Harlow--Story p420-421
    -Gangs
      -Views of Jacob Riis, 1889
        Angle--American p402-
        404
  , Juvenile
    Furnas--Americans p842-843
  -Pickpockets
    -New York City, 1891
      Cook--City p168
  -Reform
    Keller--Affairs p496-499
    Tyler--Freedom's p265-285
  -Robinson-Jewett case
    Cable--American p132-133
  -Train robbers
    Amer. Her. --New (10) p839
  -Views of Frances Trollope
    Trollope--Domestic p163-166,
      285-287
  -West
    Furnas--Americans p377-378,
    700

-Women
  Macksey--Book p136-137
"CRIME OF 1873." See COINAGE
  ACT OF 1873
"CRINOLINE AGE"
  Train--Story p270-271
CRITTENDEN, JOHN JORDAN
  Life--New (5) p96
  -Biography
    Amer. Her. --New (7) p E232-
    233
  -Compromise
    Amer. Her. --New (7) p E233
    Harlow--Story p302
CROCKER, CHARLES
  Boardman--Civil p143
  Boardman--Gilded p66-67
  Lewis--Big p49-123
CROCKER, HANNAH MATHER
  -"Observation on the real rights
    of women"
    Warren--Pictorial p69
CROCKETT, DAVID ("DAVY")
  America's Hist. p389
  Boardman--Virginia p97
  Boorstin--Americans p293, 295,
    327-333
  Cable--American p94, 96-97, 135
  Hine--American p85-87, 192, 268-
    270
  Life--Sweep (4) p52, 60, 96
  Reader's--Story p172
  200 Years (1) p237-238, 240-241
  , as legislature candidate
    Commager--Heritage p263-266
  -Biography
    Amer. Her. --New (7) p E233
  -Defense of Alamo
    Commager--Heritage p592-598
  , on Lowell's women employees,
    1834
    Angle--American p259-262
CROFFUT, WILLIAM A.
  , on Commodore Vanderbilt
    Burner--Amer. (1) p346-350
CROGAN, GEORGE
  America's Hist. p315
CROKER, RICHARD
  See also TAMMANY HALL
  Amer. Her. --New (11) p912, 914
  Weisberger--Amer. p182-183
  , on Tammany Hall and democracy
    Cook--City p204-205
CROLY, JANE CUNNINGHAM
  Adelman--Famous p204
  Macksey--Book p265-266
CROMPTON, GEORGE
  -Loom industry

Marzio--Nation p203-207
CROMPTON, WILLIAM
Marzio--Nation p203
CROOK, GEORGE, General
Amer. Her. --Indians p342, 347,
386-388, 399, 408
CROOK, WILLIAM H.
, on impeachment trial of Andrew
Johnson, 1868
Angle--American p352-357
CROPS AND GRAINS
See also AGRICULTURE; CERE-
ALS; FARMERS AND FARM-
ING; names of crops and grains
Wright--Every. p144-145
-Food
Wright--Every. p141
-Mortgage system, post-war
South
Harlow--Story p357-358
-New York state
Van Wagenen--Golden p65-74,
78-79, 84-85
-Sowing
Van Wagenen--Golden p223-
224
CROQUET
Davidson--Life (2) p62-63
Dulles--History p191-192, 202,
264-265
Partridge--As p150
Ross--Taste p92, 94-95
-1876
Hilton--Way p104
, for women
Boardman--Civil p200
CROSBY, FRANCES JANE
("FANNY")
Adelman--Famous p215-216
Bonte--America p119
Macksey--Book p214
CROSMAN, HENRIETTA
Blum--Stage. Profile 15
CROSS, BENJAMIN
Howard--Our p134-136
"CROSS OF GOLD." See
BRYAN, WILLIAM JENNINGS
CROSWELL, HARRY
-Libel case
Morris--Ency. p582
CROUCH, WILLIAM NICHOLLS
Howard--Our p172
CROW INDIANS
Andrews--Indian Leaders p104-
107, 116, 172; see also index
p175
Boardman--Virginia p119
Brown--Westerners p55, 59-60,

77, 241, 244, 246
DeVoto--Year p60, 153-154, 164,
171-172
Gilbert--Trail. p68-69
CRUSADES
Borden--Portrait (2) p65-76
, and culture
Amer. Her. --New (6) p486-496
CRYSTAL PALACE EXPOSITION
(New York, 1853)
Portraits--Americans p44
Reader's--Story p250
CUBA
See also SPANISH-AMERICAN
WAR
Amer. Her. --New (12) p994-1023
Amer. Her. --90's p106-119
Boardman--Gilded p185-187
Borden--Portrait (2) p69, 71-72
Carman--History (2) p267, 272,
274, 286-296, 302-306, 331, 335-
336
Collins--Story p289
Life--Reaching (8). See index
p172
Reader's--Story p444-445
-1840's and 1850's
Harlow--Story p276
-Annexation plan
Life--New (5) p53-54
-Expedition, 1898
Morris--Ency. p289
-Question, 1895
Morris--Ency. p286
, Revolt in
Dulles--United p164-166
-Sea power and sugar
Butterfield--Amer. p276-277
CUDGELING (sport)
200 Years (1) p306-307
CUFFE, PAUL
Boardman--Virginia p132-133
CUISINE. See FOOD
CULTS. See "UTOPIAS"
CULTURE
See also ART; BOOKS AND
READING; DRAMA; LITERA-
TURE; etc.
Amer. Her. --90's p9-10
Borden--Portrait (1) p200-201
Lynes--Taste. p6, 20, 153-155, 179
, and democracy
Trachtenberg--Demo. p333-
366
-Centers
Jones--Age p191-192
-Chicago, Ill.
Amer. Her. --90's p26

-Clubs
　　Lynes--Taste. p155-157
-Common heritage
　　Life--New (5) p8, 17
, for the masses
　　Borden--Portrait (1) p201-203
, Foreign importation of
　　Jones--Age p278-283
-Frontier
　　Life--New (5) p24
, Immigrant
　　Jones--Age p182
, in age of energy
　　Jones--Age p180-182
-Indiana
　　Wright--Culture p106-107
-Kentucky
　　Wright--Culture p79
-Literary taste, early 1800's
　　Hunt--Life p146-147
-Machine age
　　Amer. Her. --New (11) p958-
　　977
, Mexican-Californian
　　Life--Sweep (4) p130-131
, Mexican-Texan
　　Life--Sweep (4) p94-95
, Middle-class
　　Jones--Age p182-183
-New England
　　Life--New (5) p9-10, 12
-North vs. South
　　Life--New (5) p7
-South
　　Boorstin--Americans p170
　　Life--New (5) p16-17
　　, and pro-slavery sentiment
　　　　Tyler--Freedom's p524-
　　　　527
, Urban
　　Life--New (5) p58, 62-63
　　Life--Sweep (4) p26-27
-West
　　Carman--History (1) p381-384
　　-Towns
　　　　Hine--American p260-267
CUMBERLAND ROAD. See
NATIONAL ROAD
CUMBERLAND ROAD BILL
　Veto, 1822
　　Morris--Ency. p160-161
CUMING, FORTESCUE
　, on Federalists and Democrats,
　1807
　　Angle--American p158-159
　, on travelers, western highways,
　1807
　　Angle--American p157-158

CURES. See MEDICINE; REMEDIES
CURIOSITY
-Views of Frances Trollope
　　Trollope--Domestic p127-128,
　　385-386
CURRENCY
See also BIMETALLISM; COIN-
AGE ACT
　Boardman--Gilded p18-20, 181-185
　Carman--History (2) p244-248
　Dowdey--Experiment. See index
　p445
　Dulles--United p73-74, 140-142
　Handlin--This p123, 135-136, 140,
　209
　Keller--Affairs p191-195, 380-384
　Life--New (5) p120-121, 138-139
　Life--Union (6) p151-153
　, Confederate
　　Dowdey--Experiment p27, 50,
　　92, 209
-Issue, 1869
　　Morris--Ency. p250
, Portraits on ("no living person"
rule)
　　White--American p60-61
-Ratio ("Sixteen to one")
　　Harlow--Story p450-452, 463-
　　465, 471-475
-Views of William M. Gouge
(1830's)
　　Walker--Reform p70-71
CURRIER AND IVES
　Amer. Her. --New (11) p919-930,
　E379
　Boardman--Jackson. p155
　Bode--Anatomy p87-91
　Furnas--Americans p576-578
　Garrison--Lost p45-48
　Larkin--Art p207, 215
　Life--Reaching (8) p18-31
　Lynes--Taste. p58, 66-70, 79, 125
　, Romanticism of
　　Amer. Her. --New (11) p919-
　　930
CURTAINS
-1825-1860
　　Train--Story p269
CURTIN, ANDREW GREGG
　Meredith--World p148-150, 152-
　153
CURTIS, CYRUS H. K.
　Boardman--Gilded p165-166
　Morris--Ency. p584, 588
-Magazines
　　Nostalgia p78-81
CURTIS, GEORGE WILLIAM
　Boardman--Civil p88-89

Bode--Anatomy p216-318
Butterfield--Amer. p240
Lowens--Music p251
Lynes--Taste. p35, 109-110, 115
, on "Brook farm" life
   Tyler--Freedom's p182-183
CURTIS, U. (Brigadier general,
Volunteers)
Dannett--Noble p358-360
CURTIS, WILLIAM EDMUND
Amer. Her. --90's p62-63
CURZON, LADY. See LEITER,
MARY VICTORIA, LADY CURZON
CUSHMAN, CHARLOTTE SAUNDERS
Adelman--Famous p158-159, fac-
ing 168
Boardman--Jackson. p157-158
Morris--Ency. p590-591
-Biography
   Morris--Ency. p648
CUSHMAN, PAULINE
Amer. Her. --New (8) p E269
Young--Women p95, 235-244
-Biography
   Young--Women p369-370
CUSPIDORS. See SPITTOONS
CUSTER, ELIZABETH BACON
Brown--Westerners p229-239
Hilton--Way p29-31
CUSTER, GEORGE ARMSTRONG,
LIEUT. COL.
Andrews--Indian leaders p121,
150-152, 157, 159
Boardman--Gilded p94
Brown--Westerners p195, 198,
201-202, 229-240, 247-248, 256
Harlow--Story p370-372
Hilton--Way p29-30, 91, 148, 199-
200
Hine--American p141, 198-200,
204, 278
Life--Union (6) p144-147
Randel--Centennial. See index
p467
200 Years (2) p64-65, 67
Watkins--Gold p108-111
-Battle of the Washita, 1874
   Ridge--America's p576-579
-Gordon stockade and Way
  museum
   Vanderbilt--Living p191
-"Last stand," 1876
   Amer. Her. --Indians p347,
   368-369, 371
   Amer. Her. --New (9) p784-
   787, 796
   Bonte--American p132
-Massacre

Angle--American p363-365
Collins--Story p248
-View of Indians
   Andrews--Indians p81-84
CUSTIS, WASHINGTON PARKE
Boardman--Jackson. p158
CUSTOMHOUSES
-California, contraband
   Johnson--Pictorial p68-69
"CUT NOSE" (Santee Sioux Indian)
Amer. Her. --New (9) p778-779
CUTLER, MANASSEH
-"Description of life as a con-
gressman, 1801
   Angle--American p140-143
CUTTS, ADELE
Peacock--Famous p175-189
CUYLER, THEODORE
-Biography
   Amer. Her. --New (11) p E379
CYCLORAMAS. See DIORAMAS;
PANORAMAS, MOVING

D

DABNEY, THOMAS
-Hardships
   Commager--Heritage p796-800
DAGUERRE, LOUIS J.
Boardman--Jackson. p102
DAGUERROTYPES
Furnas--Americans p300, 578, 591
Langdon--Everyday (2) p237-238
Larkin--Art p195-197, 226
Life--Sweep (4) p68-78
Woodward--Way p255-256
, Cosmic
   Wilson--American p274-276
-History
   Butterfield--Amer. p114-116
DAHLGREN, JOHN ADOLPHUS
Amer. Her. --New (8) p E269
-Gun
   Wilson--American p190-191
DAKOTA INDIANS
DeVoto--Year p60, 489
DAKOTAS
Brown--Westerners. See index
p286
Drury--Midwest p168-169
Hine--American. See index p362
Life--Steel (7) p31, 35, 51, 56, 59
-"Propaganda for immigrants,"
  by George A. Batchelder
   Ridge--America's p619-621
DALY, (JOHN) AUGUSTIN
Boardman--Gilded p148-149

Morris--Ency. p591-592
Randel--Centennial p314, 335-336
-Theatrical productions
  Blum--Theatre p32-33, 45
DAMROSCH, LEOPOLD
  Marzio--Nation p415
  , on rivalry of musicians
    Angle--American p418-420
DAMS
  , Earthen
    Van Wagenen--Golden p133-
    135
DANA, CHARLES A.
  Brooks--Flower. p243-245, 374-
  376
  Our literary p72-73
  , and Transcendental music
    Lowens--Music p250-252
  -Biography
    Amer. Her. --New (11)
    p E379-380
DANA, RICHARD HENRY
  Amer. Her. --New (5) p E161-162
  Boardman--Jackson. p148
  Brooks--Flower. p55, 111-116,
  154-155, 162-165, 189, 235, 244,
  308, 502-503
  Our literary p58-59
DANA, RICHARD HENRY II (The
Younger)
  Brooks--Flower. p308-312, 391-
  392
  -"The American hide and tallow
  trade," 1840
    Ridge--America's p467
  , on California, 1836-1837
    Commager--Heritage p516-
    521
  , on life at sea
    Burner--America (1) p235-
    240
    Wright--Ency. p182-183
  , on runaway slave
    Commager--Heritage p494-
    499
  -"Two years before the mast"
    Bode--Anatomy p221-225
DANCERS AND DANCING
  See also BALLET; INDIANS--
  Dancers and dancing
  Cable--American p111-113
  Carson--Polite p197-198
  Davidson--Life (2) p10-12
  Dulles--History p76-78, 151-152,
  159, 161-162, 170-171, 179, 254,
  275-277
  Handlin--This p127, 134, 136, 141-
  143, 162, 165, 205, 252, 264, 347

Ross--Taste p83, 87
Walker--Every. p81-83, 174
Wilson--Folkways p111-113
-1876
  Hilton--Way p52-53, 112-113
-1880's
  Woodward--Way p337-338
-Balls
  Dulles--History p231-254
  Dulles--United p92
  -1824-1825
    Dreppard--Pioneer p100
  , "Fancy-dress"
    Jones--Age p134-135
  -Waldorf Hotel, 1897
    Cable--American p279
  , Barn ("Bran")
    Walker--Every. p81-83
  -Cakewalk
    Chase--America's p439-440
  -Calinda
    Chase--America's p312-314
  -"Dance House" (Leadville, Colo-
  rado, 1879)
    Ross--Taste p86
  -Halls
    Dulles--History p98, 165, 170-
    171, 179, 220-221
    -"Girls" ("Hurdy-gurdy wom-
    en," Idaho)
      Ross--Westward p127-128
  -Lessons
    Schwartz--When p94-95
  -Shakers
    Chase--America's p227, 230
  -Views of Frances Trollope
    Trollope--Domestic p134-135,
    155-156, 299, 301
  -West Point
    Life--New (5) p58
  -Women
    Warren--Pictorial p154
"DANDIES" (fops)
  Wilson--Early p162
  -Views of Frances Trollope
    Trollope--Domestic p154, 335,
    350-351, 386-387
DANGERFIELD, GEORGE
  , on War of 1812
    Miers--American p116-121
"DANIEL WEBSTER" (ship)
  Young--Women p176-177, 187
DANISH WEST INDIES
  See also names of Danish immi-
  grants
  Boardman--Civil p85-86
  Morris--Ency. p280, 307
DA PONTE, LORENZO

Boardman--Jackson. p160-161
DARBY, WILLIAM
-"Primitivism in the lower Mississippi Valley," 1818
Ridge--America's p399-401
"DAREDEVILS." See "BARN-STORMERS"
DARLING, FLORA
Macksey--Book p273
DARROW, CLARENCE S.
-"Realism in literature and art"
Harris--Land p279-288
DARTMOUTH COLLEGE
Mussey--Old p33
Nye--Cultural p177, 181, 187-188
Tyler--Freedom's p255-256
-Case, 1819
Boardman--Virginia p59-60
Morris--Ency. p158
DARWIN, CHARLES
Boardman--Gilded p111-112
Kraus--U.S. p384-385
Life--Reaching (8) p8-10, 13
DARWINISM
Borden--Portrait (2) p21-22
Carman--History (2) p349-350, 355, 359-360, 369
Dulles--United p120-121
Jones--Age p15-16, 21-24
Life--Reaching (8) p8, 10-13
Randel--Centennial p450-452
DATES. See CHRONOLOGY
DAUGHTERS OF THE AMERICAN REVOLUTION
Macksey--Book p273
DAVENPORT, E.
-"The farmer and the dude," 1897
Cook--City p7-8
DAVENPORT, FANNY
Adelman--Famous p228
Boardman--Civil p167-168
DAVENPORT, JOE
Handlin--This p386-389
DAVENPORT, IOWA
Treasury Amer. p257, 261-262
DAVIDSON, JAMES D.
-"Frenzied speculation in the Southwest," 1836
Ridge--America's p298-299
DAVIE, JOHN L.
, on "Big Four"
Lewis--Big p370-376, 379-384
DAVIS, ALEXANDER JACKSON
Boardman--Civil p173
Boardman--Jackson. p163
Lynes--Taste. p28-31

DAVIS, ANDREW JACKSON
-"Poughkeepsie seer"
Tyler--Freedom's p80-82
DAVIS, DAVID
Life--New (5) p112-113
-"Opinion in the Milligan case," 1866
Angle--By p278-287
DAVIS, JAMES
, as an Iron puddler
Commager--Heritage p961-967
DAVIS, JEFFERSON
Amer. Her. --New (8) p E269-270
Boardman--Civil p32, 45-46, 58-59
Carman--History (1). See index p. vii
Dowdey--Experiment. See index p445-446
Harlow--Story p292, 301, 322-323, 327, 334
Jordan--Civil. See index p213
Life--New (5). See index p157
Life--Sweep (4) p105, 108, 122, 136-137
Linton--Bicentennial. See index p440
Morris--Ency. See index p746
Randel--Centennial p242-246
200 Years (2). See index p352
-Biography
Amer. Her. --New (7) p E233-234
Morris--Ency. p648-649
-Confederate presidency
Carman--History (1) p634
-Inauguration, address, 1862
Angle--By p254-260
Collins--Story p208
-Credo
Dowdey--Experiment p190
-Imprisonment
Keyes--Hope p256
-Letters to Robert E. Lee, 1865
Davie--Profile p286
, on case for confederacy, 1862
Angle--By p252-254
, on secession of Mississippi
Angle--By p255-259
Hurd--Treasury p89-91
-Resolutions, 1860
Morris--Ency. p226
-Tribute to Robert E. Lee
Jordan--Civil p210
DAVIS, PAULINA WRIGHT
Gurko--Ladies p89, 138-139, 150, 160, 171, 245
DAVIS, REBECCA HARDING
Adelman--Famous p202

DAVIS, RICHARD HARDING
-Biography
Amer. Her. --New (12) p E415
, on San Juan's Hill, 1898
Angle--American p442-444
DAVIS, VARINA HOWELL
Dowdey--Experiment. See
index p446
DAVIS FAMILY (Jefferson Davis')
Dowdey--Experiment. See
index p446
DAVISSON, ANANIAS
Chase--America's p189-192, 204
Lowens--Music p140-142, 144
DAWES ACT OF 1887
Borden--Portrait (2) p50-51
Dulles--United p43
Life--Steel (7) p53
Morris--Ency. p439
Ridge--America's p588-591
DAWSON, NICHOLAS "CHEYENNE"
-"Arrival of the emigrants in
California, " 1841
Ridge--America's p482-484
DAWSON, SARAH MORGAN
, on Confederates' burning cotton
Commager--Heritage p687-689
-Sacking of home
Commager--Heritage p689-695
DAY, BENJAMIN H.
Wright--Every. p239-240
DAY, CLARENCE
, on homes, 1879
Cook--City p119-121
DEADWOOD, DAKOTA (territory)
Watkins--Gold p107-108, 110-
111
-1876
Randel--Centennial p148-149,
338
-Life
Watkins--Gold p114-115
-Population, 1877
Watkins--Gold p114
DEAF
-1876
Hilton--Way p88
-Education
Boorstin--Americans p45
-Women, teachers, etc.
Macksey--Book p73
DEAF-MUTES
-Education
Tyler--Freedom's p294-296
, Schools for
Hunt--Life p199
DEATH
See also CEMETERIES; FU-

NERALS; etc.
Bode--Anatomy p273-274
Schwartz--When p177, 180
Walker--Every. p41, 242
-Poetry
Cable--American p172
DEATH RATE
Hunt--Life p207-209
DEBATE
See also LINCOLN-DOUGLAS
DEBATES
, Public
Ross--Taste p36
DE BOUCHERVILLE, THOMAS
VERCHERES
, on surrender of Detroit, 1812
Angle--American p178-179
DE BOW, JAMES D. B.
Bode--Anatomy p263-265
Portraits--Americans p65
DEBS, EUGENE VICTOR
Boardman--Gilded p80-81
Butterfield--Amer. p266
Furnas--Americans p711, 723, 726,
728, 824-828
Harlow--Story p409-411, 509
Life--Reaching (8) p89-93
Morris--Ency. See index p746
-Biography
Morris--Ency. p649
DEBT
Hunt--Life p169-170
, Imprisonment for
Tyler--Freedom's p283-285
-Relief, 1817-1848
Morris--Ency. p518-519
DEBUTANTES
-"Coming out" balls
Cable--American p283-284
DECATUR, STEPHEN
See also TRIPOLI, WAR WITH
Boardman--Virginia p50-51
Butterfield--Amer. p65
Morris--Ency. p142
Treasury Amer. p162
-Algerine expedition
Morris--Ency. p154
-Biography
Morris--Ency. p649-650
DECORATION DAY
-1876
Hilton--Way p197
"DECREE OF TRIANON, " 1810
Morris--Ency. p138
DEER
Van Wagenen--Golden p95-96
DEERBORN WAGON
-Views of Frances Trollope

Trollope--Domestic p26-27
DEERE, JOHN
  Boardman--Jackson. p91
  -Steel plow
    Reader's--Story p263
DE FOREST, LEE
  -Biography
    Wilson--American p362-363
  -Wireless
    Wilson--American p363, 366
DEIDESHEIMER, PHILIP
  -"Square set" invention
    Watkins--Gold p77, 170, 191,
    193
DEISM
  , End of
    Nye--Cultural p214-215
DELAND, MARGARET
  Sochen--Herstory p225-227
DELANO, ALONZO
  , on Sacramento, 1849
    Angle--American p253-255
DELAWARE
  Carman--History (1) p782
DELAWARE AND HUDSON RAIL-
  ROAD
  Boardman--Jackson. p95-96
DELAWARE--HUDSON CANAL
  Van Wagenen--Golden p157-158
DELAWARE INDIANS
  Andrews--Indian leaders. See
    index p183
  DeVoto--Year p40, 197, 272, 350,
    391
DELAWARE RIVER
  -Views of Frances Trollope
    Trollope--Domestic p259, 333-
    335, 347, 424
DELMONICO, LORENZO
  Portraits--Americans p118-119
  -First dining car
    Ross--Taste p273
  -First restaurant, N. Y.
    Portraits--Americans p119
DE LOME LETTER. See DU PUY
  DE LOME, ENRIQUE
DEMENS, P. A. (TVERSKOY,
  pseud.)
  , on America, 1895
    Handlin--This p349-370
DEMOCRACY
  See also JACKSONIAN DEMOC-
    RACY; JEFFERSONIAN DEMOC-
    RACY
  Grimsted--Notions p86-98
  Handlin--This p124, 128, 154, 169-
    171, 173-175, 177-179, 252, 337-
    338

Trachtenberg--Demo. p350-366
  -1830-1860
    Billington--Far. See index
    p315
  , Bourbon
    Keller--Affairs p554-558, 564,
    580, 586
  , Broadening of, 1827
    Morris--Ency. p165-166
  , Frontier
    Carman--History (1) p378-379
  -Growth
    Kraus--U. S. p349-351
  -Views of Alexis de Tocqueville,
    1835
    Reader's--Story p504
DEMOCRATIC PARTY
  See also "BARNBURNERS"
  Alden--Pioneer p186-188, 193, 240,
    249-250, 257-261, 268, 277, 284-285
  Boardman--Gilded p15-17, 181-184
  Boardman--Jackson. See index
    p207
  Carman--History (1) p413, 425-
    430, 563, 608, 698, 733-734, 746-
    751
  Carman--History (2) p229-230
  Dulles--United. See index p. v
  Handlin--This p207-208, 247, 342,
    362, 384-388
  Harlow--Story. See index p808
  Keller--Affairs. See index p613
  Kraus--U. S. p454, 457-458
  Life--New (5). See index p157
  Life--Union (6). See index p173
  Linton--Bicentennial. See index
    p440
  -1822-1848
    Life--Sweep (4). See index
    p157
  -1877-1890
    Life--Steel (7). See index
    p157
  , and Federalist, 1807
    -Views of Fortescue Cuming
      Angle--American p158-159,
      361
  -Conventions
    Whitney--American. See
      index p361
    -1860, Charleston, S.C.
      Holzman--Stormy p37-38
      Kraus--U. S. p477-478
      Life--New (5) p89-92
    -Dilemma, 1860
      Amer. Her. --New (7) p609
  -Disunity
    Kraus--U. S. p467-468

, Independent
, Appeal of, 1854
Angle--By p192-198
-Silver Democrats, 1895
Morris--Ency. p264
-South
Life--Steel (7) p106-107
, Solid
Butterfield--Amer. p223
-Views of Fortescue Cuming
Angle--American p158-159
DEMOCRATIC REPUBLICANS
See also DEMOCRATIC PARTY
Alden--Pioneer p174-175, 181-182
Life--Growing (3) p154-155
Linton--Bicentennial. See index
p440
DEMOREST, ELLEN L. C.
Lynes--Taste. p77-79
Macksey--Book p265
Warren--Pictorial p124
DENOMINATIONS. See names of
denominations
DENTISTRY
Schwartz--When p174
Walker--Every. p80
-1876
Hilton--Way p87-88
-Tooth powder, 1876
Hilton--Way p88
-Women
Macksey--Book p148-149
-Women, first (Cincinnati, O.)
Robertson--Book p201
DENVER, COLORADO
Billington--Far p260, 265, 267,
285-287, 290-291
Brown--Westerners p157, 164,
166-169, 211, 223
-Gold mining
Watkins--Gold p52-61, 262
, and prices
Amer. Her. --New p732-733
DEPARTMENT STORES
Boardman--Civil p134
Harris--Land p71-98
Portraits--Americans p42, 45
Reader's--Story p288
Walker--Every. p123-124
-1876
Hilton--Way p171-172
, First, 1848 (New York City)
Robertson--Book p48
, Largest in world (Cast Iron
Palace, N. Y., 1876)
Hilton--Way p171
-"Two weeks in department
stores, " by Annis M. MacLean

Harris--Land p71-98
DEPENDENT PENSION ACT, 1890
Morris--Ency. p261
DEPEW, CHAUNCEY M.
Butterfield--Amer. p314
-Toast to women
Hurd--Treasury p103-105
DEPRESSIONS. See BUSINESS
DEPRESSIONS; PANICS
DE QUILLE, DAN
, on Comstock lode, 1859
Commager--Heritage p578-582
DERBY, ELIAS HASKET ("KING")
Furnas--Americans p306-307, 647-
648
DESERET (state)
See also MORMONS; YOUNG,
BRIGHAM
Billington--Far p204-205
Tunis--Frontier p123
DESERT, GREAT AMERICAN
Hine--American p74-75, 77, 156-
157
-Views of Sarah Royce
Commager--Heritage p562-571
DESERT LAND ACT, 1877
Amer. Her. --New (9) p774
Amer. Her. --New (10) p845-846
American 200 p79
Carman--History (2) p202-203
DESIGN. See ART--Design
DESKS
, old school
Wilson--Vanish. p162
, roll-top
Wilson--Vanish. p107
DE SMET, PIERRE JEAN
Boardman--Jackson. p66
Jones--Shaping p120
DESTINY, AMERICA'S MANIFEST.
See "MANIFEST DESTINY"
DETECTIVES. See SPOTTERS
DE TOCQUEVILLE, ALEXIS
Reader's--Story p340
, on conservation
Reader's--Story p502
, on democracy, 1835
Reader's--Story p504
, on freedom
Reader's--Story p500
DETROIT, MICHIGAN
Drury--Midwest p63-67
-Mayors
-Views of William T. Stead
Cook--City p206-208
-Politics, 1893
-Views of Melvin G. Holli
Cook--City p194-195

-Surrender, 1812
   Angle--American p178-179
DEW, THOMAS RODERICK
-Biography
   Amer. Her. --New (7) p E234
, on proslavery arguments
   Boardman--Jackson. p110
DEWES, W. B.
-"The military phase: the
   "Runaway scrape," 1852"
   Ridge--America's p432-433
DEWEY, GEORGE, Admiral
Life--Reaching (8) p126, 132-133
-Biography
   Amer. Her. --New (12) p E415-
   416
   Morris--Ency. p650
-Victory at Manila Bay
   Angle--American p438-442
   Commager--Heritage p980-
   984
DEWEY, JOHN
Boardman--Gilded p119-120
Life--Reaching (8) p14, 16
Portrait--Americans p143-145
, and "Progressive education"
   Dulles--United p121-122
-Biography
   Amer. Her. --New (11) p E380
-"How to teach manners in the
   school-room"
   Harris--Land p219-228
-"School and society," 1899
   Davie--Profile p322-323
DEWEY, MELVIL
Randel--Centennial p425-428
"DEWEY (NELSON) HOMESTEAD"
(Cassville, Wisconsin)
Vanderbilt--Living p169
DEWOLFE, ELSIE (LADY MENDL)
Lynes--Taste. See index p352
DIALECT
, Humorous
   Burner--America (1) p270-
   272
DIAMOND FRAUD
Gilbert--Trail. p204-206
DIAZ, PORFIRIO
-Biography
   Amer. Her. --New (12) p E416
DICEY, EDWARD
, on Civil war recruitment,
   Boston
   Commager--Heritage p675-
   677
DICKENS, CHARLES
-"Martin Chuzzlewit," 1844
   Commager--Heritage p289-300

, on locomotives, 1842
   Angle--American p205-207
-Travels to Baltimore, Harris-
   burg, 1842
   Commager--Heritage p380-383
DICKINSON, ANNA ELIZABETH
Young--Women p310
-Biography
   Young--Women p370
, on Civil war draft riots
   Commager--Heritage p696-702
DICKINSON, EMILY ELIZABETH
Adelman--Famous p200
Dulles--United p114
Heath--Women (4) p17
Morris--Ency. p576
Mumford--Brown p26-29, 53
Our literary p171-173
Reader's--Story p414, 419
Warren--Pictorial p130-131
-Biography
   Amer. Her. --New (11) p E380-
   381
   Morris--Ency. p651
, on Mt. Holyoke Seminary, 1847
   Angle--American p271-273
DICKSON, WILLIAM K.
Reader's--Story p470
DIET
See also COOKERY; FOOD
Boardman--Jackson. p174
Ross--Taste p226
-1830's
   Lynes--Domestic. p186-187
-Nutrition
   Furnas--Americans p901-902
, Pioneer
   Lynes--Domestic. p26
-Prairies
   Lynes--Domestic. p33-34
DIGGER INDIANS
DeVoto--Year p61, 165, 181, 300,
   303, 337-342, 366, 410, 412, 421,
   429, 448, 491
Gilbert--Trail. p101, 106, 111, 166
, and fur trade
   Gilbert--Trail. p52-56, 60-61,
   64, 72, 74-75, 77
DILLON, SIDNEY
-"Driving the golden spike," 1892
   Ridge--America's p568-570
DIME MUSEUMS
Partridge--As p164
"DIME NOVELS"
See also ALGER, HORATIO,
   JR.; NOEL, MARY
Boardman--Civil p195-196
Boardman--Gilded p133-134

Cable--American p152, 398
Dulles--United p107
Hart--Popular p153-156
Hine--American p273-277, 279, 297
Mott--Golden p148-151
Nye--Unembar. p200-210
Our literary p128-129
-1875-1876
   Randel--Centennial p312-313, 347-348
, Early
   Treasury--Amer. p366-368
DIME STORES
Wilson--Vanish. p137
DIMOCK, SUSAN
Macksey--Book p148
DIMSDALE, THOMAS J.
"Justice in the mining camps," 1884
Ridge--America's p546-548
DINGLEY TARIFF
Harlow--Story p475
DINING ROOMS
Langdon--Everyday (2) p183-185
Lynes--Domestic. See also index p176-199, 300
DINNERS
Hunt--Life p222-227
Langdon--Everyday (2) p188
Tunis--Young p111-112
-1830's
   Train--Story p174
, Everyday
   Wilson--Folkways p145-147
, Formal
   Wilson--Folkways p148-149
, Sunday (Georgia, 1899)
   Schwartz--When p139
DIORAMAS
Furnas--Americans p569-570
DIPLOMACY
, post-Civil war
   Dulles--United p157-158
DISASTERS
See also Earthquakes; Fires and fire protection, names of disasters
Furnas--Americans p624
Linton--Centennial p440
-1876
   Randel--Centennial. See index p468
-Middlewest
   Drury--Midwest p87-88
   Furnas--Americans p358
-Sinkings
   Furnas--Americans p358

-Steamboat explosions
   Furnas--Americans p295-296
DISCIPLES OF CHRIST
Boardman--Virginia p171-172
Morris--Ency. p551-552
Reader's--Story p102
DISCIPLINE
See also SCHOOLS--Discipline
Schwartz--When p66-67
DISCRIMINATION
See also names of nationalities, races, religions
Life--Reaching (8) p60, 64-67
, against immigrants
   Life--New (5) p8, 71-72
, Racial
   Life--New (5) p15, 68, 74
, Religious
   Life--New (5) p71
DISEASES
See also names of diseases; MEDICINE; REMEDIES
Furnas--Americans p373, 779, 842-843, 908-909
Handlin--This p107-108, 154
-1876
   Hilton--Way. See index p212
-New York City (one block, 1864)
   Cook--City p137
DISHWASHING
-1876
   Hilton--Way p36
-First dishwasher, 1889 (Shelbyville, Ind.)
   Robertson--Book p50
DISOBEDIENCE
, Punishments for
   Schwartz--When p66-67
DISTILLERIES AND BREWERIES
Furnas--Americans p457-458
Van Wagenen--Golden p216-219
DISTRIBUTION--PREEMPTION ACT, 1841
Amer. Her. --New (6) p E198
Bartlett--New p240
Hine--American p160-161, 208, 253
Morris--Ency. p438
Reader's--Story p74
Ridge--America's p405-406
DIVERS, BRIDGET
Young--Women p94-95, 327-328, 345
DIVERSIONS. See AMUSEMENTS; SPORTS AND GAMES; etc.
DIVINITY. See CLERGYMEN;

RELIGION
DIVORCE
Bartlett--New p363
Cable--American p232, 234, 264-
265
Furnas--Americans p489
Gurko--Ladies p61, 66, 97, 157,
163-164, 173, 202-206, 208, 222,
234, 282-285, 308
Keller--Affairs p470-472
-1880-1899
Sochen--Herstory p202
-Legislation for women
Tyler--Freedom's p460
DIX, DOROTHEA LYNDE
Adelman--Famous p150-151
Amer. Her. --New (6) p E199
Boardman--Jackson. p131
Cable--American p240
Carman--History (1) p525
Dannett--Noble. See index
p414
Dolin--Great p74-83
Harlow--Story p255
Heath--Women (4) p7
Life--Sweep (4) p61, 66
Macksey--Book p112-113
Neidle--America's p29-30
Reader's--Story p294-295, 338
Sochen--Herstory p122
Tyler--Freedom's p298, 304-307
Warren--Pictorial p105, 109
Young--Women. See index
p386
-Biography
Young--Women p370-371
, on insane
Commager--Heritage p419-
421
200 Years (1) p298-299
DIXIE. See EMMETT, DANIEL
DECATUR
DIXON, GEORGE WASHINGTON
Chase--America's p261, 263
DOANE, W. H.
Furnas--Americans p664-665
DOCTORS. See PHYSICIANS
DODD, ANNA BOWMAN
-"The Republic of the future"
Harris--Land p192-202
DODD, SAMUEL C. T.
Portraits--Americans p19
DODGE, DAVID LOW
Tyler--Freedom's p400-401, 405
DODGE, GRACE
Macksey--Book p273-274
Warren--Pictorial p143
DODGE, GRENVILLE MELLEN

Brown--Westerners p175, 183-184,
188, 197
-"Building the Union Pacific"
Commager--Heritage p832-837
Ridge--America's p562-564
-Driving of the Golden Spike
Davie--Profile p165-167
, on labor problems
Davie--Profile p164
-"The race against promontory"
Ridge--America's p567-568
DODGE, MARY ELIZABETH MAPES
Adelman--Famous p217
Boardman--Civil p156-157
DODGE CITY, KANSAS
Bartlett--New p112, 229, 416-417,
428
Dulles--History p180
Hine--American p127-128, 258, 311
-1875-1876
Randel--Centennial p149-150
DOG SLEDS
Marzio--Nation p163
"DOG TROTS." See "BREEZE-
WAYS"
DOLLS
Dreppard--Pioneer p135
McClinton--Antiques p292-301;
see also index p347
-Carriages
McClinton--Antiques p155, 165
, Cloth
McClinton--Antiques p338-339
-Clothes
McClinton--Antiques p198-201
-"Golliwoog," first, 1895
Robertson--Book p79
-Houses
McClinton--Antiques p302-328
-"Fairy Villa," (Museum of
City of N. Y., 1864)
McClinton--Antiques p311-
314
, Famous
McClinton--Antiques p309-
318
-Peddler
Ross--Taste p85
DOMESTIC MANNERS. See
ETIQUETTE
DOMESTIC SERVICE. See SER-
VANTS; SLAVES AND SLAVERY
DOMESTICITY. See FAMILIES
AND FAMILY LIFE
DONALD, DAVID
, on Dred Scott decision
Miers--American p178-183
DONATION LAND ACT, 1850

Ross--Westward p111
DONELSON, ANDREW JACKSON
("JACK")
, and Eaton affair
    Phillips--That p54, 58, 62-64,
    75, 78-81, 84, 91-92, 99-102,
    108-109, 111, 116
DONELSON, EMILY DONELSON
, and Eaton affair
    Phillips--That p58-60, 62-63,
    67, 74-75, 91-93, 97, 99-101,
    110, 116, 142
DONIPHAN, ALEXANDER W.
DeVoto--Year. See index p515
-Biography
    Amer. Her. --New (7) p E234-
    235
-"Doniphan's Thousand"
    Life--Sweep (4) p104, 109-
    110, 116
-Expedition, 1846-1847
    Morris--Ency. p204
DONNELLY, IGNATIUS
    Furnas--Americans p710, 728-
    729, 799
DONNER LAKE. See TRUCKEE
LAKE
DONNER PARTY, 1846
    Amer. Her. --New (7) p E235
    America's Hist. p368
    Billington--Far p110-114
    Boardman--Jackson. p55
    DeVoto--Year. See index p515
    Downey--Our p279-289
    Life--Sweep (4) p134-135
    Ridge--America's p484-486
, and Virginia Reed Murphy,
    1846
    Commager--Heritage p535-
    542
-Starvation and death
    Commager--Heritage p535-
    542
-"The tragedy of the Donner
    party," by Patrick Breen
    Ridge--America's p484-486
-Views of Patrick Breen
    Angle--American p229-231
DOOLITTLE, AMOS
    Mussey--Old p126
DOREMUS, SARAH PLATT
HAINES
    Adelman--Famous p166
"DORION WOMAN" (Indian)
    Ross--Westward p104
DORR REBELLION
    Life--Sweep (4) p86
    Morris--Ency. p186

DOS PASSOS, JOHN
    "Builders for a golden age"
    Treasury Amer. p135-147
"DOUBLE STANDARD"
    Cable--American p264-265
DOUBLEDAY, ABNER
    Harlow--Story p437
-Biography
    Amer. Her. --New (11) p E381
-Defense of Fort Sumter
    Commager--Heritage p733-738
DOUGHTY, THOMAS
    Boardman--Virginia p155
    Larkin--Art p200-201; see also
    index p523
DOUGLAS, JAMES
    Case--Empire p57-69
-"British strength in the Oregon
    country," 1839
    Ridge--America's p493-495
DOUGLAS, STEPHEN ARNOLD
    See also "FREEPORT DOCTRINE"
    Alden--Pioneer p249-250, 257-261,
    268
    Amer. Her. --New (7) p555
    Boardman--Civil p2, 14-16, 21-22,
    27-28
    Boardman--Jackson. p196-197
    Borden--Portrait (1) p216, 219-
    220, 223-225, 228
    Carman--History (1). See index
    p. viii
    Harlow--Story p291-297, 299-300,
    308
    Holzman--Stormy p37-38
    Kraus--U.S. See index p. iii
    Life--New (5). See index p157
    Linton--Bicentennial. See index
    p441
    Meredith--World p48-49, 51
    Morris--Ency. See index p747
    200 Years (1). See index p346
    Viewpoints p75
, and Anti-Nebraskans
    Butterfield--Amer. p144-145
, and Le Compton
    Morris--Ency. p223-224
, and the Lincolns
    Randall--Mary p191-192, 233
-Bill to organize Nebraska, 1854
    Angle--By p191-192
-Biography
    Amer. Her. --New (7) p E236-
    237
    Morris--Ency. p651-652
, on slaves and slavery
    Angle--American p272-274
DOUGLASS, FREDERICK

Boardman--Gilded p100
Boardman--Jackson. p120
Morris--Ency. p516
200 Years (1) p268-269, 309
, and women's rights movement
    Gurko--Ladies p102, 105, 112,
      231-232, 247, 280, 313
-Biography
    Amer. Her. --New (7) p E235-
    236
    Morris--Ency. p652
-"The cause of the negro peo-
ple, " 1864
    Trachtenberg--Demo. p52-65
-"The north star"
    Reader's--Story p360
DOW, JOY WHEELER
Lynes--Taste. p7, 140, 167-169
DOW, LORENZO
Chase--America's p209-211
, and Peggy Dow
    Earle--Two cent. (2) p. xxiii;
    facing p758, 760
DOW, NEAL
Boardman--Jackson. p130
DOW, PEGGY
, and Lorenzo Dow
    Earle--Two cent. (2) p. xxiii;
    facing p758, 760
DOWNING, ANDREW JACKSON
Boardman--Jackson. p164
Bode--Anatomy p43, 46-58
Cable--American p159
Lynes--Domestic. See index
    p300
Lynes--Taste. See index p352
Reader's--Story p237
Ross--Taste p17, 21, 135, 145,
    150
-"Highland Gardens" (home)
    Lynes--Taste. p23-24, 53
"DOWSERS" (water-witches)
Wilson--Early p113
DRAFT AND DRAFT RIOTS. See
CIVIL WAR--Draft
DRAGOONS
DeVoto--Year p515
DRAINAGE
-1876
    Hilton--Way p17
, Agricultural
    Van Wagenen--Golden p209-
    210
DRAKE, DANIEL, DR.
Boorstin--Americans p119
, on declamatory literature
    Boorstin--Americans p307-
    308

DRAKE, EDWIN L.
Harlow--Story p384-385
Portraits--Americans p7-8
DRAMA
See also THEATER
Cable--American p326-327
Nye--Cultural p265-267
200 Years (1) p306-307
-1876
    Randel--Centennial p29-30, 59,
    82-83, 314, 335-340
, Americanism in
    Grimsted--Melodrama p3, 17-
    18, 135-145, 150-169, 204-206,
    209-210
, and joke books, 1880's
    Peck--Nineteenth n. p.
-Benefits
    Grimsted--Melodrama p62-63
-"Bunker Hill"
    Grimsted--Melodrama p76-77,
    147
, Class structure in
    Grimsted--Melodrama p192-
    193, 204-210
-Comedy
    See also DRAMA--Farce
    Grimsted--Melodrama p7, 122,
    163-165, 167, 177, 183-199
, Democracy in
    Grimsted--Melodrama p156-
    165, 205-210, 220
, Domesticity in
    Grimsted--Melodrama p156-
    165, 205-210, 220
, Economic views in
    Grimsted--Melodrama p161,
    187-188, 197-199, 224
, Equestrian
    Grimsted--Melodrama p80-81,
    101, 238
, Family relationships in
    Grimsted--Melodrama p12-14,
    173-176, 179-186, 227-229, 235-
    237, 243-248
-Farce
    Grimsted--Melodrama p75, 99,
    235-240, 251, 253, 256
, Gothic
    Grimsted--Melodrama p16-17,
    250, 252
-Illinois
    Commager--Heritage p384-388
, Indians in
    Grimsted--Melodrama p61-62,
    151, 194, 215-218, 227
-Melodrama
    Dulles--History p215-217

, Military
  Grimsted--Melodrama p17-18,
  76-77, 156-157, 159, 202-203,
  226-227
-Religious attitudes
  Grimsted--Melodrama p4-7,
  15, 23-34, 40, 45, 50, 112-113,
  154, 179, 222-226, 247-248
, Shakespearean
  Dulles--History p110-112, 116,
  172-173, 219, 236-237
, Social comment in
  Grimsted--Melodrama p158-
  165, 167, 184-203, 215-218,
  222, 224-225, 235-240
-Views of nature in
  Grimsted--Melodrama. See
  index p283 (under Nature,
  Views of)
DRAMATISTS (PLAYWRIGHTS)
  Boardman--Civil p165
  Boardman--Jackson. p158-159
  Boardman--Virginia p146-147
  Furnas--Americans p322, 567-
  569, 757
  Grimsted--Melodrama. See
  index p280
  Morris--Ency. p590-592
DRAPER, EBENEZER
  Tyler--Freedom's p170-171
DRAPER, GEORGE
  Tyler--Freedom's p170-171
DRAPER, JOHN W.
  Boardman--Civil p175
  Boardman--Jackson. p102
  Reader's--Story p307
DRAWING
, for children
  McClinton--Antiques p58-61,
  90-92
DRED SCOTT DECISION, 1857
  Amer. Her. --New (7) p559-560,
  E237
  Boardman--Civil p20-22
  Bonte--America p113
  Borden--Portrait (1) p222-223
  Butterfield--Amer. p150-151
  Carman--History (1) p619-620,
  625, 696
  Collins--Story p205
  Harlow--Story p295-296
  Kraus--U.S. p465-467, 472, 475
  Life--New (5) p73-74, 77
  Morris--Ency. p221-222
  Reader's--Story p340
  200 Years (1) p279, 281, 285,
  288, 343
-"Chief Justice Roger B. Taney

for the Supreme Court"
  Heffner--Doc. p125-133
-Views of David Donald
  Miers--American p178-183
DRESEL, OTTO
  Howard--Our p217-218
DRESS. See CLOTHING AND
DRESS
DRESS MATERIALS. See FABRICS
DRESSER, PAUL
-Biography
  Amer. Her. --New (12) p E416
DRESSLER, MARIE
  Blum--Stage Profile p37
DRESSMAKERS
  Wilson--Early p78-79
DREW, DANIEL ("UNCLE DAN")
  Boardman--Civil p132-133
  Dulles--United p55
  Harlow--Story p393-395
  Life--Steel (7) p129
  Treasury Amer. p315
DREW, JOHN
  Blum--Stage Profile 6
  Boardman--Civil p165-166
DREW, LOUISA LANE (MRS. JOHN)
  Adelman--Famous p207
  Warren--Pictorial p157
DREW FAMILY
  Boardman--Civil p165-166
DRILLING MACHINERY
  Tunis--Frontier p155, 157
  Van Wagenen--Golden p223-225
DRINKS AND DRINKING. See
  ALCOHOLISM; BEVERAGES;
  LIQUOR; names of drinks
DRIVERS, ANIMAL (Livestock
  "Drovers")
  Wilson--Early p127-133
  Wright--Every. p141-142
DROUILLARD, GEORGE
  Brown--Westerners p40-41, 46,
  50, 55-56
"DROVERS." See DRIVERS, ANI-
MAL
DRUGS
  See also MEDICINE; REMEDIES;
  SQUIBB, EDWARD ROBINSON,
  DR.
  Cable--American p148
  Nostalgia p20-23
-1870's
  Randel--Centennial p324-327
-"Hard," during Civil War
  Garrison--Lost p65-67
"DRUMMERS" (Salesmen to store-
keepers)
-1876

Hilton--Way p152
DRYDEN, JOHN
  -Insurance
    Nostalgia p29-32
DUANE, WILLIAM J.
  Boardman--Jackson. p19-20
DUBOIS, WILLIAM E. B.
  Boardman--Gilded p101-102
DUBUQUE, IOWA
  Treasury Amer. p261
  -1860
    Ross--Taste p271
DUCHESNE, ROSE PHILIPPINE,
SISTER
  Neidle--America's p75
DUCKETT, ELIZABETH WARING
  -"Narrative," 1863
    Andrews--Women p30-65
DUDZIK, JOSEPHINE
  Neidle--America's p75
DUELS
  Boorstin--Americans p206-212,
  216
  Carson--Polite p114-128
  Furnas--Americans p528-531
  Hunt--Life p154-157
  Tunis--Young p108-109
  -New Orleans, 1840
    Downey--Our p255-268
DUFFIELD, GEORGE C.
  -"The beginning of the Long
  Drive," 1866
    Ridge--America's p592-595
DUFFUS, R. L.
  Furnas--Americans p371-372, 415,
  672, 779-780, 892-893, 896, 922-
  923
"DUGOUTS" (Sod houses)
  Bartlett--New p215-218, 352-353
  Hine--American p163
  Lynes--Domestic. p31-33
  Reader's--Story p238
  , Cottonwood
    Tunis--Frontier p109-110
DUKE, JAMES BUCHANAN
  -Biography
    Morris--Ency. p653
"DUKE HOMESTEAD" (Durham,
N. C.)
  Vanderbilt--Living p130
DU MAURIER, GEORGE
  Furnas--Americans p885-886
DUN, ROBERT GRAHAM
  Portraits--Americans p13
DUNBAR, WILLIAM
  Amer. Her. --New (6) p E199
DUNCAN, ISADORA
  Warren--Pictorial p154

DUNCAN, JAMES M.
  Garrison--Lost p96-97
DUNIWAY, ABIGAIL SCOTT
  Ross--Heroines. See index p179-
  180
  Ross--Westward p137-154
  Warren--Pictorial p121-122
DUNIWAY, BEN
  Ross--Heroines p159-160, 165-167
DUNLAP, WILLIAM
  Grimsted--Melodrama. See
  index p280
  Nye--Cultural p265
DUNNE, FINLEY PETER
  Furnas--Americans p611-612,
  877-878
  -Biography
    Amer. Her. --New (12) p E416
DU PONT, ELEUTHERE IRENEE
  Amer. Her. --New (5) p E162
  Boardman--Virginia p92
  Marzio--Nation p237-239
  -Powder mills
    America's Hist. p303
DU PONT, HENRY
  Life--New (5) p74
  -"Winterthur" (home, Winter-
  thur, Del.)
    Vanderbilt--Living p76-79
DU PONT, PIERRE SAMUEL
  Boardman--Virginia p91-92
DU PONT, THOMAS COLEMAN
  -Biography
    Morris--Ency. p653
DU PONT COMPANY
  Davie--Profile p254-256
DU PUY DE LOME, ENRIQUE
  -Biography
    Amer. Her. --New (12) p E416-
    417
DURAND, ASHER B.
  Boardman--Civil p159
  Boardman--Jackson. p152-153
  Bode--Anatomy p68-69
  Larkin--Art p204-205; see also
  index p523
DURANT, THOMAS CLARK
  Brown--Westerners p171-185
DURRIE, GEORGE H.
  Bode--Anatomy p88-89
  Larkin--Art p206-207, 215
DURYEA, CHARLES EDGAR
  Ross--Taste p174
DURYEA, FRANK
  -Automobile racing, 1895
    Angle--American p417-418
    White--American p135-139
DURYEA BROTHERS

-Biography
Amer.Her. --New (12) p E417
-First automobiles
Wilson--American p324-325
DVORÁK, ANTONIN
, in America
Chase--America's p387-391
DWIGHT, JOHN SULLIVAN
Brooks--Flower. p192, 229, 243-
244, 250, 268, 271, 374-376, 383
Howard--Our p218-219
Lowens--Music p228, 250-253,
255-257, 259-260, 262
Our literary p73
DWIGHT, TIMOTHY
Boardman--Virginia p139
DYES
Van Wagenen--Golden p266-267

E

EADS, JAMES BUCHANAN
Amer.Her. --New (8) p E271
Boardman--Civil p144-145
EAKINS, THOMAS
Boardman--Civil p160-161
Furnas--Americans p633-634
Hine--American p130
Larkin--Art p277-279; see also
index p523
Mumford--Brown p8, 211-217
Walker--Every. p122, 169-170
-Biography
Amer.Her. --New (12) p E417
Morris--Ency. p653-654
EAMES, EMMA
-Biography
Amer.Her. --New (12) p E417
EARLE, ALICE MORSE
Adelman--Famous p245
EARLY, JUBAL ANDERSON
("JUBILEE"), GENERAL
Amer.Her. --New (8) p E271
Boardman--Civil p54-55
Dowdey--Experiment p15, 357,
374, 398
Garrison--Lost p21-24
, and Sheridan
Pratt--Civil p53-54
-Raids, Civil war
Morris--Ency. p243
EARTHQUAKES
-"Charleston," 1886
Keyes--Hope p278
EASTER
Partridge--As p137-139
Walker--Every. p35

-Parades
Ross--Taste p256
-New York city, 1890's
Ross--Taste p253
EASTERN STAR, ORDER OF
Carson--Polite p251
-"Rob Morris memorial" (La
Grange, Ky.)
Vanderbilt--Living p121
EASTLAKE, CHARLES LOCKE
Lynes--Taste. See index p353
Train--Story p321-322
EASTMAN, GEORGE
America's Hist. p554-555
Portraits--Americans p156-157
Wilson--American p266-271
, as philanthropist
Wilson--American p270-271
-Birthplace (Rochester, N.Y.)
Vanderbilt--Living p56
-Photography
Life--Steel (7) p38, 46-47
Marzio--Nation p515-550
Nostalgia p43-46
Reader's--Story p273
EASTMAN, SETH
Amer.Her. --New (6) p E199
EATING. See FOOD; names of
food, meals
EATON, JOHN HENRY
Amer.Her. --New (5) p E162
Carman--History (1) p365, 426-
427, 430, 788
Phillips--That. See index p178-
179
EATON, MARGARET O'NEALE
TIMBERLAKE (later BUCHIGNANI)
("PEGGY"; "BELLONA")
See also names of individuals in-
volved in "Eaton affair":
BRANCH; BUCHANAN; BUCHIG-
NANI; CALHOUN; (Mr. & Mrs.),
CALL (Mr. & Mrs.); CAMP-
BELL; CLAY; COFFEE; CRAW-
FORD; DONELSON; INGHAM
(Mr. & Mrs.); KENDALL; KEY
Amer.Her. --New p394, 396, 405;
E162-163
Borden--Portrait (1) p163
Butterfield--Amer. p84-85
Carman--History (1) p427-430
Life--Sweep (4) p35-37, 40
Linton--Bicentennial p103, 111
Morris--Ency. p169-170
Peacock--Famous p69-79
Phillips--That. See index (under
O'Neale, Peggy) p181-182
200 Years p228

EBENEZER COMMUNITY, NEW
YORK
  Tyler--Freedom's p131-132
"ECLECTIC READERS"
  Drury--Midwest p130-131
ECLIPSES
  Trollope--Domestic p293-295
  -1895, South Carolina
    Schwartz--When p186
  -Views of Josiah Quincy
    Commager--Heritage p364-
    367
ECONOMY (ECONOMICS)
  Keller--Affairs. See index
    p614
  Life--Sweep (4) p157
  Reader's--Story p279-285
  Whitney--America. See index
    p362
  -1800-1899
    Reader's--Story p285
  -1849-1865
    Life--New (5). See index
    p157
  -1877-1890
    Life--Steel (7). See index
    p157
  -1890's
    Jones--Age p381-382
    Life--Reaching (8). See
    index p173
  , and Civil war
    Carman--History (1) p685-
    692
  -Power, concentration of
    Morris--Ency. p497
  -Progress, post-Civil war
    Dulles--United p31-32
  -West
    Hine--American. See index
    p362
EDDY, MARY BAKER GLOVER
  Adelman--Famous p242-243;
    facing 240
  Boardman--Gilded p159-160
  Bonte--America p155
  Heath--Women (4) p16
  Macksey--Book p115-116
  Morris--Ency. p553
  Mumford--Brown p43-44
  Warren--Pictorial p131
  -Biography
    Morris--Ency. p654
  -Home (Amesbury, Mass.)
    Vanderbilt--Living p16
"E.D.E.N.", MRS." See
  SOUTHWORTH, EMILY
EDISON, LEWIS, JR.

Lowens--Music p184-193
EDISON, THOMAS ALVA
  See also PHONOGRAPHS
  Amer. Her.--New (6) p E199
  America's Hist. p552-553
  Boardman--Civil p146
  Boardman--Gilded p58-59
  Morris--Ency. p537-540
  Portraits--Americans p34
  Randel--Centennial p178-179, 186
  Reader's--Story p269
  200 Years (2) p85
  Wilson--American p286-287
  -Biography
    Morris--Ency. p654-655
  -Birthplace (Milan, Ohio)
    Vanderbilt--Living p148
  -Electric pen
    Wilson--American p294
  -Incandescent light
    Davie--Profile p208-209
    Life--Steel (7) p34, 38-41, 49
    Nostalgia p24-27
  -Inventions
    See also names of inventions
    Wilson--American p288-289
  -"The phonograph and its future"
    Trachtenberg--Demo. p228-236
  -Views of Alfred O. Tate, 1885
    Angle--American p383-386
  -"War of the currents"
    Garrison--Lost p105-108
"EDISON EFFECT"
  Wilson--American p294
EDITORS
  -Newspaper & periodical
    Morris--Ency. p581-586
EDMONDS, SARAH EMMA (FRANK-
LIN THOMPSON, pseud.)
  Dannett--Noble p48-50, 83, 109-
    110, 135, 139, 173, 220, 227, 392-
    397
  Warren--Pictorial p109-110
EDUCATION
  See also ACADEMIES; COL-
    LEGES AND UNIVERSITIES:
    SCHOLARS AND SCHOLARSHIP;
    SCHOOLS
  Alden--Pioneer p172, 210-211,
    221-222, 280, 294
  Boardman--Civil p180-184
  Boardman--Gilded p115-122
  Boardman--Jackson. p108, 111-
    112, 125, 129, 134-140, 160, 185
  Boardman--Virginia p112-113,
    162-167
  Cable--American p114-115, 148
  Davidson--Life (2) p352-360

Furnas--Americans. See index
p985-986
Handlin--This. See index p583
Harlow--Story p250-254
Hunt--Life p124-138
Keller--Affairs. See index
p614
Keyes--Hope p217-218
Kraus--U.S. p366,372-373
Morris--Ency. p555-557
Reader's--Story p129-134
Wright--Every. p190-202
-1860-1880
    Carman--History (2) p364
-1865-1899
    Dulles--United p104-106
-1876
    Hilton--Way p54-71
-1890's
    Life--Reaching (8) p13-14, 16,
    38-39
, and American faith
    Tyler--Freedom's p227-264
-California
    Wright--Culture p140-153
, Children's
    McClinton--Antiques p15-18,
    79, 90-93, 95-96
-Common school revolution
    Carman--History (1) p514-
    518
, during Civil war
    -North
        Carman--History (1) p688-
        689
    -South
        Carman--History (1) p737-
        738
, Elementary and secondary
    Randel--Centennial p72-73,
    397-401
, Errors of: "Thoughts," by
Horace Mann
    Davie--Profile p322
, German interest in
    Weisberger--Amer. p130
-Girls', 1876
    Hilton--Way p57, 125
, Higher, 1870's
    Randel--Centennial. See
    index p468
-Lessons, taking
    Schwartz--When p94-95
-Letter of Thomas Jefferson to
Peter Carr, 1817
    Davie--Profile p313-315
, Need for
    -Views of Horace Mann

    200 Years (1) p299
-Negroes, 1876
    Hilton--Way p60-62, 128-129
    Reader's--Story p131-132
, Organized--growth
    Collins--Story p155
, Parental
    Walker--Every. p41-42, 243
-Pestalozzi system
    Train--Story p342
, Progressive
    Reader's--Story p133
    Tyler--Freedom's p245-250
    , and John Dewey
        Dulles--United p121-122
, Public
    Boardman--Jackson. p134-135
    Nye--Cultural p169-170
, Sectarian
    Furnas--Americans p749
-Segregation
    Furnas--Americans p518-519,
    847
-Views of Frances Trollope
    Trollope--Domestic. See
    index p. vi
-Views of Horace Mann
    200 Years (1) p299
-West
    Hine--American p238-251
-Women
    Cable--American p146-147,
    182-183, 166-167
    Carman--History (1) p523-524
    Davidson--Life (2) p360-362
    Furnas--Americans p481, 492,
    740-745
    Gurko--Ladies. See index
    p323
    Handlin--This p221, 270-272,
    280-281
    Hunt--Life p76-77
    Life--Reaching (8) p39
    Life--Sweep (4) p65-66
    Lynes--Domestic. p60-62
    Macksey--Book p67-69, 73
    Reader's--Story p131
    Sochen--Herstory p139-142
    Tyler--Freedom's p250-254
    Walker--Every. p120-121
    Warren--Pictorial p69-79, 128
    Wright--Culture p70, 77, 85,
    104, 109, 152-153, 224-226
    -1830-1865
        Adelman--Famous p127-130
    -Cincinnati, Ohio
        Wright--Culture p104
    , Lack of

Life--Sweep (4) p65-66
-West
   Hine--American p248-249, 328
EDWARDS, HADEN
  Bartlett--New p97-98
EDWARDS, NINIAN W.
 , and Abraham Lincoln
   Randall--Mary p65, 67, 85
EGGLESTON, EDWARD
  Boardman--Civil p151-152
  Mott--Golden p199-200
  Randel--Centennial p. ix-x, 109,
   385, 448-449
EGGLESTON, GEORGE CARY
 , on money
  Commager--Heritage p711-714
EGGLESTON, SARAH DABNEY
  Andrews--Women p320
EGYPT
 -American military service to,
  1870's
   White--American p84-87
EISFELD, THEODOR
  Howard--Our p216-217
"EL DORADO"
 , Search for, in West
   Amer. Her. --New (9) p724-739
ELECTIONS
  See also POLITICAL CAM-
  PAIGNS; POLITICS; and related
  subjects
  Mussey--Old p88
 -Australian ballot
   Keller--Affairs p529-530
 , Congressional
   -1811
     Morris--Ency. p140
   -1859
     Morris--Ency. p225
   -1866
     Keller--Affairs p58-60, 67,
     70
     Morris--Ency. p247
   -1867
     Keller--Affairs p71, 81
   -1878
     Keller--Affairs p265
     Morris--Ency. p254
   -1890
     Morris--Ency. p262
   -1894
     Keller--Affairs p570-571
 -Laws
   Keller--Affairs p242, 522-531
 , Presidential
   Dulles--United p128-129
   Life--Reaching (8). See
   index p175

Life--Sweep (4) p159
Linton--Bicentennial. See
 index p441
Whitney--American. See
 index p362
-Electoral votes
  See also ELECTORAL
  COUNT ACT
  Linton--Bicentennial. See
  index p441
 -1800-1896
  Whitney--American p352-353
 -1800
   Boardman--Virginia p12-14
   Borden--Portrait (1) p132
   Butterfield--Amer. p33
   Carman--History (1) p308-309,
   309, 311
   Harlow--Story p157-158
   Life--Growing p41
   Linton--Bicentennial p58
   Morris--Ency. p130
   -Electoral tie, 1801
     Morris--Ency. p130-131
 -1804
   Boardman--Virginia p23-24
   Carman--History (1) p323-
   324
   Harlow--Story p170-171
   Life--Growing p59-60
   Linton--Bicentennial p61
   Morris--Ency. p133-134
 -1808
   Boardman--Virginia p33
   Carman--History (1) p338-
   339
   Harlow--Story p174
   Linton--Bicentennial p66
   Morris--Ency. p137
 -1812
   Boardman--Virginia p37
   Carman--History (1) p347
   Linton--Bicentennial p71
   Morris--Ency. p144
 -1816
   Boardman--Virginia p52
   Carman--History (1) p399
   Harlow--Story p222
   Linton--Bicentennial p78
   Morris--Ency. p155
 -1820
   Boardman--Virginia p62
   Carman--History (1) p400,
   409
   Harlow--Story p222
   Linton--Bicentennial p84-85
   Morris--Ency. p160
 -1824

Boardman--Jackson. p5
Boardman--Virginia p66
Borden--Portrait (1) p156-
157
Butterfield--Amer. p75
Carman--History (1) p409-
411, 784
Harlow--Story p222-223
Life--Growing (3) p152-153
Linton--Bicentennial p90-91
Morris--Ency. p164
-1828
Boardman--Jackson. p7-8
Borden--Portrait (1) p161
Butterfield--Amer. p81
Carman--History (1) p385,
416-417, 426, 438, 784
Harlow--Story p224
Linton--Bicentennial p96
Morris--Ency. p167
-1832
Boardman--Jackson. p20-21
Carman--History (1) p440-
442, 784
Harlow--Story p231-232
Linton--Bicentennial p102-
103
Morris--Ency. p174
-1836
Boardman--Jackson. p27-28
Carman--History (1) p444-
445, 784
Harlow--Story p233
Linton--Bicentennial p108
Morris--Ency. p178
-1840
Boardman--Jackson. p33-34
Borden--Portrait (1) p171-
172
Carman--History (1) p450-
452, 596-597, 784
Harlow--Story p237-238
Linton--Bicentennial p115
Morris--Ency. p183
Wright--Every. p35-37
-1844
Billington--Far p143-144
Boardman--Jackson. p36-38
Borden--Portrait (1) p211-
212
Butterfield--Amer. p110-111
Carman--History (1) p562-
563, 597-598, 784
Harlow--Story p267-268
Linton--Bicentennial p123
Morris--Ency. p191
-1848
Boardman--Jackson. p192-

193
Butterfield--Amer. p122-123
Carman--History (1) p600-
601, 784
Harlow--Story p283-284
Life--New (5) p34
Linton--Bicentennial p132-
133
Morris--Ency. p209
-1852
Boardman--Civil p11-12
Harlow--Story p289
Life--New (5) p50
Linton--Bicentennial p141
Morris--Ency. p216
-1856
Boardman--Civil p18-19
Borden--Portrait (1) p222
Carman--History (1) p513,
617-619, 785
Harlow--Story p294-295
Life--New (5) p71-72
Linton--Bicentennial p149
Morris--Ency. p221
-1860
Boardman--Civil p24-25, 27-
28
Borden--Portrait (1) p227-
228
Borden--Portrait (2) p8-9
Butterfield--Amer. p158-
159
Carman--History (1) p629-
633, 785
Harlow--Story p298-300
Jordan--Civil p23, 33
Life--New (5) p92-94
Linton--Bicentennial p158
Morris--Ency. p226
-1864
Boardman--Civil p73
Borden--Portrait (1) p234-
235
Butterfield--Amer. p176-
177
Carman--History (1) p698,
713, 785
Carman--History (2) p863
Harlow--Story p328
Holzman--Stormy p140-143
Jordan--Civil p165, 178-179
Keller--Affairs p27
Life--New (5) p119-120
Life--Union (6) p87
Linton--Bicentennial p180
Morris--Ency. p244
-1868
Boardman--Civil p87

Butterfield--Amer. p194-195
Carman--History (1) p733-
734, 785
Carman--History (2) p34-35,
863
Harlow--Story p344-345
Holzman--Stormy p181-184
Keller--Affairs p81-84
Life--Union (6) p149-152
Linton--Bicentennial p197
Maurois--Illus. p203
Morris--Ency. p249
-1872
Boardman--Civil p89-90
Carman--History (1) p743-
744, 785
Carman--History (2) p44-45,
863
Harlow--Story p348
Holzman--Stormy p187
Keller--Affairs p262
Life--Union (6) p154-155
Linton--Bicentennial p205
Morris--Ency. p251
-1876 (disputed)
Bonte--America p136
Borden--Portrait (2) p16-17
Butterfield--Amer. p220-221
Carman--History (1) p746-
751, 785
Carman--History (2) p47-51,
245, 863
Collins--Story p247
Dulles--United p131-133
Harlow--Story p349-351
Hilton--Way p201
Holzman--Stormy p205
Keller--Affairs p262-264,
546
Life--Steel (7) p7-10
Life--Union (6) p157
Linton--Bicentennial p213
Maurois--Illus. p204, 206
Morris--Ency. p252-253
-1880
Carman--History (2) p232-
233, 238, 246, 863
Harlow--Story p452-453
Keller--Affairs p250, 266
Life--Steel (7) p14
Linton--Bicentennial p219-
220
Morris--Ency. p255-256
-1880's
Keller--Affairs p545-562
-1884
Butterfield--Amer. p238-
239

Carman--History (2) p236-
240, 417, 863
Dulles--United p136-137
Harlow--Story p455-457
Holzman--Stormy p214-219
Life--Steel (7) p15-16
Linton--Bicentennial p227
Morris--Ency. p257
-1888 (disputed)
Butterfield--Amer. p252-253
Carman--History (2) p238,
241, 247, 417, 462, 863-864
Harlow--Story p462-463
Linton--Bicentennial p231
Morris--Ency. p260
-1892
Carman--History (2) p248,
254-255, 864
Harlow--Story p466
Keller--Affairs p568, 571
Linton--Bicentennial p237
Morris--Ency. p262-263
-1896
Amer. Her. --90's p30-35,
130-138
Butterfield--Amer. p274-
275
Carman--History (2) p257-
265, 363, 864
Dulles--United p152-154
Harlow--Story p474-475
Keller--Affairs p565, 580-
587
Linton--Bicentennial p246
ELECTORAL COUNT ACT, 1887
Morris--Ency. p258
ELECTRIC CHAIR
-First used, 1890 (Auburn, N.Y.)
Robertson--Book p53
-Sing Sing prison
Garrison--Lost p105-108
ELECTRIC FANS
-First, 1882 (N.Y.)
Robertson--Book p53
ELECTRIC HEATING SYSTEMS
-First, 1887
Robertson--Book p53-54
ELECTRIC LIGHTS
Train--Story p338
-Lamps
Reader's--Story p269
, Evolution of
Wilson--America p290-291
, First successful, 1879
Collins--Story p252
Robertson--Book p54
ELECTRIC MOTORS
Life--Steel (7) p74

, First, (1837, Rutland, Vt.)
  Robertson--Book p55
ELECTRIC RAILWAYS. See
RAILWAYS
ELECTRICITY
  Boardman--Gilded p58-59
  Carman--History (2) p75-76
  Life--Steel (7) p35, 39-41, 48-49,
  74
  Reader's--Story p269
  Walker--Every. p45-47, 72-73,
  113, 130, 220
  -1829-1846
    Morris--Ency. p531
  -1890's
    Life--Reaching (8) p34-35,
    100-101
  -Enumerating machine,
    Hollerith's
    Portraits--Americans p68
  , from magnetism
    Wilson--American p110-111
  -Power
    Nostalgia p47-50
    -1891-1899
      Morris--Ency. p498
  -"War of the currents"
    Garrison--Lost p105-108
ELEVATED RAILROADS
  Furnas--Americans p675-676,
  801
  Handlin--This p352, 398-399
  Ross--Taste p274
  -New York City
    Partridge--As p101
ELEVATORS
  Davidson--Life (2) p170
  Furnas--Americans p624-625
  Ross--Taste p152, 166
  , First, installed by W. E. Hale
    Life--Steel (7) p36
  , Grain
    Furnas--Americans p797-798
  , Safety
    Life--America's p143-144
ELIOT, CHARLES WILLIAM
  Boardman--Civil p183-184
  Harlow--Story p427
  Portraits--Americans p142
  Randel--Centennial p408-410
  -Biography
    Morris--Ency. p635-636
  -Inaugural address, as Harvard
  president, 1869
    Davie--Profile p322
  , on Harvard and Yale
    Hurd--Treasury p106-109
ELLICOTT, JOSEPH

-"Holland Land Company," 1809
    Ridge--America's p238-240
-Mills
    Wright--Every. p124-125
ELLIOTT, CHARLES WYLLIS
  Lynes--Taste. p103, 105-106
ELLIS ISLAND
  Marzio--Nation p135
  200 Years (2) p78-79
ELLSWORTH, HENRY L.
  Boardman--Jackson. p61
  -"Land promotion on the prai-
  ries," 1838
    Ridge--America's p300-303
"ELM CITY" (chip)
  Young--Women p178, 183, 187
ELMIRA, NEW YORK
  -1876
    Randel--Centennial p244-245,
    288, 337-338, 448
  -Prison camp
    Randel--Centennial p244-245
ELOCUTION. See SPEECH
ELSSLER, FANNY
  Boardman--Jackson. p159
ELY, EUGENE
  Treasury Amer. p344-345
ELY, EZRA STILES
  , and Eaton affair
    Phillips--That p69-72, 76, 80-82
ELY, RICHARD THEODORE
  Life--Reaching (8) p15
  -Biography
    Amer. Her. --New (11) p E381
  -"Pullman: a social study"
    Harris--Land p118-132
EMANCIPATION
  Furnas--Americans p514-515, 750
  Life--New (5) p116-119, 140-141
  Life--Union (6) p110-111, 113-114,
  121, 128
  -North
    Life--Growing p124-129
  -South
    Life--Growing p124-125, 133
EMANCIPATION PROCLAMATION,
1863
  Amer. Her. --New (8) p E271-272
  Angle--American p320-322
  Angle--By p264-266
  Boardman--Civil p69-70
  Bonte--America p126
  Butterfield--Amer. p172
  Carman--History (1) p681, 694,
  696-697
  Collins--Story p220
  Commager--Heritage p659-661,
  664-665

Davidson--Life (2) p390-391
Davie--Profile p118-119
Harlow--Story p318, 329-330
Heffner--Doc. p147-149
Jordan--Civil p104, 112-113, 118-120
Keyes--Hope p253, 264, 266-267
Kraus--U.S. p497-498
Life--New (5) p116-118
Morris--Ency. p238-239
Reader's--Story p151
200 Years (2) p25, 31
-Views of F. B. Carpenter
    Commager--Heritage p659-661
-Views of Paul M. Angle
    Miers--American p188-192
EMBARGO ACTS
Boardman--Virginia p26-27
Borden--Portrait (1) p140-141
Butterfield--Amer. p48-49, 51
Carman--History (1) p338, 340, 471
Harlow--Story p174
Kraus--U.S. p311-314
Life--Growing (3) p63, 97, 107
Linton--Bicentennial p64, 66-67
Morris--Ency. p136-137, 147-148
Tunis--Young p92
Wright--Every. p52
EMBREE, ELIHU
Amer. Her. --New (6) p E199
EMERSON, LUTHER ORLANDO
Howard--Our p261
EMERSON, RALPH WALDO
Amer. Her. --New (6) p E199-200
Boardman--Civil p149
Boardman--Jackson. p141-143
Bode--Anatomy p205-208
Brooks--Flower. See index p542
Carman--History (1) p522, 537-539, 604, 626-627
Handlin--This p225-227
Harlow--Story p244-245, 259
Larkin--Art p150; see also index p524
Morris--Ency. p567, 585
Our literary p62-65
Randel--Centennial. See index p468
Reader's--Story p410-411
Tyler--Freedom's p56-59; see also index p595
Wright--Every. p237-238
, and music
    Lowens--Music p261-262
, as lyceum lecturer
    Commager--Heritage p440-442
-Biography

Morris--Ency. p656
-"Concord hymn"
    Davie--Profile p55
-Eulogy on Robert Burns
    Hurd--Treasury p87-89
-"A fertility of projects for the salvation of the world"
    Commager--Heritage p413-416
-"Frenzied speculation in the Northwest," 1836
    Ridge--America's p299-300
, in Concord
    Brooks--Flower. p196-209
, on man the reformer
    200 Years (1) p298
, on peace
    Tyler--Freedom's p408
, on reform and reformers
    200 Years (1) p298
, on self-reliance
    Grimsted--Notions p61-69
-Oratory
    Boorstin--Americans p316-317
-Wood-notes
    Brooks--Flower. p252-267
EMIGRATION
, Arguments for, 1818
    Commager--Heritage p261-262
-Regulations
    Marzio--Nation p121
-West, 1840's
    DeVoto--Year. See index p515-516
EMINENT DOMAIN LAW
Keller--Affairs p390-391
EMMETT, DANIEL DECATUR
Chase--America's p259-260, 263, 267-277
Howard--Our p181-184
, and "Dixie"
    Bonte--America p119
    Krythe--Sampler p100-112
-Biography
    Amer. Her. --New (7) p E237
EMORY, WILLIAM
Gilbert--Trail. p156, 174-181
"EMPRESARIO" SYSTEM (in Texas)
Billington--Far p20-21, 119, 135
ENERGY
See also ELECTRICITY; related subjects
Boardman--Gilded p57-58
ENGINEERING
See also "ARMY ENGINEERS"
Wilson--American p144-145
-Education
    Boardman--Virginia p81-82
ENGINES

, First to use petroleum as fuel
  Wilson--American p322
ENGLAND AND ENGLISH
  Carman--History (1). See index
    p. ix
  , and Civil war
    Kraus--U.S. p491-492
  -British designs in California,
    1847
      Ridge--America's p489-490
  -Immigrants
    Furnas--Americans. See
      index p986
ENGLISH LANGUAGE
  Handlin--This p140, 144, 206,
    209-211, 250, 259, 376
ENGRAVERS AND ENGRAVINGS
  Furnas--Americans p572-575, 859
  -Banknotes
    Furnas--Americans p572-573
  -New England
    Mussey--Old p126-127
  Prints
    Furnas--Americans p572-578
ENTERPRISE
  -Views of Frances Trollope
    Trollope--Domestic. See
      index p. vi
ENTERTAINMENT
  See also types of entertainment,
    e.g.: BURLESQUE; CIRCUS;
    DRAMA; EXPOSITIONS; FAIRS;
    MINSTRELS; MOTION PIC-
    TURES; MUSIC; SPORTS AND
    GAMES; THEATER; VAUDE-
    VILLE; etc.
  Amer. Her. --90's p97-105, 122-
    126
  Boardman--Civil p196-199
  Burner--America's p251-274
  Life--New (5) p58, 62-65
  Nye--Cultural p145
  Wilson--Early p120-121
  Wilson--Folkways p99-107
  Wright--Every. p228-245
  -1876
    Hilton--Way p164-166, 179-180
  -Advertisements
    Dreppard--Pioneer p101-102
  , Children's, 1876
    Hilton--Way p34, 36-53
  , Immigrants in
    Marzio--Nation p420-430
  , Rural
    Hunt--Life p103-104
    Life--New (5) p24-25, 58, 64-65
ENVIRONMENT
  -1800-1850

Sochen--Herstory p106-107
, Waste of
  Sochen--Herstory p194-197
-West
  Hine--American. See index
    p363
EPIDEMICS
  See also SMALLPOX
  Boardman--Civil p113, 179
  Boardman--Jackson. p170
  Hunt--Life p207-211
  -1876
    Hilton--Way p84-87
  -Measles
    Ross--Heroines p83
EPIDEMIOLOGY
  Furnas--Americans p908-910
EPISCOPALIANS
  Boardman--Virginia p170-171
  Hunt--Life p121-122
EPITAPHS
  Bartlett--New p367-368
  Mussey--Old p104
EQUALITY
  See also WOMEN--Equal rights;
    etc.
  Handlin--This p169, 220, 356, 367-
    369, 398
  , and the Constitution
    Carson--Polite p83
  -Views of Frances Trollope
    Trollope--Domestic. See
      index p. vi
EQUITABLE LIFE ASSURANCE
SOCIETY
  -Founding and advertising
    Portraits--Americans p72
"ERA OF GOOD FEELINGS" (1813-
1820)
  Amer. Her. --New (5) p370, 376,
    391
  Harlow--Story p221-222
  Heffner--Doc. p94-97
  Linton--Bicentennial p79, 84
ERICKSON, EVARTS
  -"When New England saw the
    serpent"
      Treasury Amer. p298-299
ERICSSON, JOHN
  Amer. Her. --New (8) p E272
  Wilson--American p204-205
ERIE, LAKE
  Tunis--Frontier p91-93
  -Views of Frances Trollope
    Trollope--Domestic p384-385,
      389-390
ERIE CANAL
  Alden--Pioneer p160-161

105

Amer. Her. --New (5) p433-434;
E163
Bartlett--New p58, 121, 153, 311-
312, 314, 317, 379
Boardman--Jackson. p94-95
Boardman--Virginia p89
Butterfield--Amer. p77
Cable--American p99-100
Carman--History (1) p361, 363,
463-465, 472, 686
Collins--Story p147
Davidson--Life (2) p196, 214-223
Furnas--Americans p285-290,
344-345, 794
Handlin--This p155-156, 204, 212
Harlow--Story p198-199
Keyes--Hope p236
Langdon--Everyday (2) p127-137
Life--Growing p158-159
Reader's--Story p194-195, 259-
260
Tunis--Frontier p91-93
Tunis--Young p144-146
Wilson--American p72-77
Wright--Every. p86-88, 120
-Locks and acqueducts
Wilson--American p74-75
-near Little Falls
Keyes--Hope p232-233
-Opening, 1825
Keyes--Hope p192-193
Linton--Bicentennial p92-93
-Reduces shipping costs
Reader's--Story p281
-"Ride," by Thomas S. Wood-
cock, 1836
Angle--American p195
-"Travel, on the Erie Canal,"
1836, by Jacob Schramm
Ridge--America's p292-294
-Views of Carl Carmer
Miers--American p126-131
-Views of Frances Trollope
Trollope--Domestic p286,
369-373
ERIE RAILROAD
Boardman--Civil p138-139
Brown--Westerners p171
Furnas--Americans p347-348,
649-651, 819
-"Erie war" (stock speculation),
1867
Butterfield--Amer. p202-203
Harlow--Story p393-394
ESCALATORS
First, 1892 (N. Y.)
Robertson--Book p59
ESKIMOS

, Alaskan
-Awls, late 1800's
Marzio--Nation p15
ESSAYS
Bode--Anatomy p203-218
"ESSEX JUNTO"
Morris--Ency. p133
ESTERHAZY, COUNTESS. See
GRIFFIN, MRS. CHARLES
ETHERIDGE, ANNA
Young--Women p113, 125, 136, 200-
201, 322, 344
-Biography
Young--Women p371-372
"ETHICAL CULTURE" (Society)
Randel--Centennial p438, 443-444
ETIQUETTE
See also SOCIAL CALLING
Burner--America (1) p241-250
Cable--American p209-216, 218-
223
Carson--Polite p171
Furnas--Americans. See index
(under Manners) p996
Handlin--This p100, 124, 138, 141,
143
Lynes--Domestic. p64-73; see
also index (under Manners) p304
Ross--Taste p289-291
Tunis--Young p107-108
Walker--Every. p42-43, 242-244
-1876
Randel--Centennial. See
index (under Manners and
customs) p471
-Books and reading
Cable--American p105, 147-148,
162
Carson--Polite p167-184
Hart--Popular p88
Lynes--Domestic. p70-73, 180-
181
, City
Lynes--Domestic. p35-36
, Country
Lynes--Domestic. p35-36
-"Good manners," by Eliza M.
Lavin
Harris--Land p216-219
-Men
Wilson--Folkways p34-35
-Pregnancy
Cable--American p161
-Social forms
Harris--Land p215-228
, Table
Cable--American p214
Carson--Polite p178-181

Lynes--Domestic. p180-184
-Views of Frances Trollope
Wright--Every. p71-72
-Teaching, in schoolroom
Harris--Land p219-228
-Views of Frances Trollope
Cable--American p84, 87, 93,
111, 140-141
Davie--Profile p382-383
Trollope--Domestic. See
index p. v
Wright--Every. p68-74
-White House
Cable--American p83-85
-Women
Cable--American p167-168
Furnas--Americans p487-488,
565
Wilson--Folkways p32-33
EUROPE
See also names of countries,
nationalities
, and Civil war
Kraus--U.S. p498-499
Morris--Ency. p233
-Confederacy
Dowdey--Experiment. See
index p447
"EUSTACE DIAMONDS" (ship)
Young--Women p23
EVANGELISM.
See also CAMP MEETINGS;
CIRCUIT RIDERS; CLERGY-
MEN
Bonte--America p157
Furnas--Americans p330-331,
663-665
-Universities and colleges, New
England
Tyler--Freedom's p29-31
EVANS, AUGUSTA JANE
Boardman--Civil p157
Mott--Golden p126-127
-St. Elmo
Hart--Popular p118-120
EVANS, GEORGE HENRY
Boardman--Jackson. p86
EVANS, MANDA EVANICH
Neidle--America's p103-105
EVANS, OLIVER
Amer. Her. --New (5) p E163
Boardman--Virginia p84
Reader's--Story p257-258
Wilson--American p148
EVARTS, WILLIAM MAXWELL
-Biography
Morris--Ency. p656-657
EVERETT, EDWARD
Boardman--Civil p72-73

Brooks--Flower. p73-88, 100-103,
120-121, 127-128; see also index
p542
Our literary p48-49
-Biography
Amer. Her. --New (7) p E237
, on John Adams and Thomas
Jefferson
Hurd--Treasury p53-55
EVERITT, SUSAN
Hilton--Way p122-123
EVOLUTION
Boardman--Civil p174-176
Boardman--Gilded p122-123, 157-
158
Jones--Age p19-30
, Pessimism of
Jones--Age p351-358
EWELL, RICHARD STODDERT
Amer. Her. --New (8) p272-273
EWING, THOMAS
Amer. Her. --New (5) p E163
EXCURSIONS
, Train
Wilson--Vanish. p177
EXECUTIONS. See HANGINGS
EXERCISING. See GYMNASIUM
EXPANSION
Life--Sweep (4). See index p157
-to 1876
Life--Union (6) p158
-1820-1876
Bartlett--New p83-114
-1890's
Life--Reaching (8). See index
p173
, Continental
Carman--History (1) p552-577
, Ideology of
Hollingsworth--Amer. p9-17
-Map
Borden--Portrait (1) p135
EXPATRIATES
, in literature
Our literary p164-165
EXPLORATION AND DISCOVERY
See also GEOGRAPHY; SURVEYS;
names of explorations
Boardman--Civil p177-178
Boorstin--Americans p223-241
-1876
Hilton--Way p91-94
-Male predominance
Bartlett--New p343-344
, Scientific
America 200 p31-33
-West
Amer. Her. --New (6) p511-514
EXPLORERS

Boardman--Civil p177-178
-Women
Macksey--Book p238-239, 244-
245
EXPORTS AND IMPORTS
Boardman--Gilded p55
, American 1880-1896 (exports)
Keller--Affairs p590
EXPOSITIONS
See also names of expositions;
FAIRS
Walker--Every. p53, 70-73, 126,
170
EXPRESS INDUSTRY
Furnas--Americans p378-381

F

FABRICS
See also COTTON; WOOL; etc.
Langdon--Everyday (2) p241-260
-Broadcloth
Van Wagenen--Golden p258-
259
, Home-woven
Van Wagenen--Golden p265-
266
FACTORIES
Amer. Her. --New (5) p426-428
Harlow--Story p204-210
Hunt--Life p98-99
-New England
-Views of Thomas C. Cochran
Miers--American p121-126
, Northern
Reader's--Story p280-281
, Organization of
Boorstin--Americans p20-25
-Owners and workers
Carman--History (1) p488-
496, 703
-Production, 1808-1818
Morris--Ency. p494
-Towns
-New Hampshire
Trachtenburg--Demo.
p160-183
-Views of Harriet Martineau,
1837
Burner--America (1) p295-
298
FAIR, JAMES G.
Watkins--Gold p77, 79
"FAIR OAKS" (SEVEN PINES)
, Battle of
Dannett--Noble p149, 165,
173, 178-180, 186

Young--Women p183-186
FAIRFAX SEMINARY HOSPITAL
(Alexandria, Va.)
Dannett--Nobel p86, 230, 239, 281,
284, 381
FAIRS
-1893
Amer. Her. --90's p122
Reader's--Story p250-251
Walker--Every. p84-86
, Agricultural
Baordman--Virginia p79
, First
Van Wagenen--Golden p47-
48
, Centennial
Wilson--American p218-219
, Country
Dulles--History p279-282
Furnas--Americans p474-475
Partridge--As p44-49
-Middlewest
Drury--Midwest p87
, County
Bonte--America p102
Collins--Story p285
Ross--Taste p87
-Cultural importation
Jones--Age p279-280
, Market
Cable--American p124-125
-Pennsylvania, 1824
Life--Sweep (4) p24-25
, Trade
Life--Growing (3) p52-53
FAIRY TALES
-Book collecting
McClinton--Antiques p106-107
FALCONS
Hilton--Way p97-98
FAMILIES AND FAMILY LIFE
Bartlett--New p171, 361-363
Handlin--This. See index p584
Keller--Affairs. See index p615
Schwartz--When p17-19
-1876
Hilton--Way p13-33
Randel--Centennial p74-75,
308-309
-1890
Amer. Her. --90's p6-7
-19th century
Life--Steel (7) p142-143
-"Democratic traumas"
Grimsted--Notions p221-230
-Hartford, Conn., 1836
Life--Sweep (4) p32-33
-New England

Mussey--Old p106
-Relations
   Walker--Every. p29, 42-43,
   233, 244
, Victorian, typical
   Cable--American p210-220
, Views of Frances Trollope
   Trollope--Domestic. See
   index p. vi
FANS
   Ross--Taste p223, 225
FAR EAST
   Boardman--Virginia p72-73
FARGO, WILLIAM G.
   Boardman--Jackson. p100-101
FARM IMPLEMENTS
   Bartlett--New p203, 205-206
   Boardman--Virginia p79
   Cable--American p180-181
   Carman--History (2) p209-211
   Collins--Story p283
   Dreppard--Pioneer p49-56
   Drury--Midwest p78-80
   Furnas--Americans p673-674
   Hilton--Way p158-159
   Langdon--Everyday (2) p303-325
   Life--Steel (7) p35, 57, 59, 135
   Marzio--Nation p148-155
   Reader's--Story p263
   Ross--Taste p62
   Van Wagenen--Golden p220-238
   Walker--Every. p105-106
  -1820-1860
     Morris--Ency. p480
  -1825-1860
     Train--Story p274-276
  -Mowers, 1868
     Viewpoints p111
  -Scythes and cradles, old North-
   west
     Tunis--Frontier p77-78
  -Tractors, First, 1889
     Robertson--Book p190
FARMERS' ALLIANCE
   Harlow--Story p464-465
   Keller--Affairs p572, 574, 576-578
FARMERS AND FARMING
   See also AGRICULTURE; COUN-
   TRY LIFE
   Handlin--This. See index p584
   Life--Sweep (4) p11, 22-25, 139
   Reader's--Story p112-113
   Schwartz--When p27, 36-37, 195-
   196
   Treasury Amer. p264-273
   Trollope--Domestic. See
   index p. vi
   Walker--Every. p74-107

Wilson--American p234-241
Wright--Every. p137-158
-1877-1890
   Life--Steel (7). See index
   p157
-1890's
   Carman--History (2) p206-225
   Life--Reaching (8). See index
   p173
, and country towns
   Partridge--As p31-49
, and Populist movement
   Harlow--Story p462-465
, and seasons
   Partridge--As p10-11
-Buildings
   Wilson--Vanish. p15
, Changing
   Wilson--Vanish. p14-79
-Debts
   Dulles--United p71
-Difficulties
   Borden--Portrait (2) p27-28
-Expansion
   Dulles--United p69-70
-"The farmer and the dude," by
  E. Davenport (1897)
   Cook--City p7-8
-"The farmer and the man"
  (poetry)
   Cook--City p14
-Farmyards
   Partridge--As p8
-Frontier homes, tools
   Life--America's p102-103
-Frontier, technology (1865-1880)
   Ridge--America's p613-635
-Horsepower
   200 Years p98-99
-Labor
   Boardman--Jackson. p91
-Markets, 1870's
   Randel--Centennial p316-317
-Mass production
   Wilson--American p240-241
-Middle West
   Bartlett--New p189-211
-Mortgaging
   Keller--Affairs p385-386
-Old Northwest
   Tunis--Frontier p74-79
-Organization
   Borden--Portrait (2) p28
-Population, 1845-1860
   Van Wagenen--Golden p21, 25
-Prairies
   Wright--Every. p152-153
-Revolt

Reader's--Story p344
-Technology
  Marzio--Nation p148
-Tenant farming
  Boardman--Gilded p90-91
  Keller--Affairs p384-385
-West
  Boardman--Civil p93-98
  Carman--History (1) p482-487
  Harlow--Story p368-371
  Ridge--America's p615-618
FARNHAM, ELIZA W.
  Adelman--Famous p166
FARRAGUT, DAVID GLASGOW,
ADMIRAL
  Amer. Her. --New (8) p E273
  Boardman--Civil p44, 56
  Bonte--America p125
  Dannett--Noble p338-340
  Holzman--Stormy p74-76
  , at Mobile Bay
    America's Hist. p460-461
    Collins--Story p230
    Pratt--Civil p36
  -Biography
    Morris--Ency. p657
FARRAR, MRS. JOHN
  Lynes--Domestic. See index
  p301
  , on nursing homes
    Cable--American p105-106
  -"Young lady's friend"
    Cable--American p105-106,
    153, 167, 213-214, 221
FASHION
  See also ACCESSORIES;
    CLOTHING AND DRESS
  Dulles--United p92
  Lynes--Taste. p26-27, 31, 76-78
  Reader's--Story p440
  , in portrait painting
    Ross--Taste p169
  -Men
    Ross--Taste p233-235
    -1840's
      Ross--Taste p236
    -1850, 1859
      Ross--Taste p236
  -New York
    Ross--Taste p176
  -Views of Anna Cora Mowatt
    Grimsted--Notions p161-196
  -War
    Ross--Taste p172
  -Women
    Dulles--United p103
    Macksey--Book p266
    -Skirt lengths

      Ross--Taste p158
  -Widows
    Ross--Taste p172
"FATHER ABRAHAM"
  Howard--Our p261-262
FAY, AMY
  Macksey--Book p214
FEATHERS
  -Dusters
    Wilson--Vanish. p97
  , Ostrich
    White--American p140-143
FEATS, UNUSUAL
  Boardman--Gilded p177-178
FEDDE, ELIZABETH
  Neidle--America's p76-79
FEDERALISTS
  Alden--Pioneer p141-144, 152-154,
  174-175
  Collins--Story p165
  Kraus--U.S. p272-280, 282-283,
  286-300, 307-312, 322-323, 329
  , and Democrats, 1807
    -Views of Fortescue and Cuming
      Angle--American p158-159
  -Views of Fisher Ames
    Walker--Reform p34-35
FELTON, REBECCA
  , on country life in Georgia
    Commager--Heritage p376-380
FEMALE LABOR REFORM ASSOCI-
ATION
  Warren--Pictorial p94-95
  Young--Women p14-15
FEMALE SEMINARY (Elizabethtown,
Ohio)
  Furnas--Americans p741-742
FEMININITY. See WOMEN--
Femininity
FEMINISTS. See WOMEN--Legal
status
FENCES
  See also BARBED WIRE
  Furnas--Americans p686-688
  Wilson--American p235
  -Problem, on Great plains
    Ridge--America's p613-615
  , Rail
    Wilson--Vanish. p75
  -Stiles
    Wilson--Vanish. p76
  , Stump
    Van Wagenen--Golden p32-33
  -West
    Hine--American p132-134, 157-
    158
FENIANS (Irish nationalists)
  Furnas--Americans p702-703

Keller--Affairs p87-90, 93
-Uprising, 1866
Morris--Ency. p280
FENNIMORE, JAMES ("OLD
VIRGINIA")
Watkins--Gold p66, 69-70, 73-74,
81
FENTON, CHRISTOPHER WEBBER
Reader's--Story p226
FERN, FANNY. See WILLIS,
SARA PAYSON
FERREE, BAR
, on architecture and environment
Cook--City p98-100
FERRIES
Handlin--This p290-291
Wilson--Vanish. p172
-Ferryboats, 1876
Hilton--Way p161-162
-Idaho, 1863
Nation in motion p32
-Indiana
Nation in motion p32
-Kentucky
Nation in motion p32
-New York
Nation in motion p33
-Pennsylvania, 1825
Nation in motion p33
, River
Tunis--Frontier p70-71
-South Dakota
Nation in motion p33
-Views of Frances Trollope
Trollope--Domestic. See
index p. vi-vii
-Virginia
Nation in motion p34
FERRIS WHEELS
Furnas--Americans p761-762
-First, World's Columbian
Exposition, 1893
Butterfield--Amer. p261
Drury--Midwest p42-43
Life--America's p140-141
Life--Reaching (8) p99
White--American p124-126
FERTILITY. See CHILDBEARING
FERTILIZERS
Furnas--Americans p475-476
Marzio--Nation p156-157
FESTIVALS
See also FAIRS
-California
Johnson--Pictorial p72-73
, Farm
Dulles--History p273
FETTERMAN, WILLIAM J.

Boardman--Civil p108-109
FEVER
-Views of Frances Trollope
Trollope--Domestic. See
index p. vii
FICTION
See also "DIME NOVELS"; NOV-
ELISTS; names of authors
Furnas--Americans p322-323, 717-
718; 724-725
-1850's
Mott--Golden p122-132
-1890's
Jones--Age p342
-Civil war
Nye--Unembar. p29, 34, 239
, Detective
Nye--Unembar. p244-246
, Domestic, as "soap operas"
Bode--Anatomy p169-172, 176-
177
-"Females in distress"
Warren--Pictorial p69-70
, for women
Hart--Popular p57, 90-92
-Golden age
Jones--Age p222
, Gothic
Bode--Anatomy p164
, Historical
Mott--Golden p211-212, 215
Nye--Cultural p254-255
-1830-1870
Mott--Golden p88-95
-Naturalism
Morris--Ency. p574-575
, Popularity of
Hart--Popular p183
-Propaganda
Morris--Ency. p575-576
, Pulp, for boys
See also ALGER, HORATIO,
JR.
Trachtenberg--Demo. p285-
298
, Reading of
Cable--American p151
-"Reform," 1848-1860
Morris--Ency. p570
, Religious and moral
Boardman--Gilded p132-133
Bode--Anatomy p145-148
-Romances
Hart--Popular p96, 104-105, 141
Mott--Golden p207-213
-Types, Popular
Hart--Popular. See index
p339

, Utopian
  Hart--Popular p169-173
-Views of E. Marion Crawford
  Amer. Her. --90's p83-84
FIELD, CYRUS WEST
  See also ATLANTIC CABLE
  Amer. Her. --New (11) p E381-382
  Life--New (5) p16
  Morris--Ency. p657-658
  -Atlantic cable
    Commager--Heritage p941-947
FIELD, DAVID DUDLEY
  -Biography
    Morris--Ency. p658
FIELD, ERASTUS SALISBURY
  -"Historical monument of the
    American republic" (painting)
    Larkin--Art p230-231
FIELD, EUGENE
  Nye--Unembar. p124-125
FIELD, MARSHALL
  Boardman--Civil p134
  -Biography
    Morris--Ency. p658
FIELD, STEPHEN JOHNSON
  Butterfield--Amer. p269
  Morris--Ency. p658-659
FIELDS, JAMES T.
  See also TICKNOR AND FIELDS
  Bode--Anatomy p113-114
  Brooks--Flower. p478-480,
    482, 503, 531
  , on "Scarlet letter" publication,
    1849
    Angle--American p273-275
"FIFTY-FOUR FORTY OR FIGHT"
  Butterfield--Amer. p111
  Harlow--Story p270
"FIFTY-NINERS"
  , Rush of, 1859
    Billington--Far p260-264
    Ridge--America's p541-542
FIGHTS AND FIGHTING
  , Boys'
    Schwartz--When p98
  -"Rough and tumble"
    Dulles--History p73-75
  -West
    Davidson--Life (2) p22
"FILCHERS"
  Wilson--Early p167-168
FILLMORE, ABIGAIL POWERS
  Melick--Wives p37
  200 Years p338
FILLMORE, MILLARD
  Butterfield--Amer. p135
  Carman--History p513, 617-618
  Harlow--Story p278, 284, 288-289
  Kraus--U.S. p439, 457-458

Life--New (5) p30, 38, 72
  Morris--Ency. p209, 214-216, 221
  200 Years (1) p267, 288, 338-339
  -Biography
    Amer. Her. --New (7) p E237-
      238
    Morris--Ency. p659
    Whitney--American p113-117
  -Cabinet
    Carman--History (1) p790-791
  -Presidency
    Linton--Bicentennial p136-141
    Reader's--Story p333
FILMS. See MOTION PICTURES
FINANCE
  Boardman--Gilded p49-50
  Life--Sweep (4). See index p157
  Life--Union (6). See index p173
  -1850-1875
    Boardman--Civil p129-133
  -1890's
    Life--Reaching (8). See index
      p173
  -Capitalism
    Dulles--United p60-61
  -Federal revenue sources (1800,
    1836, 1845, 1890)
    Morris--Ency. p503
  , National public
    Morris--Ency. p502-503
  -Views of Edward Kellogg (1840's-
    1860's)
    Walker--Reform p87-88
FINANCIERS
  See also names of financiers
  Furnas--Americans p647-654,
    705, 893
  Reader's--Story p283
FINE ARTS. See ART; DRAMA;
  MUSIC; PAINTERS AND PAINT-
  INGS; SCULPTURE; etc.
FINK, ALBERT
  Marzio--Nation p186
FINK, MIKE
  Boardman--Virginia p109
  Boorstin--Americans p335-336
  Drury--Midwest p120
  Hine--American p51-52, 268-270
  Reader's--Story p172
FINLAY, CARLOS, DR.
  Hilton--Way p86-87
FINNEY, CHARLES GRANDISON
  Amer. Her. --New (6) p E200
  Nye--Cultural p228
  -"Lectures on revivals of religion"
    Boorstin--Americans p319-320
  , on revivals
    Burner--America (1) p184-
      187

-"Sinners bound to change their
own hearts"
    Grimsted--Notions p77-85
FIREARMS. See GUNS
FIRECRACKERS. See FIREWORKS
FIREPLACES
  Tunis--Frontier p80
  Van Wagenen--Golden p205-206
  , Kitchen
    Wilson--Vanish. p38-39
  , Parlor
    Partridge--As p9
FIRES AND FIREFIGHTING
  Boardman--Civil p113-114
  Bonte--America p134
  Davidson--Life (2) p128-131
  Furnas--Americans p531-535
  Harlow--Story p425-427
  Life--Sweep (4) p30-31, 76
  Linton--Bicentennial. See index
  p441
  Ross--Taste p120
  Train--Story p287-288
  -1854
    Viewpoints p107
  -1872
    Cook--City p150-151
  -1876
    Hilton--Way p166-170
    Randel--Centennial. See
    index p468
  -1880's
    Peck--Nineteenth n. p.
  -Companies
    Walker--Every. p113-114
  -Labor and equipment
    Marzio--Nation p360-361
  -Man-drawn engines
    Wilson--Vanish. p160
  , Relics of
    Dreppard--Pioneer p150-155
  -Views of M. Bugbee, 1873
    Cook--City p151-154
FIREWORKS
  Schwartz--When p127
  -Independence Day, 1860's and
  1870's
    Train--Story. p319 (facing)
FIRKINS, BUTTER
  Van Wagenen--Golden p107-110
FISCAL BANK OF THE U.S.
  Boardman--Jackson. p35-36
FISH, HAMILTON
  Amer. Her.--New (6) p E274
  Randel--Centennial p205-206, 211,
  213
FISH (as food)
  Furnas--Americans p463-464

FISHER, DOROTHY CANFIELD
  -"The washed window"
    Treasury Amer. p148-151
FISHING AND FISHERMEN
  -1876
    Hilton--Way p100-101
  -Equipment (1880's)
    Peck--Nineteenth n. p.
  , Game--Florida reef
    Jones--Shaping p303-311
FISK, JAMES ("Gentleman Jim")
  Amer. Her.--New (10) p865
  Boardman--Civil p132-133
  Butterfield--Amer. p202-203
  Carman--History (1) p704-706, 744
  Carman--History (2) p5-7
  Dulles--United p55
  Furnas--Americans p649-650
  Harlow--Story p346
  Jones--Age p121-122
  Life--Steel (7) p128-129
  Reader's--Story p283
FISK UNIVERSITY
  Randel--Centennial p423-424
FISKE, JOHN
  Boardman--Gilded p112-113
  Life--Reaching (8) p8-9, 15, 66-67,
  128-129
  Randel--Centennial p60, 63, 428-
  429, 450-451
  -Biography
    Amer. Her. --New (11) p E382
FISKE (MRS.) MARY AUGUSTA
DAVEY
  Blum--Stage Profile 5
FISKE, MINNIE MADDERN
  Warren--Pictorial p157
FITCH, JOHN
  Harlow--Story p197
FITZGERALD, EMILY (Mrs. Jen-
kins)
  Randel--Centennial p73-77, 87,
  134, 194
FITZPATRICK, THOMAS ("TOM")
  Amer. Her. --New (6) p E200-201
  Billington--Far p44, 55, 57-60, 64,
  93, 96
"FIVE AND DIME STORES"
  See also WOOLWORTH'S
  Nostalgia p36-39
  Portraits--Americans p47-49
"FIVE CIVILIZED TRIBES." See
INDIANS--Five civilized tribes";
and names of tribes
"FIVE NATIONS." See IROQUOIS
INDIANS
FLAGG, EDMUND
  , on Mississippi river race

Wright--Every. p82-83
FLAGG, WILSON
  Randel--Centennial p369-370
FLAGLER, HENRY M.
  Furnas--Americans p787-793, 800,
  810
FLAGS
  -"The American flag"
    Burner--America (1) p171-172
  -Confederacy
    Jordan--Civil p77, 199, 201
    Life--New (5) p135
  -Union
    Life--New (5) p110
  -United States
    Jordan--Civil p2, 45, 206
FLAT IRONS. See IRONING
FLATBOATS
  See also BATEAUX; TEAM-
    BOATS
  Bartlett--New p144-145, 307-308
  Furnas--Americans p301
  Langdon--Everyday (2) p94-96
  , across Westward rivers
    200 Years (1) p200-201
FLATHEAD INDIANS
  Billington--Far p79-80
  Boardman--Jackson. p74-75
FLAX
  Langdon--Everyday (2) p241-247
  Van Wagenen--Golden p85, 184,
    249-257, 263
  , Retting of
    Van Wagenen--Golden p252-
    253
FLEMING, WILLIAMINA PATON
  Adelman-Famous p245
FLETCHER, ALICE
  Macksey--Book p151
  , on Indian music
    Chase--America's p403-405,
    408, 413, 421
FLEXNER, THOMAS
  , on artists; "Ash Can School"
    Miers--American p279-283
FLIES
  See also FLY SWATTERS;
    WINDOW SCREENS
  Hilton--Way p73
  Lynes--Domestic p129-132
FLINT, TIMOTHY
  -"Frontier society in the
    Mississippi valley," 1826
    Ridge--America's p401-403
  -"Keelboat ride," 1816
    Angle--American p193-196
  , on frontiersmen
    Commager--Heritage p266-269

  -"Routes to the West in the
    1830's"
    Ridge--America's p289-292
  -"Travel on the Ohio river,"
    1826
    Ridge--America's p278-279
  -Views of Frances Trollope
    Trollope--Domestic. See
    index p. vii
FLIRTATION
  Partridge--As p145-146
FLOGGING
  , in Navy, 1840
    Commager--Heritage p303-308
FLOOD, JAMES C.
  Life--Steel (7) p54
FLORIDA
  Andrews--Indian Leaders p57-60,
    67, 71-73
  Boardman--Virginia p20-21, 57-59
  Carman--History (1) p344-345,
    386-387, 429, 634, 783
  Furnas--Americans p784-787
  -1876
    Randel--Centennial p44-45, 250-
    251, 257, 322
  -Acquisition
    Harlow--Story p190
    Kraus--U.S. p336-337
  , East and West
    Amer. Her. --New (5) p366
  , Cession of, 1819
    Morris--Ency. p157-158
  -Game fishes of Florida reef
    Jones--Shaping p303-311
  -Gulf coast
    Furnas--Americans p784-786
  -Lake Worth
    Furnas--Americans p789-790
  -Palm Beach
    Furnas--Americans p789-790
  -St. Petersburg
    Furnas--Americans p792-793
  -Silver Springs, 1886
    Viewpoints p44
  -Tampa
    -Bay Hotel
      Lynes--Taste. p87-88
  , West
    Annexation, 1810
      Morris--Ency. p138
      Ridge--America's p253-254
    -The United States Claims West
      Florida," by James Madison
      Ridge--America's p253-254
FLOUR AND FLOUR MILLS
  Handlin--This p111-112, 114-115,
  120, 351, 353

Life--Steel (7) p35
-World's largest (Gallego, in
 Richmond, Va.)
  Dowdey--Experiment p17
FLOWER, GEORGE
, on American liberty
  Kraus--U. S. p333-334
FLOWERS
 See also GARDENS
 -Language and sale
  Cable--American p159
 -Views of Frances Trollope
  Trollope--Domestic. See
  index p. vii
FLOYD, JOHN, DR.
 -"Early propaganda for Oregon,"
  1821
  Ridge--America's p439-441
FLY SWATTERS
 Wilson--Vanish. p104
"FLYING CLOUD" (clipper ship)
 Carman--History (1) p474-475
 Collins--Story p150
FLYNN, ELIZABETH GURLEY
 Reader's--Story p432
FLYNN, TOM
 -Arguments against temperance
  Burner--America (1) p285-287
FLYNT, JOSIAH WILLARD
 Furnas--Americans p678
 Our literary p183
FOKE LUSTE HAJO (Seminole
Indian)
 Andrews--Indian leaders p73
FOLK HYMNS. See SONGS, Gospel
FOLKLORE
 Walker--Every. p50-51, 65, 94-
  95, 112, 114, 118-121
FOLSOM, FRANCES
 Boardman--Gilded p25-26
FOOD
 See also COOKERY; names of
  food, meals
 Boardman--Jackson. p173-174
 Boardman--Virginia p186
 Carson--Polite p85-87, 97, 143-
  144, 179-181
 Furnas--Americans p458-467,
  900-901
 Handlin--This. See index p584
 Hunt--Life p216-223
 Partridge--As p127
 Portraits--Americans p111-112
 Ross--Taste p72-77
 Tunis--Young p109-111
 Wilson--Folkways p145-155
 -1800's, early
  Hunt--Life p101-102

-1825-1860
 Train--Story p273-274
-1860-1899
 Train--Story p329-331
-1876
 Randel--Centennial. See
  index p468
-Cranks and cults
 Furnas--Americans p439-441,
  900
-Diet
 Lynes--Domestic. See index
  p304
-Immigrant introductions
 Marzio--Nation p583-584
-Industries
 See also COTTONSEED OIL;
  MEAT PACKING; WHEAT
 Life--Steel (7) p30, 34-35
-Menus
 Furnas--Americans p462-467,
  693, 901-903
-Preservation
 Boardman--Civil p123-124
 Boardman--Jackson. p173
 Furnas--Americans p690-692
 Walker--Every. p34-35
-Riots, Civil war (Richmond, Va.)
 Commager--Heritage p703-705
-Supply, and eating habits
 Nye--Cultural p129-132
-Views of Frances Trollope
 Trollope--Domestic. See
  index p. vii
-West
 Ross--Heroines p23-24, 63-64
 Train--Story p310-311
FOOT-RACES. See RUNNING
FOOT WARMERS
 Wilson--Vanish. p46-47
FOOTBALL
 See also CAMP, WALTER
 Boardman--Civil p201
 Boardman--Gilded p174
 Davidson--Life (2) p69
 Dulles--United p100-101
 Furnas--Americans p814-815
 Handlin--This p371-373, 396
 Jones--Age p343-344
 Partridge--As p156
 Reader's--Story p486-487
 Ross--Taste p89
 Walker--Every. p153
 -1876
  Randel--Centennial p319-320
 , College
  Life--New (5) p60-61
 , First intercollegiate

Reader's--Story p486
, Moral factors in
  Harris--Land p339-343
-Rules
  Hilton--Way p109-110
-Views of Amos Alonzo Stagg
  Angle--American p413-414
-Views of Charles Joseph Paul
  Bourget
  Davie--Profile p388
FOOTE, ANDREW HALL
  Amer. Her. --New (8) p E274
FOOTE, ARTHUR WILLIAM
  Howard--Our p310-313
FOOTWEAR. See SHOES
"FOPS." See "DANDIES"
FORBES, ALEXANDER
  -"The mission frontier in
  California, 1839
  Ridge--America's p349-354
"FORCE ACTS"
  See also KU KLUX KLAN
  Amer. Her. --New (5) p E163-164
  Harlow--Story p230, 343-344
  , and Henry Clay
  Collins--Story p179
FORD, HENRY
  Portraits--Americans p39-40
  , and Greenfield Village
  America's Hist. p560-563
  -Biography
  Morris--Ency. p660
  -"Gasoline buggy"
  Commager--Heritage p967-973
  -Selden patent squabble
  White--American p127-134
FORD'S THEATRE (Washington,
D.C.)
  -Lincoln's assassination
  Meredith--World p221-223
FORECLOSURES
  -Sales
  Tunis--Frontier p85-86
FOREFATHERS
  , and posterity
  -Views of John Quincy Adams
  Hurd--Treasury p42-44
FOREIGN AFFAIRS
  See also special subjects
  Boardman--Gilded p34-38
  Heffner--Doc. p80-82
  -1849-1865
  Life--New (5) p53-55, 139, 141
  -1866-1899
  Morris--Ency. p280-292
  -1898
  Hollingsworth--Amer. p68-75
  -Ideals and self-interest

  Hollingsworth--Amer. p76-88
  -Trade
  Morris--Ency. p487-488
FOREST
  Bartlett--New p238-239, 244
  -1870's
  Randel--Centennial p274-275
  -Culture and cutting
  Morris--Ency. p439
  -Preservation
  Jones--Age p323-324
  -Views of Frances Trollope
  Trollope--Domestic. See
  index p. vii
  -West
  Hine--American. See index
  p363
FORMAD, MARIE K., DR.
  Neidle--America's p204
FORREST, EDWIN
  Amer. Her. --New (6) p E201
  Boardman--Jackson. p156
  Bode--Anatomy p13-18
  Grimsted--Melodrama. See
  index p281
  Morris--Ency. p590
  -Biography
  Morris--Ency. p660
FORREST, NATHAN BEDFORD,
GENERAL
  Amer. Her. --New (8) p E274-275
  Boardman--Civil p82-83
  Meredith--World p121
  Young--Women p149, 242-243, 247,
  273
FORSYTH, JOHN
  Amer. Her. --New (5) p E164
"FORT HILL" (Calhoun's home,
Clemson, S.C.)
  Vanderbilt--Living p131
FORT WAYNE TREATY OF 1809
  Ridge--America's p256-258
FORTEN, CHARLOTTE
  Sochen--Herstory p189
  -"Life on the sea islands"
  Trachtenberg--Demo. p112-124
FORTIETH PARALLEL SURVEY
  Gilbert--Trail. p200-204, 206,
  214, 228
FORTS AND GARRISONS
  Bartlett--New. See index p479
  Dowdey--Experiment. See index
  p447
  Tunis--Frontier p111, 117, 141
  -Abraham Lincoln
  Brown--Westerners p236, 238-
  239
  Randel--Centennial p127-129,

132
-Belknap
 Brown--Westerners p204-205
-Bernard
 DeVoto--Year p164-182, 433, 447
-Bridger
 Billington--Far p103-104, 108-
 110, 199, 208, 214-215, 276
 DeVoto--Year. See index p518
-Brown
 DeVoto--Year p128-130, 188-192
-Buford
 Brown--Westerners p251-252
-Cobb
 Brown--Westerners p197-201
-Dearborn
 Drury--Midwest p27-28
 -Indian massacre, 1812
 -Views of Linai T. Helm
 Angle--American p174-177
-Donelson
 Jordan--Civil p65, 73-76, 80-81,
 210
-Fisher
 Holzman--Stormy p148-156
-Hall
 Billington--Far p63, 65-66, 80,
 93, 104
 DeVoto--Year. See index
 p516
-Hays
 Brown--Westerners p197, 234
-Jackson
 Holzman--Stormy p73-75
-Phil Kearney
 Andrews--Indians p42, 60, 69,
 72-73, 131, 159-160, 162-163,
 172
 Brown--Westerners p191, 244,
 268
-Lapwai
 Randel--Centennial p75-76
-Laramie
 Amer. Her. --New (6) p525-
 526
 Andrews--Indian leaders p149,
 153, 158-160
 Andrews--Indians p109-110
 Billington--Far p64, 66, 103,
 207
 Brown--Westerners p88, 91-
 98, 124-125, 139, 190-191, 194,
 197
 DeVoto--Year. See index
 p516
 Vanderbilt--Living p192
-Leavenworth
 Brown--Westerners p73, 91-92,

124, 140, 152, 235
 DeVoto--Year. See index p516
 Vanderbilt--Living p190
-Lyon, Colorado
 -Indian wars
 Amer. Her. --New (9) p780-
 781
-McHenry
 Landmarks--Liberty p20-25
 -Bombardment, 1814
 Wright--Every. p55
-Monroe
 Holzman--Storm p50-65
-Moultrie
 -Seized by South Carolina
 Young--Women p37
-Niagara
 Vanderbilt--Living p54-55
-Nisqually
 Vanderbilt--Living p209
-Osage
 Vanderbilt--Living p176
-Parker's
 , and Elder John Parker
 Amer. Her. --Indians p379-
 380
-Pickens
 Boardman--Civil p33
-Pierre
 Brown--Westerners p75-76, 241
-Pillow
 -Massacre, 1864
 Meredith--World p121, 123
-Rice
 Brown--Westerners p242, 244
-Riley
 Brown--Westerners p233-234
-Ross
 Johnson--Pictorial p80-81, 217
 Life--Sweep (4) p131, 136
 Vanderbilt--Living p207
-Sedgewick
 Meredith--World p204
-Smith
 Billington--Far p231, 279, 282-
 283
 Brown--Westerners p124, 145,
 148, 151
-Snelling
 Vanderbilt--Living p170
-Sumter
 America's Hist. p416-419
 Boardman--Civil p33-34
 Borden--Portrait (1) p231-232
 Butterfield--Amer. p164-165
 Brown--Westerners p206-207,
 261
 Jordan--Civil p13, 34, 41-45,

137, 184, 206
Kraus--U. S. p485-486
Landmarks--Liberty p26-29
Life--New (5) p79, 96, 98-99,
122, 142
Morris--Ency. p230
Young--Women p4, 37, 40-41
  -Bombardment, 1861
    Amer. Her. --New (7)
    p618-619
    Bonte--America p121
    Collins--Story p210
    Keyes--Hope p228, 230-
    231, 234
    200 Years (2) p10-12
    -Views of Abner Double-
    day
      Commager--Heritage
      p733-738
    -Views of Emma E.
    Holmes
      Angle--American
      p311-315
    -Views of Mary Boykin
    Chestnut
      Commager--Heritage
      p729-733
  -Flag raising, 1865
    -Views of Mary Cad-
    walader Jones
      Commager--Heritage
      p788-791
  -Union
    Billington--Far p56-57, 59-60,
    64-65
    Brown--Westerners p77-78
  -Vancouver
    Billington--Far p42, 44, 71-73,
    80-81, 96, 105
    Brown--Westerners p58, 65
    , and Dr. McLoughlin
      Case--Empire p27-39, 41-
      69
  -Wallace
    Brown--Westerners p233-234
  -Walsh
    Brown--Westerners p249-250
  -Wayne
    -Indian protest against treaty
    1810, by Tecumseh
      Ridge--America's p258-260
FORTUNE TELLERS
  Wilson--Early p121
  -Views of James W. Buel
    Cook--City p266
"FORTY-NINERS"
  See also ARGONAUTS;
  CALIFORNIA--GOLD RUSH

Billington--Far p222-232
Bonte--America p109
Kraus--U. S. p435-437
Life--Sweep (4) p134, 140-141,
146-147, 149
Tunis--Frontier p131-136
-Camps
  Tunis--Frontier p134-135
-Effect on Mormons
  Billington--Far p203-204
-Food
  Train--Story p310-311
-Judges and Justice
  Amer. Her. --New (6) p478-481
-Sickness
  Billington--Far p227-228, 237
FOSTER, ABIGAIL KELLEY
  Gurko--Ladies p116-117, 132, 135,
  137-139
  Warren--Pictorial p85
FOSTER, C. C.
  , on N. Y. city, by gaslight, 1850
    Burner--America p301-310
FOSTER, STEPHEN COLLINS
  Amer. Her. --New (6) p E201
  Boardman--Jackson. p176
  Bode--Anatomy p24-29
  Bonte--America p119
  Chase--America's p285-300; see
  also index p718
  DeVoto--Year p134-136, 252, 480
  Howard--Our p184-198
  Morris--Ency. p615
  Reader's--Story p392-393
  Wright--Every. p235-236
  -Biography
    Morris--Ency. p660-661
  -Songs
    Bode--Anatomy p26-28
    Burner--America (1) p265-269
"FOUR HUNDRED"
  Cable--American p275, 278, 287,
  334-335
  Lynes--Taste. p167
  Walker--Every. p129-130
FOURIER, CHARLES
  Boardman--Jackson. p123
  Borden--Portrait (1) p181-183
  Hine--American p265
  Life--Sweep (4) p62-63
  -"Fourierism"
    Carman--History (1) p526-529
    Tyler--Freedom's p176, 183-
    184
    -Phalanxes
      Tyler--Freedom's p217-220
FOURTH OF JULY. See INDE-
PENDENCE DAY

FOWL. See BIRDS AND FOWL;
names of types
FOWLE, ELIDA RUMSEY
Young--Women p86, 203-204
FOWLER, D. S.
Ross--Taste p12, 23-24, 146
FOWLER, LYDIA FOLGER
Furnas--Americans p446-447
FOWLER, ORSON SQUIRE
Furnas--Americans p438-439,
458, 735
, and "Octagon house"
White--American p37-40
FOX, MARGARET AND KATHER-
INE
Boardman--Jackson. p189-190
Tyler--Freedom's p82-83
FOY, EDDY
Blum--Stage Profile 29
FRANCE
See also FRENCH
Boardman--Civil. See index
p212
, and Civil war
Dowdey--Experiment. See
index p447
Life--New (5) p139-141
-Immigrants
Handlin--This p128, 133, 138,
147, 165, 300
FRANCHISE. See SUFFRAGE
FRANKLIN, CHRISTINE
Macksey--Book p151
FRANKLIN, JOHN
-Expedition, 1845
Boardman--Civil p177-178
"FRANKLIN HOUSE" (Washington,
D. C.)
Phillips--That p3-6, 11-12, 15,
20-22, 30-31, 38, 47, 58
FRATERNAL ORDERS (LODGES)
See also names of orders
Bartlett--New p345-346, 438
Dulles--History p254-256
Dulles--United p101
Furnas--Americans p508-509,
523, 703
Walker--Every. p101-102
FRATERNITIES
-Greek-letter college
Cable--American p164-165,
317
Carson--Polite p186
Furnas--Americans p747-748
Macksey--Book p274
Walker--Every. p119-120
FRAUDS
, Diamond

Garrison--Lost p168-171
FRAZEE, JOHN
Boardman--Virginia p156-157
Larkin--Art p103-105; see also
index p525
FRAZER RIVER MINES (California)
Billington--Far p244-248
Ridge--Far p244-248
Watkins--Gold p46-49
FREDERIC, HAROLD
Boardman--Gilded p127-128
FREDERICKSBURG, VIRGINIA
, in Civil war
America's Hist. p440-441
Dowdey--Experiment p41, 196,
240, 244, 250, 275, 330, 344
Jordan--Civil p5, 108-109, 114,
120-121, 135, 191, 211
Meredith--World p157
Morris--Ency. p238
Pratt--Civil p34
"FREE LOVE"
Furnas--Americans p500-501,
643-647
, At Oneida, N. Y.
Cable--American p195
FREE RELIGIOUS ASSOCIATION
Randel--Centennial p443
FREE SOIL PARTY
See also LECOMPTON CONSTI-
TUTION, 1857; POTTAWATOMIE
MASSACRE
Amer. Her. --New (7) p E238
Boardman--Civil p11-12, 15-16
Carman--History (1) p601, 608-
614
Harlow--Story p284
Life--Sweep (4) p136
FREEDMEN
Butterfield--Amer. p188-189
Carman--History (1) p586-587,
715-716, 723-724, 726-727, 734,
746
FREEDMEN'S BUREAU
Boardman--Civil p79
Borden--Portrait (2) p6-7, 14-15
Carman--History (2) p24-25
Harlow--Story p339
Keller--Affairs p64-65
Life--Union (6) p114, 128-131, 136
Linton--Bicentennial p186, 189,
191-192, 194, 204, 274
Morris--Ency. p247
FREEDOM OF RELIGION. See
RELIGIOUS FREEDOM
FREEDOM OF THE PRESS
, in North
Tyler--Freedom's p501-508

, in South
Tyler--Freedom's p521-524
FREEMAN, ALICE ELVIRA
Bonte--America p155
FREEMAN, MARY ELEANOR
WILKINS
Amer. Her. --New (11) p E382
Sochen--Herstory p224-225
FREEMAN, THOMAS
Amer. Her. --New (6) p E201-202
FREEMAN FAMILY
, and the frontier, 1862
Andrews--Indians p59-60
FREEMASONRY. See MASONIC
ORDER
"FREEPORT DOCTRINE" (of Stephen
Douglas)
Amer. Her. --New (7) p E228
Harlow--Story p297
FREIGHT SERVICE
Furnas--Americans. See index
p988
-Great Plains
Ridge--America's p552-554
-Rates
-Wabash and Minnesota cases
Life--Steel (7) p136
-West
Tunis--Frontier p138-139
FREIGHT WAGONS. See
CONESTOGA WAGONS
FREMONT, JESSIE BENTON
Butterfield--Amer. p107, 148-149
Gilbert--Trail. p157, 160, 163-
164, 173
Life--Sweep (4) p132-134
Peacock--Famous p123-147
Tunis--Frontier p120
FREMONT, JOHN CHARLES
Amer. Her. --New (6) p E202
Billington--Far p162-167, 183-
185, 195, 226
Boardman--Jackson. p55-56
Brown--Westerners p96-97, 115,
124, 126
Butterfield--Amer. p107, 148-149
Carman--History (1) p571, 617-
619, 698
DeVoto--Year. See index p516
Gilbert--Trail. See index p234
Harlow--Story p271-272, 295
Hine--American. See index
p363
Johnson--Pictorial p55, 76, 79,
86-87, 90, 120
Life--New (5) p71-72, 112
Life--Sweep (4) p104, 132-135
Linton--Bicentennial. See index

p441
Morris--Ency. p200-202, 428
Tunis--Frontier p120, 123
200 Years (1) p250, 252-253, 257,
261, 288
-Biography
Morris--Ency. p661-662
-"Buffalo hunting on the Fremont
expedition," 1843
Davie--Profile p146-149
-Expeditions
Reader's--Story p76-77
Wilson--American p100-101
, in High Sierras
Commager--Heritage p530-535
-"John C. Frémont advertises the
West: The Bumble Bee," 1845
Ridge--America's p373-375
FREMSTAD, OLIVE
Neidle--America's p223
FRENCH, DANIEL CHESTER
Amer. Her. --New (11) p E382-383
Larkin--Art p279-282; see also
index p525
FRENCH
See also FRANCE; HUGUENOTS
-Home life
Drury--Midwest p153-154
, in cities and villages
Drury--Midwest p144-155
"FRENCH BALL"
Cable--American p231
FRENEAU, PHILIP
Nye--Cultural p259-261
FRICK, HENRY CLAY
Life--Steel (7) p34, 96-97, 135
FRIENDS, SOCIETY OF. See
QUAKERS
FRIETSCHE (FRITCHIE), BARBARA
Amer. Her. --New (8) p E275
Dolin--Great p40-47
FROHMAN, CHARLES
Boardman--Gilded p148-149
-Theatrical productions
Blum--Theatre p39
FRONTIER
See also PLAINS; WEST
Amer. Her. --New (6) p454-538;
E186-222
Boardman--Gilded p13, 83-90
Boardman--Virginia p79-80, 93-
95, 196-197
Carman--History (1) p378-384
Dulles--History p67-83
Handlin--This p112, 114-115, 139,
153
Walker--Every. p90-103
-1876

Randel--Centennial p89-91, 111-
  112
, and American democracy
  Ridge--America's p11-13
-Arts and skills
  Life--America's p98-112
-Definition
  Hine--American p322
, Disappearance of
  -Views of Ray A. Billington
    Miers--American p253-258
-Emergence of traits
  Ridge--America's p8-11
, Last
  Dulles--United p34-51
-Life
  Kraus--U.S. p428-429
  Life--New (5) p24-25
  Reader's--Story p70
-Methodists, California
  Wright--Culture p136-137
, Significance of
  Amer. Her. --New (6) p468
  Ridge--America's p16
-Views of Frederick Jackson
  Turner
    Amer. Her. --New (9) p776
    Amer. Her. --90's p87
    Bartlett--New p401, 421-422,
      444-446
    Heffner--Doc. p169-170
-Views of Maria D. ("Grand-
  mother") Brown
    Burner--America (1) p227-230
, War on
  Hine--American p318-319
-West
  Reader's--Story p69-74
  Tyler--Freedom's p15-21
FRONTIERSMEN
  Cable--American p134-135
  Commager--Heritage p251-272
  Jones--Shaping p239-251
  Life--New (5) p22-23
  Ridge--America's p6-8
  Wilson--Early p14
  -1802
    -Views of F.A. Michaux
      Angle--American p155-156
    -Views of Timothy Flint
      Commager--Heritage p266-269
FROST, ARTHUR BURDETT
  Larkin--Art p255; see also
    index p525
FROTHINGHAM, OCTAVIUS
  BROOKS
  Randel--Centennial p442-443
FRUIT

Furnas--American p776-777, 781,
  901
Handlin--This p251, 317, 351, 404
-Pies
  Furnas--Americans p460-461
-Stands
  Wilson--Vanish. p135
, Wild, N.Y. state
  Van Wagenen--Golden p99-100
"FRUITLANDS"
  Boardman--Jackson. p125
  Commager--Heritage p424-432
  Tyler--Freedom's p172-175
FRY, WILLIAM HENRY
  Chase--America's p328-333
  Howard--Our p238-247
  Lowens--Music p212-222
FUEL
  See also names of fuel
  , Kitchen
    Lynes--Domestic. p119-120
FUGITIVE SLAVE ACT
  Amer. Her. --New (7) p E238-239
  Boardman--Civil. See index
    p212
  Boardman--Jackson. p197-198
  Borden--Portrait (2) p217-219
  Harlow--Story p288-289
  Keyes--Hope p248
  Kraus--U.S. p445, 452
  Life--New (5) p34, 36-37, 39, 51-
    52, 82
  Linton--Bicentennial p49, 57, 91,
    134, 145-146, 158, 186
  Tyler--Freedom's p536-542
FULLER, GEORGE
  Larkin--Art p266-268; see also
    index p525
  Mumford--Brown p194-199
FULLER, LOIE
  Macksey--Book p229
  Warren--Pictorial p154
FULLER (SARAH) MARGARET
  (MARCHIONESS OSSOLI)
  Adelman--Famous p145-146
  Amer. Her. --New (6) p E202
  Brooks--Flower. See index
    p542
  Carman--History (1) p523-526,
    537
  Gurko--Ladies p. vi, 11, 70-82,
    123, 137, 139, 305
  Heath--Women (4) p8
  Life--Sweep (4) p60-61, 64
  Lowens--Music p254-255
  Macksey--Book p86, 185
  Morris--Ency. p662
  Neidle--America's p29

Our literary p71-72
Sochen--Herstory p128-130
Tyler--Freedom's p54-56, 430;
  see also index p596
Warren--Pictorial p74, 81-83
FULLING MILLS
Van Wagenen--Golden p265-266
FULTON, ROBERT
Boardman--Virginia p82-83
Harlow--Story p197
Life--America's p68
Life--Growing (3) p160-161
Treasury Amer. p184-185
-Biography
  Morris--Ency. p662-663
-Boats and submarines
  Reader's--Story p196, 261-262
-"Mr. Fulton's folly": New
  York--Albany
  Davie--Profile p199-201
FULTON, SAMUEL
-Last years and death
  Wilson--American p70
FUNDAMENTALISM. See
RELIGION--Fundamentalism
FUNERALS
  See also CEMETERIES; EPI-
  TAPHS; TOMBSTONES
  Cable--American p171-172,
  174-176
  Walker--Every. p41, 242-243
    -Etiquette
      Carson--Polite p171, 173-
      175
"FUNNY PAPERS." See COMIC
STRIPS
FUR TRADE
  See also MOUNTAIN MEN;
  names of companies
  Bartlett--New p85-91, 256-257
  Billington--Far p41-68
  Boardman--Jackson. p51-52, 63-
  65
  Boardman--Virginia p104-107
  Boorstin--Americans p59-61
  Brown--Westerners p37, 52-69,
  91, 93, 152, 157
  DeVoto--Year p18-19, 51-66, 115,
  141, 148, 360-363
  Furnas--Americans p306, 362-
  363
  Gilbert--Trail. See index p234
  Handlin--This p110, 114-116, 121
  Life--America's p100-101
  Tunis--Young p140
  , and Digger Indians
    Gilbert--Trail. p52-56, 60-61,
    64, 72, 74-75, 77

-Central Rockies, 1849
  Ridge--America's p393-396
-Characteristics
  Billington--Far p44-55
-Decline, 1839
  Ridge--America's p396-398
-Desert Southwest, 1831
  Ridge--America's p389-393
-"Fur trade on the Upper Mis-
  souri," 1813, by John C. Lutting
  Ridge--America's p379-382
-Goods traded
  Life--America's p100-101
-Northwest
  Commager--Heritage p505-508
  Reader's--Story p164-166
-"Rendezvous"
  Amer. Her. --Indians p350
  Bartlett--New p258
  Billington--Far. See index
  (under Rendezvous) p230
  Boorstin--Americans p60-61,
  228-229
  Ridge--America's p393-398
  Tunis--Frontier p112-113
  -1839
    -Views of Adolph Wislizenus
      Angle--American p223-
      226
  -"Decline of the fur trade; the
    final rendezvous," by Os-
    burne Russell
    Ridge--America's p396-398
-Rockies, 1833
  -Views of Charles Larpenteur
    Angle--American p220-223
-Upper Missouri, 1831
  Ridge--America's p379-382
-West
  Carman--History (1) p369-371
  Hine--American p44-58; see
  also index p363
  -1814
    -Views of Alexander Ross
      Davie--Profile p144-145
  -1820-1845
    Ridge--America's p376-398
FURNACES
  Walker--Every. p213-214
  -1876
    Hilton--Way p18, 20
  , Central
    Furnas--Americans p428-429
  , Coal-fueled hot-air
    Marzio--Nation p498
FURNESS, CLIFTON
  , on etiquette of letter writing
    Burner--America (1) p244-249

FURNITURE
  Boardman--Virginia p185
  Handlin--This p140, 254, 393, 400
  Lynes--Taste. See index p353
  Marzio--Nation p497
  Reader's--Story p223-225
  Wilson--Folkways p127-129
  Wilson--Vanish. p106
  -1825-1860
    Train--Story p267-270
  -1860-1900
    Train--Story p320-324
  -1876
    Hilton--Way p18
  -"Belter"
    Gowans--Images p323-325, 327
  , Children's
    See also CHAIRS, Children's
    McClinton--Antiques p139-155
  -Cooper's
    Gowans--Images p432
  -Eastlake
    Gowans--Images p336
  -Empire
    Gowans--Images p243-244,
    254, 259
    Ross--Taste p116-117
  -Factories and industry
    Gowans--Images p298-300
    Marzio--Nation p211-223
  , Farm
    Walker--Every. p75-76
  -Gothic revival
    Gowans--Images p307
  -Grand Rapids, Mich.
    Gowans--Images p346-347
  -Greek revival
    Life--America's p72-73
  , Italianate
    Gowans--Images p323-324
  -Kitchen cabinets
    Carman--History (1) p426
  , Neo-classical
    Gowans--Images p243-244,
    254, 259
  , Pioneer
    Dreppard--Pioneer p245-246,
    254, 258-260, 262, 265-268
  -Post Civil war
    Gowans--Images p336
  , Richardsonian
    Gowans--Images p357-358, 362
  , Row house
    Walker--Every. p215-224
  , School
    Dreppard--Pioneer p225
  -Texas
    Tunis--Frontier p98-99

  -Upholsterers, nativity
    Marzio--Nation p213-214
  , Victorian
    Life--America's p134-135
    Train--Story p320-324
    Walker--Every. p19-25
  , Early
    Gowans--Images p299, 301
  , High
    Gowans--Images p301, 330-
    331, 352
  , Late
    Gowans--Images p375,
    384

G

"GADSBY'S HOTEL." See FRANK-
LIN HOUSE
GADSEN, JAMES
  -Biography
    Amer. Her. --New (1) p E239
GADSEN PURCHASE, 1853
  Amer. Her. --New (7) p E239
  Harlow--Story p276-277
  Morris--Ency. p216, 429
"GAG RULE" (Congress)
  Amer. Her. --New (5) p E164
  Borden--Portrait (1) p209-210
  Life--Sweep (4) p66-67
  Morris--Ency. p179-180
GAGE, MATILDA
  Macksey--Book p80
GALE, JOE
  Case--Empire p87-95
GALL, CHIEF (Oglala Indian)
  Andrews--Indian leaders p86-87,
  151-153, 159
  Brown--Westerners p245-246, 251
GALLATIN, ALBERT (Abraham Al-
fonse Albert)
  Boardman--Virginia p16-17
  Butterfield--Amer. p37
  Harlow--Story p165-166, 177
  Life--Growing p58-59
  Morris--Ency. p147
  -Biography
    Morris--Ency. p663
GALLAUDET, THOMAS HOPKINS
  Tyler--Freedom's p294-296
GALVESTON ISLAND
  Hunt--Life p163-164
GAMBLING
  See also CARD-PLAYING; HORSE
  RACING; LOTTERIES
  Dulles--History p67, 154-155, 168-
  169

Handlin--This p118, 141, 326-331
Hunt--Life p175-183
Keller--Affairs p509-510
-Games
　Hunt--Life p181-183
-Vicksburg, 1835
　Burner--America (1) p300-301
GAME
　See ANIMALS, Wild: HUNTING
　AND TRAPPING
GAMEBOARDS
　-"Nellie Bly"
　Portraits--Americans p53
GAMES
　See also AMUSEMENTS; SPORTS
　AND GAMES
　Schwartz--When p76-77, 81, 85
　-1876
　　Hilton--Way p43-48
　-1880's
　　Peck--Nineteenth n. p.
　, and pastimes
　　Wilson--Folkways p108-110
　, Children's
　　Hilton--Way p43-48
　　McClinton--Antiques. See
　　index p347
　, Historical
　　McClinton--Antiques p225-227
　, Kissing
　　Schwartz--When p117
　-Lists. See PARKER BROTHERS
　-McLoughlin Brothers
　　McClinton--Antiques p231-233
　-Manufacturers. See names of
　　manufacturers
　, Parlor
　　Cable--American p204-207
　　-"The mansion of happiness"
　　　Cable--American p206-207
GAMING. See GAMBLING
"GANDER-PULLING" (sport)
　Dulles--History p75, 160-161
"GANDY DANCERS"
　Bartlett--New p167-168
GANGS
　Grimsted--Notions p245-259
　Handlin--This p324-325
GAOLS. See PRISONS AND
　PRISONERS
GARCIA, CALIXTO
　Amer. Her. --New (12) p E418
GARD, WAYNE
　-"How they killed the buffalo"
　　Treasury Amer. p292-297
GARDENS
　See also FLOWERS; LANDSCAPE
　GARDENING; VEGETABLES

Handlin--This p124, 319, 346-347
Ross--Taste p150-151
-Ornaments and furniture
　Dreppard--Pioneer p194, 196
, Public
　Boardman--Virginia p188
GARDINER LUCEUM (Maine)
　-1821-1832
　Randel--Centennial p404-405
GARDINI, CARLO
　-Views on America, 1880's
　　Handlin--This p343-349
GARDNER, ISABELLA STEWART
　("BELLE")
　Amer. Her. --New (11) p E383
　-"Fenway court"
　　Amer. Her. --New (11) p978-988
GARDNER, JAMES TERRY
　Gilbert--Trail. p200, 214
GARFIELD, JAMES ABRAM
　Boardman--Gilded p20-21
　Butterfield--Amer. p230
　Carman--History (2) p30, 46, 228,
　233-235, 238, 240, 276
　Keller--Affairs. See index p616
　Life--Steel (7) p14, 17, 26, 28, 42
　Linton--Bicentennial p220
　Morris--Ency. p251, 255-256
　200 Years (2) p314-315; see also
　index p353
　-Assassination, 1881
　　Butterfield--Amer. p231
　　Collins--Story p255
　　Garrison--Lost p76-79
　　Harlow--Story p454-455
　　Life--Steel (7) p13-14
　　Morris--Ency. p256
　-Biography
　　Morris--Ency. p663-664
　　Whitney--American p173-178
　-Presidency
　　Amer. Her. --New (10) p877
　　Reader's--Story p334
　-Reply to Macaulay on Constitu-
　tion
　　Davie--Profile p73-74
　-Tribute by James G. Blaine
　　Hurd--Treasury p112-113
GARFIELD, LUCRETIA
　Melick--Wives p48
GARLAND, HAMLIN
　Amer. Her. --New (11) p E383-384
　Boardman--Gilded p128-129
　Dulles--United p116
　Harlow--Story p432
　-Era of the little red school-
　house, 1870's
　　Davie--Profile p306

, on wheat harvesting, Iowa
   Commager--Heritage p864-872
GARMENT TRADE. See CLOTHING
INDUSTRY
GARRISON, WILLIAM LLOYD
   Amer. Her. --New (6) p E203
   Brooks--Flower. See index
   p543
   Carman--History (1) p531-533,
   561, 632, 639
   Furnas--Americans. See index
   p988
   Gurko--Ladies. See index p323
   Harlow--Story p255-256, 282
   Kraus--U.S. p445-446
   Life--Growing p127, 129-130, 132
   Morris--Ency. p181, 515, 585
   Our literary p84-85
   200 Years (1) p266, 267, 274
   , and abolition
      Alden--Pioneer p225-229
      Boardman--Jackson. p115
      Carman--History (1) p531-532
      Commager--Heritage p483-486
      Reader's--Story p339
      200 Years (1) p298
   -Biography
      Morris--Ency. p664
   -Mobbing by Boston conserva-
   tives
      -Views of Thomas Low Nichols
         Commager--Heritage p483-
         486
   , on peace and nonresistance
      Tyler--Freedom's p408, 410-
      414
GARRISONS. See FORTS AND
GARRISONS
GAS AND GASLIGHTS
   Furnas--Americans p429-430,
   566, 672, 806
   Walker--Every. p48, 113, 214
   Wilson--Vanish. p161
GASOLINE PUMPS
   , First (Fort Wayne, Ind., 1885)
      Robertson--Book p126
GATES
   , Old wooden
      Wilson--Vanish. p82
GATLING, RICHARD J.
   Boardman--Civil p147
GAY, MARY AND HARRIS
   Warren--Pictorial p112
"GAY NINETIES"
   See also "VICTORIANISM"
   Butterfield--Amer. p260-261
   Keyes--Hope p281-287
   Life--Reaching (8) p44-57

GEER, ELIZABETH
   -Diary of a woman on the Ore-
   gon trail, 1848
      Davie--Profile p149-150
GENEALOGY
   Cable--American p287
   Handlin--This p300-301
   -Societies
      Furnas--Americans p604-605
GENERAL FEDERATION OF
WOMEN'S CLUBS
   Walker--Every. p142
GENERAL LAND OFFICE
   Bartlett--New p73-77
GENERAL STORES
   See also COUNTRY STORES
   Langdon--Everyday (2) p139
   Wilson--Vanish. p138-139
"GENTRY." See ARISTOCRACY
GEOGRAPHY
   Boardman--Virginia p177
GEOLOGY AND GEOLOGISTS
   Boardman--Civil p176-177
   Boardman--Gilded p162-163
   Boardman--Jackson. p168
   Morris--Ency. p532
   Nye--Cultural p90-92
GEORGE, HENRY
   Boardman--Gilded p113-114
   Borden--Portrait (2) p29
   Carman--History (2) p388-389
   Furnas--Americans. See index
   p989
   Mott--Golden p167-168
   Mumford--Brown p44-46
   Our literary p162-163
   -Biography
      Morris--Ency. p664
   -"City and country," 1898
      Cook--City p6
   -"Progress and poverty"
      Hart--Popular p174-176
GEORGIA
   Carman--History (1) p326-327,
   364, 782
   Handlin--This p117, 120-122, 126,
   161-162, 203, 340-341
   Harlow--Story p227-228
   Hunt--Life. See index p291
   Life--New (5) p95, 136-137
   Life--Steel (7) p100-103, 106-107
   Life--Union (6). See index p173
   -Country life
      -Views of Rebecca Felton
         Commager--Heritage p376-
         380
   -"Expansionist sentiment," 1812,
   by D.B. Mitchell

Ridge--America's p254-256
-"A Georgia town in 1807"
   Woodward--Way p160-197
-Gold mines and mining
   Watkins--Gold p21-22
, in Civil war
   Dowdey--Experiment. See
   index p447
-Indian treaties, violation of
   Life--Sweep (4) p42, 44
-Plantation life
   Burner--America (1) p215-
   218
-Savannah
   Vanderbilt--Living p136-137
-"Scenes," by Augustus B.
   Longstreet
   Grimsted--Notions p109-118
GEORGIA FEMALE COLLEGE
   Wright--Every. p196
GERMAN SEPARATISTS. See
SEPARATISTS
GERMANIA SOCIETY
   Howard--Our p212-216, 273,
   281
GERMANS
   Alden--Pioneer p206-207
   Boardman--Jackson. p182-183
   Davidson--Life (2) p346-348
   Furnas--Americans p390-391;
   see also index p988
   Kraus--U.S. p394-395
   Marzio--Nation p277
   Reader's--Story p320-321
   Weisberger--Amer. See index
   p392
-1876
   Randel--Centennial. See
   index p469
, and beer
   Cable--American p313
   Weisberger--Amer. p142-143
, and music
   Weisberger--Amer. p135, 137-
   141
-Characteristics and spirit
   Weisberger--Amer. p123, 138-
   140
-Immigrants
   Bartlett--New p152-156
   Handlin--This p120, 138, 201,
   208, 233, 237, 252-253, 255-
   260, 263-269, 291, 325-326,
   346, 368, 383-389
, in Illinois
  -Views of Gustave Koerner,
   1833
    Angle--American p263-

265
, in Texas
   Weisberger--Amer. p121-122
-Population, in West
   Bartlett--New p151
-Sabbath
   Cable--American p313
-Views of Herman Melville
   Kraus--U.S. p394-395
GERMANY
, Cultural interest in
   Nye--Cultural p236-237
, Intellectual influences of
   Life--Reaching (8) p10, 14-16
GERONIMO (Apache Indian)
   Amer. Her. --Indians p388, 398-399
   Andrews--Indian leaders p167-168,
   176-177
   Boardman--Gilded p95-96
   Life--Steel (7) p53
   Reader's--Story p85
GERRYMANDER, 1812-1813
   Butterfield--Amer. p51
"GETTYSBURG ADDRESS," 1873
   Amer. Her. --New (8) p E275-276
   Angle--By p269
   Butterfield--Amer. p173
   Collins--Story p224
   Commager--Heritage p764-765
   Davie--Profile p280
   Heffner--Doc. p147
   Keyes--Hope p401
   Maurois--Illus. p161-162
   Meredith--World p183
   Reader's--Story p153
GETTYSBURG--BATTLE
   America's--Hist. p442-447
   Boardman--Civil p51-52, 71-72
   Bonte--America p128
   Carman--History (1) p655, 657,
   666-668, 681
   Collins--Story p223
   Commager--Heritage p758-764
   Dannett--Noble p234, 246, 248-249,
   251, 253, 257
   Dowdey--Experiment. See index
   p447
   Harlow--Story p318-319
   Jordan--Civil. See index p213
   Kraus--U.S. p506-508
   Life--Union (6) p14-15, 64-65, 88,
   92, 98-99
   Maurois--Illus. p158-161, 165
   Meredith--World p177-183
   Morris--Ency. p241
   Pratt--Civil p39-42
   Reader's--Story p153-154
   Treasury Amer. p224-241

Viewpoints p81
Young--Women p284-285
  -Battlefield
    Landmarks--Liberty p34-37
  -Northern version
    Davie--Profile p279-280
  -Southern version
    Davie--Profile p277-278
  -Views of Frank A. Haskell
    Angle--American p322-325
    Treasury--Amer. p225-241
GHOSTS
  Woodward--Way p350-353
GIACOSA, GUISEPPE
  , on America, 1898
    Handlin--This p390-407
GIBBONS, ABIGAIL
  Adelman--Famous p149
  Macksey--Book p112
GIBBONS, JAMES
  Morris--Ency. p665
GIBBONS VS. OGDEN CASE
  Amer. Her. --New (5) p372-373;
  E164
GIBBS, JOSIAH WILLARD
  Boardman--Gilded p122
  Morris--Ency. p532-533
  Randel--Centennial p453-454
  Wilson--American p298-305
  -Biography
    Morris--Ency. p665-666
  -Importance of work
    Wilson--American p300-301
  -"Phase rule"
    Wilson--American p303
GIBSON, CHARLES DANA
  Amer. Her. --New (12) p E418-
  419
  Life--Reaching (8) p44, 56
  -Drawings
    See also "GIBSON GIRL"
    Treasury Amer. p320-337
"GIBSON GIRL"
  Furnas--Americans p886-887
  Life--Reaching (8) p44, 46, 49-
  50, 55
  Ross--Taste p179
  Treasury Amer. p320-337
GIDDINGS, JOSHUA R.
  -Resolutions, 1842
    Morris--Ency. p185
GIESLER-ANNEKE, MATHILDE
FRANZISKA
  Neidle--America's p41-43
GIFT COUPONS
  , First, 1865 (New York)
    Robertson--Book p77
GILBERT, ANNE HARTLEY

Adelman--Famous p207
GILCHRIST, WILLIAM WALLACE
  Chase--America's p338-339
  Howard--Our p303
"GILDED AGE" (1870-1899)
  Amer. Her. --New (11) p976-977
  Boardman--Gilded p4-5; see also
    index p196-202
  Bonte--America p138
  Borden--Portrait (2) p51-54
  Dulles--History p230-234
  Harlow--Story p432-433
  Hart--Popular p157-179
  Jones--Age. See index p536
  Life--America's p130-144
  , Deflation of
    Mumford--Brown p23
  -Views of Leland D. Baldwin
    Miers--American p215-219
GILES, WILLIAM BRANCH
  Butterfield--Amer. p37
GILLETTE, WILLIAM
  Blum--Stage Profile 10
GILLMORE, QUINCY A.
  Holzman--Stormy p124-125
GILMAN, CHARLOTTE PERKINS
  Sochen--Herstory p220-221
GILMAN, DANIEL COIT
  Morris--Ency. p557
  Randel--Centennial p60, 101, 354,
  400-403, 414, 418
  -Biography
    Morris--Ency. p666
GILMORE, PATRICK SARSFIELD
  Furnas--Americans p661-662
  Howard--Our p297-298
GILPIN, WILLIAM
  Hine--American p143
GILSON, HELEN LOUISE
  Young--Women p99, 179, 182, 213,
  300
  -Biography
    Young--Women p372
GIRDNER, JOHN H.
  , on city noise, 1896
    Cook--City p158-159
GIRL SCOUTS OF AMERICA
  -Founding. See LOW,
    JULIETTE GORDON
GIRLS
  Handlin--This p182, 194, 261, 270-
  272, 380, 399
  -"Girl friends"
    Schwartz--When p200-201
  , Working, 1868
    Trachtenberg--Demo. p149-159
GLACIARIUMS (ice-skating rinks)
  -1876

Hilton--Way p98
GLADDEN, WASHINGTON
  Randel--Centennial p19-20, 192-
    193, 458
GLASS, HUGH
  See also OWENS, MIKE
  Boardman--Virginia p109-110
  Hine--American p51-52
GLASS
  Dreppard--Pioneer p189-191
  Handlin--This p111, 351, 353, 364
  Nostalgia p51-53
  -Sandwich
    Reader's--Story p228
  , Tiffany
    Life--America's p136-137
    Reader's--Story p229
    Ross--Taste p138-139
GLAZIER, WILLARD
  , on Pittsburgh
    Cook--City p22, 24
GLEASON, FREDERICK GRANT
  Chase--America's p338-339
  Howard--Our p303-304
GLIDERS
  , First controlled flight (Otay
    Mesa, Ca., 1884)
    Robertson--Book p78
GLIEG, GEORGE R.
  , on burning of Washington by
    British, 1814
    Angle--American p180-182
GLOVES
  -1890's
    Ross--Taste p216
  -"Mitts"
    Earle--Two cent. (2) p760
  -"Perkale and linen"
    Earle--Two cent. (2) p759
GODEY'S LADY'S BOOK
  Boardman--Jackson. p187
  Bode--Anatomy p261-263
  Cable--American p111, 150-151,
    170-171
  Tyler--Freedom's p436-438
  Walker--Every. p200-201
  Warren--Pictorial p124-125
  Woodward--Way p301
GODKIN, EDWIN LAWRENCE
  -Biography
    Morris--Ency. p666
GODOY, MANUEL DE
  Bartlett--New p45-46
GODPARENTS
  Cable--American p162
"GO-GETTERS"
  Portraits--American p1-41
GOLD

America 200 p50-53
Boardman--Gilded p47-48, 182-183
Bonte--America p143
Carman--History (1) p704-705
Carman--History (2). See index
  p. x
Dulles--United p35-38
Hine--American. See index p363
Life--Sweep (4) p134, 140, 146-147
Life--Union (6) p151-153
Train--Story p306
200 Years (1) p211, 231, 260, 262
Wilson--American p164-167
-Chronology, 1841-1899
  Watkins--Gold p280
-Discovery
  See also CALIFORNIA--Gold
  -Idaho
    Watkins--Gold p87-90
  -Montana, 1863-1864
    Commager--Heritage p582-
    585
    Ridge--America's p544-546
  -North Carolina
    Watkins--Gold p21
-"Gold bugs"
  Amer. Her. --90's p60-63
-Production, 1849-1852
  Hine--American p113
-Reserve
  Morris--Ency. p263
"GOLD CORNER" (1869 scandal)
  Butterfield--Amer. p202-203
  Harlow--Story p346
GOLD MINES AND MINING
  See also names of states and
  areas
  Amer. Her. --New (6) p474-477
  America's Hist. p489-501
  Commager--Heritage p549-578,
    582-585
  Keyes--Hope p196-197
  Wright--Culture p125-131
  , and priority rule
    Boorstin--Americans p504
  , as "Nature's great lottery"
    -Views by "Dame Shirley,"
      1852
      Angle--American p255-258
  -"Big bonanza"
    Watkins--Gold p79-80
  -"Blue Bucket mine" legend
    Case--Empire p283-295
  -Camps
    -Women, lack of
      Amer. Her. --New (6) p482-
      483
  -Foreigners, discrimination

against
  Wright--Culture p128-131
-Georgia, 1829
  Watkins--Gold p21-22
, High cost of
  Amer. Her. --New (9) p732-735
-Life of miners
  Johnson--Pictorial p94, 104
  -Views of Daniel B. Woods
    Davie--Profile p156-157
-Prospectors
  Hine--American p113, 115-116,
  118, 124, 126, 130, 162, 323
-Spanish myths
  Watkins--Gold p121, 124-125,
  136
-Techniques
  Johnson--Pictorial p95, 108-
  111
  Ridge--America's p533-535
  Train--Story p313-316
  Tunis--Frontier p133-134
  -Hydraulicking
    Bartlett--New p268-272
  -Lode mining
    Watkins--Gold p248
  -Placer mining
    Watkins--Gold p175-176,
    247-248
  -Sluice mining
    Watkins--Gold p90, 184-187
  -Washington territory
    Billington--Far p243-246
GOLD RUSH. See CALIFORNIA--
Gold rush; KLONDIKE GOLD RUSH;
"PIKE'S PEAK OR BUST"
GOLD STANDARD
  Amer. Her. --90's p60-62
  Harlow--Story p346, 450-452,
  463-465, 468-469, 471-473
  Life--Reaching (8) p86-87, 106,
  111-112
  Linton--Bicentennial p238, 242,
  245, 256
"GOLDEN AGE" (Amer. renais-
sance)
  -Views of Jay Leyda
    Miers--American p158-161
"GOLDEN SPIKE"
  Amer. Her. --New (10) p834-835
  America's Hist. p525-527
  Angle--American p357-358
  Brown--Westerners p186
  Butterfield--Amer. p198-199
  Collins--Story p240
  Davie--Profile p165-167
  "Driving of the golden spike, " by
  Grenville M. Dodge

Keyes--Hope p384-385
Golden spike ceremony, 1831
  Ross--Taste p277
  Landmarks--Liberty p38-39
  Ridge--America's p568-570
  Tunis--Frontier p143-144
  -Views of Sidney Dillon
    Ridge--America's p568-570
GOLDFIELD CONSOLIDATED
MINES COMPANY
  Watkins--Gold p171
GOLDMAN, EMMA F.
  Amer. Her. --New (12) p E419
  Neidle--America's p168-171
  , on William Jennings Bryan
    Miers--American p229-234
GOLF
  Boardman--Gilded p175
  Davidson--Life (2) p69
  Dulles--History p242-243
  -Beginnings, 1880's
    Ross--Taste p95
  -Clubs, first (Foxburg, Pa.)
    Reader's--Story p490
GOMPERS, SAMUEL
  Boardman--Gilded p76
  Harlow--Story p404-405
  Life--Reaching (8) p61-62, 67
  Life--Steel (7) p81-83
  Marzio--Nation p376
  Morris--Ency. p523
  Nostalgia p66-69
  Reader's--Story p500
  -Biography
    Morris--Ency. p666-667
  , on American Federation of
    Labor, 1886
      Angle--American p392-395
  , on the Socialists, 1890's
    Davie--Profile p127
GOOD LIFE COLONY. See
BROOK FARM
GOODNIGHT, CHARLES
  Boardman--Civil p99-100
  Brown--Westerners p203-213
GOODRICH, SAMUEL
  , on life in Connecticut
    Commager--Heritage p355-359
GOODRIDGE FAMILY
  Andrews--Women p226-228
GOODWIN, NAT C.
  Blum--Stage Profile p16
GOODYEAR, CHARLES
  Amer. Her. --New (5) p E164
  Boardman--Jackson. p101
  Bonte--America p108
  Life--New (5) p11
  Wilson--American p124-129

-Biography
Morris--Ency. p667
-Rubber industry
Nostalgia p33-35
-Rubber vulcanization
Reader's--Story p266-268
GORDON, JOHN B., GENERAL
Young--Women p277-278
GORGAS, JOSIAH
Dowdey--Experiment. See
index p447
GORRIE, JOHN
Garrison--Lost p187-189
Portraits--Americans p125
GOSHORN, ALFRED
Randel--Centennial p188-189,
285, 303
GOSIUTE INDIANS
Amer. Her. --Indians p306, 390
GOSPEL SONGS. See SONGS,
Gospel
"GOTHIC REVIVAL"
See also ARCHITECTURE--
Gothic revival
Boardman--Jackson. p162-164
Gowans--Images. See index
p496
Lynes--Taste. See index p354
GOTTSCHALK, LOUIS MOREAU
Boardman--Civil p163-164
Chase--America's p302-323
Howard--Our p205-210
, as first musical "matinee idol"
Lowens--Music p223-233
-Troubles, as pianist, 1853
Angle--American p281-282
GOUGAR, HELEN
Warren--Pictorial p141
GOUGE, WILLIAM M.
, on currency, 1830's
Walker--Reform p70-71
-"Short history of paper money"
Walker--Reform p71-77
GOUGH, JOHN BARTHOLOMEW
Boardman--Jackson. p130-131
GOULD, JAY
Amer. Her. --New (10) p864-865
Boardman--Civil p132-133
Boardman--Gilded p51
Butterfield--Amer. p202-203
Carman--History (2) p5-6, 86-88
Dulles--United p55-56
Harlow--Story p346
Life--Steel (7) p32, 80-81, 83, 86,
128-129, 135
Randel--Centennial p171-172, 177,
186, 327
Reader's--Story p283

GOVERNMENT
See also CORRUPTION, Govern-
ment; ELECTIONS; POLITICS;
names of localities, presidents,
etc.
Handlin--This p169-170, 234, 277,
283, 284, 338
Hine--American. See index p363
-Early 1800's
Hunt--Life p248-258
, as a service institution
Boorstin--Americans p249-256
, City and local
Keller--Affairs. See index
p616-617
, Federal
Keller--Affairs. See index
p617
-Organization
Randel--Centennial p262-263
, State
Keller--Affairs. See index
p617
-"Function of state govern-
ments, " by James Bryce
Davie--Profile p66
-Views of Frances Trollope
Trollope--Domestic. See
index p. viii
"GRACE" (Blessing). See PRAYER
--Grace
GRAHAM, ISAAC
-"Suppression of the Americans,"
by Charles Wilkes, 1845
Ridge--America's p470-472
GRAHAM, LLOYD
-"Blundin the hero of Niagara"
Treasury Amer. p274-279
GRAHAM, SYLVESTER
Alden--Pioneer p220-221
Boardman--Jackson. p174
Downey--Our p291-302
Furnas--Americans p439-441
Garrison--Lost p160-163
Ross--Taste p60
GRAHAM CRACKERS
Garrison--Lost p160-163
-First, 1830
Reader's--Story p124
GRAIN
See also CEREALS; CROPS;
names of grain
Bartlett--New p195-197
-Flails and flailers
Van Wagenen--Golden p240-
242, 244
Wilson--Early p152, 154
, Harvesting of

Van Wagenen--Golden p226,
228-231
GRAM, HANS
Boardman--Jackson. p171
GRAMOPHONES. See PHONO-
GRAPHS
GRANARIES
Tunis--Frontier p77-78
GRAND OPERA HOUSE (N. Y.
City)
Furnas--Americans p649-650
GRANGER MOVEMENT
Boardman--Gilded p65
Borden--Portrait (2) p28
Butterfield--Amer. p225
Carman--History (2) p223, 225
Drury--Midwest p89-90
Dulles--History p274-278
Harlow--Story p375-377
Hilton--Way p155-156
Life--Steel (7) p78, 80, 136
Morris--Ency. p248
Randel--Centennial p106
Reader's--Story p345
Walker--Every. p101-102, 140
Wilson--American p240
-Laws and cases
Keller--Affairs p176-177
Life--Steel (7) p136
Randel--Centennial p277-278
GRANITE INDUSTRY
-New England
Boorstin--Americans p17-20
GRANT, ELLEN ("NELLIE")
(Ellen Grant Sartoris)
Meredith--World p234-238
GRANT, JULIA
Dannett--Noble p274-276, 283, 388
Melick--Wives p44-45
GRANT, ULYSSES SIMPSON
See also "STALWARTS"
Amer. Her. --New (8) p E276-277
Boardman--Civil p42-44, 52-55,
87-92; see also index p212
Boardman--Gilded p4-5, 7-8
Brown--Westerners. See index
p286
Butterfield--Amer. p114, 194-195
Carman--History (1). See index
p. xi
Carman--History (2). See index
p. x
Dannett--Noble. See index p414
Dowdey--Experiment. See index
p447
Drury--Midwest p121
Holzman--Stormy. See index
p275

Keller--Affairs. See index p617
Kraus--U.S. p432, 493-494, 507-
513
Life--Steel (7) p8, 11-14, 17-18, 22
Life--Sweep (4) p105-107, 112
Life--Union (6). See index p173-
174
Maurois--Illus. p157-162, 170,
172-173, 203-206, 246
Morris--Ency. See index p751
Randel--Centennial. See index
p469
Reader's--Story p148-149, 152
200 Years (2) p310-311; see also
index p353
Young--Women. See index p386-
387
, and nickname "Unconditional
surrender"
Pratt--Civil p21-22
, and radicals
Carman--History (2) p43, 45-46
, and railroads
Meredith--World p200-203
, and Vicksburg
Pratt--Civil p32-34, 42-44
-Appointment as supreme com-
mander, 1864
-Views of John G. Nicolay
Angle--American p329-330
, as lieutenant general
Meredith--World p186-191
, at Centennial
Hilton--Way p184-186
-Biography
Morris--Ency. p667-668
Whitney--American p157-164
-Birthplace (Point Pleasant, Ohio)
Vanderbilt--Living p148
-Cabinet
Carman--History (1) p739-740,
744, 792-793
-Contrast with Lee
-Views of Bruce Catton
Miers--American p202-205
-Home (Galena, Illinois)
Vanderbilt--Living p165
, in Civil war
Amer. Her. --New (8) p671-684
America's Hist. p462-467
Harlow--Story p315-317, 319-
321
, in the wilderness, 1864
Pratt--Civil p49-50
-Last days
Butterfield--Amer. p246-247
-Letters to Robert E. Lee
Commager--Heritage p783-788

-Political mistakes
  Collins--Story p246
-Presidency
  Amer. Her. --New (10) p875-
  877
  Dulles--United p129-131
  Harlow--Story p344-351
  Linton--Bicentennial. See
  index p442
  Reader's--Story p333
-Publishing aid by Samuel
Clemens
  White--American p111-114
-Scandals in administration
  Harlow--Story p344-347
-War council (Bethesda Church,
Va.,) 1864
  -Viewpoints p84
GRASS, CHIEF (Indian)
  Andrews--Indians p120
GRASSHOPPERS
-Plague of Plains, 1874
  Amer. Her. --New (9) p773
  Commager--Heritage p860-
  864
  Hilton--Way p151-152
-Views of Stuart Henry
  Commager--Heritage p860-
  861
GRASSI, G. H.
-Views on America, 1819
  Handlin--This p137-150
GRATZ, REBECCA
  Macksey--Book p69
GRAUPNER, GOTTLIEB
  Boardman--Virginia p150-151
GRAUPNER, JOHANN CHRISTIAN
  Hoard--Our p130-133
GRAVES, MARY
  DeVoto--Year p309-310, 339,
  345-347, 386, 408-410, 417
GRAVESTONES. See TOMB-
STONES
GRAY, ASA
  Boardman--Civil p174-175
  Boardman--Jackson. p168
  Gilbert--Trail. p128-129, 178
  Reader's--Story p307, 309
GRAY, ELISHA
  Portraits--Americans p34
  Randel--Centennial p178-179
  White--American p104-105
GRAYSON, P. W.
, on individualism
  Grimsted--Notions p45-60
, on justice, law and lawyers
  Grimsted--Notions p45-60
-"Vice unmasked"

Grimsted--Notions p45-60
"GREAT AMERICAN DESERT."
  See DESERT, GREAT AMERI-
  CAN; PLAINS--GREAT PLAINS
  Boardman--Virginia p102-103
  Boorstin--Americans p229-231
  -"Beginnings of ... legend, 1810,"
  by Zebulon Montgomery Pike
  Ridge--America's p370-371, 373
GREAT ATLANTIC & PACIFIC TEA
COMPANY. See A & P
"GREAT AWAKENING" (2) (REVIV-
AL)
  Bartlett--New p43-44, 368
  Boardman--Virginia p169-170
  Boorstin--Americans p319-320
  Life--Hunt p120-121
  Nye--Cultural p215-216, 219
  Treasury--Amer. p121-122
GREAT BRITAIN
  See also ENGLAND AND ENG-
  LISH; etc.
  Boardman--Civil. See index
  p212
  Boardman--Virginia. See index
  p213
  -Attitude in Civil war
  Life--New (5) p112, 117, 139-
  141, 147
  -Declaration of war, 1812
  Morris--Ency. p141
  -Tensions, 1838
  Morris--Ency. p180-181
GREAT CENTRAL RAILWAY STA-
TION (Chicago)
  Drury--Midwest p33
"GREAT DIAMOND HOAX"
  Boorstin--Americans p234-236
"GREAT FALLS TAVERN" (Mary-
land)
  Vanderbilt--Living p81
GREAT LAKES
  Furnas--Americans p285-286, 673-
  674, 695-699
  -Transportation
  Carman--History (1) p461-462
  -Trip by Ellen Glasgow, 1835
  Angle--American p196-199
"GREAT MEDICINE ROAD." See
OREGON TRAIL
GREAT MIGRATION. See MIGRA-
TION
GREAT NATIONAL ROAD. See
NATIONAL ROAD
GREAT NORTHERN RAILWAY
  Dulles--United p56
"GREAT PLAINS"
  Bartlett--New p110, 112, 130, 213,

262-263
Boardman--Civil p94-95, 143-144
Boardman--Gilded p84-88
Furnas--Americans p683-687
Gilbert--Trail. p162
Handlin--This p215-216
Hine--American. See index p367
Reader's--Story p81
-Settlements
    Collins--Story p279
    Dulles--United p47-48
GREAT SIOUX RESERVATION
Brown--Westerners p251, 256-258
"GREAT SURVEYS." See SUR-
VEYS; names of surveys
"GREAT WESTERN STORE"
(Homer, N.Y., 1813)
Boardman--Virginia p190
GREATOREX, ELIZA
Adelman--Famous p185
"GREEK REVIVAL"
See also ARCHITECTURE--
"Greek Revival"
Boardman--Jackson. p162-163
Gowans--Images. See index p496
Life--America's p70-80
Lynes--Taste. See index p354
GREEKS
-Immigrants
Life--Reaching (8) p60-62, 65
GREELEY, HORACE
Boardman--Civil p68-69, 89-90
Boardman--Jackson. p185-186
Butterfield--Amer. p208-209
Carman--History (1). See index
    p. xi
Furnas--Americans. See index
    p990
Gurko--Ladies. See index p323
Keller--Affairs. See index p617
Life--New (5) p13, 34, 87
Life--Sweep (4) p61, 64, 66, 88, 138
Life--Union (6) p154-155
Morris--Ency. p244, 250-251, 438,
    520, 583
Ross--Heroines p79, 176-177
, and Karl Marx
    Treasury Amer. p248-255
-Biography
    Amer. Her. --New (7) p E239-
    240
    Morris--Ency. p668
-Open letter to President, 1862,
and Lincoln's reply
    Davie--Profile p275-277
GREEN, DUFF
, and Eaton affair
    Phillips--That p67, 73, 80-81,

110, 114, 118-119, 128-129
GREEN, HENRIETTA ("HETTY")
Macksey--Book p165
Ross--Taste p251, 254
GREENAWAY, KATE
-Books, illustrated
    McClinton--Antiques p70, 72-
    74, 115, 177
GREENBACKS AND GREENBACK
PARTY
Amer. Her. --New (10) p884-885
Boardman--Gilded p18-19
Butterfield--Amer. p224-225
Carman--History (1) p675, 704,
    733, 740-741
Carman--History (2) p42, 245-
    246, 283
Harlow--Story p325, 349, 450, 468
Holzman--Stormy p190-191, 207,
    215-219, 223
Keller--Affairs p170, 280-282,
    547, 550, 572
Life--Reaching (8) p84, 86, 93
Life--New (5) p120-121
Life--Steel (7) p16-17, 25, 77
Morris--Ency. p255
Randel--Centennial p75, 193-195
"GREENFIELD VILLAGE" (Henry
Ford museum, Dearborn, Mich.)
Vanderbilt--Living p157-161
"GREENHORNS"
Marzio--Nation p244-245
GREENHOW, ROSE O'NEAL
Warren--Pictorial p110
Young--Women p29, 51, 108, 110-
    111
GREENOUGH, HORATIO
Boardman--Jackson. p154-155
Bode--Anatomy p93-95
Brooks--Flower. p160, 187, 307,
    450-453, 472-473, 477
Larkin--Art p181-183; see also
    index p526
Morris--Ency. p601
"GREENS"
Van Wagenen--Golden p98-99
GREENSBORO, NORTH CAROLINA
, in Civil war
    Dowdey--Experiment p391, 411-
    414
GREGG, JOSIAH
Brown--Westerners p103-117
-"Caravans on the Santa Fe
trail," 1844
    Ridge--America's p376-379
, on Santa Fe, 1831
    Angle--American p234-235
, on trader's start on Santa Fe

trail
  Angle--American p231-234
GREGG, WILLIAM
  Boardman--Jackson. p79
  Woodward--Way p354
GRIDLEY, CHARLES VERNON
  Life--Reaching (8) p132-133
GRIERSON, BENJAMIN HENRY
  Amer. Her. --New (8) p E277
GRIERSON, FRANCIS
  -"The valley of the shadows"
    Grimsted--Notions p327-344
GRIESINGER, KARL THEODOR
  , on America, 1859
    Handlin--This p252-269
GRIFFIN, MRS. WILLIAM P.
  Young--Women p176-178, 182, 184
GRIFFITHS, JOHN W.
  Wilson--American p156-157
GRIGGS, NORRIS
  , on Indians
    Andrews--Indians p139-142,
    155-156
  -Ride
    Andrews--Indians p147-148
GRIMKE, ANGELINA
  Adelman--Famous p131
  Boardman--Jackson. p119
  Gurko--Ladies. See index p323
  Warren--Pictorial p83, 118
GRIMKE, SARAH MOORE
  Adelman--Famous p130-131
  Boardman--Jackson. p119
  Gurko--Ladies. See index
    p323-324
  Warren--Pictorial p83-85, 118
GRIMKE SISTERS (ANGELINA AND
  SARAH)
  Furnas--Americans p489-493
  Life--Sweep (4) p65
  Macksey--Book p86, 111
  Neidle--America's p28-29
  Reader's--Story p433
  Sochen--Herstory p122-124,130-131
  Tyler--Freedom's p442-445, 451,
    453
  -Biography
    Amer. Her. --New (7) p E240
GRINDSTONES
  Wilson--Vanish. p59
"GRINGOS"
  -Alta California
    Tunis--Frontier p128-129
GRINNELL, HENRY
  -Expedition, 1850's
    Boardman--Civil p177-178
GRINNELL UNIVERSITY ("Peo-
  ple's College")

Boorstin--Americans p158
GROCERS AND GROCERY STORES
  Handlin--This p256-260
  Hilton--Way p154-155
GROS VENTRES INDIANS
  Gilbert--Trail. p72
GROSCH, ALLAN AND HOSEA
BALLOU
  Watkins--Gold p67-69, 90
GRUNDY, FELIX
  Amer. Her. --New (5) p E165
GUADALUPE HIDALGO TREATY
  Amer. Her. --New (7) p E254
  Billington--Far p190-191
  Borden--Portrait (1) p212-214
  Carman--History (1) p572-573,
    601
  Harlow--Story p276
  Hine--American p106-107, 120,
    167, 210
  Johnson--Pictorial p91
  Kraus--U.S. p433
  Morris--Ency. p207-208
GUITEAU, CHARLES J.
  Collins--Story p256
  Life--Steel (7) p13-14
GULF COAST
  -1876
    Randel--Centennial p44-45
GUNDALOWS (BOATS)
  Langdon--Everyday (2) p5-6, 18
GUNNISON, J. W.
  -"The cooperative experiment:
    the governmental system," 1852
    Ridge--America's p517-519
GUNPOWDER
  -Trade
    Marzio--Nation p237-239
GUNS
  See also COLT, SAMUEL
  Dreppard--Pioneer p42-47
  Hine--American. See index p363
  Marzio--Nation p520-529
  Wilson--American p188-195
  -1880's
    Peck--Nineteenth. n. p.
  -Artillery
    Meredith--World p164-169
  -Civil war
    See also GUNS--Confederacy;
      ...--Union; TORPEDOS--
      Civil war
    Jordan--Civil p44, 63, 133, 141,
      164, 182-183
  -Colt
    Tunis--Frontier p104-105, 151
  -Confederacy
    Dowdey--Experiment p19, 32,

39, 41, 48, 57, 93-94, 105, 129, 327, 376-377
Life--New (5) p137, 146-147
, Frontier
  Life--America's p100
-Gatling (1862)
  Life--America's p95
  Wilson--American p194-195
-Marksmanship
  Boardman--Virginia p187
, Parrott
  Wilson--American p192-193
-Rifles
  Dreppard--Pioneer p39-40
  Marzio--Nation p232-236
-Six-shooters, cowboys'
  Train--Story p298-299
-Union
  Life--New (5) p74, 120-121, 137
GUTHRIE, SAMUEL
  Boardman--Jackson. p170
GYMNASIUMS
-Apparatus, 1880's
  Peck--Nineteenth, n. p.
, First, 1825
  Davidson--Life (2) p32
-Supplies, (1880's)
  Peck--Nineteenth. n. p.

H

H. H., pseud. See JACKSON, HELEN FISKE HUNT
HABBERTON, JOHN
  Mott--Golden p159-160
"HABEAS CORPUS"
  Carman--History (1) p690-692, 739
HACKETT, JAMES HENRY
  Boardman--Jackson. p158
HADLEY, PIETY LUCRETIA
-Civil war experiences
  Andrews--Women p416-420
HAGUE CONFERENCE, 1ST, 1899
  Amer. Her. --New (12) p E420
  Morris--Ency. p291-292
HAH-KET-HOME-MAK (Cheyenne Indian)
  Andrews--Indian leaders p144
HAHNEMANN, SAMUEL AND HAHNEMANNISM
  Boardman--Jackson. p171
  Hunt--Life p214
HAIDA INDIANS
-Bowl, carved (c1870)
  Marzio--Nation p14-15

HAIRDRESSING
  Earle--Two cent. (2) p522-523, 527-531
  Partridge--As p143
  Ross--Taste p204
  Train--Story p171, 327
-Men's long hair
  White--American p17-19
, Military hair-cuts
  Burner--America (1) p253-254
HAIRPIECES. See WIGS AND WIG-MAKERS
HALE, EDWARD EVERETT
  Brooks--Flower. p73, 173, 204, 252, 485-486
-Boyhood, in New England
  Commager--Heritage p371-376
HALE, GEORGE ELLERY
  Wilson--American p352-353
HALE, JOHN PARKER
  Life--New (5) p50-51
-Bill to outlaw rioting, debate on
  Grimsted--Notions p312-326
-Biography
  Amer. Her. --New (7) p E240-241
HALE, SARAH JOSEPHA
  Adelman--Famous p164
  Amer. Her. --New (6) p E204
  Boardman--Jackson. p187
  Macksey--Book p69
  Tyler--Freedom's p436-438
  Warren--Pictorial p124-125
HALE, WILLIAM HARLAN
  Treasury Amer. p248-255
HALE FAMILY
  Brooks--Flower p485-486
"HALF-BREEDS" (Grant opponents)
  Harlow--Story p452-453
HALIBURTON, THOMAS CHANDLER
  Boardman--Jackson p150
HALL, ANNE
  Macksey--Book p206
HALL, BASIL, Captain
-Views of Frances Trollope
  Trollope--Domestic. See index p. viii
HALL, G. STANLEY
  Portraits--Americans p75-77
HALL, JAMES
  Bartlett--New p140, 146-147
HALL, SAMUEL READ
  Tyler--Freedom's p237-238
"HALL OF FAME" (for famous Americans)
-Names
  Harris--Land p205-312
HALLECK, FITZ-GREENE

Our literary p20
HALLECK, HENRY W., GENERAL
  Amer. Her. --New (8) p E277
  Life--Union (6) p13, 17-18, 35-39,
    60
HALLEY'S COMET
  Schwartz--When p185-186
HALLOWEEN
  Partridge--As p24
  Schwartz--When p128
HALLS
  Lynes--Domestic. p236-238
HALSTEAD, MURAT
  , on Lincoln's nomination, 1860
    Angle--American p301-307
    Commager--Heritage p637-642
HALSTED, WILLIAM STEWART
  Reader's--Story p295, 298
HAMILTON, ALEXANDER
  Butterfield--Amer. p42-45
  Life--Sweep (4) p138
  Linton--Bicentennial p42, 44, 46-
    47, 49-51, 53, 55-56, 59, 61
  -Burr duel, and death of
    Angle--American p143-144
    Butterfield--Amer. p42-43
    Life--Growing p81-82
  -Views of Gouverneur Morris
    Hurd--Treasury p44-46
HAMILTON, ELIZABETH SCHUYLER
  Butterfield--Amer. p43
HAMILTON, WILLIAM HENRY
  Life--Growing p96, 98, 102, 106,
    110-111, 113
HAMLIN, HANNIBAL
  Amer. Her. --New (8) p E277
  Life--New (5) p92-93
HAMMOCKS
  Peck--Nineteenth. n. p.
  Ross--Taste p146-147, 149
HAMMOND, GEORGE HENRY
  Wilson--American p230
HAMMOND, JAMES HENRY
  -Biography
    Amer. Her. --New (7) p E241
HAMMOND, WILLIAM A.
  Dannett--Noble p95-97, 109,
    151, 193-194
HAMPTON, WADE
  Amer. Her. --New (8) p E277
  Butterfield--Amer. p223
  Randel--Centennial p232, 251-
    254, 421
"HAMPTON" (Towson, Md.)
  Vanderbilt--Living p84
HAMPTON INSTITUTE
  Furnas--Americans p752-753
HANBY, BENJAMIN RUSSELL

See also SONGS--Darling Nellie
  Gray
  Howard--Our p261
HANCOCK, CORNELIA
  Young--Women p99, 287-289, 300,
    307-308, 322, 329, 344
  -Biography
    Young--Women p372
HANCOCK, WINIFRED SCOTT
  Amer. Her. --New (8) p E277-278
  Boardman--Gilded p20-21
  Brown--Westerners p233-234
HAND-SHAKING
  Harris--Land p218-219
  -Views of Frances Trollope
    Trollope--Domestic p100-101,
      121, 144, 282, 425
HAND-WRINGERS
  Wilson--Vanish. p100
"HANDCART (HANDCUT) BRI-
  GADES" (Mormons, 1856)
  Billington--Far p206-207
HANDEL AND HAYDN SOCIETY
  (Boston)
  Howard--Our p133
HANDICAPPED
  Hilton--Way p88-90
  , Mentally
    Hilton--Way p89-90
  -Schools
    Reader's--Story p338
HANDICRAFTS. See CRAFTS AND
  CRAFTSMANSHIP; SAMPLERS;
  SPINNING; WEAVERS AND WEAV-
  ING; names of crafts
HANDWRITING. See PENMANSHIP
HANGINGS
  Hine--American p303-307
  Trollope--Domestic p163-166,
    286-287
HANNA, MARCUS ALONZO
  ("MARK")
  Amer. Her. --New p E420
  Amer. Her. --90's p30-35, 130-138
  Boardman--Gilded p182-183
  Butterfield--Amer. p274-275
  Harlow--Story p472, 474-476
  Life--Reaching (8) p104-106, 111-
    112, 133, 138
  Morris--Ency. p265
  -Biography
    Morris--Ency. p670-671
HANNIBAL, MISSOURI
  Drury--Midwest p15-16
HAPGOOD, HUTCHINS
  Our literary p183
HAPPINESS
  Trachtenberg--Demo. p70-71

HARDEE, (WILLIAM) JOSEPH
  Amer. Her. --New (8) p E278
  Meredith--World p192-196
HARDING, CHESTER
  Amer. Her. --New (6) p E204
  Boardman--Jackson. p154
  Boardman--Virginia p154-155
  Larkin--Art p123-124; see also
    index p527
HARGER, CHARLES N.
  -"The Long drive"
    Ridge--America's p597-599
HARLAN-YOUNG PARTY
  DeVoto--Year. See index p517
HARLAND, JOHN MARSHALL
  -Biography
    Morris--Ency. p671
HARLAND, MARION, pseud. (Mrs.
  Edward Payson Terhune)
  Adelman--Famous p265
"HARMONISTS" (HARMONY SOCI-
  ETY) (Pennsylvania)
  See also "RAPPITES"
  Hunt--Life p242-243
  Life--Sweep (4) p59, 63-64
  Reader's--Story p320
HARNESS ROOMS
  Wilson--Vanish. p21
HARNESS SHOPS
  Van Wagenen--Golden p201-202
  Wilson--Vanish. p65, 129
HARNETT, WILLIAM M.
  Reader's--Story p378
HARNEY, WILLIAM S.
  Amer. Her. --New (6) p E204
HARPER, ELLEN WATKINS
  Warren--Pictorial p88
HARPER, ROBERT GOODLOE
  Amer. Her. --New (6) p E204
HARPER, WILLIAM RAINEY
  Morris--Ency. p556
  -Biography
    Morris--Ency. p671-672
HARPER AND BROTHERS
  Bode--Anatomy p132, 155-156, 221
  Mott--Golden. See index p342
HARPER'S BAZAAR
  Lynes--Taste. p76-77, 100, 103,
    107-108
HARPER'S FERRY, WEST VIR-
  GINIA. See BROWN, JOHN
HARPER'S MAGAZINE
  Bode--Anatomy p259-261
  Randel--Centennial p355-356
HARPER'S WEEKLY
  Life--Steel (7) p14, 18, 20, 22, 26,
    93, 109
"HARRIGAN AND HART" SHOWS

  Howard--Our p647-649
HARRIMAN, EDWARD H.
  Amer. Her. --New (10) p872-873
  Boardman--Gilded p66-67
  Carman--History (2) p88-89, 95-97
  Reader's--Story p283
HARRIS, ELIZA
  Dannett--Noble p101, 150, 184, 214,
    327
HARRIS, JOEL CHANDLER
  Amer. Her. --New (11) p E384
  Harlow--Story p431
  Morris--Ency. p573
  Our literary p136-137
HARRIS, TOWNSEND
  Boardman--Civil p13
HARRISON, ANNA
  Melick--Wives p30
HARRISON, BENJAMIN
  Bonte--America p142
  Butterfield--Amer. p253, 255-256
  Harlow--Story p462-463, 466
  Keller--Affairs. See index p618
  Life--Reaching (8) p58-59; see
    also index p173
  Linton--Bicentennial p115-116
  Morris--Ency. p260-263, 283-284
  200 Years (2) p91, 320-321
  -Biography
    Morris--Ency. p672
    Whitney--American p199-205
  -Presidency
    Linton--Bicentennial p231
    Reader's--Story p334
  -Views of Philip Hone, on candi-
    dacy, 1840
    Commager--Heritage p618-619
HARRISON, BURTON
  Dowdey--Experiment. See index
    p448
HARRISON, CAROLINA
  Melick--Wives p52-53
HARRISON, JONATHAN BAXTER
  -"Study of a New England factory
    town"
    Trachtenberg--Demo. p161-183
  -"View of working class"
    Trachtenberg--Demo. p160-183
HARRISON, WILLIAM HENRY
  Alden--Pioneer p188-189
  Amer. Her. --New (5) p E165
  Boardman--Jackson. p33-35
  Boardman--Virginia p40-41, 113-
    115
  Butterfield--Amer. p104-106
  Harlow--Story p176, 178, 237-238
  Morris--Ency. p139-140, 144-145,
    148, 178, 182-184

200 Years (1) p330-331; see also
 index p347
, and Eaton affair
    Phillips--That p154
    -Cabinet resignations
       Morris--Ency. p184-185
-"The battle of the Thames,"
 1813
    Ridge--America's p268-270
-Biography
    Morris--Ency. p672-673
    Whitney--American p89-93
-Home, "Grouseland," or "White
 house of the West"
    Vanderbilt--Living p153
-"Log cabin campaign"
    Burner--America (1) p166-170
-Presidency
    Dulles--United p138-140
    Phillips--That p155
    Reader's--Story p333
HART, JOEL TANNER
    Amer. Her. --New (5) p E165
HART, THOMAS
    Butterfield--Amer. p93
HARTE, BRET
    Amer. Her. --New (11) p E384-
    385
    Boardman--Civil p151-152
    Harlow--Story p432
    Hart--Popular p143-144
    Morris--Ency. p573, 587
    Mott--Golden p198-199
    Our literary p126-127
    Reader's--Story p414
HARTFORD, GEORGE HUNTINGTON
    Portraits--American p46
    Ross--Taste p60
HARTFORD, CONNECTICUT
    Boardman--Virginia p49-50
    -Family life, 1836
       Life--Sweep (4) p32-33
HARTFORD CONVENTION, 1814-
 1815
    Boardman--Virginia p49-50
    Borden--Portrait (1) p143-145
    Butterfield--Amer. p59
    Kraus--U.S. p323-324
    Morris--Ency. p153
"HARTFORD WITS." See
"CONNECTICUT WITS"
HARVARD COLLEGE (UNIVERSITY)
    Boardman--Gilded p115-116
    Furnas--Americans. See index
    p990
    Handlin--This p145, 247, 371-373
    Our literary p157
    Tyler--Freedom's p254-255

-1815
    Brooks--Flower. p28-45
-1876
    Randel--Centennial p407-411
-Law school
    Boorstin--Americans p37-38
-Library catalog
    Randel--Centennial p428-429
-Views of Charles W. Eliot
    Hurd--Treasury p106-109
HARVARD OBSERVATORY
    Wilson--American p272-273
HARVESTERS
    Wilson--American p236-237
HARVEY, WILLIAM HOPE
    Mott--Golden p170-171
HASKELL, FRANK ARETAS
, on Battle of Gettysburg, 1863
    Angle--American p322-325
    Treasury Amer. p225-241
-"The third day at Gettysburg"
    Treasury Amer. p227-241
HASSAM, CHILDE
    Larkin--Art p304-305; see also
    index p527
HASTINGS, JAMES K.
    Watkins--Gold p134-135
HASTINGS, LANSFORD W.
    Billington--Far p96-97, 107-110,
    195, 226
    DeVoto--Year. See index p517
    -"John A. Sutter and his fort"
       Ridge--America's p472-477
HASTINGS, THOMAS
    Chase--America's p161-162
    Howard--Our p141-142
HATCH ACT, 1887
    Morris--Ency. p259
    Reader's--Story p115
HATRACKS
    Wilson--Vanish. p86
HATS AND HATTERS
    Earle--Two cent. (2) p576-579
    Furnas--Americans p435, 537,
    667, 684
    Van Wagenen--Golden p128-129
, Beaver
    Tunis--Frontier p110-111
, Cowboys'
    Train--Story p297-298
, Sportsman's, 1880's
    Peck--Nineteenth. n.p.
-Stetson
    Tunis--Frontier p149
, Tipping of
    Carson--Polite p172
    Harris--Land p216-218
, Women's

Ross--Taste p207, 209
HATTON, JOSEPH
  Randel--Centennial p77-84, 337
HAUPT, HERMAN
  Boardman--Civil p141
  Young--Women p198-200, 204-205
HAUSER, WILLIAM
  Chase--America's p197-198
HAWAIIAN ISLANDS
  America's Hist. p546-549
  Boardman--Gilded p188-189
  Borden--Portrait (2) p67-68
  Dulles--United p163-164
  Keyes--Hope p278
  Life--Reaching (8). See index
    p173
  Linton--Bicentennial. See index
    p442
  -1875-1876
    Randel--Centennial p157-158
  -1893
    Morris--Ency. p285
  -Annexation
    Amer. Her. --New (12) p E420-
      421
    Carman--History (2) p281-286
    Collins--Story p278
    Morris--Ency. p289-290
  -Reciprocity treaty, 1887
    Morris--Ency. p282
  -Sugar and sea power
    Butterfield--Amer. p276
  -Treaty, 1875
    Morris--Ency. p281
"HAWKERS"
  -New York City
    Tunis--Young p116-117
  , Railroad
    Furnas--Americans p349-350
HAWKES, FRANKLIN LISTER,
BISHOP
  Meredith--World p24-27
HAWLEY, HARRIET FOOTE
  Dannett--Noble p302-303, 316-
    317, 391
HAWLEY, JOSEPH
  Randel--Centennial p225, 285,
    291, 301, 303, 315, 363, 438-439
HAWTHORNE, NATHANIEL
  Amer. Her. --New (5) p E165-
    166
  Boardman--Civil p151
  Boardman--Jackson. p145
  Brooks--Flower. See index
    p543
  Carman--History (1) p529, 541-
    542, 545-548
  Harlow--Story p244, 259

Hart--Popular p91-94
Life--Sweep (4) p60, 62
Morris--Ency. p568
Mott--Golden p130-131
Our literary p77-83
Reader's--Story p411
Treasury Amer. p300-309
-Biography
  Morris--Ency. p673
-"The celestial railroad"
  Grimsted--Notions p204-214
-"The Hawthornes in Paradise"
  Treasury Amer. p300-309
, in Salem
  Brooks--Flower. p210-227
, on Abraham Lincoln
  Commager--Heritage p650-652
, on piracy
  Commager--Heritage p233-235
-"Scarlet letter" publication of,
  1849
  -Views of James T. Fields
    Angle--American p273-275
HAWTHORNE, SOPHIA PEABODY
  Our literary p79
  Treasury Amer. p300-309
HAY, JOHN MINTON
  Amer. Her. --New (12) p E421-422
  Morris--Ency. p291, 573
  Randel--Centennial p216-227, 357
  -Biography
    Morris--Ency. p673-674
  , on Lincoln
    Kraus--U.S. p504-505
HAY, GRAIN AND FEED STORES
  Wilson--Vanish. p133
HAYDEN, FERDINAND VANDIVEER
  Boardman--Civil p176-177
  Gilbert--Trail. p182, 189, 190-192,
    197, 212
  Randel--Centennial p263-264, 279
HAYDEN SURVEY, 1876
  Gilbert--Trail. p182-183, 188-189,
    191-197, 214
  Randel--Centennial p263-264
HAYES, LUCY
  Butterfield--Amer. p220-221
  Life--Steel (7) p11, 17
  Melick--Wives p46-47
HAYES, RUTHERFORD BIRCHARD
  Amer. Her. --New (8) p E278, 279,
    708-710
  Boardman--Gilded p9-10, 17-18
  Bonte--America p136-137
  Butterfield--Amer. p220-221
  Carman--History (1) p646-751, 793
  Carman--History (2) p43, 47-50,
    228, 230-231, 246

Harlow--Story p349-351
Keller--Affairs. See index p618
Life--Steel (7) p6-11; see also
  index p157
Maurois--Illus. p204, 206
Morris--Ency. p252-255, 281-
  282, 522
Randel--Centennial p36, 105, 220-
  236, 253, 302
200 Years (2) p312-313
, and opposing Congress
  Keyes--Hope p271
, and Spoils system
  Morris--Ency. p255
-Biography
  Morris--Ency. p674
  Whitney--American p165-171
-Cabinet
  Carman--History (1) p793
-Civil service reform
  Harlow--Story p448-449
-Presidency
  Dulles--United p133-134
  Linton--Bicentennial p212, 214-
    218
  Reader's--Story p334
-Visit of Joseph (Indian)
  Davie--Profile p110-111
HAYING BEES
  Life--Sweep (4) p22-23
"HAYMARKET" RIOTS (Chicago)
  Boardman--Gilded p75, 78-79
  Butterfield--Amer. p248-249
  Carman--History (2) p146-147
  Collins--Story p259
  Commager--Heritage p1001-1003
  Dulles--United p83-85
  Furnas--Americans p711, 715-716
  Harlow--Story p407-409
  Keller--Affairs p404, 446, 487,
    489-490, 559
  Life--Steel (7) p83-84, 94-95
  Morris--Ency. p522-523
HAYNE, ROBERT YOUNG
  Amer. Her. --New (5) p E166
  Boardman--Jackson. p12-13
  Butterfield--Amer. p86-87
  Life--Sweep (4) p14-17
HAYRIDES
  Partridge--As p12
HAYS, WILLIAM SHAKESPEARE
  Howard--Our p644-645
"HAYSEEDS"
  Wilson--Early p162-163
HAYSTACKS
  Wilson--Vanish p67-68
HAYWARD, WILLIAM D. ("BIG
  BILL")

Furnas--Americans p829-830
HAZELTINE, NELLIE
  Peacock--Famous p257-263
HEADE, MARTIN JOHNSON
  Reader's--Story p376
HEADLEY, JOEL
  Bode--Anatomy p247-249
HEALTH
  See also HYGIENE; SANITATION
  Bartlett--New p159, 364-366
  Handlin--This p101, 109-110, 127,
    154, 160-161, 214, 304
  Lynes--Domestic. See index
    p302
  , and sports' growth
    Dulles--History p183-185
HEALY, GEORGE
  Larkin--Art p239; see also index
    p528
HEALY, JAMES A., Bishop
  Randel--Centennial p447, 461-462,
    (facing 19)
HEARN, LAFCADIO
  Case--America's p435-438
HEARST, GEORGE
  Amer. Her. --New (11) p E385
  Life--Steel (7) p130
  Watkins--Gold p72, 88, 90, 93, 113,
    116-119, 191
HEARST, PHOEBE APPERSON
  Adelman--Famous p256-257
  Warren--Pictorial p142
HEARST, WILLIAM RANDOLPH
  Boardman--Gilded p164
  Carman--History (2) p371
  Furnas--Americans p701, 857-858,
    860-867
  Harlow--Story p429-430
  Life--Reaching (8) p37, 41, 130-
    131, 140
  Reader's--Story p360-361
  Walker--Every. p187, 191-195
HEATING
  See also FIREPLACES; STOVES
  Boardman--Jackson. p172
  Furnas--Americans p427-429
  Langdon--Everyday (2) p223-226
  Schwartz--When p31-32
  Walker--Every. p22, 24-25, 47,
    213-214
  Wilson--Folkways p136-137
  -1876
    Hilton--Way p14, 18, 20, 35
  , with "cow-chips"
    Lynes--Domestic. p33-34
HEDGE, FREDERICK H.
  Brooks--Flower. p191, 229, 240,
    268

HEDGE'S CLUB
  Brooks--Flower. p268
HEINEMANN, BARBARA
  Neidle--America's p64-66
HEINRICH, ANTON PHILIP
  Howard--Our p226-238
  -Musical triumph
    Lowens--Music p203-211
HEINTZELMAN, SAMUEL P.
  Life--New (5) p112-113
HEINZ, H.J.
  Hilton--Way p176-177
HELD, ANNA
  Blum--Stage Profile 38
"HELDERBERG WAR, " 1845
  Morris--Ency. p192
HELM, EMILIE TODD
  Randall--Mary p188-190
HELM, LINAI T.
  , on Indian massacre at Fort
    Dearborn, 1812
    Angle--American p174-177
HELPER, HINTON ROWAN
  -Biography
    Amer. Her. --New (7) p E241
HEMANS, FELICIA
  Bode--Anatomy p189-193
HEMMINGWAY, ELIZA R.
  , on Lowell factories, women's
    workday
    Sochen--Herstory p96-97
HEMP
  Handlin--This p115-116, 119
HENRY, ANDREW
  Bartlett--New p86, 257-258
  Brown--Westerners p57-58, 61
HENRY, JOSEPH
  Boardman--Jackson. p166
  Kraus--U.S. p385
  Morris--Ency. p531, 536
  Randel--Centennial p265-267
  Reader's--Story p263, 309
  Wilson--American p108-113
  -Biography
    Morris--Ency. p674-675
HENRY, O.
  -"The trimmed lamp"
    Harris--Land p88-98
HENRY, STUART
  , on grasshopper plague
    Commager--Heritage p860-861
HENRY, WILLIAM S.
  -"Origins of the Mexican war:
    the Nueces skirmish, " 1846
    Ridge--America's p503-504
HENRY STREET SETTLEMENT,
  N. Y.
  Warren--Pictorial p148-149

HENTZ, CAROLINE LEE
  Bode--Anatomy p177-179, 273-274
HERALDRY
  Carson--Polite p187, 246
"HERALDS" (Bell-ringers)
  Wilson--Early p24-25
HERBERT, VICTOR
  Amer. Her. --New (12) p E423
  Howard--Our p653-654
HEREDITARY ASSOCIATIONS
  Carson--Polite p246
"THE HERMITAGE" (Andrew Jack-
  son's home, Nashville, Tenn.)
  Vanderbilt--Living p122-123
HERMITS
  Wilson--Early p118-120
HERNDON, WILLIAM
  -Hatred of Mary Lincoln, and
    Herndon-Welk manuscripts
    Randall--Mary p49-52, 132, 144-
      145, 440-442, 462
  -Lectures on Ann Rutledge
    Randall--Mary p430-442
  , on Abraham Lincoln
    Commager--Heritage p628-632
HEROES AND HEROINES
  See also names of individuals
  Boorstin--Americans p327-362
  , Folk
    Boardman--Virginia p97
    Reader's--Story p172-173
  , Sea
    Macksey--Book p244-245
  , Stage
    Grimsted--Melodrama. See
      index p281
  , Western
    Hine--American p268-282, 324,
      343
HERON, MATILDA
  Adelman--Famous p187-188
HERVIEU, AUGUSTE JEAN JACQUES
  -Views of Frances Trollope
    Trollope--Domestic. See
      index p. viii
HERZ, HENRI
  Howard--Our p204
  -Views on America, 1846
    Handlin--This p185-203
HETCH HETCH VALLEY,
  CALIFORNIA
  Hine--American p187-188, 293,
    332, 339
HEWITT, ABRAM STEVENS
  Meredith--World p140-143
HEWITT, HORATIO DAWES
  Howard--Our p169-170
HEWITT, JAMES

, as professional musician
  Lowens--Music p197, 200-202
HEWITT, JOHN HILL
  Chase--America's p176-179
  Howard--Our p164-169
HEWITT, SOPHIA HENRIETTE
  Howard--Our p170
HEWITT FAMILY
  Howard--Our p169-170
HICKOK, JAMES BUTLER ("WILD
BILL")
  Boardman--Civil p198
  Hine--American p141, 268, 274
  Randel--Centennial p133, 146-147
  Reader's--Story p173
HICKS, EDWARD
  Larkin--Art p229-230; see also
  index p528
HICKS, J.D.
 , on Populism
  Miers--American p219-224
HICKS, THOMAS
  Larkin--Art p197-198
"HICKSITES" (Quakers)
  Wright--Every. p211
HIDATSA INDIANS
  Boardman--Virginia p118-119
"HIGGINSON'S REVIVAL" (skating)
  Dulles--History p184
HIGH SCHOOLS
  Nye--Cultural p162-163
  Portraits--Americans p141-142
  -1876
    Hilton--Way p59-60
HIGHER EDUCATION. See COL-
LEGES AND UNIVERSITIES
HIGHWAY MARKERS
  Wilson--Vanish. p182
HIGHWAYS
  See also ROADS; names of
  roads and highways
  Carman--History (1) p325, 375,
  458-460
  -Legislation (1806, 1822, 1857,
  1893)
    Nation in motion p123
HILDRETH, RICHARD
  Boardman--Jackson. p146-147
  Morris--Ency. p570
HILL, AMBROSE POWELL
  Amer. Her. --New (8) p E279
  Dowdey--Experiment p28, 214,
  238, 275, 318, 350, 354, 374, 382
HILL, BENJAMIN
  Holzman--Stormy p191-192
  Randel--Centennial p243-244
HILL, DANIEL HARVEY
  Amer. Her. --New (8) p E279

HILL, JAMES J. ("JIM")
  Amer. Her. --New (9) p802-808
  Amer. Her. --New (10) p872-873
  Boardman--Gilded p66-67, 79-80
  Carman--History (2) p89-90, 95-97
  Dulles--United p56
  Life--Steel (7) p31, 129, 131
  Morris--Ency. p431
  Reader's--Story p283
 -Biography
  Morris--Ency. p675-676
HILL, THOMAS
 -"Album of biography and art, "
  1881
    Cable--American p244-245
HILL, TIMOTHY DWIGHT
  Wright--Culture p137-138
HILL, URELLI CORELLI
  Howard--Our p151-154
HIMES, JOSHUA VAUGHAN
  Wright--Every. p215
HIMMELWRIGHT, A. L. A.
 , on high buildings, 1883
  Cook--City p100-101
"HIRAM HOUSE" (settlement house),
Cleveland, O., 1896
  Cook--City p237
"HIRED GIRLS" AND "HIRED
MEN." See SERVANTS
HISTORIANS
  See also names of historians
  Boardman--Jackson. p146-148
  Bode--Anatomy p236-249
  Furnas--Americans p551-552
  Harlow--Story p247
  Morris--Ency. p569-570, 578
  Treasury Amer. p397
 -New England
    Our literary p50-53
 , of Boston
    Brooks--Flower. p322-342
HISTORICAL NOVELS. See FIC-
TION, Historical
HISTORY
  Boardman--Gilded p120-121
 -"History and how to write it, "
  by Dixon Wecter
    Treasury Amer. p394-399
 , in textbooks
    Nye--Cultural p159
 , Teaching of
    Randel--Centennial p10-11, 88
 -Writing, 1830-1870
    Mott--Golden p88-97
HITCHCOCK, EDWARD
  Boardman--Jackson. p168
HITCHCOCK, ETHAN ALLEN
  DeVoto--Year. See index p517

HOAR, GEORGE
 Amer. Her.--New (11) p E385
HOBBS, LUCY
 Macksey--Book p148-149
"HOBBYHORSES"
 McClinton--Antiques p156-163
HOBOES. See TRAMPS
HODJIAGE-DE (Indian)
 Marzio--Nation p18
HOE, RICHARD MARCH
 Boardman--Jackson. p102
 Morris--Ency. p583-584
 -Biography
  Morris--Ency. p676
HOFFMAN, CHARLES F.
 -Travel on National Road, 1833
  Angle--American p202-205
 -"Travel on the Old National
 Road," 1835
  Ridge--America's p276-278
HOFSTADTER, RICHARD
 -"The myth of the happy yeoman"
  Treasury Amer. p264-273
HOGE, JANE (MRS. A. H.)
 Dannett--Noble p220, 223, 226, 272,
 330, 334, 390
 Young--Women p21, 152-153, 155,
 225, 264, 309, 311
 -Biography
  Young--Women p373
HOGS
 Bartlett--New p191-192, 210
 Handlin--This p110, 115, 217, 251,
 353
 , and pork
  Furnas--Americans p455-456,
 498
HOLBROOK, AGNES SINCLAIR
 , on Chicago slums
  Cook--City p130-131
HOLBROOK, JOSIAH
 Boardman--Jackson. p139
 Reader's--Story p309
HOLDER, C. F.
 -"Game-fishes of the Florida
 reef"
  Jones--Shaping p303-311
HOLDING COMPANIES
 Keller--Affairs p435-436
 , and anti-trust laws
  Harlow--Story p391-392
HOLIDAYS
 See also names of holidays
 Boardman--Civil p199
 Cable--American p163-164
 Carson--Polite p90
 Dulles--History p162-167, 204
 Partridge--As p22-29, 136-139

HOLLADAY, BEN
 Bartlett--New p303-304
 Brown--Westerners p152, 158, 163,
 166-169
HOLLAND, JOHN PHILIP
 Furnas--Americans p702-703
HOLLAND, JOSIAH GILBERT
 Boardman--Civil p157-158
 Nye--Unembar. p106-107
 Randel--Centennial. See index
 p469
HOLLAND
 -Immigrants
  Handlin--This p300
HOLLAND LAND COMPANY
 -Views of Joseph Ellicott
  Ridge--America's p238-240
HOLLERITH, HERMAN
 Portraits--Americans p67-68
HOLLEY, MARIETTA. See ALLEN,
 SAMANTHA
HOLLI, MELVIN G.
 , on Detroit politics
  Cook--City p194-195
"HOLLOW HORN BEAR" (Bruel
 Dakota-Sioux Indian)
 Andrews--Indian leaders p155
HOLMES, EMMA E.
 , on Confederates taking Fort
 Sumter, 1861
  Angle--American p311-315
HOLMES, MARY JANE
 Bode--Anatomy p177, 179-181
 Mott--Golden p125-126
HOLMES, NATHANIEL
 -"The case for St. Louis," 1875
  Cook--City p43
HOLMES, OLIVER WENDELL
 Amer. Her.--New (11) p E385-386
 Boardman--Jackson. p148
 Brooks--Flower. p343-358; see
 also index p544
 Cable--American p137, 147, 189
 Harlow--Story p244-246
 Keller--Affairs. See index p618
 Life--Reaching (8) p15-17
 Morris--Ency. p542, 568
 Our literary p94-97
 Reader's--Story p294-295
 -"The autocrat of the breakfast
 table"
  Brooks--Flower. p478-498
 -Biography
  Morris--Ency. p676-677
 -Motion pictures
  Wilson--American p295
 -Tribute to Dorothy Quincy Jack-
 son

Hurd--Treasury p114-116
HOLSTEIN, ANNA
  Dannett--Noble p210-211, 257, 291,
  293, 295
  -Biography
    Young--Women p373
"HOLY WILDERNESS" (Black Hills,
S.D.)
  Watkins--Gold p106-119
HOME FURNISHINGS
  See also FURNITURE
  Boardman--Jackson. p172-173
  Bode--Anatomy p51-59
  Furnas--Americans. See index
  p988
  Lyons--Domestic. See index
  (under Furnishings) p301
  Partridge--As p125
  -1825-1860
    Train--Story p269-270
  -1876
    Hilton--Way p18
    Randel--Centennial p129, 309,
    375, 377-380
  -Artistic craze
    Lynes--Domestic. p140
  -"Gingerbread" and bric-a-brac
    Larkin--Art p249-251
  , Oriental
    Ross--Taste p134
  , Post Civil war
    Drury--Midwest p88-89
  , Turkish
    Ross--Taste p136, 141
  , Typical, Chicago 1870's
    Woodward--Way p300-303
  , Victorian
    Amer. Her. --New (11) p948-
    953
    Life--Steel (7) p138, 141
    Ross--Taste p134-135
  -Western mining towns
    Train--Story p307-308
HOME INDUSTRIES. See CRAFTS
AND CRAFTSMANSHIP; SPINNING
AND SPINNING WHEELS; WEAVERS
AND WEAVING; etc.
HOME LIFE. See FAMILIES AND
FAMILY LIFE
HOME MISSIONARY SOCIETY. See
AMERICAN HOME MISSIONARY
SOCIETY
HOMEOPATHY
  Boardman--Jackson. p171
  Furnas--Americans p443-445
HOMER, WINSLOW
  Amer. Her. --New (11) p E386
  Boardman--Civil p160-161

Carman--History (2) p376-378
Furnas--Americans p628, 630-634
Larkin--Art p222-223, 272-277;
  see also index p528
Mumford--Brown p200-203
Reader's--Story p381
-Biography
  Morris--Ency. p677
-Biography and illustrations
  Trachtenberg--Demo. p320-331
-Engravings (reproductions)
  Trachtenberg--Demo. p321-331
-Paintings--"New England sum-
mer"
  Treasury Amer. p386-393
HOMES
  See also HOUSES; types of homes;
  names of famous homes
  Boardman--Jackson. p172-173
  Handlin--This. See index p587
  Larkin--Art p159-164, 167-170
  Schwartz--When p27
  Wilson--Folkways p120-144
  Wilson--Vanish. p80-122
  -Conveniences and furnishings
    Boardman--Virginia p184-185
  , Country, 1876
    Hilton--Way p27-33
  -Equipment
    Wilson--Folkways p126-131
  -Views of Clarence Day, 1879
    Cook--City p119-121
"HOMESPUN" AGE
  Van Wagenen--Golden. See
  index p271-280
HOMESTAKE MINING COMPANY
  Watkins--Gold p13-14, 113, 115-
  119, 264, 274-277
HOMESTEAD ACT, 1862
  Alden--Pioneer p166, 260, 264-265
  Amer. Her. --New (10) p845
  Bartlett--New p78, 113, 214, 241
  Boardman--Civil p95-96
  Boardman--Gilded p85
  Carman--History (2) p207-209
  Commager--Heritage p844
  Dulles--United p35
  Furnas--Americans p253, 695-
  696, 795
  Harlow--Story p369
  Hine--American p110, 144, 160-
  162, 322, 331
  Keyes--Hope p258
  Life--New (5) p90, 92, 121
  Life--Steel (7) p57-58
  200 Years (2) p59
  Reader's--Story p74, 115, 327-328
  Tunis--Frontier p153-154

Whitney--American p151-152
Wilson--American p235
, and "bleeding" Kansas
    Tunis--Frontier p153
, and cattlemen
    Amer. Her. --New (9) p758-
    790
HOMESTEAD STRIKE, 1892
    Collins--Story p269
    Harlow--Story p408-409
    Jones--Age p383-385
    Life--Steel (7) p34, 96
HOMESTEADERS AND HOME-
STEADING
    Bartlett--New p215, 233
    Dulles--United p46-50
    Hine--American p144, 161-162,
    165, 172, 174, 208, 325-326
    Marzio--Nation p158-159
    Walker--Every. p96-103
    Wilson--American p235
    -Cherokee Strip, 1893
        -Views of Seth K. Humphrey
            Angle--American p371-375
    -Kansas (life, 1877)
        Ridge--America's p624-630
    -Life
        Dulles--United p48-50
    -Massacre, 1892
        Morris--Ency. p523
    -"Sod houses"
        White--American p99-103
    , Trickery of
        -Views of Albert Richardson
            Commager--Heritage p844-852
HOMOSEXUALITY
    Cable--American p235-236
HONE, PHILIP
    Amer. Her. --New (5) p E166
    Furnas--Americans p452-453,
    455, 465-466, 490
    , on American life
        Cable--American p97-98, 109-
        111, 291
    , on Harrison's candidacy, 1840
        Commager--Heritage p618-619
    , on Jenny Lind, 1850
        Angle--American p279-281
    , on John Quincy Adams' death
        Commager--Heritage p623-625
    , on New York
        Commager--Heritage p399-410
HONEYBEES. See BEES (Insects)
HOOD, JOHN BELL, GENERAL
    Amer. Her. --New (8) p E279
    Boardman--Civil p56
    Life--Union (6) p13, 86-88, 98,
    106-107

HOOD, THOMAS TRAPS
    , in Civil war, 1864
        Pratt--Civil p60
HOOKER, JOSEPH ("FIGHTING
JOE")
    Amer. Her. --New (8) p E279-280
    Carman--History (1) p663-64,
    666, 669
    Jackson--Civil p84, 106, 114, 118,
    120-121, 133, 135-136, 141, 144,
    154
    Young--Women p212, 220, 234, 272-
    273
HOOKWORM
    Furnas--Americans p335-336
HOOPS (game)
    McClinton--Antiques p204-205
HOOSAC TUNNEL
    Keller--Affairs p166-167
"HOPEDALE COMMUNITY" (Mas-
sachusetts)
    Handlin--This p224-225
    Tyler--Freedom's p166-175
"HOPEWELL VILLAGE" (Birds-
boro, Pa.)
    Vanderbilt--Living p74
HOPI INDIANS
    Amer. Her. --Indians. See index
    p421
    -Village, Arizona, 1876
        Marzio--Nation p14
HOPKINS, JOHNS
    Portraits--Americans p134
HOPKINS, MARK
    Boardman--Civil p143
    Boardman--Gilded p66-67
    Lewis--Big p124-155
HOPKINS, MARY SHERWOOD
    Lewis--Big. See index p.iii
HOPKINS, TIMOTHY
    Lewis--Big. See index p.iii
HOPKINSON, JOSEPH
    Howard--Our p107, 118-119
HOPP, E.O.
    -Views on America, 1870's
        Handlin--This p324-333
HOPPER, DE WOLF
    Blum--Stage Profile 31
HOPS
    Van Wagenen--Golden p80-81
HORN, CHARLES EDWARD
    Howard--Our p156-158
"HORNET" (ship)
    Jones--Shaping p61-62
"HORNSWOGGLERS"
    Wilson--Early p174-175
HORSE RACING
    Boardman--Civil p201

Boardman--Jackson. p158
Boardman--Virginia p187-188
Davidson--Life (2) p34-35
Dulles--History p70, 72-73, 139-
141, 171, 174, 226, 240-241
Hunt--Life p175-181
Life--New (5) p58, 61
Life--Reaching (8) p49
Nye--Cultural p145-146
Partridge--As p157
Viewpoints p118
-1870's
   Randel--Centennial p79-80, 321
-Advertisements
   Dreppard--Pioneer p102-103
-New York city
   Tunis--Young p121
-Race-tracks, law, 1892
   Cook--City p181-182
HORSECARS (Street railroads)
Furnas--Americans p674-675, 801
, First, 1832
   Harlow--Story p424
-1876
   Hilton--Way p163
HORSELESS CARRIAGES
-Patent by George B. Selden
   Wilson--American p321
HORSES
Bartlett--New p194, 247-248
Furnas--Americans. See index
p991
Handlin--This p116-118
, and horsemen
   Brown--Westerners. See
   index p286
-"Belle Meade," home of thor-
oughbreds, Nashville, Tenn.
   Vanderbilt--Living p124-125
, Carriage
   Wilson--Vanish. p31
-Collars
   Wilson--Vanish. p25
, Conestoga
   Langdon--Everyday (2) p75
-Curry combs
   Wilson--Vanish. p26
-Hitching posts
   Wilson--Vanish. p126-127
, in country towns
   Partridge--As p35
, in theater
   Boardman--Jackson. p156
-Livery stables
   Wilson--Vanish. p128
, of plains
   Jones--Shaping p157-167
, Shoeing of

Wilson--Vanish. p26
-Sidesaddles
   Wilson--Vanish. p130
-Troughs
   Wilson--Vanish. p125
, Western
   Tunis--Frontier p147-148
-Whips
   Wilson--Vanish. p27
, Wild (Broncos, or bronchos)
   Train--Story p302-303
, Work (draft)
   Furnas--Americans p302, 344,
   456-457
   Wilson--Vanish. p22-24
HORSESHOE BEND, BATTLE OF,
1814
Life--Growing (3) p105-106
Ridge--America's p270-273
HOSACK, DAVID
Hunt--Life p203, 207, 213
HOSIERY
Van Wagenen--Golden p267
HOSMER, HARRIET
Adelman--Famous p218-219
Macksey--Book p206
HOSPITALS
Hunt--Life p199-200
-Civil war
   Commager--Heritage p683-687
   -Ships, women in
      Young--Women p176-187
, Confederate
   Dowdey--Experiment p303-305
HOSTETTER, DAVID
, and almanac
   Furnas--American p904-906
"HOT DOGS"
Furnas--Americans p391-392
, First sold, Coney Island, N.Y.
   Dulles--United p100
HOTELS
See also INNS AND INNKEEPERS;
TAVERNS
Boardman--Jackson. p165-166
Cable--American p101, 108-109,
221, 236
Carson--Polite p85, 88
Furnas--Americans. See index
p991
Handlin--This p127, 186, 232, 238,
255, 291, 300, 302, 304-305, 319,
346-349, 406
Lynes--Taste. p81-89
Ross--Taste p68-72
Wilson--Folkways p179-181
-1876
   Hilton--Way p140-141

Randel--Centennial. See index
p469
-"Alpine Hotel" (Markleeville, Ca.,
1885)
Nation in motion p78
-"American plan"
Boorstin--Americans p144-145,
147
, as "palaces of the public"
Boorstin--Americans p134-147
-California (1880's)
Johnson--Pictorial p158-159
, Commercial
Wilson--Vanish. p156
-"European plan"
Boorstin--Americans p144-145
-Food and meals
Partridge--As p131
-"Gilded age"
Jones--Age p129-131
-Maryland, c1842
Nation in motion p79-80
-Plumbing
Partridge--As p132
-"Reading rooms"
Boorstin--Americans p140
-Rooms, typical
Woodward--Way p288-290
-Views of Frances Trollope
Trollope--Domestic. See
index p. viii, ix
-West
Hine--American p263
, Women in
Carson--Polite p93
HOTHLEPOYA. See (MENAWA)
(Creek Indian)
HOTZE, HENRY
Dowdey--Experiment p170-171,
210, 213-214, 269, 291, 295-296,
366-367
HOUGH, FRANKLIN B.
Randel--Centennial p274-275, 281
HOUSE OF REPRESENTATIVES
Davidson--Life (2) p328-329
Keyes--Hope p232-233
-1822
Life--Sweep (4) p50-51; see
also index p157
HOUSE ON HENRY STREET. See
HENRY STREET SETTLEMENT
HOUSE RAISING (bees)
Bartlett--New p216-217
Household articles
Dreppard--Pioneer p88
HOUSEKEEPING
See also SERVANTS
Handlin--This p195, 236-237, 274

Hilton--Way p13-33
Lynes--Domestic. p55-64
-1872
Trachtenberg--Demo. p136-148
-Changes
Trachtenberg--Demo. p71-73
-Old Northwest
Tunis--Frontier p79-80
-Women
Lynes--Domestic. p157-158
HOUSES
See also ARCHITECTURE; DUG-
OUTS; LOG CABINS; names of
famous houses; etc.
Dreppard--Pioneer p20-24
Handlin--This. See index p587
Lynes--Domestic. See index
p303
Walker--Every. p14-15, 212
-1825-1860
Train--Story p263-267
-1860-1899
Train--Story p317-320
-1870's
Randel--Centennial p28, 50, 67,
377-378
-1876 (similar)
Hilton--Way p17
, Adobe
Furnas--Americans p370-371
, and yards
Wilson--Folkways p120-125
-Attics
Walker--Every. p25-26
, "Balloon frame"
Bode--Anatomy p39
Boorstin--Americans p148-152
Furnas--Americans p622-623
Life--America's p112
Lynes--Domestic. p99
Marzio--Nation p488-489
Reader's--Story p239
-Bathrooms
Life--America's p80
-Bedrooms
Walker--Every. p24-25, 223-
224
-Cabins
Bartlett--New p182, 184-186,
188
-Cellars
Walker--Every. p16
-Cottages
Cable--American p304
-Middlewest, 1850's
Drury--Midwest p82
-Dining rooms
Walker--Every. p21-22, 220

-Exteriors
  Walker--Every. p14, 75, 211-213
-False fronts
  Reader's--Story p238
-Floor plans
  Walker--Every. p16-26, 75, 213-224
-Gothic revival
  Gowans--Images p307, 309-310
  Larkin--Art p167-170
-Greek revival
  Larkin--Art p159-164
, Hexagonal (Milton, Wisc.)
  Vanderbilt--Living p168
-Kitchens. See KITCHENS
-Large town houses
  Wilson--Vanish. p81
-Living rooms
  Walker--Every. p217-220
-New England, revived
  Gowans--Images p352, 358, 364, 369, 378
, Octagonal
  Life--America's p96
, Old farm
  Wilson--Vanish. p35-37
-Parlors
  Walker--Every. p17-20, 217
-Plan books
  Lynes--Taste. p176-177
-Porches
  Walker--Every. p15-16
-Rooms
  See also HOUSES--names of rooms; KITCHENS
  Wilson--Folkways p120-123
-Row houses
  Furnas--Americans p425-426
  Walker--Every. p209-210
-Shanties
  Lynes--Domestic. p24
-Shingled
  Life--America's p142
-Styles
  See also ARCHITECTURE
  Walker--Every. p15-16, 211-213
-West
  Train--Story p293-295, 306-308
"HOUSES OF ASSIGNATION"
  Cable--American p232
HOUSES OF REFUGE. See REFORM SCHOOLS
HOUSING
  Boardman--Gilded p107-108, 152-153

Boardman--Virginia p184-185
Furnas--Americans. See index p991
Trollope--Domestic. See index p. ix
Wright--Every. p223-225
-Immigrants
  Marzio--Nation p478-479, 488
HOUSTON, SAM
  Alden--Pioneer p236-239
  Billington--Far p127-136, 139-141, 150-151
  Boardman--Jackson. p41-42
  Harlow--Story p266
  Kraus--U.S. p420-421, 451
  Life--New (5) p35, 56, 96
  Life--Sweep (4) p44, 82-84, 86, 92, 98-99, 103, 137
-Battle of San Jacinto
  Commager--Heritage p599-602
-"The battle of San Jacinto, "
  1836
  Ridge--America's p434-436
-Biography
  Amer. Her. --New (7) p E241-242
  Morris--Ency. p677-678
-"General Sam Houston, " by Alexander Hynds
  Jones--Shaping p77-90
-Home (memorial, Huntsville, Texas)
  Vanderbilt--Living p187
-"Sam Houston stands firm, "
  1836
  Ridge--America's p433-434
-Views of Marquis James
  Miers--American p143-148
HOUSTON, TEXAS
  Randel--Centennial p45-47
HOVLAND, CJERT GREGORUSSEN
-"Propaganda for immigrants. "
  An American letter
  Ridge--America's p622-623
HOWE, ELIAS
  Amer. Her. --New (5) p E166-167
  Boardman--Jackson. p101
  Bonte--America p108
  Harlow--Story p208
  Portraits--Americans p22-23
  Wilson--American p132-133
-Biography
  Morris--Ency. p678
HOWE, JULIA WARD
  See also SONGS--Battle hymn of the republic
  Adelman--Famous p174-176
  Amer. Her. --New (8) p E280

Bonte--America p119
Brooks--Flower. p485-487
Heath--Women (4) p12
Howard--Our p259
Young--Women p46, 54, 80, 177,
    300, 311
-Biography
    Young--Women p373-374
HOWE, SAMUEL GRIDLEY
Boardman--Jackson. p137-138
Tyler--Freedom's p296-298
HOWELLS, WILLIAM DEAN
Amer. Her. --New (11) p965, 967,
    970, E386-387
Boardman--Civil p150-151
Boardman--Gilded p125-126
Carman--History (2) p345-347
Dulles--United p114-117
Furnas--Americans. See index
    p992
Morris--Ency. p574
Our literary p158-161
Randel--Centennial. See index
    p470
-Biography
    Morris--Ency. p678-679
-"Letters of an altrurian
    traveller"
    Harris--Land p345-362
-"Mark Twain"
    Jones--Shaping p235-238
, on New England authors,
    1865-1880
    Angle--American p423-427
, on Ohio neighborliness
    Commager--Heritage p275-
    279
, on Third Avenue El, N. Y.
    City, 1890
    Cook--City p52
-"A Sennight of the centennial"
    Trachtenberg--Demo. p84-100
HOWLAND, ELIZA WOOLSEY
Dannett--Noble. See index p415
HOWLAND, JOSEPH
Dannett--Noble p43, 74, 77-78, 81,
    124, 132, 181-183, 196, 354-355,
    360, 375
HOWLAND, MARY WOOLSEY
Dannett--Noble p67, 75-76, 277-
    280, 355
HOXIE, VINNIE REAM
Adelman--Famous p247-248
HOYT, JOHN W.
Randel--Centennial p399-400, 429
HUBBARD, ELBERT GREEN
Amer. Her. --New p E423
HUBBARD, GRAF J. A. VON

-Views on America, 1871
    Handlin--This p297-324
HUDSON RIVER AND VALLEY,
NEW YORK
Treasury Amer. p172-191
-Art and legend
    Treasury Amer. p190-191
-Life
    Treasury Amer. p186-187
, of gentry, patroon and ladies
    Treasury Amer. p180-181,
    189
-"The lordly Hudson," by Carl
Carmer
    Treasury Amer. p173-191
-Mansions
    Treasury Amer. p188
, Steam on
    Treasury Amer. p184-185
HUDSON RIVER SCHOOL. See
PAINTERS AND PAINTINGS--
Hudson River school
HUDSON'S BAY COMPANY
Billington--Far. See index p317
Boorstin--Americans p59
Hine--American p45-46, 48, 57, 89,
    91-93, 288, 319
Life--Sweep (4) p87-88, 91
Ross--Heroines p64
-1840's
    DeVoto--Year p59-61, 226, 360,
    362
, "American threat to," by John
McLoughlin, 1844
    Ridge--America's p495-496
-Canada
    Brown--Westerners p51-52,
    58, 65, 77
-"Fort Nisqually," Tacoma,
Wash.
    Vanderbilt--Living p209
, in the Rockies, 1825
    Ridge--America's p386-389
-"McLoughlin House" (Oregon
City, Ore.)
    Vanderbilt--Living p208
-Oregon--Willamette valley set-
tlement
    Ridge--America's p450-452
-"...Reaction," 1838
    Ridge--America's p450-452
"HUGO REID ADOBE" (California,
1839)
Ross--Taste p12, 115
HUGUENOTS
Handlin--This p300-301
HULL, ISAAC
, on "Constitution" and

"Guerrière," 1812
   Angle--American p182-185
HULL, WILLIAM
   200 Years (1) p187-188
   -"The American invasion of
   Canada," 1812
      Ridge--America's p267-268
   , in War of 1812
      Morris--Ency. p141-142
HULL HOUSE (Chicago, Ill.)
   See also ADDAMS, JANE
   Boardman--Gilded p160-161
   Commager--Heritage p912-915
   Reader's--Story p344
   Warren--Pictorial p148
   -"Twenty years at Hull House,"
   by Jane Addams
      Cook--City p79-81
HULSEMANN, CHEVALIER
   -Letter, 1850
      Morris--Ency. p215
HUMANITARIANISM. See
REFORM
HUMFREVILLE, J. L.
   -"The Indian problem: a mili-
   tary viewpoint," 1899
      Ridge--America's p637-638
HUMOR
   See also CARTOONS; COMIC
   STRIPS
   Boardman--Jackson. p186-187
   Furnas--Americans p391, 729-
   730, 877-878
   Hunt--Life p107-113
   Walker--Every. p171-174
   , Dialect
      Burner--America (1) p270-
      274
      Walker--Every. p172-173
   -Views of Frances Trollope
      Trollope--Domestic. See
      index p. ix
   -West
      Hart--Popular p141-145
HUMORISTS
   See also names of humorists
   Boardman--Jackson. p150
   -"Cracker barrel philosophers"
      Boardman--Gilded p133
HUMPHREY, HEMAN
   -"Domestic education"
      Grimsted--Notions p228-230
HUMPHREY, SETH K.
   , on Cherokee Strip homesteading
   rush, 1893
      Angle--American p371-375
HUMPHREYS, DAVID
   Boardman--Virginia p71

"HUNDRED SLAIN" BATTLE, 1866
   Brown--Westerners p180, 244
HUNGARIANS
   Furnas--Americans p835-836
   -Immigrants
      Handlin--This p368
"HUNKERS" (Democratic party
faction)
   Morris--Ency. p102
HUNT, HARRIET K.
   Tyler--Freedom's p431-432
HUNT, RICHARD MORRIS
   Amer. Her. --New (11) p E387
   Furnas--Americans p771-773
   Lynes--Taste. See index p355
   Randel--Centennial p376-377
   -"Town houses"
      Larkin--Art p247-249
HUNT, WILLIAM M.
   Larkin--Art p266-267; see also
   index p529
HUNT, WILSON PRICE
   Hine--American p47-49
HUNTER, DAVID, GENERAL
   -Rebuke, by Henrietta Lee
      Andrews--Women p200-204
HUNTER, ROBERT MERCER
   Dowdey--Experiment. See index
   p448
HUNTER, WALTER
   Wilson--American p131
HUNTING AND TRAPPING
   See also FUR TRADE
   Amer. Her. --New (6) p514
   Dulles--History p43, 70-71, 148,
   159, 202, 273
   Handlin--This p114, 116, 134, 326,
   361
   Keyes--Hope p247
   Treasury Amer. p160-161
   -1870's
      Randel--Centennial p124-125
   -1876
      Hilton--Way p97-98
   -Beavers
      Downey--Our p231-238
      Tunis--Frontier p113
   , Frontier
      Dulles--History p70-71
   , in Currier and Ives prints
      Life--Reaching (8) p22-23
   -Rocky mountains
      Commager--Heritage p508-516
   -"Trapper's guide"
      Gilbert--Trail. p70-71
   -West, 1820-1845
      Ridge--America's p376-398
HUNTINGTON, COLLIS PORTER

Boardman--Civil p143
Boardman--Gilded p66-67
Brown--Westerners p171, 176-177
Butterfield--Amer. p204
Furnas--Americans p375-376, 781
Hine--American p115-116, 146-
147, 152-155, 167
Lewis--Big p211-282
Life--Steel (7) p30, 129, 131
Randel--Centennial p174-175
Wright--Culture p166-167
HUNTINGTON FAMILY (railroads)
Lewis--Big. See index p. iii
HURD-MEAD, KATE
Macksey--Book p150
"HURDY-GURDIES"
Wilson--Vanish. p150
HUSKING BEES (corn)
Bonte--America p102
Partridge--As p13
Ross--Taste p87
HUSSEY, OBED
Portraits--Americans p27-28
-Reapers
Langdon--Everyday (2) p314-
317, 320-323
HUTCHINSON FAMILY (singers)
Chase--America's p173-176
Howard--Our p173-174
HUXLEY, NELLIE
Randel--Centennial p59-66, 87
HUXLEY, THOMAS HENRY
Randel--Centennial. See index
p470
HYATT, JOHN W.
Boardman--Civil p147
HYDE, HENRY B.
Portraits--Americans p71-72
HYDROGRAPHY
Morris--Ency. p531-532
HYGIENE
See also SANITATION
Alden--Pioneer p162-163
Furnas--Americans p339, 428,
908-910
, Male
Cable--American p238-239
HYMNS
Bartlett--New p354, 356
Furnas--Americans p584-587,
663-665
Lewis--It p123-141
Wright--Culture p186-188
, Folk
Reader's--Story p392-393
HYNDS, ALEXANDER
-"General Sam Houston"
Jones--Shaping p77-90

HYPNOTISM
Cable--American p193

I

I. W. W. (INDUSTRIAL WORKERS
OF THE WORLD; "WOBBLIES")
Harlow--Story p411
"ICARIA" SETTLEMENT (Texas)
Tyler--Freedom's p220-223
ICE INDUSTRY
Boardman--Virginia p72-73
Boorstin--Americans p11-16
Furnas--Americans p692
Tunis--Young p94
White--American p20-21
-Beginning, 1805
Cable--American p94
-Houses
Lynes--Domestic. p123
Wilson--Vanish. p17
-Makers
-Patent model, Gorrie's
Portraits--Americans p125
-Rockland Lake
Portraits--Americans p123
-Shipping, and Frederic Tudor
White--Americans p20-21
-Trade, Oceangoing
Furnas--Americans p309-310
-Wagons
Wilson--Vanish. p142
ICEBOATING
Life--Reaching (8) p27
ICEBOXES
Boorstin--Americans p11
Lynes--Domestic. p122-126
Tunis--Young p110
, Wooden
Wilson--Vanish. p41
ICE-CREAM
Davidson--Life (2) p140-141
Lynes--Domestic. p125
Ross--Taste p56, 58
-Cones
, First, 1896 (N.J.)
Robertson--Book p85
-Freezers
Wilson--Vanish. p102
, First, 1846
Ross--Taste p56
, Making of, 1876
Hilton--Way p23-24
-Sodas
First, 1874 (San Antonio, Tex.)
Furnas--Americans p459
Reader's--Story p125

ICE-SKATING
-1876
  Hilton--Way p98-99
-1880's
  Peck--Nineteenth. n. p.
IDAHO
  Handlin--This p314, 316
  Life--Steel (7) p51-52, 59
  -Population, 1862, 1890
    Watkins--Gold p87, 90
  -"Sporting women"
    Ross--Westward p122-136
IDE, SIMON
  -"The Bear flag revolt," 1880
    Ridge--America's p501-503
IDEALISM
  , Age of
    Carman--History (1) p500-550
  -Power of ideas
    -Views of Daniel Webster
      Hurd--Treasury p51-53
IDLENESS. See LEISURE
ILES, ELIJAH
  , on pioneers, 1821
    Angle--American p207-210
ILIFF, JOHN W.
  , as "cattle king"
    Amer. Her. --New (9) p764-
    765
ILLEGITIMACY
  -Children
    Keller--Affairs p463
ILLINOIS
  Boorstin--Americans p94, 155,
  163, 422
  Carman--History (1) p359, 782
  Furnas--Americans. See index
  p992
  Handlin--This p110, 209, 266,
  354, 365
  Life--Steel (7) p11, 31, 52, 74,
  135-136
  -1876
    Randel--Centennial p36, 106-
    107
  -Frontiersmen, 1817
    Views of Morris Birkbeck
    Davie--Profile p146
  -Galena
    Treasury Amer. p256-257, 261
  , Germans in
    Views of Gustave Koerner
    Angle--American p263-265
  -Nauvoo
    Boorstin--Americans p63-64
    Tunis--Frontier p121-123
    Mormon's exodus
    Ridge--America's p509-512

-New Salem
  Drury--Midwest p94-95
-Prairies
  -English settlers, 1818
    Ridge--America's p280-281
-"Recollections of Lincoln coun-
try, " 1858-1863
  Grimsted--Notions p326-344
-River valley
  -Indians
    Andrews--Indian leaders
    p78
-Rock River
  Andrews--Indian leaders p81
ILLINOIS CENTRAL RAILROAD
  Amer. Her. --New (5) p440-441
  Boardman--Civil p139-140
  , and settlement
    Bartlett--New p240, 325-327
  -Irish and German labor
    Marzio--Nation p186-187
ILLITERACY
  -1840-1860
    Bode--Anatomy p116
ILLNESS. See SICKNESS
ILLUSTRATIONS
  -1863-1877
    Trachtenberg--Demo. p101-108
  -Architecture, from Classic to
  Gothic" (1820-1860)
    Grimsted--Notions p38-44
  -"Carriers to the far frontier"
    200 Years (1) p197-212
  -"The child's world"
    Grimsted--Notions p231-237
  -"Dream and reality"
    Grimsted--Notions p132-138
  -"The face of America"
    Grimsted--Notions p297-303
  -"Golden age"
    Larkin--Art p254-257
  -"Majorities and minorities"
    Grimsted--Notions p99-105
  -"Man in nature," 1820-1860
    Grimsted--Notions p70-75
  -"Play"
    Grimsted--Notions p197-203
  -"Things in the saddle"
    Grimsted--Notions p260-266
IMMIGRANTS AND IMMIGRATION
  See also names of countries and
  nationalities
  Alden--Pioneer p205-207, 252-
  253, 289-290
  Amer. Her. --New (5) p E167
  America's Hist. p530-535
  Boardman--Civil p116-118, 127-
  178, 184-185

Boardman--Gilded p102-106
Boardman--Jackson. p181-183
Cable--American p289-290
Cook--City p65-92
Davidson--Life (2) p150-151,
   404-412
Furnas--Americans. See index
   p992
Handlin--This. See index p587-
   588
Life--Reaching (8) p59-81
Linton--Bicentennial. See index
   p443
Nye--Cultural p121-123
200 Years (2) p75-80
Walker--Every. p131-133, 163,
   173-174, 224-225
-1800-1820
   Morris--Ency. p445
-1820-1860
   Carman--History (1) p509-511
   Weisberger--Amer. p113
-1820-1890
   Davie--Profile p169
-1820-1895
   Cook--City p68
-1820-1899
   Morris--Ency. p446
-1830-1870
   Reader's--Story p319-320
-1854-1899
   Life--Reaching (8) p59-60;
   see also index p173
-1860-1899
   Borden--Portrait (2) p41-42
-1860-1899
   Harlow--Story p412-413
-1865-1870's
   Life--Union (6) p158, 160-161
-1865-1873
   Collins--Story p243
-1870's-1880's
   Dulles--United p95-96
-1876
   Randel--Centennial. See
   index p470
-1880's
   Keyes--Hope p275
-to 1897
   Cook--City p69-71
, and Genetics
   Furnas--Americans p373-374,
   841-842
, as "melting pot"
   Cable--American p306
, as strikebreakers
   Life--Steel (7) p75, 78
-Cities

Life--Reaching (8) p61-63
, Control of
   Amer. Her. --New (10) p887-
   889
-"Cycles"
   Marzio--Nation p372
-Debarkation, typical (1833,
   1840's)
   Weisberger--Amer. p148-149
-Disillusionment
   Weisberger--Amer. p156-157
, in labor market
   Life--Steel (7) p74-76, 81-82
   Marzio--Nation p364
Labor, British
   Marzio--Nation p354
Labor, Irish
   Marzio--Nation p356
-Laws
   Handlin--This p153, 173, 201,
   247-248, 295, 365-366, 384
   Marzio--Nation p300-301
   -1819-1860
      Morris--Ency. p445
-Letters of "settling in"
   Weisberger--Amer. p152-155
-Nationalities
   Cook--City p73
   Life--Reaching (8) p60-64, 66-
   69
-Occupational groups (1850-1891)
   Cook--City p288
, Policies on
   Keller--Affairs p445-447
, Propaganda for (railroad ad-
   vertising)
   Ridge--America's p621-622
, Reasons for (1830's-1850's)
   Boardman--Jackson. p182-183
-Receiving stations
   See also ELLIS ISLAND;
   STATEN ISLAND
   Marzio--Nation p131-135
Settlements--Map, 1850
   Alden--Pioneer p206
-Transportation from N.Y. to
   San Francisco (1840's-1850's)
   Marzio--Nation p120
-Typical "Migration" journey
   Weisberger--Amer. p150-151
-Typical ship voyage (1847-1848)
   Weisberger--Amer. p146-147
, Unrestricted
   Keyes--Hope p274-275
-Views of Carl Wittke
   Miers--American p244-248
-Views of Josiah Strong, 1898
   Cook--City p67

-Views of Julian Ralph
  Cook--City p76
-Westward movement
  See also WEST
  Life--Reaching (8) p60-61
-Women. See WOMEN--
Immigrants
IMMIGRATION RESTRICTION
LEAGUE, 1894
  Life--Reaching (8) p67, 69
  Reader's--Story p330
IMMORALITY. See VICE
IMPERIALISM
  Boardman--Gilded p185-190
  Butterfield--Amer. p287
  Dulles--United p156-177
  Heffner--Doc. p194-204
  Jones--Age p401-402
IMPORTS. See EXPORTS AND
IMPORTS
IMPRESSIONISM (Art)
  Boardman--Gilded p135-137
  Lynes--Taste. p149-150, 155, 158
IMPRESSMENT
  Boardman--Virginia p202-203
-American sailors by British,
1807
  Harlow--Story p172-173
IMPRISONMENT. See PRISONS
AND PRISONERS
INAUGURATIONS. See names of
presidents
INCOME
  , Farm, 1840-1860
    Bode--Anatomy p116
  , Manufacturing, 1840-1860
    Bode--Anatomy p116
  , Range of, 1800
    Boardman--Virginia p184
INCOME TAX
  Harlow--Story p325, 465-466,
  470-471
-1894
    Butterfield--Amer. p268-269
INDEPENDENCE, MISSOURI
  DeVoto--Year p54, 58, 65-66, 83,
  87
-1846
    DeVoto--Year p115-122, 130
-Emigration
    DeVoto--Year p137-148
INDEPENDENCE DAY (Fourth of
July)
  Burner--America (1) p162-164
  Cable--American p142-143
  Partridge--As p22-23
  Randel--Centennial. See index
  (under Fourth of July) p468

Schwartz--When p126-127
Walker--Every. p83
-Celebration
  Hilton--Way p197-199
-1876
    Hilton--Way p198-199
    Trachtenberg--Demo. p66-
    82
-Fireworks, 1860's & 1870's
    Train--Story p319 (facing)
, of wrong date
    Boorstin--Americans p373-
    390
-Deaths of Adams and Jeffer-
son, 1826
    Linton--Bicentennial p94
-Views of Frances Trollope
    Trollope--Domestic p86-87
INDEPENDENT ORDER OF GOOD
TEMPLARS
  Furnas--Americans p508-509
INDEPENDENT TREASURY ACT
  Morris--Ency. p182, 184, 196, 506
"INDEX OF AMERICAN DESIGN"
  Burner--America (1) p127-128
"INDIAN QUEEN." See FRANKLIN
HOUSE
INDIAN REMOVAL ACT, 1830
  Life--Sweep (4) p42, 44
INDIAN TRADE AND INTERCOURSE
ACT OF 1834
  Boardman--Jackson. p68-69
INDIAN TRUST FUND
-Misuse by Russell
    Brown--Westerners p163
INDIANA
  Boorstin--Americans p94, 256
  Carman--History p344, 359, 782
  Furnas--Americans. See index
  p992
  Tunis--Young p135-137
-Indianapolis
    Drury--Midwest p108
-Prophet's Town
    200 Years (1) p183
INDIANS
  See also ALLOTMENT ACT,
  1887; names of tribes and indi-
  viduals; headings beginning with
  Indian
  Bartlett--New p13, 19-37, 101, 121,
  175, 260
  Boardman--Civil p104-110
  Boardman--Gilded p84, 93-97, 100,
  122
  Boardman--Virginia. See index
  p210, under American Indians
  Carman--History (1). See index

p. xiii
Dulles--United p35, 40-43
Harlow--Story. See index p812
Life--Steel (7) p52-53
Life--Sweep (4) p42-45; see also
   index p157
Life--Union (6) p139-140, 143-147
Linton--Bicentennial. See index
   p443
Ross--Heroines. See index p180
Schwartz--When p17-18
Walker--Every. p90-93
-1830-1860
   Billington--Far. See index
   p317
-1840's
   DeVoto--Year. See index
   p517-518
-1860's-1870's
   Sochen--Herstory p191-194
-1876
   Hilton--Way p91-92, 199-200
   Randel--Centennial. See
   index p470
-1890
   Amer. Her.--90's p129
-Agriculture
   Van Wagenen--Golden p87
, and missions
   Tunis--Frontier p125
   200 Years (1) p238
, and "war hawks," 1811
   200 Years (1) p183-184
, and mountain men
   Gilbert--Trail. p55-56, 60-61,
   64, 68-69, 72, 74, 77, 97, 100-
   101, 106, 111
, and naturalists
   Gilbert--Trail. p127
, and Pony Express
   200 Years p209
, and War of 1812
   200 Years (1) p184, 191
-Appearance
   Handlin--This p133-134, 314,
   333
-Artifacts and customs
   Gilbert--Trail. p27, 42-43,
   144-151
-Arts and crafts
   Life--America's p122-123
   Reader's--Story p220-221
-Barrier, 1860-1890
   Ridge--America's p572-591
-Battle of the Washita, 1874
   Ridge--America's p576-579
-California
   Amer. Her.--Indians p304-
      306, 320-321
   Boardman--Jackson. p75
, Eclipse of
   Johnson--Pictorial p120-121
, Canadian
   Amer. Her.--Indians p288-289
-Children (1891)
   Viewpoints p124
-Citizenship
   Life--Steel (7) p53, 59
-Congressional Peace Commis-
   sion of 1867
   Ridge--America's p574-576
-Conversion (Christianizing)
   See also INDIANS, and mis-
   sions
   Hine--American p228
-Cowboy conflict
   Life--Steel (7) p55, 62-63
-Creed (George Catlin)
   Sochen--Herstory p192-193
-Crusade for, by women
   Warren--Pictorial p133
-Dances and dancing
   Amer. Her.--New (6) p506-509
   -Dog dance
      Andrews--Indian leaders
      p103
   -"Ghost dance"
      Amer. Her.--Indians p348,
      370-371
      Amer. Her.--New (9) p799
      Andrews--Indian leaders
      p164
      Hine--American p201-202,
      204, 221
   -Seneca eagle dance
      Andrews--Indian leaders
      p43
, Desert
   Amer. Her.--Indians p322-323
-Drama
   Grimsted--Melodrama p61-62,
   151, 194, 215-218, 227
-Fighters and scouts
   Brown--Westerners p188-202
   Marzio--Nation p330-331
   Wilson--Early p15
-Five Civilized Tribes
   See also following tribes:
   CHEROKEE, CHICKASAW,
   CHOCTAW, CREEK,
   SEMINOLE INDIANS
   Boardman--Jackson. p69-70
   Tunis--Frontier p88
-Formation of territory
   America 200 p38
   Tunis--Frontier p87

-Government policy
  Gilbert--Trail. p24
  Keller--Affairs p153-156, 457-
    461
  Ridge--America's p587-591
  Sochen--Herstory p107-109
  Weisberger--Amer. p224-227
  , after 1887 (Dawes Act)
    Life--Steel (7) p17, 53
  -Humanitarian solution, 1879
    Ridge--America's p585-586
  -Injustices suffered
    Keyes--Hope p277-278
  -Migration
    Amer. Her. --Indians. See
      index (under Migration)
      p422
  -Military viewpoint, by Nelson
    A. Miles, J. L. Humfreyville
    Ridge--America's p583-585,
      637-638
  -Removal
    America 200 p35-37
    Ridge--America's p281-286
  , Treatment of
    Carman--History (2) p180-
      185
    Keyes--Hope p260-261, 263
-Illinois River valleys
  Andrews--Indian leaders p78
-Kansas
  Andrews--Indians p99, 101, 144
-Lands
  , Ceded by (map)
    Brown--Westerners p196
  , Ownership of
    Boorstin--Americans p259-
      264
  -Rights
    Amer. Her. --Indians. See
      index (under land rights)
      p421
  , Taking of
    Life--Steel (7) p17, 52-53, 56
-Laws and ceremonies
  Amer. Her. --New (6) p506
-Leaders
  See also names of Indians
-Life, wandering
  Amer. Her. --New (6) p498-499
-"Little Big Horn" battle
  Amer. Her. --New (9) p784-
    786, 796
  Ridge--America's p579-581
-Massacres
  -Chivington, 1864
    Ridge--America's p572-574
  -Fort Dearborn, 1812

    Angle--American p174-177
-Grattan
    Amer. Her. --New (6) p526-
      527
-Minnesota, 1862
    Amer. Her. --New (9) p778-
      779
    Andrews--Indian leaders
      p95-97
-"Mountain meadows"
    Ridge--America's p524-527
-Oregon missionaries, 1847
    Ross--Westward p46-52
-Waiilatpu, Wash.
    Ross--Heroines p83-89
-Medicine
    Furnas--Americans p338
-"Messiah craze"
    Keyes--Hope p281
-Minnesota
  -Massacres, 1862
    Amer. Her. --New (9) p778-
      779
-Morality
    Ross--Westward p101-103
-Music
    See also SINGERS AND SING-
    ING, Indian
    Howard--Our p613-622
  -Dakotas (Teton Sioux)
    Chase--America's p416-
      422
  -General characteristics
    Chase--America's p406-
      409
  -Iroquois and Chippewas
    Chase--America's p409-
      416
  -Papago
    Chase--America's p427-
      429
  -Pawnee
    Chase--America's p421-
      423
  -Pueblo
    Chase--America's p423-
      427
  , Study of
    Howard--Our p616-617
  -Views of Alice C. Fletcher
    Chase--America's p403-
      429
-Musical instruments
    Howard--Our p621
-Nebraska
    Andrews--Indian leaders. See
      index p176
-Northeast

Andrews--Indian leaders p172
-Northwest
    Amer. Her. --Indians p277-284
    Boardman--Civil p109
    -Artists
        Amer. Her. --Indians p294-
        295
    -Defeat of tribes
        Amer. Her. --Indians p330-
        331
, of Spanish lands
    Andrews--Indian leaders p67
-Ohio valley
    Andrews--Indian leaders p47-
    53
    Andrews--Indians p202, 206
-Oregon
    See also INDIANS--Massacres
      --Oregon missionaries
    Amer. Her. --Indians p327
, Peace with
    See also INDIANS--Treaties
      Amer. Her. --Indians p400
-Plains
    Amer. Her. --Indians p356-
    365; see also index p423
    Amer. Her. --New (6) p497-
    509; E212-213
    Dulles--United p35, 41-43
    Hine--American p127-129, 144,
    149-150, 157, 194, 196, 201,
    204, 285
    200 Years (2) p61-68
    -Amusements
        Amer. Her. --New (6)
        p502-503, 506-509
    -Art
        Amer. Her. --New (6) p504-
        505
    , Clearing of
      Tunis--Frontier p144
    , Southern
      Amer. Her. --Indians p389
      Andrews--Indians p117
    -Toys
      Amer. Her. --New (6) p503
-Population
    Hunt--Life p21
    -1890
      200 Years (2) p67
    -Post Civil-war
      Maurois--Illus. p193
, Prairie
    Amer. Her. --Indians p254-255
-Reservations
    See also names of reservations
    Hine--American p95-96, 111,
    129, 169, 192-194, 196-198, 200-

201, 204, 285, 312
    Life--Steel (7) p52-53, 58
-Scalping. See SCALPING
-Southeast
    Andrews--Indian leaders p55-
    74
    -Lakes and swamps
      Andrews--Indian leaders
      p62-65
-Southwest
    Amer. Her. --New (9) p796-797
    Andrews--Indian leaders
    p116
-Survival
    Handlin--This p138, 217
-Tennessee valley
    Andrews--Indian leaders p85-
    86
-Trade, goods offered
    Gilbert--Trail. p74, 77
-"The tragedy of Indian removal"
    Ridge--America's p283-286
-Treaties
    Amer. Her. --Indians p424
    Boardman--Virginia p113-114
    Reader's--Story p82-85
    Tunis--Frontier p68, 87, 99
    -Treaty of Fort Laramie
      Amer. Her. --New (6) p E219
      Borden--Portrait (2) p48
    -Violation, Georgia
      Life--Sweep (4) p42, 44
    -West
      Hine--America p95, 192-
      193, 198
-Views of Frances Trollope
    Trollope--Domestic. See
      index p. ix
-Views of J. L. Humfreville
    Ridge--America's p637-638
-Views of Norris Griggs
    Andrews--Indians p155-156
-Views of Thomas J. Morgan,
  1891
    Davie--Profile p97-98
-Walla Walla council
    Amer. Her. --Indians p328-329
-Wars
    See also INDIANS--names of
     battles; specific Indian tribes
    Amer. Her. --Indians. See
     index (under Hostilities) p421
    Boardman--Gilded p94-96
    Brown--Westerners p188-202
    Carman--History (2) p177-181
    Handlin--This p115, 300, 313
    Hine--American p141, 194-195,
    201, 204, 207, 213, 216, 296, 301,

311, 315, 319, 324
Life--Steel (7) p52-53
Watkins--Gold p91, 124-217, 235
, Border
   Dulles--United p42-43
-Comic views of Bill Nye
   Burner--America (1) p345-346
-Fort Lyon, Colorado
   Amer. Her. --New (9) p780-781
, Last, with whites
   Amer. Her. --New (9) p777-789
   Maurois--Illus. p193
-Modoc war of 1872-1873
   Johnson--Pictorial p120-121
, Renunciation of
   Harlow--Story p812
-"Wagon Box Battle"
   Amer. Her. --New (9) p782-783
-Washington (state)
   Andrews--Indian leaders p163-164
-Weapons
   Handlin--This p126
-West
   See also INDIANS--California;
   --Northwest; --Oregon;
   --Reservations; --Southwest
   Harlow--Story p371-374
   Hine--American. See index p364
, and Blacks
   Hine--American p195, 206-208
, and law
   Hine--American p182, 192, 196, 201, 311, 314
-Assimilation
   Hine--American p192-201, 220, 257, 314
-Diseases
   Hine--American p94
-Fur trade
   Hine--American p45, 52-58, 191
-Labor
   Hine--American p121-122
-Last stand
   Andrews--Indian leaders p167-169
-Late 19th century
   Borden--Portrait (2) p48-50
-Property and land
   Hine--American p161, 192
-Religion

Hine--American p89, 202, 236
-Slavery
   Hine--American p89
-Women
   Handlin--This p134
   Ross--Westward p93-109
, and corps of discovery
   Gilbert--Trail. p27
, Captives by
   Ross--Westward p103
-"Wounded Knee" battle
   Amer. Her. --Indians p348
   Amer. Her. --New (9) p799
INDIVIDUALISM
   Boardman--Gilded p112-113
   Hine--American. See index p364
-1840-1860
   Morris--Ency. p553
, and frontier
   Carman--History (1) p378-380
, and race
   Hine--American p191, 206
, and religion
   Hine--American p227, 324
, and society
   Hine--American p238, 246, 251, 257, 259, 267
-Definitions and meanings
   Hine--American p169, 296, 321-325
, in arts
   Hine--American p281, 289, 295, 298
, "Rugged, " as myth
   Sochen--Herstory p99-101
-Types
   Hine--American p113, 121, 124, 126, 130-131, 142, 270-272, 282
-Views of P. W. Grayson
   Grimsted--Notions p45-60
INDUSTRIAL REVOLUTION
   Alden--Pioneer p161-163, 203-205
   Amer. Her. --New (5) p E167
   Furnas--Americans p303-305, 836
   Marzio--Nation p197-207
   200 Years (2) p76-85
INDUSTRIAL SCIENCE. See
   INDUSTRIALISM: INVENTIONS
INDUSTRIAL WORKERS OF THE
   WORLD. See I. W. W.
INDUSTRIALISM
   See also INVENTIONS; LABOR;
   RAILROADS; etc.
   Carman--History (2) p55-83
   Hine--American. See index p364
   Sochen--Herstory p92-98
   Wright--Every. p134-135
, and inventions

Jones--Age p157-158
, Development of
  Jones--Age p155-158
-North
  -Views of Arthur C. Cole on
  Daniel Webster and N. indus-
  try
    Miers--American p169-173
, Scope of
  Borden--Portrait (2) p39
-"Takeoff"
  Borden--Portrait (2) p34-35
INDUSTRIALISTS
  See also names of individuals
  Carman--History (1) p492-494
  Life--Steel (7) p36-37
  Reader's--Story p283
, Early
  Life--New (5) p10-11, 13, 16-
  17, 74
-Early careers, lack of educa-
tion
  Randel--Centennial p186
-Personal characteristics
  America's Hist. p523-524
, Role of
  Borden--Portrait (2) p37-38
INDUSTRY
  See also BUSINESS; COMMERCE;
  CRAFTS AND CRAFTSMEN;
  MANUFACTURING; etc.
  Amer. Her. --New (5) p377-389
  Amer. Her. --New (10) p814-843
  Boardman--Civil p5-6, 119-124
  Boardman--Gilded p39-60
  Boardman--Jackson. p77-81
  Boardman--Virginia p68-71
  Handlin--This p105, 111, 126, 153,
  244, 295, 316, 334, 336, 353
  Kraus--U.S. p391-392
  Life--New (5). See index p157
  Life--Sweep (4) p8, 10-12, 138-
  139
  Maurois--Illus. p124-125
  Morris--Ency. p494-498
  Reader's--Story p282
-1825-1860
  Train--Story p285-287
-1850's
  Harlow--Story p289-291
-1860-1899
  Train--Story p337-340
-1865-1899
  Dulles--United p52-68
-1876
  Wilson--American p214-215
-1877-1890
  Life--Steel (7). See index

  p157
, Government aid to
  Carman--History (2) p58-64
-Growth
  Bonte--America p112
  Keyes--Hope p223-224
  Life--Steel (7) p29-37, 128
, Causes of
  Harlow--Story p381-382
-Mergers
  Boardman--Gilded p52
-Monopolies
  Boardman--Gilded p52-53
-National market stimulus
  Carman--History (1) p487-492
-North
  200 Years (1) p223
  -Civil war
    Life--Union (6) p19, 70-71
-Northeast
  Harlow--Story p205-210
, Pioneer
  Van Wagenen--Golden p161-179
-South
  Kraus--U.S. p409-410
-South, post-Civil war
  Life--Union (6) p121, 128-129
-West
  Train--Story p313-316
INEQUALITY. See CLASSES: IN-
TOLERANCE. WOMEN--Equal
rights; etc.
"INFATIGABLE" (ship)
-Voyage, 1844
  Ross--Heroines p129-146
INGALLS, JEREMIAH
  Chase--America's p137-139
INGELOW, JEAN
  Mott--Golden p114
INGERSOLL, CHARLES JARED
  Boardman--Virginia p141
INGERSOLL, EBON CLARK
  -Views of Robert G. Ingersoll
  Hurd--Treasury p126-129
INGERSOLL, ROBERT GREEN
("ROYAL BOB")
  Amer. Her. --New (11) p E387-
  388
  Furnas--Americans p880-881
  Hart--Popular p162-163
  Life--Reaching (8) p10-11, 13-14
  Randel--Centennial p80-82, 218
, on James Blaine's nomination
  Hurd--Treasury p126-129
-Rock drills
  Life--Steel (7) p30
INGHAM, SAMUEL
, and Eaton affair

Phillips--That p58, 75, 84, 89,
91, 95-96, 113, 117, 119-121,
127, 129
INGHAM, MRS. SAMUEL
, and Eaton affair
Phillips--That p59, 62, 74, 84,
96, 98, 108
INGRAHAM, JOSEPH HOLT
Bode--Anatomy p145-148, 256
, on approval of slavery
Commager--Heritage p462-463
, on social classes among slaves
Commager--Heritage p467-470
INMAN, ARTHUR C.
-Letters on South, battles post-
Civil war
Burner--America (1) p335
INNESS, GEORGE
Boardman--Civil p159-160
Boardman--Gilded p135-136
Boardman--Jackson. p152-153
Larkin--Art p212-213, 271-272;
see also index p530
Reader's--Story p376
INNS AND INNKEEPERS
See also HOTELS; TAVERNS;
names of inns
Boardman--Virginia p189-190
Handlin--This p106, 112-113, 118-
119, 157-158
Harlow--Story p195-196
Langdon--Everyday (2) p85-86
-1872
Viewpoints p113
-Old Northwest
Tunis--Frontier p73-74
-"Teamster's stands"
Bartlett--New p293-294
INOCULATION, SMALLPOX. See
SMALLPOX
INSANE
Boorstin--Americans p44
Cable--American p239-240
Hunt--Life p197-199
-1876
Hilton--Way p89
, Care of
Tyler--Freedom's p302-307
-Views of Dorothea Dix
Commager--Heritage p419-
421
200 Years (1) p298-299
INSECTS
Furnas--Americans p785, 908-
909
Gilbert--Trail. p126-127
Trollope--Domestic. See index
p. ix

INSTALLMENT BUYING
-1876
Hilton--Way p24-25
INSTRUMENTS
Dreppard--Pioneer p95-96
INSURANCE
Keller--Affairs p173-174
Nostalgia p28-32
-1870's
Randel--Centennial p175-178
, Life
Boardman--Civil p134-135
Portraits--Americans p69-72
-1895
Nostalgia p31
INTEGRATION
Life--Union (6) p136-137
INTELLECTUAL LIFE
See also BOOKS AND READING;
COLLEGES AND UNIVERSITIES;
CULTURE; DRAMA; EDUCA-
TION; LIBRARIES; LITERA-
TURE; MUSIC, etc.
Boardman--Civil p149-150
Boardman--Jackson. p141-144
Boardman--Virginia p134-136
Hine--American p222, 250-251,
258, 261
Life--New (5) p9-10, 12
Life--Sweep (4) p59-62
"INTERFEROMETER"
, of Albert A. Michelson
Wilson--American p314-315,
318-319
INTERIOR DECORATION. See
FURNITURE; HOUSE FURNISH-
INGS; etc.
INTERMARRIAGE
See also MISCEGENATION
Handlin--This p106-107, 135, 162-
163, 284, 291
INTERNATIONAL COUNCIL OF
WOMEN
Gurko--Ladies p298-299
INTERSTATE COMMERCE ACT,
1887
Collins--Story p262
Dulles--United p66
Harlow--Story p396-397
Keller--Affairs p306, 422, 424-429
Morris--Ency. p258-259
-Breakdown
Dulles--United p66-67
INTERSTATE COMMERCE COM-
MISSION
Butterfield--Amer. p245
Harlow--Story p396-397
Keller--Affairs p312, 422, 425,

429-430
INTOLERANCE
Cable--American p242-243
Furnas--Americans. See index
p993
Life--Sweep (4) p10
, Religious
Furnas--Americans p523-528
Harlow--Story p258
INVENTIONS AND INVENTORS
See also names of inventions,
inventors
Alden--Pioneer p202-203
America's Hist. p550-563
Boardman--Civil p146-148
Boardman--Gilded p57
Boardman--Virginia p79, 82
Bonte--America p104
Cable--American p107-108, 126-
127
Handlin--This p146, 303, 336
Life--America's p94-95, 140-141
Life--Steel (7) p38-49
Life--Sweep (4) p28, 52, 138-139
Mumford--Brown p34-36
Portraits--Americans p20-40
Reader's--Story p257-274
200 Years (2) p96-97
Walker--Ency. p45-73, 105-107,
114, 212, 214
-1807-1818
Morris--Ency. p535-539
-1863-1896
Jones--Age p157-158
-1870's
Randel--Centennial p178-180
-1876
Hilton--Way p24
-1880's-1890's
Life--Steel (7) p29-31
, and gadgets
Boardman--Gilded p180
, "and tinkerers"
Amer. Her. --New (10) p818-
821
-Civil War, naval war
Amer. Her. --New (8) p690-
691
-Patents, number of
Boardman--Jackson. p101
-Post-Civil war
Warren--Pictorial p123
, Uses of
Trachtenberg--Demo. p227-
236
-Women
Macksey--Book p165
INVESTMENTS AND INVESTORS

Hine--American p113-115, 128,
160, 164-165, 199, 253, 258-259,
262, 264, 329, 332
Life--Steel (7). See index p157
-1849-1860
Morris--Ency. p506
-1870's
Randel--Centennial p137-138
-Gambling. See "BUCKET SHOPS"
IOWA
Carman--History (1) p377, 783
-1876
Randel--Centennial p39, 107-
108, 401
-"Fever," 1843, 1855
Ridge--America's p403-405;
452-453
-Land sale, 1850
Ridge--America's p406-407
-Life
-Views of Maria D. ("Grand-
mother") Brown
Commager--Heritage p279-
283
-Mason City
Harris--Land p235-241
-"Migration to the Upper Valley";
the Iowa fever, 1855
Ridge--America's p403-405
-Norwegians, 1863-1865
Angle--American p366-369
-"Squatters"
Tunis--Frontier p100-101
-vs. speculators, 1838, by
Hawkins Taylor
Ridge--America's p407-408
-Wheat
Harris--Land p230-233
Views of Hamlin Garland
Commager--Heritage p864-
872
IOWA TERRITORIAL CONVENTION
-"Demand for land reform pre-
emption," 1837
Ridge--America's p405-406
"IRANISTAN" (Home of Phineas T.
Barnum, near Bridgeport, Conn.)
Viewpoints p148
IRELAND, JOHN, ARCHBISHOP
Weisberger--Amer. p165, 167
IRISH, HAMILTON
-Biography
Morris--Ency. p659
IRISH
See also FENIANS
Alden--Pioneer p206-207
Cable--American p98-99
Davidson--Life (2) p346-347, 349-

350
Furnas--Americans. See index
p993
Handlin--This p121, 138, 208, 210,
233, 237, 256, 258, 264, 298, 326,
368, 381-382, 386, 389, 404
Hine--American p94, 115, 148-
149, 220, 234, 304, 307, 316
Keller--Affairs p540-541
Kraus--U.S. p392, 395-396
Marzio--Nation p121
Partridge--As p105
Reader's--Story p319-321, 326-
327
Weisberger--Amer. See index
p392
-1832
-Views of Charles J. Latrobe
Angle--American p262-263
-Immigrants
Bartlett--New p150-158
Life--Reaching (8) p61-63, 65,
69
, in politics
Marzio--Nation p386-387, 390-
391
Weisberger--Amer. p178-185
, Labor of
Marzio--Nation p356
-Population, in West, 1870
Bartlett--New p151
, Prejudice against
Cable--American p300-301
-Song
Burner--America (1) p312
IRON
See also STEEL; TREDEGAR
IRON WORKS, Richmond, Va.
Boardman--Civil p120-121
Boardman--Jackson. p79-80
Carman--History (1) p489, 704
Carman--History (2) p69-72
Life--New (5) p10, 120, 137, 146-
147
Life--Steel (7) p33, 100, 103-104
Wilson--American p162-163
-1876
Randel--Centennial p167, 181,
371
, in building construction
Boardman--Civil p172-173
-Progress, 1840-1850
Morris--Ency. p495-496
-Pig-iron production
-South, 1880's-1890's
Life--Steel (7) p104
-Progress, 1840-1850
Morris--Ency. p495-496

-Reorganization, 1816-1830
Morris--Ency. p494
-Smelting
Langdon--Everyday (2) p297-
298
-Working conditions, 1861
Sochen--Herstory p97-98
"IRONCLADS." See SHIPS
IRONING
-Flatirons
Wilson--Vanish. p101
"IRONSTONE" (chinaware)
Dreppard--Pioneer p167-168
IRONWORK
, Ornamental
Furnas--Americans p623-624
IROQUOIS INDIANS
See also SULLIVAN, JOHN L.
Andrews--Indian Leaders p13, 28-
30, 45-46
Van Wagenen--Golden p170-171
IROQUOIS TRAIL
Bartlett--New p13-14
IRRIGATION
, of Mormons
Bartlett--New p222, 386
, Western proposals for policies,
1890
Ridge--America's p642-644
IRVING, WASHINGTON
Amer. Her. --New (5) p E167-168
Boardman--Jackson. p144
Boardman--Virginia p188-189
Brooks--Flower. See index
p544
Harlow--Story p243
Hart--Popular p82-84
Morris--Ency. p566
Mott--Golden p70-73
Nye--Cultural p256-257
Our literary p10-11
Reader's--Story p409-410
, and Sir Walter Scott
Our literary p12-15
-Biography
Morris--Ency. p680
, on Burr's trial for treason,
1807
Angle--American p144-146
-Popularity
Bode--Anatomy p202-203
-Views of James Grant Wilson,
1855
Angle--American p275-278
IRWIN, HARRIET
Macksey--Book p166
IRWIN, MAY
Blum--Stage   Profile 22

Macksey--Book p232
ITALIANS
 -Immigrants
   Bartlett--New p162-163
   Handlin--This p303, 368, 402-
   406
   Life--Reaching (8) p60-63, 65,
   68-69
   , Employment of
     Marzio--Nation p362-363
ITALY
 , Controversy with, 1891
   Morris--Ency. p284
ITINERANTS
 See also CLERGYMEN:
   JUDGES: PEDDLERS; etc.
 Wilson--Early p37-51
IVES, JAMES MERRITT. See
 CURRIER & IVES

J

JACKSON, ANDREW ("OLD
HICKORY")
 See also "THE HERMITAGE";
   JACKSONIAN DEMOCRACY
 Alden--Pioneer. See index p. v
 Amer. Her.--New (5) p390-406,
   E168-169
 Bartlett--New. See index p480
 Boardman--Jackson. See index
   p208
 Boardman--Virginia p28-29, 43-
   44
 Bonte--America p101
 Borden--Portrait (1) p61-62
 Butterfield--Amer. p64, 78-85,
   90-93, 114-115
 Davidson--Life (2) p330-331
 Harlow--Story p224-233
 Kane--Gone p183-205
 Keyes--Hope p237-240
 Kraus--U.S. p321, 325, 337,
   342-343, 347-348, 350-351, 353-
   368, 370, 421, 479
 Life--Growing. See index p173
 Life--Sweep (4). See index
   p158
 Maurois--Illus. p118-129
 Reader's--Story p58-59
 Tunis--Young p149-150
 200 Years (1) p214-235, 326-327;
   see also index p348
 , and Calhoun
   Morris--Ency. p169
 , and Eaton affair
   See also JACKSON, ANDREW--

Cabinet
   Phillips--That. See index
   p180
 -"The battle of Horseshoe Bend,"
   1814
   Ridge--America's p270-273
 -Biography
   Alden--Pioneer p182-183
   Morris--Ency. p680-681
   Whitney--American p27-40, 65-
   80
 -Birthplace (Raleigh, N.C.)
   Vanderbilt--Living p126
 -Cabinet
   Amer. Her.--New (5) p394, 396
   Morris--Ency. p167, 170
 -Diplomacy
   Morris--Ency. p170-171
 -Inaugurations
   Commager--Heritage p611-616
   Ross--Taste p247
   Wright--Every. p33-35
   -First inaugural address, 1801
   (text)
     Heffner--Doc. p67
 -Indian policy
   Morris--Ency. p171
 -Maysville road veto
   Morris--Ency. p169
 , on integrity of Union
   Hurd--Treasury p59-61
 , on National Bank, including
   message to Senate, 1832
   Walker--Reform p64-70
 , on state's rights, Union integrity
   Hurd--Treasury p59-61
 , on theory of secession, 1832
   Angel--By p165-180
 -"Our Union...," 1830
   Morris--Ency. p168-169
 -Presidency
   Alden--Pioneer p183-187
   Linton--Bicentennial p97-108,
   189-197
   Reader's--Story p332
 -"Proclamation against nullifica-
   tion," 1832
   Angle--By p183-187
 -Rout of British, New Orleans,
   1815
   Angle--American p188-192
   Commager--Heritage p243-247
 -Society during administration
   Carson--Polite p99, 102-103
 -Veto on National Bank renewal,
   1832
   Heffner--Doc. p87-93
   Walker--Reform p64-70

-Views of Anne Royall, 1829
  Angle--American p210-212
-Views of Arthur Schlesinger,
Jr.
  Miers--American p138-143
-Views of Frances Trollope
  Trollope--Domestic. See
  index p.ix
JACKSON, DOROTHY QUINCY
-Views of Oliver Wendell Holmes
  Head--Treasury p114-116
JACKSON, GEORGE K.
  Howard--Our p133-134
JACKSON, HELEN HUNT ("H.H.,"
pseud.)
  Adelman--Famous p200
  Boardman--Gilded p96-97
  Our literary p174
  Randel--Centennial p354-355
  Warren--Pictorial p133
-"The thrill of Western rail-
  roading," 1878
  Ridge--America's p570-571
JACKSON, PATRICK TRACY
  Boardman--Virginia p69-70
JACKSON, RACHEL DONELSON
  Life--Growing (3) p155
  Melick--Wives p28
  Phillips--That p30, 38-42, 50-52,
  56, 58, 63, 69, 89
JACKSON, THOMAS JONATHAN
("STONEWALL")
  Amer. Her. --New (8) p E280-281
  Boardman--Civil p46-47
  Dowdey--Experiment. See
  index p448
  Harlow--Story p312, 317-319
  Jordan--Civil. See index p213
  Life--Sweep (4) p105-106, 112
  Life--Union (6). See index p174
  Linton--Bicentennial. See index
  p192(facing), 443
  Morris--Ency. p236-237
  , and General Lee
  Pratt--Civil p19, 28-29
  -Biography
  Morris--Ency. p681
  -Death
  Andrews--Women p180-181
  , in Civil war
  Carman--History (1) p656,
  659, 662-664
  -Shrine, Fredericksburg, Va.
  Vanderbilt--Living p105
JACKSON, WILLIAM HENRY
  Gilbert--Trail. p191-192, 196-197,
  220-221, 226
"JACKSONIAN DEMOCRACY"

("JACKSONIANS")
  Alden--Pioneer p168, 183-184
  Amer. Her. --New (5) p390-406
  Boardman--Jackson. p31-32
  Borden--Portrait (1) p162, 148-
  179
  Butterfield--Amer. p81
  Carman--History (1) p421-425,
  514
  Collins--Story p177
  Heffner--Doc. p85-87
  Our literary p102-103
  Tyler--Freedom's p21-22
JACOBI, MARY PUTNAM
  Adelman--Famous p236
JAEGER, GUSTAV
  Furnas--Americans p896-897
JAILS. See PRISONS AND
PRISONERS
JAMES, EDWIN
-"Journey along the Red river,
  1823"
  Ridge--America's p371-373
JAMES, HENRY
  Amer. Her. --New (11) p965, E388
  Boardman--Civil p150-151
  Boardman--Gilded p124, 126-127
  Carman--History (2) p338, 340-
  342
  Dulles--United p117-118
  Morris--Ency. p574
  Our literary p166-170
  Randel--Centennial p349, 356-357
  Reader's--Story p414, 416
-Biography
  Morris--Ency. p681-682
JAMES, JESSE
  Boardman--Civil p203
  Boardman--Gilded p176
  Reader's--Story p173
  , and Frank James
  Hine--American p154-155, 310-
  311
JAMES, MARQUIS
  , on Sam Houston
  Miers--American p143-148
JAMES, REUBEN
  Wright--Every. p51
JAMES, WILLIAM
  Amer. Her. --New (11) p E388-
  389
  Boardman--Gilded p119, 126, 190
  Carman--History (2) p350-352
  Life--Reaching (8) p16-17
JAMES RIVER, VIRGINIA
  , in Civil war
  Dowdey--Experiment. See
  index p448

"JANE" (Indian woman)
Ross--Westward p104, 109
JANIN, LOUIS
Watkins--Gold p114-115, 248
JANSON, ERIC
Tyler--Freedom's p132-137
JAPAN AND JAPANESE
See also PERRY, MATTHEW
GALBRAITH
-West
Hine--American p219-220
JARVES, JAMES JACKSON
Lynes--Taste. p37-38, 48-50,
59-62; see also index p355
Mumford--Brown p185-187
JARVIS, JOHN W.
Larkin--Art p125-127; see also
index p530
JASON LEE MISSION
-Founding, 1834
Ridge--America's p449-450
JAY, WILLIAM
, on arbitration
Tyler--Freedom's p409
JAY COOKE & COMPANY
-Bankruptcy
Butterfield--Amer. p211
JEANES, ANNA T.
Adelman--Famous p211
"JEFF DAVIS" (ship)
-Piracy
Dowdey--Experiment p126
JEFFERSON, JOSEPH
Commager--Heritage p384-388
JEFFERSON, THOMAS
Boardman--Virginia. See
index p214
Butterfield--Amer. p34-35, 80
Carman--History (1). See
index p. xiv
Furnas--Americans. See index
p993
Handlin--This p125-127
Harlow--Story. See index
p812-813
Kane--Gone p149-168
Kraus--U.S. See index p. v
Life--Growing (3) p41, 54-73;
see also index p174
Maurois--Illus. p100-105
Morris--Ency. See index p755
Reader's--Story p55, 58
200 Years (1) p318-319; see
also index p348
Wright--Every. See index p253
, and judiciary
Borden--Portrait (1) p133-139
Reader's--Story p58
, and Republicans
Collins--Story p168
, and West
Gilbert--Trail. See index
p235
, as architect
See also "MONTICELLO"
Nye--Cultural p271-272
Reader's--Story p234-235
Treasury Amer. p135-147
Wright--Every. p225
-Biography
Morris--Ency. p682-683
-Cabinet
Carman--History (1) p316, 787
Life--Growing p58-59
-Ideas
Carman--History (1) p311-315
-Inaugural
Kraus--U.S. p299
-First inaugural address, 1801
Angle--By p154-159
Commager--Heritage p215-
217
Hurd--Treasury p40-42
-Letter of Mrs. Samuel
Harrison Smith
Angle--American p139-
140
-Instructions to Lewis and Clark,
1804
Davie--Profile p140
-Life, in White House
Commager--Heritage p221-226
-Lottery, to pay debts, 1826
Garrison--Lost p80-83
-Meetings with Mandan Indians
Gilbert--Trail. p44
-Memorials
Landmarks--Liberty p50-51,
76-79
, on democracy
Angle--By p152-159
See also "JEFFERSONIAN
DEMOCRACY" and "JEF-
FERSONIANS"
, on education
-Letter to Peter Carr, 1817
Davie--Profile p313-315
, on freedom
Reader's--Story p500
, on politics
Walker--Reform p10-16, 45-53
-Peace policy
Butterfield--Amer. p48-49
-Presidency
Alden--Pioneer p140-153
Carman--History (1) p309-338

Reader's--Story p332
-Program
      Borden--Portrait (1) p132-133
-Society during administration
      Carson--Polite p97
-Views of Edward Everett
      Hurd--Treasury p53-55
-Views of Frances Trollope
      Trollope--Domestic. See
      index p. ix
"JEFFERSONIAN DEMOCRACY"
 AND "JEFFERSONIANS"
      Alden--Pioneer p141-156
      Angle--By p152-154
      Butterfield--Amer. p31-32
      Carman--History (1) p312, 330
      Harlow--Story. See index p813
      Tyler--Freedom's p14-15
JEHOVAH'S WITNESSES
      Reader's--Story p102
"JELL-O"
 , First, 1845
      Reader's--Story p125
JEMISON, MARY
      Boardman--Virginia p121
JENKINS, E. JEFF
 -"The rush for free land," 1880
      Ridge--America's p623-624
JENNEY, WILLIAM LE BARON
      Amer. Her. --New (11) p E389
      Boardman--Gilded p141-142
JENSEN, CARL CHRISTIAN
      Commager--Heritage p905-912
JENSEN, GERARD E.
      "A boyhood in the nineties.
      Reminiscence of Norwich,
      Connecticut"
      Amer. Her. --90's p90-96
JENSEN, OLIVER
 -"Farewell to steam"
      Treasury Amer. p198-215
JERVIS, JOHN B.
      Boardman--Jackson. p97
JESUITS
      Handlin--This p137, 146, 148-
      149, 248
      Hine--American p45, 89, 94, 228
JEWELRY
      Ross--Taste p228-230
 -1840-1880
      Dreppard--Pioneer p80, 83-84
 -1880's
      Peck--Nineteenth n. p.
 , Children's
      McClinton--Antiques p62
 , Indian-Mexican design
      Life--America's p122
JEWETT, SARAH ORNE

Adelman--Famous p239
Amer. Her. --New (11) p E389-390
Morris--Ency. p573
Our literary p175
JEWS
      See also JUDAISM; THEATRE,
      Yiddish; names of individuals
      Bartlett--New p143, 160-162
      Boardman--Civil p186-187
      Cable--American p219, 333, 342
      Davidson--Life (2) p342, 347
      Furnas--Americans. See index
      p993
      Handlin--This p258-260, 270-273,
      319, 349
      Hine--American p235-236
      Holzman--Stormy p133, 222-223
      Life--Reaching (8) p60-62, 65
      Marzio--Nation. See index p660
      Morris--Ency. p552
      Reader's--Story p99-100
      Weisberger--Amer. p164-165
 -1800's, early
      Hunt--Life p123
 -1870's
      Randel--Centennial p99, 444-
      446, 449
 -Immigrants
      -Characteristics & trades
      Marzio--Nation p362
 -Refuge planned
      Boardman--Virginia p147
 , Sephardic (Iberian peninsula)
      Furnas--Americans p392-393,
      705
 -Women
      Handlin--This p270-272
JICARILLA APACHE INDIANS
      Amer. Her. --Indians p376-377,
      398
"JINGOISM"
      Borden--Portrait (2) p68-69
      Hollingsworth--Amer. p27-28, 31-
      33, 50-51
      Whitney--American p196
JOHN BROWN'S RAID. See BROWN,
 JOHN
"JOHN DONKEY" (weekly comic)
      Woodward--Way p261
"JOHNNY APPLESEED." See
 "APPLESEED, JOHNNY"
JOHNS HOPKINS UNIVERSITY
      Randel--Centennial p60, 65, 395,
      402-403
 -Hospital
      Reader's--Story p296
JOHNSON, ANDREW
      Amer. Her. --New (8) p E281-282

Boardman--Civil p77-78, 83, 87
Butterfield--Amer. p185, 187
Carman--History (1). See index
p. xiv
Dulles--United p9-10, 12, 14-18,
20-21, 30
Harlow--Story p328, 337, 339-342,
345
Holzman--Stormy p141, 160-171
Keller--Affairs. See Index p619
Keyes--Hope p255-257
Maurois--Illus. p125, 170, 177-
179, 217
Morris--Ency. p244-249
200 Years (2) p308-309; see also
index p353
, and Congress
Dulles--United p20-21
, and radicals
Angle--By p288-289
Carman--History (2) p25-34
Dulles--United p12
-Views of Howard K. Beale
Miers--American p205-212
, and reconstruction
Borden--Portrait (2) p5-7
-Annual message to Congress,
1866
Angle--By p290-296
-Biography
Whitney--American p149-156
-Cabinet
Carman--History (1) p792
-Impeachment
Borden--Portrait (2) p9-10
Collins--Story p237
Holzman--Stormy p165-171
Keyes--Hope p256-257
Morris--Ency. p248
, and Judge Armor Bingham
Meredith--World p228-230,
232-233
-Regrets of George Julian
Commager--Heritage p824-
827
-Views of William H. Crook
Angle--American p352-357
-Presidency
Reader's--Story p333
JOHNSON, EASTMAN
Amer. Her. --New (12) p E423-
424
Reader's--Story p379
JOHNSON, ELIZA
Melick--Wives p43
JOHNSON, ELLEN
Macksey--Book p113
JOHNSON, GERALD W.

-"Great man eloquent"
Treasury Amer. p192-197
JOHNSON, JOHN
Van Wagenen--Golden p209-210
JOHNSON, RICHARD M.
Amer. Her. --New (5) p E169
Life--Sweep (4) p40
, and Eaton affair
Phillips--That p12, 50, 91, 121-
122
JOHNSTON, ALBERT SIDNEY,
GENERAL
Amer. Her. --New (8) p E282
Boardman--Civil p43-44
Life--Union (6) p13, 35-39
Morris--Ency. p198, 235-236
JOHNSTON, JOSEPH EGGLESTON,
GENERAL
Amer. Her. --New (8) p E282
Boardman--Civil p55-56
Dowdey--Experiment. See index
p448-449
Jordan--Civil. See index p213
Life--Union (6). See index p174
-Biography
Morris--Ency. p683-684
JOHNSTON, WILLIAM G.
-"The first wagon train into
California, " 1849
Davie--Profile p152-155
JOHNSTOWN (PA.) FLOOD, 1889
Boardman--Gilded p178
Collins--Story p264
Keyes--Hope p278-279
Walker--Every. p189-190
JOINERS
Van Wagenen--Golden p112-113
JOINT COMMITTEE OF FIFTEEN,
1865
Morris--Ency. p246-247
JOINT CONGRESSIONAL COMMIT-
TEE ON RECONSTRUCTION, 1866
Boardman--Civil p79-80
JOLLY, JOHN (Cherokee Indian)
Life--Sweep (4) p44
JONES, ANNIE
Brown--Westerners p230
JONES, CASEY
Reader's--Story p173
JONES, J. B.
, on Confederate cabinet
Commager--Heritage p678-680
, on food riots (Richmond, Va.,
Civil war)
Commager--Heritage p703-705
, on scarcity (Richmond, Va.,
Civil war)
Commager--Heritage p705-710

JONES, JOHN S.
  Brown--Westerners p157-158
JONES, JOSEPH STEVENS
  Boardman--Jackson. p158
  Grimsted--Melodrama p145n,
    148-149, 152, 154, 156n, 164-
    165, 199, 258
JONES, MARY CADWALADER
  , on Fort Sumter flag raising
      Commager--Heritage p788-
      791
JONES, MARY HARRIS ("MOTHER
  JONES")
  Marzio--Nation p380
  Neidle--America's p117-123
  Sochen--Herstory p183-184
  Warren--Pictorial p145-146
JONES, SAM
  -"Golden rule," as mayor of
    Toledo, O.
      Commager--Heritage p1004-
      1008
JONES, THOMAS AP CATESBY
  -Biography
      Amer. Her. --New (7) p E242
JONES, WILLIAM R.
  Amer. Her. --New (12) p E424
JOPLIN, SCOTT
  Chase--America's p440-443
JORDAN, LEONIDAS M.
  Jordan--Civil p5, 81, 91-92, 96-
    97, 159-160, 162, 172
"JOSEPH, CHIEF" (Nez Perce
  Indian) (HINMATON-YALAKTIT)
  Amer. Her. --Indians p313-316
  Amer. Her. --New (9) p798-799
  Andrews--Indian leaders p166-
    168, 170-171
  Boardman--Gilded p95
  Davie--Profile p109-110
  Hine--American p91, 96, 197-198
  Reader's--Story p85
  -"The last stand of Chief
    Joseph," by Alvin M. Joseph,
    Jr.
      Treasury Amer. p280-291
  -Visit to President Hayes
      Davie--Profile p110-111
JOSEPHY, ALVIN M., JR.
  -"The last stand of Chief Joseph"
      Treasury Amer. p280-291
JOURNALISM AND JOURNALISTS
  See also MAGAZINES; NEWS-
    PAPERS; names of journalists
  Amer. Her. --New (11) p938-939
  Boardman--Civil p194-195
  Boardman--Jackson. p185-186
  Furnas--Americans p556-558,

    856-861
  Life--Reaching (8) p35-41
  Walker--Every. p128-131, 136,
    156-157, 175-177, 187, 195-196
  -Columnists
      Walker--Every. p195-196
  , Country
      Partridge--As p40
  -Women
      Macksey--Book p190
  , Yellow
      Harris--Land p62-70
      Walker--Every. p168, 188-200
  -"Familiar glimpses of yellow
    journalism," by James Cree-
    land
      Harris--Land p62-72
JOURNALS. See MAGAZINES
JOY, JAMES FREDERICK
  Portraits--Americans p17
"JUBILEES"
  -"Jubilee singers," 1871-1876
      Hilton--Way p164, 166
JUDAH, THEODORE DE HONE
  Johnson--Pictorial p134
  Lewis--It p3-48
JUDAISM
  , Conservative
      Morris--Ency. p553
JUDGES
  Keller--Affairs p358-359, 364-366
  Wilson--Early p30-31
  -"Forty-Niners"
      Amer. Her. --New (6) p478-481
JUDICIARY
  , and Thomas Jefferson
      Reader's--Story p58
  , Federal
      Boardman--Virginia p159-160
JUDICIARY ACT
  Morris--Ency. p131
  -Repeal
      Morris--Ency. p131
JUDSON, ADONIRAM
  Boardman--Virginia p167-168
JUDSON, E. Z. C.
  Boardman--Jackson. p151
JUDSON, JACOB
  , on a soldier's life, 1898
      Angle--American p448-449
JUKEBOXES
  , First, 1889 (San Francisco, Ca.)
      Robertson--Book p90
"JULIA" (Indian woman) (MRS.
  PETER SKENE)
  Ross--Westward p103, 109
JULIAN, GEORGE
  Life--New (5) p56

-Regrets Johnson impeachment
   Commager--Heritage p824-827
JULIEN, LOUIS ANTOINE
   Howard--Our p219-225
JULY 4TH. See INDEPENDENCE
   DAY
JUMEL, ELIZA BOWEN
   -Roger Morris--Jumel mansion
   (N. Y. city)
      Vanderbilt--Living p39
JUNG, C. G.
   Bode--Anatomy p171-172, 176-
   177, 189
JURIES
   , Country
      Partridge--As p39
JUSTICE
   -Views of P. W. Grayson
      Grimsted--Notions p45-60

K

"KACHINAS" (Indian religious
   spirits)
   Amer. Her. --Indians p127, 134-
   135
KAIPOLEQUA (Sauk Indian)
   Andrews--Indian leaders p81
KANE, ELISHA KENT
   Our literary p109
KANE, PAUL
   Hine--American p287-288, 343
KANSAS
   See also KANSAS-NEBRASKA
   ACT
   Brown--Westerners p73, 183,
   195-196, 209, 212, 215, 233
   Carman--History (1) p614-615,
   622-623, 646, 783
   Drury--Midwest p165-168
   Furnas--Americans p683
   Harlow--Story p291-298
   Kraus--U. S. p452-453
   Life--New (5). See index
   p157-158
   Tunis--Frontier p105, 117, 142,
   153-154, 156
   -1855
      Morris--Ency. p218-219
   -1876
      Randel--Centennial p37, 113-
      114
   -Abilene
      Tunis--Frontier p157
   , and James Buchanan
      Treasury Amer. p216-223
   , and slavery

      Gurko--Ladies p197-198
   , and suffrage
      Gurko--Ladies p216-218, 220-
      221, 227, 232
   , as free state
      Kraus--U. S. p468-469
   -Barber Co. looting
      Commager--Heritage p857-860
   , "Bleeding"
      Boardman--Civil p15-16, 18
      Borden--Portrait (1) p220-221
      Morris--Ency. p220-221
      , and "Bully" Brooks
         Butterfield--Amer. p146-147
      , and homesteading
         Tunis--Frontier p153
         -Life on a homestead, 1877
            Ridge--America's p624-
            630
   -"Border ruffians," 1856
      Morris--Ency. p220
   -Ghost towns
      Boorstin--Americans p298
   -Senators
      Lewis--It p149-176
   -Sod houses, 1877
      -Views of Howard Ruede
         Angle--American p369-371
   -Views of T. A. McNeal
      Commager--Heritage p857-860
KANSAS CITY, MISSOURI
   Drury--Midwest p158-160
   Handlin--This p299, 383-389
KANSAS-NEBRASKA ACT, 1854
   Amer. Her. --New (7) p E242-243
   Boardman--Civil p14-15
   Borden--Portrait (1) p219-220
   Carman--History (1) p609, 611-613
   Collins--Story p203
   Drury--Midwest p164-165
   Harlow--Story p291-296
   Hine--American p109
   Kraus--U. S. p450-452, 454, 465,
   472
   Life--New (5) p56-57, 67-68, 71
   Linton--Bicentennial p144-145,
   149-150
   Morris--Ency. p217
   Tunis--Frontier p153
   200 Years (1) p275-276, 340
   Whitney--American p120, 123,
   141-142
KAUSA INDIANS
   DeVoto--Year p138, 145, 152, 154
KEARNEY, DENNIS
   Furnas--Americans p700-701
KEARNY, STEPHEN WATTS
   Boardman--Jackson. p45-46

Brown--Westerners p91-92, 98-99,
106, 109-118, 152
Carman--History (1) p570
DeVoto--Year. See index p518
Gilbert--Trail. p171-172
Hine--American p100, 102-103
Life--Sweep (4) p104, 108-110,
133-134
Morris--Ency. p201-202
-Arrival in California
DeVoto--Year p356-359, 372
-Biography
Amer. Her. --New (7) p E243
-Expedition, 1847
Morris--Ency. p201
"KEARSAGE" AND "ALABAMA"
(ships)
Collins--Story p229
KEELBOATS
Bartlett--New p309-310, 320
Langdon--Everyday (2) p93-94
, on Mohawk
Langdon--Everyday (2) p6-7
-Ride, by Timothy Flint, 1816
Angle--American p193-196
KEELY, JOHN
, and "mystery motor"
White--American p106-110
KEENE, LAURA
Adelman--Famous p186-187
KEIL, WILLIAM
Tyler--Freedom's p125-128
KELAWATSET INDIANS
Gilbert--Trail. p100
KELLEY, FLORENCE
Warren--Pictorial p145
KELLEY, HALL JACKSON
Boardman--Jackson. p51-52
Case--Empire p55, 61, 73
-"Propaganda for Oregon," 1830
Ridge--America's p441-444
KELLEY, OLIVER HUDSON
Harlow--Story p375
KELLOGG, CLARA LOUISE
Adelman--Famous p250
Randel--Centennial p341-342
KELLOGG, JOHN HARVEY
Randel--Centennial p317-318
KELLY, EDMOND
-Good government clubs, New
York City
Cook--City p201
KELLY, FLORENCE
"Sweating systems," Chicago,
1896
Cook--City p252-253
KELLY, JOHN ("HONEST")
Holzman--Stormy p215-216

Weisberger--Amer. p180-181
KELLY, MYRA
Neidle--America's p251-253
KELLY, WILLIAM
Train--Story p285-286
KEMBLE, FRANCES ANNE
("FANNY")
Boardman--Jackson. p157
Chase--America's p232-234, 247,
266, 280
, on slavery
Commager--Heritage p465-467
KENDALL, AMOS
Amer. Her. --New (5) p E169
Life--Sweep (4) p40-41
Morris--Ency. p582
, and Eaton affair
Phillips--That p50, 65-66, 95,
104-105, 109, 116, 120
KENEDY, MIFFLIN
, and King ranch
Hine--American p126
KENLY, JOHN R.
, on Battle of Monterey and
Zachary Taylor, 1846
Angle--American p238-241
KENNEDY, JOHN F.
Our literary p29
KENO
Handlin--This p327-331
KENSETT, (JOHN) FREDERICK
Boardman--Civil p160
Bode--Anatomy p64, 67-68
Reader's--Story p377
KENT, JAMES
Boardman--Virginia p181-182
Morris--Ency. p582
-Biography
Morris--Ency. p684
KENTUCKY
Furnas--Americans. See index
p994
Handlin--This p110-112, 116-117,
119-121, 234
Life--Growing (3) p136-137, 152
Life--Union (6) p16, 19, 35-36, 38,
60-61
, in Civil war
Dowdey--Experiment. See
index p449
-Louisville
Bartlett--New p145-146, 403
Tunis--Frontier p90-91
-Music
Wright--Culture p77-78
-Textbooks. See TEXTBOOKS--
Kentucky
-Views of F.A. Michaux, 1802

Angle--American p153-155
-Views of Frances Trollope
  Trollope--Domestic. See
  index p. x
KENTUCKY MUSICAL SOCIETY
  Boardman--Virginia p149-150
KEOKUK (Sauk and Fox Indian)
  Amer. Her. --Indians p202, 210
  Andrews--Indian leaders p80-81
KETCHUM, RICHARD M.
  -New England summer
    Treasury Amer. p386-393
"KETTLEDRUMS" (receptions)
  Cable--American p215
  Lynes--Domestic. p242-244
KETTLES
  , Lard
    Wilson--Vanish. p55
KEY, FRANCIS SCOTT
  See also SONGS--"Star spangled
  banner"
  Howard--Our p122-124
  Reader's--Story p88
KEY, PHILIP BARTON
  , and Eaton affair
    Phillips--That p155-156, 161
"KICKING BIRD" (Kiowa Indian)
  Andrews--Indian leaders p134
KIER, SAMUEL M.
  Portraits--Americans p4-5
KILDEER MOUNTAIN
  Brown--Westerners p241-242,
  269
KILGORE, CARRIE BURNHAM
  Adelman--Famous p213
KILPATRICK, JUDSON H.
  Lewis--It p47-66
KIMBALL, MARTHA GERTRUDE
  Adelman--Famous p185-186
KINDERGARTEN
  -1876
    Hilton--Way p58-59
KINETOSCOPIC RECORDS
  -1894
    Viewpoints p173
KING, CLARENCE
  Gilbert--Trail. p182, 189, 196-
  197, 200-202, 204-206, 212, 214
KING, RICHARD
  See also KING RANCH
  Boardman--Civil p99-100
KING, RUFUS
  See also MISSOURI COMPRO-
  MISE, and Rufus King
  Boardman--Virginia p23-24
KING, W. S.
  Young--Women p128-130, 135
KING RANCH

, and Mifflin Kenedy
  Hine--American p126
, and Richard King
  Hine--American p126
-Size and purchase price
  Hine--American p98, 126
KINGSBURY, F. T.
  -"The tendency of men to live in
  cities," 1895
    Cook--City p11-13
KIOWA INDIANS
  Amer. Her. --Indians p380-381, 389
  Andrews--Indian leaders p118-
  122, 125, 127, 132, 134, 137-141,
  143, 150, 168
  Boardman--Jackson. p73-74
  Brown--Westerners p82, 195-196,
  201, 204, 207-208
  DeVoto--Indians p54, 245, 260
KIPLING, RUDYARD
  -"Market for votes," 1899
    Cook--City p196-197
  , on Chicago, Ill.
    Cook--City p37-39
  , on Chinese in San Francisco,
  Ca.
    Cook--City p87-89
  -Popularity in America
    Mott--Golden p184-188
KIRBY, MRS. WILLIAM
  Andrews--Women p116-126
KIRKLAND, JOSEPH
  , on Chicago sweatshops, 1891
    Angle--American p399-400
KISH-KAL-WA (Shawnee Indian)
  Andrews--Indian leaders p51
KITCHENS
  Langdon--Everyday (2) p196-201
  Lynes--Domestic. p115-134; see
  also index p303
  Marzio--Nation p493
  Partridge--As p14
  Ross--Taste p124
  Walker--Every. p22-24, 220-221
  -1876
    Hilton--Way p20-23
    Randel--Centennial p315-316
  -Lost arts
    Van Wagenen--Golden p4-5
  -Plans of Catherine Beecher
    Marzio--Nation p493
  -Plans, Beecher's and Stowe's,
  1869
    Portraits--Americans p62
  -Utensils
    Train--Story p329
KITES
  McClinton--Antiques p216-222

KITTREDGE, WALTER
  Krythe--Sampler p150-157
KLIKITAT INDIANS
  Boardman--Virginia p119-120
"KNICKERBOCKER BASEBALL
  CLUB"
  Boardman--Jackson. p178-179
"KNICKERBOCKER CLUB" (Society,
  arts & letters, 1871)
  Ross--Taste p50
"KNICKERBOCKER SCHOOL"
  (literature, 1809-1860)
  Morris--Ency. p566-567
KNIGHT, JOSEPH PHILIP
  Howard--Our p159-160
KNIGHT, MARGARET
  Macksey--Book p165
KNIGHTS OF LABOR
  Amer. Her. --New (10) p828-829
  Boardman--Gilded p75-76
  Bonte--America p140
  Butterfield--Amer. p228
  Carman--History (2) p144-148,
    152, 254
  Dulles--United p76-81, 83, 87
  Furnas--Americans p711, 713-
    714, 828-829
  Harlow--Story p404, 413
  Keller--Affairs p395-397
  Life--Steel (7) p77-78, 80-86
  Morris--Ency. p522
  Reader's--Story p342
  200 Years (2) p86
KNIGHTS OF ST. CRISPIN
  Boardman--Civil p126
KNIGHTS OF THE GOLDEN CIR-
  CLE
  Furnas--Americans p409-410
KNITTING
  Van Wagenen--Golden p267
KNIVES
  Tunis--Frontier p104
  -1880's
    Peck--Nineteenth. n. p.
  -Sharpeners (persons)
    Schwartz--When p54-55
"KNOW NOTHING PARTY"
  Amer. Her. --New (7) p E243
  Boardman--Civil p17-18
  Boardman--Jackson. p184-185
  Cable--American p98, 242
  Carman--History (1) p512-513,
    613, 617
  Furnas--Americans p523-528
  Harlow--Story p258
  Kraus--U. S. p454, 457
  Life--New (5) p8, 71-72
  Morris--Ency. p218

Tyler--Freedom's p389-395
Weisberger--Amer. p168, 173-174
-"Plug Uglies"
  Life--New (5) p72
KNOWLTON, CHARLES
-"The fruits of philosophy"
  Cable--American p226-227
KODAK, EASTMAN
  Wilson--American p268-269
KOERNER, GUSTAV PHILIPP
  Weisberger--Amer. p123-124, 130
  , on Germans in Illinois, 1833
    Angle--American p263-265
  , on Spanish-Americans war, 1898
    Angle--American p436-438
KOREN, ELSE ELISABETH
  Neidle--America's p95-96
KOSSUTH, LOUIS
  Kraus--U. S. p442-443
KOTZEBUE, AUGUST VON
  Grimsted--Melodrama p10-15, 108-
    109, 212, 228, 250, 252, 254, 258
KRIMMEL, JOHN LEWIS
  Amer. Her. --New (5) p E169
KU KLUX KLAN
  See also "FORCE ACTS"
  Amer. Her. --New (8) p E282-283
  Boardman--Civil p82-83
  Bonte--America p133
  Butterfield--Amer. p190-191
  Cable--American p242
  Carman--History (1) p738-739
  Carman--History (2) p39-40
  Collins--Story p236
  Commager--Heritage p821-824
  Dulles--United p26-28
  Handlin--This p340-341
  Harlow--Story p343-344
  Maurois--Illus. p181
  -1870-1871
    Morris--Ency. p250
  -1871
    Angle--American p349-352
  -1876
    Randel--Centennial p194, 229,
      247, 350, 359-360
  -Views of Albion Tourgée
    Commager--Heritage p821-824
KURZ, RUDOLPH FRIEDRICH
  Hine--American p288-289, 291

                        L

LA BONTE, LOUIS
  Case--Empire p29-39
LABOR
  See also CONTRACT LABOR;

NATIONAL LABOR UNION;
STRIKES; etc.
Boardman--Civil p124-128
Boardman--Gilded p73-82
Boardman--Jackson. p84-88
Boardman--Virginia p76-77
Boorstin--Americans. See
 index p506
Carman--History (2) p131-168
Handlin--This. See index p589
Keller--Affairs. See index
 p620
Kraus--U.S. p397-398
Life--Growing (3) p125, 127, 129,
 131, 143
Life--New (5) p12, 15, 72, 120-
 121, 137
Life--Steel (7). See index p158
Nostalgia p66-69
Reader's--Story p338
Tyler--Freedom's p211-216
-1800's, early
 Hunt--Life p98-103
-1868
 Butterfield--Amer. p201
-1876
 Randel--Centennial p470
-Agitation
 Keyes--Hope p225
, and classes
 Borden--Portrait (2) p24-25
 Furnas--Americans p711-714,
 719, 723
, and literature
 Furnas--Americans p717-719,
 725-730
, and management
 Harris--Land p99-132
-British influence
 Marzio--Nation p375
, Child
 Carman--History (1) p494-496
, Domestic
 See also SERVANTS; etc.
 Furnas--Americans p480-483,
 697
, Immigrant
 Carman--History (2) p133-140
 Furnas--Americans. See
 index p994
 Life--Reaching (8). See
 index p174
 Marzio--Nation p352-381
 Weisberger--Amer. p268-269
 -British
 Marzio--Nation p354
 -Irish
 Marzio--Nation p356

, Industrial
 Carman--History (1) p494-496,
 704
-Leaders
 -Women
 Warren--Pictorial p94-95
-Length of day
 -"Eight-hour" day
 Harlow--Story p403-404
 -"Ten-hour" day
 Holzman--Stormy p26-28
 Morris--Ency. p520
-Marx, Karl
 Carman--History (2) p150-151,
 158
-Model towns
 Furnas--Americans p817, 821-
 823
-Organization
 See also LABOR UNIONS
 Borden--Portrait (2) p25-26
 Carman--History (1) p497-499
 Furnas--Americans. See
 index p994
 Life--Steel (7) p73-97
-Parties, 1828-1834
 Morris--Ency. p519
-Physical work
 Sochen--Herstory p116-117
-Pro-labor politics
 Walker--Reform p61-63
-Radicals
 Marzio--Nation p380
, Reaction against
 Butterfield--Amer. p250-251
-Reform
 Furnas--Americans p451-454
 Keller--Affairs p280-281
 200 Years (2) p84
 -1840-1852
 Morris--Ency. p520
-Strikes
 Borden--Portrait (2) p62
 Carman--History (1) p498
 Furnas--Americans. See
 index p994
 200 Years (2) p86-87, 89, 272
-"View of working class," by
 Jonathan Baxter Harrison
 Trachtenberg--Demo. p160-183
-Violence and terrorism
 Furnas--Americans. See
 index p994
 , in Western mines
 Jones--Age p385-386
-West
 Hine--American. See index
 p365

, in towns
  Hine--American p257-260
-Women
-1880-1860
  Sochen--Herstory p89-118
-1890
  Life--Reaching (8) p39
  Carman--History (1) p495-
  496, 524
  Geiko--Ladies p26-29, 148,
  223, 228-229
  Life--Reaching (8) p38-40
  Life--Steel (7) p82, 84-85, 103
  Lynes--Domestic. p43-44, 153-
  154
  Wilson--Folkways p80-82
  Life--Steel (7) p82, 84-85, 103
-Working conditions, 1876
  Hilton--Way p125-126
LABOR DAY
  Walker--Every. p240
LABOR-SAVING DEVICES
-Post Civil-war
  Drury--Midwest p78-80
LABOR UNIONS
  Boardman--Gilded p75-76, 79-81
  Boardman--Jackson. p84-88
  Furnas--Americans. See index
  p1012
  Harlow--Story p402-406; see also
  index p813
  Keyes--Hope p270
  Life--Steel (7). See index (under
  Unions) p160
  Morris--Ency. p518
  Reader's--Story p342-343
-First national
  Boardman--Jackson. p84
-Growth
  Davie--Profile p127
-Membership, 1897
  Davie--Profile p130
, Miners'
  See also WESTERN FEDERA-
  TION OF MINERS
  Watkins--Gold p211-213, 215,
  218
-West
  Hine--American p134-135,
  138, 217-220, 308-310, 313,
  315, 321, 323-324
-Women
  Life--Steel (7) p77, 81, 85
  Sochen--Herstory p183-184
  Warren--Pictorial p94, 113, 143
LACE AND LACE-MAKING
  Earle--Two cent. (2) p559-560
LACROSSE (game)

-1828
  200 Years (1) p307
LADD, WILLIAM
  Amer. Her. --New (6) p E204-205
, and American Peace Society
  Tyler--Freedom's p404-406
LADIES. See WOMEN
LADIES' BOOKS. See BOOKS AND
  READING--Women
LADIES' GUNBOAT ASSOCIATION
  (Georgia, 1862)
  Andrews--Women p296-298
LADIES' HOME JOURNAL
  Carman--History (2) p373-374
  Harlow--Story p430-431
  Lynes--Taste. See index p356
  Walker--Every. p197, 215-217
"LADIES' WAR"
  See also EATON, PEGGY
  O'NEALE TIMBERKAJE
  Phillips--That p61, 95
LA FARGE, JOHN
  Boardman--Gilded p138
  Carman--History (2) p376
  Larkin--Art p296-299; see also
  index p531
  Mumford--Brown p205-208
-Biography
  Morris--Ency. p684-685
LAFAYETTE, MARQUIS DE
  Boardman--Virginia p199
, and Mississippi river accident,
  1825
  White--American p27-34
LA FOLLETTE, ROBERT MARION
, and railroads
  Commager--Heritage p1008-
  1011
-Biography
  Morris--Ency. p685
"LAISSEZ FAIRE" DOCTRINE
  Dulles--United p63-84
  Randel--Centennial. See index
  p470
-Protest against
  Dulles--United p65-66
LAKE, HANDSOME (Indian)
  Boardman--Virginia p120-121
LAKE ERIE BATTLE
  See also PERRY, OLIVER
  HAZARD
  Angle--American p185-188
  Boardman--Virginia p46-47
  Collins--Story p188
  Keyes--Hope p192-193
  Morris--Ency. p145
LAMAR, LUCIUS QUINTUS
  CINCINNATUS

Meredith--World p28-32
Randel--Centennial p243-244, 246, 255, 258
LAMB, MARTHA JOANNA READE
Adelman--Famous p216
LA MOUNTAIN, JOHN
Holzman--Stormy p56-57
LAMPS
See also ELECTRIC LIGHTS; LANTERNS
Dreppard--Pioneer p206-215
Furnas--Americans p419, 671-672
-1880's
  Peck--Nineteenth. n. p.
-Kerosene
  Hilton--Way p13-14
  Wilson--Vanish. p52
-Whale-Oil
  Woodward--Way p253
LANCASTER, JOSEPH
-Schools
  Wright--Culture p103-104
LANCASTER-CUMBERLAND ROAD.
See NATIONAL ROAD
LAND
See also DONATION LAND ACT; GENERAL LAND OFFICE; HOMESTEAD ACT: INDIANS--Lands; SOIL; WEST--Land
Handlin--This. See index p589
Jones--Age p302-303
Keller--Affairs p186-187, 384-394
Life--New (5) p14, 16-17, 121
Life--Steel (7). See index p158
Life--Sweep (4) p11, 14-15, 41-44
-Advertising
  Handlin--This p267, 269
  -1865
    Partridge--As p72
  -1876
    Hilton--Way p160-161
-Burnings (clearings)
  Van Wagenen--Golden p32-33
-Grants
  Furnas--Americans p695, 794
-Influence and culture
  Mumford--Brown p59-60
, Love of
  Partridge--As p1-6
-Open range. See CATTLE--Open range
-Policies
  , and George Perkins Marsh
    America 200 p83
-Promotion, in prairies
  Ridge--America's p300-303
, Public
  Boardman--Civil p95-96, 139-

141
Boardman--Virginia p75-76, 95-97
Life--Growing p153-154
-Laws regarding purchase
  Boardman--Virginia p95-97
-Old Northwest
  Tunis--Frontier p69-70
-Sales
  America 200 p39-43
-Reform
  -Views of George Henry Adams
    Walker--Reform p83-87
-"Rush"
  Boorstin--Americans p72-78
  -"The rush for free land, "
    1871, by E. Jeff Jenkins
    Ridge--America's p623-624
-Speculation
  Bartlett--New p8, 28, 43, 59-60, 62
  Boardman--Virginia p75, 96-97
-"The land system, the problem of speculation, 1867, " by Albert D. Richardson
  Ridge--America's p618-619
-Value, by area
  Hunt--Life p23
-West. See WEST AND WESTWARD MOVEMENT--Land
LAND ACTS
Amer. Her. --New (6) p E205
Carman--History (1) p366
Morris--Ency. p436-438
LAND-GRANT COLLEGES. See COLLEGES AND UNIVERSITIES, Land-grant
LANDLORDS
Trollope--Domestic p24, 37-38
LANDMARKS, HISTORIC
See also names of landmarks, and individuals
Boardman--Gilded p178-179
LANDSCAPE GARDENING
Dreppard--Pioneer p192-193
, Romantic
  Larkin--Art p173-174
LANDSCAPE PAINTING. See PAINTERS AND PAINTING--Landscape
LANE, CHARLES
Tyler--Freedom's p172-175
LANE, HARRIET
Peacock--Famous p161-174
LANE, JAMES H.
Lewis--It p148-176
LANE, JOSEPH
-Biography

Amer. Her. --New (7) p E243-244
LANEY, LUCY
　Sochen--Herstory p206
LANGDELL, CHRISTOPHER COLUMBUS
　Portraits--Americans p20
　-Biography
　　Morris--Ency. p685
LANGFORD, NATHANIEL PITT
　, on Montana vigilantes
　　Commager--Heritage p582-585
LANGLEY, SAMUEL PIERPONT
　Amer. Her. --New (12) p E425
　Garrison--Lost p112-116
　Wilson--American p342-343
LANGUAGES
　Boardman--Virginia p166-167
　Boorstin--Americans p277-289
　Handlin--This p206-207, 209
　-Changes, affectations, malapropisms
　　Carson--Polite p94, 143-144, 146-148, 153, 189
　, Foreign
　　, of immigrants
　　　Marzio--Nation p245
　　-Word-borrowing
　　　Boorstin--Americans p288-289
　-Provincialisms
　　Carson--Polite p188
　, Snobbery in
　　Cable--American p223
LANIER, JAMES F.D.
　-Home (Madison, Ind.)
　　Vanderbilt--Living p154
LANIER, SIDNEY
　Chase--America's p341-345
　Morris--Ency. p576
　Our literary p134-135
　Randel--Centennial p43(facing), 291, 353-354, 390-391
LANTERNS
　Dreppard--Pioneer p208
LARCOM, LUCY
　Adelman--Famous p199-200
　Furnas--Americans p386, 552-553
　Macksey--Book p164
　Sochen--Herstory p94-95
　Warren--Pictorial p93
LARIMER, WILLIAM, GENERAL
　Boorstin--Americans p119-121, 151
LARKIN, OLIVER W.
　, on artists
　　Miers--American p162-166

LARKIN, THOMAS O.
　Amer. Her. --New (6) p E205
　DeVoto--Year p20-21, 41, 55, 71-72, 108, 125, 195, 218-223, 255, 273-276, 455
　Johnson--Pictorial p78-79, 83, 218
LARPENTEUR, CHARLES
　, on fur trade in Rockies, 1833
　　Angle--American p220-223
LASKER, ALBERT
　, on early advertising, 1898
　　Angle--American p386-389
LATHES
　, Stocking
　　Reader's--Story p258
LATIN AMERICA
　Boardman--Virginia p62-65
　Morris--Ency. p161
"LATIN FARMERS" (German scholar-farmers)
　Weisberger--Amer. p123
LATROBE, BENJAMIN HENRY
　Amer. Her. --New (5) p E170
　Boardman--Virginia p159-160
　Larkin--Art p92-94, 96; see also index p531
　Morris--Ency. p602-603
　Nye--Cultural p272-273
　Ross--Taste p10, 13, 18, 126
　-Biography
　　Morris--Ency. p686
LATROBE, CHARLES J.
　, on Irish, 1832
　　Angle--American p262-263
　-Trip on steamboat, 1832
　　Angle--American p199-202
LATTER-DAY SAINTS. See MORMONS
LAUNDRY. See WASHING MACHINES
LAVIN, ELIZA M.
　-"Good manners"
　　Harris--Land p216-219
LAW, ANDREW
　, and musical pirates
　　Lowens--Music p85-88
LAW, GEORGE
　Meredith--World p56-59
LAW AND LAWYERS
　See also special subjects, e.g. JUDGES; VIGILANTISM; etc.
　Boardman--Virginia p181-182
　Boorstin--Americans. See index p507
　Handlin--This p118, 134, 148-150, 169-170, 176, 204, 235, 248, 276, 367, 390
　Keller--Affairs. See index p620

Randel--Centennial. See index
p470
Walker--Every. p114-115
Wilson--Early p108
-California
    Jones--Shaping p104
-Codification
    Keller--Affairs p347-348, 419
, Country
    Partridge--As p38-39
-Enforcement
    Furnas--Americans p377-378,
    699
    -Views of Frances Trollope
        Trollope--Domestic. See
        index p. x
-Kentucky
    Wright--Culture p67
-Views of Joseph Hodges Choate
    Hurd--Treasury p109-110
-Views of P.W. Grayson
    Grimsted--Notions p45-60
-West
    Hine--American. See index
    p365
-Women lawyers
    Macksey--Book p124-126
-Women's equality
    Life--Sweep (4) p64-65
LAW SCHOOLS
Boorstin--Americans p37-38
Hunt--Life p130-131
LAWN TENNIS. See TENNIS,
Lawn
LAWRENCE, JAMES
Treasury Amer. p168
LAZARUS, EMMA
Adelman--Famous p226-227
Dolin--Great p132-143
-Poem on Statue of Liberty
    Cook--City p65
    Life--Reaching (8) p61
LEA, ISAAC
Boardman--Jackson. p168-169
LEAD MINES AND MINING
Carman--History (1) p374-375
Tunis--Young p141
LEADVILLE, COLORADO
-Healy House, and Dexter cabin
    Vanderbilt--Living p193
-Life
    Watkins--Gold p94-98, 233-234,
    251-252
-Silver mining
    Collins--Story p280
LEAGUE OF INTERNATIONAL
BROTHERHOOD
Tyler--Freedom's p421-423

LEAGUE OF NATIONS, PROPOSED
(1826)
-First, as proposed by Simon
    Bolivar, 1826
    Harlow--Story p223
LEARNING. See COLLEGES AND
UNIVERSITIES; EDUCATION;
SCHOOLS; etc.
LEASE, MARY ELLEN
Butterfield--Amer. p259
Dulles--United p146
Life--Reaching (8) p109
Warren--Pictorial p139-141
LEATHER
See also SHOEMAKERS; TANNERS
AND TANNING
Van Wagenen--Golden p182, 185-
191, 201
LEAVITT, MARY
Macksey--Book p81, 276
LECLERCQ, JULES
Randel--Centennial p49-57, 337
LECOMPTON CONSTITUTION (of
"Free Soilers," 1857)
Harlow--Story p296
Morris--Ency. p222-224
LECTURES
Cable--American p153-154
Furnas--Americans p490, 560-561,
881
, Popular
    Dulles--History p92-95, 257-
    260
LEE, ("MOTHER") ANN
Boardman--Jackson. p126-127
LEE, HENRIETTA
-Rebuke to General Hunter
    Andrews--Women p200-204
LEE, JASON (DANIEL), REV.
Case--Empire p60-69, 71-83
Tunis--Frontier p114-115
, and J.H. Frost--"Founding the
Jason Lee Mission," 1834
    Ridge--America's p449-450
LEE, JOHN D.
-"The mountain meadows massa-
cre," 1877
    Ridge--America's p524-527
LEE, ROBERT EDWARD, GENERAL
See also "STRATFORD" (birth-
place)
Amer. Her.--New (8) p666, 671,
678, 680-684, E283-284
Andrews--Women. See index
p461
Boardman--Civil p40; see also
index p213
Butterfield--Amer. p178-179

Carman--History (1); see index
p. xv
Dannett--Noble. See index p416
Dowdey--Experiment. See index
p449
Harlow--Story. See index p813
Jordan--Civil. See index p213
Kraus--U.S. p432, 475, 489, 495,
506, 510, 512-513
Life--Union (6) p174-175
Linton--Bicentennial. See index
p443
Maurois--Illus. p148-162, 156-
157, 172-173, 177
Meredith--World p179
Morris--Ency. See index p757
Reader's--Story. See index p515
200 Years (2). See index p353
Viewpoints p83
Young--Women. See index p387
, and Stonewall Jackson
Pratt--Civil p19, 28-29
-Biography
Morris--Ency. p686-687
-Chapel, Lexington, Va.
Vanderbilt--Living p112
-Character and description
Dowdey--Experiment p29, 284-
285, 298, 378-379
Jordan--Civil p151, 184, 196
-Contrast with Grant
-Views of Bruce Catton
Miers--American p202-205
-Death
Jordan--Civil p210
-"Farewell to the Army of
Northern Virginia," 1865
Angle--By p275
, in Mexican war
Life--Sweep (4) p106
-Invasion of Pennsylvania
Commager--Heritage p756-758
-Last battles, 1865
Commager--Heritage p778-782
Pratt--Civil p61-62
-Letters
Commager--Heritage p795-796
, from Ulysses S. Grant
Commager--Heritage p783-
788
, to Jefferson Davis, 1865
Davie--Profile p286
-Surrender at Appomattox Court
House, 1865
Collins--Story p226
Commager--Heritage p782-788
Pratt--Civil p62
-Views of Armistead L. Long

Angle--American p336-338
-Tribute by Jefferson Davis
Jordan--Civil p210
LEE, MRS. ROBERT EDWARD
Dowdey--Experiment p35, 195,
238, 319
LEECHES
, Bleeding by, 1876
Hilton--Way p79, 81
"LEFT HAND" (Indian). See
"NAWAT" (Arapahoe Indian)
LEGAL TENDER ACT OF 1862
Boardman--Civil p130-131
Holzman--Stormy p190
LEGARE, HUGH LEGARE
Boardman--Virginia p205
LEGENDS
Hilton--Way p42-43
LE GRAND, JULIA
-Diary and philosophy
Andrews--Women p356-357
LEIDY, JOSEPH
Boardman--Civil p177
LEISURE
See also names of leisure-time
pursuits
Dulles--History p85-86, 203-204,
209
, and prestige
Furnas--Americans p486-488
-Late 19th century
Borden--Portrait (2) p59-63
LEITER, MARY VICTORIA, LADY
CURZON
Peacock--Famous p264-287
L'ENFANT, PIERRE CHARLES
Harlow--Story p250
LENG, JOHN
Randel--Centennial. See index
p470
LENOX, EDWARD H.
-"Propaganda for Oregon":
Peter H. Burnett
Ridge--America's p453-454
LESLIE, MRS. FRANK
Adelman--Famous p247
LESLIE'S ILLUSTRATED NEWS-
PAPER
Walker--Every. p176, 178
LESUEUR, CHARLES
Amer. Her.--New (6) p E205
LETTERMAN, JONATHAN, DR.
Young--Women p186, 188, 214-215,
220-221, 252, 272
LETTERS AND LETTER-WRITING
See also DIARISTS; names of
letter-writers
Wilson--Folkways p185-187

-Etiquette
  Carson--Polite p175
  -Views of Clifton Furness
    Burner--America (1) p244-
    249
LEUTZ, EMANUEL
  Bode--Anatomy p75-77
LEWIS, DIO
  Furnas--Americans p450, 538,
  638-639
LEWIS, ESTELLE ANNE BLANCHE
  Adelman--Famous p181-182
LEWIS, IDAWALLEY ("IDA")
  Dolin--Great p92-97
  Macksey--Book p244-245
LEWIS, JOHN
  Randel--Centennial p2, 66-73,
  286-287, 289, 295, 297-298
LEWIS, MERIWETHER
  See also LEWIS & CLARK
    EXPEDITION
  Boardman--Virginia p98-101
  Brown--Westerners p38-50, 55,
  60, 68, 70, 73, 79, 87, 124, 195
  Butterfield--Amer. p41
  Gilbert--Trail. See index p235
  Life--Growing p69, 79-82, 85-86,
  88-89
  Maurois--Illus. p102, 105
  -Biography
    Morris--Ency. p687-688
  -"The gates of the Rocky moun-
  tains," 1805
    Davie--Profile p142
  , on two escapes, 1805
    Angle--American p160-163
LEWIS, WILLIAM B.
  Amer. Her. --New (5) p E170
  , and Eaton affair
    Phillips--That. See index
    p181
LEWIS & CLARK EXPEDITION
  Amer. Her. --Indians p252, 254,
  284, 308-310, 339
  Amer. Her. --New (6) p511-513,
  E205-206
  Bartlett--New p3, 49, 55, 85, 129,
  253-254, 343
  Boardman--Virginia p98-101,
  118-119
  Brown--Westerners p38-51
  Carman--History (1) p324, 326,
  369
  Davie--Profile p140-143
  Harlow--Story p169-176
  Hine--American. See index
  p365
  Kraus--U.S. p411-412

Life--Growing (3) p68-69, 79-83,
  86, 88-90
Morris--Ency. p133, 421
Nye--Cultural p92-93
Reader's--Story p72-73, 163
Ridge--America's p357-364
Ross--Heroines p34-51
200 Years (1) p174, 300-301
Warren--Pictorial p65, 67
Wilson--American p40-43
-"The expedition crosses the
  Divide," 1805
  Ridge--America's p359-361
-Instructions, by Thomas Jeffer-
son
  Davie--Profile p140
-"Lewis and Clark reach the
  Rocky Mountains," 1805
  Ridge--America's p357-359
-"Meeting with Shoshoni Indians,"
  1805
  Ridge--America's p361-363
-Pacific Ocean reached, 1805
  Ridge--America's p363-364
  -Views of William Clark
    Angle--American p163-164
-"The problems of river travel,"
  1805
  Ridge--America's p359
-Trail followed
  America's Hist. p349-357
  -Map of routes
    Gilbert--Trail. p35-36
LEXINGTON, KENTUCKY
  Boardman--Virginia p198
  Wright--Culture. p64; see also
    index p267
LHEVINNE, ROSINA, MME.
  Neidle--America's p240-241
LIBERAL REPUBLICAN PARTY
  Boardman--Civil p89-90
  Carman--History (2) p44-45, 229
  Harlow--Story p348
"THE LIBERATOR" (newspaper)
  Harlow--Story p256
  -First issue, 1831
    Heffner--Doc. p106-108
LIBERIA
  See also AMERICAN COLINIZA-
    TION SOCIETY
  Boardman--Virginia p131-132
  Hunt--Life p237-238
  Tyler--Freedom's p476-481
LIBERTY
  See also FREEDOM OF THE
    PRESS; etc.
  -1854
    Angle--By p191-198

-"Personal liberty laws," of
  Northern states
    Life--New (5) p34, 37
-Views of Alexis de Toqueville
    Reader's--Story p500
-Views of Frances Trollope
    Trollope--Domestic. See
      index p. vii
-Views of Henry Ward Beecher
    Hurd--Treasury p96-98
LIBERTY BELL
  Landmarks--Liberty p44-45
  -Legend of "pealing" date
    Boorstin--Americans p380-382
"LIBERTY LINE." See UNDER-
  GROUND RAILROAD
LIBERTY PARTY
  See also FREE SOIL PARTY
  Amer. Her. --New (6) p493,
    E206-207
  Boardman--Jackson. p117
  Carman--History (1) p596-597,
    601
  Kraus--U. S. p435, 447
  Morris--Ency. p182
LIBRARIES
  See also AMERICAN LIBRARY
    ASSOCIATION
  Handlin--This p145, 231
  Hart--Popular p183
  Morris--Ency. p578-579
  -1800's, late
    Harlow--Story p429
  -1800-1860
    Morris--Ency. p571
  -1859
    Tyler--Freedom's p161
  -1876
    Hilton--Way p41, 69-70
    Randel--Centennial p425-429
  , "Coonskin"
    Wright--Culture p117-118
  , Freedom
    Tyler--Freedom's p160
  -Gifts of Andrew Carnegie
    Davie--Profile p259
    Dulles--United p105
  , Home (rooms)
    Lynes--Domestic. p238-240
  -Mechanics and apprentices
    Hart--Popular p67
  , Private
    Brooks--Flower. p119-120
  , Subscription
    Wright--Culture p117-119
LIBRARY JOURNAL
  Randel--Centennial p425-427
LICK, JAMES

-Observatory
    Reader's--Story p310
    Wilson--American p277
"LICKLADLES" (flatterers)
  Wilson--Early p182-183
LIDE, ELI H.
  -"A South Carolina planter moves
    Westward," 1836
    Ridge--America's p297-298
"LIFE-CARS"
  Wilson--American p161
LIFE INSURANCE. See INSUR-
  ANCE, LIFE
LIGHT AND LIGHTING
  See also CANDLES AND CANDLE-
    MAKERS; EDISON, THOMAS A.;
    LAMPS; LANTERNS
  Furnas--Americans p429, 671-
    672, 805-806
  Langdon--Everyday (2) p226-231
  Partridge--As p83, 116
  Wilson--American p290-294
  Wilson--Folkways p132-135
  -1876
    Randel--Centennial p30, 182-
      183
  , Gas
    Davidson--Life (2) p162-163
    Lynes--Domestic. p260
  , Incandescent
    Life--Steel (7) p38-41
    Lynes--Domestic. p260-263
    Nostalgia p24-27
  , Speed of
    Morris--Ency. p533
    Wilson--American p313
LIGHTHOUSES
  -1876
    Hilton--Way p143-144
  -Alabama, 1872
    Nation in motion p22
  -California, 1855, 1856, 1874
    Nation in motion p24
  -Connecticut, 1801
    Nation in motion p24
  -Delaware, 1858
    Nation in motion p24
  -Florida, 1852, 1872
    Nation in motion p24-25
  -Hawaii, 1899
    Nation in motion p25
  -Illinois, c1860
    Nation in motion p25
  -Louisiana, 1881, 1890
    Nation in motion p25-26
  -Maine, 1830, 1854, 1858, 1869
    Nation in motion p26
  -Massachusetts, 1800, 1816, 1849,

1860
   Nation in motion p27
-Michigan 1861, 1874
   Nation in motion p27-28
-New York, 1883
   Nation in motion p28
-North Carolina, 1872
   Nation in motion p28
-Rhode Island, 1816, 1856, 1858,
   1862, 1868, 1869, 1871, 1875
   Nation in motion p29-30
-South Carolina, 1858
   Nation in motion p30
-Texas, 1897
   Nation in motion p30
-Virginia, 1881, 1895
   Nation in motion p30
-Washington, 1857
   Nation in motion p31
LILIUOKALANI, QUEEN OF
HAWAII
   Amer. Her. --New (12) p E425-
   426
   Butterfield--Amer. p276
   Carman--History (2) p283-284
   Life--Reaching (8) p128-129
LIME BURNING
   Van Wagenen--Gold p210-212
LINCOLN, ABRAHAM
   See also CIVIL WAR; EMAN-
   CIPATION PROCLAMATION;
   RECONSTRUCTION
   Alden--Pioneer. See index
   p. vi
   Amer. Her. --New (7) p608-619
   Amer. Her. --New (8) p655-665,
   E284-285
   Boardman--Civil. See index
   p213
   Bonte--America p118
   Butterfield--Amer. p152, 158-
   159, 162-163, 172-173, 176-177,
   181
   Carman--History (1). See index
   p. xv
   Dannett--Noble. See index p416
   Davie--Profile. See index p412
   DeVoto--Year. See index p519
   Dowdey--Experiment. See index
   p449
   Drury--Midwest p92-100
   Furnas--Americans. See index
   p995
   Harlow--Story. See index p813-
   814
   Holzman--Stormy. See index
   p276

Jordan--Civil. See index p213
Keller--Affairs. See index
   p620-621
Kraus--U.S. See index p. v. 1
Life--New (5). See index p158
Life--Union (6). See index p174
Maurois--Illus. See index p295
Meredith--World. p50, 80-83, 92,
   146-147, 151
Morris--Ency. See index p757
Portraits--Americans p15
Reader's--Story. See index
   p515
200 Years (2) p306-307; see also
   index p353
Young--Women. See index p387
-Acceptance speech, 1858
   Hurd--Treasury p73-77
-Achievements
   Amer. Her. --New (8) p660-661
, and Illinois Central Railroad
   Portraits--Americans p16
, and militia
   Davie--Profile p274-275
, and negroes
   Country--Lincoln p30-41
, and Ninian W. Edwards
   Randall--Mary p65, 67, 85
, and Polk
   Butterfield--Amer. p117
, and "Trent affair"
   White--American p46-49
, and Walt Whitman
   Our literary p118-119
, as a father
   Randall--Mary p117-119, 306-
   307
-Assassination
   Amer. Her. --New (8) p662-663
   Bonte--America p130
   Butterfield--Amer. p180
   Collins--Story p232
   Keyes--Hope p254-255
   Morris--Ency. p245
   Reader's--Story p156
   200 Years (2) p52-53
-"The story of ... and the pur-
suit of the assassins"
   Jones--Shaping p190-205
   -Views of Gideon Wells
      Angle--American p338-342
      Commager--Heritage p668-
      672
-Biography
   Amer. Her. --New (7) p E244
   America's Hist. p468-479
   Morris--Ency. p688

Whitney--American p133-147
-Birthplace
   Landmarks--Liberty p8-9
   -Abraham Lincoln National
   Park (Hodgenville, Ky.)
   Vanderbilt--Living p115
-Burial place, controversy over
   Randall--Mary p421
-Cabinet
   Carman--History (1) p692-695,
   791-792
   -Views of Samuel Portland
   Chase
      Commager--Heritage p661-
      664
   -Views of Thurlow Weed
      Commager--Heritage p647-
      650
-Chronology
   Country--Lincoln p94
-Cooper Union speech
   Morris--Ency. p226
-Courtship of Mary Owens
   Randall--Mary p22-25
-Early years, 1832-1848
   Country--Lincoln p10-23
-Everett letter and reply
   Davie--Profile p280
-Funeral train
   Garrison--Lost p126-140
-"Gettysburg address," 1863
   Angle--By p269
   Commager--Heritage p764-
   765
   Hurd--Treasury p92-93
   Meredith--World p177-183
-Home (Springfield, Ill.)
   Randall--Mary p102-222
   Vanderbilt--Living p163
, in cartoons
   Amer. Her. --New (8) p658-
   659
, in Washington
   Amer. Her. --New (8) p657
-Inaugurations
   Angle--By p213-214
   Collins--Story p209
   -First inaugural address,
   1861
      Angle--By p215-224
      Commager--Heritage p645-
      647
      Heffner--Doc. p136-143
      Morris--Ency. p229
      Randall--Mary p231-233
   -Second inaugural address,
   1865
      Angle--By p271-273

Commager--Heritage p666-
668
Davie--Profile p286, 288
Heffner--Doc. p153-154
Hurd--Treasury p94-96
Morris--Ency. p245
-Legitimacy questioned
   Randall--Mary p463-465
-Letter to Mrs. Bixby
   Commager--Heritage p666
-"Lincoln Village," New Salem
State Park (near Petersburg,
Ill.)
   Vanderbilt--Living p162-163
-Love of Shakespeare and theatre
   Randall--Mary p45
-"A Man for the ages"
   Country--Lincoln p86-89
-Memorial
   Landmarks--Liberty p52-55
-"Message to Congress," 1861
   Angle--By p238-251
-Military leadership
   Borden--Portrait (1) p232-233
-Nomination, 1860
   Jones--Shaping p168-175
   -Views of Murat Halstead
      Angle--American p301-307
      Commager--Heritage p637-
      642
, on land and property
   America 200 p55-56
   Reader's--Story p504-505
, on Mexican war
   DeVoto--Year p519
-Pardon of a sentinel
   -Views of L. E. Chittenden
      Commager--Heritage p653-
      659
-"Peoria speech"
   Morris--Ency. p218
-Personal and private life
   Country--Lincoln p75-85
-Pioneer Village (Rockport, Ind.)
   Vanderbilt--Living p154
-Presidency
   Borden--Portrait (1) p233-234
   Collins--Story p231
   Country--Lincoln p58-74
   Langdon--Everyday p362
   Linton--Bicentennial p158-188;
   see also index p443
   Reader's--Story p333
   , and Union
      Angle--By p237-238
      Country--Lincoln p50-57
-"A Reception by," by C. Van
Santvoord

Jones--Shaping p176-178
-Reconstruction program
　Dulles--United p7-8
-Religion
　Randall--Mary p163-164, 318,
　463
-Reply to Greeley's letter, 1862
　Davie--Profile p277
-Society during presidency
　Carson--Polite p103-104
-Tributes
　Country--Lincoln p90-93
　Amer. Her. --New (8) p66
-Views of Benjamin P. Thomas
　Miers--American p183-188
-Views of John Hay
　Kraus--U.S. p504-505
-Views of Nathaniel Hawthorne
　Commager--Heritage p650-652
-Views of William Herndon
　Commager--Heritage p628-632
-Visit to Army headquarters,
Harper's Ferry, 1862
　Viewpoints p78
LINCOLN-DOUGLAS DEBATES
　Amer. Her. --New (7) p560-561,
　E244-245
　Angle--American p294-298
　Boardman--Civil p21-22
　Borden--Portrait (1) p224-225
　Butterfield--Amer. p152-153
　Carman--History (1) p625
　Collins--Story p206
　Country--Lincoln p24-29
　Harlow--Story p296-297
　Hurd--Treasury p77-81
　Kraus--U.S. p472-474
　Linton--Bicentennial p152-153
　Morris--Ency. p224-225
　Randall--Mary p191-195
　Whitney--American p131, 134, 142
　-Views of Carl Schurz
　　Commager--Heritage p632-637
LINCOLN, MARY TODD
　Life--New (5) p76, 103, 106-108
　Melick--Wives p39-42
　Meredith--World p84
　Young--Women p51, 87, 144,
　331-335, 338
　, and Lyman and Julia Trumbull
　　Randall--Mary p181-186
　, as family seamstress
　　Randall--Mary p110-111
　, as first lady
　　Randall--Mary p242, 248-415
　, as widow
　　Randall--Mary p419-429
　-Characteristics

Randall--Mary p108-109, 112-
　113, 140, 154, 245-247
-Clothes, selling of
　Randall--Mary p443-457
-Debts
　Randall--Mary p426, 428
-Early life, Springfield, Ill.
　Randall--Mary p13-20, 39
-Effect of three children's deaths
　Randall--Mary p159-160, 164,
　310-315, 460
-Engagement, broken
　Randall--Mary p48-64
-Expenditures, as first lady
　Randall--Mary p284-291
-Girlhood, Lexington, Ky.
　Randall--Mary p31-39
-Illness and death
　Randall--Mary p475-480
-"In-law" problems
　Randall--Mary p148-191
-Letter-writing
　Randall--Mary p424-428
-Life abroad
　Randall--Mary p452-457, 473-
　476
-Life, in Chicago
　Randall--Mary p422-473
-Life, in Washington (as Con-
gressman's wife)
　Randall--Mary p125
-Love of literature
　Randall--Mary p45-46
-Married life
　, Early, in Springfield, Ill.
　　Randall--Mary p91-121
　-Love and happiness
　　Randall--Mary p131
-Meeting and courtship, with
Lincoln
　Randall--Mary p25-30, 40
-Mental illness and recovery
　Randall--Mary p465-471
-Pension fight
　Randall--Mary p427, 454-455,
　478
-Persecution and abuse
　Randall--Mary p217, 219, 315,
　422, 428, 478
　-Biographers, influenced by
Herndon
　　Randall--Mary p51-52
　-Hatred by Herndon
　　Randall--Mary p49-50, 440-
　　442, 462
-Relations with son Robert
　Randall--Mary p465-470
-Religion

Randall--Mary p318
-Wedding
  Randall--Mary p85-89
LINCOLN, NANCY HANKS
Adelman--Famous p113
LINCOLN, "TAD"
-Youth and death
  Randall--Mary p458-460
"LINCOLN-TALLMAN HOUSE"
Vanderbilt--Living p168
LIND, JENNY
Amer. Her. --New (6) p488-489,
  E207
Bode--Anatomy p19, 32-36, 254-
  255
Cable--American p152
Collins--Story p159
Davidson--Life (2) p36-37
Dulles--History p125-127, 135,
  237
Howard--Our p202-204
Life--New (5) p62
Neidle--America's p219-220
Viewpoints p165
Wright--Every. p233-234
-Views of Philip Hone
  Angle--American p279-281
LINDERMAN, FRANK B.
, on Battle of Rosebud, Montana
  Commager--Heritage p852
LINE BOATS
Marzio--Nation p176
LINEN DUSTERS
Wilson--Vanish. p183
LINN, W. A.
, on telegraph boys, N. Y. city
  Cook--City p276-277
LINOTYPE MACHINES
Bonte--America p140
Nostalgia p54-57
Reader's--Story p359-360, 363
"LION HOUSE" (Mt. Vernon of the
Mormons, Salt Lake City, Utah)
Vanderbilt--Living p194
LIPPARD, GEORGE
Bode--Anatomy p149, 162-168
Boorstin--Americans p381-382
LIQUOR
See also ALCOHOLISM; DIS-
  TILLERIES AND BREWERIES;
  names of liquors
Furnas--American p457-458
Handlin--This p118, 259-260, 263-
  264, 377, 397
, and patent medicines
  Furnas--Americans p904-906
-Licensing and prohibition
  Furnas--Americans p511-513

LISA, MANUEL
Boardman--Virginia p104
Brown--Westerners p55-56
Gilbert--Trail. p54-56, 60, 127
Hine--American p48-50
LISTER, JOSEPH, DR.
Hilton--Way p82-84, 196
LITCHMAN, CHARLES
Life--Steel (7) p77
LITERACY
-1840-1860
  Bode--Anatomy p116
-Late Victorian
  Gowans--Images p372-375,
  395-396
LITERATURE
See also AUTHORS; BOOKS AND
  READING; PUBLISHERS AND
  PUBLISHING; types of literature;
  names of authors; etc.
Amer. Her. --New (6) p495-496
Boardman--Civil p149-158
Boardman--Gilded p124-134
Boardman--Jackson. p142-151
Boardman--Virginia p136-144,
  146-148
Davie--Profile p328-349
Furnas--Americans. See index
  p995
Handlin--This p145, 247, 277
Harlow--Story p242-248
Reader's--Story p409-416
Tunis--Young p127-128
-1876
  Randal--Centennial p247-362
-1880's
  Mott--Golden p172-183
-1890's
  Life--Reaching (8) p91-92, 114,
  117, 121, 123
  Mott--Golden p183-193
, Anti-slavery
  Our literary p85-86
-Boston, Mass.
  Our literary p58-59, 92-93
, Declamatory
  Boorstin--Americans p307-324
, Dutch, along Hudson river
  Our literary p8-9
-Frontier life contribution
  Our literary p24-25
-"Immoral literature," by
  Thomas DeWitt Talmage
  Harris--Land p272-279
-Individual struggle for self-
realization
  Carman--History (1) p541-550
-Industrialization

Borden--Portrait (2) p56-57
    Harlow--Story p431
-"Local colorists"
    Harlow--Story p431-432
-Middlewest
    Our literary p22-23
-New England
    Morris--Ency. p567-568
    Our literary p6-7, 40-101,
    150-151
-New York, 1850's
    Our literary p106-107
, of America's rediscovery
    Morris--Ency. p572-574
-Philadelphia, 1800
    Our literary p4-5
, Popular
    -1840-1860
        Morris--Ency. p571
-Realism
    Borden--Portrait (2) p57-59
    Harris--Land p279-286
    Our literary p158-161
    Reader's--Story p414-416
    -1865-1892
        Morris--Ency. p574
    -Views of Howard Mumford
    Jones
        Miers--American p275-279
, Regional
    Our literary p138-141
    Jones--Age p217-218
    Nye--Cultural p247-248
-Short stories, Animal
    Mott--Golden p162-164
-South
    Morris--Ency. p569
    Our literary p26-29
    , Post Civil war
        Dulles--United p33
-Subjects
    Nye--Cultural p244-246
-Views of Frances Trollope
    Trollope--Domestic. See
    index p.x
-West
    Hart--Popular p140-156
    Wright--Culture p120-121
    -Post Civil war
        Our literary p124-125
-Women
    Macksey--Book p184-186, 190
LITHOGRAPHS
    Bode--Anatomy p89-91
    Furnas--Americans p576-578,
    628-630
    Larkin--Art p113, 140-141, 168
    Lynes--Taste. p54, 58, 67-70, 125

, and popular art
    Boardman--Jackson p155
, Political
    Life--Sweep (4) p52-53
"LITTLE BEST" AFFAIR, 1811
    Morris--Ency. p139
"LITTLE BIG HORN" BATTLE
(Montana), 1877
    Andrews--Indian leaders p150-
    152, 159-160
    Boardman--Gilded p94
    Ridge--America's p579-581
"LITTLE CROW" (Santee Sioux
Indian)
    Amer. Her.--New (9) p778-779
    Andrews--Indian leaders p94-96
"LITTLE RAVEN" (Araphahoe Indian)
    Andrews--Indian Leaders p118-
    119, 121, 123, 129, 134
LITTLE ROCK, ARKANSAS
-Territorial capitol
    Vanderbilt--Living p177
"LITTLE TURTLE" (MICHIKIM-
KIVA) (Miami Indian)
    Andrews--Indian leaders p48, 96
LIVERMORE, MARY ASHTON
    Adelman--Famous p203-204
    Dannett--Noble p35-37, 160, 220,
    223, 231, 272, 330, 334, 336, 338,
    390, 392
    Sochen--Herstory p162, 164
    Young--Women p21, 42, 44, 46, 70,
    79, 97, 152-155, 225, 253-257, 264,
    309-311
    -Biography
        Young--Women p375
LIVESTOCK
    See also CATTLE; DRIVERS,
    ANIMAL; names of domestic
    animals
    Bartlett--New p191-194
    Boardman--Jackson. p90-91
    Furnas--Americans p350, 372,
    377, 472-476
    Van Wagenen--Golden p21, 101
    -1840's-1850's
        Boardman--Jackson. p90-91
    , Western, and cowboys
        Furnas--Americans p683-688
LIVING ROOMS
    Lynes--Domestic. p231-234
    -Leisure occupations
        Lynes--Domestic. p251-252
LIVINGSTON, CORA
    Peacock--Famous p80-89
LIVINGSTON, EDWARD
    Boardman--Virginia p181-182
    Hunt--Life p190, (facing), 193

Morris--Ency. p688-689
LIVINGSTON, ROBERT R.
  Boardman--Virginia p82-83
  Life--Growing (3) p59, 78, 160
  , and John Livingston, family feud
    Reader's--Story p262
LLOYD, HENRY DEMAREST
  Boardman--Gilded p113-115
  Borden--Portrait (2) p29-30
  Carman--History (2) p389-390
  Furnas--Americans. See index
    p995
"LOAFERS" ("Do-Nothings")
  Wilson--Early p166
LOBBYING
  Harlow--Story p448
  -1870's
    Randel--Centennial p173-175
LOCKE, DAVID ROSS (Petroleum
  V. Nasby)
  Boardman--Civil p156
  Walker--Every. p172-173
  , on Reconstruction (comic views)
    Burner--American (1) p342-
    345
LOCKWOOD, BELVA ANN
  Adelman--Famous p252
  Butterfield--Amer. p217
  Life--Steel (7) p16
  Macksey--Book p125-126
  Reader's--Story p436
  Warren--Pictorial p132-133
"LOCOFOCOS" (labor party)
  Boardman--Jackson. p86
  Handlin--This p208-209
  Morris--Ency. p176
LOCOMOTIVES. See RAILROADS
  --Locomotives
LODGE, HENRY CABOT, SR.
  Butterfield--Amer. p287
  Life--Reaching (8) p66-67, 130,
    134, 137
  , on Americanism
    Hurd--Treasury p116-118
LODGES
  Boardman--Gilded p169-170
"LOG CABIN AND HARD CIDER"
  (slogan, 1840)
  Morris--Ency. p183
LOG CABINS
  Lynes--Domestic. p24-31
  Van Wagenen--Golden p49-55
  -1802
    -Views of F.A. Michaux
      Angle--American p156
LOG-ROLLING
  Bonte--America p102
  Van Wagenen--Golden p38-39

LOGAN, JOHN A.
  Life--Steel (7) p12-13
LOGAN, OLIVE
  -"About nudity in the theaters"
    Trachtenberg--Demo. p200-
    312
LOGGING. See LUMBER AND
  LUMBERING; related subjects
"LONE STAR REPUBLIC." See
  TEXAS
"LONE WOLF" (Kiowa Indian)
  Andrews--Indian leaders p120,
    128-129, 135
  Brown--Westerners p201
LONG, ARMISTEAD L.
  , on Robert E. Lee's surrender,
    1865
    Angle--American p336-338
LONG, CRAWFORD, DR.
  Boardman--Jackson. p170-171
  Reader's--Story p294-295
  Wilson--American p104-105
LONG, JOHN DAVIS
  , on Theodore Roosevelt and Navy
    Commager--Heritage p979-980
LONG, STEPHEN HARRIMAN
  Amer. Her. --New (6) p E207
  Boardman--Virginia p102
  Hine--American p74-75, 78, 156,
    192, 284
  -"The Great American Desert"
    legend grows
    Ridge--America's p373
"LONG BEAR" (Indian)
  -Death
    Andrews--Indians p144-145
"LONG BULLET" (sport)
  Dulles--History p73
"LONG DRIVES." See CATTLE--
  "Long Drives"
"LONG NINE" (group Illinois legis-
  lators)
  Drury--Midwest p95
LONGFELLOW, HENRY WADS-
  WORTH
  Amer. Her. --New (11) p E390
  Boardman--Civil p152-153
  Boardman--Jackson. p148-149
  Bode--Anatomy p189, 197-200
  Brooks--Flower. See index
    p545
  Furnas--Americans. See index
    p996
  Harlow--Story p244-245
  Hart--Popular p127-130
  Morris--Ency. p569
  Nye--Unembar. p101-103
  Our literary p54-57

-Biography
　Morris--Ency. p569, 689
, in Cambridge
　Brooks--Flower. p147-171,
　303-308, 316-318, 321
LONGMERE, MRS.
　-Trip across Cascades, 1853
　　Ross--Heroines p20-22
LONGSTREET, AUGUSTUS B.
　Boardman--Jackson. p150
　-Georgia scenes
　　Grimsted--Notions p109-118
LONGSTREET, JAMES, GENERAL
("OLD PETE")
　Amer. Her. --New (8) p E285
　Dowdey--Experiment. See index
　p449
　Jordan--Civil p58, 84, 98, 108,
　133, 136, 138, 140-141
　Life--Union (6) p13, 55-56, 64-
　65, 81-82, 84, 92, 106-107
LONGWORTH, NICHOLAS
　Drury--Midwest p128-129
"LOOKING GLASS" (Nez Perce
Indian)
　Andrews--Indian leaders p173
LOOKOUT MOUNTAIN, TENNESSEE
, in Civil war
　　Jordan--Civil p141-145
LOPEZ, NARCISCO
　-Filibustering expeditions, 1851
　　Morris--Ency. p215
LOS ANGELES, CALIFORNIA
　Furnas--Americans. See index
　p996
　Johnson--Pictorial p126-127
　-Early settlers, 1845
　　Jones--Shaping p103
LOTTERIES
　Keller--Affairs p233, 418, 509-
　510
LOUGHBOROUGH, MARY ANN
, on Vicksburg, 1863
　　Angle--American p325-328
LOUISIANA
　See also NEW ORLEANS, LA.
　Alden--Pioneer p231-232
　Boardman--Virginia p124-125,
　128-129
　Carman--History (1). See
　index p. xvi
　Handlin--This p110-111, 126,
　133-135, 137, 336-337, 341
　Hine--American p70, 73-74, 80,
　82, 100, 111
　Hunt--Life. See index p293
　Keller--Affairs p204-205, 216,
　223-225, 229, 578

Life--Steel (7). See index p158
Maurois--Illus. p100, 102, 105
Randel--Centennial p230-232
Tunis--Young p78-79
, and Civil war
　Dowdey--Experiment p14, 45,
　61, 73, 94, 115, 131, 226, 272,
　301
　Life--Union (6). See index
　p174
-Criminal code
　Hunt--Life p193
-Planters, luxury among
　Commager--Heritage p447-449
LOUISIANA PURCHASE, 1803
　Alden--Pioneer p145-149, 179, 231
　Amer. Her. --New (5) p366-367,
　407
　Boardman--Virginia. See index
　p214-215
　Boorstin--Americans p257-259,
　261, 265, 268
　Borden--Portrait (1) p134-135
　Brown--Westerners p37-38
　Butterfield--Amer. p40-41
　Carman--History (1) p321-324,
　344-345, 372, 459, 554, 563
　Collins--Story p169
　Gilbert--Trail. p16-17, 34-36
　Harlow--Story p167-169
　Heffner--Doc. p80
　Hine--American p47, 54, 69-70,
　80, 107, 109, 320
　Jones--Shaping p59-60
　Keyes--Hope p202-204
　Kraus--U.S. p301-302, 304-307
　Life--Growing (3) p78-79, 86, 98,
　125
　Linton--Bicentennial p60-61, 70,
　131
　Morris--Ency. p132-133
　Tunis--Frontier p68
　200 Years (1) p174-175, 181
　Whitney--American p29, 38-39,
　45, 50
　Wright--Every. p48-49
　-Change of flags
　　-Views of C.C. Robin
　　　Angle--American p159-160
　　-Views of John Bakeless
　　　Miers--American p107-111
LOVE
　See also COURTSHIP; MAR-
　RIAGE
　Bode--Anatomy p269-273
　Schwartz--When p19-20
LOVEJOY, ELIJAH P., REV.
　Boardman--Jackson. p116

, and abolition
    Butterfield--Amer. p97
    Commager--Heritage p487-489
, Murder of
    -Views of Wendell Phillips
      Hurd--Treasury p61-63
LOVEJOY, JULIA
    Hine--American p224, 226, 236-
    237, 341
LOVING, OLIVER
    Brown--Westerners p205, 208
LOW, CHARLES P.
    , on "going to sea, " 1842
      Angle--American p214-217
LOW, JULIETTE GORDON
    Dolin--Great p144-153
    , and Girl Scouts of America
      Heath--Women (4) p23
LOW, LYDIA
    Ross--Heroines p14
LOWE, THADDEUS S. C.
    Meredith--World p110-113
    Morris--Ency. p537
    Wilson--American p185-187
LOWELL, FRANCIS CABOT
    Boardman--Virginia p69-70
    Harlow--Story p207
    Reader's--Story p259
LOWELL, JAMES RUSSELL
    Amer. Her. --New (11) p E390-
    391
    Boardman--Civil p153
    Brooks--Flower. See index
    p545
    Butterfield--Amer. p240
    Cable--American p147
    Harlow--Story p245-246
    Our literary p90-91
    , and "My Maryland, my Mary-
    land"
      Krythe--Sampler p142-149
    -The Bigelow papers
      Grimsted--Notions p215-220
    -Biography
      Morris--Ency. p689
    -Essays
      Brooks--Flower. p503-504,
    512-525
LOWELL, JOSEPHINE SHAW
    Adelman--Famous p235
    Warren--Pictorial p143, 145
LOWELL, MASSACHUSETTS
    Furnas--Americans p303, 476-480
    Holzman--Stormy p26-29; see
    also index p276
    -Textile mills
      Boardman--Jackson. p78-79
      Harlow--Story p209-210

Tunis--Young p61
Wilson--American p88-89
Wright--Every. p132-133
-Amusements, mill workers
    Dulles--History p92-93
-Women employees
    Warren--Pictorial p91-94
    -Views of Davy Crockett,
    1834
      Angle--American p259-
    262
    -Views of Eliza R. Hem-
    mingway, 1845
      Sochen--Herstory p96-
    97
LOWENSTEIN, ISIDORE
    -Views on America, 1837
      Handlin--This p179-185
LOWER CLASS. See POVERTY;
SERVANTS; SLAVES AND SLAV-
ERY
LOYOLA, MARY, SISTER
    Ross--Heroines. See index p180
    Ross--Westward p77-92
LOZIER, CLEMENCE SOPHIA
    Adelman--Famous p184
LUCAS, LENA BROOKE
    Andrews--Women p207-208
LUCHICH, ANTHONY F.
    Marzio--Nation p242
LUDLOW, NOAH
    , on actors, 1842
      Angle--American p278-279
LUKENS, REBECCA
    Macksey--Book p163-164
LUMBER AND LUMBERING
    See also SAWMILLS
    Furnas--Americans p696, 830-831
    Life--Steel (7) p54, 57-58, 100,
    103-104, 106, 128
    -"Follers" (cut trees), burning
    of
      Van Wagenen--Golden p30-31
    -Logging camps
      Schwartz--When p196-197
    -Michigan
      Drury--Midwest p66-67
    -Minnesota
      Weisberger--Amer. p212-213
LUNCHES
    Ross--Taste p58
    Walker--Every. p227, 229
LUNDY, BENJAMIN
    Amer. Her. --New (6) p E207
    Boardman--Jackson. p116
    Carman--History (1) p530-531
LUNNY, ROBERT M.
    -"The great sea war"

Treasury Amer. p162-171
LUTHERANS
    Weisberger--Amer. p163-164,
    166
LUTTING, JOHN C.
    -"Fur trade on the Upper Mis-
    souri," 1813
        Ridge--America's p379-398
LYCEUMS
    See also CHAUTAUQUA
    Alden--Pioneer p211
    Boardman--Jackson. p139
    Boorstin--Americans p314-318
    Cable--American p153-154
    Furnas--Americans p561-562
    Harlow--Story p253-254
    Ross--Taste p44
    Tyler--Freedom's p262-264
    Wright--Ency. p236-237
    -Lecturers
        -Emerson, Ralph Waldo
            Commager--Heritage p440-
            442
LYELL, CHARLES, SIR
    , on slaves and slavery, 1846
        Angle--American p287-289
LYMAN, THEODORE
    , on Lee's victory at Cold Har-
    bor, 1864
        Angle--American p331-333
LYNCHINGS
    Furnas--Americans p848-849
    Harris--Land p147-158
LYON, MARY
    Adelman--Famous p128
    Dolin--Great p68-73
    Furnas--Americans p741-743
    Heath--Women (4) p6
    Macksey--Book p68
    Neidle--America's p30
    Reader's--Story p131, 433
    Sochen--Herstory p140
    Tyler--Freedom's p252-253, 429,
    437
    Warren--Pictorial p72-73
    -Biography
        Morris--Ency. p689
LYON, PETER
    -"The honest man"
        Treasury Amer. p310-319

M

McALLISTER, WARD
    Cable--American p274-275, 311,
    334
    Walker--Every. p129-130

, on idle rich, 1890
    Commager--Heritage p889-895
, on society, New York city
    Cook--City p267
McARTHUR, JOHN, JR.
    Furnas--Americans p613-614
McCARTHY, HARRY B.
    , and "Bonnie blue flag"
        Krythe--Sampler p133-141
MACAULAY, THOMAS BABINGTON,
1st BARON MACAULAY
    -"Your Constitution is all sail
    and no anchor"
        Davie--Profile p73
MACLAY, EDGAR S.
    -"Laurels of the American tar
    in 1812"
        Jones--Shaping p61-76
McCLELLAN, GEORGE BRINTON,
GENERAL ("LITTLE MAC")
    Amer. Her. --New (8) p639, 642-
    647; E285
    Boardman--Civil p41-42, 45-48,
    73-74
    Carman--History (1) p656, 659-
    663, 693-694, 698
    Dannett--Noble. See index p416
    Dowdey--Experiment. See index
    p450
    Harlow--Story p311-313, 315, 317-
    318, 328
    Holzman--Stormy p65-72
    Jordan--Civil. See index p213-
    214
    Kraus--U.S. p432, 491-495, 497,
    499-500, 511
    Life--New (5) p104-106, 118-120
    Life--Union (6) p12, 17, 51-57, 60-
    61, 63, 71, 94-95, 97
    Maurois--Illus. p153-154, 157,
    161, 170
    Meredith--World p92-96
    Young--Women. See index p387
    , at Richmond, 1862
        Pratt--Civil p18-19
McCLINTOCK, MARY ANN
    Gurko--Ladies p2, 96, 101, 105, 107
McCLURE, SAMUEL SIDNEY
    Amer. Her. --New (12) p E427
    Boardman--Gilded p165-166
McCLURE'S
    Furnas--Americans p869-870
McCORMICK, CYRUS HALL
    Amer. Her. --New (5) p E170-171
    Bartlett--New p204-206, 409
    Boardman--Jackson. p91-92
    Drury--Midwest p53
    Morris--Ency. p536

Portraits--Americans p25-31
Reader's--Story p263
-Biography
  Morris--Ency. p690
-Reapers
  Amer. Her. --New (5) p384-385
  Langdon--Everyday (2) p316-
  325
  Life--New (5) p75-121
  Nostalgia p8-12
  Portraits--Americans p25
  Wilson--American p139-
  143
-War with N. Y. Central
  Wilson--American p142-
  143
McCOY, JOSEPH G.
-"First of the 'cow towns, '
  Abilene," 1874
  Ridge--America's p595-597
McCULLOCH VS. MARYLAND,
1819
  Amer. Her. --New (5) p371-372,
  E171
  Morris--Ency. p158-159
McDONALD, JOHN, GENERAL
  Randel--Centennial p203
MacDOWELL, EDWARD ALEXAN-
DER
  Chase--America's p346-364
  Howard--Our p323-344
  -Biography
  Morris--Ency. p690-691
McDOWELL, EPHRAIM
  Reader's--Story p294, 298
  -Medical shrine, Danville, Ky.
  Vanderbilt--Living p121
McDOWELL, IRVIN, GENERAL
  Boardman--Civil p40-41
  Life--Union (6) p32-33, 53-54
  Young--Women p107-109, 111,
  113, 115, 117-119, 128, 141, 205,
  234
McDOWELL, MARY E.
  Warren--Pictorial p150
McGREADY, JAMES
  Boardman--Virginia p170
McGUFFEY, WILLIAM HOLMES
  Amer. Her. --New (6) p E207-208
  Boardman--Jackson. p138-139
  Woodward--Way p234-241
  Wright--Every. p190-191
  -Biography
  Morris--Ency. p691
McGUFFEY READERS
  Bartlett--New p390-392
  Commager--Heritage p928-931
  Davie--Profile p308-312

Dulles--United p104-105
Furnas--Americans p548-550
Harlow--Story p253
Hine--American p241-243, 249,
321
Kraus--U. S. p375
McClinton--Antiques p82-83
Wright--Culture p215-222
Wright--Every. p190-192
-Views of Herbert Quick
  Commager--Heritage p928-931
McGUIRE, JUDITH BROCKEN-
BROUGH
  Andrews--Women p71-104, 155-
  189, 372-412
  , on Confederate evacuation of
  Richmond, 1865
  Angle--American p334-336
"MACHINE AGE"
  Trachtenberg--Demo. p209-226
  Wilson--American p242-255
  , Beginning of
  Bonte--America p147
MACHINERY
  See also FARM IMPLEMENTS;
  INVENTORS AND INVENTIONS;
  etc.
  Handlin--This p125, 351
  Keller--Open p83
  -1876
  Randel--Centennial p294, 374-
  375
  -Interchangeable parts
  Wilson--American p250-251
  -Lathes, planers and milling
  machines
  Wilson--American p246-249
McINTIRE, SAMUEL
  Boardman--Virginia p159-161
McINTOSH, WILLIAM (Creek
Indian)
  Amer. Her. --Indians p219, 221-
  222, 224-225
  Andrews--Indian leaders p66
McKAY, CHARLOTTE E.
  Dannett--Noble p205, 235, 346,
  355, 387
McKAY, DONALD
  Boardman--Jackson. p82-83
  Reader's--Story p179
  Wilson--American p158-159
McKAY, LAUCHLAN, CAPTAIN
  Wilson--American p160
MacKENZIE, ALEXANDER
  Gilbert--Trail.p25
McKENZIE, KENNETH
  Boardman--Jackson. p64
McKIM, MEAD, AND WHITE

Walker--Every. p128, 146-147
McKINLEY, IDA
  Melick--Wives p54
McKINLEY, WILLIAM B.
  Amer. Her. --New (12) p E427-
  428
  Amer. Her. --90's p30-35, 117-
  119, 130-138
  Boardman--Gilded p181-186, 188
  Butterfield--Amer. p254-255,
  274, 280-281, 286
  Carman--History (2). See index
  p. xvi
  Dulles--United. See index p. xi
  Harlow--Story. p472-475
  Keller--Affairs. See index p621
  Life--Reaching (8). See index
  p174
  200 Years (2) p322-323; see also
  index p353
  , and Manifest Destiny
    -Views of Julius W. Pratt
      Miers--American p259-265
  -Biography
    Morris--Ency. p691
    Whitney--American p207-214
  -Election campaign
    Collins--Story p276
  -Presidency
    Linton--Bicentennial p244-255
    Reader's--Story p334
  -Views of G. W. Stevens, 1896
    Angle--American p461-463
  -War message, 1898
    Davie--Profile p288-290
  , with business, and Cuba
    Hollingsworth--Amer. p59
McKINLEY TARIFF, 1890
  Carman--History (2) p242-243
  Collins--Story p263
  Harlow--Story p463-464
McLANE, LOUIS
  Amer. Her. --New (5) p E171
MacLAREN, GUY
  , on Chatauqua in South Dakota
    Commager--Heritage p932-
    938
MacLEAN, ANNIE M.
  -"Two weeks in department
  stores"
    Harris--Land p72-88
McLOUGHLIN, JOHN, DR.
("White Headed Eagle")
  Hine--American p45-46, 48,
  52, 89, 92, 94-95
  Kraus--U.S. p413-414
  Life--Sweep (4) p91
  Ross--Heroines p64, 66, 147

-"The American threat to the
Hudson's Bay Company," 1844
  Ridge--America's p495-496
, and Fort Vancouver
  Case--Empire p27-39, 41-69
-"The Hudson's Bay Company
reaction," 1878
  Ridge--America's p450-452
McLOUGHLIN BROTHERS
  -List of games
    McClinton--Antiques p231-233
  -Paper dolls
    McClinton--Antiques p322, 324-
    325
"McLOUGHLIN HOUSE" (Oregon
City, Oregon)
  Vanderbilt--Living p208
McLURE, MARGARET A. E.
  , in Civil war
    Andrews--Women p336-343
McMASTER, JOHN BACH
  Boardman--Gilded p120-121
McNEIL, T. A.
  Commager--Heritage p857-860
MACON BILL NUMBER TWO, 1810
  Borden--Portrait (1) p142
  Harlow--Story p174-175
  Kraus--U. S. p317
  Morris--Ency. p137-138
McPEEK, MRS. ALLIE
  -Experiences, 1864
    Andrews--Women p284-285
MacREADY, WILLIAM C.
  Boardman--Jackson. p156-158
MACY, R. H. & CO., INC. (New
York City)
  Boardman--Civil p134
  Reader's--Story p288
  -First store, c1869 (New York
  City)
    Portraits--Americans p45
MACY, ROWLAND HUSSEY
  Portraits--Americans p45
MADISON, DOROTHY PAYNE TODD
("DOLLEY")
  Adelman--Famous p103-104,
  (facing) 112
  Butterfield--Amer. p50
  Cable--American p83, 85, 90, 164
  Dolin--Great p48-58
  Earle--Two cent. (2) p758, 784,
  787, xxiv
  Hunt--Life. See index p293-294
  Macksey--Book p102
  Maurois--Illus. p106
  Melick--Wives p18-22
  200 Years (1) p189, 195, 321
  Warren--Pictorial p63-65

, and Peggy Eaton
  Phillips--That p4, 11, 14, 16
MADISON, JAMES
  Alden--Pioneer p142-143, 154-
    155, 175-176
  Boardman--Virginia. See index
    p215
  Butterfield--Amer. p50
  Carman--History (1). See index
    p.xvi
  Harlow--Story. See index p814
  Hunt--Life p261-270; see also
    index p293
  Kraus--U.S. See index p. vi
  Life--Growing (3) p58-59, 76;
    see also index p174
  Maurois--Illus. p92-93, 97, 99-
    100, 106, 112-114
  Morris--Ency. p758
  Phillips--That p11, 13-15
  200 Years (1) p186, 320-321; see
    also index p348
  , and war of 1812
    Bonte--America p89
  -Biography
    Morris--Ency. p692
    Whitney--American p41-47
  -Cabinet
    Carman--History (1) p787
  -Presidency
    Borden--Portrait (1) p141-142
    Linton--Bicentennial p66-79
    Reader's--Story p332
    , Society during
      Carson--Polite p97-98
  -"The United States claims West
    Florida," 1810
    Ridge--America's p253-254
  -War message to Congress, 1812
    Davie--Profile p270-271
MAFIA INCIDENT (New Orleans,
  1891)
  Collins--Story p267
MAGARAC, JOE
  Walker--Every. p50-51
MAGAZINES
  See also CHILDREN'S MAGA-
    ZINES; names of magazines
  Boardman--Gilded p163, 165-166
  Boardman--Jackson. p187-188
  Boardman--Virginia p142-143
  Bode--Anatomy p115-116, 259-
    265
  Borden--Portrait (2) p59-61
  Brown--Westerners. See index
    p286
  Cable--American p150
  Carman--History (2) p373-374

Dulles--United p107-108
Furnas--Americans p323, 559-
  560, 668
Handlin--This p144, 197, 356-357,
  379-383
Harlow--Story p247-248
Hunt--Life p144-146
Kraus--U.S. p377-378
Life--Reaching (8) p37-39
Morris--Ency. p584-585
Mott--Golden p204-206
Nostalgia p78-81
Reader's--Story p358-360
Walker--Every. p24, 121, 167,
  175-187, 196-206
-1800's, late
  Harlow--Story p430-431
-1840's
  Lynes--Taste. p10
-1880's-1890's
  Amer. Her. --New (11) p964
-1890's
  Jones--Age p343
-California
  Wright--Culture p154-155
, Circulation of, 1860
  Bode--Anatomy p116
, Cosmopolitan
  Jones--Age p280-281
, Farm
  Boardman--Virginia p79
-Kentucky
  Wright--Culture p71
, Little
  Jones--Age p347
, Non-political-number (1840-
  1860)
  Bode--Anatomy p116
-Northwest territory
  Wright--Culture p112-115
-Popular
  Hart--Popular p86, 89
  Wright--Every. p238-239
-Publishing
  Jones--Age p223-224
-Revolution
  Keller--Affairs p566
-South, Fiction in 1880's
  Life--Steel (7) p108-109
-Toys noted in
  McClinton--Antiques. See
    index p348
-Women editors
  Tyler--Freedom's p436-440
, Women's
  Warren--Pictorial p123-125
MAGIC
  See also CONJURERS

192

-1880's
　Peck--Nineteenth n. p.
-Equipment and supplies
　Peck--Nineteenth n. p.
MAGIC LANTERNS AND MEGA-
SCOPES
, and slides (1880's)
　Peck--Nineteenth n. p.
MAGOFFIN, JAMES
　Brown--Westerners p99, 104,
　106, 111-115, 177, 224, 269
　De Voto--Year. See index p519
MAGOFFIN, SAMUEL
　Brown--Westerners p99, 104,
　106, 112-117
　DeVoto--Year p116, 251-253, 262-
　263, 320-323, 382, 401-402, 404
MAGOFFIN, SUSAN SHELBY
　Brown--Westerners p99, 104,
　106, 112-117
　DeVoto--Year p116, 251-253, 261-
　263, 289, 320-323, 349, 380-382,
　401-402, 404, 511
MAHAN, ALFRED THAYER,
CAPTAIN
　Amer. Her. --New (12) p E428
　Boardman--Gilded p38
　Dulles--United p160-161
　Life--Reaching (8) p129, 134, 139
　-Biography
　　Morris--Ency. p692
　-"The United States looking out-
　　ward, " 1890
　　Heffner--Doc. p198-204
MAHONEY, MARY E.
　Reader's--Story p436-437
MAIL-ORDER SERVICE
　Boardman--Civil p133
　Boardman--Gilded p54
　Nostalgia p62-65
　Reader's--Story p288
　Walker--Every. p104-105
, and R.F.D.
　Portraits--Americans p53-58
-Catalogs
　Ross--Taste p61
, in patterns
　Lynes--Taste. p78
MAIL SERVICE. See POSTAL
SERVICE
MAINE
　See also FUR TRADE
　Furnas--Americans p511-513
　Mussey--Old p71-72
　-Boundary dispute
　　Carman--History (1) p453-454
　-Portland
　　Mussey--Old p29-30

MAINE (ship)
　Amer. Her. --New (12) p E428
　Butterfield--Amer. p278-280
　Life--Reaching (8) p132, 140
　Linton--Bicentennial p250-251
　Reader's--Story p364, 444
, Sinking of, 1898
　Collins--Story p287
　Keyes--Hope p284
　Morris--Ency. p287-288
MAIZE. See CORN
MAJORITIES
, and minorities--illustrations
　Grimsted--Notions p99-105
MAJORS, ALEXANDER
　Brown--Westerners p152, 157-159,
　163-164, 166, 186
　-"Freighting on the Great
　Plains"
　　Ridge--America's p552-554
"MA-KA-TAI-ME-SHE-KIA-KIAK"
(Indian). See "BLACK HAWK"
"MAKERS" (occupations)
　Wilson--Early p74
MALARIA
　See also CINCHONA BARK
　Garrison--Lost p187-189
MALIN, DAVID (Indian boy)
　Ross--Heroines p74, 81-82, 89-90
MALLORY, STEPHEN RUSSELL
　Dowdey--Experiment. See index
　p449-450
　Life--New (5) p133-134, 137
MANASSAS
　See also BULL RUN, BATTLE
　OF
　Dowdey--Experiment. See index
　p450
MANDAN INDIANS
　Amer. Her. --Indians p260-263
　Andrews--Indian leaders p111-113
　Boardman--Virginia p118-119
　Brown--Westerners p39, 43-44,
　58, 79-80
　Gilbert--Trail. p27-28, 69, 127,
　134, 143-145, 147
　-Meetings with Jefferson
　　Gilbert--Trail. p44
"MANGAS COLORADAS" ("RED
SLEEVES") (Apache Indian)
　Amer. Her. --Indians p385
　Boardman--Civil p107
"MANIFEST DESTINY, " 1845
　See also EXPANSION; SLAVES
　AND SLAVERY, and Manifest
　Destiny; names of presidents,
　etc.
　Amer. Her. --New (6) p515, E208

America's--Hist. p341-348
Billington--Far p143-167
Boardman--Gilded p37-38
Boorstin--Americans p273-274
Brown--Westerners p99, 106, 114,
117, 129, 170
Butterfield--Amer. p111, 287
Carman--History (1) p552-554,
561, 563, 597, 611
Carman--History (2) p268, 282,
284-285
DeVoto--Year p3, 8, 10, 29, 37, 39,
47-48, 55, 112, 139, 155, 227, 246,
265, 286, 461
Gilbert--Trail. p155, 158-160,
170-171
Harlow--Story p264-277, 282,
525-528, 531-541
Kraus--U.S. p417-418, 430, 441
Life--Sweep (4) p90, 101, 129, 132
Linton--Bicentennial p124-126,
142, 148
Morris--Ency. p193
Tunis--Frontier p129
200 Years (1) p245, 255
, and McKinley
-Views of Julius W. Pratt
Miers--American p259-265
, and New Mexico
DeVoto--Year p8-9
, and Philippines
Hollingsworth--Amer. p25-28
-"Spirit of 1845, " by John L.
O'Sullivan
Ridge--America's p490-491
MANILA BAY
, Battle of
See also DEWEY, GEORGE
Collins--Story p288
Commager--Heritage p980-984
Morris--Ency. p288-289
-Views of Joseph L. Stickney
Angle--American p438-442
MANN, HORACE
Alden--Pioneer p221-222
Amer. Her. --New (5) p E171-172
Boardman--Jackson. p135-136
Carman--History (1) p515-516,
604
Furnas--Americans. See index
p996
Harlow--Story p252
Kraus--U.S. p374-375
Morris--Ency. p556
Portraits--Americans p146
Tyler--Freedom's p238-239
-Biography
Morris--Ency. p692-693

, on education, "the great equal-
izer"
200 Years (1) p299
, on Massachusetts school law,
1846
Davie--Profile p305-306
-"Thoughts" (errors of education)
Davie--Profile p322
MANNERS. See ETIQUETTE
MANNES, CLARA DAMROSCH
Neidle--America's p234-235
MANORS. See MANSIONS
MANSFIELD, ARABELLA
Macksey--Book p124-125
MANSFIELD, RICHARD
Blum--Stage. Profile 2
Marzio--Nation p412-413
"MANSION HOUSE" (Home of Dr.
Hanson Chapline), Wheeling, W. Va.
Vanderbilt--Living p114
MANSION HOUSE HOSPITAL
(Alexandria, Va.)
Dannett--Noble p92-93, 95
MANSIONS
See also names of mansions
Boardman--Gilded p153
Larkin--Art p246-249
-Greek revival
-"Rosemount Mansion" (Fork-
land, Ala.)
Vanderbilt--Living p140
, of Byrd family (Westover, Va.)
Life--New (5) p148-149
, Southern
Life--New (5) p148-149
MANTELL, ROBERT B.
Blum--Stage. Profile 4
MANUFACTURING
See also FACTORIES; INDUSTRY;
names of manufacturers; etc.
Alden--Pioneer p203, 252, 265, 293
Boardman--Virginia p68-69
Carman--History (1). See index
p. xvi
Furnas--Americans p302-304,
673-674
Hunt--Life p24-25
Walker--Every. p177-181
Reader's--Story p280-281
, Rise of
Kraus--U.S. p330-331, 391,
409, 463
-Women
Macksey--Book p170
MAPLE SUGAR
Van Wagenen--Golden p108, 110,
169, 174
-Sap buckets

Van Wagenen--Golden p107-108
-Vermont
Mussey--Old p86
MAPS
-1820's
Wilson--American p94-95
MARBLES
McClinton--Antiques p206-209
-Games (Ring Hole), N. Y. City,
1890
Schwartz--When p85
MARBURY VS. MADISON
Amer. Her. --New (5) p370, E172
Boardman--Virginia p18-19
Davie--Profile p68-70
Harlow--Story p166-167
Morris--Ency. p131-132
-"Chief Justice John Marshall
for the Supreme Court," 1803
Heffner--Doc. p74-79
MARCY, WILLIAM L.
Life--New (5) p52-54
-Biography
Amer. Her. --New (7) p E245
"MARDI GRAS"
Life--Steel (7) p118-119
MARIA. CRISTINA, QUEEN OF
SPAIN
, and Peggy Eaton
Phillips--That p144-147, 149-
150
MARICOPA INDIANS
DeVoto--Year p352-353, 372
MARKETS AND MARKETING
-Need for foreign (1890's)
Hollingsworth--Amer. p41-60
-New York City
Partridge--As p106
-West
Hine--American p159-161, 167,
170-172, 176, 319, 333-334
MARKHAM, EDWIN
Dulles--United p114
Furnas--Americans p865-866
MARLOWE, JULIA
Blum--Stage. Profile 13
MARRIAGE
See also WEDDINGS
Cable--American p170-171, 198-
199
Furnas--Americans. See index
p996
Handlin--This. See index p590
Schwartz--When. p20, 200-201
-1876
Randel--Centennial p57-58
, Contract
Warren--Pictorial p101

-Status
Keller--Affairs p467-468
, European, to wealthy American
women
Boardman--Gilded p154-155
, for foreign titles
Hart--Popular p181-182
-Manuals
Lynes--Domestic. p206-207,
213-215
-Views of Frances Trollope
Trollope--Domestic. See
index p. xi
-Women, legal position of
Keller--Affairs p368-470
MARRIED WOMAN'S PROPERTY
ACTS (New York City)
Gurko--Ladies p86-90, 95, 111, 138,
173, 175-183, 196, 201-202, 212
MARRYAT, FREDERICK
, on American children
Burner--American (1) p193-196
, on conservation
Reader's--Story p502
, on women
Burner--American (1) p196-200
MARSH, CALVIN W.
Bode--Anatomy p201-202
MARSH, DR.
Jones--Shaping p91-93
MARSH, GEORGE PERKINS
Brooks--Flower. p411-413
Mumford--Brown p72-79
, and land policies
America 200 p83
MARSH, OTHNIEL L. C.
Boardman--Civil p175-176
Randel--Centennial p61-62, 125,
402, 451
Reader's--Story p307
MARSHALL, JAMES WILSON
See also CALIFORNIA--Gold--
Discovery
Amer. Her. --New (6) p469-471
Boardman--Jackson. p57
Brown--Westerners p120, 130-132
Jones--Shaping p109-110
Tunis--Frontier p131-132
Watkins--Gold p26-27
, on discovery of gold, California,
1849
Davie--Profile p151-152
MARSHALL, JOHN, CHIEF JUSTICE
Amer. Her. --New (5) p370-374,
E172
Boardman--Virginia p18-19, 30-
31, 59-60
Butterfield--Amer. p37

Carman--History (1). See index
p. xvi
Garrison--Lost p68-69
Harlow--Story p164, 188-189
Kraus--U.S. p296, 307, 309-310,
331-332, 343, 355, 365
Life--Growing (3) p84-85, 133,
148-149, 155
Morris--Ency. See index p759
Reader's--Story p58
-Biography
Morris--Ency. p694
-Influence
Collins--Story p172
, on Constitution
Commager--Heritage p226-229
, on Supreme Court
Davie--Profile p68
Heffner--Doc. p70-73
MARTIN, JOHN STUART
-"When the President disap-
peared"
Treasury Amer. p338-343
MARTINEAU, HARRIET
Amer. Her. --New (5) p E172-173
Gurko--Ladies p271-272
, on factory life
Commager--Heritage p367-371
, on Shakers
Tyler--Freedom's p164
, on slaves and slavery, 1834
Angle--American p283-287
MARTINI, SIMONE
Lynes--Taste. p280-281
"MARVEL, IK." See MITCHELL,
DONALD G.
MARX, KARL
, and Horace Greeley
Treasury Amer. p248-255
MARY SHARP COLLEGE (Win-
chester, Tenn.), c1860
Viewpoints p149
MARYLAND
See also BALTIMORE, MARY-
LAND
Carman--History (1) p781-782
Furnas--Americans. See index
p996
Hunt--Life. See index p294
, in Civil war
Andrews--Women p31-36, 57-
59
Dowdey--Experiment p18,
113, 115, 207, 212, 214, 225,
232, 280
MARYSVILLE, CALIFORNIA
Woodward--Way p274-276
MASKS

-1880's
Peck--Nineteenth n. p.
MASON, JAMES H.
Boardman--Civil p66-67
MASON, JAMES MURRAY
Dowdey--Experiment. See index
p450
Life--New (5) p140-141
-Biography
Amer. Her. --New (7) p E245-
246
MASON, MRS. JAMES ("MISS
CHEW")
Dowdey--Experiment p132, 135-
136
MASON, JOHN Y.
-Biography
Amer. Her. --New (7) p E246
MASON, LOWELL
Boardman--Jackson. p160
Boardman--Virginia p151
Bode--Anatomy p19-24
Cable--American p152
Chase--America's p151-161
Furnas--Americans. See index
p996
Howard--Our p136-141
MASON, TIMOTHY
Chase--America's p187
MASON, WILLIAM
Chase--America's p333-334
Furnas--Americans p588-589
Howard--Our p274-280
MASON AND DIXON LINE
Amer. Her. --New (7) p E246
MASON JARS (food preservation)
Lynes--Domestic. p125
MASONIC ORDER
See also ANTI-MASONIC PARTY
Bartlett--New p345-346
Boardman--Jackson. p21
Burner--America (1) p187-189
Carson--Polite p250-251
Handlin--This p131-133, 359-360
MASS PRODUCTION
See also names of products
Boardman--Gilded p59-60
Lynes--Taste. See index p356
Marzio--Nation p508-519, 563-565
MASSACHUSETTS
See also BOSTON; etc.
Boardman--Virginia p70-72
Carman--History (1) p782
Furnas--Americans. See index
p997
Handlin--This p224, 244, 262, 336
Hunt--Life. See index p294
-1876

Randel--Centennial p95-97, 401
-Consumer expenditure patterns,
1874-1875
Cook--City p289
-School law
-Views of Horace Mann, 1846
Davie--Profile p305-306
-State Board of Education
Reader's--Story p129-130
-Worcester
Mussey--Old p48
MASSACHUSETTS EMIGRANT AID
SOCIETY, 1854
Morris--Ency. p217
MASSACRES
See also INDIANS--Massacres
-"Besieged by the Utes, the
Massacre of 1879"
Jones--Shaping p252-262
-Chivington (Sand Creek, Colo.)
Borden--Portrait (2) p49
200 Years (2) p62, 64
-Fort Pillow, 1864
Meredith--World p121, 123
-Marais des Cygnes, 1854
200 Years (1) p276
-Pottawatomie Creek, Kansas,
1856
200 Years (1) p281
-River Raisin, Canada, 1812
200 Years (1) p 190
-Sack of Lawrence, 1856
200 Years (1) p278-279
-Whitman massacre, Oregon,
1847
200 Years (1) p249
MATCHES
, Long wooden
Wilson--Vanish. p105
-"Lucifer, " 1820's (tinderboxes)
Lynes--Domestic. p25
, Phosphorous, first (1836)
Train--Story p287
MATHEMATICS
Handlin--This p146, 276, 281-282
-1870-1884
Morris--Ency. p533
-1876
Hilton--Way p65-66
, and mathematicians
Nye--Cultural p85
MATTRESSES
-Corn shucks and straw
(Missouri, 1890)
Schwartz--When p29-30
MAURY, MATTHEW FONTAINE
Boardman--Civil p178-179
Boardman--Jackson. p169

Harlow--Story p202
Reader's--Story p177
MAXIMILIAN, FERDINAND
Gilbert--Trail. p118-119, 121, 131,
133, 138-139
-Reception at Mexico City
Collins--Story p238
MAYORS
-Detroit
-Views of William T. Stead
Cook--City p206-208
-Women
-First, 1887 (Argonia, Kan-
sas)
Robertson--Book p203
MEAD, GEORGE GORDON, GEN-
ERAL
Amer. Her. --New (8) p E285-286
Boardman--Civil p51-52
Life--Union (6) p12-13, 63-65, 77,
84, 98-99
Young--Women p272-274, 276, 278-
280, 292, 318
MEADOWS (PASTURES)
Van Wagenen--Golden p83-89
MEALS. See FOOD; names of
meals
MEAT PACKING INDUSTRY
(STOCKYARDS)
Boardman--Gilded p48-49
Furnas--Americans p683
Harlow--Story p386
Life--Steel (7) p34-35, 131, 135
-1876
Randel--Centennial p35-36,
55-56, 139
, and refrigerator car
Wilson--American p228-233
-Chicago, Ill.
Boardman--Gilded p48-49
Drury--Midwest p53
Wilson--American p232-233
-Hams
Handlin--This p110, 114-115,
121
-Labor unions
Marzio--Nation p281
MECHANIZATION. See "MACHINE
AGE"
MEDICAL SCHOOLS
Hunt--Life p130, 211
Train--Story p343
Wright--Every. p197-198
MEDICINE
See also DISEASES: DRUGS;
PHYSICIANS; REMEDIES; etc.
Bartlett--New p356, 365-377
Boardman--Civil p72, 179

Boardman--Jackson. p170-171
Boardman--Virginia p178-181
Dreppard--Pioneer p229-231
Furnas--Americans. See index
  p997
Handlin--This p142, 145, 215
Morris--Ency. p542-543
Ross--Taste p62-63
Walker--Every. p39-41, 182
Wilson--Folkways p73-74
-Advertising
  Handlin--This p214-215
, Alcohol in, 1876
  Hilton--Way p76-77
-Books, for women
  Warren--Pictorial p126-127
-Civil war
  Andrews--Women p49n, 61,
  117, 133
, Folk
  Furnas--Americans p338-339,
  441-442, 498
, Herbal
  Furnas--Americans p338, 442-
  443, 498
, Homemade, 1876
  Hilton--Way p21-22, 75, 77-79
-Housewives'
  Ross--Taste p62
, Mail-order
  Train--Story p342
, Patent
  Cable--American p238-239,
  258-259
  Furnas--Americans p904-906
  Harlow--Story p420
  -1876
    Hilton--Way p75-77
-Regulation of practice
  Keller--Affairs p411-412, 417
-Research
  Harlow--Story p419-420
-West
  Ross--Heroines p11-12
-Women
  Bartlett--New p350
MEDICINE SHOWS
  Furnas--Americans p560-561
MEDIOCRITY
  Lynes--Taste. p16-17, 49
MEEK, JOSEPH L.
  Case--Empire p147, 161
  Ross--Heroines p29-30, 63, 90-91
MEGASCOPES. See MAGIC LAN-
  TERNS AND MEGASCOPES
MELLIMELLI, SIDI SOLIMAN
  Wright--Every. p64
MELLON, THOMAS

  Wright--Every. p104
MELODEONS
  Bode--Anatomy p21
MELODRAMA. See DRAMA--
  Melodrama
MELVILLE, HERMAN
  Alden--Pioneer p253-255
  Boardman--Jackson. p145-146
  Carman--History (1) p541-542,
  545, 547-548
  Harlow--Story p243-244
  Life--Sweep (4) p60
  Morris--Ency. p568
  Our literary p110-111
  Reader's--Story p411-414
  Wright--Every. p172-173, 176-181
, and Walt Whitman
  Our literary p114-115
-Biography
  Amer. Her. --New (7) p E246-
  247
  Morris--Ency. p694
-Moby Dick
  Our literary p112-113
, on Germans
  Kraus--U. S. p394-395
MEMMINGER, CHRISTOPHER
GUSTAVUS
  Dowdey--Experiment p14, 50-51,
  75, 92, 105, 153, 209, 262-263, 283,
  315, 358, 364
  Life--New (5) p133-134, 138
MEN. See names of special groups;
  names of individuals
MENDL, LADY. See DE WOLFE,
  ELSIE, LADY MENDL
"MENEWA" (MENAWA; HOTHLEPOYA)
(Creek Indian)
  Amer. Her. --Indians p221-222,
  225, 227-228
  Andrews--Indian leaders p64, 66
  Life--Sweep (4) p45
"MENIALS." See SERVANTS;
  SLAVES AND SLAVERY
MENKEN, BERTHA (ADAH
ISAACS MENKEN)
  Adelman--Famous p188
, in Virginia City
  Dulles--History p173-174
MENLO PARK, NEW JERSEY
  Wilson--American p286-287
MEN'S CLUBS. See CLUBS,
  Men's
MENUS
  See also COOKERY; DINNERS;
  FOOD; etc.
, Banquet, 1890's
  Ross--Taste p75

MERCANTILE AGENCY, N. Y.
-Ledger, 1850's
    Portraits--Americans p14
MERCER, ASA
    Ross--Heroines p28-29
    Ross--Westward p113-120
MERCHANDISING
    Furnas--Americans. See index
    p997
    -New York City
    Partridge--As p106-108
MERCHANT MARINE
    Carman--History (1) p475-476,
    686
    Morris--Ency. p488-489
"MERCHANT PRINCES"
    Wilson--Early p59-65
MERCHANTS
    See also SHOPS AND SHOP-
    KEEPERS; names of compa-
    nies
    Handlin--This p104, 106-107,
    109-110, 128, 180-181, 232
MERGENTHALER, OTTMAR
    -Biography
    Morris--Ency. p694-695
    -Linotype machine
    Nostalgia p54-57
    Reader's--Story p359-360,
    362-363
MERGLER, MARIA JOSEPHA
    Neidle--America's p202-203
"MERRIMAC" (ship)
    See also "MONITOR AND
    MERRIMAC," Battle of
    Dowdey--Experiment p24, 74,
    162, 178, 184, 186, 188, 212
    Harlow--Story p312-313
    Wilson--American p198-199
    Wilson--American p202-203
MERRIMAC MANUFACTURING
    COMPANY
    Wilson--American p88
"MERRY-GO-ROUNDS"
    -Country fairs
    Partridge--As p45
"MESSAGE TO GARCIA"
    Amer. Her. --New (12) p E429
    Keyes--Hope p285-286
METAL CONSTRUCTION
    Gowans--Images p258, 322,
    326-327, 332, 347, 351
METEORITES
    -Views of Nathaniel Bowditch,
    1807
    Wilson--American p45
METEOROLOGY AND METEOROL-
OGISTS

-1831-1861
    Morris--Ency. p531
METHODISTS
    See also CIRCUIT RIDERS
    Bartlett--New p369-372, 375
    Boardman--Jackson. p132-133
    Boardman--Virginia p167-172
    Carman--History (1) p504-506,
    509, 556, 585
    Chase--America's p207-211
    Furnas--Americans p585, 639
    Handlin--This p119, 148, 243, 259-
    260, 358
    Hine--Americans p89, 223-224,
    226-227, 236, 244, 288
    Hunt--Life p120-121, 174
    Morris--Ency. p551
    Nye--Cultural p230-231
    Wright--Culture p98-99
    Wright--Every. p207-210
    -Colleges and universities
    Wright--Culture p143-145
    , on California frontier
    Wright--Culture p136-137
METROPOLITAN MUSEUM OF ART
    Larkin--Art p251-253
    Lynes--Taste. p57, 64, 142, 160-161
METROPOLITAN OPERA COMPANY
    Neidle--America's p220-221
METROPOLITAN OPERA HOUSE
    (N. Y. City)
    Dulles--History p238-239
    Partridge--As p162
    Warren--Pictorial p152-154
    -Opening, 1883
    Dulles--United p92
METZ, CHRISTIAN
    Boardman--Jackson. p127
MEXICAN WAR
    See also SOLDIERS--Mexican
    War
    Alden--Pioneer p241-245
    Amer. Her. --New (7) p561-579
    Boardman--Civil. See index
    p214
    Boardman--Jackson. p44-49
    Bonte--America p107
    Borden--Portrait (1) p212
    Butterfield--Amer. p112-113
    Carman--History (1) p568-573
    DeVoto--Year. See index p519
    Harlow--Story p273-276, 282-283,
    301, 306, 316
    Hine--American. See index
    p366
    Johnson--Pictorial p78-79, 86-91
    Kraus--U. S. p431-433
    Life--Sweep (4) p100-127; see

also index p158
Linton--Bicentennial p126-132
Morris--Ency. p196-209
Reader's--Story p442-443
200 Years (1). See index p348
Whitney--American p104-105,
107-109, 121, 139, 151, 159
, and peace advocates
  Tyler--Freedom's p415-417
, and Texas
  Commager--Heritage p587-606
-Ante-bellum period
  Morris--Ency. p209-227
-Battles and campaigns
  -Buena Vista
    DeVoto--Year p85, 401,
    406, 470, 472, 479
    Viewpoints p72
  -Camargo and Cerralvo
    DeVoto--Year p282
  -Cerro Gordo
    DeVoto--Year p404, 472-
    473, 477
  -Chapultepec
    DeVoto--Year p473-474,
    479
  -Churubusco
    DeVoto--Year p473
  -Contreras
    DeVoto--Year p473
  -El Brazito
    DeVoto--Year p480-481
  -Jalapa
    DeVoto--Year p473
  -Mexico City. See MEXICO
  CITY
  -Monterey
    DeVoto--Year p283-286,
    469-471
  -Palo Alto
    DeVoto--Year p190-191,
    202, 209, 215, 254, 282-283
    Morris--Ency. p197
  -Puebla
    DeVoto--Year p473
  -Resaca de la Palma
    DeVoto--Year p178, 192,
    202, 207, 254
    Morris--Ency. p197
  -Saltillo
    DeVoto--Year p470
  -San Pasqual
    DeVoto--Year p108, 357-
    359, 372-373, 455
  -Santa Clara
    DeVoto--Year p412
  -Vera Cruz
    DeVoto--Year p404, 472, 474

  Viewpoints p73
-Casualties and cost, 1849
  Morris--Ency. p208
-End, and executions
  Life--Sweep (4) p126-127
, in California
  Amer. Her. --New (7) p568-569
-Mexican view, 1850
  Ridge--America's p506-508
-Mission to Santa Anna
  Morris--Ency. p198
-Origins, 1846
  Amer. Her. --New (7) p566-567
  Morris--Ency. p193
  -Declaration of war
    Morris--Ency. p196-197
    -President Polk's decision,
    and war message
      Davie--Profile p273-274
      Ridge--America's p504-
      505
  -"Nueces skirmish"; "Origins
  of the Mexican war," by
  William S. Henry, 1846
    Ridge--America's p503-504
-"Rebel yell"
  Life--Sweep (4) p107
-Taos revolt
  DeVoto--Year p394-395
-Texas
  Commager--Heritage p587-606
-West
  Billington--Far p168-192
MEXICO
  Alden--Pioneer p230-238, 241-245
  Boardman--Jackson. p40-49
  Boardman--Virginia p103-104
  Hine--American. See index
  p366
  Life--Sweep (4). See index
  p158
, and America
  DeVoto--Year p520
, and Civil war
  Dowdey--Experiment. See
  index p450
  -Southern Confederate migra-
  tion
    White--American p56-59
-Borderlands
  Billington--Far p1-22
-Immigration
  , from Mexico
    Handlin--This p368
  -Restrictions, 1830
    Ridge--America's p422-423
-Mexicans
  Hine--American. See index

p366
-"Mexico's distrust of Texans, "
by Manuel Mier y Téran, 1828
Ridge--America's p419-422
MEXICO CITY, MEXICO
, Assault on
Amer. Her. --New (7) p572-573
DeVoto--Year p468-470, 474-
475
Morris--Ency. p206-207
-Capture by General Winfield
Scott
Commager--Heritage p602-606
-"Mill of the King, " Mexico City,
by Lieut. Robert Anderson,
1847
Angle--American p246-248
MEYER, ANNIE
Macksey--Book p68
MEYNELL, ALICE
Adelman--Famous p266-267
MIAMI CANAL, OHIO
Furnas--Americans p290-291
Tunis--Frontier p92-93
MIAMI INDIANS
Andrews--Indian leaders p29,
45, 47-49, 78
"MICANOPY" (Indian)
Andrews--Indian leaders p68
MICHAUX, F.A.
-Letters on America, 1802
Angle--American p153-157
Handlin--This p109-122
-"The Ohio Valley frontier in
1802"
Ridge--America's p242
, on Kentuckians, 1802
Angle--American p153-155
, on log cabins
Angle--American p156
MICHELSON, ALBERT ABRAHAM
Boardman--Gilded p122-123
Reader's--Story p310
Wilson--American p309-315
-Biography
Morris--Ency. p695
-"Ether drift"
Wilson--American p314-315
-"Interferometer"
Wilson--American p314-315,
318-319
MICHIGAN
Carman--History (1) p373-374,
783
Hunt--Life p17, 21-22
MICHIGAN, UNIVERSITY OF
Davidson--Life (2) p362-363
MICHIKIMKIVA. See "LITTLE

TURTLE" (Miami Indian)
MICROSCOPY
Jones--Age p329-330, 332-333
"MIDDLE BORDER" COUNTRY
Bartlett--New p187, 212-214, 422
MIDDLE CLASS
Dulles--United p94
-Culture
Hart--Popular p85-88
-Life
Jones--Age p44-45
-Women
Hart--Popular p86-87
MIDDLE WEST. See MIDWEST
"MIDNIGHT JUDGES"
-Adams' Federalist judges, 1801
Harlow--Story p166
MIDWEST
Jones--Age p64-72
-Cities of Middle border
Treasury Amer. p256-263
, in literature
Our literary p22-23, 130-133
-Politics
Jones--Age p70
-Settlers
Jones--Age p69
MIDWIVES
Hunt--Life p213
Schwartz--When p21
MIER Y TERAN, MANUEL
-"Mexico's distrust of the
Texans, " 1828
Ridge--America's p419-422
MIERS, EARL SCHENCK
, on Sherman and Civil war
Miers--American p192-197
MIGRATION
Mussey--Old p114
-Causes and impetus
Ridge--America's p294-297
Weisberger--Amer. p114-116
-"Causes for migration: Eng-
land's rural decay, " 1889
Ridge--America's p294-295
-"Great migration of 1816"
Ridge--America's p274-276
-"Great migration, " 1843
Case--Empire p109-121
, Internal, 1870-1890
Morris--Ency. p443
, over the Appalachians
Alden--Pioneer p157-173
, Pioneers'
Boardman--Virginia p96
, to upper valley, 1855
Ridge--America's p403-405
, Westward

Ridge--America's p5-6
-1830's-1840's
Wright--Culture p124-125
MIGRATORY WORKERS
Furnas--Americans p830-832
MILBURN, WILLIAM HENRY
, as circuit rider, West Virginia
Commager--Heritage p269-272
MILDAMS
Van Wagenen--Golden p133-135
MILES, NELSON, COLONEL
Andrews--Indian leaders p152,
168-169, 177
Boardman--Gilded p94-95
-"The Indian problem: the
militarist's solution," 1879
Ridge--America's p583-585
MILITARY BADGES
-Civil war
Jordan--Civil. front, back,
cover pages
MILITARY DRAFT. See CIVIL
WAR--Draft and draft riots
MILITARY UNIFORMS
Reader's--Story p459
-Civil war
Jordan--Civil. front, back,
cover pages
Meredith--World p86-89
Reader's--Story p146
-U.S. Navy, 1830's
Linton--Bicentennial.
(facing) p88
MILK
Handlin--This p114, 117
, Scarcity of, Civil war
Andrews--Women p23
-Bottles
, First, 1879
Robertson--Book p98
-Vacuum pan, Borden's, for
condensing
Portraits--Americans p112
MILKMAIDS
Wilson--Early p151-152
"MILLENNIALISM"
Tyler--Freedom's p70-78
MILLER, ALFRED JACOB
Amer. Her. --New (6) p E208
Boardman--Jackson. p153
Hine--American p286-287
MILLER, ELIZABETH SMITH
Gurko--Ladies p67, 142-145,
147, 153
MILLER, FRANKLIN
, on discrimination vs. Chinese
Cook--City p86-87
MILLER, HENRY

Blum--Stage. Profile 25
MILLER, JOAQUIN
Morris--Ency. p573
-Cabin (Rock Creek Park, Wash.,
D.C.)
Vanderbilt--Living p85
MILLER, LEWIS
Cable--American p125
MILLER, NATHAN
, on Eli Whitney
Miers--American p112-116
MILLER, PERRY
-"The garden of Eden and the
Deacon's meadow"
Treasury Amer. p118-122
MILLER, SAMUEL FREEMAN
Morris--Ency. p468
-Biography
Morris--Ency. p695
MILLER, WILLIAM
Boardman--Jackson. p133
Hine--American p228
Tyler--Freedom's p70-78
, and "Miller madness"
Chase--America's p220-221
MILLERISM AND MILLERITES
See also "MILLENIALISM";
SEVENTH DAY ADVENTISTS
Chase--America's p220-221
Morris--Ency. p553
Tyler--Freedom's p74-78
MILLIGAN CASE, 1866
Angle--By p278-287
MILLIKAN, ROBERT
-Biography
Wilson--American p328-329
MILLINERS. See HATS AND HAT-
TERS
MILLIONAIRES
America's Hist. p537-538
Furnas--Americans p647-654
Ross--Taste p251-252, 254-255
Wright--Every. p99-100
-Club, and politics
Amer. Her. --New (11) p909-
910
, in "Horatio Alger" age (mid
1880's)
Keyes--Hope p273
MILLIS, WALTER
-"The Spanish fleet comes out to
die"
Amer. Her. --90's p113-116
MILLS, CLARK
Boardman--Civil p161
Morris--Ency. p601-602
, and "Jackson" statue
Bode--Anatomy p96-97

MILLS, ROBERT
  Boardman--Jackson. p162-163
  Boardman--Virginia p159-160
  Larkin--Art. See index p534
MILLS AND MILLING
  See also LOWELL, MASSA-
    CHUSETTS--Textile mill;
    WHEELS, Mill
  Cable--American p94, 295
  Handlin--This p111-112, 147
  Treasury Amer. p153-155
  Van Wagenen--Golden p127-128,
    130-133, 135-140
  , and Nathaniel Stevens
    Langdon--Everyday (2) p252-
    255
  , Combination
    Reader's--Story p259
  , Grist
    Handlin--This p159, 166, 168
  -"The mills of early America, "
    by Eric Sloane
    Treasury Amer. p152-155
  , Old grain
    Wilson--Vanish. p152-153
MILLSTONES
  Treasury Amer. p153
  Van Wagenen--Golden p137-138
"MILTON HOUSE" (Milton, Wisc.)
  Vanderbilt--Living p168
MIND, POWER OF
  -Views of Daniel Webster
    Hurd--Treasury p51-53
MINERAL SPRINGS
  -Appalachian Mts. , 1830's
    200 Years (1) p307
MINERALS
  See also names of minerals
  -Geologic history
    Watkins--Gold p175-176
"MINER'S LAW"
  Watkins--Gold p48, 156, 239-240,
    243-248
MINES AND MINING
  See also types of mining;
    localities
  Bartlett--New p263-272, 434-439
  Boardman--Gilded p47-48
  Handlin--This p113, 307, 315,
    317-318, 320
  Life--Steel (7) p52-55, 79, 86,
    88-89, 104
  -1860-1864
    Morris--Ency. p430
  -1870's
    Randel--Centennial p106, 125,
    137-139, 161, 181-182
  -Arizona

Billington--Far p249-251
-California. See CALIFORNIA--
  Gold mines and mining
-Camps
  -Amusements
    Dulles--History p168-181
  -Government organization
    Ridge--America's p546-548
  -Justice, 1884
    Ridge--America's p548-551
  -Laws
    Boorstin--Americans p78,
    82-86
  -Life
    See also MINING--Towns
    Watkins--Gold p36-38, 74-76
  -West
    -Society, Makeup of
      Hine--American p119-120
-Fatalities, 1839-1899
  America 200 p101
-Frontier, 1849-1876
  Ridge--America's p530-551
-Life
  See also MINES AND MINING
    --Camps--Life; MINES AND
    MINING--Towns
  Watkins--Gold p201-205, 229-
    230
-Mules, use of
  Watkins--Gold p190-194
, Placer
  See also MINES AND MINING
    --Camps
  Watkins--Gold p12, 36-37, 87,
    176-189
-Stock swindles
  Watkins--Gold p260-262
-Terminology, glossary of
  Watkins--Gold p278-279
-Towns
  Dulles--United p36-38
  Life--America's p110-111
  Watkins--Gold p59, 231-236
-West
  Boardman--Civil p101-103
  Hine--American p112-124;
    see also index p366
  -Companies
    Hine--American p162-163,
    262, 329, 332
  -Labor violence in Western
    mines
    Jones--Age p385-386
  -Mexicans, exclusion of
    Hine--American p120-121
  -Minorities
    Hine--American p194, 210,

214-216, 220, 233, 235-236
MINETAREE INDIANS
Brown--Westerners p44, 46
Gilbert--Trail. p28, 117-119
MINISTERS. See CLERGYMEN
MINNESOTA
Carman--History (1) p377-378,
783
Furnas--Americans p695-696
Randel--Centennial p108-110, 381
-Bonanza farming
-Views of C.C. Coffin
Ridge--America's p630-631
-Indian massacres and uprisings
Amer. Her. --New (9) p778-
779
Andrews--Indian leaders p95-
97
-Minneapolis
-Street cars, 1892
Cook--City p61
-St. Paul, 1892
Cook--City p26-28
Treasury Amer. p260, 263
, Scandinavians in
Weisberger--Amer. p207-209
MINNESOTA, UNIVERSITY OF
Randel--Centennial p419-420
MINORITIES
See also names of minorities;
special subjects
Harris--Land p133-158
, and majorities--illustrations
Grimsted--Notions p99-105
-West, labor in
Hine--American p206-210,
214-217, 219-220
MINSTRELS
See also BRYANT, DAN
Boardman--Gilded p170-171
Boardman--Jackson p174-175
Cable--American p112, 250-251
Chase--America's p259-300
Dulles--History p98, 122, 128-131
Grimsted--Melodrama p75, 191-
192
Howard--Our p176-184, 643-644
Marzio--Nation p418-421
Nye--Unembar. p162-167
Partridge--As p163
Reader's--Story p465
Walker--Every. p162-163
-1876
Hilton--Way p179-180
Randel--Centennial p337
-1898
Viewpoints p176
-Antecedents; first troupes

Chase--America's p259-264,
267-268
-Songs
See also SONGS--(names of
songs)
Burner--America (1) p269-270
Chase--America's p277-282
Howard--Our p179-182
Reader's--Story p393-394
MIRRORS
Train--Story p269-270, 308
, Largest, 1854
Toss--Taste p252
MISCEGENATION
Handlin--This p162-163
"MISFITS"
Wilson--Early p163
MISSIONARY RIDGE, BATTLE OF
Collins--Story p215
MISSIONS AND MISSIONARIES
Furnas--Americans p363
Handlin--This p308-309
Life--Sweep (4) p88-91, 94, 111,
131, 136, 140
Reader's--Story p97
-California
Amer. Her. --Indians p318-319
America's Hist. p380-385
Gilbert--Trail. p113
Jones--Shaping p99, 111
-1800's
Vanderbilt--Living p202-206
-1839
Ridge--America's p349-354
-Alta
Tunis--Frontier p124-125
, and agriculture
Billington--Far p6-7
-"Camino Real"
Vanderbilt--Living p202-206
, Death of
Johnson--Pictorial p58-59, 61
-Hawaii
Wright--Every. p220
-Oregon
Boardman--Jackson. p52
Case--Empire p55
Ridge--America's p447-450
Ross--Westward p23-92
Tunis--Frontier p114-115
Wright--Every. p219
, and Cayuse Indians
Amer. Her. --Indians p210-
211, 327
-Wives, first. See SPALD-
ING, ELIZA; WALKER,
MARY; WHITMAN, NARCISSA
-"Origin of the missionary

invasion, by William Walker,
1892
  Ridge--America's p447-448
-Societies
  See also AMERICAN HOME
    MISSIONARY SOCIETY
  Tyler--Freedom's p31-32
-Sonoma
  Johnson--Pictorial p57
-West
  Hine--American. See index
    p366
  Tunis--Frontier p114-120
MISSISSIPPI
  Carman--History (1) p369, 634,
    782
  Handlin--This p234, 336, 340-341
, in Civil war
  Jordan--Civil. See index
    p214
  Life--Union (6) p8, 38, 62,
    130-134
-Natchez
  Vanderbilt--Living p178-181
  -1835
    Cable--American p157
-pre Civil war
  America's Hist. p404-409
, Secession of
-Views of Jefferson Davis
  Hurd--Treasury p89-91
MISSISSIPPI RIVER AND VALLEY
  Boardman--Virginia p20-22, 83-
    84, 101-102
  Drury--Midwest p9-25
  Handlin--This p110-111, 133, 217,
    249, 333, 336, 339
  Hine--American p52, 74, 80, 110-
    111, 156, 158, 205, 261, 269
  Life--Growing p140-141, 160,
    162, 166-167
  Life--Steel (7) p104, 112, 114-115,
    124-125
  Trollope--Domestic. See
    index p.xi
-1810-1845
  Ridge--America's p399-413
-1876
  Randel--Centennial p42-43, 161
, as "highway"
  Reader's--Story p196-197
-Boats
  See also STEAMBOATS
  Kane--Gone p206-237
  Lynes--Taste.p89-93, 125
-Commerce
  America's Hist. p335-337
, in Civil war

Jordan--Civil. See index
  p214
-Life, Picture of
  -Views of Mark Twain
    Wright--Every. p84-85
-Primitivism, 1818
  Ridge--America's p399-401
-Race
  -Views of Edmund Flagg
    Wright--Every. p82-83
-Settlements
  Kraus--U.S. p424-428
-Society, on frontier, 1826
  -Views of Timothy Flint
    Ridge--America's p401-403
-Views of Frances Trollope
  Wright--Every. p84-85
MISSOURI
  Carman--History (1) p359-373,
    403-405, 782
  Handlin--This p266, 287, 333, 423
  Hine--American. See index
    p366
  Life--Growing (3) p121, 123-124,
    146
  Life--New (5) p10, 19-29, 21, 24,
    55-56, 68-69, 94, 99
  Tunis--Frontier p97-98, 142, 153
, in Civil war
  Jordan--Civil. See index
    p214
-Jefferson City
  Drury--Midwest p157
-"Lake country folk"
  Bartlett--New p171-172
-Saint Louis
  Tunis--Frontier p71, 95-98,
    110-112, 140
-Statehood
  Amer.Her.--New (5) p376
  America's Hist. p361, 363
-Westport Landing
  Billington--Far p28, 107, 206,
    227, 261
MISSOURI COMPROMISE, 1820
  Amer.Her.--New (5) p E173
  Borden--Portrait (1) p153-155
  Butterfield--Amer. p70
  Carman--History (1) p373, 403-
    405, 597, 611, 619-620, 641
  Harlow--Story p217-218
  Kraus--U.S. p345-346, 434, 450-
    451, 456, 466
  Life--Growing (3) p121-124, 132
  Linton--Bicentennial p84, 108, 124,
    131, 133, 138, 144, 150
  Morris--Ency. p159-160
  200 Years (1) p268-269, 275, 285

Tyler--Freedom's p472-473
Whitney--American p50, 55, 111,
115-116, 135, 141
, and Rufus King
Collins--Story p173
-Slaves and slavery
DeVoto--Year p477-478
MISSOURI INDIANS
Brown--Westerners p40, 73
MISSOURI RIVER
Bartlett--New p245-246, 255, 309
Boardman--Jackson. p63-64
Boardman--Virginia p97-99
Brown--Westerners. See index
p287
Handlin--This p115, 126, 286-
289, 299, 313, 384
Life--New (5) p20-23, 68
Tunis--Frontier p98, 109, 111,
122, 138
-"Fur trade on the Upper
Missouri," 1813 by John C.
Lutting
Ridge--America's p379-382
-Schoolcraft and Cass on Upper
Missouri, 1820
Angle--American p166-170
-Steamboat travel, dangers of
Wright--Every. p83-84
"MISTIPPE" (Creek Indian)
Andrews--Indian leaders p64-65
MITCHELL, D. B.
-"Expansionist sentiment in
Georgia," 1812
Ridge--America's p254-256
MITCHELL, DONALD G. (IK
MARVEL)
Bode--Anatomy p202-214
Brooks--Flower. p65, 409-411
MITCHELL, MARGARET JULIA
("MAGGIE")
Adelman--Famous p209
MITCHELL, MARIA
Adelman--Famous p181
Boardman--Jackson. p167-168
Dolin--Great p98-104
Heath--Women (4) p11
Macksey--Book p150-151
Reader's--Story p437
Warren--Pictorial p74-75
MITCHELL, ORMSBY MacKNIGHT
Boardman--Jackson. p167
MITCHELL, SAMUEL LATHAM
Boardman--Virginia p175-176
"MOBILE BAY"
, and Farragut
Collins--Story p230
Pratt--Civil p56

MOBILITY
Davidson--Life (2) p364-366
Lynes--Domestic. p5-17; see
also index p305
MOBS. See RIOTS; CIVIL WAR--
Draft--Riots
MODESTY
-Views of Frances Trollope
Trollope--Domestic. See
index p. xi
MODJESKA, HELENA
Marzio--Nation p412-413
MODOC INDIANS
Boardman--Civil p109
MOHAWK INDIANS
Andrews--Indian leaders p22, 28,
30, 35-36, 38, 40
MOJAVE INDIANS
Boardman--Jackson. p73-74
Brown--Westerners p62-64
Gilbert--Trail. p97, 100
"MOLLY B' DAMN"
Ross--Westward p125, 133
"MOLLY MAGUIRES" (Pa. Irish
coal miners' group)
Boardman--Civil p126-127
Carman--History (2) p144, 150
Randel--Centennial p193-194
MONEY
See also CURRENCY; SPECIE
CIRCULAR, 1836
Carman--History (1) p366-367,
674-675, 678
-1876
Hilton--Way p172
Randel--Centennial. See
index p471
-Bimetallic standard
Harlow--Story p451
-Cartoons
Life--Steel (7) p25
, Confederate
Life--New (5) p138-139
-"Greenbacks"
Boardman--Civil p130-131, 133
, Love of
-Views of Frances Trollope
Trollope--Domestic. See
index p. xi
-Old Northwest
Tunis--Frontier p85-86
-Panorama of legal tender
Reader's--Story p281
, Paper
Carman--History (1) p366-367,
674-675, 678
-Short history
-Views of William M.

Gouge
Walker--Reform p71-77
, Sound
Harlow--Story p468-469, 472
-Views of George Cary Eggleton
Commager--Heritage p711-714
-West
Carman--History (1) p366-367
"MONEY-BACK GUARANTEES"
-1876
Hilton--Way p157-158
"MONGERS" (dealers and traders)
Wilson--Early p71-74
MONHEGAN ISLAND, MAINE
-Mackerel fishing
Commager--Heritage p320-322
"MONITOR" (ship)
Life--Union (6) p34, 42-43
Wilson--American p200-201, 204-
205
"MONITOR AND MERRIMAC"
(Battle of), 1862
Amer.Her. --New (8) p286
Angle--American p316-320
Bonte--America p124
Collins--Story p227
Commager--Heritage p746-749
Keyes--Hope p268-269
Morris--Ency. p236
MONONGAHELA RIVER
Handlin--This p109-112
MONOPOLIES
Amer.Her. --90's p11, 127
Life--Reaching (8). See index
p174
Life--Steel (7). See index p158
-Growth
Dulles--United p61-62
MONROE, ELIZABETH
Life--Growing (3) p146
Melick--Wives p23-25
, and society
Cable--American p85
MONROE, JAMES
See also MONROE DOCTRINE
Alden--Pioneer p174-176, 178-
179
Boardman--Virginia. See index
p215
Bonte--America p96
Carman--History (1). See
index p.xviii
Harlow--Story p167-168, 190-
193, 222
Hunt--Life. See index p294
Kraus--U.S. p305, 327-329,
339-341
Life--Growing (3). See index

p174
Linton--Bicentennial p80-91
Maurois--Illus. p114-117
Morris--Ency. See index p760
200 Years (1) p323-324; see also
index p349
-Biography
Morris--Ency. p696
Whitney--American p49-56
-Cabinet
Carman--History (1) p788
-Law office & museum (Freder-
icksburg, Va.)
Vanderbilt--Living p104
, on famous warning, 1823
Angle--By p160-164
-Presidency
Reader's--Story p332
-Society during presidency
Carson--Polite p98
MONROE, JOHN
Holzman--Stormy p92-93
MONROE DOCTRINE, 1823
Amer.Her. --New (5) p368-370,
E173-174
Angle--By p162-164
Boardman--Gilded p34-35
Bonte--America p96
Borden--Portrait (1) p155-156
Carman--History (1) p387-391,
679, 684
Davie--Profile p80-82
Harlow--Story p192-193
Heffner--Doc. p83-84
Keyes--Hope p204-206
Kraus--U.S. p337-340
Life--Growing (3) p150-151
Maurois--Illus. p115-116
Morris--Ency. p161-162
Whitney--American p50-51, 54-55,
61, 196
, of James Monroe
Collins--Story p174
Hurd--Treasury p49-50
, Reaffirmation of
Hollingsworth--Amer. p29-40
-Views of Dexter Perkins
Miers--American p131-136
MONROE FORT, VIRGINIA
Jordan--Civil p34, 83-84, 101, 153,
186-187, 210-211
MONROE-PINKNEY TREATY, 1806
Morris--Ency. p134
MONTANA
Handlin--This p313-314, 316
Hine--American p96, 113, 118, 128,
151, 186, 198
Life--Steel (7) p31, 52, 54-56, 59

-Gold mines and mining
  Amer.Her.--New (9) p733-738,
  740
  Ridge--America's p544-546
  Watkins--Gold p90-93
-Rosebud battle
  -Views of Frank B. Linde-
  man
    Commager--Heritage p852
-Tonopah mining
  Watkins--Gold p167-169,171
-Vigilantes
  Hines--American p304-307
  -Views of Nathaniel Pitt
  Langford
    Commager--Heritage p582-
    585
MONTEREY, CALIFORNIA
  Johnson--Pictorial. See index
  p223
  , as provincial capital
    Johnson--Pictorial p74-75
  , Battle of
    Morris--Ency. p203
  , and Zachary Taylor, 1846
    -Views of John R. Kenly
      Angle--American p238-
      241
  -Early settlers, 1844
    Jones--Shaping p102-103
  -Gold
    -Views of Walter Colton
      Commager--Heritage p555-
      559
MONTEZ, LOLA
  Life--New (5) p9
  Warren--Pictorial p96
MONTGOMERY, ALABAMA
  Life--New (5) p95,98,131-132,
  134-135
  -Convention, 1861
    Morris--Ency. p228-229
MONTGOMERY, ZEBULON
  -Expedition, Rocky Mountains
    Ridge--America's p364-368
MONTGOMERY WARD & COMPANY
  Amer.Her.--90's p20-21
  Boardman--Gilded p54
  Reader's--Story p288
  -First catalog, and advertising
    Hilton--Way p32,155,157-158
    Portraits--Americans p55
"MONTICELLO" (home of Thomas
Jefferson, Charlottesville, Va.)
  America's Hist. p254-263
  Handlin--This p125-127
  Life--Growing (3) p64-75
  Vanderbilt--Living p107

MONTLEZUN, BARON DE
  -Views on America, 1816-1817
    Handlin--This p123-137
MOODY, DWIGHT LYMAN
  Amer.Her.--New (11) p917-918
  Boardman--Gilded p159-160
  Furnas--Americans p663-664
  Life--Reaching (8) p10,12-13,33
  Reader's--Story p101
  -Biography
    Amer.Her.--New (11) p E391
    Morris--Ency. p696-697
MOODY, WILLIAM VAUGHAN
  Boardman--Gilded p131-132
MOODY AND SANKEY (evangelists)
  Randel--Centennial p1-2
MOORE, CLEMENT CLARKE
  Boardman--Virginia p141
MOORE, JULIA A.
  Randel--Centennial p358-359
MORALITY
  See also PUNISHMENT; RELI-
  GION
  Burner--America (1) p287-291
  Carson--Polite p105,145-154
  Furnas--Americans. See index
  p998
  -1865
    Jones--Age p9-10
  , and politeness
    Carson--Polite p91-92
  , of art and architecture
    Lynes--Taste. p24-25,27,97,
    101,103,111,150-151,163
  -"Public mores"
    Keller--Affairs p128-131,507-
    517
  -Views of Charles Grandison
  Finney
    Grimsted--Notions p77-85
  -Women, lack of knowledge
    Sochen--Herstory p146,180
MORAN, THOMAS
  Randel--Centennial p264-265,384
MORAVIANS
  -Northwest territory
    America's Hist. p285,287
MORGAN, CHARLES HILL
  Portraits--Americans p128
MORGAN, HOUSE OF
  Carman--History (2) p86-87,94-
  95,109-114
MORGAN, JOHN HUNT
  Amer.Her.--New (8) p E286-287
MORGAN, JOHN PIERPONT
  Amer.Her.--New (10) p868-869
  Amer.Her.--90's p60-63,138-141
  Boardman--Gilded p50-51,141

Carman--History (2) p90, 94-95, 107-113, 116, 249-250
Dulles--United p60-61
Harlow--Story p391-398, 417
Life--Reaching (8) p87, 106, 150-151
Life--Steel (7) p34, 99, 104, 131
Morris--Ency. See index p760
Reader's--Story p283
    -Biography
        Morris--Ency. p697
MORGAN, LEWIS HENRY
    Boardman--Civil p175
    Boardman--Gilded p122
MORGAN, SARAH FOWLER
    -Diary
        Andrews--Women p345-352
MORGAN, SHUBEL, pseud. See BROWN, JOHN
MORGAN, THOMAS J.
    -The present phase of the Indian question," 1891
        Davie--Profile p97-98
MORGAN, WILLIAM
    Carman--History (1) p422-423
MORISON, ELTING
    , on Teddy Roosevelt
        Miers--American p265-269
MORMON BATTALION
    Brown--Westerners p99, 118-121, 126, 131-132, 149
    DeVoto--Year. See index p520
MORMONS
    See also "BEE HIVE HOUSE"; DESERET (State of); NAUVOO, ILLINOIS; OHIO--Kirtland; names of Mormons
    Alden--Pioneer p209-210
    Amer. Her. --New (6) p527-528, E208-209
    America's Hist. p370-372
    Bartlett--New p82, 107, 222, 298, 358-359, 380-388
    Boardman--Jackson. p124-126
    Boorstin--Americans p62-65
    Borden--Portrait (1) p198-200
    Brown--Westerners. See index p287
    Cable--American p195, 281
    Carman--History (1) p507-509, 513
    Furnas--Americans p496, 522-523
    Hine--American. See index p366
    Life--Steel (7) p51-52, 58-59
    Life--Sweep (4) p59, 61-63
    Linton--Bicentennial. See

index p444
    Maurois--Illus. p137-139
    Reader's--Story p74, 76, 102
    Tunis--Frontier p86, 121-123
    Wright--Every. p212-214
    -1830
        Morris--Ency. p552
    -1846-1847
        Tunis--Frontier p122-123
    -1847-1860
        Ridge--America's p509-529
    -1876
        Randel--Centennial. See index p471
    -Agriculture. See AGRICULTURE
    --Mormons
    , at winter quarters
        DeVoto--Year p431-438
    -Book of Mormon
        Bartlett--New p380-383
        Tunis--Frontier p121
        Tyler--Freedom's p89-92
    -Comparison with other emigrations
        DeVoto--Year p93-94, 103, 111, 113, 115, 149-150, 441-443
    -Cooperative experiment: the economy
        Ridge--America's p515-517
        -Governmental system
            Ridge--America's p517-519
    -Diseases
        DeVoto--Year p487, 494-495, 498, 504-506, 512
    -Entertainment
        DeVoto--Year p435-437, 444
    , Establishment of
        Tyler--Freedom's p93-94
    -Expansion, over Great Basin, 1852
        Ridge--America's p519-520
        -"Parawon City, 1855," by Frederick Piercy
            Ridge--America's p520-521
    -"Forty-Niners," effect on
        Billington--Far p203-204
    -"Handcart brigades," 1856
        Billington--Far p206-207
        Ridge--America's p521-524
    -Ideology and history
        DeVoto--Year p76-98
    , in Illinois
        -Nauvoo
            Tunis--Frontier p121-122
            Tyler--Freedom's p101-106
            , Expulsion from, 1846
                DeVoto--Year p72-76,

318-320, 333, 368-369
  Ridge--America's p509-
   512
, in Iowa
  DeVoto--Year p90-98
  Drury--Midwest p161
, in Missouri
  Tyler--Freedom's p97-100
, in Ohio
  Tunis--Frontier p121
  Tyler--Freedom's p94-100
, in Utah
  See also SALT LAKE CITY,
   UTAH
  DeVoto--Year p450-454
  Harlow--Story p272-273
  Ridge--America's p512-515
  Tunis--Frontier p123
  -"Bee Hive House," "Lion
  House"
    Vanderbilt--Living p194-
    195
  -Deseret
    See also DESERET (STATE
    OF)
    DeVoto--Year p454, 459,
    462, 480
    Tyler--Freedom's p106-
    107
  -Pioneer party's passage to
  Salt Lake
    DeVoto--Year p439-444,
    462-464
  -Views of Brigham Young,
  1846
    Davie--Profile p112-113
  -Irrigation of
    Bartlett--New p222, 386
-Meeting with Jim Badger
  DeVoto--Year p447-448
-"Mormon War of 1857," by
John Pulsipher
  Ridge--America's p527-529
-Music
  Wright--Culture p188-190
-Oregon Trail, first mileposts
  DeVoto--Year p444-446
-"Pipe Spring National Monu-
ment" (near Fredonia, Ari-
zona)
  Vanderbilt--Living p198
, Popular fear of
  DeVoto--Year p121, 137-141,
  146-147, 198, 222, 235-242,
  305, 313-317
-Respect for Cooke
  DeVoto--Year p370-372, 411
-Social conditions (life)

Billington--Far p210-211
-Speculation in real estate
  DeVoto--Year p82, 485-487
-War of 1812
  Ridge--America's p527-529
-Westward movement
  Billington--Far p193-217
  -Preparation for final exodus
    DeVoto--Year p438
-Women
  Bartlett--New p358-359
  Handlin--This p307, 311
  Neidle--America's p98-100
MORPHY, PAUL
  Meredith--World p60-65
MORRILL, JUSTIN SMITH
  Hine--American p246
  Portraits--American p133
MORRILL ACT OF 1862
  America 200 p57
  Bartlett--New p113, 241, 389-390,
  397
  Boardman--Civil p181
  Davie--Profile p315-316
  Dulles--United p105
  Furnas--Americans p746-747
  Harlow--Story p369-370
  Randel--Centennial p213, 395, 404-
  405, 418-419
  Reader's--Story p115, 130
MORRIS, CLARA
  Adelman--Famous p273-274
MORRIS, ESTHER HOBART
  Warren--Pictorial p120-121
MORRIS, GEORGE POPE
  Chase--America's p171-172
MORRIS, GOUVERNEUR
  Life--Growing (3) p39, 41
  , on Alexander Hamilton
    Hurd--Treasury p44-46
MORSE, JEDIAH
  Boardman--Virginia p177
MORSE, SAMUEL FINLEY BREESE
  Amer. Her. --New (5) p E174
  Boardman--Jackson. p99-100
  Boardman--Virginia p154-155
  Furnas--Americans. See index
  p998
  Harlow--Story p201
  Keyes--Hope p213
  Kraus--U.S. p381-382, 385
  Life--Sweep (4) p50-51, 68, 71, 138
  Morris--Ency. p536, 600
  Mussey--Old p121
  Reader's--Story p264, 266-267,
  375
  Train--Story p284
  Wilson--American p116-121

-Biography
  Morris--Ency. p699
-Inventions
  Wilson--American p117-123
-Telegraph
  Collins--Story p157
  Commager--Heritage p389-394
  -Morse code
    Reader's--Story p265
MORTALITY. See DEATH-RATE
MORTON, J. STERLING
  -"My last buffalo hunt," 1861
    Andrews--Indians p159-165
MORTON, WILLIAM THOMAS
GREEN, DR.
  Boardman--Jackson. p171
  Commager--Heritage p304-399
  Wilson--American p106-107
MOSBY, JOHN SINGLETON
  Amer. Her. --New (8) p E287
MOSQUITOES
  Furnas--Americans p335
"MOTHER JONES." See JONES,
MARY HARRIS
"MOTHER LODE" MEMORIAL
(Columbia, Ca.)
  Vanderbilt--Living p207
MOTHER-OF-PEARL
  Marzio--Nation p224
MOTHERS
  -"Letters to mothers," by
  Lydia Sigourney
    Grimsted--Notions p223-227
  -Views of Lydia Sigourney
    Grimsted--Notions p223-227
MOTION PICTURES
  Bonte--America p141
  Morris--Ency. p539
  Reader's--Story p470
  Wilson--American p295-297
  , and Alexander Black
    Wilson--American p296-297
  -Camera
    Reader's--Story p269
  -Development, by Leland Stan-
  ford
    Garrison--Lost p151-154
  , First, 1896 (New Orleans)
    Robertson--Book p38
  -Sport event, first, 1894
    Robertson--Book p70-71
  -Studio, first, 1893 (West
  Orange, N.J.)
    Robertson--Book p71
  -Views of Oliver Wendell
  Holmes
    Wilson--American p295
  -Women, first

    Macksey--Book p232-233
MOTLEY, JOHN LOTHROP
  Boardman--Civil p153-154
  Brooks--Flower. p43, 119, 194,
  327, 334-342, 384, 466, 483, 504,
  515
  Morris--Ency. p569-570
  Our literary p52
  -Biography
    Morris--Ency. p699
"MOTOR BUGGIES." See
AUTOMOBILES
MOTORING ASSOCIATIONS
  , First, 1895 (Chicago, Ill.)
    Robertson--Book p107
MOTT, JAMES
  Gurko--Ladies p52-54, 99-100,
  114, 138, 159
MOTT, LUCRETIA COFFIN
  Adelman--Famous p167-168
  Amer. Her. --New (6) p E209
  Boardman--Virginia p193
  Gurko--Ladies. See index p324-
  325
  Heath--Women (4) p5
  Life--Sweep (4) p64-65
  Macksey--Book p86, 110-111
  Neidle--America's p30
  Reader's--Story p433-434
  Warren--Pictorial p85, 88-90, 97-
  99, 117
  , in anti-slavery movement
    Tyler--Freedom's p446-447
  , in peace movement
    Tyler--Freedom's p420
  , in women's rights movement
    Tyler--Freedom's p452, 455
MOTTOES
  -1876
    Hilton--Way p17
MOUNT, WILLIAM SIDNEY
  Boardman--Jackson. p154
  Bode--Anatomy p72-74
  Furnas--Americans p579-580
  Larkin--Art p216-218; see also
  index p535
  Lynes--Taste. p40-42
  Meredith--World p52-55
  Reader's--Story p378
MOUNT HOLYOKE FEMALE
SEMINARY
  Reader's--Story p433
    -Views of Emily Dickinson,
    1847
      Angle--American p271-273
"MOUNTAIN MEADOWS MASSA-
CRE," 1877
  -Views of John D. Lee

Ridge--America's p524-527
"MOUNTAIN MEN"
See also names of individuals
Bartlett--New p89-91, 102, 107-
108, 256
Billington--Far p41-68
Boardman--Virginia p107-110
Brown--Westerners p58, 60-62,
91, 95, 139, 207
Commager--Heritage p508-511
DeVoto--Year. See index p520
Gilbert--Trail. See index
p235
Reader's--Story p163-171
Tunis--Frontier p112-113
-West
America's Hist. p358-359
, Wild freedom of
-Views of William Brandon
Treasury Amer. p156-
161
MOUNTAINS
, as frontier barriers
Boardman--Virginia p93
-Climbers, women
Macksey--Book p260
-West
Hine--American p179-180
"MOVING DAY" (May 1st)
Cable--American p190-191
Life--Sweep (4) p28-29
MOVING PANORAMAS. See
PANORAMAS, MOVING
MOVING PICTURES. See MOTION
PICTURES
MOWATT, ANNA CORA
Boardman--Jackson. p159
Bode--Anatomy p6, 12-13
-"Fashion" (comedy)
Grimsted--Notions p161-196
"MUCKRAKERS"
See also names of individuals
Borden--Portrait (2) p74-75
Carman--History (2) p390-391
Furnas--Americans. See index
p998
Miers--American p234-239
, Newspaper
Walker--Every. p202-205
"MUD WAGONS." See PASSEN-
GER WAGONS
"MUGWUMPS" (Independent Re-
publicans)
Butterfield--Amer. p240-241
Harlow--Story p457
Keller--Affairs p550-552, 584,
586
Life--Steel (7) p15-16

MUIR, JOHN
Boardman--Civil p177
Hine--American p177, 184-189,
250, 332, 339
MULATTOES. See QUADROONS
MULES
Bartlett--New p209
Train--Story p311, 330
MUNICIPAL GOVERNMENT. See
CITIES--Government
MUNICIPAL REFORM. See Cities
--Reform
MUNITIONS. See GUNS
MUNN VS. ILLINOIS
Harlow--Story p396
Randel--Centennial p277-278, 281
fn 23
MUNSEY, FRANK A.
Boardman--Gilded p165-166
Carman--History (2) p374
MUNSEY'S MAGAZINE
Furnas--Americans p868-869
MURAL PAINTINGS. See PAINT-
ERS AND PAINTINGS, Mural
MURDER
Hine--American p303-304, 312,
315
Keller--Affairs p491-492
MURFREE, MARY
Our literary p139
MURPHY, VIRGINIA REED
, on Donner Lake, 1846
Commager--Heritage p535-542
MURRIETA, JOAQUIN
Amer. Her. --New (6) p E209
Hine--American p212-214, 268,
310-311
Johnson--Pictorial p122-123
MUSEUMS
See also names of localities,
names of museums
Furnas--Americans p563-564
Lynes--Taste. See index p357
-1876
Randel--Centennial p383-384
-Views of Frances Trollope
Trollope--Domestic. See
index p. xi
MUSIC
See also BANDS; COMPOSERS;
CONCERTS; HYMNS; INDIANS--
Music; SONGS
Boardman--Civil p162-164, 199-
200
Boardman--Gilded p145-148, 171-
172
Boardman--Jackson p159-161,
174-176

Boardman--Virginia p149-151
Cable--American p152
Furnas--Americans. See index
p999
Handlin--This. See index p592
Morris--Ency. p614-622
Nye--Cultural p274-276
Tunis--Young p128
Wright--Every p234-236
-1870's
   Partridge--As p165
-1870's-1890's
   Harlow--Story p434-435
-1876
   Randel--Centennial. See
   index p471
-Advertising
   Handlin--This p188
, and democracy, 1830-1899
   Lowens--Music p265-270
, and religion
   Bode--Anatomy p21-23, 26
, and transcendentalism, 1835-
1850
   Lowens--Music p249-263
, Centennial
   Hilton--Way p185-186
-Conductors
   Boardman--Civil p162-163
-Conservatories
   Morris--Ency. p620
-Covers
   -"New costume polka," 1851
      Viewpoints p105
-Criticism, after 1880
   Jones--Age p224
-Culture
   Howard--Our p269-293
-Education
   Furnas--Americans p587-588
-Fasola Folk
   See also MUSIC--Shape-note
   system
   Chase--America's p183-206
, Instrumental
   Furnas--Americans p581-583
-Kentucky
   Wright--Culture p77-78
-Lack of aesthetics
   Chase--America's p166
-Lessons, 1876
   Hilton--Way p68-69
, Martial
   Reader's--Story p393
-National consciousness
   Howard--Our p226-252
-Negroes
   Howard--Our p624-632

-Spirituals
   Boardman--Civil p164
   Chase--America's p-232-
   258
   -First publications
      Chase--America's p239-
      240, 243-246
   , Folk tradition of
      Chase--America's p249-
      255
   -Manner of singing
      Chase--America's p232-
      233, 236, 238-239, 246,
      250-254
   -Relation to African music
      Chase--America's p254-
      257
   , West African
      Boardman--Virginia p150
-Pirates
   , and Andrew Law
      Lowens--Music p85-88
, Popular
   Boardman--Jackson. p174-175
   Bode--Anatomy p19-37
   Harlow--Story p248
   Howard--Our p642-655
   Randel--Centennial. See
   index (under Popular) p472
   Ross--Taste p41-42
   -1876 ("hits")
      Hilton--Way p51
   -1890's
      Jones--Age p340-341
-Publishers
   Morris--Ency. p615, 620
, Ragtime
   Boardman--Gilded p171-172
   Chase--America's p433-443
   Furnas--Americans p855-856
   -1890's
      Reader's--Story p394
   -c1895
      Howard--Our p657
, Religious
   -Mormons
      Wright--Culture p188-190
, Secular
   -Background
      Howard--Our p150-210
-Shape-note system
   Chase--America's. See index
   p730
   -Tune-books
      Lowens--Music p121-137
-Teachers
   Howard--Our p270-280, 289-
   292

-Theater
  Grimsted--Melodrama p16, 54,
    64-65, 91, 99, 106-107, 238-241
-Views of Frances Trollope
  Trollope--Domestic. See
    index p. xi
-Westward expansion
  Howard--Our p269-274
MUSIC BOXES
  McClinton--Antiques p286-288
  Wilson--Vanish. p89
MUSICAL INSTRUMENTS
  Cable--American p153
  Dreppard--Pioneer p75
  Furnas--Americans p582-583,
    586-587
  Marzio--Nation p266-273
  -1880's
    Peck--Nineteenth. n. p.
  , Indian
    Howard--Our p621
  , Popular
    Wright--Every. p236
MUSICAL TOYS
  McClinton--Antiques p282-288
MUSICIANS
  See also COMPOSERS
  -Debuts
    Morris--Ency. p618
  -Immigrants, 1848
    Howard--Our p211-225
  , Rivalry of, 1875-1899
    -Views of Walter Damrosch
      Angle--American p418-420
  -Women
    Macksey--Book p214
MUSSEY, ELLEN
  Macksey--Book p68
MUYBRIDGE, EDWARD
  Wilson--American p295

N

NAILS
  , Iron
    Furnas--Americans p623
NAISMITH, JAMES
  Boardman--Gilded p175
  Reader's--Story p489
NAMES
  -Changes
    -New York City, 1898
      Cook--City p78-79
  , Derogatory
    Carson--Polite p186, 195-196
  , for children
    Cable--American p162-163

, Occupational
  Wilson--Early p156-162
, Place
  Boorstin--Americans p299-306
  Marzio--Nation p248
NAPOLEON I
  Alden--Pioneer p145-147, 151-152
  -Deception, decrees, 1810
    Morris--Ency. p138
NASBY, PETROLEUM V. See
  LOCKE, DAVID ROSS
"NASHOBA" COLONY, TENNESSEE
  Neidle--America's p35
  Tyler--Freedom's p206-211
  , and Frances Trollope
    Trollope--Domestic. See
      index p. xi
NASHVILLE CONVENTION, 1850
  Morris--Ency. p214
NAST, THOMAS
  Harlow--Story p422
  Holzman--Stormy p190-191, 200,
    207-208, 218-219
  Keller--Affairs p47-48, 138, 246,
    270, 536
  Life--Steel (7) p12, 18-27, 79, 101,
    137
  Marzio--Nation p408-409
  Reader's--Story p361
  Walker--Every. p36, 133, 202-203
  -Biography
    Morris--Ency. p699-700
  -Cartoons
    -America
      Larkin--Art p259-260
    -Attacks on Tammany
      Butterfield--Amer. p206-
        207
    -Political zoo, Republican
      elephant, 1874
        Butterfield--Amer. p219-
          220
"NAT TURNER'S REBELLION."
  See TURNER, NAT
NATHANIEL RUSSELL HOUSE
  (Charleston, S.C.)
    Reader's--Story p235
NATION, CARRIE AMELIA MOORE
  Amer. Her. --New (11) p E391
  Bartlett--New p349-350
  Macksey--Book p116-117
NATIONAL BANK, 1832
  -Views of Andrew Jackson
    (including message to Senate),
    1832
      Walker--Reform p64-70
NATIONAL BANK ACT OF 1863
  Boardman--Civil p131

Harlow--Story p325-326
NATIONAL BANKING SYSTEM,
1864
   Morris--Ency. p239-240
NATIONAL CHARACTERISTICS.
See AMERICANS--Characteristics;
NATIONALITIES
NATIONAL FAIR, 1846
   DeVoto--Year p211-217, 238
NATIONAL FARMER'S ALLIANCE,
1877
   Amer. Her. --New (10) p854-855
   Carman--History (2) p251-252
NATIONAL GRANGE OF THE PA-
TRONS OF HUSBANDRY. See
GRANGER MOVEMENT
NATIONAL INDEPENDENT PARTY
   Holzman--Stormy p207
   Keller--Affairs p280-282
NATIONAL LABOR UNION
   Carman--History (2) p143
   Dulles--United p76-77
   Harlow--Story p403-404
   Life--Steel (7) p77-78
   -Organization, 1866
      Morris--Ency. p521
NATIONAL LEAGUE, 1876
   Dulles--History p190, 224-225
   Hilton--Way p102-104
NATIONAL MUSEUM, 1876
   Randel--Centennial p265-266
NATIONAL PERIOD
   , Early
      Morris--Ency. p130-141
NATIONAL PUBLISHING COMPANY
   Furnas--American p734-735
NATIONAL REPUBLICAN PARTY
   Boardman--Jackson. p20-21
   Life--Growing (3) p154
   Morris--Ency. p164, 167, 173-175
NATIONAL ROAD (CUMBERLAND
ROAD)
   Amer. Her. --New p430-431, E161,
   169-170
   America's Hist. p273-274
   Bartlett--New p278, 281, 287, 295
   Boardman--Virginia p55-56, 86-
   87
   Bonte--America p100
   Butterfield--Amer. p77
   Carman--History (1) p361-362,
   367, 459-460, 462
   Davidson--Life (2) p210-211
   Drury--Midwest p101-110
   Harlow--Story p194-195
   Langdon--Everyday (2) p66-81
   Tunis--Frontier p70-72, 74, 93
   Tunis--Young p79-80

Wright--Every. p79
-Travel, by Charles Fenno Hoff-
man, 1830's
   Angle--American p202-205
   -1835
      Ridge--America's p276-278
NATIONAL TRADES UNION
   Boardman--Jackson. p84
   Morris--Ency. p519-521
NATIONAL UNION PARTY
   Keller--Affairs p55, 57-60, 66, 70
NATIONAL WOMAN'S LOYAL
LEAGUE
   Gurko--Ladies p211-212
NATIONAL (AMERICAN) WOMAN'S
SUFFRAGE ASSOCIATION
   Amer. Her. --New (11) p E391-392
   Furnas--Americans p643-645
   Gurko--Ladies. See index p235
   Sochen--Herstory p175, 201, 231-
   232, 244, 267
   Warren--Pictorial p117
NATIONALISM
   See also PATRIOTISM
   Bode--Anatomy p. xii-xiii, 49-50,
   58-59, 65-66, 83-84
   Cable--American p92
   Handlin--This p154, 172
   Hine--American p226-227, 249-
   250, 281, 320-322, 324, 328, 333
   Kraus--U.S. p329-333
   , after War of 1812
      Amer. Her. --New (5) p364-376
      Harlow--Story p186-189, 221
   , Diplomatic
      Borden--Portrait (1) p151-152
   , Economic, 1816
      Borden--Portrait (1) p150
   , Legal
      Borden--Portrait (1) p150-151
   -South
      Carman--History (1) p636
NATIONALITIES
   See also names of nationalities
   Alden--Pioneer p205-206
   -Ethnic stereotypes
      Marzio--Nation p277
   -Group identities
      Marzio--Nation p245
NATIVE AMERICAN PARTY, 1842
   Boardman--Jackson. p184-185
   Butterfield--Amer. p127
   Morris--Ency. p187
NATIVE AMERICANS. See
INDIANS
NATIVISM
   See also INTOLERANCE
   Boardman--Civil p17-18, 117-118

Boardman--Jackson. p183-185
Carman--History (1) p509, 511-512, 613
Furnas--Americans. See index p999
Life--Reaching (8) p60, 63-67, 69
Morris--Ency. p187
Tyler--Freedom's p363-364, 376-377, 385-390
, Political
See also "KNOW-NOTHING PARTY"; NATIVE AMERICAN PARTY
Tyler--Freedom's p389-395
NATURAL RESOURCES
, and energy
Jones--Age p301-302
, Exhaustion of
Mumford--Brown p77-80
-Exploitation
Dulles--United p53-55
-West
Hine--American p124, 177-179, 182-183, 186-187, 222, 270, 330, 332
NATURALISTS
See also names of naturalists
Gilbert--Trail. See index p235
Jones--Age p310-317
Wilson--American p96-101
NAUVOO, ILLINOIS. See MORMONS--Illinois--Nauvoo
NAVAHO INDIANS
Amer. Her. --Indians. p394-395; see also index p422
Amer. Her. --New (9) p797
Boardman--Jackson. p73-74
Brown--Westerners p205
DeVoto--Year p48, 324, 327, 350, 369, 376-380, 383, 401, 406
-Names, War
Amer. Her. --Indians p382
NAVAL ACT OF 1883
Collins--Story p274
NAVIGATION
Boardman--Jackson. p169
-Instruments
Marzio--Nation p117
NAVY. See CONFEDERACY--Navy; U.S. NAVY
NAVY DEPARTMENT, 1876
Randel--Centennial p262, 271-273
"NAWAT" ("LEFT HAND")
(Arapahoe Indian)
Andrews--Indian leaders p129
"NAWKAW" (Winnebago Indian)
Andrews--Indian leaders p84

NAYLOR, ISAAC
-"The battle of Tippecanoe," 1811
Ridge--America's p260-262
NEAGLE, JOHN
Amer. Her. --New (5) p E174
Larkin--Art p127; see also index p535
"NEAMATHLA" (Seminole-Creek Indian)
Andrews--Indian Leaders p73
NEBRASKA
See also ANTI-NEBRASKANS; KANSAS-NEBRASKA ACT
Bartlett--New p113, 336-337
Carman--History (1) p614, 783
Drury--Midwest p160-165
Hine--American. See index p366
Life--New (5) p55-56, 67, 121
Tunis--Frontier p117, 133, 154, 156, 160
-1876
Randel--Centennial p39, 113
-Bill to organize, by Stephen A. Douglas, 1854
Angle--By p191-192
-Omaha
Brown--Westerners p124, 161, 168, 173, 186, 192
Handlin--This p288-291
Tunis--Frontier p142-143
-Slaves and slavery
-Extension bill
Angle--By p193-198
NEEDLEWORK. See types of needlework; CHILDREN'S NEEDLE-WORK; SAMPLERS
NEGROES
See also AMERICAN COLONIZA-TION SOCIETY; "BLACK CODES"; MUSIC--Negroes "QUADROONS"; SLAVES AND SLAVERY
Bartlett--New p127-130, 208-209
Boardman--Civil p210; see also index (under Blacks)
Boardman--Gilded. See index (under Blacks) p197
Boardman--Jackson. See index (under Blacks) p206
Boardman--Virginia. See index (under Blacks) p212
Boorstin--Americans p109, 179-190
Carman--History (1). See index p. xviii
Furnas--Americans. See index p999
Handlin--This. See index p592

Keller--Affairs. See index
p623
Life--Growing (3). See index
(under Blacks) p172
Life--New (5) p15, 68, 74, 104,
117, 149
Life--Steel (7). See index
(under Blacks) p156
Life--Union (6). See index
(under Blacks) p172
Lynes--Domestic. p159, 165, 174
Walker--Every. p89-90, 172-173
Weisberger--Amer. p227-232
-1876
  Randel--Centennial. See
  index p472
-Alabama, 1881
  -Views of Booker T. Washington
    Commager--Heritage p922-
    924
, and Ku Klux Klan, 1871
  Angle--American p349-352
, and Civil war
  Dowdey--Experiment. See
  index p451
  Sochen--Herstory p170-172
, and community
  Boorstin--Americans p190-
  192
, anti-Negro prejudice
  Furnas--Americans. See
  index p999
, as Christians
  Hunt--Life p123
, as Congressmen, 1870's
  Butterfield--Amer. p222
, as entertainers
  Marzio--Nation p420-421
, as immigrants
  Boorstin--Americans p179-
  190
-"The cause of the negro peo-
ple, " 1864
  Trachtenberg--Demo. p52-65
-Characteristics
  Hunt--Life p111-113, 123
-Chronology, 1850-1865
  Young--Women p296-297
-Churches
  Boorstin--Americans p196-
  199
-Classes
  Cable--American p301-302
-Clubs
  Macksey--Book p275
-Colonization movement
  See also AMERICAN

COLONIZATION SOCIETY
Boorstin--Americans p183, 185,
187, 189
Furnas--Americans p317-321
Hunt--Life p233-238
, and William Thornton
  Hunt--Life p234-235
-Education
  Furnas--Americans. See
  index p999
, Emancipated
  Trachtenberg--Demo. p111-
  124
-Exodus, schemes for
  Alden--Pioneer p226
-Folklore
  Our literary p136-137
-Freedom, and cause of people,
1864
  Trachtenberg--Demo. p51-65
-Frontier, life on, 1862
  Andrews--Indians p59-60
-Humor
  Hunt--Life p111-113
, in Census
  Boorstin--Americans p180, 184
, in theater audiences
  Grimsted--Melodrama p52-53,
  112n
, in Union league
  Commager--Heritage p816-821
, Language of
  Boorstin--Americans p170, 191
-Law of slavery
  Boorstin--Americans p199-206
-Legislators
  Dulles--United p24-25
-Life
  Kraus--U.S. p408
-Lynchings
  Harris--Land p147-158
-Music. See MUSIC--Negroes
-New Orleans
  Life--Steel (7) p120-121
-New York City
  -Views of Jacob A. Riis
    Cook--City p92-94
, on stage
  Grimsted--Melodrama p190-
  192, 193n, 194, 239-240
-Politicians, 1870's
  Life--Steel (7) p107
  -"Black parliament"
    -Views of James S. Pike
      Angle--American p346-
      349
-Population
  , 1830-1850

Boardman--Jackson. p103-
104, 111
-1850-1860
Boardman--Civil p10-11
-1899 (ten largest cities)
Cook--City p22
, Post Civil war
Harlow--Story p335-344, 360
Young--Women p303-305
-Religion
Cable--American p186-187
-South
Sochen--Herstory p203-207
-Southwest
Burner--America (1) p218-
220
-Suffrage. See EMANCIPATION
PROCLAMATION; SUFFRAGE,
Negro
-Uprisings
Alden--Pioneer p200-201
Boorstin--Americans p183-
185
-Views of Frances Trollope
Trollope--Domestic. See
index p. xi-xii
-Vital statistics
See also NEGROES--
Population
Kraus--U.S. p408
-Wealth, 1887
Cable--American p301
-West
Hine--American. See index
(under Blacks) p360
, and Indians
Hine--American p195,
206-208
-Women
See also TRADE AND
TRADERS--Negroes--Women
Handlin--This p133
, as reformers
Warren--Pictorial p85-88
, Professional
Sochen--Herstory p188-189
NEOCLASSICISM
, Forms and spirit of
Gowans--Images p243-255
"NEOQUAQUOIT" (Fox Indian)
Andrews--Indian leaders p82
"NESTERS." See HOMESTEAD
ACT, 1862
NETHERLANDS. See HOLLAND
NEVADA
Randel--Centennial p118-119
Tunis--Frontier p129, 132, 135-
137, 139, 141

-Johntown
Watkins--Gold p65-67
-Mines and mining
See also COMSTOCK LODE
Watkins--Gold p161-164
-Camps
Commager--Heritage p715-
719
-"Treasure Hill" Silver Mines
Watkins--Gold p164-167
-Washoe district
Billington--Far p251-259
NEVINS, ALLAN
, on "Age of Enterprise"
Miers--American p239-244
NEW ENGLAND
See also names of N.E. states
Boardman--Virginia. See index
p215
Furnas--Americans. See index
p999
Handlin--This. See index p592
Jones--Age p57-64
-1876
Randel--Centennial p94-99
-Fine arts
Jones--Age p59-60
-Inhabitants
, Character of
Hunt--Life p36-37
, in Middlewest
Drury--Midwest p77-78
-Intellectual life
Jones--Age p59-62
Life--Sweep (4) p60-62
-Literature
Harlow--Story p243-244
Jones--Age p61-63
-Rural decay
Ridge--America's p294-295
-Summer
, by Richard M. Ketchum
Treasury Amer. p386-393
-Paintings, by Winslow Homer
Treasury Amer. p286-293
-Weather
-Views of Samuel L. Clemens
Hurd--Treasury p105-106
NEW ENGLAND EMIGRANT AID
CO.
Carman--History (1) p615
NEW ENGLAND WOMEN'S SUF-
FRAGE ASSOCIATION
Furnas--Americans p642-643
NEW HAMPSHIRE
Carman--History (1) p782
Hunt--Life. See index p294
Mussey--Old p71, 73-75

-Portsmouth
    Holzman--Stormy p217-218
NEW HARMONY, INDIANA (COM-
MUNITY)
    Alden--Pioneer p223
    Amer. Her. --New (6) p E209
    Boardman--Virginia p193-194
    Borden--Portrait (1) p182
    Davidson--Life (2) p345-346
    Drury--Midwest p132
    Hine--American p264-265
    Linton--Bicentennial p92-93
    Neidle--America's p34, 36
    Reader's--Story p320
    Tyler--Freedom's p196-206
    Vanderbilt--Living p156
NEW HAVEN, CONNECTICUT
-1810-1820
    Mussey--Old p28
-1876
    Randel--Centennial p61-63
NEW JERSEY
    Carman--History (1) p780, 782
    Handlin--This p143, 222, 224,
    262, 354
-Red Bank
    Handlin--This p222-224
NEW MEXICO
    Boardman--Virginia p103-104
    Brown--Westerners. See index
    p287
    Carman--History (1) p565
    Harlow--Story p272, 275-276,
    285-287, 371
    Hine--American p100, 102, 106-
    107, 109, 120, 195, 214, 267
    Life--New (5) p32-36, 38-39, 54
    Whitney--American p104-105,
    110, 115, 124, 234, 248
, Acquisition of (and Texas,
    California)
    DeVoto--Year p6, 13-15
, and "Manifest destiny," 1840's
    DeVoto--Year p8-9
-Battle of Sacramento
    DeVoto--Year p400-401
, Conquest of
    DeVoto--Year p187, 227-235,
    243-271
, Disaffection in
    DeVoto--Year p251, 267-271
-Indians
    DeVoto--Year p153, 244-245,
    376-380
-Mines and mining
    Watkins--Gold p124-125, 129-
    130, 132-133, 274
-Occupation by "Army of the

West"
    DeVoto--Year p268-269, 323-
    327
-Organization as territory, 1850
    DeVoto--Year p475-476, 479
, Revolt in
    DeVoto--Year p394-395
-Santa Fé
    Tunis--Frontier p103-108, 132
    -Trade
        DeVoto--Year p116-117
-Taos
    DeVoto--Year. See index
    p523
, under Spain and Mexico
    DeVoto--Year p13, 16-18, 29,
    50, 69, 72, 105
"NEW NATIONALISM"
    Alden--Pioneer p175-177
NEW ORLEANS, LOUISIANA
    Bartlett--New p85, 151-152, 307-
    308, 321
    Boardman--Virginia. See index
    p215
    Carman--History (1) p353, 657,
    665, 711-712, 730
    Davidson--Life (2) p117
    Handlin--This p110-112, 133-136,
    162-163, 201-203, 250, 333, 337
    Holzman--Stormy p70-71, 76-80,
    96-103
    Hunt--Life. See index p294
    Life--Growing (3) p106-107, 118-
    119, 124, 134, 143
    Life--Steel (7) p31, 104-105, 112-
    125
    Tunis--Frontier p68, 80, 88, 90-91
    Vanderbilt--Living p182-185
    Weisberger--Amer. p158-159
-1883
    Cable--American p297
, Battle of
    America's Hist. p318-320
    Boardman--Jackson. p3-4
    Butterfield--Amer. p60-61
    Keyes--Hope p238
    Linton--Bicentennial p76-77
    Morris--Ency. p151-152
    Reader's--Story p89
    Wright--Every. p58
    , and Andrew Jackson, 1815
        Angle--American p188-192
        Collins--Story p193
-Capture, 1862
    Collins--Story p228
-Civil war
    See also NEW ORLEANS,
    Battle of

Andrews--Women p353-371
Dowdey--Experiment. See
 index p451
Jordan--Civil p45, 83, 87, 90,
 94-96, 122, 153
Life--Union (6). See index
 p175
-Dueling, 1840
 Downey--Our p255-268
-"The foreign city," by Charles
 Dudley Warner, 1889
 Cook--City p34-35
-French quarter
 Life--Steel (7) p116-117
-Rioting, Reconstruction days
 Collins--Story p233
-Rivermen
 Life--Steel (7) p124-125
-Theater. See Theater--New
 Orleans
NEW ORLEANS (ship)
 Bartlett--New p317-318
"NEW THEOLOGY," 1876
 Randel--Centennial p457-459
NEW YEAR'S DAY
 Cable--American p163-164
 Carson--Polite p198
 Partridge--As p136-137
 Walker--Every. p239-240
-1876
 Hilton--Way p176-178
 Randel--Centennial p1-3, 67-
 68, 200
NEW YORK (state)
 Boardman--Virginia. See index
 p215
 Carman--History (1) p782
 Furnas--Americans. See index
 p1000
 Handlin--This p164, 193, 266,
 346, 353-354, 365, 368
 Hunt--Life. See index p294
-1876
 Randel--Centennial p99-100
-Census, 1845, 1855
 Van Wagenen--Golden. See
 index p176
-Garden City
 Furnas--Americans p677, 810,
 817-818
-Plattsburg, Battle of, 1814
 Collins--Story p189
-Wheat
 Van Wagenen--Golden p66-68,
 76-78
NEW YORK CENTRAL
-War with Cyrus McCormick
 Wilson--American p142-143

NEW YORK CENTRAL RAILROAD
 Boardman--Civil p139
-War with Cyrus McCormick
 Wilson--American p142-143
NEW YORK CITY
 Boardman--Jackson p181-182
 Boardman--Virginia. See index
 p215
 Davidson--Life (2) p109
 Furnas--Americans. See index
 p1000
 Handlin--This. See index p592-
 593
 Hunt--Life. See index p294
 Life--New (5) p10-11, 60-62, 78,
 97, 103, 126-127
 Life--Reaching (8). See index
 p174
 Life--Steel (7). See index p158
 Life--Union (6). See index p175
 Lynes--Domestic. See index
 p305
 Ross--Taste p250
 Tunis--Young p113-121
 Wright--Every. p117-122
-1807-1836
 Life--Growing (3) p48-49, 52-
 53
-1867
 Cook--City p9-10
-1868
 Cable--American p217
-1876
 Randel--Centennial. See index
 p472
, and Frances Trollope
 Trollope--Domestic. See
 index p. xii
-Baths and bathing
 -Free rain, 1894
 Cook--City p141
-"The Bend"
 -Views of Jacob A. Riis, 1890
 Cook--City p292
-Board of Health
 Cable--American p292
-The Bowery
 Life--Steel (7) p48-49
-Broadway
 Partridge--As p99
 -1836
 Ross--Taste p270
, By gaslight
 -Views of C.C. Foster, 1850
 Burner--America (1) p301-
 310
-Carriages
 Tunis--Young p118-119

-Central Park
　See also OLMSTED,
　　FREDERICK LAW
　Boardman--Civil p114-115
　Davidson--Life (2) p166-167
　Mumford--Brown p87-88, 90
　Reader's--Story p248
　Ross--Taste p148, 150
　-1865
　　Portraits--Americans
　　p91-92
　-1869
　　Ross--Taste p270
-Citizens association, 1868
　Cook--City p218
-City hall, c1860
　Landmarks--Liberty p18-19
　Viewpoints p150
-Corruption
　Carman--History (1) p707-709
-Crowded conditions, 1875
　Cook--City p155-157
-Crystal Palace
　Ross--Taste p248
-Draft riots
　Carman--History (1) p649-650
-Election and naturalization
frauds
　-Views of John Davenport,
　1894
　　Cook--City p195
-Good government clubs
　-Views of Edmond Kelly,
　1894
　　Cook--City p20
-Greenwich Village
　Tunis--Young p115
-Growth
　Carman--History (1) p464,
　473-474
　Collins--Story p151
-Harbor
　-"Hell gate," 1876
　　Randel--Centennial p268-
　　270
-Hawkers
　Tunis--Young p116-117
-Horse racing
　Tunis--Young p121
-Housing
　Partridge--As p121-122
-"Human and heroic," by Walt
Whitman, 1889
　Cook--City p37
-Immigrants
　Partridge--As p104-105
-Irish in politics
　Weisberger--Amer. p170-171,

173, 178-191
-Life
　Life--Sweep (4) p26-29
　-1850
　　-Views of Anna Cora Mowatt
　　Grimsted--Notions p161-
　　196
　-1890's
　　-Views of Henry Collins
　　Brown
　　　Angle--American p408-
　　　413
　-Contrast with ancient Athens
　　Trachtenberg--Demo. p246-
　　247
-Newsboys
　Partridge--As p103
-"Niblo's Gardens"
　Woodward--Way p210-212
-"North and South from Brooklyn
Bridge," (poetry) by Marion
Wilcox, 1894
　Cook--City p10
-Panic of 1873. See PANIC OF
1873--New York City
-Park Theatre (1st and 2nd)
　Dulles--History p101, 103
　Ross--Taste p105-106, 120, 142
-Pleasure gardens
　Tunis--Young p121
-Police
　-"Recollections of a New York
　city Chief of Police," 1888
　　Cook--City p197-199
-Poverty, 1890
　-Views of Jacob Riis
　　Commager--Heritage p895-
　　901
-Railroad Commission bill
　Cook--City p58-59
-Railways, Electric
　-Third Avenue El
　　-Views of William Dean
　　Howells
　　　Cook--City p52
-Sanitation
　-Views of Josiah Strong
　　Cook--City p138
-Slums. See SLUMS--New York
city
-Society
　Cable--American p272-280
　Hunt--Life p69-70
　Nye--Cultural p111-112
　-Views of Ward McAllister
　　Cook--City p267
-Streets
　200 Years (2) p80

, Conditions on, 1893
    Cook--City p144-145
-Telegraph boys. See
TELEGRAPH--Boys--New
York city
-Theater. See THEATER--New
York city
-Thieves and thievery
   -Views of Jacob A. Riis,
   1890
    Cook--City p283-284
-"The Tombs"
   Furnas--American p417-418
-Transportation
   Tunis--Young p117-119
   -Transit, 1867
    See also NEW YORK CITY
    --Railways, Electric
   Cook--City p60
-Views of C. C. Foster
   Burner--America (1) p301-
   310
-Views of Philip Hone
   Commager--Heritage p399-
   410
-Waldorf Hotel
   Ross--Taste p72
-Wall Street
   Furnas--Americans p652-653
   -1817
    Hunt--Life p69
   -"Barons," 1865-1872
    Butterfield--Amer. p202-
    203
-Water supply
   Tunis--Young p116
NEW YORK CONSTITUTIONAL
CONVENTION
  -Views of David Buel, Jr.
   Walker--Reform p55-61
NEW YORK DECORATIVE ART
SOCIETY, 1880's
  Ross--Taste, p284
NEW YORK GALLERY OF FINE
ARTS
  Lynes--Taste p40-41
"NEW YORK" GROUP (women's
reform)
  Gurko--Ladies p225-226, 228,
  234
NEW YORK HERALD
  Bode--Anatomy p252, 254-255
  Langdon--Everyday (2) p175-
  180
  Walker--Every. p128-129
  -Yellow journalism
   Woodward--Way p206-208
NEW YORK JOURNAL

Furnas--Americans p856-858,
  860-864
Walker--Every. p157, 187, 191-
  195, 202
NEW YORK LEDGER
  Bode--Anatomy p257-258
NEW YORK PHILHARMONIC
SOCIETY
  Boardman--Jackson. p159-160
  Chase--America's p326-330
NEW YORK STOCK EXCHANGE
  Davidson--Life (2) p144
  -"Black Penny," 1869
   Collins--Story p241
NEW YORK SUN
  Langdon--Everyday (2) p171-174
NEW YORK TRIBUNE
  Furnas--Americans p427, 449,
  558-559, 641, 742, 863
  Harlow--Story p348
  Langdon--Everyday (2) p179-182
NEW YORK WORLD
  Furnas--Americans p859-863
  Life--Reaching (8) p36-37, 41, 131
  Walker--Every. p130, 191-192,
  194-195
NEWCOMB, SIMON
  Randel--Centennial p262, 272, 279,
  420-421
NEWHALL, JOHN B.
  -"An Iowa land sale," 1840
   Ridge--America's p406-407
NEWMARKET
  , Battle of
   Commager--Heritage p765-771
NEWPORT, RHODE ISLAND
  Boardman--Gilded p154
  Dulles--History p149-153, 202, 241
  Handlin--This p346-347, 371
  Mussey--Old p54
NEWSBOYS
  Furnas--Americans. See index
  p1000
  -1833
   Viewpoints p106
  -New York city
   Partridge--As p103
NEWSPAPERS
  See also "PENNY PRESS"; names
  of newspapers
  Boardman--Gilded p163-165
  Boardman--Jackson. p185-186
  Boardman--Virginia p191-192
  Bode--Anatomy p116, 250-258
  Borden--Portrait (2) p59
  Dulles--United p108-109
  Furnas--Americans. See index
  p1000

Handlin--This. See index p593
Harlow--Story p247-248, 428-430
Hunt--Life p149-150
Kraus--U.S. p377-379
Life--Reaching (8) p35-37, 131-
  132
Life--Sweep (4) p26, 52, 59-60, 78
Morris--Ency. p581-586
Wright--Every. p239-240
-1800-1835
  Hart--Popular p67
-1810-1840
  Leyden--Everyday (2) p154-
  155
-1835-1860
  Amer. Her.--New (11) p937-
  938
-1840-1860
  , Daily
    Bode--Anatomy p116
  , Weekly
    Bode--Anatomy p116
-1840's
  Butterfield--Amer. p126-127
-1876
  Randel--Centennial p11, 362-
  364
, "Booster"
  Boorstin--Americans p124-
  134
-California
  Wright--Culture p154-155
-Cincinnati, Ohio
  Trollope--Domestic. See
    index p.iv
-Circulation
  Walker--Every. p187-188
-Circulation drive
  Reader's--Story p364
-Columns
  Nye--Cultural p251-252
-Color supplement, First, 1893
  (N.Y. city)
  Robertson--Book p117
, Illustrated
  Reader's--Story p359-360
-Northwest territory
  Wright--Culture p111-114
-Photographs, First, 1880
  (N.Y. city)
  Robertson--Book p118
-Power of press
  Reader's--Story p358-361
, Southern
  Boorstin--Americans p216-
  217
, Syndicates
  Morris--Ency. p585

-Views of Frances Trollope
  Trollope--Domestic. See
    index p.xii
-Weeklies
  See also NEWSPAPERS--
  1840-1860, Weekly
  Bode--Anatomy p255-258
-Westward expansion
  Morris--Ency. p562
NEWTON, JOHN, LIEUTENANT
COLONEL
  Randel--Centennial p268-269
NEZ PERCE INDIANS
  Amer. Her.--Indians p308-310,
  313-316
  Andrews--Indian leaders p116,
  166-175
  Billington--Far p79-80, 82-83
  Boardman--Gilded p95
  Boardman--Jackson p74
  Boardman--Virginia p119
  Brown--Westerners p48-50, 249
  Gilbert--Trail. p32
  Hine--American p57, 89, 194, 197
  Ross--Heroines p65, 67, 88-89
  Treasury--Amer. p280-291
  Tunis--Frontier p114-115, 144
    -Outbreak, 1877
    Bartlett--New p110-111
NIAGARA FALLS, NEW YORK
  -1854, 1866
    Viewpoints p108, 119
  , and tightrope walker, 1859
    White--American p41-42
  -Cable crossing by Blondin, 1859
    Treasury Amer. p274-279
NICARAGUA
  -Clayton-Bulwer treaty
    Carman--History (1) p574-575
NICHOLS, CLARINA HOWARD
  Tyler--Freedom's p457-458
NICHOLS, JESSE C.
  Portraits--American p93
NICHOLS, MARY GROVE
  Warren--Pictorial p81
NICHOLS, THOMAS LOW
  , on Garrison's mobbing by Bos-
  ton conservatives
    Commager--Heritage p483-486
  , on reform
    Commager--Heritage p416-419
NICOLAY, JOHN G.
  , on Grant appointment as su-
  preme commander
    Angle--American p329-330
  , on Lincoln learning of Bull Run,
  1861
    Angle--American p315-316

, on "old time" religion, 1835
  Angle--American p265-268
-"The story of the assassination
  of President Lincoln and the
  pursuit of the assassins"
  Jones--Shaping p190-205
NICOLLET, JOSEPH N.
  Boardman--Jackson. p65-66
NIGHTINGALE, FLORENCE
  Young--Women p4, 9, 18-19, 61,
  102-103, 179, 193
NILES, HEZEKIAH
  Morris--Ency. p582
NINETEENTH CENTURY
-Chronology
    -1859
      Young--Women p26
    -1860
      Young--Women p26-27
    -1861
      Young--Women p39, 48,
      58, 67, 82-83, 105, 117,
      127, 139
    -1862
      Young--Women p139-140,
      157, 173-174, 190, 206-
      207, 218, 245
    -1863
      Young--Women p233, 245-
      246, 259-260, 270-271,
      284, 306
    -1864
      Young--Women p315-317,
      325
    -1864-1883 (illustrations)
      Trachtenberg--Demo.
      p184-194
    -1865
      Young--Women p340-341
-Personalities
  Dreppard--Pioneer p111-115
-Summary of progress, 1890's
  Life--Reaching (8) p140,
  149-166
-"Taboo" topics
  Cable--American p225-232
NOAH, MORDECAI MANUEL
  Boardman--Virginia p146-147
NOEL, MARY
  -Dime novels
    Treasury Amer. p366-373
"NO-GOODS" (Rascals)
  Wilson--Early p175-178
NOISE
  , City
    -Views of John H. Girdner,
    1896
      Cook--City p158-159

-Effect on nerves
  Trachtenberg--Demo. p242-245
NOME, ALASKA
  Watkins--Gold p153-156
NOMENCLATURE. See NAMES
NONIMPORTATION ACT, 1806
  Carman--History (1) p335, 338
NONINTERCOURSE ACT, 1809
  Boardman--Virginia p34-35
  Bonte--America p89
  Carman--History (1) p340, 342,
  472
  Harlow--Story p174-175
  Kraus--U.S. p316-317
  Morris--Ency. p137
NONRESISTANCE MOVEMENT
  Tyler--Freedom's p411-415
NORBERTINE, SISTER
  Ross--Heroines p149-150
NORDICA, LILLIAN
  Adelman--Famous p248-249
NORFOLK, VIRGINIA
  , in Civil war
    Dowdey--Experiment p24, 40-
    41, 72, 74, 161, 163, 178, 180
  -Occupation, 1861-1862
    Commager--Heritage p749-752
NORMAL SCHOOLS
  Furnas--Americans p546-547
  Train--Story p288-289
  -Lexington, Mass.
    Furnas--Americans p546-547
NORRIS, BENJAMIN FRANKLIN
  ("FRANK")
  Boardman--Gilded p128
  Furnas--Americans. See index
  p1000
  -Biography
    Amer. Her.--New (11) p E392-
    393
NORTH
  Boardman--Jackson. See index
  p210
  Boardman--Virginia p60-61, 187-
  188
  Carman--History (1). See index
  p. xvix
  -1849-1865
    Life--New (5). See index
    p158
  -Life
    Kraus--U.S. p463-464
  -Pre Civil war
    America's Hist. p394-401
NORTH AMERICAN PHILANSTERY
  (PHALANX), Red Bank, N.J.,
  1843-1854
  Boardman--Jackson. p123

Handlin--This p222-224
NORTH AMERICAN REVIEW
    Brooks--Flower. p111-134
NORTH CAROLINA
    Carman--History (1) p634, 782
    Handlin--This p117, 120-122, 361
    Hunt--Life. See index p295
    Life--New (5) p99, 136-137
    Randel--Centennial p101, 422-423
    , in Civil war
        Dowdey--Experience p10, 22,
        94, 144, 158, 166, 179, 226,
        255, 292, 310, 323, 377, 395
    -Wilmington
        Holzman--Story p149, 152,
        154-155
NORTH CAROLINA TEMPERANCE
SOCIETY
    Boardman--Jackson. p130
NORTHEAST
    Life--New (5) p9-15, 33, 52, 68-
    69
    -1850's
        Life--New (5) p12-13
NORTHEND, MARY HAROLD
    , on Salem, school and plays
        Commager--Heritage p360-364
NORTHERN CONFEDERACY
    -Scheme, 1803-1804
        Morris--Ency. p133
NORTHERN PACIFIC RAILROAD
    Bartlett--New p113, 158, 243,
    289, 322, 328-331
    Boardman--Civil p140
    Hine--American p96, 151, 164,
    181, 198-199
    Life--Steel (7) p31-32, 54
NORTHWEST
    Life--New (5) p10-15
    -1850's
        Life--New (5) p13-15
    -Chicago, and railroads
        -Views of Julian Ralph, 1893
            Cook--City p45, 47
    , Speculation in, 1836
        Ridge--America's p299-300
    -Women, "imported"
        Ross--Westward p113-120
NORTHWEST COMPANY
    Carman--History (1) p369-370,
    378, 555-556
    DeVoto--Year p57, 61
    Hine--American p45-48
NORTHWEST CONSPIRACY
    Amer. Her. --New (8) p E288
NORTHWEST ORDINANCE
    Hine--American p65-66, 319,
    322

NORTHWEST TERRITORY
    America's Hist. p284-291
    Boardman--Virginia p95-96, 112-
    113
    -Theater. See THEATER--
    Northwest Territory
NORTON, ANDREWS
    Brooks--Flower. See index p546
NORTON, CHARLES B., GENERAL
    Randel--Centennial p283-285
NORTON, CHARLES ELIOT
    Brooks--Flower. p453-459; see
    also index p546
NORWEGIANS
    Handlin--This p204-212, 214-217
    Marzio--Nation p245
    -Family home in Iowa, 1863-1865
        -Views of Gro Svendsen
            Angle--American p366-369
NORWICH UNIVERSITY
    , as first civilian engineering
    school
        Boardman--Virginia p81
NOTION STORES
    Wilson--Vanish. p136
NOTT, CHARLES C.
    -"Causes for migration: New
    England's rural decay," 1889
        Ridge--America's p294-295
NOVELISTS
    See also FICTION; names of
    novelists
    Boardman--Jackson. p144-147,
    151
    Carman--History (1) p542-548
    Life--Sweep (4) p60
    , Antislavery
        Hart--Popular p110-113
    -Detective writers
        -Women, First
            Robertson--Book p49
    , of manners
        Morris--Ency. p574
    , Religious
        Hart--Popular p117-121, 163-
        169
    , Sensational
        Hart--Popular p98-99
    , Temperance
        Hart--Popular p108-110
    -Women
        Cable--American p151
        Hart--Popular p91-98
    , First
        Robertson--Book p49
NOYES, JOAN HUMPHREY
    Alden--Pioneer p224
    Amer. Her. --New (6) p E209-210

Boardman--Jackson. p127
Cable--American p194-195, 227
Tyler--Freedom's p184-195
-Communal society
    Wilson--American p92
-"Stirpiculture"
    Cable--American p194
NUDITY
  Cable--American p270-271
, and sculpture
    Cable--American p156, 158
, of women
    Trachtenberg--Demo. p299-
    312
NULLIFICATION
  See also CALHOUN, JOHN C.
  Amer. Her. --New (5) p399-401,
  E174-175
  Boardman--Jackson. p13-17
  Borden--Portrait (1) p165
  Butterfield--Amer. p86-87
  Collins--Story p176, 179
  Harlow--Story p229-230
  Life--Sweep (4) p12-19
  Linton--Bicentennial p102-104
  Morris--Ency. p171-173
  Whitney--American p76-77, 96-
  97
-Views of Charles M. Wiltse
    Miers--American p174-178
NURSES AND NURSING
  See also ARMY NURSING
  CORPS
  Warren--Pictorial p105-106
-1876
    Hilton--Way p70
-Civil war
    Dannett--Noble. See index
    p413-419, under names of
    women, hospitals
    Harlow--Story p322-323
    Young--Women. See index
    p385-389, under names of
    women
-Homes
    -Views of Mrs. John Farrar
      Cable--American p105-106
-Profession
    Warren--Pictorial p133-135
NUTS
  Van Wagenen--Golden p100
NUTTALL, THOMAS
  Boardman--Virginia p103
  Gilbert--Trail. See index p235
NYE, BILL
-Comic views of Indian wars
  (1870's)
    Burner--America (1) p345-346

O

OAKLEY, ANNIE
  Hine--American p268, 277-278
  Macksey--Book p229, 256
  Reader's--Story p173
-Biography
    Amer. Her. --New (11) p E393
-"Oakley Plantation House"
  (Francesville, La.)
    Vanderbilt--Living p186
OATMAN, OLIVE
, as Indian captive
    Amer. Her. --Indians p384
OBERLIN COLLEGE
  Boardman--Jackson. p137
  Drury--Midwest p61
  Furnas--Americans p492, 519,
  744-745
  Gurko--Ladies p126-134, 190
  Hine--American p182, 248-249
  Kraus--U.S. p446
  Warren--Pictorial p76-77
  Wright--Culture p108-110
  Wright--Every. p196
-Education of women
    Tyler--Freedom's p433
-Founding
    Tyler--Freedom's p257-258
O'BRIEN, WILLIAM S.
  Furnas--Americans p376-377
OBSERVATORIES. See ASTRONOMY
  AND ASTRONOMERS
OCCUPATIONS
-New England
    Mussey--Old p108-110
, Rapidity of
    Bartlett--New p447-448
-Trends
    Morris--Ency. p527
OCEANOGRAPHY
  Boardman--Jackson. p169
  Morris--Ency. p531-532
OCHS, ADOLPH SIMON
  Boardman--Gilded p164-165
-Biography
    Amer. Her. --New (11) p E393
    Morris--Ency. p700
OCONALUFTEE INDIAN VILLAGE
  (Cherokee, N.C.)
  Vanderbilt--Living p130
O'CONNELL, ANTHONY, SISTER
  Neidle--America's p75
ODDIE, TASKER L.
  Watkins--Gold p167-168
OFFENBACH, JACQUES
  Randel--Centennial. See index
  p472

OFFICEHOLDERS
   Handlin--This p170-171, 180-181,
   277-278, 284, 369, 384-387
OGDEN, PETER SKENE
   -"The Hudson's Bay Company
   invades the Rockies," 1825
   Ridge--America's p386-389
OGDEN, WILLIAM B.
   Boardman--Jackson. p78
   Boorstin--Americans p116-119
   Drury--Midwest p29-30
OGLALO INDIANS.   See SIOUX
INDIANS
OGLE, CHARLES
   , on Martin Van Buren
   Cable--American p102, 104
O'HENRY (WILLIAM SYDNEY
PORTER)
   -Biography
   Amer. Her. --New (12)
   p E429
OHIO
   Boardman--Virginia p96, 115,
   131, 164, 173
   Boorstin--Americans.   See
   index p510
   Carman--History (1) p782
   Furnas--American.   See index
   p1001
   Handlin--This p110-111, 120,
   164, 166, 351, 353
   Hunt--Life.   See index p295
   Linton--Bicentennial.   See
   index p445
   Tunis--Frontier p68-70, 74, 93,
   95
   Tunis--Young p135-136, 138-139,
   144-145
   -Cities, industrial
      Jones--Age p373-374
   -Constitution
      -Backwoods democracy, 1819
         -Views of John Bradbury
         Ridge--America's p248-
         251
   -Kirtland
      Tunis--Frontier p121
   -Life
      -Views of "Grandmother
      Brown"
         Commager--Heritage p279-
         283
      -Views of William Cooper
      Wells, 1813-1840
         Burner--America (1) p223-
         227
   -Nationality of settlers
      Wright--Culture p81-82

   -Neighborliness
      Commager--Heritage p275-279
   -Politics
      Jones--Age p372-373
      -Frontier
         Ridge--America's p247-248
         Wright--Culture p88
   -Routes to "country"
      America's Hist. p273-283
   -Sandusky
      Drury--Midwest p61-62
   -Toledo
      -"Golden rule," and Mayor
      Sam Jones
         Commager--Heritage p1004-
         1008
   -Zanesville
      Drury--Midwest p104
OHIO CANAL
   Tunis--Frontier p93
OHIO COMPANY
   Bartlett--New p61, 79-81, 403
OHIO RIVER AND VALLEY
   Amer. Her. --New (5) p412-413,
   429, 431, 433-434
   Boardman--Virginia.   See index
   p216
   Drury--Midwest p119-120
   Handlin--This p109-116, 153
   Tunis--Frontier p69-70, 90-91
   -Indians
      Amer. Her. --Indians p202, 206
      Andrews--Indian leaders p45,
      47-53
   -"The Ohio Valley Frontier,"
   1802, by F. A. Michaux
      Ridge--America's p242-245
   -"Travel on the Ohio river,"
   1826
      Ridge--America's p278-279
   -Views of Frances Trollope
      Trollope--Domestic.   See
      index p. xii
OIL INDUSTRY
   Boardman--Gilded p44-47
   Dulles--United p58-59
   Furnas--Americans p649, 671-672,
   721-722
   Handlin--This p295, 335, 352-353
   Life--Steel (7) p30, 34, 128, 131-
   134
   Nostalgia p40-42
   Wilson--American p168-171
   -First well ("Drake"), Pennsyl-
   vania, 1859
      America's Hist. p522-523
      Harlow--Story p384-385
      Nation in motion p81

Vanderbilt--Living p75
 -Rig
      Portraits--Americans p7
 -"Rock oil"
      Portraits--Americans p2-9
 -Views of Andrew Carnegie,
      1862
      Angle--American p376-378
OKLAHOMA TERRITORY
 See also "SOONERS"
 America 200 p89-90
 Hine--American p74, 100, 169,
      193, 196, 279
 -"Land rush," 1889
      America 200 p89
      Commager--Heritage p872-875
      Dulles--United p50-51
      Keyes--Hope p279
      Reader's--Story p84
      Ridge--America's p631-633
      Tunis--Frontier p161
 -"Sooners" (settlers)
      Boardman--Gilded p86
 -Views of William Allen White
      Commager--Heritage p872-876
OLCOTT, CHAUNCEY
 Blum--Stage. Profile 35
"OLD IMMIGRANTS"
 Alden--Pioneer p202, 205-207,
      247, 252-253, 260, 293
"OLD IRONSIDES" (ship). See
 "CONSTITUTION" (ship)
OLD NATIONAL ROAD. See
 NATIONAL ROAD
"OLD NORTHWEST"
 Boardman--Jackson. p60-61
 Tunis--Frontier p69-87
 -People
      Tunis--Frontier p82-83
 -Politics
      Kraus--U.S. p455
 -Towns
      Tunis--Frontier p84-85
"OLD THREE HUNDRED" (first
 Texas colonists)
 Hine--American p81-82
OLDS, RANSOM E.
 Wilson--American p326
"O'LEARY, MRS., AND COW"
 MYTH
 Woodward--Way p315
OLEOMARGARINE
 Keller--Affairs p413-414
OLIN, S.H.
 , on school boards, 1895
      Cook--City p193-194
OLIVER, HENRY KEMBLE
 Howard--Our p147

OLMSTED, DENISON
 Boardman--Jackson. p166-167
OLMSTED, FREDERICK L.
 Dannett--Noble p148, 158, 161, 165,
      182, 194, 220-221, 259
 Mumford--Brown p79, 82-85, 88-94
 Portraits--Americans p90-92
 Randel--Centennial p380-381
 Ross--Taste p148, 150
 Walker--Every. p121-122
 Young--Women p80, 126, 176-177,
      182-184, 290
 -Biography
      Amer.Her.--New (11) p E393-394
 , on needed parks, 1871
      Cook--City p114-115
OLNEY, RICHARD
 Harlow--Story p410, 529
 Life--Reaching (8) p90-91, 93
 -Biography
      Amer. Her.--New (12) p E429-
      430
OLNHAUSEN, MARY PHINNEY VON
 Dannett--Noble p92-94, 229-230, 291
 Young--Women p193-196
 -Biography
      Young--Women p375-376
OLSON, JONAS
 Tyler--Freedom's p137-138
OLYMPIC GAMES
 Reader's--Story p495
OMAHA INDIANS
 Brown--Westerners p40, 73
 DeVoto--Year p433-434, 437
OMNIBUS BILLS
 Morris--Ency. p248, 260
OMNIBUSES
 Furnas--Americans p467-468
ONE HUNDREDTH MERIDIAN
 , Excursion to
      Brown--Westerners p177-178
O'NEALE, PEGGY. See EATON,
 MARGARET O'NEALE TIMBER-
 LAKE
O'NEALE, WILLIAM
 Phillips--That p2-3, 15, 38, 104, 150
O'NEALE FAMILY
 Phillips--That. See index p181-
      182
"O'NEALE HOUSE." See "FRANK-
 LIN HOUSE"
ONEIDA COMMUNITY, NEW YORK
 Alden--Pioneer p224
 Amer. Her.--New (6) p E210
 Cable--American p194-195, 227
 Life--Sweep (4) p62-63
 Reader's--Story p338
 Tyler--Freedom's p184-195

O'NEILL FAMILY (theatrical)
  Marzio--Nation p412
"ONONDAGA" (gunboat), 1864
  Meredith--World p197-198
"OPEN DOOR" POLICY
  Carman--History (2) p312-313
  Collins--Story p292
  Hollingsworth--Amer. p100-117
OPERA
  Boardman--Civil p162
  Boardman--Gilded p146-147
  Boardman--Jackson. p160-161
  Cable--American p152, 285-286
  Chase--America's p329-332
  Dulles--History p100, 238-239
  Grimsted--Melodrama p91, 107-
  110, 238-241, 254, 258-261
  Marzio--Nation p415
  Ross--Taste p41, 255
  Walker--Every. p158, 166
  -1876
    Randel--Centennial p340-342
OPERA HOUSES
  See also METROPOLITAN
  OPERA HOUSE
  Dulles--History p257-258, 307
OPIUM
  -Use during Civil war
    Garrison--Lost p65-67
"OPOTHLE-YOHOLE" (Creek
Indian)
  Andrews--Indian leaders p61
OPTIC, OLIVER
  -Biography
    Amer. Her. --New (11) p E394
ORANGES
  -California (1870's-1880's)
    Johnson--Pictorial p168-169
ORATORY. See SPEECHES;
names of orators
ORCHESTRAS
  Furnas--Americans p581, 661-
  663
  Marzio--Nation p414-415
  Morris--Ency. p614, 814
  Walker--Every. p166
ORD, MRS.
  Young--Women p333-334
ORDER OF AMERICAN KNIGHTS,
1854
  Boardman--Civil p71
ORDER OF SONS OF LIBERTY,
1863
  Boardman--Civil p71
ORDER OF THE HEROES OF
AMERICA
  Dowdey--Experiment p298-299
ORDER OF THE PATRONS OF

HUSBANDRY. See GRANGER
MOVEMENT
ORDER OF THE STAR SPANGLED
BANNER
  Boardman--Civil p17-18
ORDER OF UNITED AMERICANS
  Boardman--Civil p118
"ORDINARIES." See TAVERNS
ORDNANCE
  Wilson--American p188-195
  -West Point foundry
    Wilson--American p188-189
OREGON (ship)
  , at Guantanamo Bay, 1898
    Angle--American p444-448
OREGON TERRITORY
  See also MISSIONS AND MIS-
  SIONARIES--Oregon; "SOUTH
  PASS"
  Alden--Pioneer p239-241
  Amer. Her. --New (6) p515-518,
  521-522
  Bartlett--New p101-104
  Billington--Far. See index p320
  Boardman--Jackson. p38-39, 50-
  54, 63-64
  Brown--Westerners p38, 65, 82,
  91-102, 106, 132, 195
  Carman--History (1) p554-558,
  565; see also index p. xix
  Hine--American. See index
  p367
  Keyes--Hope p242
  Life--Sweep (4). See index p159
  Linton--Bicentennial. See index
  p445
  Ross--Heroines. See index p180
  -1803
    Case--Empire p13-25
  -1813-1828
    Case--Empire p27-39
  -1820-1845
    Ridge--America's p439-461
  -1828-1829
    Case--Empire p41-54
  -1828-1834
    Case--Empire p55-69
  -1834-1836
    Case--Empire p71-83
  -1836-1840
    Case--Empire p85-95
  -1840's
    Collins--Story p184
  -1840-1843
    Case--Empire p97-108
  -1843-1859
    Case--Empire p311-322
  -1844-1852

Case--Empire p179-190
-1845
Case--Empire p135-146
-1845-1854
Case--Empire p191-202
-1846
DeVoto--Year p364-465; see
also index p520
Morris--Ency. p195-196
-1847-1848
Case--Empire p147-161
-1848-1849
Case--Empire p163-177
-1852
Case--Empire p257-268
-Acquisition, demand for
DeVoto--Year p8-10, 18-20
-American occupation
Harlow--Story p269-270
-Applegate cutoff
DeVoto--Year p289
-Bill, 1849
Morris--Ency. p208
-"Bitter road to"
Tunis--Frontier p114-120
-Boundary settlement
DeVoto--Year. See index
p520
-"British strength in the Oregon
country," 1839 by James Doug-
las
Ridge--America's p493-495
-"Capital controversy," 1850-
1852
Case--Empire p243-255
-"The demand for all Oregon,"
by Thomas Hart Benton, 1846
Ridge--America's p497-498
-Dispute with Great Britain
DeVoto--Year p5-6, 12
Morris--Ency. p187-188
-Election of 1876, disputed
Harlow--Story p350
-Explorations
Gilbert--Trail. p163-165
-"Fever," in Iowa, 1843
Ridge--America's p452-453
-First American "invaders"
Ridge--America's p444-447
-Government, origins of, 1843
Ridge--America's p460-461
-"Great Migration" (Emigration),
1843
Case--Empire p109-121
Commager--Heritage p521-530
DeVoto--Year p360-361, 490
Life--Sweep (4) p87-88, 145
Ridge--America's p456-459

-Caravan organization
Ridge--America's p454-456
-Indians
-"Treaty of Table Rock," 1853
Case--Empire p269-281
-Missionaries. See MISSIONS
AND MISSIONARIES--Oregon
-Portland, 1850
Case--Empire p217-230
-Propaganda
, for 1821, by Dr. John Floyd
Ridge--America's p453-454
, for 1830, by Hall Jackson
Kelley
Ridge--America's p441-444
-Territorial status, 1848
DeVoto--Year p475-480, 490
-Treaty of 1846 with Great
Britain
Harlow--Story p270
Hine--American p93-94, 109,
288
Morris--Ency. p428
-Wagon trains
Tunis--Frontier p115-116, 118-
119
-Willamette river
See also MISSIONS AND
MISSIONARIES--Oregon
Ross--Heroines p17, 89-90, 120,
126-127, 147
-Women
See also MISSIONS AND
MISSIONARIES--Oregon;
PIONEERS--Women--West;
WOMEN--Pacific Northwest
Ross--Westward p3-22
OREGON TRAIL
See also OREGON--"Great
Migration," 1843
Amer. Her. --New (6) p524-529;
E210-211
Bartlett--New p107, 112, 135, 226,
364
Boardman--Jackson. p53-54
Boardman--Virginia p107-108
Butterfield--Amer. p107
Commager--Heritage p521-530
Hine--American p76, 91, 111, 141,
262, 286
Kraus--U.S. p413-418
Life--Sweep (4) p87-88, 90, 145
Tunis--Frontier p116-118, 120
200 Years (1) p206, 236, 249-250
-Diary of Elizabeth Geer, 1848
Davie--Profile p149-150
-Survey
Gilbert--Trail. p157, 160-163

-Views of Samuel Parker, 1835
  Angle--American p226-229
, Women on
  Davie--Profile p149-150
ORGANIZATIONS
  See also ASSOCIATIONS; CLUBS
  Trollope--Domestic p65-69
ORGANS
  Furnas--Americans p586-587
, Parlor, 1890's
  Train--Story p321
, Pipe
  Furnas--Americans p659-661
, Pump
  Wilson--Vanish. p90
ORIENTALS
  See also CHINESE; JAPAN AND
   JAPANESE
  Lynes--Taste. p170-171, 174
-West
  Hine--American p121, 149,
  214-220
"ORIGINAL PACKAGE CASE."
See BROWN VS. MARYLAND
ORMSBY, WATERMAN L.
  -"The Butterfield Overland
  Mail," 1858
  Ridge--America's p555-558
ORNAMENTS. See BADGES AND
ORNAMENTS
ORPHAN ASYLUM SOCIETY OF THE
CITY OF NEW YORK, 1806
  Boardman--Virginia p193
  Cable--American p90
  Hunt--Life p196
ORPHANS
  -1876
  Hilton--Way p68
  -Asylums
  Hunt--Life p196-197
ORR, J.A.
  -"Migration to the Texan repub-
  lic," 1845
  Ridge--America's p436-438
ORR, JOHN R.
  Boardman--Civil p185-186
"ORUKTOR AMPHIBOLOS"
(steam dredge), 1804
  Life--America's p68
OSAGE INDIANS
  Amer. Her. --Indians p251-252,
  254, 412
  Andrews--Indian leaders p12, 74,
  116
  Hine--American p54, 253
OSBORNE, SUSAN M.
  Adelman--Famous p255
"OSCEOLA" (ASSEOLA; Seminole

Indian)
  Andrews--Indian leaders p58-59,
  68, 70-71, 75
  Bonte--America p103
  Life--Sweep (4) p43-44
  Reader's--Story p85
OSSOLI, MARCHIONESS. See
FULLER, (SARAH) MARGARET
OSTEND MANIFESTO, 1854
  Amer. Her. --New (7) p E247
  Life--New (5) p54, 71
  Morris--Ency. p218
, and Pierre Soulé
  Amer. Her. --New (7) p E247
O'SULLIVAN, JOHN LOUIS
  Amer. Her. --New (6) p E211
  -"The spirit of Manifest Destiny,"
  1845
  Ridge--America's p490-491
OTIS, ELISHA GRAVES
  Boardman--Civil p145
  Portraits--Americans p44
OTIS, EMILY MARSHALL
  Peacock--Famous p90-101
OTO INDIANS
  Brown--Westerners p40, 73
  Gilbert--Trail. p124
OTTENDORFER, ANNA UHL
  Neidle--America's p48-50, 137
OULD, MATTIE
  Peacock--Famous p230-238
"OURAY" (Ute Indian)
  Andrews--Indian leaders p114-115
OUTBOARD MOTORS
, First, 1896 (New York)
  Robertson--Book p121
OUTHOUSES
  Ross--Taste p131
  Wilson--Vanish. p34
OUTLAWS
  See also BANDITS
  -West
  Hine--American. See index
  p367
OVENS
  Tunis--Frontier p80
OVERLAND COMPANIES
  See also BUTTERFIELD OVER-
  LAND STAGE COMPANY;
  POSTAL SERVICE--Overland
  mail
  Boorstin--Americans p68-72
, Organization of
  Boorstin--Americans p68-69
OVERLAND TRAIL. See OREGON
TRAIL
OVERTON, JOHN
  Phillips--That p38-40, 50, 54, 101-

102, 109, 116
OWEN, MARIE
  Macksey--Book p137
OWEN, ROBERT DALE
  Alden--Pioneer p223
  Amer. Her. --New (6) p E211
  Boardman--Jackson. p86
  Boardman--Virginia p193-194
  Borden--Portrait (1) p180-182
  Carman--History (1) p526-527
  Furnas--Americans p495-496
  Hine--American p264-265
  Hunt--Life p245-246
  Reader's--Story p320
  Tyler--Freedom's p196-206
  , and New Harmony
      Weisberger--Amer. p128
  , on birth control
      Cable--American p225-226
  , on communitarian movement
      Burner--America (1) p287-
      291
"OWENITES"
  Reader's--Story p320
OWENS, BETHENIA
  Ross--Westward p155-171
OWENS, MARY S.
  Country--Lincoln p14-16
  -Courtship by A. Lincoln
      Randall--Mary p22-25
OWENS, MIKE
  Nostalgia p51
  -Glass industry
      Nostalgia p51-53
"OXBOW ROUTE." See BUTTER-
FIELD OVERLAND STAGE COM-
PANY
OXEN
  Bartlett--New p194-195
  Van Wagenen--Golden p39-48,
      239-240
  -"Buck and Bright"
      Tunis--Frontier p100-101
OYSTERS
  Hunt--Life p220-221
  Woodward--Way p212-214

P

"PACER" (Kiowa-Apache Indian)
  Andrews--Indian leaders p143
PACIFIC COAST
  Furnas--Americans p316-363
PACIFIC FUR COMPANY
  Amer. Her. --New (6) p514
  Bartlett--New p258
  Carman--History (1) p370-372, 378

Gilbert--Trail. p58-59
PACIFIC RAILROAD ACTS, 1862,
1864
  Amer. Her. --New (10) p833
  Commager--Heritage p833
  Hine--American p144, 146
  Reader's--Story p115
PACIFIC RAILWAY CONVENTION
  Bartlett--New p409-410
PACKER, ASA
  Langdon--Everyday (2) p295-299
PACKER, WILLIAM F.
  Furnas--Americans p606-607
PACKET SHIPS
  See also BARGES AND PACKET
    BOATS
  Boardman--Virginia p71-72
  Marzio--Nation p176-177
  Tunis--Frontier p92-93
  Tunis--Young p94-95
  Wright--Every. p118-120
PACKING INDUSTRY. See MEAT
PACKING INDUSTRY
"PADDLE-WHEELERS"
  Reader's--Story p186
  Wilson--Vanish. p174
  , Transatlantic
      Furnas--Americans p357-358
PAGE, THOMAS NELSON
  Amer. Her. --New (11) p970-971;
    E394-395
  Life--Steel (7) p108, 111
PAINE, JOHN KNOWLES
  Chase--America's p334-338
  Howard--Our p298-303
  Randel--Centennial p63-64, 291,
    343
PAINE, TOM
  Butterfield--Amer. p37
PAINTER, HETTIE K.
  Young--Women p329-330
PAINTERS AND PAINTING
  Amer. Her. --90's p64-79
  Boardman--Civil p159-161
  Boardman--Gilded p135-138
  Boardman--Virginia p151-152
  Bode--Anatomy. See index p289
  Furnas--Americans. See index
    p1001
  Handlin--This p145-146, 245, 282,
    368
  Harlow--Story p249
  Jones--Age p224-225
  Kraus--U.S. p380-381
  Lynes--Taste. See index p358
  Morris--Ency. p509-601
  Nye--Cultural p280-290
  Our literary p38-39

Reader's--Story p374-381
Tunis--Young p124-126
Walker--Every. p18, 63, 122, 169-171, 178
-1800's, late
  Harlow--Story p434
, at Centennial exhibition
  Randel--Centennial p82, 382-386
-"Dusseldorf school"
  Bode--Anatomy p75-77
-Genre (everyday life)
  Bode--Anatomy p71-75, 86-87
  Larkin--Art p214-231
, Historical
  Larkin--Art p134
-Hudson River school
  Boardman--Civil p159-160
  Boardman--Jackson. p152-153
  Boardman--Virginia p155
  Harlow--Story p249
-Impressionists, first American
  Larkin--Art p304-307
-Instruction, for children
  McClinton--Antiques p93-96
, Landscape
  See also PAINTERS AND PAINTINGS--Hudson River school
  Boorstin--Americans p236-241
  Furnas--Americans p574, 579, 632-633
  Larkin--Art p140, 143, 200-213
  Morris--Ency. p600, 604
  Nye--Cultural p289-290
  Reader's--Story p376-377
-"Man in nature" (illustrations)
  Grimsted--Notions p70-75
-"Masterpieces by nobodies"
  Dreppard--Pioneer p144-147
-Miniatures
  Boardman--Virginia p156
, Mural
  Jones--Age p250-251
  -1890's
    Amer. Her. --90's p67
    -Cassatt's "Modern Women"
      Portraits--Americans p147, 150
, of cities, 1890's
  Amer. Her. --90's p78-79
, Panoramic
  Boorstin--Americans p237-239
-Portraits
  Boardman--Civil p159-160
  Boardman--Jackson. p154
  Boardman--Virginia p151-155
  Larkin--Art p117-127, 192-194

Morris--Ency. p599-600, 603-604
Nye--Cultural p282-289
, Fashion
  Ross--Taste p169
, of children
  McClinton--Antiques. See index p349
, of common man
  Reader's--Story p378-379
, of men
  Amer. Her. --90's p76-77
, of women
  Amer. Her. --90's p72-75
-Prints
  Larkin--Art p139-141
-Romantic period
  Jones--Age p218-219
-Seascapes
  Furnas--Americans p632-633
  Larkin--Art p138-139
-Victorian era
  Life--Steel (7) p142-145
-West
  Boardman--Jackson. p153-154
  Larkin--Art p207-210
PALACE HOTELS (San Francisco, Calif.)
  Jones--Age p129-130
  Lynes--Taste. p81-89, 123
PALEONTOLOGY
  Morris--Ency. p530, 532
"PALES." See FENCES
PALMER, ALICE FREEMAN
  Adelman--Famous p233
PALMER, AMELIA
  Ross--Taste p169
PALMER, BERTHA HONORE
  Carson--Polite p144
  Portraits--Americans p149-150
PALMER, ERASTUS DOW
  Boardman--Civil p161-162
PALMER, JOHN WILLIAMSON
  -"Pioneer days in San Francisco"
    Jones--Shaping p137-155
PALMER, MRS. POTTER
  Cable--American p286-287
  Drury--Midwest p43
  Ross--Taste p12, 126, 134-135, 161, 230, 257
PALMER, NATHANIEL BROWN
  Amer. Her. --New (5) p E175
  Garrison--Lost p62-63
  Reader's--Story p179
PAN-AMERICAN UNION
  Amer. Her. --New (12) p E430-431
PANAMA

-Congress, 1826
   Harlow--Story p223
-Debate, 1826
   Morris--Ency. p165
-Route
   Billington--Far p224-225,
   277-278
PANAMA CANAL
   Amer. Her. --New (12) p1025,
   E430
   Bonte--America p156
   Carman--History (2) p319-322
   -Views of James Shenton
      Miers--American p269-274
PANIC OF 1819
   Amer. Her. --New (5) p E175
   Borden--Portrait (1) p152-153
   Butterfield--Amer. p100
   Carman--History (1) p436
   Linton--Bicentennial p82
   Morris--Ency. p157
PANIC OF 1837
   Amer. Her. --New (5) p E175
   Billington--Far p69, 90, 134, 145,
   193, 269
   Boardman--Jackson. p29-30
   Carman--History (1) p443, 445-
   447, 449, 473
   Collins--Story p180
   Harlow--Story p233-236
   Kraus--U.S. p365
   Linton--Bicentennial p111-112
   Morris--Ency. p178-179, 506
   Wright--Every. p106-107
PANIC OF 1857
   Billington--Far p260-261
   Boardman--Civil p135
   Carman--History (1) p475, 620-
   621
   Harlow--Story p291
   Life--New (5) p72-73, 78
   Linton--Bicentennial p151
   Morris--Ency. p223, 506
PANIC OF 1873
   Boardman--Civil p135-136
   Butterfield--Amer. p210-211
   Carman--History (1) p710, 741
   Collins--Story p244
   Life--Steel (7) p22, 24-25, 74,
   79, 88
   Linton--Bicentennial p207, 270,
   272, 318, 325, 330
   Morris--Ency. p251
   -New York city
      -Views of Samuel Gompers
         Commager--Heritage p885-
         889
PANIC OF 1893

Collins--Story p270
Harlow--Story p466-467
Keyes--Hope p281-283
Life--Reaching (8) p38-85, 88-91,
   93, 149-150
Morris--Ency. p263
PANORAMAS, MOVING
   See also DIORAMAS
   Boardman--Jackson. p177
   Dulles--History p124, 155-156
   Nye--Unembar. p186-188
PAPAGO INDIANS
   Amer. Her. --Indians p396-397
PAPER DOLLS
   Dreppard--Pioneer p135
   McClinton--Antiques p321-328
   -McLoughlin Bros.
      McClinton--Antiques p322, 324-
      325
PAPER-WORK, CUT
   Earle--Two cent. (2) p669-671
   McClinton--Antiques p195-196
PARADES
   Dulles--History p256
   Walker--Every. p87-88, 239-241
PARASOLS
   Ross--Taste p222
PARK THEATRE (N.Y.)
   -First and second
      Dulles--History p101, 103, 105-
      106, 120, 142
PARKER, CYNTHIA ANN
   Boardman--Civil p106-107
   , as Indian captive
      Amer. Her. --Indians p379-380
PARKER, JOHN ("ELDER")
   , and Parker's fort
      Amer. Her. --Indians p379-380
PARKER, HORATIO WILLIAM
   Howard--Our p313-319
PARKER, JAMES CUTLER DUNN
   Howard--Our p295-296
PARKER, NATHAN H.
   -"Migration to the Upper Valley:
   the Iowa fever," 1855
      Ridge--America's p403-405
PARKER, QUANAH (Comanche
Indian)
   Amer. Her. --Indians p379-381,
   389
   Amer. Her. --New (9) p797
   Andrews--Indian leaders p180-181
   Boardman--Civil p106-107
PARKER, SAMUEL
   Ross--Heroines p55-56
   Tunis--Frontier p114-115, 120
   , on Oregon trail, 1835
      Angle--American p226-229

PARKER, THEODORE
  Amer. Her. --New (6) p E211
  Boardman--Jackson. p143-144
  Brooks--Flower. p120, 175, 194,
    244, 246, 249, 268-271, 427-428
  Carman--History (1) p504-505,
    511, 526, 537, 604, 626
  Randel--Centennial p437-438, 443
  Tyler--Freedom's p61-63
  -Biography
    Morris--Ency. p702
PARKER BROTHERS GAMES
  -Partial list, to 1900
    McClinton--Antiques p238-240
PARKHURST, CHARLES, DR.
  Cable--American p246
PARKMAN, FRANCIS
  Alden--Pioneer p255-256
  Boardman--Civil p153-154
  Boardman--Jackson. p61-62,
    147-148
  Brown--Westerners p88, 91-100,
    118, 124, 192
  DeVoto--Year. See index p521
  Furnas--Americans p551-552
  Morris--Ency. p570
  Our literary p52-53
  -Biography
    Morris--Ency. p702-703
PARKS, RICHARD ("SILVER DICK")
  Butterfield--Amer. p263
PARKS
  See also AMUSEMENT PARKS
  America 200 p74
  Boardman--Civil p114-115
  Boardman--Gilded p163
  Mumford--Brown p90-95
  Ross--Taste p148-150
  , Needed, 1871
    -Views of Frederick L.
      Olmsted
      Cook--City p114-115
PARLOA, MARIA
  Adelman--Famous p239
"PARLOR HOUSES"
  See also PROSTITUTION
  Ross--Westward p130-133
  -Piano players ("Professors")
    Ross--Westward p130-131, 135
PARLORS
  Bode--Anatomy p51-57
  Langdon--Everyday (2) p210-216
  Lynes--Domestic. p138-154; see
    also index p305
  , Victorian
    Life--America's p86
  -"What-nots"
    -Views of Mark Twain

    Bode--Anatomy p52-55
PAROLE. See PROBATION AND
PAROLE
PARRINGTON, VERNON LOUIS
  -Biography
    Amer. Her. --New (11) p E395-
    396
PARRISH, LYDIA G.
  Dannett--Noble p326-328
PARTIES
  Boardman--Gilded p153-154
  Schwartz--When p111
  -1876
    Hilton--Way p51-52, 112-113
  -1890's
    Ross--Taste p256, 258-260
  , Birthday
    Schwartz--When p120
  , Small town
    Dulles--History p45-46, 251-
    252
PARTON, SARA PAYSON ("FANNY
FERN")
  -"Little ferns"
    Grimsted--Notions p238-244
PARTRIDGE, ALDEN, CAPTAIN
  -Academy
    Hunt--Life p132-133
"PARTY BOSSES." See POLITICS
  --Political bosses
PASSENGER ACTS. See U.S.
PASSENGER ACTS
PASSENGER PIGEONS. See
PIGEONS, PASSENGER
PASSENGER WAGONS (Mud wagons)
  , Hack
    Marzio--Nation p172-173
PASTEUR, LOUIS
  Hilton--Way p82
PASTOR, TONY (ANTONIO)
  Marzio--Nation p430
PASTORS. See CLERGYMEN
PASTURES. See MEADOWS
PATCH, SAM
  Reader's--Story p173
  White--American p41-47
PATENT OFFICE HOSPITAL (U.S.
GENERAL HOSPITAL)
  Dannett--Noble p81-83, 131-132
PATENTS
  Borden--Portrait (2) p37
  Partridge--As p87
  Reader's--Story p258-259
  -Injustice of system
    Langdon--Everyday (2) p325
PATRIOTIC SOCIETIES
  See also HEREDITARY SOCI-
  ETIES; names of societies

Boardman--Gilded p170
Cable--American p287
PATRIOTISM
    Boardman--Jackson. p190
    Handlin--This p104, 130, 172-173,
    275, 331, 337, 378-379
    Hunt--Life p273-279
    -Views of Sir Henry Lodge, Sr.
        Hurd--Treasury p116-118
"PATRONS" (wealthy rancheros)
    Tunis--Frontier p105-107
PATRONS OF HUSBANDRY. See
  GRANGER MOVEMENT
"PATROONS" (Negro boatmasters)
    Langdon--Everyday (2) p14-15
PATTERNS
    , Paper, 1870's
        Ross--Taste p298
PATTERSON, ELIZABETH
(ELIZABETH BONAPARTE)
    Peacock--Famous p39-60
PATTERSON, JOHN HENRY
    Portraits--American p73-74
    -Biography
        Amer. Her. --New (12) p E431
PATTI, ADELINA
    Neidle--America's p220
PATTIE, JAMES OHIO
    Boardman--Jackson. p64-65
    -"Fur trade in the desert
    Southwest," 1831
        Ridge--America's p389-393
PAUL, CHARLES JOSEPH
    , on America, 1893
        Handlin--This p370-383
PAULDING, JAMES KIRKE
    Boardman--Jackson. p144-145
    Boardman--Virginia p136-138
    Our literary p20-21
PAWNEE INDIANS
    Amer. Her. --New (6) p514-515
    Andrews--Indians. See index
    p176
    Billington--Far p36-38, 101
    Boardman--Jackson. p73
    Boardman--Virginia p119
    Brown--Westerners p74, 91, 109,
    179-180
    DeVoto--Year p54, 140-141, 152-
    153, 161, 165, 171, 244, 296, 310
    -Slaughter, 1873
        Andrews--Indians p171-173
PAYNE, JOHN HOWARD
    See also SONGS--Home sweet
    home
    Boardman--Virginia p147
    Bonte--America p119
    Garrison--Lost p84-88

Grimsted--Melodrama. See
    index p283
Krythe--Sampler p40-61
PEABODY, ELIZABETH PALMER
    Adelman--Famous p183
    Brooke--Flower. p226-231, 236,
    245, 268, 270, 383, 413, 437, 460
    Our literary p71
    Warren--Pictorial p73
PEABODY, GEORGE
    Amer. Her. --New (5) p E175-176
PEABODY, JAMES H.
    Watkins--Gold p217-219
PEACE
    See also names of supporters
    Borden--Portrait (1) p188-190
    -Movement
        Tyler--Freedom's p400-423
PEACE DEMOCRATS. See
  "COPPERHEADS"
"PEACE JUBILEES" (Postwar
musical spectacles)
    Furnas--Americans p661
    Reader's--Story p393
PEALE, CHARLES WILLSON
    Boardman--Virginia p151-153
    Larkin--Art. See index p537
    Nye--Cultural p280-281
PEALE, RAPHAELLE
    Reader's--Story p379
PEALE, REMBRANDT
    Nye--Cultural p285
PEALE'S MUSEUM
    Boardman--Virginia p152-153
    Furnas--Americans p563-564
    Vanderbilt--Living p83
PEANUT BUTTER
    , First, 1890
        Reader's--Story p125
PEARSALL, RACHEL
    -Reminiscences, end of Civil war
        Andrews--Women p236-245
PEARY, ROBERT EDWIN
    Morris--Ency. p703
PECK, ANNIE
    Macksey--Book p260
PECK, JOHN M.
    Hine--American p244-245, 341
"PECK'S BAD BOY"
    Furnas--Americans p729
PECO INDIANS
    Brown--Westerners p113
"PECOS BILL"
    Hine--American p268-269
"PEDAGOGUES." See TEACHERS
PEDDLERS
    See also ANTIQUES; names of
    occupations, products

236

Furnas--Americans p299-300, 393
Lynes--Domestic. p126-129
Marzio--Nation p216
Mussey--Old p107
Partridge--As p21
Schwartz--When p54-55
Wilson--Early p39-51
Wilson--Folkways p164-165
Woodward--Way p203-205
-1876
   Hilton--Way p170
, Itinerate
   Boardman--Virginia p190
-Wagons
   Wilson--Vanish. p151
"PEEP MACHINES"
   Bonte--America p141
PEFFER, WILLIAM ALFRED
   Butterfield--Amer. p262
   Life--Reaching (8) p108-110
"PEG-LEG ANNIE"
   Ross--Westward p125-126
PEIRCE, CHARLES SANDERS
-Biography
   Morris--Ency. p703-704
PELTRY TRADE. See FUR
TRADE
PEMBERTON, JOHN CLIFFORD,
GENERAL
   Boardman--Civil p52-53
   Dowdey--Experiment p245, 247,
   249-250, 252, 275, 279, 281-282,
   284, 286, 311, 352, 356
   Life--Union (6) p61-62
PENAL CODES
-Early models
   Boardman--Virginia p182
   Tyler--Freedom's p268-269
PENCIL BOXES
, Children's
   McClinton--Antiques p97-98
"PENDARVIS" (Cornish restoration,
Mineral Point, Wisconsin)
   Vanderbilt--Living p166
"PENDLETON ACT," 1883 (Civil
Service reform)
   Dulles--United p134
   Harlow--Story p455
   Morris--Ency. p256-257
   Reader's--Story p61
PENITENTIARIES. See PRISONS
PENMANSHIP
   Cable--American p116-117, 152
   Dreppard--Pioneer p65-66
   McClinton--Antiques p87-89
PENNELL, JOSEPH
   Larkin--Art p255
PENNIMAN, JAMES H.

, on crowding of schools, 1890's
   Cook--City p221-223
PENNSYLVANIA
   Carman--History (1) p782
   Furnas--Americans. See index
   p1002
   Handlin--This p112-113, 158-160,
   262, 333
   Hunt--Life. See index p295
-Confederate invasion, by Lee,
1863
   Commager--Heritage p756-758
   Life--Union (6) p16, 63-64, 98
-Fairs, 1824
   Life--Sweep (4) p24-25
-McConnel's Town
   -1817
      Commager--Heritage p259-
      261
-Pittsburgh
   Tunis--Frontier p70, 73, 80,
   90, 93-94
PENNSYLVANIA ACADEMY OF
FINE ARTS
   Larkin--Art p114
PENNSYLVANIA CANAL
   Langdon--Everyday (2) p119-127
PENNSYLVANIA DUTCH (GERMANS)
-Amusements, including holidays
   Ross--Taste p81-82
PENNSYLVANIA RAILRAOD
   Boardman--Civil p138
PENNSYLVANIA SYSTEM (CANALS
AND RAILROADS)
   Tunis--Frontier p93-94
"PENNY PRESS," 1830's
   Bode--Anatomy p252
   Kraus--U.S. p377
   Reader's--Story p358
PENNYROYAL DISTILLING INDUSTRY
   Drury--Midwest p104
PENSIONS
   See also DEPENDENT PENSION
   ACT
, Veterans', and President Cleve-
land
   Harlow--Story p459-460
PEOPLE'S PARTY. See POPU-
LISM
PERCIVAL, JAMES GATES
   Boardman--Virginia p141-142
   Brooks--Flower. p66, 155, 157-
   159, 162, 186
PERFECTIONISM (PERFECTION-
ISTS)
   Boardman--Jackson. p127
   Life--Sweep (4) p59, 62-63
   Tyler--Freedom's p185-195

PERFUME
  Ross--Taste p227
PERIODICALS. See MAGAZINES;
 NEWSPAPERS
"PERIPATETICS" (professional
 wanderers)
  Wilson--Early p38-39
PERKINS, CHARLES CALLAHAN
  Howard--Our p295-296
PERKINS, JACOB
  Mussey--Old p120
  Portrait--Americans p124
PERRY, MATTHEW CALBRAITH
 ("OLD BRUIN"), COMMODORE
  Amer. Her. --New (6) p211-212
  Boardman--Civil p12
  Boardman--Virginia p46-47
  Life--New (5) p55
  , and Japan
    Butterfield--Amer. p138-139
    Collins--Story p161
    Harlow--Story p277-278
    Keyes--Hope p264-265
    Morris--Ency. p216
    Reader's--Story p460
    Viewpoints p21
    Wright--Every. p166
  -Biography
    Morris--Ency. p704
PERRY, NORA
  Adelman--Famous p202
PERRY, OLIVER HAZARD
  See also LAKE ERIE BATTLE,
  1813
  Boardman--Virginia p46-47
  Bonte--America p93
  Harlow--Story p178
  Mussey--Old p26
  -Biography
    Morris--Ency. p704
PERSECUTION. See ANTI-
 CATHOLICISM; INTOLERANCE;
 MORMONS; etc.
"PERUKERS." See WIGS AND
 WIGMAKERS
PESTALOZZI, JOHANN HEINRICH
  Furnas--Americans. See index
  p1002
  Nye--Cultural p166-167
  -Educational theory
    Tyler--Freedom's p245-246
"PET BANKS," 1832
  Harlow--Story p234
"PETALSHARO" (Pawnee Indian)
  Amer. Her. --Indians p247-249
  Andrews--Indian leaders p102
PETERSBURG, VIRGINIA
  , in Civil war

  Dowdey--Experiment p238, 256,
  327, 344-345, 348, 351, 353, 356
  Jordan--Civil. See index p214
  Meredith--World p204-207
  Viewpoints p85
PETERSON, HENRY
  Bode--Anatomy p256-257
PETITION, RIGHT OF
  Tyler--Freedom's p509-512
PETROLEUM INDUSTRY
  Boardman--Civil p121-123
  Carman--History (2) p72-75
  Harlow--Story p384-386
  Marzio--Nation p242
  Morris--Ency. p496
  -1870's
    Randel--Centennial p182-185
PETS
  -1876
    Hilton--Way p47
"PETTICOAT WAR"
  Amer. Her. --New (5) p394, 396
PETTICOATS. See CLOTHING
 AND DRESS--Petticoats
PETTIGREW, SUSAN
  -"Susan Pettigrew makes a
  journey," 1836
    Woodward--Way p198-243
"PETTIS RESOLUTION," 1860
  Jones--Shaping p171-173
PEWTER AND PEWTERERS
  Dreppard--Pioneer p179, 181-182
PEYOTE
  Hine--American p201-202, 221
"PHALANSTERIES" (Utopias)
  Alden--Pioneer p224
PHANTASCOPE, JENKINS'
  Wilson--American p297
PHELPS ELIZABETH STUART
  Hart--Popular p120-121
  -"The tenth of January"
    Trachtenberg--Demo. p249-274
PHILADELPHIA, PENNSYLVANIA
  Boardman--Virginia. See index
  p216
  Davidson--Life (2) p107
  Furnas--Americans. See index
  p1002
  Handlin--This. See index p594
  Hunt--Life. See index p295
  Life--Growing (3) p123, 129-131
  Life--New (5) p97, 120, 122, 124-
  125
  Life--Sweep (4). See index p159
  -1876
    Randel--Centennial. See
    index p472
  , as intellectual center, 1800

Nye--Cultural p113
-"The city of bodily comforts, "
1871
Cook--City p24-26
-Election, 1815
Butterfield--Amer. p62-63
-Growth
Nye--Cultural p125-128
-July 4th, 1819
Life--Growing (3) p30-31
-Masonic Temple
Viewpoints p151
-Second Street, 1800
Viewpoints p102-103
-Society
Cable--American p280
Nye--Cultural p111-113
-Views of Frances Trollope
Trollope--Domestic. See
index p. xiii
PHILADELPHIA AND READING
RAILROAD
-1876
Randel--Centennial p165-166
PHILANTHROPY. See CHARITIES
PHILHARMONIC SOCIETY (Boston)
Boardman--Virginia p150-151
-Founding, 1810
Howard--Our p131-132
PHILIPPINES
Amer. Her. --90's p117-119
Boardman--Gilded p187-190
Carman--History (2) p281, 284,
294-296, 299, 302, 311-312
Keyes--Hope p286
Life--Reaching (8). See index
p175
-1898-1899
Dulles--United p169-171
Morris--Ency. p290-291
, and foreign policy
Hollingsworth--Amer. p25,
68-75, 89-95
-Three years' war
Butterfield--Amer. p284-287
PHILLIPS, WENDELL
Furnas--Americans p713-714
Life--New (5) p52, 112-113
Mussey--Old p115
Our literary p85
, on Elijah Lovejoy's murder
Hurd--Treasury p61-63
PHILOSOPHY
Boardman--Gilded p118-120
PHONOGRAPHS
Boardman--Gilded p147-148
Lynes--Domestic. p253-254
Marzio--Nation p499

Portraits--Americans p34, 36
Reader's--Story p269
Wilson--Vanish. p92-93
, Berliner's, 1888
Portraits--Americans p36
, Edison's
Trachtenberg--Demo. p228-
236
-Tin-foil, c1878
Portraits--Americans p35
, Evolution of
Wilson--American p292-293
-"Sound-recording apparatus, "
1886 patent
Robertson--Book p165
PHOTOGRAPHY
See also DAGUEROTYPES;
MOTION PICTURES; EASTMAN,
GEORGE
Boardman--Civil p175, 202
Boardman--Jackson. p102
Furnas--Americans p578, 591, 859
Life--Steel (7) p46-47
Life--Sweep (4) p68-79
Marzio--Nation p545-549
Nostalgia p43-46
Reader's--Story p273
Walker--Every. p115, 131, 170-
171, 178-179
Wilson--American p264-271
-1880's
Woodward--Way p335
-Cameras and supplies, 1880's
Peck--Nineteenth n. p.
, Kodak
Life--Steel (7) p46-47
-Celebrities, 1839-1849
Life--Sweep (4) p69-73
-Civil war portraits. See
BRADY, MATHEW B.
-"Great surveys"
See also JACKSON, WILLIAM
HENRY
Gilbert--Trail. p191-196, 218
-Locomotion, animal
Wilson--American p295
-Portrait studio, first, 1840
(N.Y. city)
Robertson--Book p128
, Traveling, country fairs
Partridge--As p47
PHRENOLOGY
Alden--Pioneer p220
Boardman--Jackson. p189
Borden--Portrait (1) p185-186
Cable--American p112, 192, 240
Furnas--Americans p445-449
-Views of Frances Trollope

Trollope--Domestic p68-69
PHYFE, DUNCAN
  Amer. Her. --New (5) p E176
  Reader's--Story p223-224
PHYSICAL CULTURE
  See also HEALTH
  Cable--American p136-137
  Furnas--Americans. See index
    p1002
PHYSICIANS
  See also CRANKS AND QUACKS;
    MEDICINE; names of physicians;
    etc.
  Furnas--Americans. See index
    (under Medicine) p997
  Handlin--This p101, 118, 145, 274,
    279, 367-368, 372
  Hunt--Life p201-214
  Reader's--Story p294
  Schwartz--When p21, 175-176
  Wilson--Early p108, 110
  -1876
    Hilton--Way p79-82
  , Country
    Partridge--As p36-37
  -Women
    Macksey--Book p148-150
    Warren--Pictorial p77-79,
      126-128
    -Civil war
      Warren--Pictorial p109
PHYSIOLOGISTS
  Wilson--American p102-103
PIANOS
  Boardman--Virginia p150
  Bode--Anatomy p21
  Carson--Polite p155-162
  Handlin--This p125, 167, 185-186,
    190, 195, 197, 205, 351
  Lynes--Domestic. p252-253
  Marzio--Nation p499
  Morris--Ency. p614
  Reader's--Story p393
  Tunis--Young p128
  -1876
    Randel--Centennial p345
  , Player
    Wilson--Vanish. p91
"PIAZZAS" (Verandas)
  Furnas--Americans p422-424
PICKERING, EDWARD CHARLES
  Wilson--American p276
PICKERING, JOHN, JUDGE
  -Impeachment, 1804
    Morris--Ency. p133
PICKERING, TIMOTHY
  Life--Growing (3) p39-40
PICKETT, GEORGE EDWARD

Amer. Her. --New (8) p E288
  Boardman--Civil p51-52
PICNICS
  Dulles--History p51, 157, 162, 277-
    278
  Walker--Every. p83-84, 235
  -1876
    Hilton--Way p51-52
  -Maine
    Life--New (5) p64-65
PICO, PIO
  Billington--Far p89, 160-162, 166-
    167, 183-184
PICTOGRAPHS
  Gilbert--Trail. p174
"PICTURESQUENESS"
  -Concepts and definition
    Gowan--Images p319-320, 329-
      331, 350
PIEDMONT PLATEAU
  Bartlett--New p126-127
PIERCE, EDWARD
  Holzman--Stormy p56, 58-59
PIERCE, FRANKLIN
  Boardman--Civil p11-13
  Butterfield--Amer. p135
  Carman--History (1) p525, 608-
    609, 611-612, 615, 617
  Harlow--Story p276, 289, 294-295
  Kraus--U.S. p448-449, 453
  Life--New (5) p66; see also
    index p159
  Morris--Ency. p216-221
  200 Years p277, 340-341, 343
  -Biography
    Amer. Her. --New (7) p E247
    Morris--Ency. p705
    Whitney--American p119-125
  -Cabinet
    Carman--History (1) p791
  -Presidency
    Linton--Bicentennial p141-148
    Reader's--Story p333
PIERCE, JANE
  Melick--Wives p38
PIERCE MILL (Washington, D.C.)
  Vanderbilt--Living p85
PIERCE FAMILY (Western traders)
  Boardman--Virginia p105
PIERCY, FREDERICK
  -"Mormon expansion: Parowan
    City," 1855
    Ridge--America's p520-521
PIERREPONT, EDWARDS
  Holzman--Stormy p127-128
PIETISM
  Bartlett--New p369
"PIG WAR" (1859 incident)

America's Hist. p367
PIGEONS, PASSENGER
    Bartlett--New p192, 250-252
    Van Wagenen--Golden p97-98
PIKE, JAMES SHEPHERD
    , on "Black Parliament," S.C.,
    1873
        Angle--American p346-349
        Commager--Heritage p811-816
PIKE, ZEBULON MONTGOMERY
    Amer. Her. --New (6) p512-513,
    p E212
    Boardman--Virginia p39-40, 101-
    102
    Gilbert--Trail. p102-103
    Hine--American p74-75, 130
    Life--Growing (3) p83, 85
    Tunis--Frontier p103
    -"Beginnings of the 'Great
    American desert' legend," 1810
        Ridge--America's p370-371
    -Expeditions, 1805
        Morris--Ency. p134
    -"Pike's party crosses the
    Rockies," 1807
        Ridge--America's p365-368
    -Pike's party is captured by the
    Spaniards," 1807
        Ridge--America's p369-370
    -Pike's Peak
        Angle--American p164-166
        Boardman--Virginia p101-102
    -"Zebulon Montgomery Pike
    reaches the Rocky Mountains,"
    1806
        Ridge--America's p364-365
"PIKE'S PEAK OR BUST" (Gold
    rush)
    Kraus--U.S. p469-470
"PILLORY & STOCKS"
    Wilson--Folkways p221-224
PIMA INDIANS
    Amer. Her. --Indians p396-397
    DeVoto--Year p352-353, 370, 372,
    386
PINCKNEY, CHARLES COTES-
WORTH
    Boardman--Virginia p23-24
PINCKNEY MANSION-RUINS
(Charleston, S.C.)
    Viewpoints p150-151
PINKERTON, ALLAN
    Dowdey--Experiment p173-174,
    201
    Meredith--World p124-129, 131
PINKHAM, LYDIA E.
    Cable--American p238, 258
    Furnas--Americans p905-907

Macksey--Book p164-165
Randel--Centennial p324-325
Warren--Pictorial p126
PINS
    Keyes--Hope p211
"PIONEER HOME" (Dayton, Ohio)
    Vanderbilt--Living p151
PIONEERS
    See also FRONTIER; WOMEN--
    Pioneers; names of localities,
    nationalities
    Boardman--Virginia p79-80
    Lynes--Domestic. p21, 23-24, 26,
    29-31, 38
    -Middlewest, Life of
        Drury--Midwest p71-76
    -Plains travel
        Partridge--As p76
    -Views of Elijah Iles, 1821
        Angle--American p207-210
    -West
        200 Years (1) p302-303
        -1830-1860
            Billington--Far p69-90
"PIP SQUEAK" OR BELLOWS TOYS
    McClinton--Antiques p277-281
"PIPE SPRING NATIONAL MONU-
MENT" (near "Winsor Castle,"
Fredonia, Arizona)
    Vanderbilt--Living p198
PIRACY
    Hunt--Life p160-165
    Wilson--Early p168-174
    -Views of Nathaniel Hawthorne
        Commager--Heritage p233-235
PIROGUES (large canoes)
    Langdon--Everyday (2) p92
    Tunis--Frontier p67
PITCHERS
    , and basins
        Wilson--Vanish. p50
PITTSBURGH, PENNSYLVANIA
    Boardman--Virginia. See index
    p216
    Davidson--Life (2) p118-119
    Handlin--This p109-111, 113, 115,
    165-166
    Wright--Culture p82-83
    -Views of Willard Glazier, 1885
        Cook--City p22, 24
PITTSFIELD (ILL.) UNION
    Bode--Anatomy p253-254
PITTSBURGH WAGONS. See
CONESTOGA WAGONS
PLACE NAMES. See NAMES,
Place
PLAINS. See GREAT PLAINS
PLAINS INDIANS

America's Hist. p510-515
Boardman--Jackson. p71-76
Brown--Westerners. See index
p287
PLANTATIONS AND PLANTERS
See also COTTON; MANSIONS,
Southern; SUGAR CANE
Carman--History (1) p360, 477-
479, 583, 590, 712-713, 717-718
Handlin--This p122, 126, 153, 160-
161, 249-252, 334, 337
-"Belle Meade" (Nashville, Tenn.)
Vanderbilt--Living p124-125
-Civil war
Jordan--Civil p14, 30-31, 38-39,
132
-Economy
Life--Growing (3) p122, 125-
126, 134-141
-Hardships, 1865
-Views of Myrta Lockett Avary
Commager--Heritage p808-
811
-Life
Wright--Every. p137-151
-Louisiana
, Luxury in
Commager--Heritage p447-
449
-"Oakley Plantation House, " St.
Francisville, La.
Vanderbilt--Living p186
-Mississippi
-Model, of Thomas Dabney
Commager--Heritage p475-
479
-South Carolina
Commager--Heritage p454-456
PLANTS
See also FLOWERS; names of
plants
Gilbert--Trail. p37-39, 123-125,
178
, Domestic
Bartlett--New p195-199
-Prints
Dreppard--Pioneer p195-198
PLATT, ORVILLE HITCHCOCK
-Biography
Amer. Her. --New (12) p E431
PLATT, THOMAS C.
Harlow--Story p446
PLATTE RIVER
Tunis--Frontier p112-113, 117,
136, 138
PLAYGROUNDS
, of asphalt, 1896
Cook--City p107-108

, Vacant lot
Wilson--Vanish. p163
PLAYHOUSES. See THEATER
PLAYING CARDS. See CARD-
PLAYING
PLAYS. See DRAMA
PLAYWRIGHTS. See DRAMATISTS
PLEASANT HILL SETTLEMENTS
(Kentucky)
Tyler--Freedom's p151-152
PLEASURES. See AMUSEMENTS;
SPORTS AND GAMES; types of
entertainment
PLOWS
Bartlett--New p198-199, 201-204
Reader's--Story p114, 263
Van Wagenen--Golden p155, 221-
227
PLUM CREEK (NEBRASKA) BATTLE
Andrews--Indians p117-119
PLUMBERS AND PLUMBING
See also BATHROOMS
Cable--American p236-237, 248-
249
PLURAL MARRIAGE. See MOR-
MONS
POE, EDGAR ALLAN
Alden--Pioneer p215-216
Boardman--Jackson. p187-188
Brooks--Flower. See index p547
Harlow--Story p243, 246
Morris--Ency. p569, 585
Motte--Golden p108-109
Our literary p31-35
Randel--Centennial p17-18, 361
Reader's--Story p413
-Biography
Amer. Her. --New (7) p E247-
248
Morris--Ency. p705-706
-Home, Baltimore, Md.
Vanderbilt--Living p83
POETS AND POETRY
See also names of poets
Boardman--Gilded p131-132
Boardman--Jackson. p148-151
Bode--Anatomy p188-200
Cable--American p151
Dulles--United p111, 114
Furnas--Americans p323, 550-552
Harlow--Story p244-246
Mott--Golden p103-114
Nye--Cultural p259-261
Nye--Unembar. p94-126
Our literary p54-57
-"The American flag"
Burner--America (1) p171-173
-"Bivouac of the dead"

Andrews--Women p120-121
-Broadsides
  Nye--Unembar. p88-90, 113-
  114
-Changing fashions
  Morris--Ency. p576-577
-Civil war
  Burner--America (1) p318-322
  Nye--Unembar. p105, 110,
  113-114
  -"Three hundred thousand
  more"
    Burner--America (1) p319-
    320
  -"The women of the South"
    Burner--Women p131
-"Concord hymn," by Ralph
Waldo Emerson
  Davie--Profile p55
-"Enlisted today"
  Burner--America (1) p318-319
-Family life
  Burner--America (1) p251-253
-"The farmer is the man"
  Cook--City p14
-Kentucky
  Wright--Culture p70
-"Mannahatta," by Walt Whitman
  Cook--City p4-5
-New England
  Hart--Popular p135-137
-Nonsense rhymes
  Schwartz--When p93
-"North and south from Brooklyn
Bridge"
  Cook--City p10
-"The Orphans"
  Burner--America (1) p249-250
-"Paddy on Sambo as a soldier"
  Burner--America (1) p320-321
, Pessimism in
  Jones--Age p358-366
, Political
  Cook--City p194-195
, Pre-Civil war
  Hart--Popular p125-127
-"Squeak the fife and beat the
drum"
  Burner--America (1) p163-164
-Temperance
  Burner--America (1) p284-285
POINSETT, JOEL
  Amer. Her. --New (6) p E213
"POLICE GAZETTE"
  Cable--American p151-152, 246,
  298
POLICEMEN
  Boardman--Civil p113

Cable--American p318-319
Davidson--Life (2) p152
Handlin--This p140, 148, 187, 325,
  377-378
Harris--Land p266
Wilson--Early p32-33
-Lodging houses
  -Views of Jacob Riis
    Commager--Heritage p901-
    905
-"Recollections of a N. Y. Chief
of police," by George W. Wall-
ing, 1888
  Cook--City p197-199
, Traffic (first, 1860)
  Train--Story p340
POLISH
  Furnas--Americans p836-837
  Handlin--This p368
POLITICAL CAMPAIGNS
  See also PRESIDENTIAL ELEC-
  TIONS; etc.
-1822-1824
  Morris--Ency. p163-164
-1825-1828
  Morris--Ency. p167
-1831-1832
  Morris--Ency. p173-174
-1835-1836
  Morris--Ency. p178
-1893-1840
  Morris--Ency. p182-183
-1840
  Davidson--Life (2) p332-334
  Walker--Reform p80-81
-1843-1844
  Morris--Ency. p190-191
-1847-1848
  Morris--Ency. p208-209
-1851-1852
  Morris--Ency. p216
-1856
  Morris--Ency. p221
-1860
  Country--Lincoln p42-49
  Morris--Ency. p226-227
-1862
  Morris--Ency. p263
-1864
  Morris--Ency. p244
-1868
  Morris--Ency. p249
-1872
  Morris--Ency. p251
-1876
  Morris--Ency. p252-253
  Randel--Centennial p116, 214-
  216

-1880
    Morris--Ency. p255-256
-1884
    Morris--Ency. p257
-1888
    Morris--Ency. p260
-1896
    Morris--Ency. p264-265
POLITICAL PARTIES
  See also POLITICS--"Political
  bosses"; PRESIDENTIAL ELEC-
  TIONS; names of political
  parties; etc.
  Amer. Her. --New (5) p401, E176-
  177
  Dulles--United p147-148
  Harlow--Story p444-448
  Life--New (5) p57, 72-73, 89-93
  Life--Steel (7). See index
  p158-159
  Life--Sweep (4). See index
  p159
  Warren--Pictorial p139-141
  Whitney--American. See index
  p368
  -1800-1896
    Reader's--Story p56-57
  -Conventions
    -1832 (first national)
      Harlow--Story p223-234
    -1860 (caucuses)
      Commager--Heritage p637-
      642
    -1864
      Pratt--Civil p52-53
    -Machines
      Keller--Affairs p25-27,
      249-258, 522, 536-538,
      552-564, 581-582
    -Politics
      Keller--Affairs. See
      index p624
    -Two party system established
      Harlow--Story p231-233
POLITICS
  See also GOVERNMENT; homes
  of localities, related subjects
  Boardman--Gilded p14-33, 181-185
  Handlin--This. See index p595
  Keller--Affairs. See index p624
  Life--New (5) p13, 28-29, 93
  Life--Steel (7). See index p159
  -1824-1860
    Commager--Heritage p607-642
  -1859
    Kraus--U.S. p476-477
  , and newspapers
    Bode--Anatomy p250-251

-Change
  -Views of Thomas Jefferson
    Walker--Reform p45-53
-Chicago
  -Views of Julian Ralph, 1892
    Cook--City p185
-Cities
  Cook--City p177-214
-"Dark horses"
  Whitney--American p104, 120,
  122, 163
-Ethnic influences
  Marzio--Nation p395
-Immigrants
  Cable--American p293
  Marzio--Nation p386-387, 390-
  392, 395-396
-Morality
  -Views of Thomas Jefferson
    Walker--Reform p10-16
, of conformity and revolt
  Carman--History (2) p227-265
-"Political bosses"
  See also names of bosses;
  TAMMANY HALL, etc.
  Harlow--Story p446-447
  Keller--Affairs p246-249, 255-
  258, 522, 538-542
  Life--Reaching (8) p40-42, 104
  Life--Steel (7) p11-14, 17, 106-
  107
  -1898
    Cook--City p201-202
  -Politicians, as orators
    Life--New (5) p26-27
  -Post-Civil war
    Life--Union (6) p150-152
  , Pro-labor, 1829
    Walker--Reform p61-63
  -Radicalism
    Marzio--Nation p396
  , Symbols of, 1840
    Walker--Reform p80-81
  -Satire
    Keller--Affairs p268-270
-"Ticket-making"
  Boorstin--Americans p429
, Western
  , in Bingham's paintings
    Butterfield--Amer. p118-
    121
POLK, JAMES KNOX
  Amer. Her. --New (6) p E213-214
  Amer. Her. --New (7) p546-550
  Billington--Far. See index p320
  Boardman--Jackson. See index
  p210
  Borden--Portrait (1) p211-215

Carman--History (1) p364, 563-
572, 598-600, 604
DeVoto--Year. See index p521
Harlow--Story p267-268
Kraus--U.S. p417, 423, 429-435
Life--Sweep (4) p90-91; see also
index p159
200 Years (1) p335; see also
index p349
Viewpoints p76
-"American designs on Califor-
nia, " 1845
Ridge--America's p498-501
-Biography
Morris--Ency. p706
Whitney--American p101-106
-Cabinet
Carman--History (1) p576-
578, 598, 790
-"Doctrine"
Morris--Ency. p192-193
-Home (Columbia, Tenn.)
Vanderbilt--Living p124
-Presidency
Linton--Bicentennial. (facing)
122-132
Reader's--Story p333
-War message, 1846
Davie--Profile p273-274
Ridge--America's p504-505
POLK, SARAH
Melick--Wives p34-35
POLLOCK, ROBERTA
, Ride of
Andrews--Women p148-154
POLYGAMY
See also MORMONS
DeVoto--Year p80-81, 85
Handlin--This p310-311, 313, 358
Hine--American p175, 231, 267
POLYMERS
Wilson--American p380-381
PONCA INDIANS
Hine--American p196
POND, SILVANUS BILLINGS
Howard--Our p146
"PONY EXPRESS"
Billington--Far p287-290
Brown--Westerners p152, 158-
163, 166, 168, 172, 197, 255
Collins--Story p163
Commager--Heritage p546-548
Davidson--Life (2) p258, 265-
267
Harlow--Story p363-365
Hine--American p141-142, 276-
277, 323
Johnson--Pictorial p138-139

Kraus--U.S. p471
Ross--Taste p276
Tunis--Frontier p139, 141-142
200 Years (1) p208-209
Wilson--Early p126-127
-1860 (establishment)
Drury--Midwest p159-160
-1860-1869
Carman--Hist. (2) p198
-1872
Ridge--America's p561-562
-Views of Samuel Clemens
Commager--Heritage p546-548
Davie--Profile p162-164
Ridge--America's p561-562
POOLROOMS
Wilson--Vanish. p157
"POOLS" (in corporations)
Harlow--Story p390
POOR. See POVERTY
POPE, JOHN
Amer. Her. --New (8) p E288-289
Life--Union (6) p12, 38, 55-57
POPERY
, Fear of
Furnas--Americans p523-528
POPPENHEIM, MRS. C.C.
-"Reminiscences"
Andrews--Women p246-256
"POPULAR SOVEREIGNTY"
Life--New (5) p32, 38-39, 56, 71,
74, 77, 90-91
POPULATION (including Census)
Boardman--Civil p4-5, 10-11, 93-
94, 111-113, 116, 203-204
Boardman--Gilded p93-94
Boardman--Jackson. p180, 198-199
Boardman--Virginia p8, 96, 124,
194-195, 197-198, 202
Handlin--This p130, 139, 153, 201,
205-206, 321
Kraus--U.S. p390-391
Morris--Ency. p442-443
Randel--Centennial p93-94, 100,
151-152
-1800-1860
Carman--History (1) p501
-1801
Carman--History (1) p321
-1810
Linton--Bicentennial p68
-1810-1860
Hunt--Life p19
-1820
Linton--Bicentennial p84
-1830-1840
Bartlett--New p190
-1840

Linton--Bicentennial p115
-1840-1860
  Bode--Anatomy p116
-1850
  Linton--Bicentennial p136
-1850-1860
  Life--New (5) p9
-1850-1899
  Dulles--United p89
-1860
  Alden--Pioneer p252-253
-1870
  Linton--Bicentennial p200
-1880
  Linton--Bicentennial p219
-1890
  Butterfield--Amer. p257
  Linton--Bicentennial p234
-1890's
  Life--Reaching (8). See
   index p175
, by state
  Life--Hunt p20-21
-Cities
  Boardman--Gilded p106
  Nye--Cultural p124
, Control of
  Burner--America (1) p288-
   289
-Density
  Hunt--Life p21-22
  , per square mile, 1870,
   1876, 1880
    Randel--Centennial p152
-Ethnic classes, by state
  Life--Hunt p19-20
, Foreign born
  Marzio--Nation p196
  , Location of, 1840-1860
   (map)
    Weisberger--Amer. p168-
     169
  -Ratio of native to, 1875
   Life--Union (6) p160
  -Total, European-born, by
   country, 1890
    Cook--City p66
-Growth
  Life--Union (6) p158
-Immigrants
  Amer. Her. --90's p128
-North-South ratio
  Life--Union (6) p8, 19
, Rural and urban
  , by size of place, 1860-1890
   Cook--City p289
  , Ratio, 1870
   Life--Union (6) p163

-West
  Carman--History (1) p358-
   359
  Hine--American. See
   index p367
  -Increase, 1870-1890
   Dulles--United p50-51
POPULISM (POPULIST PARTY;
PEOPLE'S PARTY)
  Amer. Her. --New (10) p856-860
  Boardman--Gilded p28-33, 183-184
  Borden--Portrait (2) p30-31
  Butterfield--Amer. p257, 259, 268
  Carman--History (2) p225, 248,
   253-254, 256-258, 262-264
  Dulles--United p73-74, 87, 140,
   142-147, 151-155, 160, 180, 187
  Harlow--Story p262, 465-466, 470-
   471, 473-474
  Hollingsworth--Amer. p26-27
  Jones--Age p53, 378-379
  Keller--Affairs. See index p624
  Keyes--Hope p282
  Life--Reaching (8) p175
  Linton--Bicentennial p234, 236-
   237, 245
  Morris--Ency. p262-263
  Reader's--Story p345-346
  200 Years (2) p92-94
  Warren--Pictorial p139-141
  , and agriculture
   Keller--Affairs p571-577
  -Leaders
   Dulles--United p145-147
  -Origins
   Dulles--United p74-75
  -Platform, 1892
   Commager--Heritage p1025-
    1026
   Heffner--Doc. p183-187
  -Views of J.D. Hicks
   Miers--American p219-224
  -Views of William Allen White
   Dulles--United p146-147
  -Voting percentage of candidates,
   1894
   Life--Reaching (8) p112
  -West
   Hine--American p172-173, 176,
    258-259, 333
   Keller--Affairs p575-576
PORCHES
  See also "PIAZZAS"
  Ross--Taste p144-145, 149
  , Front
   Wilson--Vanish. p83
PORK. See HOGS; MEAT PACK-
ING INDUSTRY

"PORK-BARREL" LEGISLATION
  Harlow--Story p455
PORT HUDSON, LOUISIANA
  -Hardships, 1863
      Commager--Heritage p752-753
    -Views of officer, diary
      Commager--Heritage p754-
        756
PORTER, DAVID DIXON, REAR
ADMIRAL
  Amer. Her. --New (8) p E289
  Boardman--Virginia p45-46, 51
  Bonte--America p94, 125
  Holzman--Stormy p149-157
  Jordan--Civil p122-123, 126-127,
    187, 195
  Life--Union (6) p44-45, 62
  Treasury Amer. p164
  Young--Women p251, 257-258,
    260, 343-344
PORTER, EDWIN
  -"The Fall River tragedy"
    Harris--Land p203-214
PORTER, FITZ-JOHN
  Amer. Her. --New (8) p E289
PORTER, JANE
  -Popularity in America
    Mott--Golden p64-65
PORTER, PETER BUELL
  Amer. Her. --New (5) p E177
PORTER, WILLIAM SYDNEY.
  See O'HENRY
PORTLAND RIOT, 1825
  (PROSTITUTION)
  Bruner--America (1) p298-300
PORTRAITS AND PORTRAIT
  PAINTING. See PAINTERS AND
  PAINTINGS--Portraits
POST OFFICES
  Boardman--Virginia p191
  Keller--Affairs p101, 310-311
  , Country town
    Partridge--As p32-33
  -Fraud, 1880's
    Harlow--Story p453-454
  -New York, 1845
    Viewpoints p146
POSTAL SERVICE
  Amer. Her. --New (6) p525
  Furnas--Americans. See
    index p1003
  Handlin--This p136, 144
  Langdon--Everyday (2) Prelude
  Tunis--Young p75-76
  Walker--Every. p104, 110
  -1876
    Hilton--Way p173
  -1898-1899

    Portraits--Americans p60
  , at country store, 1876
    Hilton--Way p154
  -Confederacy
    Dowdey--Experiment p19, 96-
      99, 153, 393
  -Letter rates, 1800
    Boardman--Virginia p191
  -Overland mail (coaching)
    Langdon--Everyday (2) p35,
      82-83
    Ridge--America's p555-561
    Tunis--Frontier p139-140
  -Post Office department, "Star
  routes" scandal
    Keyes--Hope p272
  -Rural free delivery
    Boardman--Gilded p54
    Portraits--Americans p59-60
  -West, early
    Ross--Heroines p53-54
POSTCARDS
  -First, 1861 (Philadelphia)
    Robertson--Book p138
POSTILIONS (coach horse-guides)
  Langdon--Everyday (2) p83-84
  -1876
    Ross--Taste p271
POTASH
  Van Wagenen--Golden p164-169
POTATO CHIPS
  Reader's--Story p125
  , First, 1853 (Saratoga Springs,
    N.Y.)
    Robertson--Book p138
POTATOES
  Van Wagenen--Golden p85-86
  -1839-1845
    Boardman--Jackson. p89
POTOMAC RIVER
  -Views of Frances Trollope
    Trollope--Domestic. See
      index p. xiii
POTTAWATOMIE MASSACRE (Free
Soilers)
  Boardman--Civil p15-16
POTTERY AND POTTERS
  Dreppard--Pioneer p170-171, 173,
    175
  McClinton--Antiques p170-171,
    174, 179-180
  Reader's--Story p226-228
  Van Wagenen--Golden p204-205
  , Britannia
    McClinton--Antiques p166-176
  -Flower pots
    Dreppard--Pioneer p197
  -Mugs

McClinton--Antiques p177-179
POTTS, DANIEL
Bartlett--New p88-89
POVERTY
Amer. Her. --New (6) p488-490
Cable--American p288-296, 298-304, 320-321
Furnas--Americans p314-316
Handlin--This p130, 133, 140
Keller--Affairs p124-126, 499-500, 503-506
Tyler--Freedom's p291-294
-New York city
Boardman--Jackson. p181-182
Cook--City p246-248
-Views of Jacob Riis, 1890
Commager--Heritage p895-901
-South
Cable--American p302-303
Carman--History (1) p584-586
, Urban
Dulles--United p93-94
"POWDER FACE" (Arapahoe Indian)
Andrews--Indian leaders p126-127
POWDER RIVER WAR. See
JOHNSON CO. WAR (Wyoming)
POWDERLY, TERENCE W.
Boardman--Gilded p75-76
Harlow--Story p404
Life--Steel (7) p80-81, 83-85
POWELL, JOAB
Case--Empire p257-268
POWELL, JOHN WESLEY
Boardman--Gilded p162-163
Davidson--Life (2) p400
Gilbert--Trail. p182, 189, 206-207, 210, 212
Hine--American p182-184, 186-187, 189, 332, 339
Morris--Ency. p264
, and arid regions
America 200 p78-79
-Biography
Morris--Ency. p706
-"Proposals for Western irrigation policies," 1890
Ridge--America's p642
POWELL SURVEY
Gilbert--Trail. p184-185, 207-212, 214, 222
POWER
See also types of power
Wilson--American p290-291
, Sources of
Walker--Every. p47-48
POWERS, HIRAM

Boardman--Jackson. p154-155
Cable--American p156, 158, 270-271
Morris--Ency. p601
, and "Greek slave" statue
Bode--Anatomy p96-100
PRAGMATISM
Boardman--Gilded p118-119
"PRAIRIE SCHOONERS" (WAGONS)
Reader's--Story p192
PRAIRIES. See GREAT PLAINS
"PRANKS"
Wilson--Folkways p114-119
PRATT, EDWIN A.
, on railroads' influence in West, 1870-1890
Angle--American p380-383
, on "Manifest destiny," and McKinley
Miers--American p259-265
PRATT, JULIUS W.
, on "Manifest destiny," and McKinley
Miers--American p259-265
PRATT, SILAS GAMALIEL
Chase--America's p340-341
Howard--Our p305-306
PRATT, ZADOC
Van Wagenen--Golden p190-191
PRAYER
-Grace
Schwartz--When p40
PREEMPTION ACTS. See
DISTRIBUTION--Preemption Acts
PREGNANCY
Cable--American p161-162
PREJUDICE
See also INTOLERANCE
Marzio--Nation p287-296
-1876
Hilton--Way p49-50, 67-68, 88-89
, against minorities
Cable--American p300-301
, in migrant labor
Marzio--Nation p370, 384-385
-Views of Booker T. Washington
Hurd--Treasury p118-120
PRE-RAPHAELISM
-Views of John Ruskin, 1851
Reader's--Story p504
PRESBYTERIANS
Boardman--Virginia p169-171
Carman--History (1) p382-383, 506, 509, 530, 565, 585
Furnas--Americans. See index p1003
Handlin--This p147, 164, 211, 259-

260, 313
Hine--American p90, 184, 226-227,
244-246
Nye--Cultural p227
Wright--Culture p98-99
Wright--Every. p210-211
-Oregon
Billington--Far p81-85
-Pennsylvania
Wright--Culture p84-85
PRESCOTT, WILLIAM HICKLING
Boardman--Jackson. p147
Bode--Anatomy p240-245
Brooks--Flower. See index
p547
Morris--Ency. p569
Our literary p51
-Biography
Morris--Ency. p706-707
-"Ferdinand and Isabella"
Brooks--Flower. p135-146
PRESIDENTIAL ELECTIONS. See
ELECTIONS, Presidential
PRESIDENTIAL SUCCESSION ACT,
1886
Morris--Ency. p258
PRESIDENTS--UNITED STATES
See also names of presidents
Jones--Age p374-375
Life--Hunt p259-272
Reader's--Story p332-333
, and cabinets
Morris--Ency. p402-404
-Assassinations
Whitney--American p134, 146,
174, 208, 214
-Cuisine
Ross--Taste p74-76
, "Doughface" (slavery sympa-
thizers)
Butterfield--Amer. p135, 149
-Inaugurations
-Age at, and age at death
Davie--Profile p76-79
-Parties
Ross--Taste p246-247
-Wives, list of
Whitney--American p357-358
PRESS. See NEWSPAPERS; PENNY
PRESS"; PRINTERS AND PRINT-
ING; PUBLISHERS AND PUBLISH-
ING
PRESTON, ANN
Adelman--Famous p184-185
PREUSS, CHARLES
Gilbert--Trail. p161-162, 164,
166
PRICE, STERLING

DeVoto--Year. See index
p521
PRICES
See also individual products and
subjects
-1876
Hilton--Way p172
-1880's
Dulles--United p70-71
-Views of Frances Trollope
Trollope--Domestic. See
index p. xiii
, Wholesale
-Effect of wars
Morris--Ency. p510
PRIMERS
McClinton--Antiques p80
, Patriotic
Life--New (5) p114
"PRINCETON" (ship)
-Guns
Garrison--Lost p120-121
PRINTERS AND PRINTING
See also PUBLISHERS AND
PUBLISHING
Furnas--Americans p321-322
Marzio--Nation p229-231
Reader's--Story p363
-Presses and type
Boardman--Jackson. p101-102
Langdon--Everyday (2) p156-
158
-1880's
Peck--Nineteenth n. p.
PRISONS AND PRISONERS
See also CONVICTS: PROBA-
TION AND PAROLE; PUNISH-
MENT
Handlin--This p169, 184-185, 220,
235
Keller--Affairs p125-128, 496-498
-Civil war
See also ANDERSONVILLE
(GEORGIA) PRISON; ST.
LOUIS PRISON FOR
SOUTHERN WOMEN
Andrews--Women. See index
p463
Butterfield--Amer. p191
Dowdey--Experiment p87-90,
125-127, 298, 305, 307-308,
334, 379
Jordan--Civil p152-153, 203
-Reform
Furnas--Americans p483-485
Harlow--Story p255
Life--Hunt p188-193
Life--Sweep (4) p66

Tyler--Freedom's p273-274
-1817-1848
  Morris--Ency. p518-519
-Auburn system
  Tyler--Freedom's p274-
  277, 282
-Pennsylvania system
  Tyler--Freedom's p277-
  278, 282
-Silent system
  Furnas--Americans p484-485
-Views of Frances Trollope
  Trollope--Domestic p224,
  286n, 347, 368, 391
PRITCHARD, JAMES A.
  Boorstin--Americans p69-71
PRIVACY
  Lynes--Domestic. See index
  p306
PRIVATEERS
  See also PIRACY
  Boardman--Virginia p47-48
  Collins--Story p191
  Furnas--Americans p359
  Tunis--Young p93
  -Yankee captures prize, 1812
    Commager--Heritage p233-
    235
PRIZE FIGHTING. See BOXING
PROBATION AND PAROLE
  Keller--Affairs p497-498
PROBITY
  , Lack of
    -Views of Frances Trollope
      Trollope--Domestic. See
      index p. xiii
PROCTOR AND GAMBLE
  -1876
    Hilton--Way p170
PROFANITY
  Life--Hunt p186-187
PROFITEERING
  Wilson--American p216-217
PROGRESSIVE EDUCATION. See
  EDUCATION, Progressive
"PROGRESSIVES"
  Borden--Portrait (2) p73-76
PROHIBITION
  -1876
    Randel--Centennial p114, 136,
    310-311
PROHIBITION PARTY
  Carman--History (1) p521-522,
  613-614
  Furnas--Americans p739-740,
  917-919
  Warren--Pictorial p141
PROJECTORS. See PHANTA-

SCOPE, JENKINS'
"PROLETARIATS"
  Alden--Pioneer p207-208
PROPERTY ACTS
  , Women's
    See also MARRIED WOMAN'S
    PROPERTY ACT OF N.Y.
    Gurko--Ladies p89, 146, 185,
    268, 272, 276
"THE PROPHET" (Shawnee Indian)
("ELKSWATAWA"; "TENSKWATAWA")
  Andrews--Indian leaders p48-49
  Boardman--Virginia p115
  Reader's--Story p85
  200 Years (1) p183
PROSPECTORS. See GOLD MINES
AND MINING
PROSPERITY
  , Dream of
    Wright--Every. p95-107
PROSTITUTION
  Bartlett--New p353, 427-428, 436
  Cable--American p132-133, 229-
  231, 252-253
  Sochen--Herstory p115-116
  -Brothels
    Bartlett--New p428-429
    , in "Gilded Age"
      Jones--Age p131
    -Portland riot, 1825
      Burner--America (1) p298-300
PROTECTIVE TARIFF. See
TARIFF, Protective
PROTESTANTS
  See also names of denominations
  Boardman--Virginia p170-172
  Carman--History (1) p383, 502,
  504-514, 556
  Handlin--This p147-148, 250, 259-
  260, 358
  Hine--American p94, 106, 222, 226-
  229, 234-237, 323-324
  Keller--Affairs p138-139, 484-485
  , and Spanish-American war
    Jones--Age p401-402
  -Denominations
    Alden--Pioneer p169-170
    -California
      Wright--Culture p137-140
PRUDENTIAL COMPANY
  Nostalgia p28-32
PRUDERY
  Handlin--This p101, 182-183, 190
  -Women
    Handlin--This p182
PRYOR, ROGER
  Young--Women p31, 40-41, 330-
  331

PRYOR, MRS. ROGER
  Young--Women p29, 31-32, 37, 40-
  41, 330-331
PSALMODY
  Lowens--Music p81, 125, 284-285
PUBLIC DOMAIN
  -1803-1853
    Morris--Ency. p419
  -Distribution
    Morris--Ency. p439
  -West
    Hine--American. See index
    p368
PUBLIC HEALTH
  Boardman--Civil p113, 179
  Keller--Affairs p123-124, 499-
  500
  Walker--Every. p122-123
PUBLIC OPINION
  -First poll, 1824 (Wilmington,
  Del.)
    Robertson--Book p141
PUBLIC RELATIONS
  See also ADVERTISING
  Handlin--This p189, 191-193
PUBLIC SPEAKERS. See
  SPEAKERS
PUBLIC UTILITIES
  See also types of public utilities
  Keller--Affairs p340-342
PUBLIC WELFARE
  Keller--Affairs p189, 501-506
PUBLISHERS AND PUBLISHING
  Boardman--Virginia p143
  Bode--Anatomy p110-115
  Furnas--Americans p321-322,
  477, 449, 734-736
  Jones--Age p222-224
  Morris--Ency. p579
  Walker--Every. p167-169
  -1802-1860
    Morris--Ency. p570-571
  -1810-1850
    Hart--Popular p90
  -1820-1850
    Hart--Popular p90
  -1880'-1890's
    Reader's--Story p359-360
  -Books, 16 categories of (1835)
    Hart--Popular p90
  -Children's books and toys
    McClinton--Antiques p100,
    116-117, 120-121, 131-132
  -"Great revolution"
    Mott--Golden p76-79
  , Subscription
    Furnas--Americans p734-
    736

PUEBLO INDIANS
  DeVoto--Year p263, 269, 271, 324-
  325, 379-380, 394-395
  -Alta California
    Tunis--Frontier p126-127
PUGILISM. See BOXING
PULITZER, JOSEPH
  Boardman--Gilded p164
  Carman--History (2) p370-371
  Furnas--Americans p858-861,
  867-868
  Harlow--Story p428-430
  Life--Reaching (8) p36-37, 41, 131
  Reader's--Story p360-361
  Walker--Every. p191-192, 194-195
  -Biography
    Amer. Her.--New (11) p E395-
    396
    Morris--Ency. p707
PULLMAN, GEORGE MORTIMER
  See also PULLMAN CARS;
    PULLMAN STRIKE
  Boardman--Civil p143
  Butterfield--Amer. p266-267
  Furnas--Americans p352, 821-
  824, 827
  Life--Reaching (8) p88-90, 105
  Lynes--Taste. p94-96
  Portraits--Americans p94-95
  Randell--Centennial p127, 168-169
  Ross--Taste p273
  Wilson--American p222-227
PULLMAN, ILLINOIS
  Portraits--Americans p94, 97
  , as social study
    Harris--Land p118-132
PULLMAN CARS
  Amer. Her.--New (10) p840-841
  Garrison--Lost p136-140
  Handlin--This p286, 301, 366
  Hine--American p263
  Lewis--Big p322-324
  Lynes--Taste. p89, 94-96, 175
  Marzio--Nation p564-565
  Train--Story p331-332
  Wilson--American p222-225
  -1876
    Randel--Centennial. See
    index p473
  -1894
    Viewpoints p48
  -Dining cars, first, 1863
    Robertson--Book p151
  -"Hotel cars"
    Drury--Midwest p36-38
  -Upper births
    Wilson--Vanish. p176
PULLMAN COMPANY

Boardman--Gilded p80-81
Furnas--Americans p822-825
PULLMAN STRIKE, 1894
Butterfield--Amer. p266-267
Collins--Story p271
Dulles--United p85-88
Harlow--Story p409-410
Life--Reaching (8) p88-90, 105
Life--Steel (7) p92-93
Morris--Ency. p523
-Views of George Mortimer
Pullman
Angle--American p395-397
-Views of Henry David
Miers--American p224-229
-Workmen's case
Angle--American p397-399
PULSIPHER, JOHN
-"The Mormon War of 1857"
Ridge--America's p517-529
PULZSKY, FERENC AURELIUS
, on America, 1852
Handlin--This p232-252
PUMPS AND PUMPERS
, Fire
Furnas--Americans p532-535
, Hand
Wilson--Vanish. p63
PUNISHMENT
See also HANGINGS; PILLORY
AND STOCKS; PRISONS AND
PRISONERS; etc.
Hunt--Life p157-159
Schwartz--When p66-67
, Church
Wilson--Folkways p205
, Home
Wilson--Folkways p202
, Official
Wilson--Folkways p218-220
, Personal
Wilson--Folkways p206-217
, Schools'
Train--Story p341
Wilson--Folkways p204
PURITANISM
Dulles--History p86, 101, 205
-"Purity crusade"
Keller--Affairs p515-516
PURSES. See "RETICULES"
PUSHCARTS
Wilson--Vanish. p149
PUTNAM, MARY TRAILL SPENCE
Adelman--Famous p177
PUTNAM-JACOBI, MARY C.
Warren--Pictorial p127-128
PUTNEY (VERMONT) COMMUNITY
Tyler--Freedom's p187-189, 195

PUZZLES
, Children's
McClinton--Antiques p227, 321
PYLE, HOWARD
Larkin--Art p256; see also index
p538

Q

"QUAD CITIES" (4 towns on Miss.
river)
Drury--Midwest p20
"QUADROONS"
-New Orelans
Cable--American p88
QUADRUPLE ALLIANCE, 1815
Harlow--Story p191-192
QUAKERS
Boardman--Virginia p171
Gurko--Ladies p2, 10, 37, 51-54, 85,
105, 109-112, 116, 145
Handlin--This p158, 187-188, 260
-Discipline and work
Tyler--Freedom's p150-151
-Split, 2 sects
Wright--Every. p211
QUANTRILL, WILLIAM CLARKE
Amer. Her.--New (8) p E289-290
"QUARTER RACING"
Dulles--History p72-73
"QUARTERONS"
Handlin--This p162-163
QUAY, MATTHEW
Life--Steel (7) p11
QUICK, HERBERT
, on McGuffey readers
Commager--Heritage p928-931
-"The tragedy of the wheat"
Harris--Land p230-247
QUIDOR, JOHN
Reader's--Story p379
QUILTS AND QUILTING BEES
Bonte--America p102
Life--Sweep (4) p22
Marzio--Nation p169-170
Wright--Every. p230
QUINCY, JOSIAH
Boorstin--Americans p37, 44
, on eclipse
Commager--Heritage p364-367
QUOTATIONS
-"Americanisms"
Boorstin--Americans p281-282
-Proverbs and sayings
Wilson--Folkways p198-200

R

R.M. &W. See PONY EXPRESS
RABINOWITCH-KEMPNER, LYDIA, DR.
  Neidle--America's p210
RACES
  See also NATIONALITIES
  , and genteel tradition
    Jones--Age p201-212
  -Minorities--West
    See also INDIANS; MEXICO--
    Mexicans; RAILROADS--West,
    and racial minorities
    Hine--American p190-221; see
    also index p368
  -Prejudice
    -Views of Booker T. Washing-
    ton
      Hurd--Treasury p118-120
  -Relations
    See also BLACK CODES
    Harris--Land p267
    Life--Union (6) p111-113, 124,
    134-137
    -Civil war
      Andrews--Women. See
      index p463
      Borden--Portrait (2) p8
RACES, ATHLETIC
  Train--Story p291
RADICAL REPUBLICANS
  Amer. Her. --New (8) p701-710
  Boardman--Civil p64-65, 76-77,
  79-80, 82-83
  Dulles--United p8-10
  Harlow--Story p338-345, 347
  Holzman--Stormy p116, 140, 142,
  159, 162-165, 172, 175, 177
  Life--Union (6) p110-117, 130
RADICALS
  See also ANARCHISTS
  Dulles--United p12, 16-18, 20-22,
  26, 28-30
  Furnas--Americans. See index
  p1004
  Jones--Age p379-380
  Keller--Affairs p47-52, 55-57
  -Acts, 1867
    Butterfield--Amer. p187
  , in Congress, 1866
    Butterfield--Amer. p187
  , in Grant's administration
    Carman--History (2) p43, 45-
    46
  -Germans, Austrians and Jews,
  in politics
    Marzio--Nation p396

, Post Civil war
    Carman--History (1) p719-739,
    745-746, 752-753
    Carman--History (2) p20-40
RADIO
  -First signalling, 1866 (Washing-
  ton, D.C.)
    Robertson--Book p143
  -Invention
    Morris--Ency. p538
RAEDER, O.M.
  , on America, 1847
    Handlin--This p204-219
RAFTS
  Langdon--Everyday (2) p90-92
  , and lugs (from Maine)
    Langdon--Everyday (2) p3-4
"RAG-PICKERS"
  Harris--Land p269
RAGTIME. See MUSIC--Ragtime
RAILROADS
  See also PULLMAN CARS; names
  of railroads
  Amer. Her. --New (5) p436-441;
  E177
  Angle--American p204-205, 263,
  267, 281, 287, 293
  Bartlett--New p243, 323, 325, 330-
  331
  Boardman--Civil p132-133, 138-
  144
  Boardman--Gilded p61-67, 75-77,
  79-81, 85-87
  Boardman--Jackson. p95-98
  Boorstin--Americans. See index
  p512
  Cable--American p100, 220, 299-
  301
  Carman--History (1). See index
  p. xxii
  Carman--History (2) p65-68
  Davidson--Life (2) p244-257
  Furnas--Americans. See index
  p1004
  Handlin--This. See index p596
  Harlow--Story p386-389; see also
  index p817
  Jones--Age p152-154
  Keller--Affairs. See index p625
  Langdon--Everyday (2). See
  index p395
  Life--America's p106-107
  Life--Growing (3) p156, 160, 164-
  165
  Life--Steel (7). See index p131,
  159
  Life--Union (6). See index p175
  Linton--Bicentennial. See index

p446
Nation in motion p84-107
Partridge--As p73-75, 80-81
Reader's--Story p198-200
Tunis--Frontier p94-96, 142-144, 157
200 Years (2) p69-72
Walker--Every. p49, 58-70, 139
Wright--Every. p89-93
-1825-1893
  Nostalgia p15
-1830-1840
  Reader's--Story p281
-1840-1860
  Life--New (5) p38
-1850-1865
  Life--New (5). See index p159
-1876
  Randel--Centennial. See index p473
-Advertising propaganda
  Ridge--America's p621-622
-Air brake, 1869
  Reader's--Story p265
-Alabama, 1832
  Nation in motion p85
, and Chicago
  -Views of Julian Ralph
    Cook--City p45, 47
, and mining
  America's 200 p63-64
, and Robert M. Lafollette
  Commager--Heritage p1008-1011
-Arkansas, 1850's, 1899
  Nation in motion p86
-Banks
  -Mississippi, c1836
    Nation in motion p103
-"Barons" (financiers, giants)
  See also names of individuals
  Boardman--Gilded p66-67
  Carman--History (2) p85-90
  Dulles--United p55-56
-Building of early
  Dulles--United p38-40
  Marzio--Nation p179
  Morris--Ency. p426-427
-California
  Johnson--Pictorial p132-135
  Tunis--Frontier p142
  -1850's, 1856, 1873, 1876
    Nation in motion p86-87
  -Sierra Nevada
    Johnson--Pictorial p134-135, 140-141
  -"Techachapi loop," 1876

Johnson--Pictorial p142
-Carriages and coaches
  Wilson--American p152-153
-Cars
  Lynes--Taste. p94-96, 175-176
-Civil war period
  Dowdey--Experiment p17, 41, 127, 181-182, 272, 345, 375-376
  Jordan--Civil. See index p214
  Meredith--World p98-109
-Consolidation
  See also RAILROADS, Transcontinental
  Collins--Story p261
  Morris--Ency. p432
-Depots and stations
  -1871 (first terminal)
    Ross--Taste p157
  -California, 1888, 1894
    Nation in motion p100
  -Florida, 1880's
    Nation in motion p101
  -Georgia, 1849
    Nation in motion p102
  -Massachusetts, 1884, 1898
    Nation in motion p102
  -New Jersey, 1897
    Nation in motion p103
  -New York, 1860
    Nation in motion p103
  -North Carolina, c1875
    Nation in motion p104
  -Oregon, 1892
    Nation in motion p105
  -Pennsylvania, 1856, 1870, 1872
    Nation in motion p106
  -Rhode Island, 1875, 1882
    Nation in motion p106
  -Tennessee, 1876, 1890's
    Nation in motion p107
  -Utah, 1898
    Nation in motion p107
  , Village
    Partridge--As p80-81
-Financing
  See also RAILROADS--"Barons"
  Carman--History (2) p90-97
-Georgia, 1838
  Nation in motion p87
-"Immigrant cars"
  Marzio--Nation p181, 184
  , and the Westward bound immigrant
    Marzio--Nation p178-179
-Iron T-rail, 1830
  Reader's--Story p264

-Kansas, 1867
  Nation in motion p87-88
-Labor
  See also RAILROADS--
    Strikes
  Marzio--Nation p186
  , Disputes in
    Morris--Ency. p524
  , Immigrant
    See also RAILROADS--
    West, and Immigrants
    Marzio--Nation p358-359
-Land development
  American 200 p59-64
  Hine--American p153-154, 161,
  165, 167, 173
  -Grants
    Morris--Ency. p433
  -Values
    Marzio--Nation p185, 189-
    191
-Legislation
  -1820, 1830's, 1838, 1850, 1862,
  1887, 1893
    Nation in motion p126-127
-Locomotives
  Dreppard--Pioneer p301
  Train--Story p277-278
  Treasury--Amer. p198-215
  Wilson--American p148-151
  -1831-1889
    Reader's--Story p198
  -"Best friend of Charleston"
    Wright--Every. p89-90
  -"Iron Horse"
    Lewis--Big p321-353
  -Views of Charles Dickens,
  1842
    Angle--American p205-207
  , Wood-burning
    Wilson--Vanish. p175
-Maine, 1836
  Nation in motion p88
-Maryland, 1829
  Nation in motion p88
-Massachusetts
  -Revere, 1871
    Trachtenberg--Demo. p210-
    226
-"Monopoly"
  Lewis--Big p354-412
, Narrow gauge
  America's Hist. p528-529
-New Hampshire, 1869
  Nation in motion p88
-New Jersey, 1834
  Nation in motion p88
-Ohio, 1875

  Nation in motion p89
-Palace cars
  See also PULLMAN CARS
  Furnas--Americans p352-353
-Pennsylvania, 1891
  Nation in motion p89
-Presidents
  See also RAILROADS--"Bar-
  ons"
  Maurois--Illus. p190-191
-"Railroaders"
  Wilson--Early p148, 150
-Rails
  Wilson--American p154
-Rebates
  Harlow--Story p394-395
-Refrigerator cars
  Ross--Taste p63
  Wilson--American p228-233
-"Roundhouses"
  -West Virginia, 1883
    Nation in motion p107
-Safety coupler, 1868
  Reader's--Story p265
-Shops
  -Nevada, c1870
    Nation in motion p103
  -North Carolina, 1857, 1893,
  1896
    Nation in motion p103-104
  -Pennsylvania, 1849
    Nation in motion p105-106
  -West Virginia, c1890
    Nation in motion p107
-Signals and switches
  Reader's--Story p265
-Signs
  -Connecticut, mid-19th cen-
  tury
    Nation in motion p101
, Southern
  Morris--Ency. p432-433
-Strikes
  Amer. Her. --New (10) p828-
  830
  Life--Steel (7) p79-80, 90-95
  , of 1877
    Harlow--Story p406-407
-Telegraph, 1844
  Reader's--Story p264
-Towns
  -Rowesville, S.C., 19th cent.
    Nation in motion p106
-Trains
  See also PULLMAN CARS;
  RAILROADS--Locomotives
  Amer. Her. --New (5) p386-389
  McClinton--Antiques p265-266,

269
Woodward--Way p217-220
-1876
    Randel--Centennial. See
    index p474
, First (Pennsylvania, 1832)
    Collins--Story p149
-"Lightning express"
    Viewpoints p42
-Luxuries
    Ross--Taste p273-274
-Passenger cars, first
    Train--Story p280
, Transcontinental
    See also names of railroads
    Boardman--Civil p141-143
    Boorstin--Americans p256
    Brown--Westerners p93, 124,
    147, 162, 164, 169-172, 177,
    193, 221
    Carman--History (2) p67
    Davidson--Life (2) p259, 268-
    278
    Davie--Profile p164-167
    Harlow--Story p345, 365-367
    Hine--American p105, 110, 139,
    144, 150-151, 188, 323
    Johnson--Pictorial p142
    Langdon--Everyday (2) p395
    Life--Steel (7) p30-32
    Maurois--Illus. p190-191
    Reader's--Story p199-200
    200 Years (2) p70, 72, 76, 81
        -Express, 1876
            Hilton--Way p142-143
        -"Golden Spike." See
            "GOLDEN SPIKE"
-Travel
    Hilton--Way p137-143
    -Excursion, 1872
        Trachtenberg--Demo. p195-
        208
-Tunnels. See TUNNELS,
    Railroad
-Utah
    Nation in motion p90
    -Lumber camps, 1866
        Nation in motion p107
-Views of Julian Ralph, 1893
    Cook--City p45, 47
-Virginia, 1888
    Nation in motion p90
-Warehouses
    North Carolina, 1866
        Nation in motion p103-104
-West
    See also names of railroads
    Amer. Her. --New (9) p802-808

Hine--American. See index
    p368
Morris--Ency. p430-431
-1878
    Ridge--America's p570-571
-1880
    Carman--History (2) p198
-Advertising and tourists
    Hine--American p169, 262-
    264, 326
, and agriculture
    Hine--American p33, 154,
    164, 167-170, 172, 176, 178
, and racial minorities
    Hine--American p149-150,
    194, 213, 215-217, 234, 260
, and settling of West
    Jones--Age p154-155
        -Views of Edwin A.
        Pratt
            Angle--American
            p380-381
-Building
    Hine--American p144, 146-
    149, 217, 260, 276
-Effects
    Hine--American p139, 152-
    153, 155, 167, 333
-"The thrill of Western rail-
    roading," 1878, by Helen
    Hunt Jackson
        Ridge--America's p570-571
-Wisconsin (1851's, 1870's)
    Nation in motion p90
RAILWAYS
    See also HORSECARS; TROL-
    LEYS
, Elevated
    , First, N. Y. city, 1870
        Harlow--Story p424-425
    -Third Avenue El., N. Y. city
        -Views of William Dean
        Howells, 1890
            Cook--City p52
, First electric, 1839
    Robertson--Book p152
, Street
    Davidson--Life (2) p174
    Dreppard--Pioneer p305
    Furnas--Americans p674-676,
    801-804
    Partridge--As p100
    Portraits--American p82-84
    Wilson--Vanish. p179-181
    , First, 1873
        Harlow--Story p425
        Linton--Bicentennial p103
    -Georgia (late 19th cent.)

Nation in motion p102
, Interurban
Furnas--Americans p802-
803
Wilson--Vanish. p178
-Minneapolis, 1892
Cook--City p61
-New York City
-Accidents, 1866
Cook--City p52-53
-Steam engine
Life--Steel (7) p31
-Washington, D.C., 1895
Viewpoints p49
-Strikes
Dulles--United p82-83
Wilson--American p226-227
-Traveling, nervousness
Trachtenberg--Demo. p245
-Trolleymen
Wilson--Early p143, 147
"RAIN-IN-THE-FACE" (Hunkpapa
Sioux Indian)
Andrews--Indian leaders p160
Andrews--Indians p88-91
RAINER FAMILY
Howard--Our p175
RAINEY, JOSEPH HAYNE
Butterfield--Amer. p222
RALPH, JULIAN
, on Chicago and railroads,
1893
Cook--City p45, 47
, on Chicago politics
Cook--City p185
, on immigration
Cook--City p76
RALSTON, WILLIAM C.
Garrison--Lost p168-171
Watkins--Gold p72-73, 76-80,
135, 258, 260
RAMBOUILLET DECREE, 1810
Morris--Ency. p138
RANCHERS AND RANCHING
-Frontier, 1865-1890
Ridge--America's p592-612
, Great
Bartlett--New p227-228
-"Ranchos"
-Alta California, and trade
Tunis--Frontier p127-128
-Sante Fé, houses
Tunis--Frontier p105-106
-West
Boardman--Civil p99-100
Jones--Shaping p219-234
RANDALL, JAMES RYDER
Howard--Our p260

RANDALL, SAMUEL
Randel--Centennial p234-235, 241-
242, 245
RANDOLPH, EMILY
Phillips--That p158-159, 165-166
RANDOLPH, JOHN
Amer. Her. --New (5) p E177-178
Butterfield--Amer. p36-37, 71
Carman--History (1) p327, 350,
392, 400-401
Kraus--U.S. p310-311, 356
Our literary p27
RANDOLPH, ROBERT
Phillips--That p105-106
RANDOLPH FAMILY
Phillips--That. See index p183
RAPID TRANSIT. See RAILWAYS
RAPP, GEORGE JOHANN
Hunt--Life p242-243, 245
Reader's--Story p320
Tyler--Freedom's p121-125
"RAPPITES"
See also "HARMONISTS"
Morris--Ency. p551
Reader's--Story p320
Tyler--Freedom's p121-128
Weisberger--Amer. p126-128
RAVENAL, HENRY W.
, on South's social revolution,
1865
Angle--American p343-346
RAY, CHARLOTTE
Macksey--Book p125
RAYMOND, HENRY JARVIS
Boardman--Civil p194-195
Meredith--World p116
Morris--Ency. p584
READ, DANIEL
-Musical letters, 1800's
Lowens--Music p161-177
READ, OPIE
, and "The Jucklins"
Mott--Golden p200-202
READERS
See also McGUFFEY READERS
McClinton--Antiques p82-84
REAGAN, JOHN
Dowdey--Experiment. See index
p452
REAL ESTATE
See also LAND; names of
localities
Handlin--This p264-269
-Booms and developments
Furnas--Americans. See
index p1004
REALISM
, in literature and art

-Views of Clarence S. Darrow
　Harris--Land p279-288
REAPERS AND REAPING
　Nostalgia p8-12
　Portraits--Americans p25-31
　Reader's--Story p112, 263
　Train--Story p275-276
　Wilson--American p136-143
　Wright--Every. p154-155
　-Hussey's model
　　Portraits--Americans p27
　-McCormick's model
　　Amer. Her. --New (5) p384-
　　385
　　Portraits--Americans p25
RECONSTRUCTION
　Amer. Her. --New (8) p596-711
　Boardman--Civil p75-84
　Boardman--Gilded p5-7
　Bonte--America p131
　Borden--Portrait (2) p1-11
　Carman--History (1) p712-753
　Commager--Heritage p793-830
　Davidson--Life (2) p392-393
　Furnas--Americans p750-754,
　　847-848, 850
　Handlin--This p295, 333, 338-343
　Harlow--Story p333-334, 432-435
　Keller--Affairs. See index
　　p625
　Life--Union (6). See index
　　p175
　Morris--Ency. p246-253
　Randel--Centennial. See index
　　p473
　Reader's--Story p61, 340-341
　Sochen--Herstory p172-174
　200 Years (2) p55-59
　Whitney--American p153-156,
　　161-162, 166, 176, 186
　, and Lincoln
　　Borden--Portrait (2) p4
　　Carman--History (2) p20-25
　, and Negroes
　　Amer. Her. --New (8) p710-711
　　200 Years (2) p292-293
　, and recovery
　　Dulles--United p20-31
　, and Supreme Court
　　Morris--Ency. p249-250
　-Comic views of Petroleum V.
　Nasby
　　Burner--America (1) p342-
　　345
　, Conflict over
　　Heffner--Doc. p149-154
　, Spirit of
　　Dulles--United p18-19

RECONSTRUCTION ACTS
　Amer. Her. --New (8) p290
　Carman--History (1) p730-731, 734
　Harlow--Story p341
　Life--Union (6) p115-116, 152
　Morris--Ency. p246-248
　Reader's--Story p157
RECREATION. See AMUSEMENTS:
SPORTS AND GAMES: ETC.
"RED CLOUD" (Sioux, Oglala Indian)
　Amer. Her. --New (9) p782
　Amer. Her. --Indians p42, 344-345,
　　347, 366-367
　Andrews--Indian leaders p120,
　　149-150, 153, 157
　Boardman--Civil p108-109
　Brown--Westerners p93-94, 96,
　　191-192, 194-195, 237, 244-246,
　　249, 260
　Davie--Profile p99-100
　Hine--American p150, 196, 198, 204
　200 Years (2) p63-65
"RED EAGLE" (Creek Indian)
　(WEATHERFORD, WILLIAM)
　Andrews--Indian leaders p55-57,
　　61
　Bonte--American p91
"RED JACKET" (Seneca Indian)
　Andrews--Indian leaders p41, 43
　Boardman--Virginia p120
　Davie--Profile p98-99
　, on religion
　　Hurd--Treasury p47-48
RED RIVER JOURNEY, 1823
　Ridge--America's p371-373
"RED SLEEVES." See "MANGAS
COLORADAS"
"RED STICKS" (Indian anti-
Americans)
　Amer. Her. --Indians p221, 233
REDWOOD TREES
　-California
　　Johnson--Pictorial p128-129
REED, AMY L.
　, on "Brook Farm," 1844-1847
　　Angle--American p268-271
REED, JAMES FRAZIER
　DeVoto--Year p521-522
REED, LUMAN
　Lynes--Taste. p38-40, 42, 44, 48,
　　56, 64, 150
REED, MARGARET KEYES
　DeVoto--Year p522
REED, THOMAS BRACKETT
　Butterfield--Amer. p254-255
　Life--Reaching (8) p84
　-Biography
　　Amer. Her. --New (11) p E396

REED, VIRGINIA (BLACKENSTOE, VIRGINIA)
DeVoto--Year. See index p522
REED, WALTER
-Biography
Amer. Her. --New (12) p E432
Morris--Ency. p707-708
REESE RIVER MINES
Watkins--Gold p162-164
REFORM AND REFORMERS
See also CRUSADERS; RELIGION, and reformers; SOCIAL RE-FORM: names of reform movements and reformers
Boardman--Civil p88-89, 188-191
Boardman--Gilded p109-110, 157-158
Boardman--Virginia p130-133, 192-194
Boorstin--Americans. See index p512
Borden--Portrait (1) p181-196
Carman--History (1) p518-523
Commager--Heritage p411-442
Gurko--Ladies p31-33, 94-95
Handlin--This p153, 184, 219-221, 246, 296
Harlow--Story p254-259
Keyes--Hope p216
Life--Reaching (8) p41-42, 91-92
Macksey--Book p105-121
200 Years (1) p298-299
-Views of Ralph Waldo Emerson
200 Years (1) p298
-Women
Boardman--Gilded p155-156
Life--Reaching (8) p39, 42
Macksey--Book p111-113, 116-117
Reader's--Story p432-433
Sochen--Herstory p122-128
REFORM SCHOOLS
Hilton--Way p66-67
Tyler--Freedom's p287-291
REFRIGERATION
See also ICEBOXES
Davidson--Life (2) p145
-1850's
Dreppard--Pioneer p86
, Mechanical (invention)
Garrison--Lost p187-189
REGATTAS
Dulles--History p141-143, 147, 166, 240
Ross--Taste p91, 96-97
REGIONALISM
Nye--Cultural p109-110
-1876

Randel--Centennial p102-104
"REGULATORS." See VIGILANTES
REID, HUGO. See "HUGO REID ADOBE," Calif., 1829
REID, JOHN P.
DeVoto--Year p247, 258, 377-380, 385, 396, 398, 404
RELIEF ACT OF 1821
Bartlett--New p75
RELIGION
See also CAMP MEETINGS; CHURCHES; EVANGELISM; names of denominations and individuals
Alden--Pioneer p168-170, 196, 205, 208-211, 217-218, 252, 290-291
Boardman--Civil p184-188
Boardman--Gilded p104-105, 157-160
Boardman--Jackson. See index p210
Boardman--Virginia p119-121, 167-174
Bode--Anatomy p. xiii-xiv
Borden--Portrait (1) p196-199
Carman--History (1) p503-515
Furnas--Americans. See index p1005
Handlin--This. See index p596
Keller--Affairs p136-142, 484-485
Kraus--U.S. p387-389
Life--Hunt p114-123
Reader's--Story p96
Wilson--Folkways p89-92
Wright--Ency. p203-221
-1830's
Ross--Westward p23
-1876
Randel--Centennial. See index p473
-1890's
Life--Reaching (8). See index p175
, and national liberty
-Views of Henry Ward Beecher
Hurd--Treasury p96-98
, and reformers
Harlow--Story p259
, and "Uncle Tom's Cabin"
Bode--Anatomy p186-187
, and urbanization
Borden--Portrait (2) p22
-Christianity
Bartlett--New p368-369
-Denominations
Boardman--Jackson. p133
Boardman--Virginia p167

Carman--History (1) p506-509
-1876
  Randel--Centennial p71-72,
  95, 436
, New
  Reader's--Story p102
-Freedom
  Davidson--Life (2) p336-343
-Frontier
  Cable--American p138-139
  Tyler--Freedom's p33-35
-Fundamentalism
  Furnas--Americans p327-328
  Jones--Age p20-21
-Geographical location
  Hunt--Life p123
-Growth of organized
  Collins--Story p154
, Influence of
  Trachtenberg--Demo. p77-79
-Kentucky
  Wright--Culture p79-80
, Liberal vs. conservative
  Nye--Cultural p223-226
-1847
  Morris--Ency. p553
-Literature
  Bode--Anatomy p132-148
  Mott--Golden p193-198
  Walker--Every. p168-169
-Magazines
  Bode--Anatomy p261-262
-Middlewest
  Drury--Midwest p81-82
-Music
  Bode--Anatomy p21-22, 26
  Howard--Our p592-596, 605-
  611
-Negroes
  Boardman--Virginia p172-173
-Old Northwest
  Tunis--Frontier p83-84
, "Old time"
  -Views of Thomas Low
  Nichols, 1835
    Angle--American p265-268
-Organizations
  See also names of organiza-
  tions and societies
  Walker--Every. p147-149
-Radicalism, 1876
  Randel--Centennial p442-443
-Sects and cults
  Wright--Culture p99-100
-Views of Frances Trollope
  Trollope--Domestic. See
  index p. xiv
-Views of "Red Jacket" (Indian)

Hurd--Treasury p47-48
-West
  Carman--History (1) p381-383
  Hine--American. See index
  p368
-Women
  Hunt--Life p77
  Warren--Pictorial p131
RELIGIOUS COMMUNITIES. See
UTOPIAS; names of communities
REMEDIES
  See also HERBS; MEDICINE
  Cable--American p148
  Dreppard--Pioneer p229-231
  Hunt--Life p105-106
  Schwartz--When p170-173
-Backache
  Schwartz--When p173
-Colds
  Schwartz--When p170-172
-Coughs
  Schwartz--When p172
-Cuts
  Schwartz--When p173
, Home
  Hilton--Way p21-22
  Ross--Heroines p11-12
  Schwartz--When p171-173
, in medicine cabinet
  Lynes--Domestic. p225-226
REMINGTON, FREDERIC
  Hines--American p294-297, 299
, and Western art
  Life--Steel (7) p70-71, 93
-Horses of the plains
  Jones--Shaping p156-157
REMINGTON, PHILO
-Typewriter
  Wilson--American p253-255
REMOVAL ACT OF 1830
  Amer. Her. --New (6) p E214
REMY, JULES
, on Brigham Young
  Commager--Heritage p542-546
"RENDEZVOUS. " See FUR TRADE
--"Rendezvous"
REPUBLICAN PARTY
  See also AMERICAN REPUBLI-
  CAN PARTY; RADICAL REPUB-
  LICANS; etc.
  Alden--Pioneer p258-261, 264, 267-
  268, 277-278, 296
  Amer. Her. --New (7) p609-612
  Boardman--Civil. See index
  p215
  Boardman--Gilded p5-9, 11-12,
  15-17, 181-184
  Boardman--Virginia p12-17, 23-24;

see also index p216
Borden--Portrait (1) p221-222
Carman--History (1) p409, 612-
614, 617, 698, 733-734, 746-749
Collins--Story p165
Dulles--United p151-152; see
also index p. xiv, xv
Handlin--This p339, 341-343,
384-388
Hine--American p110, 161, 231
Keller--Affairs p625
Kraus--U. S. p455-459, 468, 471,
474, 476-479
Life--New (5). See index p159
Life--Steel (7). See index p159
Life--Union (6). See index
p175
Linton--Bicentennial. See index
p446
Maurois--Illus. p206-207; see
also index p295
Whitney--American. See index
p368
-1800's
    Butterfield--Amer. p36-37
-1854
    Morris--Ency. p217-218
-1858
    Morris--Ency. p225
-1860
    Life--New (5) p92-93
-1890's
    Life--Reaching (8). See
    index p175
-Connecticut
    -Views of Abraham Bishop,
    1800
        Walker--Reform p36-45
, Domination of
    Borden--Portrait (1) p138
-Founding
    Harlow--Story p293
, "Free Soil"
    Butterfield--Amer. p143
-"Half-breeds" and "Stalwarts, "
1881
    Morris--Ency. p256
-Leaders, 1850's-1860's
    Life--New (5) p56
-Liberals, 1872
    Morris--Ency. p250
, Post-Civil war
    Carman--History (2) p20-40,
    228-229
-"The Softies"
    Maurois--Illus. p206
-"The Toughs, " 1880
    Maurois--Illus. p206

-Views of Abraham Bishop
    Walker--Reform p36-45
RESERVATIONS. See INDIANS--
Reservations
RESORTS
    See also names of resorts
    Boardman--Jackson. p188-189
    Cable--American p109-110, 283,
    332-333
    Dulles--History p64-65, 148-153,
    202
    Handlin--This p186, 346-348
    Walker--Every. p235-236
    Wright--Every. p245
-1870's
    Randel--Centennial p109, 322-
    324
-Women
    Handlin--This p347
RESOURCES. See NATURAL RE-
SOURCES
RESTAURANTS
    Furnas--Americans p463-465,
    692-693
    Partridge--As p128-130
-1876
    Randel--Centennial p22-23, 25-
    26
-New York city
    Partridge--As p130
-Specialties
    Ross--Taste p72-73
, Short-order
    Davidson--Life (2) p138-139
RESUMPTION ACT OF 1875
    Harlow--Story p450
RETAIL TRADE
    See also SHOPS AND SHOP-
    KEEPERS; etc.
    Boardman--Civil p133-134
    Boardman--Gilded p53-54
"RETICULES" ("CABAS, " "INDIS-
PENSABLES, " PURSES)
    Earle--Two cent. (2) p591-594
REVELS, HIRAM RHOADES
    Butterfield--Amer. p222
REVIVALISM
    See also CAMP MEETINGS;
    EVANGELISM
    Boardman--Jackson. p132
    Boorstin--Americans p318-320
    Chase--America's p207-231
    Handlin--This p119, 153, 243, 299,
    312
    Morris--Ency. p552
    Nye--Cultural p218-221
    Ross--Taste p49
    Trollope--Domestic p. xxxiii; see

also index p. xiv
Tyler--Freedom's. See index
   p604
Wright--Every. p217
-Frontier
   -Views of Frances Trollope
      Burner--America (1) p179-
      184
   -Views of Charles Grandison
     Finney
      Burner--America (1) p184-187
"REWARDS OF MERIT, " CHIL-
DREN's
   McClinton--Antiques p98-101
REYNOLDS, BELLE
   Young--Women p94-95, 159-167,
   171, 257, 307
-Biography
   Young--Women p376
RHETT, ROBERT BERNWELL
   Life--New (5) p51-52, 94
   Life--Sweep (4) p137-138
-Biography
   Amer. Her. --New (7) p E248
RHODE ISLAND
   See also DORR REBELLION
   Carman--History (1) p782
RICE, THOMAS DARTMOUTH
   ("DADDY, " or "JIM CROW")
   Boardman--Jackson. p174-175
   Chase--America's p264-265, 267
RICE
   Commager--Heritage p456-461
   Wright--Every. p144-145, 148-
   149
-1849
   Boardman--Jackson. p90
RICHARDS, ELLEN HENRIETTA
SWALLOW
   Adelman--Famous p244
   Macksey--Book p15-16, 151
   Reader's--Story p437
   Warren--Pictorial p126
RICHARDS, LAURA
   Macksey--Book p189
RICHARDS, LINDA
   Warren--Pictorial p135
RICHARDSON, ALBERT D.
   Watkins--Gold p55-56
   -"The land system. The
     problem of speculation, "
     1867
      Ridge--America's p618-619
   , on homesteader's tricks
     Commager--Heritage p844-
     848
RICHARDSON, HENRY HOBSON
   Carman--History (2) p381-382

Furnas--Americans p424, 620-623,
   774
Harlow--Story p433
Larkin--Art p284-290; see also
   index p539
Morris--Ency. p607-608
Mumford--Brown p115-128
Train--Story p318
-Biography
   Morris--Ency. p708
RICHARDSON, JAMES
-"Travelling by telegraph"
   Trachtenberg--Demo. p196-208
RICHES. See WEALTH
RICHMOND, VIRGINIA
   Carman--History (1) p657, 661,
   663, 670, 711
   Holzman--Stormy p120-122, 141,
   181, 184
   Life--New (5) p84, 92, 107, 133-
   134, 137, 147-148
   Life--Union (6) p16, 31, 52-55, 85-
   86, 89, 94-95
-Civil war
   Dowdey--Experiment. See
     index p452
   Jordan--Civil. See index
     p214-215
   -Campaign (Malvern Hill)
     Collins--Story p218
   -Confederate evacuation, 1865
     -Views of Mrs. John P.
     McGuire
      Angle--American p334-
      336
   , Fall of
     Meredith--World p212-217
   -Food riots, 1863
     Commager--Heritage p703-
     705
     -Views of J. B. Jones
      Commager--Heritage
      p703-705
   -General McClellan at Rich-
    mond
     Pratt--Civil p18-19
   , "On to Richmond drive"
     Dowdey--Experiment p70,
     78-79, 81, 105, 177, 183, 239,
     269, 271, 275, 280
   -Ruins, 1865
     Viewpoints p86-87
   -Scarcity
     -Views of J. B. Jones
      Commager--Heritage
      p705-710
   , Siege of, 1862
     Bonte--America p123

-Historic homes
Vanderbilt--Living p106
RICHTHOFEN, WALTER, BARON VON
-"Investment in the range cattle industry," 1885
Ridge--America's p608-610
RICKETTS, FANNY
Young--Women p135-136
-Biography
Young--Women p377
RIDDLES AND RIDDLE BOOKS
See also CHILDREN'S BOOKS AND READING--Riddle books
Schwartz--When p91-95
RIDGE, MAJOR (Cherokee Indian)
Andrews--Indian leaders p88, 93
RIFLES. See GUNS
RIIS, JACOB AUGUST
Boardman--Gilded p108-109
Our literary p182
Portraits--Americans p98-100
Randall--Mary p505
Walker--Every. p115, 131, 136, 138, 202-203
-Biography
Amer. Her. --New (11) p E396
, on city gangs in crime, 1889
Angle--American p402-404
, on N. Y. city--"The Bend," 1890
Cook--City p292
, on police lodging houses
Commager--Heritage p901-905
, on poverty, N. Y. city, 1890
Commager--Heritage p895-901
, on slums
Cook--City p123, 129, 132-135, 147, 244-245
, on strikers, 1890
Cook--City p290
RILEY, JAMES WHITCOMB
-Birthplace (Greenfield, Ind.)
Vanderbilt--Living p154
-Home (Indianapolis, Ind.)
Vanderbilt--Living p155
RIMNER, WILLIAM
Larkin--Art p186-187; see also index p539
RIO GRANDE
Hine--American p74, 80, 98-99, 101, 103, 106-107, 125-126, 213, 315
-Border dispute
Life--Sweep (4) p101-104, 113
RIOTS

See also CIVIL WAR--Draft-Riots; STAMP ACT; names of riots
Furnas--Americans. See index p1005
-Bill to outlaw, debate on, 1848
Grimsted--Notions p312-326
-Theater
Grimsted--Melodrama p65-74
RIPLEY, GEORGE
Boardman--Jackson. p124
Brooks--Flower. p229, 242-244, 268, 280, 375-376
Tyler--Freedom's p177-178, 183
RIPLEY, HORACE
Alden--Pioneers p224
RIVERS
See also names of rivers, settlements
Brown--Westerners. See index p287-288
Reader's--Story p194-196
-Boats
Amer. Her. --New (5) p408-409
Dulles--History p153-154
-Rivermen, life of
Life--New (5) p20-23
-Transportation
Life--America's p104-105
Wright--Every. p81-89
ROAD SHOWS (COMPANIES)
Boardman--Jackson. p155-156
Dulles--History p260-263
Nye--Unembar. p183-185
ROADS
See also BRIDGES, Road; HIGH-WAYS; TUNNELS, Road; TURN-PIKES; names of roads
America's Hist. p273-274
Bartlett--New p281-305
Boardman--Jackson. p93-94
Boardman--Virginia p85-89
Handlin--This p104-105, 123-124, 153, 177, 295
Harlow--Story p193-197
Keyes--Hope p226
Langdon--Everyday (2) p28-37
Life--Growing p146-148, 156
Marzio--Nation p164
Nation in motion p40-83
Walker--Every. p57, 113, 210-211
, across mountains
200 Years (1) p198-199
-Alabama
Nation in motion p41
-Arizona, 1857
Nation in motion p41
-Arkansas, 1834

Nation in motion p42
-California, 19th cent.
  Nation in motion p43
-District of Columbia, c. 1800
  Nation in motion p43
-Illinois, late 1820's, c. 1850
  Nation in motion p44
-Laws 1806, 1822, 1857, 1893
  Nation in motion p123
-Louisiana, mid 19th
  Nation in motion p45
-Maryland, 1834, c. 1820
  Nation in motion p46-47
-Massachusetts, 1897
  Nation in motion p47-48
-Montana, c. 1860
  Nation in motion p49
-New Hampshire, 1861
  Nation in motion p49
-New Jersey, 1870
  Nation in motion p50
-New Mexico, 1855
  Nation in motion p50
-New York, 1857
  Nation in motion p50
-Ohio, 1895
  Nation in motion p51
-Oklahoma, 1867
  Nation in motion p51
-Pennsylvania, 19th cent.
  Nation in motion p52
-Rhode Island, 1815
  Nation in motion p53
-Trails, Overland
  Billington--Far p91-115
-Utah, 19th cent.
  Nation in motion p54
-Views of Frances Trollope
  Trollope--Domestic. See
  index p. XIV
-Virginia, 19th cent.
  Nation in motion p55
-Wagon
  Bartlett--New p287-288
  200 Years (1) p246
-West Virginia, 1809, 1818, 1838,
1847
  Nation in motion p56-57
, Westward
  Carman--History (1) p457-460
  Life--Sweep (4) p87-90, 108,
  134, 136, 145
-Wisconsin, 1832
  Nation in motion p57
ROANOKE ISLAND, VIRGINIA
-Civil war
  Dowdey--Experiment p143,
  146, 148, 174, 324

"ROBBER BARONS"
  See also names of individuals
  Amer. Her. --New (10) p825-827,
  861-874
  Butterfield--Amer. p202-207
  Reader's--Story p283
, on rails
  Amer. Her. --New (10) p852-
  853
ROBERTS, ROBERT
, on servants
  Burner--America (1) p241-244
ROBIN, C. C.
, on Louisiana, change of flags
  Angle--American p159-160
ROBINSON, C. M.
-Views on improvement of life,
  philanthropy, in cities, 1899
  Cook--City p103-106
ROBINSON-JEWETT CASE, New
York, 1830
  Cable--American p132-133
ROCK DRILLS
, of Robert Ingersoll
  Life--Steel (7) p30
"ROCK OF CHICKAMAUGA." See
  THOMAS, GEORGE HENRY
ROCKEFELLER, JOHN DAVISON
  Amer. Her. --New (10) p870-871
  Boardman--Civil p122-123
  Boardman--Gilded p45-47
  Butterfield--Amer. p314
  Carman--History (2) p73, 98-101,
  107, 111-112, 120-121
  Dulles--United p58-59
  Harlow--Story p385-386
  Life--Steel (7) p34, 131-134
  Portraits--Americans p9
  Randel--Centennial p165, 184-186,
  377, 396, 424
  Reader's--Story p283
  200 Years (2) p82
-Biography
  Morris--Ency. p708-709
-Oil industry
  Harlow--Story p385-386
  Nostalgia p40-42
-Justification of Standard Oil
  Co.
  Angle--American p378-380
ROCKEFELLER FAMILY
-Early careers and monopoly
  Randel--Centennial p184-185
ROCKY MOUNTAIN FUR COMPANY
  Amer. Her. --New (6) p514
  Bartlett--New p87, 258
  Billington--Far p44, 55-64, 72
  Boardman--Jackson. p64

Boardman--Virginia p109
Carman--History (1) p371
DeVoto--Year p170, 243
Gilbert--Trail. p61, 64, 77, 130-131
Hine--American p51-52, 54, 58, 269
Reader's--Story p171
Tunis--Frontier p111-112
ROCKY MOUNTAINS
See also COLORADO ROCKIES
Boardman--Jackson. p153-154
Boardman--Virginia p106-107
Brown--Westerners. See index p288
-First white women to cross
Brown--Westerners p93, 98, 118, 124, 132, 145, 164, 166, 180, 183, 215, 265
Ross--Westward p23
-Fur trade, 1833
-Views of Charles Larpenteur
Angle--American p220-223
-Zebulon Montgomery expedition
Ridge--America's p364-368
ROE, EDWARD PAYSON (E. P.)
Mott--Golden p147-148
ROEBLING, JOHN AUGUSTUS
Boardman--Civil p144-145
Marzio--Nation p192-195
Mumford--Brown p97-100
-Biography
Amer. Her. --New (7) p E248-249
Morris--Ency. p709
ROEBLING, WASHINGTON AUGUSTUS
Boardman--Gilded p144-145
Larkin--Art p283-284
Life--Steel (7) p44-45
Mumford--Brown p98-101, 105
-Biography
Amer. Her. --New (12) p E432
ROEBUCK, ALVAH CURTIS
See also SEARS, RICHARD WARREN
Portraits--Americans p58-59
-Mail order business
Nostalgia p62-65
ROGERS, AGNES
-"The undimmed appeal of the Gibson girl"
Treasury Amer. p320-337
ROGERS, HARRIET
Macksey--Book p73
ROGERS, ISAIAH
Boardman--Jackson. p165-166
Lynes--Taste. p83-84

ROGERS, JOHN
Boardman--Civil p162
Bode--Anatomy p103-104
Furnas--Americans p625-628
Larkin--Art p185-186; see also index p540
Lynes--Taste. p70-75
Morris--Ency. p602
-"Rogers groups"
Lynes--Taste. p58, 70, 72-75
Randel--Centennial p129, 386-387
ROGERS, LOUISA KENDALL
-"Narrative"
Andrews--Women p286-302
ROGERS, RANDOLPH
Morris--Ency. p602
ROLLER SKATING
Dulles--History p182, 193-194, 265
-1863 (first)
Ross--Taste p88
-1880's
Peck--Nineteenth n. p.
"ROLLING SHOWS"
Dulles--History p133-134
ROMAN CATHOLICS. See CATHOLICS
"ROMAN NOSE" ("BAT") (Cheyenne Indian)
Amer. Her. --Indians p344, 346
Amer. Her. --New (9) p783
Andrews--Indian leaders p118, 120, 125, 148
ROMANTICISM
Furnas--Americans p409-411, 415-416
Jones--Age p216-220
-West
Hines--American p69, 222, 289-290, 292, 294-298, 322-323, 330-332
ROOF GARDENS
Ross--Taste p75
ROOFS
Van Wagenen--Golden p143-144
ROORBACH, ORVILLE
Bode--Anatomy p119-120, 222
ROOSEVELT, EDITH
Melick--Wives p56-57
ROOSEVELT, THEODORE
See also "SAGAMORE HILL" (home)
Brown--Westerners p260-273
Butterfield--Amer. p316-317
Furnas--Americans. See index p1005
Harlow--Story p482-483
Hine--American p136-138, 186-

187, 189, 296, 306, 336, 338
Morris--Ency. See index p767
Reader's--Story p62
200 Years (2) p324-325
, and "Rough Riders"
    Amer. Her. --90's p108
    -San Juan Hill, 1898
      Viewpoints p90-91
-Biography
    Amer. Her. --New (12) p E432-
    433
    Morris--Ency. p710
    Whitney--American p215-227
-"Frontier types"
    Jones--Shaping p239-251
, in charge of Navy, 1898
    -Views of John Davis Long
      Commager--Heritage
      p979-980
, on endurance vs. ease
    Hurd--Treasury p123-126
-"Ranch life in the far West"
    Jones--Shaping p219-234
-"The strenuous life, " 1899
    Amer. Her. --90's p84
-Views of Elting Morison
    Miers--American p265-269
ROOT, CAPTAIN
, and Eaton affair
    Phillips--That p17-20
ROOT, GEORGE FREDERICK
    Chase--America's p179-180
    Howard--Our p264-266
ROOT, JOHN WELLBORN
    Larkin--Art p247, 284-285, 289,
    311
ROSE, ERNESTINE
    Gurko--Ladies. See index p326
    Neidle--America's p30, 37-41
    Tyler--Freedom's p457
ROSE, WILLIAM
    Amer. Her. --New (6) p E214
ROSECRANS, WILLIAM S. ,
GENERAL
    Amer. Her. --New (8) p E290
    Jordan--Civil p122, 138, 140-142
    Life--Union (6) p8, 12-13, 61, 63,
    81-83, 100
    Young--Women p234-238, 243, 246,
    312
"ROSEMOUNT MANSION" (Forkland,
Ala.)
    Vanderbilt--Living p140
ROSS, ALEXANDER
-"Fur hunters of the far West, "
    1814
    Davie--Profile p144-145
ROSS, CHARLES

Randel--Centennial p330-331, 335,
340
ROSS, DAVID R. See NASBY,
PETROLEUM V.
ROSS, JOHN (Cherokee Indian)
    Andrews--Indian leaders p88, 92
    Life--Sweep (4) p44
"ROUND HILL SCHOOL" (Northamp-
ton, Mass.)
    Tyler--Freedom's p249-250
ROWAN, ANDREW S.
    Life--Reaching (8) p133
"ROWDIES"
    Handlin--This p315, 324-326
ROWING
    Boardman--Civil p201
    Dulles--History p141-143, 184, 226
ROWLAND, HENRY AUGUSTUS
    Wilson--American p277
-Biography
    Morris--Ency. p711
ROYALL, ANNE
, on "Old Hickory" Jackson, 1829
    Angle--American p210-212
ROYCE, JOSIAH
    Wright--Culture p133-134
-Biography
    Morris--Ency. p711
ROYCE, SARAH
    Brown--Westerners p124, 126-127
    Hine--American p226
    Wright--Culture p133-134
-Frontier courage
    Commager--Heritage p562-572
, on Western desert
    Commager--Heritage p562-571
ROYLE, EDWIN MILTON
-"The vaudeville theatre"
    Harris--Land p180-190
RUBBER INDUSTRY
    Nostalgia p33-35
-Inventions
    Boardman--Jackson. p101
-Vulcanization, by Charles Good-
year
    Train--Story p284
    Wilson--American p124-129
RUDOLPH, FREDERICK
    Hine--American p245-246, 248,
    341
RUEDE, HOWARD
-"Life on a Kansas homestead, "
    1877
    Ridge--America's p624-630
, on sod houses in Kansas
    Angle--American p369-371
RUFFIN, EDMUND
    Boardman--Jackson. p92

RUFFIN, JOSEPHINE
Macksey--Book p273
RUFFIN, VIOLA KNAPP
Treasury Amer. p148-151
RUGGLES, M. B.
-"Pursuit and death of John
Wilkes Booth"
Jones--Shaping p205-208
RUM
Mussey--Old p102
"RUM, ROMANISM AND REBEL-
LION"
Collins--Story p258
RUMSEY, ELIDA. See FOWLE,
ELIDA RUMSEY
RUNNING. See TRACK AND
FIELD EVENTS--Running
RURAL FREE DELIVERY. See
POSTAL SERVICE
RURAL LIFE. See COUNTRY
LIFE
RUSH, BENJAMIN
Furnas--Americans. See
index p1005
Hunt--Life p202-207, 210
Tyler--Freedom's. See index
p604
RUSH, WILLIAM
Larkin--Art p102-103
RUSH-BAGOT AGREEMENT, 1817
Amer. Her. --New (5) p365, 367,
E178
Boardman--Virginia p56-57
Harlow--Story p189-190
Morris--Ency. p156
RUSKIN, JOHN
, on Pre-Raphaelism, 1851
Reader's--Story p504
RUSSELL, CHARLES M.
Bartlett--New p233, 373-374
Hine--American p297-298
Life--Steel (7) p60-63
RUSSELL, HAMLIN
-"The extermination of the
buffalo," 1893
Ridge--America's p581
RUSSELL, HENRY
Chase--America's p166-171
Howard--Our p160-164
RUSSELL, LILLIAN
Amer. Her. --90's p99, 122, 124-
125
Blum--Stage. Profile 1
Warren--Pictorial p157
RUSSELL, OSBURNE
-"Decline of the fur trade; the
final rendezvous," 1839
Ridge--America's p396-398

RUSSELL, TILLIE
, in Civil war battle
Andrews--Women p145-147
RUSSELL, WILLIAM (British war
correspondent)
Young--Women p85, 106-109, 112,
114-115, 120-121, 125, 172, 186
RUSSELL, WILLIAM HENRY ("OWL
RUSSELL")
DeVoto--Year. See index p522
RUSSELL, WILLIAM HEPBURN
Brown--Westerners p152, 157-
168, 172, 186
RUSSELL, WILLIAM HOWARD
, on Battle of Bull Run
Commager--Heritage p738-746
RUSSELL, MAJORS, AND WADDELL
(freighting firm)
See also "PONY EXPRESS"
Bartlett--New p227, 295-299, 303
Billington--Far p273-276, 285-292
Kraus--U.S. p470-471
RUSSIA AND RUSSIANS
Boardman--Virginia p64-65
Life--Reaching (8) p60-62, 65
-Warships, in N.Y. harbor
White--American p50-55
RUTGERS, HENRY
Amer. Her. --New (5) p E178
RUTLEDGE, ANN
-False legend of Lincoln's "Love"
(Lectures on, by William Hern-
don)
Randall--Mary p430-442
RUTLEDGE FAMILY
Randall--Mary p38
RUXTON, GEORGE F.
-"Fur trade and rendezvous in
the Central Rockies," 1849
Ridge--America's p393-396
RYAN, THOMAS
Howard--Our p215
RYDER, ALBERT PINKHAM
Larkin--Art p269-271; see also
index p540
Morris--Ency. p605
Mumford--Brown p221-230
Reader's--Story p381
-Biography
Amer. Her. --New (11) p E396-
397
Morris--Ency. p711-712
RYE
-New York state
Van Wagenen--Golden p79-80
RYNNING, OLE
Furnas--Americans p385-386, 696

S

SABBATARIANISM (Sunday blue
  laws)
  Keller --Affairs p508-509
  -1876
    Randel--Centennial. See
    index p473
SABBATH
  Handlin--This p119, 125, 132,
    134, 148-150, 165, 187, 236, 253,
    259, 260-264, 385-386, 399
  Walker --Every. p33
  , and poor people
    Cable--American p296, 298
  -Germans
    Cable--American p313
  -Observance
    Dulles--History p70, 90-91,
      207-209, 266
    Furnas--Americans p390-391
    , Breaking of
      Burner--American (1)
      p176-179
      Hunt--Life p183-186
    -Rules
      See also SABBATARIAN-
      ISM
      Hilton--Way p48-49
    , Slum
      -Views of Jacob A. Riis
      Cook--City p244-245
  -Views of Frances Trollope
    Trollope--Domestic. See
    index p. XIV
  -Virginia
    Cable--American p89
SAC AND FOX INDIANS
  See SAUKS AND FOXES
"SACAJAWEA" ("BIRD WOMAN")
  (Indian)
  Amer. Her. --New (6) p E214-215
  Boardman--Virginia p101
  Brown--Westerners p44-50
  Dolin--Great p59-67
  Gilbert--Trail. p28, 31-32, 42
  Life--Growing p80-81, 88-89
  Ross--Heroines p34-51
  Ross--Westward p93-100, 108-
    109
  Warren--Pictorial p65-67
SACRAMENTO, CALIFORNIA
  -Views of Alonzo Delano, 1849
    Angle--American p253-255
SACRAMENTO RIVER AND VAL-
  LEY, CALIFORNIA
  Bartlett--New p109, 112, 222,
    266-272

Billington--Far p42-43, 76-78
  -Transportation
    Johnson--Pictorial p144-145
SADDLES
  Life--America's p118-119
  , Cowboys'
    Train--Story p298-299
    Tunis--Frontier p150-151
  -Saddlebags
    Wilson--Vanish. p169
SAFETY BRAKES
  Wilson--American p258-259
SAFFORD, MARY J.
  Young--Women p93-94, 99, 145,
    151, 155, 168
  -Biography
    Young--Women p377
"SAGAMORE HILL" (Theodore
  Roosevelt's home, L. I.)
  Vanderbilt--Living p36
SAGE, MRS. RUSSELL
  Adelman--Famous p253-254
  Warren--Pictorial p142
SAGER, CATHERINE
  Ross--Heroines p10-11, 81-82
SAGER, JOHN
  Ross--Heroines p83-85
SAILING
  Commager --Heritage p301-322
  -"Around the world alone, " by
  Slocum
    Garrison--Lost p130-135
SAILORS
  See also FISHING AND FISHER-
  MEN; WHALING
  Handlin--This p102, 107, 129, 149
  Wilson--Early p139
  -Education
    Furnas--Americans p307, 309
  -Views of Charles P. Low, 1842
    Angle--American p214-217
  -Views of Richard Henry Dana
    Burner--America (1) p235-240
SAINT-AULAIRE, FELIX ACHILLE
  Amer. Her. --New (5) p E178-179
SAINT-GAUDENS, AUGUSTUS
  Amer. Her. --New (1) p E397
  Boardman--Gilded p138-139
  Larkins--Art p298-299; see also
    index p540
  Morris--Ency. p606
  -Biography
    Morris--Ency. p712
ST. JOHN, JOHN P.
  Life--Steel (7) p16
ST. JOSEPH, MISSOURI
  Billington--Far p107, 227, 277,
    288-289

Drury--Midwest p159-160
Handlin--This p286-289
ST. LOUIS, MISSOURI
　Boardman--Virginia p104-105
　Drury--Midwest p9-14
　Hine--American. See index
　　p368
　Life--Steel (7) p30, 33, 55, 77, 90,
　　125, 128-129
　Treasury Amer. p256-257, 262
　Vanderbilt--Living p174-175
　-1832 (as port)
　　Life--Growing (3) p166-167
　-1876
　　Randel--Centennial p36-37,
　　　56, 203-205
　-"The case for St. Louis," by
　　Nathaniel Holmes, 1875
　　Cook--City p43
　-Theater. See THEATER--
　　St. Louis, Mo.
ST. LOUIS PRISON FOR SOUTHERN
WOMEN
　Andrews--Women p336-343
ST. PUAL PIONEER PRESS, 1876
　Randel--Centennial p1-3, 109
ST. VALENTINE'S DAY. See
VALENTINE DAY
"SALARY GRAB" ACT, 1873
　Harlow--Story p346
　Morris--Ency. p251
SALEM, MASSACHUSETTS
　Life--Growing (3) p44-45
　-Schools, and play
　　-Views of Mary Harrod
　　　Northend
　　　　Commager--Heritage p360-
　　　　364
SALISH INDIANS
　Andrews--Indian leaders p172
　Gilbert--Trail. p58
SALOONS. See TAVERNS
"SALT DESERT"
　DeVoto--Year p40, 166, 179-180,
　　289, 300-306, 311, 331, 334-336,
　　365
SALT LAKE CITY, UTAH
　Billington--Far p201, 277-278,
　　287, 291-292
　Handlin--This p306-307, 312-
　　313, 316
　Hine--American p77, 108, 232,
　　261, 268
　-1880
　　Cable--American p281
"SALT SULPHUR SPRINGS,"
WEST VIRGINIA, 1816
　Nation in motion p83

SALVATION ARMY, 1880
　Morris--Ency. p553
SAMBARD, SIR. See BRUNEL,
MARC
SAMOA, AMERICAN
　Borden--Portrait (2) p68
　Dulles--United p164
　-American intervention
　　Carman--History (2) p367, 270,
　　　274, 278-281
　-Berlin conference, 1889
　　Morris--Ency. p283
　, Partition of, 1899
　　Collins--Story p266
　　Morris--Ency. p292
　-Rivalry
　　Morris--Ency. p282-283
　-Treaty, 1878
　　Morris--Ency. p281
SAMPLERS
　McClinton--Antiques p188-195
　Marzio--Nation p259-260
SAMPSON, WILLIAM THOMAS,
ADMIRAL
　-Biography
　　Amer. Her.--New (12) p E434-
　　　435
　-Defeat of Cervera, 1898
　　Commager--Heritage p984-992
SAN DIEGO, CALIFORNIA
　-Early settlers, 1846
　　Jones--Shaping p103
SAN FRANCISCO, CALIFORNIA
　Amer. Her.--New (6) p484-485
　Bartlett--New p410-415
　Billington--Far p5-6, 219-220, 280-
　　285, 289
　Brown--Westerners p64, 117, 121,
　　129, 145-152, 161, 167, 184
　Davidson--Life (2) p123-125
　Furnas--Americans. See index
　　p1006
　Handlin--This p316-321
　Hine--American. See index
　　p368
　Johnson--Pictorial p126-127
　Life--Reaching (8). See index
　　p175
　Life--Sweep (4) p148-151; see
　　also index p159
　Randel--Centennial. See index
　　p473
　200 Years (2) p294-295
　-Amusements, 1849-1850
　　Jones--Shaping p150
　-Buildings, early, 1842
　　Jones--Shaping p102
　-Cable cars

Life--Reaching (8) p35
-Chinese
  Bartlett--New p168-169
  Cook--City p87-89
  -Views of Rudyard Kipling
    Cook--City p87-89
-"City of entrepreneurs," by
  Samuel Bowles, 1869
  Cook--City p29-32
-Jews
  Bartlett--New p161
-Palace Hotels. See PALACE
  HOTELS, San Francisco
-"Pioneer days in San Fran-
  cisco," by John Williamson
  Palmer
  Jones--Shaping p137-155
-Population, nationalities of
  Wright--Culture p200-201
-Prices, 1848-1849
  Jones--Shaping p140, 142
-Views of Bayard Taylor, 1849
  Commager--Heritage p572-
  578
-Vigilantes
  Hine--American p302-304
SAN JACINTO, TEXAS, BATTLE
  Ridge--America's p434-436
-Houston's victory over Mexi-
  cans
  Commager--Heritage p599-
  602
"SAN JACINTO" AND THE
  "TRENT" (ships)
  Collins--Story p212
SAN JUAN HILL, BATTLE
  See also ROOSEVELT, THEO-
  DORE
  Collins--Story p290
  Keyes--Hope p387, 389
  -Rough Riders charge, 1898
  -Views of Richard Harding
    Davis
    Angle--American p442
SANBORN, JOHN D.
  Holzman--Stormy p202-203
SAND PAINTINGS
  , Navaho
  Amer. Her. --Indians p395
SANDOW, EUGENE
  Viewpoints p174
SANGER, MARGARET
  Adelman--Famous p217-218
  Warren--Pictorial p150-151
SANITARY COMMISSION, CIVIL WAR
  Dannett--Noble p272, 292, 330
  Meredith--World p118-123
  Young--Women. See index p388

-Fairs
  Partridge--As p63
  -Great Northern fair
    Dannett--Noble p273
  -Mammoth fair
    Dannett--Noble p335
  -Manhattan fair
    Dannett--Noble p273, 277,
    279
SANITATION
  Furnas--Americans p334, 454-458,
  908-909
  Partridge--As p15
  Walker--Every. p113, 118
  , in New York city, 1898
  -Views of Josiah Strong
    Cook--City p138
  , in wealthy homes
  -Views of C. F. Wingate, 1883
    Cook--City p140
SANSOM, EMMA
  -Ride, 1863
  Andrews--Women p278-283
SANTA ANNA, ANTONIO LOPEZ
DE
  Bartlett--New p99-100
  Billington--Far p123-125, 127-
  132, 150, 188-190
  Boardman--Jackson. p41-42, 45,
  47-49
  DeVoto--Year. See index p522
  Harlow--Story p265-266, 273, 275
  Hine--American p85-87, 98, 103
  Life--Sweep (4) p97-99, 104, 107-
  108, 111-112
  -Biography
  Amer. Her. --New (7) p E249
SANTA FE, NEW MEXICO
  Billington--Far. See index p321
  Boardman--Virginia p104-105
  Brown--Westerners. See index
  p288
  -Trade, 1840's
  DeVoto--Year. See index
  p522
  -Views of Josiah Gregg, 1831
  Angle--American p234-235
SANTA FE RAILRAOD
  Bartlett--New p113, 287-288, 416
SANTA FE TRAIL
  Amer. Her. --New (6) p524, E215
  Boardman--Jackson. p63
  Boorstin--Americans p54-55, 90
  DeVoto--Year p149, 152, 188, 230,
  232
  Gilbert--Trail. p94, 102-104
  Kraus--U.S. p418
  Reader's--Story p169

Tunis--Frontier p105
, and "Army of the West"
DeVoto--Year p243-271
-Bloody history, 1846
DeVoto--Year p244-245, 299,
401, 495, 502, 504
-Caravans, 1844
Ridge--America's p376-379
-Trader's start, 1831
-Views of Josiah Gregg
Angle--American p231-234
SANTIAGO (CUBA), BATTLE
Amer. Her. --90's p112-116
Collins--Story p291
Commager--Heritage p984-995
SANTO DOMINGO AFFAIR, 1870
Morris--Ency. p281
"SANTOS" (Religious statues)
America's Hist. p377
SANTVOORD, C. VAN
-"A reception by President
Lincoln, " by C. Van Santvoord
Jones--Shaping p176-178
SARATOGA SPRINGS, NEW YORK
Boardman--Virginia p188-189
Cable--American p109-110, 333
Dulles--History p149-152, 202
Partridge--As p170-171
Ross--Taste p70-71, 268-269
SARGENT, JOHN SINGER
Boardman--Gilded p137-138
Larkin--Art p302-304; see also
index p541
Reader's--Story p384
-Biography
Amer. Her. --New (11) p E397-
398
SARGENT, LUCIUS MANLIUS
Hart--Popular p109
SARTORIS, ELLEN GRANT. See
GRANT, ELLEN ("NELLIE")
"SASSACUS" (gunboat)
Meredith--World p197-198
"SATANK" (SANTANTA, SETAN-
GYA), (Kiowa Indian)
Amer. Her. --Indians p381
Andrews--Indian leaders p118,
132, 137, 141
"SATURDAY CLUB"
Brooks--Flower. p498-525
Our Literary p98-99
SATURDAY EVENING POST
Bode--Anatomy p256-257
SATURDAYS
Walker--Ency. p32-33, 80, 235-
236
SAUKS AND FOXES (SAC AND
FOX) (INDIANS)
Andrews--Indian leaders p74-83

Boardman--Jackson. p71
Gilbert--Trail. p151
"SAVANNAH" (ship)
Dowdey--Experiment p80, 125-126
SAWMILLS
Tunis--Frontier p75-76, 85
Van Wagenen--Golden p130-132,
138-139
SAWS
Van Wagenen--Golden p28-29
SAWYER, PHILETUS
-Biography
Amer. Her. --New (11) p E398
SAWYER EXPEDITION, 1865
Andrews--Indians p13-24
SAXE, JOHN GODFREY
Nye--Unembar. p108-109
SAXE-WEIMAR-EISENACH, DUKE
OF
-Views on America, 1825-1827
Handlin--This p155-168
"SCABS" (Strikebreakers)
Harlow--Story p406
"SCALAWAGS"
Boardman--Civil p81-82
Collins--Story p235
Harlow--Story p342-343
Life--Union (6) p133-135, 137
SCALPING
-Wyoming
Andrews--Indians p49-51
SCANDINAVIANS
See also names of nationalities
Reader's--Story p320-321
Weisberger--Amer. See index
p395
-Immigrants
Bartlett--New p152, 158-160
Kraus--U.S. p392-394
Marzio--Nation p158-159
"SCARECROWS"
Wilson--Vanish. p66
SCHARFENBERG, WILLIAM
Howard--Our p154-156
SCHAUMBERJ (SCHAUMBURG),
EMILIE
Peacock--Famous p190-205
SCHLESINGER, DANIEL
Howard--Our p154
SCHOOL BOOKS. See TEXTBOOKS
SCHOOLCRAFT, HENRY ROWE
Boardman--Virginia p113
, and Lewis Cass, on Upper Mis-
souri, 1820
Angle--American p166-170
SCHOOLHOUSES
Bartlett--New p388-389
Furnas--Americans. See index
p1006

Schwartz--When p60-61
Tyler--Freedom's p235-236
-1876
  Hilton--Way p54-56, 62
-"Era of the little red school-
house," 1870's
  Davie--Profile p306
, for religious services
  Wright--Culture p182-183
, "Little red"
  Davis--Profile p306
  Partridge--As p19-20
-Maine, 1890's
  Amer. Her. --90's p56-57
, One-room
  See also SCHOOLS, Country
  Wilson--Vanish. p79
SCHOOLMASTERS. See TEACH-
ERS
SCHOOLS
  See also COLLEGES AND UNI-
  VERSITIES; EDUCATION; types
  of schools, etc.
  Dreppard--Pioneer p220-223
  Handlin--This. See index p597
  Schwartz--When p60-63
  Tunis--Young p129-130
  Walker--Every. p77, 116-117, 244
  Wilson--Folkways p92-95
  Wright--Every. p187-202
, and religion
  Nye--Cultural p151-152
, and society
  Commager--Heritage p917-938
-Boards
  -Views of S. H. Olin, 1895
    Cook--City p193-194
, Common
  Collins--Story p282
  Tyler--Freedom's p234-242
, Country
  Keyes--Hope p264-265
  -1876
    Hilton--Way p54, 56, 62-63
, Crowding of
  -Views of Henry D. Chapin,
  1895
    Cook--City p225-226
  -Views of James H. Penni-
  man, 1890's
    Cook--City p221-223
-Curriculum
  Hunt--Life p136-137
  -1876
    Hilton--Way p62-63
-Discipline
  Hunt--Life p135
-Enrollment and attendance,

1870-1890
  Cook--City p288
, Free. See SCHOOLS, Public
-Funds, Distribution of
  Tyler--Freedom's p378-379
-Furniture
  See also SCHOOLS--Supplies
  Hunt--Life p135
, Girls'
  Hunt--Life p133-134
, Graduate
  Dulles--United p119-120
-Kentucky
  Wright--Culture p85-86
, Pauper
  Tyler--Freedom's p240-241
, Private
  Tyler--Freedom's p244-245
, Public
  Amer. Her. --New (6) p494-495
  Carman--History p514-516
  Harlow--Story p251
  Morris--Ency. p556
  Tyler--Freedom's p240-242
, in cities, 1865-1899
  Harlow--Story p426-427
, Number of (1878-1898)
  Hart--Popular p183
-Improvements
  -Views of C. M. Robinson,
  1899
    Cook--City p226-229
-Supplies
  Hunt--Life p136
  , and furniture
    Dreppard--Pioneer p224-225
-Truants, 1876
  Hilton--Way p66-67
-Views of Frances Trollope
  Trollope--Domestic. See
  index p. xiv
-West
  Carman--History (1) p381
  Hine--American. See index
  p369
SCHOONERS. See SHIPS AND
SHIPPING--Schooners; "YANKEE
CLIPPERS"
SCHRAMM, JACOB
  -"Travel on the Erie Canal,"
  1836
    Ridge--America's p292-294
SCHUMANN-HEINK, ERNESTINE
  Neidle--America's p226-227
SCHURZ, CARL
  Butterfield--Amer. p204
  Life--Steel (7) p12
  Marzio--Nation p395

Randel--Centennial. See index
p473
Weisberger--Amer. p124-126,
136
-Biography
Morris--Ency. p712
, on Lincoln-Douglas debate,
1858
Commager--Heritage p632-
637
, on "Old world and the new"
Hurd--Treasury p111-112
SCHUYLER, MONTGOMERY
, on America
Larkin--Art p262
SCIENCE AND SCIENTISTS
See also INVENTIONS AND
INVENTORS; names of
scientists, special subjects
Boardman--Civil p174-179
Boardman--Gilded p122-123
Boardman--Jackson. p166-170
Boardman--Virginia p175-178
Kraus--U.S. p383-386
Morris--Ency. p529-533
Nye--Cultural p93-94
Walker--Every. p44-73
-Expeditions
Boardman--Jackson. p170
, Impact of
Walker--Every. p50-54, 59-
68, 70-73, 126-127, 170, 177-
181
-Materials
Walker--Every. p48-50
-West
Boardman--Civil p176-177
Hine--American. See index
p369
-Women
Macksey--Book p150-152, 154-
155
Warren--Pictorial p126-128
"SCISSORBILLS." See HOME-
STEADERS
SCISSORS-GRINDERS
Harris--Land p268
Schwartz--When p54
"SCORCHERS" (fast bicyclists)
Wilson--Early p114-115
SCOTCH-IRISH
See also special subjects
Bartlett--New p139-140
SCOTT, ABIGAIL. See DUNIWAY,
ABIGAIL SCOTT
SCOTT, DRED
Amer. Her. --New (7) p559
SCOTT, MRS. TAYLOR

-Saving of home (Civil war)
Andrews--Women p205-206
SCOTT, THOMAS ALEXANDER
Boardman--Civil p139
Randel--Centennial p174, 184-185
-Biography
Amer. Her. --New (12) p E435
SCOTT, SIR WALTER
Bode--Anatomy p149-154
Brooks--Flower. See index
p548
Hart--Popular. See index p544
, and Washington Irving
Our literary p12-15
-Popularity in America
Bode--Anatomy p152-153
Mott--Golden p64-70
SCOTT, WINFIELD, GENERAL
Amer. Her. --New (7) p573
Boardman--Civil p39-40
Boardman--Jackson. p46-48
Carman--History p454, 569-571,
608-609, 643, 659, 785
DeVoto--Year. See index p522
Harlow--Story p275, 289
Kraus--U.S. p432-433, 449
Life--Sweep (4) p86, 100, 104, 110-
113, 118
Morris--Ency. See index p768
Young--Women p37, 49-51, 78, 106,
112, 115, 135, 142
-Biography
Amer. Her. --New (7) p E249-
250
Morris--Ency. p712-713
-Capture of Mexico City
Commager--Heritage p602-606
SCRIBES (Writers)
Wilson--Early p104-105
SCRIMSHAW
Life--New (5) p40, 43, 45, 47
SCRIPPS, EDWARD WYLLIS
Furnas--Americans p866-867
SCULPTURE AND SCULPTORS
Boardman--Civil p161-162
Boardman--Gilded p138-140
Boardman--Jackson. p154-155
Boardman--Virginia p156-157
Bode--Anatomy p92-103, 105
Cable--American p156, 158
Carman--History (2) p379-380
Furnas--Americans p572, 581,
625-628, 636-637
Handlin--This p145-146, 166, 245
Kraus--U.S. p381-382
Larkin--Art p99-107, 177-187,
279-282
Morris--Ency. p601-602, 606

Nye--Cultural p290-292
Reader's--Story p382-383
Walker--Every. p127-128, 170
-1830's
    Lynes--Taste. p13
-1840's
    Lynes--Taste. p19
-1890's
    Harlow--Story p434
, Bisque
    Dreppard--Pioneer p72
, Folk
    America's Hist. p296-297
-"Greek slave" by Hiram
    Powers
    Bode--Anatomy p96-100
-"Rogers groups," at exhibition,
    1876
    Randel--Centennial p382, 386-
    387
-Traveling exhibition
    Lynes--Taste. p152
-Women
    Warren--Pictorial p154, 157
"SCUTCHING BEES" (flax)
    Life--Sweep (4) p22-23
SCYTHES AND CRADLES
    Langdon--Everyday (2) p305-310
    Van Wagenen--Golden p234-235
SEA
    See also SAILORS
    -Captains
        America's Hist. p304-311
    -Life
        -Account of Richard Henry
            Dana
            Wright--Every. p182-185
    -Power
        Reader's--Story p176-188
    -Travel
        Hilton--Way p143-148
SEA SERPENTS
    -New England
        Treasury Amer. p298-299
SEAFARING COMPANIES. See
    ARGONAUTS
SEAFOOD. See FISH (as food)
SEALS (animals)
    -Fur seal controversy, 1893
        Collins--Story p268
SEAMEN. See SAILORS
"SEAMSTRESSES." See DRESS-
    MAKERS
SEARLES, EDWARD T.
    Lewis--Big p142, 145-150, 152-
    153
SEARS, RICHARD WARREN
    Nostalgia p62-65

Portraits--Americans p56-57
SEARS, STEPHEN W.
    -"Jedediah S. Smith: unsung
        pathfinder of the West"
        Amer. Her. --New (6) p531-538
SEARS ROEBUCK AND COMPANY
    Boardman--Gilded p54
    Reader's--Story p288
    -Catalog prices, 1897
        Boardman--Gilded p167
    -First catalog, cover, 1894
        Portraits--Americans p57
SEASONS
    -"Lay-by" season (late summer)
        Wright--Every. p157-158
"SEATTLE" (SEALTH) (Suquamish
    Indian)
    Andrews--Indian leaders p163-164
    Davie--Profile p100, 109
SEATTLE, WASHINGTON
    , Brides for, 1860's
        White--American p68-72
SECESSION
    Amer. Her. --New (7) p615-616
    Bonte--American p120
    Borden--Portrait (1) p229-231
    Butterfield--Amer. p160-161
    Carman--History (1) p632-638
    Davidson--Life (2) p384-385
    Jordan--Civil p10-11, 24, 27, 32-
    34, 45
    Kraus--U.S. p479-482, 485
    Life--New (5) p88-109; see also
        index p159
    -1860-1861
        Morris--Ency. p228
    -Beginnings
        Angle--By p165-167
        Tyler--Freedom's p542-544
    -Justification
        -South Carolina
            Angle--By p206-311
        -Views of Jefferson Davis
            Angle--By p255-259
    -Ordinance of, South Carolina
        Angle--By p203-204
SECTIONALISM
    Amer. Her. --New (5) p374-376
    Amer. Her. --New (7) p549-554,
    557-560
    Bonte--American p98
    Cable--American p92
    Life--New (5). See index p159
    Life--Sweep (4). See index
    p159
    , Economic
        Amer. Her. --90's p8-9
SECURITIES EXCHANGES

Furnas--Americans p652-653
SEDDON, JAMES ALEXANDER
  Dowdey--Experiment. See index
    p453
SEDGWICK, CATHERINE MARIA
  Boardman--Virginia p142
  Tyler--Freedom's p440
"SEED FROM MADAGASCAR. "
  See RICE
SEGREGATION
  Boardman--Gilded p99-100
  Life--Union (6) p113, 136-137
  , and discrimination
    Furnas--Americans. See
      index p1006
SELDEN, GEORGE BALDWIN
  Garrison--Lost p53-57
  Portraits--Americans p37-38, 40
  White--American p127-134
  -Horseless carriage, patent
    Wilson--American p321
  -Internal combustion engine
    Wilson--American p321
  -"Patent squabble, " by Henry
    Ford
    White--American p127-134
SELF-RELIANCE
  -Views of Ralph Waldo Emerson
    Grimsted--Notions p61-69
SELIGMAN, JOSEPH
  Furnas--Americans p706, 708-
    709
"SELOCTA" ("SHELOKTA") (Creek
  Indian)
  Andrews--Indian leaders p57,
    60-61
SEMBRICH, MARCELLA
  Neidle--America's p225-226
SEMINARIES
  Dreppard--Pioneer p220-221
  Nye--Cultural p230
  , Women's
    Nye--Cultural p169
    Train--Story p290
SEMINOLE INDIANS
  Amer. Her. --New (5) p E179
  Andrews--Indian leaders p57-
    61, 67-73
  Boardman--Jackson. p70
  Boardman--Virginia p117
  Brown--Westerners p85, 188-
    189
  Furnas--Americans p785-786,
    789
  Hine--American p100, 192, 206
  Life--Sweep (4) p43-45
  Whitney--American p66, 73, 86,
    109

-"Simanoli" (renegades)
  Bonte--America p103
-Wars
  Amer. Her. --Indians p228, 232-
    233
  Bonte--America p103
  200 Years (1) p224, 232-233
  , and Osceola
    Collins--Story p198
  , and President Jackson
    Morris--Ency. p156
SEMMES, RAPHAEL
  , on capture of Vera Cruz, 1847
    Angle--American p243-246
SENATE
  Life--New (5) p32, 34-38, 53, 96
  -1829-1849
    Life--Sweep (4) p14-19, 48, 52,
      84
  -1850's-1870's
    -Opposition to Southerners
      Lewis--It p12-30
  -1876
    Randel--Centennial p212-213,
      232
  -Senators
    Reader's--Story p66-67
  -"Senatorial courtesy" (Civil
    service appointments)
    Harlow--Story p447-448
SENECA FALLS CONVENTION
  Gurko--Ladies. See index p326
  Morris--Ency. p208
  Reader's--Story p433-434
  200 Years (1) p299
  Tyler--Freedom's p453-454
  Warren--Pictorial p90, 97-99, 159
  -Declaration of 1848
    Sochen--Herstory p127, 131-132
  , Ladies of
    Gurko--Ladies p2-3, 6, 29, 31,
      57, 92, 96, 100, 120-121, 137,
      234, 276, 305
SEPARATISTS (of Zoar, Ohio)
  Hunt--Life p244
  Tyler--Freedom's p128-130
SEPTEK, "BIG MARY"
  Neidle--America's p103
"SEQUOYAH" (Cherokee Indian)
  Amer. Her. --Indians p219-221
  Amer. Her. --New (5) p E180
  Andrews--Indian leaders p86
  Boardman--Virginia p116-117
  Hine--American p193
  Life--Growing (3) p84
  -Cherokee alphabet
    Reader's--Story p130
SERRA, JUNIPERO

Tunis--Frontier p124-125
SERVANTS
See also SLAVES AND SLAVERY
Cable--American p280,282,324-
325
Hunt--Life p102-103
Lynes--Domestic. p155-166
Partridge--As p126
Wilson--Early p89-102
Wilson--Folkways p138-141
-Hired men
Wilson--Early p154-155
, Household
Furnas--Americans p480-483,
697
Walker--Every. p26-29
Wilson--Early p94-97
-Wages (N.Y. city, 1875)
Cook--City p242
-Views of Frances Trollope
Trollope--Domestic. See
index p. XIV
-Views of Robert Roberts
Burner--America (1) p241-244
SETON, ELIZABETH (MOTHER)
Macksey--Book p67
Warren--Pictorial p40
SET-TAIN-TE (SATANA) (Kiowa
Indian)
Andrews--Indian leaders p132
SETTLEMENT HOUSES
See also names of houses
Boardman--Gilded p160-161
Carman--History (2) p410-411
Furnas--Americans p839-840
Warren--Pictorial p148-150
-1886-1895
Cook--City p215-216
-Workers
Amer. Her. --New (11) p946
SETTLERS. See FRONTIERSMEN;
IMMIGRANTS AND IMMIGRATION;
names of nationalities and locali-
ties
"SEVEN DAYS" BATTLES
Nettle--Noble p149-150,183,187,
193,258
"SEVEN PINES." See "FAIR
OAKS" (BATTLE)
SEVENTH DAY ADVENTISTS.
See ADVENTISTS
SEVERANCE, CAROLINE
Furnas--Americans p890-891
SEWARD, WILLIAM HENRY
See also ALASKA
Amer. Her. --New (7) p553-554
Boardman--Civil p64-65; see
also index p216

Boardman--Jackson. p196-197
Butterfield--Amer. p192-193
Carman--History (1). See index
p. xxiii
Harlow--Story p329-330
Holzman--Stormy. See index
p. 278
Keller--Affairs. See index p626
Life--New (5) p31,37-38,79,93,
113-114
Life--Sweep (4) p139
Life--Union (6) p155-157
Morris--Ency. See index p769
Portraits--Americans p30
-Biography
Amer. Her. --New (7) p E250
Morris--Ency. p713
, on slavery, 1858
Hurd--Treasury p81-84
SEWING
-1876
Hilton--Way p125-126
-Views of Frances Trollope
Trollope--Domestic p281-282,
284,416n
SEWING MACHINES
Boardman--Civil p147
Dreppard--Pioneer p89
Furnas--Americans p668-670
Langdon--Everyday (2) p270-273
Marzio--Nation p505,530-537
Nostalgia p16-19
Partridge--As p84
Portraits--Americans p21-25
Reader's--Story p266
Ross--Taste p298
-1876
Hilton--Way p24-25
, Foot-powered
Wilson--Vanish. p97
-Inventions (3)
Boardman--Jackson. p101
Wilson--American p130-135
, First, 1851 (Boston)
Robertson--Book p163
-Patent model, Howe's, 1846
Robertson--Americans p22
-Patent model, Singer's, 1855
See also SINGER, ISAAC
MERRIT
Portraits--Americans p25
SEXES
, Segregation of
-Views of Frances Trollope
Trollope--Domestic. See
index p. XV
SEYMOUR, HORATIO
Life--Union (6) p149-152

SEYMOUR, SAMUEL
  Hine--American p284, 286
SHAFTER, WILLIAM RUFUS
  -Biography
    Amer. Her. --New (12) p E436
SHAKERS
  Boardman--Jackson. p125-127
  Boardman--Virginia p173
  Furnas--Americans p334, 458,
    497, 522
  Handlin--This p164-165, 358
  Hunt--Life p239-242
  Life--Sweep (4) p59, 62-64
  Tyler--Freedom's p140-165
  -Agriculture
    Tyler--Freedom's p161-163
  -Architecture
    Larkin--Art p98-99
  -Children
    Tyler--Freedom's p154-155
  -Clothing and dress
    Tyler--Freedom's p151
  -"Common" or "Gathering room"
    Life--America's p87
  -Communal life and economic
    development
    Tyler--Freedom's p160-165
  -Doctrine
    Tyler--Freedom's p146-148
  -Food
    Tyler--Freedom's p153
  -Gifts
    Tyler--Freedom's p159-160
  -Houses
    Tyler--Freedom's p151-153
  -Industry
    Tyler--Freedom's p162-163
  -Inventions
    Tyler--Freedom's p163
  -Life
    Tyler--Freedom's p150-155
  -Order of worship
    Tyler--Freedom's p155-160
  -Organization and government
    Tyler--Freedom's p148-150
  -Songs
    Chase--America's p224-231
    , and dancing
      Tyler--Freedom's p155-158
  -Views of Harriet Martineau
    Tyler--Freedom's p164
  -Village, Lebanon, Ohio
    Commager--Heritage p438-440
  -Wealth
    Tyler--Freedom's p164
SHARECROPPING
  Life--Union (6) p129-130
  Schwartz--When p18, 47

  -South
    Harlow--Story p358
SHARON, WILLIAM
  Watkins--Gold p72-73, 77, 79-80
"SHARPENERS" (men)
  Wilson--Early p87-88
SHARPSBURG, MARYLAND
  , in Civil war
    Jordan--Civil p104-106, 181
SHATTUCK, LEMUEL
  Portraits--Americans p66
SHATTUCK'S TABLES
  , of vital statistics, 1846
    Portraits--Americans p66
SHAVING MUGS
  Dreppard--Pioneer p279-281, 289
  , Occupational
    -List, 1875
      Dreppard--Pioneer p283-287
SHAW, ANNA HOWARD
  Macksey--Book p87
  Neidle--America's p43-45
SHAW, LEMUEL
  Boorstin--Americans p39-42, 47-
  48
  Furnas--Americans p453-454, 518
  -Biography
    Morris--Ency. p713-714
SHAW, OLIVER
  Howard--Our p134-136
SHAW, PAULINE AGASSIZ
  Neidle--America's p48, 50-51
SHAWNEE INDIANS
  Andrews--Indian leaders. See
    index p184
  DeVoto--Year p51, 138, 152
  Hine--American p67, 192, 201
SHEEP
  Bartlett--New p193
  Furnas--Americans p472-474
  Langdon--Everyday (2) p249-250
  Van Wagenen--Golden. See
    index p278
  -1870's
    Randel--Centennial p142, 144-
    145
  , Merino
    Furnas--Americans p473-475
  -West
    Hine--American p125, 136, 185-
    186, 266-267, 307
    Tunis--Frontier p159
"SHELOKTA. " See "SELOCTA"
  (Creek Indian)
SHENANDOAH VALLEY, VIRGINIA
  , in Civil war
    Boardman--Civil p46-47, 54-55
    Jordan--Civil p90-91, 98, 160,

165, 169, 176-178
Life--Union (6) p16, 32, 52-54,
86-87
SHENTON, JAMES
, on Panama canal
Miers--American p269-274
SHEPARD, ODELL
, on "Utopias"
Miers--American p154-158
"SHEPHERD HALL" ("MONUMENT
PLACE"), Wheeling, W. Va.
Vanderbilt--Living p114
SHERIDAN, PHILIP HENRY,
GENERAL ("LITTLE PHIL")
Amer. Her. --New (8) p E291
Boardman--Civil p54-55
Brown--Westerners p188, 194-
202, 231-232, 235-238
Dannett--Noble p295, 310-313, 331
Jordan--Civil p157, 165, 169, 176-
178, 190, 201-202
Life--Union (6) p14, 86-87
-Entertainer of Russian Grand
Duke
White--American p92-98
-Ride, 1864
Pratt--Civil p57
SHERMAN, JOHN
Butterfield--Amer. p254-255
Life--Steel (7) p13, 136-137
SHERMAN, WILLIAM TECUMSEH,
GENERAL
Amer. Her. --New (8) p673, 678-
679, 683-684; E291-292
Andrews--Women. See index
p464
Boardman--Civil p55-58
Brown--Westerners p122, 177,
180, 188-202, 236-238
Butterfield--Amer. p178-179
Dannett--Noble p281, 310, 319,
325-326, 358-359, 374, 388
Dowdey--Experiment. See
index p453
Harlow--Story p320-322, 341
Holzman--Stormy. See index
p278
Jordan--Civil. See index p215
Kraus--U.S. p508-510, 512
Life--Union (6). See index
p175
Maurois--Illus. p157, 161-162,
170, 172
Meredith--World p208-211
Morris--Ency. p242-245
200 Years (2). See index p355
Young--Women. See index p388
-Biography

Morris--Ency. p714
-"The Congressional Peace Com-
mission of 1867"
Ridge--America's p574-576
, in Carolinas, 1865
Pratt--Civil p60-61
-Letters to brother on Civil war
Burner--America (1) p322-327
-March to the sea, Atlanta, 1864
America's Hist. p458-459
Collins--Story p217
Commager--Heritage p772-776
Pratt--Civil p50-52, 54, 56, 58-
59
-Views of Earl Schenck Miers
Miers--American p192-197
SHERMAN ANTI-TRUST ACT, 1890
Carman--History (2) p127-129, 230
Collins--Story p265
Davie--Profile p126-127
Dulles--United p67
Harlow--Story p391, 397
Keller--Affairs p306, 367, 407, 422,
437
Life--Reaching (8) p84, 93
Life--Steel (7) p127, 137
Morris--Ency. p261
Reader's--Story p282, 284
SHERMAN SILVER PURCHASE ACT,
1890
Carman--History (2) p242, 247-250
Dulles--United p74
Harlow--Story p464
Life--Reaching (8) p84-85, 87
Morris--Ency. p261-263
-Effects of repeal
Watkins--Gold p80, 100, 214-215
SHERWOOD, MARY ELIZABETH
Carson--Polite p167-168
Lynes--Taste. p103-106, 115-116
SHILOH, BATTLE 1862
Amer. Her. --New (8) p638, 640-
641
Boardman--Civil p43-44
Collins--Story p213
Life--Union (6) p36-38, 92
Morris--Ency. p235-236
Pratt--Civil p22-24
Young--Women p157-172
"SHINGABA W'OSSIN" (Chippewa
Indian)
Andrews--Indian leaders p83
SHINGLES
, Shaving of
Van Wagenen--Golden p141-144
SHINN, CHARLES HOWARD
Watkins--Gold p70, 223-224, 239,
243-244

-"Governmental organization in the mining camps," 1884
   Ridge--America's p546-548
SHIPBUILDING
  Mussey--Old p25, 64
  Wilson--Early p139-141
  Wright--Every. p127-128
SHIPS AND SHIPPING
  See also names of ships
  Boardman--Jackson. p81-83
  Boardman--Virginia p71-72
  Furnas--Americans. See index p1007
  Lynes--Taste. p90-94
  Wright--Every. p117-118, 127-128
  -1870's
    Randel--Centennial p158-161, 267
  -1876
    Hilton--Way p161-162
  -Clippers
    Life--America's p91-92
  , Emigrant, crowding of
    Marzio--Nation p119
  -Ironclads, Civil war
    Dowdey--Experiment p73-74, 161-163, 172, 212, 323, 326-327
  -Ocean liners, first, 1818
    Robertson--Book p120
  -Officers. See SEA CAPTAINS
  , Palace
    Lynes--Taste. p89-94
  , Passenger, advertisements of rates, etc.
    Marzio--Nation p122-125, 127
  -Passenger trade laws
    See also U.S. PASSENGER ACTS
    Marzio--Nation p119
  -Prints
    Treasury Amer. p162-171
  -Rules of sea
    Marzio--Nation p118
  , Sailing
    Wilson--Vanish. p173
  -Schooners
    See also "YANKEE CLIP-PERS"
    Reader's--Story p181
  , used as habitations, San Francisco
    Train--Story p312-313
  -Warships
    Wilson--American p198-205

SHIPWRECKS
  Bonte--America p158
SHIRLEY, DAME. See CLAPPE, LOUISE AMELIA KNAPP SMITH
"SHIVAREES"
  Furnas--Americans p522
SHOEMAKERS AND SHOEMAKING
  See also CORDWAINERS; STRIKES
  Van Wagenen--Golden p192-202
  , Frontier
    Tunis--Frontier p81
SHOES
  Furnas--Americans p433-434, 666, 670
  Partridge--As p86
  Ross--Taste p218, 220
  Tunis--Frontier p81
  -1876
    Hilton--Way p119-120
  -1880's
    Peck--Nineteenth n. p.
  -Boots
    Tunis--Frontier p81, 150
    Van Wagenen--Golden p193, 196, 198, 267-268
  , Cowboys'
    Train--Story p295-296
  -Inventions
    Earle--Two cent. (2) p756
  , Work
    Marzio--Nation p168
SHOLES, CHRISTOPHER LATHAM
  Boardman--Civil p147
  Walker--Every. p53-54
SHOLES, LILLIAN
  , as first woman typist
    Life--Steel (7) p37
"SHOOFLIES"
  McClinton--Antiques p582
"SHOOTING MATCHES"
  , Frontier
    Dulles--History p71-72
    Life--New (5) p24-25
"SHOOTING STAR." See "TECUM-SEH" (Shawnee Indian)
SHOPS AND SHOPKEEPERS
  See also MERCHANTS
  Langdon--Everyday (2) p148-151
  -Clerks
    Wilson--Early p79-87
  -Views of Frances Trollope
    Trollope--Domestic p272, 352, 401-402
SHORT STORY WRITING
  Harlow--Story p243
SHOSHONI (SNAKE) INDIANS
  Andrews--Indian leaders p7, 53,

279

127-128, 135, 147-148, 152-153,
157, 166
Brown--Westerners p37, 44-49,
97-98, 244
DeVoto--Year p153, 164, 166-167,
172, 176, 256, 294, 296-297, 299,
306, 337, 491, 493
Gilbert--Trail. p32, 152-153
Ross--Heroines p42-46
-Meeting with Lewis & Clark,
1805
Ridge--America's p361-363
SHOW-BOATS
Dulles--History p153-154
SHURTLEFF COLLEGE (Illinois)
Hine--American p244-245
SHUTTERS
, Inside
Wilson--Vanish. p85
SICKLES, DANIEL EDGAR
("DASHING DAN"), MAJOR
GENERAL
Meredith--World p170-175
SICKNESS
See also DISEASES; EPIDEM-
ICS; MEDICINE: PHYSICIANS:
REMEDIES; etc.
Walker--Every. p38-40, 242
-1876
Hilton--Way p72-90
, among Forty-niners
Billington--Far p227-228, 237
, among pioneers
Billington--Far p87-88
-Views of Frances Trollope
Trollope--Domestic. See
index p. XV
SIDEWALKS
-1876
Hilton--Way p164
SIGNBOARDS
Dreppard--Pioneer p159-162
, Old store
Wilson--Vanish. p146-147
SIGOURNEY, LYDIA HUNTLEY
Adelman--Famous p130
Boardman--Jackson. p151
Bode--Anatomy p189-191, 193-
197
Brooks--Flower. p66, 155-157,
399
Cable--American p151, 167, 172
Hart--Popular p133-135
Mott--Golden p114
Nye--Unembar. p95-96
-"Letters to mothers"
Grimsted--Notions p223-227
-"The orphans" (Poem)

Burner--America (1) p249-250
SIKES, WIST
-"Among the poor girls"
Trachtenberg--Demo. p150-159
SILHOUETTES
Train--Story p266
Woodward--Way p216-217
SILK
-Production
Van Wagenen--Golden p180-182
SILLIMAN, BENJAMIN
Kraus--U.S. p384-385
Morris--Ency. p530-531
SILLIMAN, BENJAMIN, JR.
Boardman--Civil p174
Boardman--Virginia p175-176
SILOS
Hilton--Way p158
SILVER
Boardman--Gilded p19-20, 47-48,
182-183
Life--Reaching (8). See index
p175
, Free
Borden--Portrait (2) p31-32
Holzman--Stormy p190-191
-Debate, 1893
Butterfield--Amer. p262-
263
, Standard
Harlow--Story p450-452, 463-
465, 468-469, 471-475
, vs. Gold
Amer. Her. --New (10) p880-
886
"SILVER GRAY" WHIGS, 1850
Morris--Ency. p214
SILVER MINES AND MINING
See also LEADVILLE, COLO-
RADO; VIRGINIA CITY, NEVA-
DA; etc.
Collins--Story p280
Tunis--Frontier p136
Watkins--Gold p67-69, 92-93
-California
Commager--Heritage p578-582
-Comstock Lode
Butterfield--Amer. p201
-Deposit formations
Watkins--Gold p174-176, 176n
-Production, 1860-1863
Hine--American p113
-Ratio, "16 to 1"
Collins--Story p275
-"Silverites"
Amer. Her. --90's p60-62
SILVER PURCHASE ACT, 1890
Butterfield--Amer. p262

Linton--Bicentennial p234-235,
238, 240
SILVERWARE
Dreppard--Pioneer p181, 183, 188
SIMMONS, MICHAEL T., COLONEL
Case--Empire p297-309
SIMMS, WILLIAM GILMORE
Boardman--Jackson. p146
Life--Sweep (4) p60
Our literary p28-29
-Biography
Morris--Ency. p714
SIMPSON, GEORGE, GOVERNOR
Case--Empire p41-54
SIMS, JAMES MARION
Reader's--Story p298
SING SING PRISON
-Electric chair
Garrison--Lost p105-108
SINGER, ISAAC MERRIT
See also SEWING MACHINES
Amer. Her. --New (5) p E180
Boardman--Jackson. p101
Marzio--Nation p530, 533-537
Nostalgia p16-19
Portraits--Americans p24-25
Wilson--American p134-135
SINGERS
-Women
Warren--Pictorial p152-154
SINGING
See also CHORAL SOCIETIES;
HYMNS: SONGS
Wright--Every. p234-235
-Families and groups
Howard--Our p173-175
Life--New (5) p32
-1876
Hilton--Way p51, 164-166
, Indian
Howard--Our p618-622
-Schools
Chase--America's. See
index p730
-Connecticut
Chase--America's p184-
186
SINKS
, Dry
Wilson--Vanish. p41
, Early bathroom
Marzio--Nation p502
"SINTE MAZO" (Oglala Dakota,
Sioux Indian)
, as Buffalo nickel model
Andrews--Indian leaders
p156
SIOUX INDIANS (DAKOTA:

OGLALA)
See also GREAT SIOUX RESER-
VATION
Amer. Her. --Indians. See index
p423
Amer. Her. --New (6) p498-499,
526-527
Amer. Her. --90's p38-39
Andrews--Indian leaders p94-99,
101; see also index p18
Andrews--Indians p43-44; see
also index p176
Bartlett--New p110-111, 321
Boardman--Civil p107-109
Boardman--Gilded p94-96
Boardman--Jackson. p73
Boardman--Virginia p118
Brown--Westerners p41-42, 76,
83-84, 87, 175, 191-193, 196, 202,
233, 237, 240-244, 247, 249, 252,
255, 267
DeVoto--Year. See index p518
Gilbert--Trail. p26, 127, 148, 151
Hine--American p194, 196, 198-
202, 204, 285, 296
Life--Union (6) p145-147
200 Years (2) p63-68
Watkins--Gold p107, 109-112
-1876
Randel--Centennial p124-132
-Camp, 1891
Viewpoints p122-123
-War of 1876
Collins--Story p248
"SISTERS OF CHARITY"
Young--Women p186, 286-287
"SISTERS OF THE HOLY CROSS"
Young--Women p154-155
SITHS AND MATHOOKS
Langdon--Everyday (2) p304-305
"SITTING BULL" (Sioux Indian)
Amer. Her. --Indians p344, 347-
348, 366, 368-369, 371, 405
Amer. Her. --New (9) p784-787,
796
Andrews--Indian leaders p154
Andrews--Indians p94-95
Brown--Westerners p237, 239-
259, 261, 269
Harlow--Story p372-373
Hine--American p198, 200-202,
204, 278
Life--Steel (7) p52
Reader's--Story p85
-"The Battle of the Little Big
Horn," 1877
Ridge--America's p579
"SIX COMPANIES"

-Control of Chinese
  Bartlett--New p166-169
"SIX NUNS FROM NAMUR"
  Ross--Heroines p126-155
SKATERS AND SKATING
  See also ICE-SKATING; ROLLER
    SKATING
  Dulles--History p96-97, 184, 269
  Life--New (5) p60
  McClinton--Antiques p212-213
  Partridge--As p151
  Ross--Taste p84, 88, 93
SKENE, MRS. PETER. See
  "JULIA" (Indian woman)
SKIING
  -1876
    Hilton--Way p99-100
SKINNER, OTIS
  Blum--Stage. Profile 20
  , on theater ("Trouper's
    trials"), 1895-1896
      Angle--American p420-423
SKYSCRAPERS
  Davidson--Life (2) p170-171
  Furnas--Americans p624, 768-
    770
  Lynes--Taste. p163-164, 169
  Morris--Ency. p608
  Mumford--Brown p139-140
  , First
    Boardman--Gilded p141-142
    Train--Story p320
  , Victorian
    Life--America's p143
  -Views of Louis Sullivan
    Mumford--Brown p150-151
SLANG
  Boorstin--Americans p279-280
  , Early
    Wilson--Folkways p194-198
  , Underworld
    Burner--America (1) p310-
      312
SLATER, SAMUEL
  Amer. Her. --New (5) p E180
  Boardman--Virginia p69
  Harlow--Story p206
  -Inventions
    Marzio--Nation p197-202
  -Textile mill, Pawtucket, R.I.
    America's Hist. p303
    Vanderbilt--Living p29
SLATES, CHILDREN'S
  McClinton--Antiques p96-97
SLAVES AND SLAVERY
  See also ABOLITIONISTS;
    BROWN, JOHN; EMANCIPA-
    TION PROCLAMATION;

UNDERGROUND RAILWAY;
  names of abolitionists
  Amer. Her. --New (7) p E250-251
  Angle--By p199-202
  Billington--Far. See index p321-
    322
  Boardman--Civil. See index
    p216
  Boardman--Jackson. See index
    p211
  Boardman--Virginia p60-61, 116-
    117, 123-133
  Bode--Anatomy. See index p291
  Boorstin--Americans. See index
    p513
  Borden--Portrait (1). See index
    p246
  Burner--American p220-223
  Carman--History (1) p587-607
  Davidson--Life (2). See index
    p499
  Furnas--Americans. See index
    p1007-1008
  Handlin--This. See index p598
  Harlow--Story. See index p818
  Holzman--Stormy p54-55
  Hunt--Life p39-47
  Jordan--Civil. See index p215
  Kraus--U.S. p400, 402-409
  Life--Growing (3). See index
    p175
  Life--New (5). See index p159
  Linton--Bicentennial. See index
    p447
  Morris--Ency. p514-516
  Reader's--Story p322-325
  Schwartz--When p18
  Tunis--Young p93-94
  200 Years (1). See index p350
  Warren--Pictorial p80-81, 83-85,
    88-89, 91, 95, 102-104
  Whitney--American. See index
    p369-370
  Wilson--Early p90-92
  , Abolition of (XIIIth Amendment)
    Alden--Pioneer p226, 274-275,
      277, 287
    Angle--By p119
  -African trade
    Morris--Ency. p137
  -Amusements
    Cable--American p128-129
    Dulles--History p158-160
  , and "Manifest Destiny," 1840's
    DeVoto--Year p9, 11-12, 18-19,
      183, 188, 205-206, 208-209, 287
  -Arguments against
    Alden--Pioneer p218-230

-Arguments for
  Kraus--U.S. p448-449
  Tyler--Freedom's p513-519
  -Approval by Joseph Holt
  Ingraham
    Commager--Heritage p462-
    463, 467-470
  -South
    Alden--Pioneer p229-230
    Amer. Hist. --New (7) p586-
    588
    -Views of Thomas R. Dew
    Boardman--Jackson. p111
-Auctions
  -Views of Henry Ward
  Beecher
    Burner--America (1) p275-
    277
-Children
  Furnas--Americans p402-403
-Church attitudes
  Tyler--Freedom's p519-521
-Compromise of 1850
  DeVoto--Year p475-476
-Democrats split
  Amer. Her. --New (7) p588
-Education
  Hilton--Way p60-62
-Extension, Nebraska bill
  Angle--By p193-198
-Fugitives
  See also BURNS, ANTHONY;
  FUGITIVE SLAVE ACT
  Commager--Heritage p494-499
  Life--New (5) p36-37, 39, 52,
  80, 82-83, 137, 148-149
  Warren--Pictorial p85-86
  -"Autobiography of a fugitive
  negro," 1855
    Grimsted--Notions p304-
    311
  -Return of a fugitive, 1854
    Angle--American p289-292
  -Views of Richard Henry
  Dana, Jr.
    Commager--Heritage p494-
    495
-Houses
  Wilson--Vanish. p19
-Kansas and Nebraska
  Alden--Pioneer p257-259
  Gurko--Ladies p197-198
-Missouri Compromise
  DeVoto--Year p477-478
-"Neglected period," 1808-1831
  Tyler--Freedom's p470-472
-Number, by state
  Hunt--Life p21

-Plantations
  Wright--Every. p148-149
  -Heyward's
    Commager--Heritage p470-
    475
-Revolts
  Boardman--Jackson. p104-105
-Ships
  -Views of Rev. R. Walsh
    Commager--Heritage p449-
    454
-Slaveholders
  Wilson--Early p92-93
-Social classes
  Commager--Heritage p467-470
-South
  See also CIVIL WAR; SLAVES
  AND SLAVERY--Plantations
  Alden--Pioneer p189-194
  Carman--History (1) p477-478,
  481
  Kane--Gone p260-275
  Kraus--U.S. p406-409
  Life--New (5) p17
  Sochen--Herstory p109-112
  -Civil war
    Andrews--Women. See
    index p464
    Dowdey--Experiment p5, 17-
    18, 31, 215-216, 328, 376,
    381, 394
-Views of Fanny Kemble
  Commager--Heritage p465-467
-Views of Frances Trollope
  Trollope--Domestic. See
  index p. XV
-Views of Harriet Martineau,
1834
  Angle--American p283-287
-Views of Sir Charles Lyell,
1846
  Angle--American p287-289
-Views of Stephen A. Douglas,
1854
  Angle--American p292-294
-Views of William H. Seward
  Hurd--Treasury p81-84
-Views on America
  200 Years (1) p308-309
-West
  Borden--Portrait (1) p215
  Hine--American. See index
  p369
  Life--Sweep (4) p138-139; see
  also p159
-Wilmot Proviso
  DeVoto--Year p208, 289-292,
  476

SLEDS AND TOBOGGANS
McClinton--Antiques p213-216
-1880's
Peck--Nineteenth n. p.
SLEEPING AND PARLOR CARS.
See PULLMAN CARS
SLEIGHS AND SLEIGHING
Davidson--Life (2) p13
Mussey--Old p83-85
Ross--Taste p84, 86
Wilson--Vanish. p33
, Making of
Van Wagenen--Golden p116-
121
SLIDELL, JOHN
Boardman--Civil p66-67
Boardman--Jackson. p43-44
DeVoto--Year p16, 27-28, 69,
104-105, 108, 121, 126, 185
Dowdey--Experiment. See
index p453
Harlow--Story p274, 314
Life--New (5) p140-141
-Biography
Amer. Her. --New (7) p E251
SLIDELL MISSION, 1845
Morris--Ency. p193-195
SLOAN, JOHN
Mumford--Brown p238-240
SLOANE, ERIC
-"The mills of early America"
Treasury Amer. p152-155
SLOAT, JOHN DRAKE
DeVoto--Year p20, 195, 227, 250,
255-256, 273-274, 400-401
-Biography
Amer. Her. --New (7) p E251
SLOCUM, JOSHUA
Garrison--Lost p130-135
Reader's--Story p184
SLOGANS
, Patriotic
Burner--America (1) p165-166
, Political
Life--New (5) p51
SLUMS
Amer. Her. --New (11) p943-
946
Furnas--American. See index
p1008
Harlow--Story p418-419
Life--Reaching (8) p35, 42-43, 65,
70-75, 77-78, 80-81
Marzio--Nation p486
Portraits--American p99-101
Walker--Every. p115, 122-123,
127, 131-138
-Chicago

-Views of Agnes Sinclair Hol-
brook
Cook--City p130-131
-Children
Cable--American p294
-Immigrants
Marzio--Nation p374
-Jews
Harris--Land p177-179
-New York city, 1897
Cook--City p82-83
-New York city
Boardman--Civil p114
Boardman--Gilded p107-108
Cable--American p290
Davidson--Life (2) p146-147,
164-165
-1890's
Dulles--United p93
-1894
Cook--City p127-129
-Views of James W. Buel,
1891
Cook--City p243
-Views of Jacob A. Riis
Cook--City p123, 129, 132-
135, 147
SMALLPOX
-Inoculation
Boardman--Virginia p180
Hunt--Life p207-208
SMEDES, SUSAN DABNEY
, on Dabney's model plantation
Commager--Heritage p475-479
SMET, DE, FATHER
Ross--Heroines p130-131, 134-
135, 138, 141
SMITH, ADELAIDE W.
Dannett--Noble p274, 306, 331-332,
345, 350, 370, 382
-Biography
Young--Women p377-378
SMITH, ASHBEL
-"British designs on Texas, "
1844
Ridge--America's p487-490
SMITH, ELIZABETH
Case--Empire p125-134
Tyler--Freedom's p441-442
SMITH, ERMINE ADELLE
Adelman--Famous p210
SMITH, ERWIN
Life--Steel (7) p60, 64-69
SMITH, GERRIT
Furnas--Americans p320, 506-507
Gurko--Ladies p66-69, 138, 142,
144, 159, 214, 220, 224
SMITH, GUSTAVUS F.

Boardman--Gilded p48
Dowdey--Experiment p111-112,
114-115, 179-180, 197
SMITH, HYRUM
Wright--Every. p255
SMITH, JEDEDIAH STRONG
Amer. Her. --New (6) p530-538,
E215
Bartlett--New p87-89
Boardman--Virginia p109
Brown--Westerners p57-70, 73,
86, 97, 103, 124, 126, 184, 207
Gilbert--Trail. p61, 77, 88, 90-
91, 96-97, 100, 106-107
Hine--American p51-52, 54, 56,
76
Reader's--Story p167-169
-"Jedediah S. Smith: unsung
pathfinder of the West," by
Stephen W. Sears
Amer. Her. --New (6) p521-538
SMITH, JOSEPH
See also MORMONS
Amer. Her. --New (6) p E215-216
Bartlett--New p120, 380-384
Boardman--Jackson. p125-126
Hine--American p229-231, 233
Tyler--Freedom's p88-94
Wright--Every. p212-213
SMITH, JOSEPH F., JR.
DeVoto--Year p74-98, 121, 137-
138, 314, 318, 434, 436, 438, 440,
446, 485, 487, 506
SMITH, MARGARET BAYARD
Amer. Her. --New (5) p E180-181
Cable--American p83-85
SMITH, RICHARD PENN
Boardman--Jackson. p158-159
SMITH, SAMUEL FRANCIS
Amer. Her. --New (6) p E216
Holzman--Stormy p127-128
Howard--Our p127-128, 143
, and "America"
Krythe--Sampler p62-73
SMITH, MRS. SAMUEL HARRISON
-"Letter on Thomas Jefferson's
inauguration," 1801
Angle--American p139-140
Commager--Heritage p611-616
, on life in White House, 1801-
1808
Commager--Heritage p221-226
SMITH, SEBA
Boardman--Jackson. p186-187
SMITH, SOPHIA
Adelman--Famous p149
Macksey--Book p69
SMITH, THEOBALD

-Biography
Morris--Ency. p715-716
SMITH, WILLIAM F.
Holzman--Stormy p120, 122-124
SMITH, WILLIAM HENRY
Bode--Anatomy p6-10
"SMITHS" (occupation)
Wilson--Early p67-71
SMITHSON, JAMES
Boardman--Jackson. p166
SMITHSONIAN INSTITUTION
Amer. Her. --New (6) p E216
Kraus--U.S. p385
Reader's--Story p308-309
-1876
Randel--Centennial p265-267
-Architecture
Bode--Anatomy p42-44
-Founding, 1846
Boardman--Jackson. p166
Morris--Ency. p531
SMITHWICK, NOAH
, on Texas settlements
Commager--Heritage p589-591
SMOKEHOUSES
Wilson--Vanish. p18
SMOKING
Cable--American p256-257
Furnas--Americans p894-895
Ross--Taste p291, 293
-Rooms
Lynes--Domestic. p245
-Supplies, 1880's
Peck--Nineteenth n. p.
SMUGGLING
See also NAVIGATION ACTS
-Civil war
-South
Life--New (5) p136, 144-145
-Women
Life--New (5) p136
SNAKE INDIANS. See SHOSHONI
INDIANS
"SNEAK-BOXES" (boats)
-1876
Randel--Centennial p41-42
SNOBBISHNESS
Lynes--Taste. p88, 104-105
SNOW, ELIZA
DeVoto--Year p74, 89-90, 94
SNOW
-Blizzard of 1888
Boardman--Gilded p178
-Views of Stephen Crane
Cook--City p160-166
-Wardens
Wilson--Early p36
SNOWSHOES

Marzio--Nation p167
SNUFF
  Wilson--Folkways p75-76
  -"Dipping"
    Cable--American p85
SNUFFBOXES
  Dreppard--Pioneer p288-291
SOAP AND SOAP-MAKING
  Handlin--This p351-352
  Wilson--Vanish. p53
  -1876
    Hilton--Way p25, 27
SOCIAL CALLING (etiquette)
  Carson--Polite p170-171
  Wilson--Folkways p182-184
SOCIAL CLASSES. See
 ARISTOCRACY; CLASSES
"SOCIAL DARWINISM"
  Boardman--Gilded p112-115
  Carman--History (2) p117-120,
  126-127
  Dulles--United p120-124
  Furnas--Americans p655-656
  Life--Reaching (8) p8-10, 14-17,
  64-65, 105, 128-129
"SOCIAL GOSPEL"
  Randel--Centennial p436, 447,
  457-459
SOCIAL REFORM
  See also types of reform
  Cable--American p320-321
  Keller--Affairs. See index
  p627
  -1870's-1890's
    Dulles--United p123-125
  -1880-1899
    Reader's--Story p342
  , in literature
    Our literary p162-163
  , Labor demands for
    Life--Steel (7) p76-77, 81-83,
  85
SOCIALISM
  Furnas--Americans p722-725
  Harlow--Story p259, 411
SOCIALIST LABOR PARTY
  Furnas--Americans p710-712
SOCIETIES OF TRUTH AND
 BEAUTY
  Lynes--Taste. p147-162
SOCIETY
  See also ARISTOCRACY;
   CLASSES; "FOUR HUNDRED"
  Boardman--Civil p202-203
  Boardman--Gilded p153-155
  Dulles--History p148-152, 230-
  234
  Furnas--Americans p329, 522,

  561-562
  Partridge--As p154
  -1800
    Boardman--Virginia p183
  -1890's
    Lynes--Taste. p165-167
  , and foreign titles
    Cable--American p311
  , and newspapers
    Carson--Polite p203-210
  , and wealth
    Life--Reaching (8) p44, 46-49
  -Boston
    Cable--American p280
    Hunt--Life p70-71
  -Characteristics, to 1820
    Nye--Cultural p146-149
  , Communal
    See also names of communal
    societies
  , Customs of
    Wilson--Folkways p182-200
  , European influence of
    Cable--American p286-287
  -New York city
    Cable--American p272-280
    Hunt--Life p69-70
    Nye--Cultural p111-112
    -Views of Ward McAllister,
    1890
      Cook--City p267
  -Philadelphia, Pa.
    Cable--American p280
    Nye--Cultural p111-113
  -South
    See also PLANTATIONS AND
    PLANTERS
    Cable--American p88
    Carman--History (1) p584
    Dulles--History p57-63
    Hunt--Life p71-72
    Nye--Cultural p113-116, 140,
    232-233
  -Status
    Marzio--Nation p276-296
  -Washington, D.C.
    Cable--American p83-85
    Carson--Polite p96-107
    Hunt--Life p64-67
    Wright--Ency. p61-63
  -West
    Nye--Cultural p117-122
SOCIETY FOR THE PREVENTION
OF CRIME
  -New York city, 1894
    Cook--City p169-170
SOCIETY FOR THE PROMOTION
OF ENGINEERING EDUCATION

Jones--Age p172-174
SOCIETY OF AMERICAN ARTISTS
    Carman--History (2) p376
SOCIETY OF CALIFORNIA
PIONEERS
    Jones--Shaping p154-155
SOCIOLOGY
    Boardman--Gilded p117
SOD HOUSES
    See also "DUGOUTS"
    Lynes--Domestic. p34-37
    White--American p99-103
    -Kansas, 1877
        -Views of Howard Ruede
            Angle--American p369-371
    -Nebraska
        White--American p100-102
    -Water
        Tunis--Frontier p155-156
    -West
        Hine--American p157-158, 162-
        164
SODA
    , Substitute for, Civil war
        Andrews--Women p22
SODA FOUNTAINS
    Davidson--Life (2) p141
    Walker--Every. p241
"SODBUSTERS"
    America's Hist. p508-509
    , and cattle drives
        Tunis--Frontier p154-160
SOIL
    -Exhaustion, as cause for
    migration
        -Views of John H. Craven,
        1833
            Ridge--America's p295-297
SOLDIERS
    -Civil war
        Partridge--As p64-67
        -Confederacy
            Viewpoints p86
        -North
            Butterfield--Amer. p167
        -Return home, 1865
            Angle--American p333-334
            Partridge--As p69-71
        -South
            Butterfield--Amer. p166
        -Uniforms
            Meredith--World p86-89
    -Life
        Views of Jacob Judson, 1898
            Angle--American p448-449
    -Mexican war
        Life--Sweep (4) p120-121
SOLDIERS' AID SOCIETIES

    -Organization, 1861
        Young--Women p67-70
SONG WRITERS
    Boardman--Civil p199-200
    Howard--Our p158-172
SONGS
    See also BROADSIDES--Songs;
    MINSTRELS
    Boardman--Jackson. p174-176
    Boardman--Virginia p189
    Bonte--America p120
    Walker--Every. p30, 32, 64, 82-83,
    95, 100, 162-167
    -"America"
        Howard--Our p126-128
        Krythe--Sampler p62-73
    -"Angel of the tenements"
        Cook--City p230
    -"The Battle cry of freedom"
        Burner--America (1) p317-318
    -"Battle hymn of the Republic"
        Burner--America (1) p315-316
        Chase--America's p231
        Commager--Heritage p681-683
        Howard--Our p258-259
        Krythe--Sampler p113-132
        Meredith--World p119
        Warren--Pictorial p107-108
    -"Be kind to the loved ones at
    home"
        Burner--America (1) p251-252
    -"Beautiful dreamer"
        Burner--America (1) p267
    -"The Bonnie blue flag"
        Burner--America (1) p314-315
        Krythe--Sampler p133-141
    -California--"Acres of clams"
        Burner--America (1) p234-235
    -"Carry me back to old Virginny"
        Krythe--Sampler p158-176
    -Circus
        Dulles--History p285
    -Civil war
        See also names of songs
        Chase--America's p179-180
        Howard--Our p255-268
        Jordan--Civil p45, 76, 111, 153-
        154, 173, 181, 185, 196
        Krythe--Sampler. See index
        p240
        Morris--Ency. p616-617
    , Cowboys. See COWBOY MUSIC
    -"Darling Nellie Gray"
        Howard--Our p261
    -"Dixie"
        Burner--America (1) p313-314
        Howard--Our p255-258
        Krythe--Sampler p100-112

, First national
  Howard--Our p126-128
-Foster, Stephen
  See also names of songs
  Burner--America (1) p265-269
-"The Glorious Fourth"
  Burner--America (1) p162-163
, Gospel (including Folk-Hymnody)
  Howard--Our p605-611
  Lowens--Music p139-155
  -Writers
    Howard--Our p608-611
-Hamlet air: "Jim Crow"
  Burner--America (1) p269-270
-"Home sweet home"
  Bonte--America p119
  Garrison--Lost p84-88
  Krythe--Sampler p40-61
, in burning home, 1864
  Andrews--Women p198-199
-"Jeannie with the light brown
hair"
  Burner--America (1) p268
-"John Brown's body" (two ver-
sions)
  Burner--America (1) p316-317
-"Life is a toil"
  Burner--America (1) p252-253
-"The little old sod shanty on the
claim"
  White--American p102-103
-"The log cabin and the hard
cider candidate"
  Burner--America (1) p165-166
-Lumberjacks
  Howard--Our p637-638
-"Maryland, my Maryland"
  Andrews--Women p66-69
  Howard--Our p260
  Krythe--Sampler p142-149
-"Massa's in de cold ground"
  Burner--America (1) p265-266
, Mountain
  Howard--Our p634-635
-"My old Kentucky home"
  Vanderbilt--Living p120
-"No Irish need apply"
  Burner--America (1) p312
-"Oh, Susanna"
  Woodward--Way p264-265
-"Old Black Joe"
  Burner--America (1) p268-269
-"The old Chisholm trail"
  White--American p88-91
, Old favorite. See SONGS,
Popular; names of songs
-"The old folks at home"
  Burner--America (1) p266-267

Krythe--Sampler p74-99
, Patriotic
  See also SONGS--Civil war;
  names of songs
  Burner--America (1) p162-165,
  313-318
  Morris--Ency. p616
, Popular
  See also names of songs
  Boardman--Gilded p172
  Dulles--History p252-254, 276-
  277
  Morris--Ency. p615
  -1820-1860
    Grimsted--Notions p25-37
  -1890's
    Dulles--United p102
-Shakers
  Chase--America's p224-231
  Tyler--Freedom's p155-158
-"The Southern cross"
  Burner--America (1) p321-322
-"Star spangled banner"
  Butterfield--Amer. p56-57
  Howard--Our p121-126
  Keyes--Hope p205
  Krythe--Sampler p15-39
  Landmarks--Liberty p24-25
  Morris--Ency. p614
, Sung after supper (Tennessee,
1890)
  Schwartz--When p145
-"Sweet Betsey from Pike"
  200 Years (1) p303
-Temperance
  200 Years (1) p298
  -"Come home father"
    Burner--America (1) p284-
    285
  200 Years (1) p298
-"Tenting on the old camp
ground" (1863)
  Krythe--Sampler p150-157
-"Tilda Horn"
  Burner--America (1) p269-270
, War
  See also SONGS--Civil war;
  names of songs
  Boardman--Civil p199
-Words and music
  Harris--Land p323-333
  Schwartz--When p154-164
SONNTAG, WILLIAM
  Bode--Anatomy p87-88
SONS OF LIBERTY. See ORDER
OF SONS OF LIBERTY
"SOONERS" (Oklahoma settlers)
  Boardman--Gilded p86

SOROSIS CLUB
  Furnas--Americans p890-892
  Ross--Taste p51
SOUDER, EMILY BLISS
  Dannett--Noble p249-253, 267
  Young--Women p287, 289, 293-294
SOULE, PIERRE
  , and Ostend Manifesto
    Amer.Her. --New (7) p E247
SOUND-RECORDING APPARATUS.
  See PHONOGRAPHS
SOUSA, JOHN PHILIP
  Harlow--Story p434-435
  Howard--Our p652-653
  -Biography
    Amer.Her. --New (12) p E436-
    437
SOUTH
  See also ARCHITECTURE--South;
    CIVIL WAR--South; NEGROES;
    RECONSTRUCTION; names of
    states; special subjects
  Boardman--Civil p4-7, 65-66, 77-
    78, 96-97, 180-181
  Boardman--Gilded p6-7, 90-91, 98-
    100, 129-130
  Boardman--Jackson. See index
    p211
  Boardman--Virginia p56-57, 60-
    61, 77-78, 129-130, 187-188
  Boorstin--Americans p169-170;
    see also index p513-514
  Carman--History. See index
    p. xxiv
  Furnas--Americans p394-406
  Handlin--This p201, 333-343, 350,
    354, 368
  Harlow--Story p210-213
  Jones--Age. See index p543
  Keller--Affairs. See index p627
  Life--Growing (3). See index
    p175
  Life--New (5). See index p159
  -1828-1849
    Life--Sweep (4). See index
    p159
  -1850's
    Life--New (5) p15-17
  -1861-1876
    Life--Union (6). See index
    p175
  -1876
    Randel--Centennial. See
    index p368
  -1877-1890
    Life--Steel (7) p98-125; see
    also index p158
  -Agriculture

    Collins--Story p153
  , and Dickens' works
    Bode--Anatomy p160-162
  -Architecture
    Bode--Anatomy p41-42, 45
  -Blockade
    Collins--Story p227
  , in Stephen Foster's songs
    Bode--Anatomy p26-28
  -Industries
    Harlow--Story p358-360
  -Land and staples
    Carman--History (1) p476-482
  -Life
    See also SOUTH--Society
    Kraus--U.S. p403-406
  -Nationalism
    Carman--History (1) p636
    Kraus--U.S. p459-461
  -Nationalities
    Kraus--U.S. p400-401
  , New
    -Origins
      Dulles--United p32-33
  , Old
    Alden--Pioneer p189-201
    -Nostalgia
      Trachtenberg--Demo. p125-
      135
  -Plantations and planters. See
    PLANTATIONS AND PLANTERS
  -Politics
    Dulles--United p15-16
  -Post Civil war
    See also RECONSTRUCTION
    Burner--America (1) p325-342
    Carman--History (1) p710-719
    Carman--History (2) p11-21
    Dulles--United p5-6
    Harlow--Story p356-360
    -Economy
      Collins--Story p234
      Life--Union (6) p121, 128-
      130
    -Letters of Arthur C. Inman
      Burner--America (1) p335
    -State governments
      Dulles--United p21-23
  -Pre-Civil war
    Harlow--Story p286-287, 289-
    291, 300-302
    Kane--Gone p279-297
    Maurois--Illus. p130-145
    -Amusements
      Dulles--History p156-162
  -"Problem"
    Amer.Her. --New (7) p580-607
  -Regional distinctions

289

Furnas--Americans p414-415
-Social revolution, 1865
    -Views of Henry W. Ravenal
        Angle--American p343-346
-Society
    Cable--American p88
    Carman--History (1) p584
    Dulles--History p57-63
    Hunt--Life p71-72
-"Solid" (1877)
    Butterfield--Amer. p223
-Southerners
    Bartlett--New p118, 125-126,
    207
    , Confederate migration to
    Mexico, 1865
        White--American p56-59
-Women
    Gurko--Ladies p23, 185-186
    Life--New (5) p125, 136, 142
    , Genius of
        Andrews--Women p19-30
SOUTH CAROLINA
    Carman--History (1) p634, 782
    Handlin--This p117, 120-122, 126,
    160, 342
    Harlow--Story. See index p818
    Hunt--Life. See index p296
    Life--New (5) p94-96, 98, 136-137
    Life--Sweep (4) p11-13, 15-19
    -1876
        Randel--Centennial p231-232,
        251-253
    -Act of Nullification
        Harlow--Story p229-230
    -Declaration of causes, 1860
        Angle--By p206-211
    , in Civil war
        Dowdey--Experiment p14, 18,
        23, 51, 85, 396, 419
        Life--Union (6) p89-90, 103,
        122-123, 127-128, 130, 132-133,
        136, 157
    -Justification of secession,
    Ordinance, 1860
        Angle--By p203-205
    -Parliament, Black (post-war)
        -Views of James Shepherd
        Pike
            Commager--Heritage p811-
            816
    -Planters and plantations
        Commager--Heritage p454-456
    -Sea islands
        Trachtenberg--Demo. p111-124
    -Secession
        Morris--Ency. p228
        Young--Women p37

    -Views of Samuel Wylie
        Crawford p308-311
    -Senators, resigned
        Young--Women p36
SOUTH DAKOTA
    -Deadwood
        Amer. Her. --New (9) p738-739
    -Gold mines and mining
        Amer. Her. --New (9) p738-740
        -Black Hills gold rush, and
        Indians
            Amer. Her. --New (9) p796
    -Lead
        Watkins--Gold p108, 113, 113n,
        117-119
SOUTH PARK SETTLEMENT, SAN
FRANCISCO, CALIFORNIA, 1897
    Cook--City p239
"SOUTH PASS" (route to Oregon)
    Bartlett--New p89, 285-286
    DeVoto--Year. See index p523
    Tunis--Frontier p113, 117, 120,
    123, 132, 138
SOUTHERN COMMERCIAL CONVEN-
TION, 1859
    Morris--Ency. p225-226
SOUTHERN LITERARY MESSENGER
    Bode--Anatomy p160-162
SOUTHERN PACIFIC RAILROAD
    Furnas--Americans. See index
    p1008
    Hine--American p153, 157, 167-
    168, 263
    Lewis--Big. See index p. v
SOUTHERN RAILROAD AND STEAM-
SHIP COMPANY
    -1870's
        Randel--Centennial p170-171
SOUTHWEST
    Life--America's p114-128
    -Boundaries
        Tunis--Frontier p96
    -"Fur trade in the desert South-
    west," 1831
        Ridge--America's p389-393
    -Mines and mining
        Watkins--Gold. See index
        p287
    -Plains
        -Indians
            Andrews--Indian leaders
            p116
    , Speculation in
        Ridge--America's p298-299
SOUTHWORTH, EMMA (MRS.
E. D. E. N.)
    Bode--Anatomy p181-183, 257
    Hart--Popular p96-97

Mott--Golden p136-142
Young--Women p6, 10, 17, 68, 209
SPAIN AND SPANIARDS
Boardman--Virginia p57-59, 62-
64, 102-104
, Relations with, 1898
Morris--Ency. p287
SPALDING, ALBERT G.
, on history of baseball, 1875-
1899
Angle--American p411-413
SPALDING, ELIZA HART
Hine--American p90
Ross--Heroines p14, 58-60, 63-
64, 66, 88
Ross--Westward p23-52
Tunis--Frontier p114
SPALDING, HENRY HARMON
Hine--American p90-91, 96
Ross--Heroines p58, 64-66, 78,
88, 119
Ross--Westward p26-50
Tunis--Frontier p114
SPANISH-AMERICAN WAR
Amer. Her. --New (12) p994-1023
Amer. Her. --90's p106-116
Boardman--Gilded p186-189
Bonte--America p148-150
Borden--Portrait (2) p69-71
Butterfield--Amer. p282-283
Carman--History (2) p281, 288,
290-296, 371, 464, 467-468
Commager--Heritage p980-995
Dulles--United p166-168
Furnas--Americans p863, 865,
908-909
Jones--Age p395-404
Keller--Affairs p317, 589, 592-
594
Keyes--Hope p284-286
Life--Reaching (8). See index
p176
Linton--Bicentennial p250-254
Maurois--Illus. p218
Morris--Ency. p288-290
Reader's--Story p444-445
Schwartz--When p190-192
, and Protestants
Jones--Age p401-402
-Cost
Morris--Ency. p290
-Goals
Hollingsworth--Amer. p68-117
-McKinley's war message, 1898
Davie--Profile p288-290
-Origins
Hollingsworth--Amer. p51-67
-Results

Dulles--United p168-169
-San Juan charge
Amer. Her. --New (12) p1018-
1019
-Santiago battle
Viewpoints p89
-Views of H. H. Kohlman
Angle--American p436-438
SPARGO, JOHN
, on child labor
Commager--Heritage p954-958
SPARKS, JARED
Boardman--Jackson. p146
Boardman--Virginia p142-143
Bode--Anatomy p238-240
Boorstin--Americans p347-349,
366-367
Brooks--Flower. p122-127; see
also index p548
Our literary p50
SPEAKERS
-Women
Warren--Pictorial p80-81, 83-
85, 101, 140-141
SPECIALIZATION
, Necessary evils of
Trachtenberg--Demo. p240
"SPECIE CIRCULAR," 1836
Amer. Her. --New (5) p E181
Boardman--Jackson. p24-25
Borden--Portrait (1) p170-171
Harlow--Story p235
Morris--Ency. p177-178
SPECIE PAYMENTS, 1875-1879
Collins--Story p254
Morris--Ency. p251
SPECTROHELIOGRAPH
, of George Ellery Hale
Wilson--American p353
SPECULATION
See also LAND--Speculation
Billington--Far p19-21, 91, 153-
154, 260
Handlin--This p213, 216, 264-269,
317, 355
Partridge--As p110
Ridge--America's p618-619
-"Frenzied speculation in the
Southwest," 1836, by James D.
Davidson
Ridge--America's p298-299
-"Watered stock"
Harlow--Story p392-394
-West
Hine--American. See index
p369
SPEECH
Cable--American p244-245

-Inflections and pronunciation
  Carson--Polite p187
-Recitations
  Schwartz--When p63
-Views of Frances Trollope
  Trollope--Domestic. See
  index p. XV
SPEECHES
  Boorstin--Americans p307-324
SPELLING
  Hunt--Life p137
-Reform
  -Views of Noah Webster
    Burner--America (1) p200-
    204
SPELLING BEES
-Iowa, 1895
  Schwartz--When p110
SPENCE, JAMES
  Dowdey--Experiment p265, 294-
  295
SPENCER, HERBERT
  Boardman--Gilded p112-113
  Life--Reaching (8) p8-9, 13, 14,
  16
SPENCER, LILY
  Bode--Anatomy p86-87
SPENCER, PLATT ROGERS
  Cable--American p116, 152
SPENCER, SAMUEL R., JR.
  , on Booker T. Washington
    Miers--American p248-253
"SPENDERS"
  Wilson--Early p178, 180
SPERRY, ELMER A.
  Reader's--Story p268, 270
SPIES
  See also names of spies
-Civil war
  Dowdey--Experiment p2, 173-
  174, 211, 334-335
  Meredith--World p131-133
-Women
  Warren--Pictorial p110
SPINNING AND SPINNING WHEELS
  Dreppard--Pioneer p87
  Marzio--Nation p254, 261-265
  Van Wagenen--Golden p251, 255,
  263-264
  Wilson--Vanish. p57
"THE SPIRIT OF THE TIMES"
  (periodical)
  Grimsted--Notions p119-131
SPIRITUALISM
  Boardman--Jackson. p189-190
  Borden--Portrait (1) p197-198
  Handlin--This p240-243, 275
  Tyler--Freedom's p78-85

SPIRITUALS
-"Go down Moses"
  200 Years (1) p309
, Negro
  Boorstin--Americans p192-193
, Revival
  Chase--America's p217-219
, in oral tradition
  Chase--America's p213
SPITTOONS
  Carson--Polite p87-88
  Wilson--Folkways p75
  Wilson--Vanish. p108
"SPOILS SYSTEM"
  Amer. Her. --New (5) p E181
  Bonte--America p101
  Harlow--Story p167, 226-227
  Life--Sweep (4) p9, 39-40, 42, 46
  Morris--Ency. p167-168
  Reader's--Story p61
  , and Rutherford B. Hayes
    Morris--Ency. p255
SPOKANE INDIANS
  Ross--Heroines p106, 109-110,
  118-120, 123-124
SPOONS
  Holzman--Stormy p107, 135, 165-
  166, 177, 180, 197, 219
SPORTS AND GAMES
  See also GAMES; names of sports
  and games; special subjects
  Boardman--Civil p200-202
  Boardman--Gilded p173-175
  Boardman--Jackson. p178-179
  Boardman--Virginia p186-188
  Bonte--America p145
  Borden--Portrait (2) p61
  Cable--American p322-323
  Davidson--Life (2) p56-77
  Dreppard--Pioneer p104-106
  Dulles--United p100-101
  Furnas--Americans. See index
  p1009
  Handlin--This p326, 361, 371-375
  Harlow--Story p436-437
  Partridge--As p149-178
  Reader's--Story p483-491
  Ross--Taste p89-97
  Wright--Every. p240-245
-1830's
  Cable--American p110
-1870's
  Randel--Centennial p78-80,
  319-322
-1876
  Hilton--Way p91-111; see also
  index p215
-1890's

Dulles--History p263-269
Jones--Age p343-344
Life--Reaching (8). See
    index p176
, Children's (Indoor and outdoor)
    McClinton--Antiques p202-223
    -Salem, Mass.
        Commager--Heritage
        p360-364
-Clothing
    Wilson--Folkways p50-72
-Colleges and universities
    Cable--American p165
    Harris--Land p335-339
-Equipment, 1880's
    Peck--Nineteenth n. p.
-Frontier
    Dulles--History p71-75
, Indoor
    See also SPORTS AND
    GAMES, Children's
    Walker--Every. p30-31, 78,
    85-86, 119-120, 149-151, 233-
    234
-Middlewest
    Drury--Midwest p80-81
-Organization, Beginning of
    Dulles--History p182-189
, Outdoor
    See also SPORTS AND
    GAMES, Children's
    Walker--Every. p31-32, 84,
    119, 146, 149-157, 174, 241
, Spectator
    See also BASEBALL, FOOT-
    BALL, etc.
    Dulles--History p98, 136-147,
    200-202, 223-228
    Partridge--As p154-158
-Victorian era
    See also SPORTS AND GAMES
    --1890's
    Life--Steel (7) p146-147
, Water
    Furnas--Americans p437
-Women
    Dulles--History p191-193,
    195-196
    Furnas--Americans p816
    Macksey--Book p256, 258, 260
SPOTSWOOD HOTEL (Richmond,
Va.)
, in Civil war
    Dowdey--Experiment p37, 43,
    45, 69-70, 75, 80, 90, 221, 431
SPOTSYLVANIA, VIRGINIA, 1864
    Morris--Ency. p242-243
"SPOTTED TAIL" (Brule Sioux
Indian)
    Andrews--Indian leaders p149, 158
    Brown--Westerners p192-193, 246
    White--American p92-98
"SPOTTERS" (Detectives)
    Wilson--Early p30
SPRAGUE, CHARLES
    Nye--Unembar. p99-100
SPRAGUE, J. T.
    -"The tragedy of Indian removal"
    Ridge--America's p283-286
SPRAGUE, KATE CHASE
    Peacock--Famous p206-229
    Ross--Taste p249
SPRECKELS, CLAUS
    Randel--Centennial p157-158
"SPRING HOUSES"
    Wilson--Vanish. p16
SPRINGFIELD, ILLINOIS
    Drury--Midwest p95-100
    Life--New (5) p100, 103, 108
, as Lincoln's residence
    Randall--Mary p102-222
"SPRINGFIELD REPUBLICAN"
(newspaper)
    Langdon--Everyday (2) p169-171
"SQUATTERS"
    Handlin--This p216-217
    Tunis--Frontier p69-70, 91, 100-
    101
    -West
    Hine--American p63, 66, 160-
    161, 211, 325
"SQUATTERS COURT" (Kansas)
    Life--New (5) p68
SQUIBB, EDWARD ROBINSON, DR.
    -Drug industry
    Nostalgia p20-23
"STAASTZEITUNG" (N. Y. news-
paper)
    Neidle--America's p48-49
STABLES
    Wilson--Vanish. p20
STAGE STATIONS
    -California
        -1850
            Nation in motion p78
        -1876
            -"Stagecoach Inn" (Newbury
            Park)
                Nation in motion p78
    -New Mexico, 1858
        Nation in motion p80
STAGECOACHES AND STAGE
LINES
    See also CONCORD COACHES;
    POSTAL SERVICE--Stage
    coaches

Bartlett--New p299-303
Boardman--Virginia p88-89
Bonte--America p114
Davidson--Life (2) p212-213
Handlin--This p105, 123-124, 313-314
Kraus--U.S. p470-471
Langdon--Everyday (2) p81-89
Life--America's p61
Life--Growing (3) p146, 156, 164-165, 167
Life--New (5) p10-11
Marzio--Nation p161, 171-172
200 Years (2) p61
Wilson--Early p133-137
Wilson--Vanish. p169
-Drivers
   Langdon--Everyday (2) p79-80, 84-85
-Horses
   Langdon--Everyday (2) p84
-Robberies
   Downey--Our p317-335
-Routes, Overland (1860-1880)
   Carman--History (2) p198
-Travel
   Billington--Far. See index p322
   Hunt--Life p49-53
   -California
      Johnson--Pictorial p136-137
      Tunis--Frontier p137-138
   -"Phoenix line," 1830's
      Viewpoints p36
   -Views of Frances Trollope
      Trollope--Domestic. See index p. XV
   -West
      Davidson--Life (2) p258, 262-263
      Hine--American p139-143, 150, 277-327
STAGG, ALONZO
, on football, 1884
   Angle--American p413-414
STAGING. See THEATER
STAIRWAYS
   Langdon--Everyday (2) p217-218
"STALWARTS" (Grant's supporters)
   Harlow--Story p452-454
   Keller--Affairs p266-267, 543, 561
STANDARD OF LIVING
   Handlin--This p110, 113-114, 406
STANDARD OIL COMPANY
   Boardman--Gilded p45-46
   Carman--History (2) p97, 99-102, 111, 118, 333, 335, 374

Harlow--Story p385-386
Life--Steel (7) p34, 131-134
-Justification of, by John D. Rockefeller, 1899
   Angle--American p378-380
"STANDING BEAR" (Indian)
   Hine--American p196-197
STANFORD, JANE LATHROP
   Adelman--Famous p234-235
   Lewis--Big. See index p. v
   Macksey--Book p69
   Warren--Pictorial p143
STANFORD, LELAND
   Boardman--Civil p142-143
   Boardman--Gilded p66-67
   Brown--Westerners p171, 177, 185-186
   Garrison--Lost p151-154
   Lewis--Big p156-210
   Life--Steel (7) p33
   Portraits--Americans p137-138
   -Biography
      Morris--Ency. p716
STANFORD, LELAND, JR.
   Lewis--Big p108, 177-181, 201
STANFORD UNIVERSITY
   Lewis--Big. See index p. vi
   Portraits--Americans p138
STANHOUSE, T. B. H.
   -"The handcart migration of 1856"
      Ridge--America's p521-524
STANLEY, HENRY MORGAN
   Boardman--Civil p202-203
   Reader's--Story p364
   -Biography
      Amer. Her.--New (11) p E398-399
STANLEY, JOHN MIX
   Ross--Heroines p116-117
STANSBURY, HOWARD
   -"Mormon expansion over the Great Basin," 1852
      Ridge--America's p519-520
STANTON, EDWIN McMASTERS
   Amer. Her.--New (8) p E292
   Andrews--Women. See index p464
   Butterfield--Amer. p184
   Holzman--Stormy. See index p278
   Portraits--Americans p29
   Young--Women p103, 199, 213, 222, 272, 287, 337, 347-348
STANTON, ELIZABETH CADY
   Adelman--Famous p171-174
   Amer. Her.--New (6) p E216
   Boardman--Civil p190

Boardman--Jackson. p128-129
Furnas--Americans. See index
  p1009
Gurko--Ladies. See index p326-
  327
Harlow--Story p254-255
Heath--Women (4) p10
Life--Sweep (4) p64-65
Macksey--Book p86
Neidle--America's p30
Reader's--Story p432-434
Sochen--Herstory p122, 124-125;
  see also index p446
Warren--Pictorial p89, 97-100;
  see also index p227
, in temperance movement
  Tyler--Freedom's p448-449
, in women's rights crusade
  Tyler--Freedom's p451-453,
  459-460
, on "Woman's declaration of
  independence"
  Commager--Heritage p422-424
-"A Woman's declaration of
  independence"
  Burner--America (1) p280-282
STARR, BELLE
  Macksey--Book p136
STARR, ELLEN
  Macksey--Book p117
"STARVATION PARTIES"
  See also "BREAD RIOT"
  Dowdey--Experiment p272, 317
STATE GOVERNMENT
  -Reform
    Borden--Portrait (2) p76
  -Views of James Bryce
    Davie--Profile p66
STATEN ISLAND, NEW YORK
  -Quarantine station, 1833
    Viewpoints p103
STATES
  See also names of states
  -1803 (map)
    200 Years (1) p174
  -Readmission to Union (map)
    Dulles--United p29
  -Statehood
    , Dates of
      Reader's--Story p75
    , Western
      -Admission to Union (map)
        Dulles--Union p48
STATES' RIGHTS
  Boardman--Jackson. p12-13
  Harlow--Story p227-231
  Life--New (5). See index p159
  Life--Union (6) p110-116

Reader's--Story p59-60
-Views of Andrew Jackson
  Hurd--Treasury p59-61
STATUARY. See SCULPTURE
STATUE OF LIBERTY
  Boardman--Gilded p178-179
  Keyes--Hope p276-277
  Landmarks--Liberty p70-75
  Life--Reaching (8) p37, 61, 68, 70
  Marzio--Nation p137, 141
  Reader's--Story p329
  200 Years (2) p74-75
  , Unveiling of, 1886
    Keyes--Hope p388-389
    Maurois--Illus. p209
STEAD, WILLIAM T.
  -"If Christ came of Chicago, "
  1894
    Cook--City p62-64
  , on mayors, Detroit
    Cook--City p206-208
STEAM ENGINEERING
  Amer. Her. --New (5) p382
  Boardman--Virginia p82-83
  Boorstin--Americans p99-100
  Furnas--Americans. See index
    p1009
  Langdon--Everyday (2) p338-340
  Morris--Ency. p494-495
  -1804-1849
    Morris--Ency. p535
  , Age of
    Amer. Her. --New (5) p435-440
  -Ice-boats
    Drury--Midwest p21-22
  -Navigation
    See also STEAMBOATS;
      STEAMSHIPS
    Tunis--Frontier p90-91
STEAM RAILROADS
  Marzio--Nation p178-179
  Tunis--Young p146-147
  Wilson--American p146-147
STEAMBOATS
  Amer. Her. --New (5) p412-419;
  E181
  Boardman--Virginia p82-85
  Boorstin--Americans p98-102, 112
  Cable--American p221-222
  Carman--History (1) p460-463,
  475, 713
  Davidson--Life (2) p224-243
  Furnas--Americans. See index
    p1009
  Handlin--This p123-124, 158, 203,
  205, 231, 287, 289
  Harlow--Story p196-198
  Hunt--Life p50-56

Langdon--Everyday (2) p104-112
Life--America's p104-105
Life--Growing (3) p147, 156, 160,
162-167
Lynes--Taste. p89-94, 125-126
Morris--Ency. p422
Reader's--Story p185, 196-197
Train--Story p280-281
200 Years (1) p204-205
-1870's
    Randel--Centennial p37, 159-
    160
, First
    , Fulton's ("Clermont," 1807)
        Harlow--Story p197
    -Launching in West
        Commager--Heritage p325-
        329
, Practical
    Morris--Ency. p535
-Races
    -Mississippi river
        Commager--Heritage p340-
        348
-River travel
    Tunis--Young p142-143
    Wilson--American p70-71
    Wright--Every. p81-85
    -Excursions
        Dulles--History p164, 222
    -Hudson river
        Partridge--As p168
    -Mississippi river
        Drury--Midwest p9-11, 16-
        17
    -Ohio
        Drury--Midwest p121-122
    -Trip by Charles J. Latrobe,
    1832
        Angle--American p199-202
    , Western
        Davidson--Life (2) p232-243
-Views of Frances Trollope
    Trollope--Domestic. See
    index p. XV
STEAMSHIPS
    Boardman--Jackson. p98-99
    Dreppard--Pioneer p305
    Marzio--Nation p126, 128-129
    Reader's--Story p185
    , Transatlantic
        Furnas--Americans p357-359
    -Travel
        Hilton--Way p146-148
    , vs. sailing vessels
        -Voyages, 1867, 1872
            Marzio--Nation p126
STEEL

See also BESSMER STEEL IN-
DUSTRY: IRON AND STEEL
    Boardman--Gilded p41-44, 141-142
    Dulles--United p57-58
    Furnas--Americans p171, 768-770
    Life--Steel (7). See index p159
    Morris--Ency. p497
    Walker--Every. p48-51
    , Age of
        Amer. Her. --New (10) p815-898
    , Structural
        Wilson--American p243
STEFFENS, LINCOLN
    , on Tammany Hall
        Cook--City p192
STEINMETZ, CHARLES PROTEUS
    Life--Reaching (8) p67
STEINWAY, WILLIAM
    Marzio--Nation p210-211
STEPHENS, ALEXANDER HAMIL-
TON
    Dowdey--Experiment. p453-454
    Life--New (5) p31, 35, 132, 134, 136
    Morris--Ency. p228-229
    -Biography
        Amer. Her. --New (7) p E251-
        252
        Morris--Ency. p717
STEPHENS, ANN
    Macksey--Book p186
STEPHENS, JOHN LLOYD
    Boardman--Jackson. p169
    Our literary p109
STEPHENS, URIAH
    Life--Steel (7) p77-78, 80
STEPHENSON, JOHN
    Portraits--Americans p82-84
STEPHENSON CAR COMPANY, 1869
    -Advertising and car p82, 84
        Portraits--Americans p82, 84
STEREOSCOPES
    Wilson--Vanish. p94
STEVENS, G.W.
    , on William Jennings Bryan
        Angle--American p458-461
STEVENS, ISAAC J.
    -"Cultural conflict on the Fraser
    River, " 1858
        Ridge--America's p536-538
STEVENS, JOHN
    Boardman--Virginia p85
    Langdon--Everyday (2) p111-112,
    338-339
    -"Family feud, " and Robert R.
    Livingston
        Reader's--Story p262
STEVENS, NATHANIEL
    , and mills

Langdon--Everyday (2) p252-
255
STEVENS, ROBERT
Wilson--American p154-155
STEVENS, THADDEUS
Amer. Her. --New (8) p E292
Butterfield--Amer. p186-187
Carman--History (1) p423, 692,
720-721, 731-732
Dulles--United p14
Harlow--Story p338, 340
Keller--Affairs. See index p627
Life--Union (6) p112, 114-117
Morris--Ency. p233, 246, 556
-Biography
Morris--Ency. p717
STEVENSON, ROBERT LOUIS
Bartlett--New p334-338
Mott--Golden p160-161
, as immigrant
Cable--American p299-300
, on railroads
Hine--American p150
, on William McKinley, 1896
Angle--American p461-463
-"The Transcontinental railroad:
Across the plains"
Davie--Profile p164
Commager--Heritage p837-
844
STEVENSON, SARA YORKE
Adelman--Famous p264
STEWART, ALEXANDER TURNEY
Furnas--Americans p481, 648-
649, 677, 817-818
Portraits--Americans p42
-Mansion, New York City
Partridge--As p124
-Store: A.T. Stewart's
Partridge--As p108
STEWART, MARIA W.
Warren--Pictorial p85
STEWART, WILLIAM DRUMMOND
Gilbert--Trail. p139, 142
STICKNEY, JOSEPH L.
, on Dewey's victory at Manila
Bay, 1898
Angle--American p438-442
STOCK COMPANIES
Dulles--History p103, 213
STOCK MARKET
See also NEW YORK STOCK
EXCHANGE; SPECULATION
Furnas--Americans p652-653
, Swindles. See MINES AND
MINING--Stock swindles
, Women in
Furnas--Americans p643

Macksey--Book p165-166
Robertson--Book p206
STOCKGROWERS
See also CATTLEMEN
-West
Hine--American p129-130,
133-135,186,305-308,315,329
STOCKTON, ROBERT FIELD
Amer. Her. --New (6) p E216-217
Boardman--Jackson. p56-57
Gilbert--Trail. p171-172
Life--Sweep (4) p104, 133
STOCKYARDS. See MEAT-
PACKING INDUSTRY
STONE, CORNELIA BRANCH
-Recollections of Civil war
Andrews--Women p420-424
STONE, LUCY
Adelman--Famous p168-170
Furnas--Americans p492-493
Gurko--Ladies. See index p327
Macksey--Book p86-87
Sochen--Herstory p175, 177
Tyler--Freedom's p433-435, 442,
449, 453
Warren--Pictorial p75-77; see
also index p227
STONE RIVER, TENNESSEE--
BATTLE
Pratt--Civil p35
STORES
See also CHAIN STORES; COUN-
TRY STORES; DEPARTMENT
STORES; MAIL ORDER SER-
VICE; SHOPS AND SHOPKEEP-
ERS
, Bulk buying in
Wilson--Folkways p162-163
, Early
Wilson--Folkways p156-161
, General, 1876
Hilton--Way p75, 77, 152-155
, Novelty
Walker--Every. p124
STORY, JOSEPH
Boardman--Virginia p181-182
-Biography
Morris--Ency. p719
STOVES
See also COOKSTOVES; HEAT-
ING
Dreppard--Pioneer p233-239, 241-
242
Furnas--Americans p202, 426-
427, 429
, Cast-iron
Marzio--Nation p493-494, 498
Train--Story p324

, Coal-burning
  Furnas--Americans p427-429
  Schwartz--When p31-32
, Potbellied
  Wilson--Vanish. p143
, Wood-burning
  Schwartz--When p32
STOWE, CALVIN E.
  Boardman--Jackson. p136
STOWE, HARRIET ELIZABETH
BEECHER
  Adelman--Famous p174, facing
    193
  Boardman--Civil p152
  Bode--Anatomy p183-187
  Brooks--Flower. p117, 307, 393,
    417-421, 460, 465-467, 478, 482-
    483, 508
  Dolin--Great p84-91
  Garrison--Lost p123-129
  Heath--Women (4) p9
  Life--New (5) p50-53, 80, 84-85
  Macksey--Book p33, 111-112
  Maurois--Illus. p142-143
  Morris--Ency. p215, 570
  Portraits--Americans p62-63
  Sochen--Herstory p42, 146
  Treasury Amer. p118-122
  200 Years (1) p271, 274-275
  Warren--Pictorial p103-104
  -Biography
    Amer. Her. --New (7) p E252
    Morris--Ency. p719
  -"The lady who does her own
    work"
    Trachtenberg--Demo. p137-
      148
  -"Uncle Tom's cabin"
    Alden--Pioneer p236-237
    Butterfield--Amer. p136
    Harlow--Story p246-247
    Hart--Popular p110-112
    Kraus--U.S. p387, 447-448
    Mott--Golden p114-122
    Our literary p88-89
    Walker--Every. p160-161, 168
"STRATFORD HALL" (Lee's birth-
  place, Westmoreland Co., Va.)
  Vanderbilt--Living p101-102
STRATTON, CARL SHERWOOD.
  See "TOM THUMB"
STRAUSS, LEVI
  , and "levis"
    Tunis--Frontier p149
STREET CARS. See RAILWAYS--
  Street cars
STREET SWEEPERS. See "WHITE-
  WINGS"

STREET VENDORS
  Wilson--Early p52-57
STREETS
  Davidson--Life (2) p161
  Handlin--This p105, 124, 136, 139,
    166, 187, 302, 318, 402
  -1876
    Hilton--Way p162-163
  , Cobblestone
    Wilson--Vanish. p124
STRICKLAND, WILLIAM
  Boardman--Jackson. p163
  Boardman--Virginia p159-160
  Larkin--Art p94
STRIKES
  See also PULLMAN STRIKE,
    1894; "SCABS"
  Boardman--Gilded p76-81
  Boardman--Jackson. p85
  Furnas--Americans. See index
    p1009
  Keller--Affairs. See index p628
  Keyes--Hope p261-263
  Life--Reaching (8). See index
    p176
  Life--Steel (7). See index p159-
    160
  -"Great stike of 1877"
    Butterfield--Amer. p226-227
  , Miners'
    See also Western Federation
    of Miners
    Watkins--Gold p171, 212-215
  -Strikebreakers
    Furnas--Americans p716-717,
      826
  -Views of Jacob A. Riis, 1890
    Cook--City p290
  , Women's
    , First, 1824 (Pawtucket, R.I.)
      Boardman--Virginia p77
    , Shoemakers', 1860 (Lynn,
      Mass.)
      Butterfield--Amer. p156-
        157
STRINGHAM, SILAS
  Holzman--Stormy p62-63
STRONG, GEORGE TEMPLETON
  Furnas--Americans. See index
    p1009
  Howard--Our p344-345
  -Diary, 1836-1856
    Grimsted--Notions p267-285
STRONG, JOSIAH
  Furnas--Americans p612-613, 839
  -Biography
    Amer. Her. --New (11) p E399
  , on immigrants, 1898

Cook--City p67
, on power of saloons in cities
Cook--City p185-186
, on sanitation, N.Y. City, 1898
Cook--City p138
, on John Brown's hanging, 1859
Angle--American p299-301
-"Why the city grows"
Cook--City p15-17
STROTHER, DAVID HUNTER
, on John Brown's hanging
Angle--American p299-301
STROWGER, ALMON BROWN
, and automatic telephone ex-
change
White--American p118-120
STUART, GILBERT
Boardman--Virginia p153
Morris--Ency. p599
Nye--Cultural p281-282
Reader's--Story p375
-Biography
Morris--Ency. p719
, in Boston
Brooks--Flower. See index
p548
STUART, GRANVILLE
-"Excitement in the Montana
gold fields," 1863-1864
Ridge--America's p544-546
STUART, JAMES EWELL BROWN
("JEB")
Amer. Her. --New (8) p E292-
293
Andrews--Women p376-378
Dowdey--Experiment p29, 39, 83,
178, 187, 202, 239, 243, 270, 346-
347
Jordan--Civil p58, 88-89, 97, 108,
121, 135, 145, 156-157
Life--Union (6) p32, 54, 63-64,
97, 106-107
-Raid
Collins--Story p222
STUART, ROBERT
Boardman--Virginia p106-107
STUDEBAKER SHOP
, California, 1850's
Nation in motion p78
STURBRIDGE, MASSACHUSETTS
America's Hist. p294-295, 297
Vanderbilt--Living p16
"THE STUYVESANT"
Marzio--Nation p486
SUBLETTE, WILLIAM
Amer. Her. --New p E217
Bartlett--New p87-88
SUBMARINES

Furnas--Americans p702-703
-Civil war
Wilson--American p210-211
SUB-TREASURY BILL, 1838
-Views of Frances Wright
Walker--Reform p77-80
SUBURBS
Cable--American p159
, Garden
Gowan--Images p313-315, 319
SUBWAYS
Boardman--Gilded p68-69
Davidson--Life (2) p176-177
SUCCESS
Bode--Anatomy p274-276
Borden--Portrait (2) p20-21
, Doctrine of, 1883
Wright--Every. p98-99
"SUFFOLK SYSTEM"
Morris--Ency. p505
SUFFRAGE
See also NATIONAL (AMERICAN)
WOMAN'S SUFFRAGE ASSOCIA-
TION; WOMEN--Suffrage
Boorstin--Americans p215, 410
Davidson--Life (2) p326-335
Furnas--Americans. See index
p1010
Handlin--This p339, 341-343, 383
Keyes--Hope p221-225
Sochen--Herstory p201-203
, and Abigail Duniway
Ross--Westward p138-152
-Arguments
Gurko--Ladies. See index
p322
, Extension of
Trachtenberg--Demo. p73-75
-Views of David Buel, Jr.
Walker--Reform p54-55
-Kansas
Gurko--Ladies p216-218, 220-
221, 227, 232
-"Market for votes," by Rudyard
Kipling
Cook--City p196-197
, Negro
Gurko--Ladies p207, 212-218,
220, 223-224
Keller--Affairs. See index
p628
Life--Union (6) p112-113, 115-
116, 130-132
SUGAR
See also MAPLE SUGAR
Furnas--Americans p460-461
Handlin--This p110, 121, 133, 251,
336, 353-354

-1828-1849
   Boardman--Jackson. p89-90
-Cane
   Life--Growing (3) p124-125,
   134, 136
   Life--Steel (7) p101, 104, 114,
   123, 135
   -Louisiana
     America's Hist. p329
SULKY RACING
   Randel--Centennial p79
SULLIVAN, ANNE
   Macksey--Book p73
SULLIVAN, JAMES ("YANKEE")
   Downey--Our p303-315
SULLIVAN, JOHN LAWRENCE
   Amer. Her. --90's p100, 104
   Boardman--Gilded p174-175
   Dulles--History p227-228
   Reader's--Story p487-488
   Walker--Every. p152-165
   -Biography
     Amer. Her. --New (11) p E399-
     400
SULLIVAN, LOUIS HENRI
   Boardman--Gilded p142-143
   Carman--History (2) p383
   Harlow--Story p433-434
   Larkin--Art p284, 290-291; see
   also index p543
   Morris--Ency. p608-609
   Mumford--Brown p142-165
   -Biography
     Amer. Her. --New (11) p E400
     Morris--Ency. p720
   , on skyscrapers
     Mumford--Brown p150-151
SULLIVAN, MRS. ALGERNON
SYDNEY
   Andrews--Women p428-448
SULLY, THOMAS
   Boardman--Virginia p153-154
   Nye--Cultural p285-286
   Reader's--Story p374
SUMMER
   , Coldest, New England (1816)
     Mussey--Old p114
SUMMER RESORTS. See
RESORTS
SUMMIT SPRINGS BATTLE
   Andrews--Indians p131-133
SUMNER, CHARLES
   Brooks--Flower. See index
   p548
   Butterfield--Amer. p146-147
   Carman--History (1) p616-617,
   692, 720, 723-724, 746
   Carman--History (2) p21, 24-25,

47, 231, 270
Dulles--United p12-13
Harlow--Story p294-295, 338, 340
Keller--Affairs. See index p628
Life--New (5) p57, 68-71, 116
Morris--Ency. See index p771
Our literary p85
-Biography
   Amer. Her. --New (7) p E252-
   253
   Morris--Ency. p720
-Brooks affair
   Harlow--Story p295
   Hurd--Treasury p70-72
   Life--New (5) p70-71
   Morris--Ency. p221
SUMNER, E. V.
-"Besieged by the Utes, the
   Massacre of 1879"
   Jones--Shaping p252-262
SUMNER, WILLIAM GRAHAM
   Boardman--Gilded p117-118
   Life--Reaching (8) p10, 14-15, 138
   -Biography
     Morris--Ency. p720-721
SUNDAY. See SABBATH; SABBA-
TARIANISM
SUNDAY SCHOOL UNION
-"Picture lessons"
   Cable--American p184-185
SUNDAY SCHOOLS
   Cable--American p90, 184-185
   Furnas--Americans. See index
   p1010
   Tyler--Freedom's p259-260
   Wright--Culture p193
   -1876
     Randel--Centennial p448-449
SUN-DIALS
   Dreppard--Pioneer p71
"SUNNYSIDE" (Home of Washington
Irving, Irvington-on-the-Hudson,
N. Y.)
   Vanderbilt--Living p44
SUPERSTITION
-Folklore
   Wilson--Folkways p77-79
SUPPERS. See DINNERS
SUPREME COURT OF UNITED
STATES
   Boardman--Jackson. p22-23
   Boardman--Virginia p17-19, 59-
   60
   Keller--Affairs. See index p628
   Life--Growing (3). See index
   p175
   -1829-1849
     Life--Survey (4). See index

p160
-1876
  Randel--Centennial p276-278,
  456-457
, and Reconstruction, 1866-1868
  Morris--Ency. p249-250
-Decisions
  See also names of cases
  Carman--History (1)
  See index p. xxv
  -1803-1835
    Harlow--Story p188-189
  -1803-1899
    Morris--Ency. p463-470
  -1870's-1880's
    Dulles--United p30
-Justices
  Morris--Ency. p461-462
  -1800-1877
    Carman--History (1) p794-
    795
, on impeachment
  Garrison--Lost p109-111
-Views of John Marshall
  Davie--Profile p68
SURGEONS AND SURGERY
  See also APPENDECTOMY
  Hunt--Life p212-213
  Reader's--Story p298
  -1876
    Hilton--Way p81-83
  -Advances
    Morris--Ency. p543-544
SURNAMES. See NAMES
SURPLUS REVENUE ACT
  Morris--Ency. p436
SURRATT, MARY
  Warren--Pictorial p110-111
SURREYS
  Wilson--Vanish. p31
SURVEYS
, Great--West
  See also names of surveys
  Boorstin--Americans p231-
  232, 235, 242, 247
  Gilbert--Trail. See index
  p235
  Hine--American p74-76, 100,
  179-180
SUTRO, ADOLPH
  Marzio--Nation p241
  Watkins--Gold p72-73
SUTTER, JOHN AUGUSTUS
  Amer. Her. --New (6) p E217
  Billington--Far p77-79, 98, 162-
  163, 218-219
  Brown--Westerners p117, 119-121,
  123, 126, 128, 130, 132

DeVoto--Year. See index p523
Garrison--Lost p68-71
Johnson--Pictorial p65
Jones--Shaping p93-97, 109
Life--Sweep (4) p131, 134, 140, 146
Marzio--Nation p240-241
Watkins--Gold p26-27
, on gold discovery, 1848
  Angle--American p248-250
SUTTER'S FORT (Sacramento, Ca.)
  Billington--Far p78, 98, 165-166,
  218-219
  Jones--Shaping p96-97, 108-109
  Vanderbilt--Living p201
  -Views of Lansford Hastings
    Ridge--America's p472-477
SUTTER'S MILL
  Maurois--Illus. p139-140
  Vanderbilt--Living p201
SVENDSEN, GEORGE
, on Norwegian's family home in
  Iowa, 1863-1865
  Angle--American p366-369
SWAMPLANDS ACT OF 1850
  Bartlett--New p240-241
SWEARING. See PROFANITY
SWEATSHOPS
  -Chicago, Ill.
    -Views of Florence Kelly,
    1896
    Cook--City p252-253
    -Views of Joseph Kirkland,
    1891
    Angle--American p399-400
SWEDEN AND SWEDISH
  Furnas--Americans p696-697
  -Immigrants
    Handlin--This p205, 386
    Life--Reaching (8) p61-62
SWEDENBORG, EMANUEL
, and Swedenborgianism
  Tyler--Freedom's p79
SWEENEY, JOEL WALKER
  Chase--America's p262-263
SWEETWATER RIVER (Wyoming)
  Tunis--Frontier p112-113, 117,
  120, 123
SWIFT, GUSTAVUS
  Portraits--Americans p114
"SWIFT BEAR" (Brule Sioux Indian)
  Andrews--Indian leaders p149, 159
SWIMMING
  Furnas--Americans p437
  Wright--Every. p242-243
  -1876
    Hilton--Way p105-107
  -Lifesaving suits
    Hilton--Way p107-109

-"The old swimming hole"
  Wilson--Vanish. p77
SWISSHELM, JANE GREY
  Adelman--Famous p167
  Tyler--Freedom's p438-440, 451,
  458
SYLVIS, W. H.
  Harlow--Story p403
SYMMES, JOHN CLEVES
  -"Political divisions on the
  Ohio frontier," 1802
    Ridge--America's p247-248
SYMPHONY ORCHESTRAS
  Boardman--Gilded p145-146

T

TABLE ETIQUETTE. See
ETIQUETTE, Table
TABLEWARE. See names of
tableware
TABOR, H. A. W.
  Watkins--Gold p60, 96, 213,
  233-234
TABULATING MACHINES, 1880's
  Reader's--Story p274
  -Hollerith's census
    Portraits--Americans p67
"TAHCHEE" (Cherokee Indian)
  Amer. Her. --Indians p213
TAILOR SHOPS
  Wilson--Vanish. p141
"TALKERS"
  Wilson--Early p180-182
TALKING MACHINES. See
PHONOGRAPHS
"TALL TALES"
  Boorstin--Americans p289-295
  -Foreign travelers, on America
    200 Years (1) p304-305
  -West
    Amer. Her. --New (9) p772-773
TALLMADGE, JAMES
  Amer. Her. --New (5) p E181-182
TALLMADGE, THOMAS E.
  Randel--Centennial p365-368
"TALLYHOS" (Coaches)
  Cable--American p329
  Hilton--Way p132
TALMAGE, THOMAS DEWITT
  -Biography
    Amer. Her. --New (11) p E400
  -"Immoral literature"
    Harris--Land p272-279
"TAMASON" (Nez Perce Indian)
  Andrews--Indian leaders p175
"TAMMANY HALL"

See also CROKER, RICHARD
  Butterfield--Amer. p206-207
  Harlow--Story p421-422
  Holzman--Stormy p215-216
  Life--Steel (7) p15, 18-21
  Weisberger--Amer. p170-171, 173,
  177-191
  , and democracy
    -Views of Richard Croker
      Cook--City p204-205
    -Cartoon attacks, by Thomas
    Nast
      Butterfield--Amer. p206-207
    -Views of Lincoln Steffens
      Cook--City p192
"TAMMANY SOCIETY" (Indian
fraternal society)
  Amer. Her. --Indians p242-243
TANEY, ROGER BROOKE, CHIEF
JUSTICE
  Amer. Her. --New (5) p E182
  Boardman--Jackson. p22-23
  Butterfield--Amer. p150-151
  Collins--Story p205
  Harlow--Story p296
  Kraus--U. S. p362, 365, 466-467
  Life--New (5) p73-74, 114
  Morris--Ency. See index p771
  -Biography
    Morris--Ency. p721-722
  -Career
    Angle--By p224-227
  -Dred Scott V. Sanford
    Heffner--Doc. p125-133
  -"Opinion in the Merryman
  case," 1861
    Angle--By p227-236
TANNERS AND TANNING. See
LEATHER
TAPPAN, ARTHUR
  Boardman--Jackson. p114-115
  Tyler--Freedom's p493-494
TAPPAN, LEWIS
  Portraits--Americans p10-11
"TAPS." See BUGLE CALLS
("TAPS")
TARBELL, IDA MINERVA
  Furnas--Americans p722, 871
  -Biography
    Amer. Her. --New (12) p E439
"TARIFF OF ABOMINATIONS"
(Tariff of 1828)
  Alden--Pioneer p184-185
  Amer. Her. --New (5) p E182
  Borden--Portrait p159-161
  Carman--History (1) p416-417,
  427, 451
  Harlow--Story p229

Life--Sweep (4) p11
Morris--Ency. p166-167
TARIFFS
See also "AMERICAN SYSTEM";
  TAXATION
Amer. Her. --New (5) p398-400
Amer. Her. --New (10) p879-883
Boardman--Gilded p22-23, 25-27
Boardman--Jackson. p38-39
Boardman--Virginia p54-56, 74-
  75
Carman--History (1) p406-408;
  see also index p. xxv
Collins--Story p175
Dulles--United p137-142
Keller--Affairs p24, 53, 162-163,
  195-196, 310, 376-380, 383-384
Kraus--U. S. p346, 356, 360, 500
Life--New (5) p12-15, 92, 121
Life--Reaching (8). See index
  p176
Life--Sweep (4) p11-12, 17-19
Life--Union (6) p111, 151-152, 154
Morris--Ency. p491-492
Whitney--American. See index
  p370
-1827-1828
  See also "TARIFF OF
  ABOMINATION"
  Morris--Ency. p166-167
-1832-1860
  Morris--Ency. p491
-1861-1897
  Harlow--Story p464
, and election of 1844
  Collins--Story p183
-Commission, 1882
  Morris--Ency. p256
, Protective
  Carman--History (1). See
  index p. xxi
  Dulles--United p62-63
  Harlow--Story p148, 187-188
  Morris--Ency. p491-492
TARKINGTON, BOOTH
Boardman--Gilded p132-133
"TASTE" (Cultural)
See also related subjects
Jones--Age p12-14
Lynes--Taste. See index p361
, Sentimental
  , in Currier & Ives prints
    Collins--Story p183
TATE, ALFRED O.
, on Thomas A. Edison, 1885
  Angle--American p383-386
TAVERNS
See also INNS AND INNKEEPERS

Boardman--Virginia p189-190
Cable--American p93
Handlin--This p263, 381, 386-387
Life--America's p61-62
Ross--Taste p68
Wilson--Folkways p179-181
Wilson--Vanish. p155, 158
-Chicago, 1894
  -"Farmer Jones," by William
  T. Stead
    Cook--City p212-214
-Cities, power in
  -Views of Josiah Strong
    Cook--City p185-186
-"Gem saloon," 1854
  Ross--Taste p252
-New York city, 1899
  , Political
    Burner--America (1) p171
-Rhode Island, 1855
  Nation in motion p82
-Saloonkeepers
  Wilson--Early p59
-Sports
  Dulles--History p36-37
-Virginia, early 19th cent.
  Nation in motion p83
TAXATION
Handlin--This p234, 340, 344, 354
Keller--Affairs p22-23, 53, 107,
  114, 307-309, 324-327, 332
-Civil war
  Dowdey--Experiment p54, 209,
  263, 364-365
  Furnas--Americans p720-721
-Single tax
-South
  Life--Steel (7) p106-107, 123
-Tax law of 1862
  Partridge--As p56
TAYLOR, BAYARD
Boardman--Jackson. p58-59
Bode--Anatomy p34, 228-235
Our literary p108
Randel--Centennial. See index
  p474
-Biography
  Amer. Her. --New (11) p E400
, on California, by Isthmus of
  Panama
    Angle--American p250-253
-Visit to San Francisco, 1849
  Commager--Heritage p571-578
TAYLOR, LUCY HOBBS
Reader's--Story p437
TAYLOR, FANNY
Peacock--Famous p118-122
TAYLOR, HAWKINS

-"Squatters versus speculators in
Iowa, " 1838
 Ridge--America's p407-408
TAYLOR, MARGARET
 Melick--Wives p36
TAYLOR, ZACHARY ("Old Rough
and Ready")
 Amer. Her. --New (7) p545-554
 Billington--Far p172, 176-178,
 185, 188-189
 Boardman--Jackson. p43-45, 192-
 195
 Butterfield--Amer. p122-123
 Carman--History (1) p567, 600-
 601, 605, 790
 DeVoto--Year. See index p523
 Harlow--Story p274-275, 284-288
 Hine--American p98-101, 103
 Kraus--U.S. p432, 434-435
 Life--New (5) p6, 31, 34-39
 Life--Sweep (4). See index
 p160
 Morris--Ency. See index p771
 200 Years (1) p336-337; see
 also index p351
 , and Battle of Monterey, 1846
 -Views of John R. Kenly
 Angle--American p238-241
 , at Buena Vista, 1847
 Amer. Her. --New (7) p570-
 571
 -Biography
 Amer. Her. --New (7) p E253
 Morris--Ency. p722
 Whitney--American p107-111
 -Cabinet
 Carman--History (1) p790
 -Presidency
 Linton--Bicentennial p132-138
 Reader's--Story p333
"TAYLORISM" (shop management)
 Train--Story p340
TEACHERS
 Bartlett--New p388-389
 Furnas--Americans. See index
 p1011
 Handlin--This p120, 142-143, 221,
 272, 279, 368
 Nye--Cultural p163-165
 Schwartz--When p62, 66-67
 Tyler--Freedom's p236-237
 Wilson--Early p103
 Wilson--Folkways p92-94
 -1876
 Hilton--Way p56-57
 , as profession
 Sochen--Herstory p101-102
 , Freedom of

 Jones--Age p423-424
-Training
 Boardman--Jackson. p135-136
 Tyler--Freedom's p237-239
 Warren--Pictorial p71
, Traveling, 1876
 Hilton--Way p68-69
-Wages
 Hunt--Life p136
 -Women
 Cable--American p148
-Women
 Reader's--Story p431
 -1889-1890
 Life--Reaching (8) p38-39
TEAMBOATS (Flatboats)
 Langdon--Everyday (2) p16-17
TECHNOLOGY
 See also MACHINE AGE
 Boardman--Civil p146-148
 Boardman--Gilded p56-59
 Boardman--Jackson. p91-92, 101-
 102
 Boardman--Virginia p91-92
 Borden--Portrait (2) p37
 -1860-1899
 Train--Story p317-345
 -1880's-1890's
 Dulles--United p90-91
 , Impact of
 Walker--Every. p44-73
 -West
 Hine--American. See index
 p370
 -Women. See WOMEN--
 Technology, Role in
"TECUMSEH" (Shawnee Indian)
("SHOOTING STAR")
 Amer. Her. --Indians p202, 206-208
 Andrews--Indian leaders p46-50,
 75-76
 Boardman--Virginia p114-115
 Brown--Westerners p73, 188
 Life--Sweep (4) p40, 43
 Maurois--Illus. p105, 112
 Morris--Ency. p139-140, 142, 145-
 146, 148
 Reader's--Story p85-86
 200 Years (1) p182-183, 185, 187
 -"Indian protest against the Fort
 Wayne treaty, " 1810
 Ridge--America's p258-260
 -Support of British
 Commager--Heritage p237-238
TELEGRAPH
 See also COLLINS, PERRY
 McDONOUGH; MORSE, SAMUEL;
 WESTERN UNION

Boardman--Civil p145-146
Boardman--Jackson. p99-100
Furnas--Americans p347, 356-357, 378
Handlin--This p231, 298-310
Harlow--Story p210-202
Linton--Bicentennial p122, 165, 167, 204, 264, 276
Partridge--As p109
Trachtenberg--Demo. p241-242
Train--Story p284, 334-335, 337
Walker--Every. p51-52
Wilson--American p363-366
-1844
 Reader's--Story p264
-1880's
 Peck--Nineteenth n. p.
-Boys, New York city
 -Views of W. A. Linn, 1879
  Cook--City p276-277
-Codes, Secret, Civil war
 Meredith--World p114-117
, Collins overland
 White--American p63-67
, Electromagnetic
 Wilson--American p176-177
 , of Samuel Morse
  Commager--Heritage p389-394
  Wilson--American p116-117, 122-123
, Harmonic
 -Tuned reeds, Bell's & Gray's
  Portraits--Americans p32
, Transformer and electric motor
 Wilson--American p112-113
TELEPHONE
 See also BELL, ALEXANDER GRAHAM; VAIL, THEODORE
 Cable--American p210-211
 Davidson--Life (2) p172-173
 Furnas--American p635, 806-807
 Linton--Bicentennial. See index p447
 Marzio--Nation p610-611
 Nostalgia p58-61
 Partridge--As p116
 Portraits--Americans p32-33
 Randel--Centennial p178-180
 Reader's--Story p271
 Train--Story p336-337
 Walker--Every. p53
 Wilson--American p281-285
 Woodward--Way p299
-1876
 Hilton--Way p194-195
-Automatic exchange device

, and Almon Brown Strowger
 White--American p118-119
-Bell, Alexander Graham, and Life--Steel (7) p42-43
-Demonstrations, Salem, 1876
 Collins--Story p251
-Call-box, First public, 1880 (New Haven, Conn.)
 Robertson--Book p176
-Expansion, early
 Morris--Ency. p433
, Hand-crank
 Wilson--Vanish. p42
, in hotel rooms
 Woodward--Way p289
, Invention of
 -Gray vs. Bell
  White--American p104-105
, Private
 , First, 1877 (Boston, Mass.)
  Robertson--Book p176
, Switchboard
 , First, 1877 (Boston, Mass.)
  Robertson--Book p176
TELESCOPES
 See also CLARK, ALVIN G.; HALE, GEORGE ELLERY
 Wilson--American p352-353
TELLER, HENRY
-Biography
 Amer. Her. --New (12) p E439-440
TEMPERANCE
 See also ALCOHOLISM; AMERICAN TEMPERANCE UNION: W. C. T. U. (WOMEN'S CHRISTIAN TEMPERANCE UNION); DUNIWAY, ABIGAIL; WILLARD, FRANCES ELIZABETH and other temperance leaders
 Amer. Her. --New (6) p490-491; E217-218
 Boardman--Civil p190-191
 Boardman--Gilded p156-157
 Boardman--Jackson. p130-131
 Boorstin--Americans p45, 214
 Borden--Portraits (1) p190-191
 Cable--American p90, 254-255, 298-299
 Carman--History (1) p519-523
 Collins--Story p245
 Dulles--United p97-98
 Furnas--Americans. See index p1010
 Garrison--Lost p160-163
 Gurko--Ladies p2, 31, 33, 94-95, 107, 113, 117-119, 145-146, 156-158, 163-165, 174, 260-265

Handlin--This p190, 225, 296, 377, 385-386
Harlow--Story p255
Ross--Westward p148-150
Sochen--Herstory p134-137
Tyler--Freedom's p308-350
Walker--Every. p70, 143-144
Warren--Pictorial p83, 99, 137-138
-1876
    Randel--Centennial p20-21, 133
-Argument against, by Tom Flynn
    Burner--America (1) p285-287
-Arguments for
    Burner--America (1) p283-285
-International movement
    Tyler--Freedom's p346
-Maine law
    Tyler--Freedom's p347-350
-Origins of crusade
    Tyler--Freedom's p316-322
-Religious aspects
    Tyler--Freedom's p318-322, 336
-Societies
    See also names of societies
    Life--Sweep (4) p11, 61, 66
    Tyler--Freedom's p324, 327-328, 338-347
    , First, "Temperance Society," 1808
        Hunt--Life p173
TEMPLETON, FAY
    Blum--Stage Profile 30
TENEMENTS. See SLUMS
TENNESSEE
    Carman--History (1) p634, 664-665, 729, 782
    Handlin--This p116, 121, 234
    Hunt--Life. See index p297
    Life--New (5) p94, 99, 118, 134
    , in Civil war
        Dowdey--Experiment. See index p454
        Jordan--Civil p215
        Life--Union (6) p35-38, 61, 63, 81-84, 87-89
    -Memphis
        , in Civil war
            Dowdey--Experiment p72, 147, 157, 160, 181, 208, 210, 228-229, 250, 349
TENNESSEE RIVER VALLEY
    -Indians

Andrews--Indian leaders p85-86
TENNIS
    Dulles--History p182, 192-193, 202, 265
    Jones--Age p344
    Life--Steel (7) p146-147
    Reader's--Story p491
    -1876
        Hilton--Way p105
    -Beginning, 1874
        Ross--Taste p95
    -Equipment, 1880's
        Peck--Nineteenth. n. p.
    , Lawn
        Cable--American p322-323
        Davidson--Life (2) p69
        -1887
            Viewpoints p120
        -Equipment, 1880's
            Peck--Nineteenth. n. p.
TENNYSON, ALFRED
    -Popularity in America
        Mott--Golden p105-108
"TENSKWATAWA" (Indian). See "THE PROPHET" (Indian)
TENTS
    -1880's
        Peck--Nineteenth n. p.
TENURE OF OFFICE ACT, 1867
    Amer. Her. --New (8) p E293
    Borden--Portrait (2) p9
    Carman--History (1) p731-732, 733n
    Harlow--Story p341-342
    Life--Union (6) p116-117
TERHUNE, MRS. EDWARD PAYSON. See HARLAND, MARION, pseud.
TERRELL, MARY CHURCH
    Sochen--Herstory p206-207
TERRITORIAL EXPANSION, 1803-1899
    Davie--Profile p167-168
    Morris--Ency. p419-434
    -1876
        Randel--Centennial p150-152
TERRORISM
    See also RIOTS
    Furnas--Americans. See index p1010
TERRY, ELI
    Dreppard--Pioneer p7
TESLA, NIKOLA
    Morris--Ency. p538
    -Biography
        Morris--Ency. p722
TEXAS

306

See also "ALAMO"
Alden--Pioneer. See index p. ix
Amer. Her. --New (6) p518-522
Bartlett--New p85, 93, 99-100,
129, 154, 193-194
Billington--Far. See index
p322
Boardman--Jackson. See
index p211
Boorstin--Americans p43, 178,
253, 258, 272
Brown--Westerners. See index
p288
Carman--History (1) p558-564,
634, 783; see also index p. xxv
Furnas--Americans. See index
p1011
Handlin--This p333, 336, 340-341
Hine--American. See index
p370
Kane--Gone p238-259
Keyes--Hope p241-242
Kraus--U.S. p418-424
Life--New (5) p34-36, 39, 95, 139
Life--Steel (7) p16, 55-56, 58, 60,
70-71, 101
Life--Sweep (4) p81-86, 92-99;
see also index p160
Linton--Bicentennial. See index
p447
Morris--Ency. p176-177
Randel--Centennial p45-49, 114-
115, 120, 377-378
Tunis--Frontier p98-99, 139, 142,
145-146, 157, 160
200 Years (1). See index p351
-Abilene, as "cow town"
Ridge--America's p595-597
, and acquisition of New Mexico
and California
DeVoto--Year p6, 13-15
, and Compromise of 1850
Harlow--Story p286-287
, and Mexican War
Commager--Heritage p587-
606
Harlow--Story p273-274
-Annexation, 1846
Borden--Portrait (1) p210-
211
Collins--Story p182
DeVoto--Year p5-13
Hine--American p88, 97-98,
100, 107
Kraus--U.S. p421-424
Morris--Ency. p189, 191-192,
428
, as "Lone Star Republic"

Kraus--U.S. p418-421
-Austin's advertisement for set-
tlers, 1823
Ridge--America's p414-416
-Boundary dispute
DeVoto--Year p13-18, 20-21,
28, 68-69
, "British designs on," by Ashbel
Smith
Ridge--America's p487-489
-Civil war
, and Confederacy
Harlow--Story p300, 320
, Women in
Andrews--Women p413-427
-Comanche ravages
DeVoto--Year p153, 184-185,
202, 205, 221, 227, 230-231, 244-
245, 263
-Cultural conflict, 1833
Ridge--America's p423-426
-"Expedition"
DeVoto--Year p267-270, 280-
281, 289, 393-394, 475
-Frontier, social conditions (life)
Billington--Far p136
, Germans in
Weisberger--Amer. p121-122
-Independence movement
Hine--American p83, 85-87, 97-
98
Ridge--America's p429-430
-Lone Star flag
Amer. Her. --New (7) p564-565
-"Migration to the Texan repub-
lic," 1845, by J. A. Orr
Ridge--America's p436-438
-Mormons
DeVoto--Year p86-87, 105-107,
121, 131, 141
-"Old Three Hundred" (first
Texas colonists)
Hine--American p81-82
-Rebellion
Borden--Portrait (1) p210
-Revolution
See also TEXAS--Annexation
Alden--Pioneer p234-237
Billington--Far p117-142
Harlow--Story p264-269
, Causes of, 1835
Ridge--America's p426-429
-San Antonio
Furnas--Americans p371, 389,
459
-Settlements
Alden--Pioneer p232-235, 238
Ridge--America's p414-438

-Views of Noah Smithwick
   Commager--Heritage p589-
   591
-Texans
  -"Mexico's distrust of the
   Texans," by Mier y Teran,
   1828
    Ridge--America's p419-422
"TEXAS RANGERS"
  DeVoto--Year p130, 188, 215-216,
  281-286, 405
  Hine--American p84, 135, 212-
  213, 311, 314-315, 324
TEXTBOOKS
  Furnas--Americans p536, 548-
  549, 738-739
  Hunt--Life p137-138
  McClinton--Antiques p79-89
  Nye--Cultural p159-160
  Schwartz--When p62
  Wright--Every. p190-191
  -Kentucky
   Wright--Culture p67-68
TEXTILE INDUSTRY
  Boardman--Gilded p74-75
  Boardman--Jackson. p78-79
  Boardman--Virginia p69-70
  Furnas--Americans. See index
  p1010
  Life--Growing (3) p51
  Life--Steel (7) p35, 74, 79, 100,
  102-104
  Van Wagenen--Golden p249-250
  Wright--Every. p130-134
  -Mills
   See also names of mills,
   localities
   -Life, collapse of mill
   (Lawrence, Mass., 1871)
    Trachtenberg--Demo. p248-
    274
  -Steam, use of
   Langdon--Everyday (2) p248
  , Women in
   Warren--Pictorial p92-94
TEYA INDIANS
  Brown--Westerners p203
THALBERG, SIGISMUND
  Howard--Our p204-205
THAMES RIVER BATTLE, 1813
  Morris--Ency. p145-146
  Ridge--America's p268-270
THANKSGIVING DAY
  Hilton--Way p200-201
  Mussey--Old p92-93
  Partridge--As p25-26
  Schwartz--When p130-131
  Walker--Every. p35-36

-1858
  Ross--Taste p85
-Masquerade ball (Colorado,
  1895)
  Schwartz--When p130
-Middlewest
  Drury--Midwest p87
THAXTER, CELIA
  Adelman--Famous p201
THEATER
  See also DRAMA; names of road
  companies
  Boardman--Civil p165-168
  Boardman--Gilded p148-151
  Boardman--Jackson. p155-159
  Boardman--Virginia p144-147
  Bode--Anatomy p3-18
  Cable--American p110-111
  Davidson--Life (2) p19-21
  Dulles--History p100-121, 213-216,
  219, 234-237, 260-263
  Furnas--Americans p565-569, 689,
  757-758
  Handlin--This p104, 127, 195, 262-
  263, 307, 310, 375-379, 390
  Harris--Land p160-179
  Hunt--Life p86-92
  Nye--Cultural p267
  Nye--Unembar. p150-160
  Partridge--As p150-160
  Reader's--Story p463-464
  Tunis--Young p123-124
  Walker--Every. p129, 157-164
  Wright--Every. p228-231
  -before 1860
   Blum--Theatre p6
  -1860-1870
   Blum--Theatre p7-16
  -1868
   Cook--City p268
  -1870-1880
   Blum--Theatre p17-26
  -1876
   Randel--Centennial. See
   index p474
  -1880-1890
   Blum--Theatre p27-38
   Viewpoints p171-172
  -1890's
   Blum--Theatre p39-53
   Life--Reaching (8) p37-38, 44,
   52-53
  -"About nudity in the theaters,"
  by Olive Logan
   Trachtenburg--Demo. p300-
   312
  , Amateur
   Grimsted--Melodrama p49-51,

89-91
-Audience
 Grimsted--Melodrama. See
 index p279
-Boston, Mass.
 Grimsted--Melodrama. See
 index p279
 Mussey--Old p119
-Buildings
 Furnas--Americans p428, 565-
 566
 Grimsted--Melodrama p77-78
-California
 Wright--Culture p158-160
-Charleston, South Carolina
 Grimsted--Melodrama p107-
 109, 147, 151, 232, 249-257,
 259
, Church attacks on
 Dulles--History p89, 204-205
-Civil war period
 Blum--Theatre p13
-"Combination system," 1880's
 Blum--Theatre p27
-Companies, touring
 Dulles--United p101
 Reader's--Story p468
-Critics
 Grimsted--Melodrama. See
 index p280
, Economics of
 Grimsted--Melodrama p18-19,
 22-23, 29, 81-82, 145-149
, German
 Harris--Land p176-177
, Italian
 Harris--Land p161-168
-Little theaters, first (Cincin-
 nati, O.)
 Dreppard--Pioneer p99-100
-New Orleans, La.
 Grimsted--Melodrama. See
 index (under New Orleans)
 p13
-New York city
 Grimsted--Melodrama. See
 index p283
 -Park Theater, 1822
 Ross--Taste p48
-Northwest Territory
 Wright--Culture p119-120
-Riots
 Grimsted--Melodrama p65-74
-St. Louis, Mo.
 Grimsted--Melodrama p30,
 35, 39, 61, 107-109, 249, 255-
 257, 261
-Shows

See also Drama
 Furnas--Americans p562-564,
 569
-Societies, college
 Cable--American p316
-Stage costuming
 Grimsted--Melodrama p26, 81-
 84, 91
-Stage lighting
 Grimsted--Melodrama p49, 77,
 82, 143
-Stage scenery
 Grimsted--Melodrama p3, 16-
 17, 41, 76-84
-Staging
 Grimsted--Melodrama p76-84
, Unappreciated
 , anti-bellum
 Train--Story p291
-Views of Frances Trollope
 Trollope--Domestic. See
 index p.xvi
-Views of Otis Skinner, 1895-
 1896
 Angle--American p420-423
-Villains
 Grimsted--Melodrama p16,
 176-179, 215, 223, 242-248
-West
 Hine--American p261
-Women
 Macksey--Book p232
, Yankee
 Grimsted--Melodrama p47, 142-
 143, 186-189, 193, 245-246
, Yiddish
 Harris--Land p168-176
THEOLOGY. See RELIGION
THIRD PARTY MOVEMENTS
 See also names of movements
 and parties
 Keller--Affairs p275-283, 547-552
THOMAS, BENJAMIN P.
 , on Abraham Lincoln
 Miers--American p183-188
THOMAS, EDITH MATILDA
 Adelman--Famous p272
THOMAS, GEORGE HENRY,
 GENERAL ("OLD PAP")
 Amer. Her. --New (8) p E293-294
 Life--Union (6) p14, 82-83, 87-88,
 100-101
 Morris--Ency. See index p772
 -Biography
 Morris--Ency. p722-723
THOMAS, JESSE
 Amer. Her. --New (5) p E182
THOMAS, JULIA

Randel--Centennial p406-407
THOMAS, PHILIP E.
  Nostalgia p13-15
THOMAS, THEODORE (CHRISTIAN
FRIEDRICH)
  Boardman--Gilded p145-146
  Furnas--Americans p662-663,
  762
  Howard--Our p280-289
  Marzio--Nation p414
  Randel--Centennial p290, 298,
  342-345
  -Biography
    Morris--Ency. p723
THOMPSON, BENJAMIN
  Morris--Ency. p530
THOMPSON, FRANKLIN, pseud.
See EDMONDS, SARAH EMMA
THOMPSON, WADDY
  -British designs on California,
  1847
    Ridge--America's p489-490
THOREAU, HENRY DAVID
  Alden--Pioneer p214
  Amer. Her. --New (6) p E218
  Boardman--Civil p149-150
  Boardman--Jackson. p143
  Brooks--Flower. p286-302; see
  also index p549
  Butterfield--Amer. p117
  Carman--History (1) p537, 539-
  541
  DeVoto--Year p29-31, 33-35, 43,
  48, 50, 64, 80-81, 101
  Harlow--Story p244-245
  Life--Sweep (4) p62, 109
  Morris--Ency. p567-568
  Mumford--Brown p66-71
  Our literary p66-70
  Randel--Centennial p109, 188-
  189, 274
  Reader's--Story p411
  Tyler--Freedom's p59-61
  , and Mexican war
    DeVoto--Year p206-209, 287,
    304, 438, 494
  -Biography
    Morris--Ency. p723-724
  , on "civil disobedience"
    Tyler--Freedom's p417
  , on conservation
    Reader's--Story p502
  -Walden Pond
    Brooks--Flower. p359-373
    -Building a cabin
      Commager--Heritage p432-
      438
THORNTON, JESSY QUINN

Case--Empire p163-177
  DeVoto--Year. See index p523
THORNTON, WILLIAM
  , and negro colonization
    Hunt--Life p234-235
THRESHING AND THRESHING
MACHINES
  Reader's--Story p263
  Van Wagenen--Golden p239-248,
  265
  Wilson--Vanish. p69-71
  Wright--Every. p154-156
THURBER, CHARLES
  Amer. Her. --New (5) p E183
TICKNOR, GEORGE
  Brooks--Flower. p73-88; see
  also index p549
  Our literary p48-49
  , and Fields
    Bode--Anatomy p111-114, 132,
    154, 197-198
TIEMANN, DANIEL FAWCETT
  Meredith--World p66-69
TIFFANY, LOUIS COMFORT
  Lynes--Taste. p170, 173-175
  Reader's--Story p229
  Ross--Taste p138-139
TILDEN, HARRIET
  Randel--Centennial p379-380, 406
TILDEN, SAMUEL JONES ("HON-
EST SAM")
  Amer. Her. --New (8) p E294
  Boardman--Civil p115-116
  Boardman--Gilded p9-10
  Butterfield--Amer. p220
  Harlow--Story p349-351
  Life--Steel (7) p8-9, 23-24
  Randel--Centennial p36, 100, 221-
  236
TILE, DRAINAGE
  Van Wagenen--Golden p209-210
TILLMAN, BENJAMIN ("PITCH-
FORK BEN")
  , Profanity of
    Life--Reaching (8) p84, 88, 106
TILTON, ELIZABETH
  Gurko--Ladies p248-249
TILTON, THEODORE
  -Biography
    Amer. Her. --New (11) p E401
TIMBER. See LUMBER AND
LUMBERING; FOREST; WOOD
"TIMBER BARONS"
  Bartlett--New p240-243
TIMBER CULTURE ACT OF 1873
  Amer. Her. --New (9) p773-774
  Boardman--Civil p96
  Carman--History (2) p202

TIMBERLAKE, JOHN BOWIE
, and Peggy O'Neale (later
Eaton)
Phillips--That. See index
p183
TIMBERLAKE, MARGARET
(daughter of Peggy Eaton)
Phillips--That p45, 151, 156, 158
TIMBERLAKE, VIRGINIA
Phillips--That p31, 148, 151, 155-
156, 158, 173-174
TIMM, HENRY CHRISTIAN
Howard--Our p153-154
TINWARE AND TINSMITHS
Cable--American p200-201
Dreppard--Pioneer p178-179, 184,
187
-Cans, invention, 1839
Lynes--Domestic. p125
"TIPPECANOE AND TYLER TOO"
(slogan)
Burner--America (1) p165-166
Butterfield--Amer. p104-106
Collins--Story p181
Kraus--U.S. p368-370
-Log cabin incident, 1840
Downey--Our p239-254
TIPPECANOE BATTLE, 1811-1812
Collins--Story p196
Morris--Ency. p140, 421
Ridge--America's p260-262
-Views of Adam Walker
Angle--American p171-174
TITLES (SOCIAL)
Carson--Polite p75-76
Hunt--Life p58-59
-Views of Frances Trollope
Carson--Polite p76
TLINGIT INDIANS
-Dance mask, c1880
Marzio--Nation p20
"TOASTS"
Ross--Taste p68
TOBACCO
See also SMOKING
Boardman--Jackson. p90
Carman--History (1) p359, 479-
480, 582, 587
Furnas--Americans. See index
p1011
Handlin--This p116, 120-121, 126,
160, 488
Life--Steel (7) p79, 100-105, 128,
134-135
Wilson--Folkways p74-75
-1876
Randel--Centennial p288-289,
309-310

, Chewing
Carson--Polite p87-88
Furnas--Americans p243-244
Woodward--Way p291-292
-"Chewing Tobacco Era" (19th
cent.)
Randel--Centennial p309
-Soldiers' hunger, and Battle of
Antietam
Garrison--Lost p38-47
-Spitting
Cable--American p84
Lynes--Domestic. p67-68
-Trade names
Randel--Centennial p309
-Views of Frances Trollope
Trollope--Domestic. See in-
dex p. xvi
TOCQUEVILLE, ALEXIS DE
Amer. Her. --New (5) p E183
Boardman--Jackson. p26, 81, 132,
188, 191, 200
Carman--History (1) p492, 502-
503, 507, 509, 517, 523
, on America and Americans
Handlin--This p169-179
Kraus--U.S. p388-389
, on democracy, 1831
Wright--Every. p100-101
-"A Remarkable prophecy, " 1835
Davie--Profile p382
TODD, JOHN
, on women, limitations
Adelman--Famous p189-191
TODD, MARY. See LINCOLN,
MARY TODD
TODD FAMILY
Randall--Mary p31-33
TOILETS
, Early
Marzio--Nation p500-501
-Lavatories, 1894
Cook--City p142
-"Thundermugs" (chamber pots)
Wilson--Vanish. p48
TOLERANCE
See also special nationalities and
subjects
Handlin--This p187, 248, 260, 322-
323, 358
TOLL HOUSES
Langdon--Everyday (2) p33-34
-Illinois, 19th cent.
Nation in motion p79
"TOM THUMB" (CHARLES SHER-
WOOD STRATTON)
Boardman--Civil p198
Dulles--History p122, 124-125, 135

TOMATOES
  Furnas--Americans p462-463
  Van Wagenen--Golden p86-87
TOMBSTONE, ARIZONA
  Vanderbilt--Living p199
  Watkins--Gold p136-138, 191, 277
TOMBSTONE INSCRIPTIONS. See
 EPITAPHS
TOMPKINS, SALLY, CAPTAIN
  Andrews--Women p127-130
  Macksey--Book p149
TONQUIN (ship)
  Gilbert--Trail. p58-59
  Hine--American p47-48
TOOLS
  See also FARM IMPLEMENTS
  Dreppard--Pioneer p311
  -1880's
    Peck--Nineteenth n. p.
  , Cowboy
    Life--America's p120-121
TOOMBS, ROBERT AUGUSTUS
  Dowdey--Experiment. See
    index p454
  Life--Sweep (4) p136-138
  -Biography
    Amer. Her. --New (7) p E253-
    254
TOPONCE, ALEXANDER
  , on completion of Union Pacific,
    1869
    Angle--American p357-358
TORNADOES
  Drury--Midwest p87-88
TORPEDOES
  -Civil war
    Dowdey--Experiment p183,
    324-325, 345, 411
    Wilson--American p206-209
TORREY, JOHN
  Boardman--Jackson. p168-169
TOTEM POLES
  , and potlatches
    Amer. Her. --Indians p298-299
TOURGEE, ALBION
  , on Ku Klux Klan
    Commager--Heritage p821-824
  , on Union League
    Commager--Heritage p816-821
TOURISM. See TRAVEL AND
 TRAVELERS
TOURNAMENTS
  , Southern antebellum
    Furnas--Americans p410-411
TOUTAIN, PAUL
  Randel--Centennial p57-59
TOWN, ITHIEL
  Boardman--Virginia p90-91

TOWNS
  , Agricultural
    Bartlett--New p422-432
  , Changing
    Wilson--Vanish. p123-164
  , Country
    See also TOWNS, Agricultural
    Harris--Land p229-270
    Partridge--As p31-49
  -Life
    America's Hist. p292-303
    Wright--Every. p109-136
  -New England
    Mussey--Old p56-59
  -Old Northwest
    Tunis--Frontier p84-85
  , Small
    200 Years (2) p100-101
  -West
    Hine--American p252-255, 259,
    267, 271, 324
  , Attitudes of
    Hine--American p256-259
  -Covenanted community
    Hine--American p256-257
TOWNSEND, JOHN KIRK
  Gilbert--Trail. p121, 130-131,
    134-135
TOWSON, NATHAN
  , and Eaton affair
    Phillips--That p76-79
TOYS
  See also DOLLS
  Dreppard--Pioneer p120-135
  McClinton--Antiques. See index
    p351
  -1880's
    Peck--Nineteenth n. p.
  -Animals
    McClinton--Antiques p250-263,
    266, 277-281, 336-339
  , Cast iron
    McClinton--Antiques p266-270
  -Mechanical banks
    Dreppard--Pioneer p121-123
  -Pull toys
    Dreppard--Pioneer p133
  , Clockwork
    McClinton--Antiques p265-266,
    320-321
  , Cloth
    McClinton--Antiques p329-339;
    see also index (under Cloth)
    p346
  , Electrical
    Dreppard--Pioneer p132
  -Furniture, miniature
    Dreppard--Pioneer p129

312

-"Jack-in-the-box"
　McClinton--Antiques p279-281
-Locomotives and engines
　(1880's)
　Peck--Nineteenth n. p.
, Manufacturers of
　McClinton--Antiques p348
-"Noah's Ark"
　McClinton--Antiques p259-260
, Noted in magazines
　McClinton--Antiques. See
　index p348
, Paper
　McClinton--Antiques p320-328
-Pistols
　McClinton--Antiques p270-271
, "Push and pull"
　See also TOYS, Cast iron
　McClinton--Antiques p250-266
-Rattles
　McClinton--Antiques p28, 77,
　207
-Safes
　McClinton--Antiques p273-274
-"Snake-in-the-box"
　McClinton--Antiques p279-280
-Tops
　McClinton--Antiques p209-212
, Wooden, 1870's
　Dreppard--Pioneer p130
TRACK AND FIELD EVENTS
　Dulles--History p182, 269
-Running
　Dulles--History p73, 75, 143-
　144, 175
TRACTS. See AMERICAN TRACT
SOCIETY
TRADE AND TRADERS
　See also FUR TRADE
　Carman--History (1) p471-476
　Handlin--This. See index p600
　Langdon--Everyday (2) p138-139
　Life--Growing (3). See index
　p176
　Tunis--Frontiers p107-108
-Fairs. See FAIRS, Trade
-Negro women
　Macksey--Book p170-171
, Opposition to free
　Butterfield--Amer. p253
TRADE MARK ACT, 1870
　Keller--Affairs p184, 420-421
TRADE SOCIETIES
, Women's
　Boardman--Jackson. p87
TRADE UNIONS. See LABOR
UNIONS
TRADER, ELLA K.

Andrews--Women p131-144
TRADING POSTS
　See also names of fur companies
　Tunis--Frontier p111-112
-Map
　Tunis--Frontier p108
TRADITION
, Victorian
　Gowans--Images. See index
　p498
TRAFFIC
-Problems, 1876
　Hilton--Way p162-163
"TRAILBLAZERS"
　See also names of individuals
　Reader's--Story p163-171
-Portraits
　Gilbert--Trail. p80-87
TRAIN, GEORGE FRANCIS
　Brown--Westerners p170-178, 183,
　186-187, 215
　Furnas--Americans p642
　Gurko--Ladies p219-225, 230-231,
　233, 235-236, 246
TRAINS. See PULLMAN SLEEP-
ING CARS; RAILROADS--TRAINS
TRAMPS
　Cable--American p303
　Furnas--Americans p678-683,
　725-726
TRANSCENDENTAL CLUB
　Tyler--Freedom's p50-52
TRANSCENDENTALISM
　See also names of individuals
　Alden--Pioneer p213-214, 217, 219,
　224
　Amer. Her. --New (6) p E218-219
　Boardman--Jackson. p124, 141-144
　Carman--History (1) p536-537
　Commager--Heritage p424-432,
　440-442
　Handlin--This p219, 226-228
　Jones--Age p22-23
　Kraus--U.S. p374
　Life--Sweep (4) p61-62
　Morris--Ency. p567-568
　Our literary p60-61
　Reader's--Story p338, 410-411
　Tyler--Freedom's p47-67
-1876
　Randel--Centennial p442-443
, and music, 1835-1850
　Lowens--Music p249-263
-New England
　Harlow--Story p244-245
-"Transcendental wild oats, " by
　Louisa Alcott
　Tyler--Freedom's p172-175

TRANSCONTINENTAL RAILROAD.
See RAILROADS--Transcontinental
railroad
TRANSFORMERS, STANLEY
Portraits--Americans p86
TRANSPORTATION
See also CANALS; FLATBOATS;
HIGHWAYS; HORSES; RAIL-
ROADS; RIVERS; ROADS;
STAGE COACHES; STEAMBOATS;
STEAMSHIPS; TRAVEL AND
TRAVELERS; WATERWAYS;
Etc.
Bartlett--New p273-340
Boardman--Civil p103-104, 138-
145
Boardman--Gilded p61-71
Boardman--Jackson. p93-99,
100-101
Boardman--Virginia p81-91
Bonte--American p100, 139
Carman--History (2) p65-68
Cook--City p41-64
Dreppard--Pioneer p304, 307
Furnas--Americans. See index
p1011
Life--Growing (3) p146-147,
156-159
Life--New (5) p10-11, 120-121
Marzio--Nation p160-177
Ross--Taste p268
Wilson--Folkways p166-178
Wilson--Vanish. p165-185
-1825-1860
Train--Story p276-285
-to 1850 (map)
Harlow--Story p194
-1860-1899
Train--Story p331-337
-1880's-1890's
Borden--Portrait (2) p35-37
, beyond the Mississippi
Davidson--Life (2) p258-277
-"Carriers to the far frontier"
(illustrations)
200 Years (1) p197-212
-Development
Keyes--Hope p235
-Eastern U.S.--Map
Bartlett--New p283
-Frontier, 1850-1884
Ridge--America's p552-571
, Impact of
Walker--Every. p59-68, 70,
125
-West
Bartlett--New p284-285
Hine--American p139-155,

167, 281
Train--Story p311-313
TRANSYLVANIA COLLEGE (Lexing-
ton, Ky.)
Tyler--Freedom's p256
TRAPPING. See HUNTING AND
TRAPPING
TRAVEL AND TRAVELERS
See also BOOKS AND READING--
Travel books; WOMEN--Travel
and travelers; types of traveling;
names of travelers
Cable--American p92-93, 99-100,
220-223
Hunt--Life p52-54
Jones--Age p152-154
Keyes--Hope p212
Ross--Taste p268, 273
Wright--Every. p79-93
-1876
Hilton--Way p130-150
-Tourism
Furnas--Americans p361-362
-West
Hine--American p180-181,
263-264
-Highways, 1807
-Views of Fortescue
Cuming
Angle--American p157-
158
-"Susan Pettigrew makes a
journey," 1836
Woodward--Way p198-243
-Writers
Our literary p108-109
TRAVELING SHOWS
See also CIRCUS; names of
shows; etc.
Dulles--History p39-42, 132-133,
155-156, 161
TRAVIS, WILLIAM BARRET
Hine--American p85-87, 91
Kraus--U.S. p420-421
-Biography
Amer. Her. --New (7) p E254
-Command of "Alamo"
Commager--Heritage p598-599
-"The fall of the Alamo," 1836
Ridge--America's p430-432
, on siege of the Alamo, 1836
Angle--American p235-238
"TREASURE HILL" SILVER MINES
(Nevada)
Watkins--Gold p164-167
TREATIES
See also INDIANS--Treaties;
names of treaties

Bartlett--New. See index p485-
486
TREATY OF FORT LARAMIE.
See INDIANS--Treaty of Fort
Laramie
TREATY OF GHENT, 1814
Borden--Portrait (1) p145-146
Collins--Story p194
Harlow--Story p180-181
Kraus--U.S. p325-326
Reader's--Story p89
TREATY OF MORFONTAINE, 1800
Life--Growing (3) p36
TREATY OF NEW GRANADA, 1846
Morris--Ency. p203
TREATY OF PARIS, 1898
Morris--Ency. p290
TREATY OF SAN ILDEFONSO,
1800
Hine--American p70
TREATY OF TABLE ROCK
-Oregon country, Indians
Case--Empire p269-281
TREATY OF WASHINGTON, 1871
Harlow--Story p330
TREDEGAR IRON WORKS, Rich-
mond, Va.
Dowdey--Experiment p17, 19, 22,
65, 129, 134, 162, 179, 182-183,
191, 356, 376-377, 405
Life--New (5) p137, 146-147
TREES
See also WOOD; types of trees
Handlin--This p139, 187, 287, 289
-Views of Frances Trollope
Trollope--Domestic. See
index p.xvii
"TREMONT HOUSE" (Hotel, Boston)
Lynes--Taste. p81-84, 123
TRENHOLM, GEORGE
Dowdey--Experiment p172, 364-
365, 399-400, 403-404, 414, 420
"TRENT AFFAIR, " 1861
Amer. Her. --New (8) p E294
Boardman--Civil p66-67
Collins--Story p212
Harlow--Story p314
White--American p46-49
TRICYCLES
Dulles--History p196
McClinton--Antiques p164-165
-1880's
Peck--Nineteenth n. p.
TRINITY CHURCH
-Boston, Mass.
Larkin--Art p285-286
-New York City
Viewpoints p147

TRIPOLITAN (TRIPOLI) WAR, 1801-
1805
Butterfield--Amer. p46-47
Kraus--U.S. p300-301
Morris--Ency. p131
-Decatur's exploit
Collins--Story p195
TRIST, NICHOLAS P.
Boardman--Jackson. p48-49
DeVoto--Year p473-475, 483-484,
510
Morris--Ency. p206-207
-Biography
Amer. Her. --New (7) p E254-
255
TROLLEYS
See also RAILWAYS
Davidson--Life (2) p72
Furnas--Americans p801-804
Handlin--This p295, 352, 371
-"Carnivals" (Amusement parks)
Cable--American p298
-Excursions
Dulles--History p221-222
-Houses
-Utah, c1890
Nation in motion p107
TROLLOPE, ANTHONY
, on Americans
Cable--American p141
TROLLOPE, FRANCES ("FANNY")
Larkin--Art p147-148
Lynes--Domestic. See index
p307
Lynes--Taste. p5-6, 10, 13, 50
Neidle--America's p35
Trollope--Domestic. See index
p.XVI-XVII
, on subjects, about America, etc.
See various subjects
TROLLOPE FAMILY
Trollope--Domestic. See index
p.XVI-XVII
TROTTING RACES
Dulles--History p141, 147, 226,
269, 279-280
"TROTTING WOLF" (Kiowa Indian)
Andrews--Indian leaders p140
TRUCKEE LAKE (DONNER LAKE)
DeVoto--Year p165, 303, 331-332,
339, 342-343, 408-430, 512
TRUMBULL, JOHN
Larkin--Art. See index p544
Nye--Cultural p282-283
TRUMBULL, LYMAN
Life--New (5) p56
, and Lincolns
Randall--Mary p181-186

-Biography
  Amer. Her. --New (7) p E255
TRUNKS
  Wilson--Folkways p142-144
 , of immigrants
    Marzio--Nation p138-140
TRUSTS
  See also MONOPOLIES; SHER-
  MAN ANTI-TRUST ACT
  Boardman--Gilded p52-53
  Harlow--Story p390-391
  Keller--Affairs p435-437
  Life--Reaching (8) p64, 69, 84,
  91-92
  Life--Steel (7) p17, 131, 133-135,
  137
  Reader's--Story p282, 284
TRUTH, SOJOURNER
  Boardman--Jackson. p120
  Gurko--Ladies p139, 207, 214-215
  Macksey--Book p112
  Reader's--Story p432
  200 Years (1) p268
  Tyler--Freedom's p458
  Warren--Pictorial p87-88
 -Biography
    Amer. Her. --New (7) p E255
TUBE, COLLAPSIBLE
 , First, 1841
    Robertson--Book p41
TUBERCULOSIS
 -Remedies
    Woodward--Way p306
TUBMAN, HARRIET ROSS
  Dolin--Great p105-110
  Life--New (5) p36
  Macksey--Book p54-55, 112
  Reader's--Story p432
  Sochen--Herstory p165-166
  Warren--Pictorial p86-87
  Young--Women p300-304
 -Biography
    Amer. Her. --New (7)
    p E255-256
    Young--Women p378
TUCKERMAN, HENRY
  Bode--Anatomy p190-191, 204-
  205, 208-211
TUDOR, FREDERIC
  Boardman--Virginia p72-73
  Boorstin--Americans p11-16
  Cable--American p94
 , and ice-shipping
    White--American p20-21
TUKE, WILLIAM
  Tyler--Freedom's p301
TUNNELS
 -Illinois, 1869

Nation in motion p75
-North Carolina, 1879
  Nation in motion p98
-Weber Canyon, Utah, 1870's
  Viewpoints p43
TUNNELS, RAILROAD
-Colorado, 1881
  Nation in motion p97
-Georgia, 1849
  Nation in motion p98
-Michigan, 1891
  Nation in motion p98
-New Jersey, 1856
  Nation in motion p98
-Virginia, 1851, 1853, 1858, 1869
  Nation in motion p98-99
-West Virginia, 1849, 1858, 1868,
1870
  Nation in motion p99
TURCHIN, NADINE, MADAME
-Biography
  Young--Women p378-379
TURKEYS
  Hunt--Life p220-221
-Shootings
  Partridge--As p29
TURNER, FREDERICK JACKSON
  Bartlett--New p401, 421-422, 444-
  446
  Hine--American. See index p370
 , on closed frontiers, 1890
    Amer. Her. --90's p87
-"The significance of the frontier
in American history, " 1893
  Heffner--Doc. p169-177
-"To the frontier, " an epitaph
for old West
  Amer. Her. --New (9) p776
TURNER, JONATHAN BALDWIN
  Furnas--Americans p542, 686-687
  Portraits--Americans p132
TURNER, NAT
 -Biography
    Amer. Her. --New (7) p E256
 -Insurrections
    Carman--History (1) p533-534,
    591
    Tyler--Freedom's p487-488
"TURNERS" (Cabinet makers)
  Wilson--Early p65-67
TURNPIKES
  See also HIGHWAYS; ROADS
  Amer. Her. --New (5) p429-431
  Bartlett--New p281-284
  Boardman--Jackson. p93-94
  Boardman--Virginia p86-87
  Turner--Young p76-77
 -1811-1818

Morris--Ency. p421
"TURNVEREINE" (German social-
athletic societies)
Weisberger--Amer. p123, 126,
129, 132, 140-141
TUSKEGEE INSTITUTE
See also WASHINGTON,
BOOKER T.
Commager--Heritage p924-928
Furnas--Americans p850-852
"TUSTENNUGGEE EMATHLA"
(Creek Indian)
Andrews--Indian leaders p63
TVERSKOY, pseud. See
DEMENS, P. A.
TWACHTMAN, JOHN H.
Larkin--Art p304-306; see also
index p544
TWAIN, MARK. See CLEMENS,
SAMUEL LANGHORNE
TWEED, WILLIAM MARCY
("BOSS")
See also TAMMANY HALL;
"TWEED RING"
Amer. Her.--New (11) p913-914
Boardman--Civil p115-116
Butterfield--Amer. p205-207
Carman--History (1) p707-709
Carman--History (2) p8-10
Harlow--Story p421-422, 446-447
Keller--Affairs p49, 120, 242-
243, 257-258, 264, 269
Life--Steel (7) p18-21, 24
-Biography
Amer. Her.--New (11) p E402-
403
-Nast cartoon
Viewpoints p88
"TWEED RING"
Boardman--Civil p115-116
Cook--City p194
Harlow--Story p421-422
Morris--Ency. p250
Reader's--Story p361
TYLER, ADELINE, SISTER
Young--Women p53-54
-Biography
Young--Women p379
TYLER, JOHN
Amer. Her.--New (6) p E219
Boardman--Jackson. p33-37
Butterfield--Amer. p106
Carman--History (1) p449, 451-
452, 562-563
Harlow--Story p237-238, 267-268
Life--Sweep (4) p47, 80-81, 84-86
Morris--Ency. See index p773
200 Years (1) p332-333

-Biography
Morris--Ency. p724
Whitney--American p95-100
-Cabinet
Carman--History (1) p789-790
-Escape, from cannon explosion
Garrison--Lost p120-122
-Presidency
Garrison--Lost p30-33
Linton--Bicentennial p116-125
Reader's--Story p333
TYLER, JULIA
Melick--Wives p32-33
TYLER, LETITIA
Melick--Wives p31
TYPEWRITERS
Boardman--Civil p147
Boardman--Gilded p57
Dreppard--Pioneer p90
Marzio--Nation p538-544
Partridge--As p117
Reader's--Story p266
Train--Story p335-336
Walker--Every. p53-54
Wilson--American p252-255
Woodward--Way p326
, and Lilian Sholes
Life--Steel (7) p37
-Invention
Bonte--America p132
-Patent, 1868
Ross--Taste p298
-Remington
Marzio--Nation p539, 542-544
Wilson--American p253-255
TYPISTS
, Female, first (New York)
Robertson--Book p194
-Training course, first (New
York), 1877
Robertson--Book p194

U

"UNCLE SAM"
-Origin of nickname (Samuel
Wilson)
Boardman--Virginia p199-200
Burner--America (1) p164
"UNCLE TOM'S CABIN"
See also STOWE, HARRIET
BEECHER
Collins--Story p204
, and religion
Bode--Anatomy p186-187
-Staging, in opposition of author
Garrison--Lost p123-129

"UNDERGROUND RAILROAD"
  Amer. Her.--New (7) p E256-257
  Boardman--Civil p188-189
  Boardman--Jackson. p120-121
  Burner--America (1) p277-280
  Butterfield--Amer. p137
  Furnas--Americans p400-401
  Kraus--U.S. p446-447
  Life--New (5) p36, 82-83
  200 Years (1) p272-273, 309
  -1840
    Morris--Ency. p516
  -Historic houses (Wisconsin)
    Vanderbilt--Living p168
  -North
    Tyler--Freedom's p527-532
  , of Levi Coffin
    Commager--Heritage p489-493
  -South
    Tyler--Freedom's p532-536
UNDERTAKERS (funeral)
  Cable--American p174-175
UNEMPLOYMENT
  Bartlett--New p348
"UNIFORMITY SYSTEM OF
MANUFACTURE"
  Boorstin--Americans p30-33
UNIFORMS. See MILITARY UNI-
FORMS
UNION
  Life--Union (6) p7-9, 19, 70-71,
  80, 83
  -Army
    Life--New (5). See index
    p160
    Life--Union (6). See index
    p176
  , before Civil war
    Life--New (5). See index
    p160
  , during Civil war
    Life--New (5). See index
    p160
  , Integrity of
    -Views of Andrew Jackson
    Hurd--Treasury p59-61
  -Navy
    Life--Union (6). See index
    p176
  -Preservation
    Kraus--U.S. p357-361
    -Views of John C. Calhoun
    Hurd--Treasury p64-66
  -Southern states' readmission,
  1866-1870
    Harlow--Story p344
  -Views of Daniel Webster
    Commager--Heritage p616-618

  Wright--Every. p31-33
UNION LEAGUE
  -Views of Albion Tourgée
    Commager--Heritage p816-821
UNION PACIFIC RAILROAD
  Bartlett--New p289, 327, 330-331
  Brown--Westerners p167-188, 192,
  197, 223
  Dulles--United p39-40
  Harlow--Story p345, 366-367
  Hine--American p51, 144, 146-149,
  152, 279
  Keller--Affairs p165, 185-186, 387-
  388
  Langdon--Everyday (2) p358
  Lewis--Big. See index p. vi
  Ridge--America's p462-570
  Tunis--Frontier p142-143, 157
  -1876
    Randel--Centennial. See index
    p474
  , Building of
    -Views of Grenville M. Dodge
    Commager--Heritage p832-
    837
    Ridge--America's p562-564
  -Completion
    -Views of Alexander Toponce,
    1869
    Angle--American p357-358
  -"The hell on wheels," 1873, by
  John H. Beadle
    Ridge--America's p565-567
  -Labor problems
    -Views of Grenville M. Dodge
    Davie--Profile p164
  -"The race toward promontory,"
  by Grenville M. Dodge
    Ridge--America's p567-568
UNITARIANS
  Boardman--Virginia p172
  Carman--History (1) p504, 536
  Linton--Bicentennial p92
  Morris--Ency. p552
  Nye--Cultural p224-227
  -1876
    Randel--Centennial p443
  -Controversy
    Morris--Ency. p567
UNITED BRETHREN IN CHRIST,
1800
  Morris--Ency. p551
UNITED SOCIETY OF BELIEVERS
IN CHRIST'S SECOND APPEARING.
See SHAKERS
UNITED STATES
  , Destiny of
    Boardman--Virginia p204-205

-Growth (map)
  Kraus--U.S. p416
  Reader's--Story p75
U.S. ARMY
  Boardman--Gilded p94-96, 187-188
  Life--Growing (3). See index p176
  -Corps of Topographical Engineers
    Gilbert--Trail. See index p236
  -Topographical Corps
    Gilbert--Trail. See index p236
    Hine--American p74-76, 100
  -West
    Hine--American. See index p359
UNITED STATES CHRISTIAN COMMISSION. See CHRISTIAN COMMISSION
U.S. COAST GUARD
  -Legislation, 1843
    Nation in motion p132
U.S. CONGRESS
  Handlin--This p138, 149, 235, 263, 370, 384
  Whitney--American. See index p371
U.S. DEPARTMENT OF INTERIOR
  America 200 p45-49
UNITED STATES EXPLORING EXPEDITION
  Boardman--Jackson. p170
U.S. GENERAL HOSPITAL. See PATENT OFFICE HOSPITAL
U.S. GEOLOGICAL SURVEY
  America 200 p77-78
U.S. HOUSE OF REPRESENTATIVES
  Whitney--American p. viii, 37, 61-63, 69, 103
UNITED STATES MAGAZINE AND DEMOCRATIC REVIEW
  -"The Democratic principle"
    Grimsted--Notions p86-98
U.S. MILITARY ACADEMY. See WEST POINT
U.S. NAVAL ACADEMY. See ANNAPOLIS
U.S. NAVAL OBSERVATORY
  Reader's--Story p309
U.S. NAVY
  See also CONFEDERACY--Navy
  Boardman--Gilded p37-38, 186-187
  Life--Growing (3). See index

p176
-Gunboats (James River flotilla)
  Meredith--World p197-198
, on Barbary Coast
  Life--Growing (3) p60-61, 63
-"White Squadron, " 1889
  Collins--Story p274
UNITED STATES PASSENGER ACTS
  Marzio--Nation p121, 129
U.S. PATENT OFFICE
  See also PATENT OFFICE HOSPITAL
  Reader's--Story p258
U.S. POST OFFICE
  Boardman--Jackson. p100
UNITED STATES SANITARY COMMISSION
  Carman--History (1) p655
  Dannett--Noble. See index p418
  Harlow--Story p323
U.S. SENATE
  Whitney--American p84, 97, 129, 141, 150
U.S.S. MAINE. See MAINE (ship)
UNITED STATES STEEL CORPORATION
  Harlow--Story p391-392, 394
UNITED STATES TEMPERANCE UNION. See AMERICAN TEMPERANCE UNION
U.S. TREASURY DEPARTMENT
  Whitney--American p85-86, 194-196
  -Civil war
    -Women clerks
      Partridge--As p58-59
U.S. WAR DEPARTMENT
  -1870's
    Randel--Centennial p126-128, 270-271
U.S. WEATHER BUREAU
  Boardman--Jackson. p166
UNIVERSITIES. See COLLEGES AND UNIVERSITIES
UNIVERSITY SETTLEMENT SOCIETY
  Lynes--Taste. p157-158
UPHOLSTERERS. See FURNITURE
UPJOHN, RICHARD
  Boardman--Civil p169-170
  Boardman--Jackson. p163-164
UPPER CLASSES. See ARISTOCRACY
UPSHUR, ABEL P.
  Amer. Her. --New (6) p E219-220
  Kraus--U.S. p422-423
"THE UPSTARTS. " See "BOOSTERS"

URBANIZATION
See also CITIES; TOWNS
Boardman--Civil p111-116
Boardman--Gilded p68-69, 106-110
Boardman--Jackson. p180-182
Borden--Portrait (2) p39-44
Hine--American. See index p370
UTAH
See also MORMONS
Billington--Far p205, 212-217, 276
Brown--Westerners p60, 63, 140-143, 145, 185, 221, 224
Handlin--This p152, 309-310
Hine--American p107, 109, 111, 139, 175, 230-233, 301, 309, 325, 328
Life--New (5) p38-39, 54
-1876
Randel--Centennial p117-118, 151
-"The pioneer band reaches Utah," by William Clayton, 1847
Ridge--America's p512-515
-Salt Lake City
Tunis--Frontier p122-123, 138-139, 141
UTE INDIANS
Amer. Her. --Indians p306, 391
Andrews--Indian leaders p114, 166, 119
DeVoto--Year p54, 71, 196, 260-261, 324, 327, 376-377, 497
Gilbert--Trail. p97, 166
, Massacre by, 1879
Jones--Shaping p252-262
UTILITIES
-Westinghouse
Wilson--American p260-261
UTOPIAN SOCIALISM
Tyler--Freedom's p196-214
UTOPIAS
See also names of communities
Alden--Pioneer p223-225
Boardman--Jackson. p123-128
Carman--History (1) p526-530
Davidson--Life (2) p345-346, 372
Furnas--Americans p724-726
Hine--American p228, 234, 264-267, 324
Reader's--Story p320, 338
Tyler--Freedom's p46-224
Weisberger--Amer. p127-128
, of religious origin
Tyler--Freedom's p166-195

-Old Northwest
Tunis--Frontier p86-87
-Views of Odell Shepard
Miers--American p154-158

V

VACATIONS
Davidson--Life (2) p55
, and week-ends
Partridge--As p167
VAIL, ALFRED
Boardman--Jackson. p99-100
VAIL, THEODORE
, and telephone industry
Nostalgia p58-61
VALENTINE DAY
Walker--Every. p237-239
VALENTINES
Dreppard--Pioneer p62
VALLANDIGHAM, CLEMENT L.
Amer. Her. --New (8) p E294-295
Boardman--Civil p71-72
Butterfield--Amer. p174-175
Life--New (5) p115-116
VALLEJO, GUADALUPE
-"Life in California in the 1830's"
Ridge--America's p462-467
VALLEJO, MARIANO G.
Johnson--Pictorial p64
VAN BUREN, HANNAH
Melick--Wives p29
VAN BUREN, MARTIN
Amer. Her. --New (5) p E183-184
Boardman--Jackson. See index p212
Bonte--America p105
Borden--Portrait (1) p163-164, 170-171
Butterfield--Amer. p100-101
Carman--History (1) p443-448; see also index p. xxvii
Harlow--Story p231-233, 236, 284
Kraus--U.S. p254, 347, 354-356, 362-363, 366-370, 422, 435
Life--Sweep (4). See index p160
Morris--Ency. See index p773
200 Years (1) p328-329; see also index p351
, and Eaton affair
Phillips--That. See index p183-184
-Biography
Morris--Ency. p725
Whitney--American p81-87
-Cabinet
Carman--History (1) p789

-Clay letters
  Morris--Ency. p189-190
, on John Quincy Adams' election
  Commager--Heritage p609-611
-Presidency
  Linton--Bicentennial p108-114
  Reader's--Story p332
-Society during administration
  Carson--Polite p102
-Views of Charles Ogle
  Cable--American p102, 104
VAN CAMP, GILBERT
  Furnas--Americans p690-691
VAN DEURS, G., REAR ADMIRAL
-"Rickety flight deck, primitive
  plane...."
  Treasury Amer. p344-345
VAN ES, ELIZABETH
  Neidle--America's p269
VAN HORN, ROBERT THOMPSON
  Boorstin--Americans p131-132
VAN LEW, ELIZABETH
  Warren--Pictorial p110
, as Union spy
  Dowdey--Experiment p90-91,
  174, 307, 334-335, 337, 344, 433
VAN NESS, MARCIA BURNS
  Peacock--Famous p11-17
VAN VRIES, MARGARET HARDEN-
BROEK
  Neidle--America's p269
VANDERBILT, ALVA SMITH
-"The party," 1883
  Cable--American p274-275,
  308-309
VANDERBILT, CORNELIUS
("COMMODORE")
  Amer. Her.--New (10) p862
  Boardman--Civil p132-133
  Boardman--Jackson. p80-81
  Cable--American p274-275, 277
  Carman--History (1) p574, 704-
  705, 709
  Carman--History (2) p5-6, 85-87
  Dulles--United p56
  Harlow--Story p200, 388, 393-395,
  401
  Life--New (5) p17
  Lynes--Taste. p121-122, 131
  Randel--Centennial p18, 99, 169-
  170, 172-173, 423
  Wright--Ency. p104
-Views of William A. Croffut
  Burner--America (1) p346-350
VANDERBILT, WILLIAM HENRY
  Amer. Her.--New (10) p862-863
-"The public be damned"
  Butterfield--Amer. p234-235

VANDERBILT, WILLIAM K.
  Lynes--Taste. p121-122, 131, 139,
  142, 144
VANDERBILT FAMILY
  Furnas--Americans. See index
  p1012
-Homes
  -"Biltmore"
    Lynes--Taste. p121-122,
    131, 144, 211
  -"The Breakers"
    Life--Steel (7) p148-151
    Vanderbilt--Living p26
  -Mansion
    Ross--Taste p162
    Vanderbilt--Living p45
VANDERBILT (ship)
  Young--Women p184-185, 187
VANDERLYN, JOHN
  Boardman--Virginia p153-154
  Larkin--Art p130-131. See also
  index p545
  Nye--Cultural p283
"VAQUEROS" (first cowboys)
  Amer. Her.--New (9) p742-743
  Gilbert--Trail. p114-115
  Tunis--Frontier p127, 150
VARIETY SHOPS
  Dulles--History p98, 119-120, 217-
  218
VASSAR, MATTHEW
  Portraits--Americans p139
VASSAR COLLEGE
  Sochen--Herstory p184-187
-"Daisy chain"
  Cable--American p316-317
VAUDEVILLE
  See also VARIETY SHOWS
  Boardman--Gilded p170-171
  Dulles--History p119, 218-219
  Marzio--Nation p430
  Nye--Unembar. p167-169
  Reader's--Story p469
  Walker--Every. p163-164
-1880's-1890's
  Dulles--United p99
-1899
  Viewpoints p177
-Views of Edwin Milton Royle
  Harris--Land p180-190
VAUGHAN, CHARLES, SIR
, and Eaton affair
  Phillips--That p62, 86, 88, 113-
  114, 142
VAUX, CLAVERT
  Lynes--Taste. p32-33, 64, 99
VEGETABLES
  Van Wagenen--Golden p85-88

-Stands, New York (c1890)
Viewpoints p120-121
"VEGETARIANISM"
Alden--Pioneer p220-221
Furnas--Americans p439-441
VEHICLES
See also TRANSPORTATION;
types of vehicles
-1860
Life--America's p88-90
-1876
Randel--Centennial. See
index p475
VELOCIPEDES. See BICYCLES:
TRICYCLES
"VELOX"
Wilson--American p380
VENEZUELA
-Boundary dispute, 1895
Amer. Her. --New (12) p E441
Morris--Ency. p286
-Crisis
Dulles--United p162
VENTRILOQUISM
-Supplies, 1880's
Peck--Nineteenth n. p.
VERA CRUZ
-Capture, 1847
-Views of Raphael Demmes
Angle--American p243-246
-Expedition, by Scott, 1847
Morris--Ency. p205
-Mexican evacuation
Collins--Story p202
VERANDAS
Furnas--Americans p412, 422-
424
Lynes--Domestic. p247-248
VERMONT
Mussey--Old p71, 76-77, 100
VERTICAL RAILWAY CARS. See
ELEVATORS
VERY, JONES
Brooks--Flower. p182, 204-206,
227-228, 284, 293, 479
VESEY, DENMARK
Amer. Her. --New (6) p E220
VETERANS' PENSIONS. See
PENSIONS, Veterans'
VICE
Hunt--Life p171-187
-1876
Randel--Centennial. See
index p475
-Social evils, born in 19th
century
Langdon--Everyday (2) p274-
275

-"Vice unmasked, " by P. W.
Grayson
Grimsted--Notions p45-60
VICE-PRESIDENTS--U. S.
-List
Whitney--American p355-356
VICKSBURG (MISS.) BATTLE
Boardman--Civil p52-53
Collins--Story p214
Dowdey--Experiment. See index
p454
Harlow--Story p319-320
Jordan--Civil. See index p215
Kraus--U. S. p507-508
Life--Union (6) p40, 44-45, 61-62,
65, 81, 99
Young--Women p260-267
, and General Grant
Pratt--Civil p32-34, 42-44
-Views of Mary Ann Lough-
borough, 1863
Angle--American p325-328
-Women
Young--Women p257-269
VICTORIA, QUEEN
-Biography
Amer. Her. --New (11) p E403
"VICTORIANISM"
See also "GAY NINETIES"
Amer. Her. --New (11) p947-957
Life--America's p130-137
Life--Steel (7). See index p160
-Society of "Gay Nineties"
Life--Reaching (8) p24-27, 44-
47, 49-51, 56-57
VIELE, EGBERT L.
, on Norfolk occupation, 1861-
1862
Commager--Heritage p749-752
VIGILANTES
See also names of special groups,
e. g. "BALD-KNOBBERS";
"WHITE CAPS"
Bartlett--New p137-138
Boorstin--Americans p81-90
Furnas--Americans p377, 699-701
Keller--Affairs p225, 487-489
Watkins--Gold p244-245
Wilson--Early p15, 23
-Laws
Watkins--Gold p240-244
-West
Hine--American. See index
p370
-California--Committees
Johnson--Pictorial p114,
116, 118-119
-Montana

Hine--American p304-307
-Views of Nathaniel Pitt
Langford
    Commager--Heritage
    p582-585
-San Francisco, California
    Hine--American p302-304
VILLARD, HENRY
Boardman--Gilded p66-67
-The first major Colorado gold
discovery, 1860
    Ridge--America's p542-544
VINCENNES, INDIANA
Drury--Midwest p131-132
-Territorial capitol
    Vanderbilt--Living p153
VIOLENCE
See also CRIME AND CRIMI-
NALS; GUNS; RIOTS; VIGI-
LANTES; WARS, names of
wars and uprisings, massa-
cres
Jones--Age p375-376
Keller--Affairs p224-225, 486-
491
-West
    Hine--American. See index
    p370
    -Frontier writers
        Boardman--Jackson. p150-
151
VIOLINISTS
Furnas--Americans p582-583
VIRGINIA
See also RICHMOND, VA.
Carman--History (1) p634, 657-
664, 669-672, 747, 782
Furnas--Americans. See index
p1012
Handlin--This. See index p600
Hunt--Life. See index p297
Life--New (5) p94, 99, 118, 135,
148-149
-Civil war
    Dowdey--Experiment. See
    index p454
    Jordan--Civil. See index
    p215
    Life--Union (6). See index
    p176
-Drewry's Bluff
    Dowdey--Experiment p186-
    187, 325, 345, 348, 402
    -"Farewell to the Army of
    Northern Virginia, " 1865
        Angle--By p275
-Lexington
    Jones--Shaping p179

-1857
    Viewpoints p109
-Virginians
    Dowdey--Experiment p5-6, 9,
    18, 66
VIRGINIA CITY, NEVADA
Amer. Her. --New (9) p731
Billington--Far p256-258, 270
Dulles--United p37-38
Harlow--Story p362-363
Randel--Centennial p118-119
Vanderbilt--Living p199-200
Watkins--Gold p68-75, 77-78, 224
-Amusements
    Dulles--History p169-174, 231
-Life
    Watkins--Gold p76-78
-Views of Mark Twain
    Commager--Heritage p715-719
"VIRGINIA DYNASTY." See
ADAMS, JOHN; JEFFERSON,
THOMAS; MONROE, JAMES
VIRGINIA MILITARY INSTITUTE
Jones--Shaping p179-189
"VIRGINIUS" (ship)
-Cuban incident, 1873
    Morris--Ency. p281
VITAL STATISTICS
-Shattuck's Tables, 1846
    Portraits--Americans p66
"VOLUNTEERS, MISSOURI
MOUNTED" (1st & 2nd)
DeVoto--Year. See index p524
VON HUBNER, BARON
, on America, 1873
    Davie--Profile p386, 388
VON OLNHAUSEN, MARY PHINNEY
See OLNHAUSEN, MARY
PHINNEY VON
VOORHEES, DANIEL WOLSEY
Butterfield--Amer. p263
VOTING. See ELECTIONS;
SUFFRAGE

W

W. C. T. U. See WOMAN'S CHRIS-
TIAN TEMPERANCE UNION
"WA-BAUN-SEE" (Pottawatomie
Indian)
    Viewpoints p104
WADDELL, WILLIAM B.
Billington--Far p273-276, 285-291
Brown--Westerners p152, 157-159,
163-164, 166, 186
"WADDIES. " See COWBOYS
WADE, BENJAMIN FRANKLIN

("BLUFF BEN")
Amer. Her. --New (8) p E295
Lewis--It p13-30
Life--Union (6) p111-113
WADE-DAVIS BILL, 1864
Boardman--Civil p76-77
Borden--Portrait (2) p4-5
Morris--Ency. p246
WAGES
See also PRICES
Handlin--This p212, 258, 363,
367-369
Hunt--Life p98-101
-1850's
Boardman--Civil p127
, Miners'
Watkins--Gold p36, 67, 69, 88,
171, 176, 211-215
"WAGON DOCTORS" (repair men)
Wilson--Early p115
WAGON ROADS. See ROADS,
Wagon
WAGON TRAINS
See also RUSSELL, MAJORS,
AND WADDELL
Bartlett--New p295, 298
Boardman--Jackson. p53-54, 72-73
, Emigrant
Marzio--Nation p174-175
, First in California, 1849
Davie--Profile p152-155
-Freighting, 1876
Randel--Centennial p161-163
-Hardships
200 Years (1) p303
-Organization
Tunis--Frontier p115-116
-West
Train--Story p311-312
WAGONS
See also CONESTOGA WAGONS;
"WINDSHIP WAGONS"
Bartlett--New p290-294
Boorstin--Americans p56
Van Wagenen--Golden p116-121
, Covered
Schwartz--When p18
Wilson--Vanish. p168
, Delivery
Wilson--Vanish. p132
, Farm
Wilson--Vanish. p28-29
, "Mover"
-"Turn back Eastward, " 1887
-Views of William Allen
White
Commager--Heritage
p875-876

-Wagon works
Wilson--Vanish. p131
-"Wagoners"
Langdon--Everyday (2) p76-79
, Westward
200 Years (1) p206-207
WAITE, MORRISON REMICK
Morris--Ency. p468
Randel--Centennial p205, 220, 236,
277-278
-Biography
Morris--Ency. p726
"WAKE CHAI" (Sauk Indian)
Andrews--Indian leaders p79
WALD, LILLIAN D.
Dolin--Great p162-172
Warren--Pictorial p148-149
-Biography
Amer. Her. --New (12) p E442
WALES, PRINCE OF
-Visit to New York, 1860
Viewpoints p24
WALKER, ADAM
, on Battle of Tippecanoe Creek,
1811
Angle--American p171-174
WALKER, DAVID
Tyler--Freedom's p484-485
WALKER, ELKANAH
Ross--Heroines. See index p181
Ross--Westward p56-75
WALKER, FRANCIS A.
Randel--Centennial p19, 189-192
WALKER, JAMES
-Biography
Amer. Her. --New (7) p E257
WALKER, JOSEPH REDDEFORD
Gilbert--Trail. See index p236
WALKER, LEROY POPE
Dowdey--Experiment. See index
p455
Life--New (5) p133-134
WALKER, MARY E., DR.
Adelman--Famous p204-205
Warren--Pictorial p109
Young--Women p319-320
-Biography
Young--Women p380
WALKER, MARY RICHARDSON
Ross--Heroines. See index
p181
Ross--Westward p53-76
WALKER, ROBERT J.
Boardman--Jackson. p38-39
Life--New (5) p69, 74-75
WALKER, SARAH
Macksey--Book p170-171
WALKER, WILLIAM

Amer. Her. --New (6) p E220
Chase--America's p194-197, 200-
202, 204-205
-Filibustering expeditions, 1855
Morris--Ency. p219
-"Origin of the missionary
invasion," 1833
Ridge--America's p447-448
WALKING
-1876
Randel--Centennial p41-42, 79
, in migrations
Marzio--Nation p161, 164
, to school
Wilson--Vanish. p78
WALL COVERINGS
-1876
Hilton--Way p18
WALL PAINTINGS
Larkin--Art p226-227
WALL STREET. See NEW YORK
CITY--Wall Street
WALLACE, LEWIS ("LEW")
Mott--Golden p172-174
-Biography
Amer. Her. --New (11) p E403
WALLACK COMPANY (theatrical
stock co.)
Blum--Theatre p3-9, 17, 27, 29
WALLA WALLA INDIANS
DeVoto--Year p55, 354
WALLING, GEORGE W.
-"Recollections of a N. Y. Chief
of police," 1888
Cook--City p197-199
WALLPAPERS
Langdon--Everyday (2) p238-239
WALSH, R. , REV.
, on slave ship
Commager--Heritage p449-454
WALTERS, HENRY
-Biography
Amer. Her. --New (11) p E403-
404
WANAMKER, JOHN
Portraits--Americans p59
WAR
See also names of wars
, "Glory" of
Sochen--Herstory p158-159
, Offensive and defensive
Tyler--Freedom's p409-411
"WAR HAWKS," 1811-1812
Boardman--Virginia p36-37, 40,
54
Butterfield--Amer. p52-53
Harlow--Story p175-177
Kraus--U. S. p317-321

Morris--Ency. p140
WAR OF 1812
Alden--Pioneer p153-156
America's Hist. p313-321
Boardman--Virginia p36-49, 71-
73, 114-115, 198-199
Bonte--America p89-95
Butterfield--Amer. p54-67
Carman--History (1) p346-357
Commager--Heritage p231-249
Harlow--Story p175-181
Kraus--U. S. p321-326
Linton--Bicentennial p70-77
Maurois--Illus. p112-113
Miers--American p148-154
Morris--Ency. p141-153
Mussey--Old p25-26
Reader's--Story p86-89
Tunis--Young p92-93
200 Years (1) p179-196, 220-221
Whitney--American. See index
p371
Wright--Every. p53-57
-British blockade
Morris--Ency. p144
, British Royal Navy in
Life--Growing (3) p100-106,
108-109, 112-116
-Castlereagh's proposal, 1813
Morris--Ency. p147
-Drive on upper Canada, 1813
Morris--Ency. p146
-East coast
Life--Growing (3) p102-104,
108, 116; see also index p176
-Madison, James
Bonte--America p89
-War message to Congress,
1812
Davie--Profile p270-271
-March on Washington and Dela-
ware
Morris--Ency. p150-151
-Military losses
Morris--Ency. p153
-Naval battles
Morris--Ency. p142-143
Reader's--Story p87
-Heroes and heroics
Treasury Amer. p162-171
-Niagara campaign
Morris--Ency. p142
-Northern campaign, 1814
Morris--Ency. p149
-Peace, 1815
Commager--Heritage p248-249
-Plattsburg (N. Y.) Battle
Collins--Story p189

-Resolution of Kentucky legisla-
ture, 1811
    Ridge--America's p262-264
-Russian mediation
    Morris--Ency. p147
-Seamanship and gunnery
    Jones--Shaping p61-76
-Views of George Dangerfield
    Miers--American p116-121
WAR OF SECESSION. See CIVIL
WAR
WAR WITH MEXICO. See
MEXICAN WAR
WAR WITH SPAIN. See SPANISH-
AMERICAN WAR
WARD, AARON MONTGOMERY
    Boardman--Civil p133
    Hilton--Way p155-158
    Portraits--Americans p54-55
"WARD, ARTEMUS," pseud.
(CHARLES FARRAR BROWNE)
    Boardman--Civil p155-156
    Furnas--Americans. See index
    p1012
WARD, ELIZABETH STUART
PHELPS
    Adelman--Famous p244
WARD, JOHN QUINCY ADAMS
    Boardman--Civil p162
    Larkin--Art p185-187; see also
    index p546
WARD, LESTER FRANK
    Boardman--Gilded p117-118
    Life--Reaching (8) p14-15, 17
    -Biography
        Morris--Ency. p726
    , on American life, 1860-1862
        Burner--America (1) p230-
        234
WARD, SALLIE
    Peacock--Famous p148-160
WARD, SAMUEL RINGGOLD
    -"Autobiography of a fugitive
    negro," 1855
        Grimsted--Notions p304-311
WARD, MRS. SAMUEL
    , on peace, 1815 (N.Y. city)
        Commager--Heritage p248-
        249
WARNER, ANNA BARTLETT (AMY
LOTHROP, pseud.)
    Adelman--Famous p178
    Mott--Golden p123-124
WARNER, CHARLES DUDLEY
    Randel--Centennial p349, 389-
    390, (facing)30
    -Biography
        Amer. Her. --New (11) p E404

-"What is your culture to me?"
    Trachtenberg--Demo. p336-349
WARNER, SUSAN (ELIZABETH
WETHERELL)
    Adelman--Famous p177-178
    Bode--Anatomy p136, 172-177
    Hart--Popular p95-96
    Mott--Golden p122-123
WARREN, JOHN COLLINS
    Boardman--Virginia p180-181
WARREN, MERCY OTIS
    Boardman--Virginia p140-141
WASATCH MOUNTAINS
    DeVoto--Year p153, 180, 301, 305,
    309-312, 332-333, 335, 497-500
WASHING MACHINES
    Dreppard--Pioneer p88
    Viewpoints p111
    Walker--Every. p229-230
    -1876
        Hilton--Way p25-26
    -Washboards
        Wilson--Vanish. p99
WASHINGTON, BOOKER TALIAFERRO
    See also TUSKEGEE INSTITUTE
    Boardman--Gilded p100-101
    Borden--Portrait (2) p15-16
    Furnas--Americans p850-855
    Life--Steel (7) p85, 98, 110-111
    Treasury Amer. p149-151
    -"The American standard," 1896
        Davie--Profile p119
    -Biography
        Amer. Her. --New (11) p E404
        Morris--Ency. p726
    , on negroes in Alabama, 1881
        Commager--Heritage p922-924
    , on racial prejudice
        Hurd--Treasury p118-120
    -Views of Samuel R. Spencer,
    Jr.
        Miers--American p248-253
WASHINGTON (State and territory)
    Boardman--Virginia p119-120
    Hine--American p95-96, 113, 266
    -Gold
        Billington--Far p243-246
    -Waiilatpu
        Ross--Heroines. See index
        p181
    -Women from New England
        Ross--Westward p116-117
WASHINGTON, D.C.
    See also WHITE HOUSE
    Boardman--Virginia p2-4
    Brown--Westerners. See index
    p288
    Davidson--Life (2) p113-115

Handlin--This p123-124, 138, 145-
146, 232-233, 374, 378
Hunt--Life. See index p297
Life--Growing (3). See index
p176
Life--New (5) p30, 34-36, 39, 96,
105, 128-129
-1800 (becomes capitol)
Life--Growing (3) p39
-1857
Cable--American p172-173
-Capitol
-c1846
Viewpoints p141
-1850
200 Years (1) p177
-Building
Landmarks--Liberty p12-
17
, Burning of, by British, 1814
Butterfield--Amer. p56-57
Collins--Story p192
Commager--Heritage p239-
243
Wright--Every. p54
-Views of George R. Glieg
Angle--American p180-
182
-Entertainment and amusements
Wright--Every. p64-67
, in Civil war
Dowdey--Experiment. See
index p455
Jordan--Civil p215
Young--Women p105-116
-Defense by ransom
Garrison--Lost p21-24
-Pennsylvania avenue, 1861
Meredith--World p85
-Society
Cable--American p83-85
Carson--Polite p96-107
Hunt--Life p64-67
-1800-1801
Wright--Every. p61-63
-Manners (etiquette)
Wright--Every. p67-68
-Views of Frances Trollope
Trollope--Domestic. See
index p.xviii
-Street cars (Railways)
Viewpoints p49
WASHINGTON MONUMENT
Boardman--Gilded p178
"WASHINGTONIANS" (WASHINGTON
TEMPERANCE SOCIETY)
Amer. Her. --New (6) p E220-221
Furnas--Americans p507-508, 510

Tyler--Freedom's p328-346
WASHITA BATTLE, 1874
Ridge--America's p576-579
WASHSTANDS
Train--Story p322
WASON MANUFACTURING COMPA-
NY (Springfield, Mass.)
Viewpoints p152-153
WATER AND WATER SUPPLY
Boardman--Virginia p195-196
Davidson--Life (2) p132-134
Furnas--Americans p454-455, 458
Van Wagenen--Golden p122-140
Walker--Every. p22, 113, 214
Wilson--Folkways p149-151
, of sodbusters
Tunis--Frontier p155-156
-Old Northwest territory
Tunis--Frontier p78-79
-Power
Furnas--Americans p303-304
-"Pump logs" (wooden water
pipes)
Van Wagenen--Golden p122-126
-Systems
Life--Sweep (4) p28, 30-31
-West
Hine--American p122, 124, 130,
157-158, 182-183, 186-189, 219,
233, 241
WATER CLOSETS
-1876
Hilton--Way p16-17
WATER COOLERS
Dreppard--Pioneer p76
WATER WHEELS
See also MILLS
Treasury Amer. p154-155
"WATER-WITCHES. " See
"DOWSERS"
WATERHOUSE, BENJAMIN
Boardman--Virginia p180
WATERMELONS
Wright--Every. p72
"WATERPROOF LIME"
Reader's--Story p261
WATERVILLE COLLEGE
Holzman--Stormy p23-24
WATERWAYS
See also CANALS; RIVERS
Amer. Her. --New (5) p407-421
Life--Growing (3) p141, 147, 156,
162-163, 165-167
-Routes
Bartlett--New p306-322
-Transportation
Walker--Every. p55-57, 113
-West

Langdon--Everyday (2) p90-114
WATKINS, HARRY
  Bode--Anatomy p3-6,9-10,12-13,18
WATSON, ELKANAH
  Boardman--Virginia p79
  Furnas--Americans p285, 474-
  475, 505
WATT, JOSEPH
  Case--Empire p179-190
WATTERSON, HENRY ("MARSE")
  Life--Steel (7) p104-105
WAUD, ALFRED R.
  Viewpoints p80
WAX
  -Modeling, women in
    Macksey--Book p203
  -Waxworks
    Furnas--Americans p562-563
WEALTH
  See also MILLIONAIRES
  Amer. Her. --New (11) p904-929
  America's Hist. p536-541
  Boardman--Gilded p153-155
  Cable--American p108, 301, 311,
  343-344
  Handlin--This p129, 143, 194, 239,
  243-244, 273, 277-279, 296, 391
  Harlow--Story p397
  Hunt--Life p230-232
  Lynes--Taste. p117, 121-122, 131,
  165-166
  Ross--Taste p250-251
  -1880's
    Keyes--Hope p272-280
  -1890
    Amer. Her. --90's p10-11
    Butterfield--Amer. p257
  -California
    Wright--Culture p164-167
  , Distribution of
    Keller--Affairs p373-374
    -Views of Frances Trollope
      Trollope--Domestic p1-3,
      243-244
  -"Gentility" and flamboyance
    Life--Steel (7) p138-150
  , "Gospel of," by Andrew
  Carnegie
    Amer. Her. --90's p84-86
    Davie--Profile p259
    Dulles--United p64-65
    Heffner--Doc. p154-165
  -Life
    Walker--Every. p69, 127-131
    -"Life of idle rich," 1890
      -Views of Ward McAllister
        Commager--Heritage
        p889-895

-"Rags to riches" dream
  Cable--American p314-315
, Sanctified
  Hart--Popular p160-161
-Society
  Life--Reaching (8) p44, 46-49
-Views of Andrew Carnegie, 1889
  Davie--Profile p259
-Views of Frances Trollope
  Trollope--Domestic p43, 243-
  244
-Women
  Ross--Taste p251, 253-254
WEAPONS
  See also GUNS
  -Civil war
    Jordan--Civil p44, 54-55, 63,
    68-69, 76, 80, 83, 96, 133, 141,
    151, 164-165, 183-184
WEATHER
  -1876
    Hilton--Way p160
    Randel--Centennial. See index
    p475
  -Rainfall
    -Kansas and Nebraska
      Tunis--Frontier p156
  -Views of Frances Trollope
    Trollope--Domestic. See
    index p. IV
  -Views of Samuel L. Clemens
    Hurd--Treasury p105-106
"WEATHERFORD." See "RED
EAGLE" (Creek Indian)
WEAVER, JAMES B.
  Boardman--Gilded p30-31
WEAVERS AND WEAVING
  Van Wagenen--Golden p255-256
  -Looms
    See also COMPTON, GEORGE
    Wilson--Vanish. p58
WEBB, ANN ELIZA. See YOUNG,
ANN ELIZA
WEBB, GEORGE JAMES
  Howard--Our p142-144
WEBBER, CHARLES W.
  Boardman--Jackson. p150
WEBER AND FIELDS
  Blum--Stage Profile 14
WEBSTER-ASHBURTON TREATY,
1842
  Amer. Her. --New (6) p E221
  Amer. Her. --New (7) p624-626
  Harlow--Story p239
  Morris--Ency. p185-186
WEBSTER, DANIEL
  Amer. Her. --New (7) p620-628
  Boardman--Civil p2

Boardman--Jackson. See index
p212
Brooks--Flower. See index p549
Butterfield--Amer. p66, 108-109,
141
Carman--History (1). See index
p. xxvii
Harlow--Story p231, 237-239, 256,
267, 278
Kraus--U.S. See index p. x
Life--New (5) p13, 34, 37
Life--Sweep (4). See index p160
Meredith--World p12-17
Morris--Every. See index p774
Mussey--Old p116-117
Our literary p47
Reader's--Story p67
Treasury Amer. p192-197
200 Years (1). See index p351
, and Northern industrialism
    -Views of Arthur C. Cole
        Miers--American p169-173
-Biography
    Amer. Her. --New (7) p E257
    Morris--Ency. p727-728
-Hayne debates
    Amer. Her. --New (5) p E184
    Boardman--Jackson. p11-14
    Collins--Story p176
    Harlow--Story p230-231
    Heffner--Doc. p97-103
    Morris--Ency. p168
-Memorial (near Franklin, N.H.)
    Vanderbilt--Living p22
, on conservation
    Reader's--Story p502
, on Constitution
    Davie--Profile p70-71
, on Harrison's speech
    Commager--Heritage p621-623
, on power of mind, ideas
    Hurd--Treasury p51-53
, on Union
    Angle--American p212-214
    Butterfield--Amer. p87-89
    Commager--Heritage p616-618
    Wright--Every. p31-33
-Speech, 1850
    Commager--Heritage p626-628
WEBSTER, NOAH
    Boardman--Jackson. p138-139
    Boardman--Virginia p166-167
    Morris--Ency. p563, 581-582
    Our literary p46
    -Biography
        Morris--Ency. p728
    -Educational campaign
        Hunt--Life p139-142

, on spelling reform
    Burner--America (1) p200-204
WECTER, DIXON
    -"History and how to write it"
        Treasury Amer. p394-399
WEDDINGS
    Cable--American p169-170
    Walker--Every. p37, 242
    -Anniversaries
        Cable--American p171, 200-201
    , Frontier
        Dulles--History p78-79
    , International
        Ross--Taste p256
WEED, THURLOW
    Holzman--Stormy p113-114, 197
    -Biography
        Amer. Her. --New (7) p E257-
        258
    -on Lincoln's cabinet
        Commager--Heritage p647-650
"WEEHAWKEN" (ship)
    Garrison--Lost p94-96
WEEMS, MASON LOCKE
    Amer. Her. --New (5) p E184-195
    Boardman--Virginia p143-144
    -Moral tracts
        Cable--American p130-131
    -Washington biography, and
    cherry tree story
        Hart--Popular p49
WEIGHT-GUESSING CONTESTS
    , at country fairs
        Partridge--As p46
WELD, THEODORE DWIGHT
    Alden--Pioneer p217, 225-226, 228
    Amer. Her. --New (6) p E221
    Boardman--Jackson. p118
    Furnas--Americans. See index
    p1013
    Gurko--Ladies p43-45, 48-49, 64,
    69, 116, 191, 272
WELLES, GIDEON
    Holzman--Stormy. See index
    p279
    Meredith--World p199
    -Biography
        Amer. Her. --New (7) p E258
    , on Lincoln's assassination, 1865
        Angle--American p338-342
        Commager--Heritage p668-672
WELLS, DAVID A.
    Life--Steel (7) p35-36
WELLS, HENRY
    Boardman--Jackson. p100-101
    Hine--American p140-141, 143
WELLS, HORACE
    Boardman--Jackson. p171

WELLS, IDA B.
-"A red record"
Harris--Land p147-158
WELLS, WILLIAM COOPER
, on life in Ohio, 1813-1840
Burner--America (1) p223-227
WELLS
Wilson--Vanish. p62
-Cisterns
Furnas--Americans p454-455
, Public
Partridge--As p132
WELLS FARGO, AND CO.
Boardman--Jackson. p100-101
Hine--American p143
Randel--Centennial p161-162
Reader's--Story p193
WELSH, HERBERT
, on good government movement,
cities, 1894
Cook--City p205-206
WESLEYAN FEMALE COLLEGE
(Macon, Ga.)
-Narrative of graduate, 1860's
Andrews--Women p286-302
WEST, BENJAMIN
Boardman--Virginia p151-154
Furnas--Americans p578-579
WEST AND WESTWARD MOVE-
MENT
See also special subjects, e.g.
RAILROADS
America's Hist. p480-515
Boardman--Gilded p27-28, 83-90
Boardman--Jackson. p60-67, 88-
90, 153-154, 185-186; see also
index p212
Boardman--Virginia p35-36, 55-
56, 75-77, 93-110, 166-167
Carman--History (1) p358-384;
see also index p. xxviii
Life--Growing (3) p77-95; see
also index p176
Life--New (5). See index p160
Life--Steel (7). See index p160
200 Years (1) p236-263
Walker--Every. p88, 90-103
-1829-1849
Life--Sweep (4). See index
p160
-1890's
Life--Reaching (8). See index
p176
-Assimilation
See also RACIAL MINORITIES
Hine--American. See index
p359

, Conquest of, and Indians
Amer. Her. --New (9) p726-727
-Lawlessness
Amer. Her. --New (9) p727-
728
-Description
Jones--Age p83-89
-Exploration
Keller--Affairs p103-104
-Farmers and ranchers
Boardman--Civil p93-100, 176-
177
-Agricultural disasters
Jones--Age p91-92
-Fuel, lack of
Amer. Her. --New (9) p770
-Growth
Amer. Her. --New (10) p831-
876
-Land
Hine--American. See index
p365
Jones--Age p97-98
Keller--Affairs p386-389
, Language of
Kraus--U.S. p427
-Life
See also WEST--Society
Amer. Her. --New (6) p460-465
-Literature, post-Civil war
Our literary p124-125
-Migration
Alden--Pioneer p157-173
Amer. Her. --New (6) p454-468
America 200 p43
America's Hist. p360-366
Andrews--Indians p11-12
Butterfield--Amer. p39
Commager--Heritage p259-261
Dulles--United p34-35
Keyes--Hope p201-206
Train--Story p292-316
, Reasons for
Ridge--America's p3-5
-"Routes, 1830's," by Timothy
Flint
Ridge--America p289-292
-Trails, major
Reader's--Story p169
-Miners and Indians
Boardman--Civil p101-110
, Opening of
Amer. Her. --New (6) p510-529
-Pioneering spirit
Amer. Her. --New (9) p728-730
-"Ranch life in the far West,"
by Theodore Roosevelt
Jones--Shaping p219-234

-Schools. See SCHOOLS--West
, Separitism in
 Jones--Age p52-53
-Settlement
 Borden--Portrait (2) p44-45
 Hine--American. See index
 (under Settlement) p369
 Jones--Age p89, 97-98
 Kraus--U.S. p367, 422-423,
 434, 439, 449, 454, 457
 Tunis--Young p135-148
 -Social patterns in
  Jones--Age p96-97
 -Society
  Nye--Cultural p117-122
 , Stimuli to
  Amer. Her. --New (10)
  p849-850
-Wheat. See WHEAT--West
-Wildlife
 Hine--American p177-178,
 185-186, 331
-"Wildness, " end of
 Keyes--Hope p270-271
 Life--Steel (7) p50-59
WEST POINT (Military Academy)
 Boardman--Virginia p81
 Holzman--Stormy. See index
 p279
 Jordan--Civil p41, 45, 48-50, 59,
 63-64, 76, 90, 108
 Randel--Centennial p272
 -Clergymen
  Lewis--It p82-100
 -Dancing
  Life--New (5) p58
 , of Confederacy
  Jones--Shaping p179-189
WESTCOTT, EDWARD NOYES
 , and "David Harum"
  Mott--Golden p202-203
WESTERN DEVELOPMENT COM-
PANY
 Lewis--Big p295-296, 298, 304-
 306, 308
WESTERN FEDERATION OF
MINERS
 Hine--American p309
 Watkins--Gold p214, 217-221
WESTERN STAGE COMPANY
 Billington--Far p270, 290-291
WESTERN UNION
 Boardman--Civil p145-146
 Randel--Centennial p61, 179, 371-
 372
 White--American p65-67
WESTINGHOUSE, GEORGE
 Boardman--Civil p147

Life--Steel (7) p38, 48-49
 Nostalgia p47
 Portraits--Americans p85-86
 Reader's--Story p265, 267
 Wilson--American p256-263
-Biography
 Morris--Ency. p728
-Electric power
 Nostalgia p47-50
-Safety brake
 Wilson--American p258-259
-"War of the currents"
 Garrison--Lost p105-108
-Youth
 Wilson--American p256-257
WESTINGHOUSE UTILITIES
 Wilson--American p260-261
WESTON, EDWARD
 Randel--Centennial p41-42
WETHERELL, ELIZABETH. See
WARNER, SUSAN
WEYLER, VALERIANO
 Amer. Her. --New (12) p E442
WHALING
 Amer. Her. --New (7) p589-607
 Boardman--Jackson. p83
 Bonte--America p97
 Commager--Heritage p308-317
 Furnas--Americans p671-672
 Life--New (5) p40-47
 Mussey--Old p68-70
 Reader's--Story p182-184
 Wright--Every. p166-182
 -1825-1860 (New Bedford, Mass.)
  Amer. Her. --New (7) p590-591
 -1876
  Hilton--Way p28-29
 -Cutting and boiling
  Commager--Heritage p317-320
 -Harpooning, and art
  Life--America's p93
  -after harpooning
   Amer. Her. --New (7) p594-
   595
 -Implements
  Amer. Her. --New (7) p592
 -Preparation
  See also WHALING--Cutting
  and boiling
  Amer. Her. --New (7) p592-593
 -Travel and legends
  Amer. Her. --New (7) p596-597
 -Views of Henry T. Cheever,
 1850
  Angle--American p217-219
WHARTON, EDITH NEWBOLD
JONES
 Amer. Her. --New (11) p E404-405

Furnas--Americans. See index
   p1013
"WHATNOTS" (Bric-a-brac)
   Bode--Anatomy p51-59
   Wilson--Vanish. p88
WHEAT
   Bartlett--New p186, 196, 199-200
   Furnas--Americans p780-781
   Handlin--This p120, 125, 304
   Life--Steel (7) p35, 59, 128
   Van Wagenen--Golden. See
      index p279
   -1839-1840
      Boardman--Jackson. p89
   -Iowa
      , Farming in
         Harris--Land p230-233
      , Harvesting in, by Hamlin
         Garland
            Commager--Heritage p864-
            872
   -New York state
      Van Wagenen--Golden p66-68,
      76-78
   -Production, by state (1859,
      1879, 1899)
         Carman--History (2) p213
   -West
      Hine--American p116, 165,
      167, 169-170, 179, 194
WHEELBARROWS
   Marzio--Nation p171
WHEELER, CANDACE
   Macksey--Book p16
WHEELER, GEORGE MONTAGUE
   Gilbert--Trail. See p236
WHEELER, JOSEPH, GENERAL
   Amer. Her. --New (8) p E295-296
   Life--Reaching (8) p133-135
WHEELER SURVEY
   Gilbert--Trail. p186-187, 212-
   215, 223
WHEELOCK, JULIA SUSAN
   Dannett--Noble p199-200, 204-
   205, 233, 241, 284-285, 380, 386,
   388
WHEELS
   See also BICYCLING, etc.
   , Mill
      Van Wagenen--Golden p131-133
   -Velocipedes, monocycles, etc.
      Dreppard--Pioneer p302
   , Wooden
      Van Wagenen--Golden p118-119
WHEELWRIGHTS
   Van Wagenen--Golden p116-121
   -Wheel works (Arkansas, 1867)
      Nation in motion p78

WHIG PARTY
   See also "SILVER GRAY" WHIGS
   Alden--Pioneer p182, 187-188, 193,
   237, 240, 249-250, 253, 258
   Boardman--Civil p11-12
   Boardman--Jackson. See index
   p212
   Borden--Portrait (1) p171, 219
   Butterfield--Amer. p103-106
   Carman--History (1) p422-423, 444-
   452, 512, 562-563, 568-600, 608
   Handlin--This p199, 207-209, 244,
   247, 251
   Harlow--Story p233, 237-238, 267-
   268, 289
   Holzman--Stormy p34-35
   Life--New (5) p31-32, 34, 37-38,
   50, 53, 57, 71
   Life--Sweep (4). See index p160
   Linton--Bicentennial. See index
   p448
   Morris--Ency. p175
   Whitney--American. See index
   p372
   , End of
      Butterfield--Amer. p140
   -Gains, 1846
      Morris--Ency. p203-204
   -Grand, national banner, 1848
      Viewpoints p74
   -Northern "conscience"
      Butterfield--Amer. p117
   -Procession, Boston, 1840
      Commager--Heritage p618-621
   -Symbols of political reform
      Walker--Reform p80-82
WHIPPER, WILLIAM
   -Biography
      Amer. Her. --New (7) p E258
"WHIPPING POSTS"
   Wilson--Folkways p221
   Wilson--Vanish. p159
"WHIRLWIND" (Cheyenne Indian)
   Andrews--Indian leaders p147
   DeVoto--Year p171-172, 176, 256-
   257, 293
"WHISKY RING," 1873
   Amer. Her. --New (8) p E296
   Boardman--Civil p91
   Carman--History (1) p744
   Carman--History (2) p45
   Harlow--Story p347
   Morris--Ency. p251
   Randel--Centennial p201-207
   -Whiskey rebellion
      Bartlett--New p138-140
WHISTLER, JAMES ABBOTT
   McNEILL

Amer.Her.--New (11) p E405-406
Boardman--Civil p160-161
Morris--Ency. p603-604
Reader's--Story p384
-Biography
  Morris--Ency. p728-729
WHISTLES
, Alder (Maine, 1895)
  Schwartz--When p95-96
WHITE, ANDREW DICKSON
Randel--Centennial. See index
p475
-Biography
  Morris--Ency. p728-729
WHITE, BENJAMIN FRANKLIN
Chase--America's p196-197
WHITE, CANVASS
Reader's--Story p259, 261
WHITE, EDWARD DOUGLASS
-Biography
  Morris--Ency. p729
WHITE, ELIJAH, DR.
Billington--Far p84, 95-96
Boardman--Jackson. p53-54
WHITE, ELLEN G.H.
Warren--Pictorial p131
WHITE, HORACE
, on great Chicago fire, 1871
  Commager--Heritage p878-885
WHITE, OCTAVIUS
Hilton--Way p85-86
WHITE, STANFORD
Boardman--Gilded p143-144
Furnas--Americans p765, 771,
774-776, 818
Ross--Taste p164
WHITE, WILLIAM ALLEN
Butterfield--Amer. p287
-"Entirely personal," 1895
  Davie--Profile p364-367
, on "mover wagons" turning
eastward, 1876
  Commager--Heritage p875-876
, on Oklahoma
  Commager--Heritage p872-876
, on Populism
  Dulles--United p146-147
"WHITE CAPS" (vigilantes)
Keller--Affairs p487-489
"WHITE CITY." See COLUMBIAN
EXPOSITION, CHICAGO, 1890
"WHITE HEADED EAGLE." See
McLOUGHLIN, JOHN, DR.
"WHITE HOUSE" (Washington, D.C.)
Jordan--Civil p112-113, 209
Vanderbilt--Living p86-90
Whitney--American p345-351
Wright--Every. p65

-1807
  Viewpoints p140-141
, Burning of
  See also WASHINGTON, D.C.
    --Capitol, Burning of
  Phillips--That p14
-Dinners
  Carson--Polite p106
-Early years
  Phillips--That p3-4
-Redecoration, by presidents
  Cable--American p102
, Views of
  Angle--American p137-139
"WHITE HOUSE OF THE CONFED-
ERACY" (Richmond, Va.)
Dowdey--Experiment p108-110, 127-
128, 141, 156, 234
Jordan--Civil p26, 103
"WHITE WINGS" (street sweepers)
Wilson--Early p34
WHITMAN, ALICE CLARISSA
Ross--Heroines p67, 69-72, 92
WHITMAN, MARCUS
America's Hist. p365
Billington--Far p81-83, 104
Butterfield--Amer. p107
Hine--American p90-91, 94
Life--Sweep (4) p88-89, 91
Ross--Heroines. See index p181
Ross--Westward p24-50
Tunis--Frontier p114-118
-"Whitman's ride," 1842-1843
  Ross--Heroines p78
WHITMAN, NARCISSA PRENTISS
America's Hist. p365
Hine--American p90-91, 94
Ross--Heroines. See index
p181-182
Ross--Westward p23-52, 67, 110-
111
Tunis--Frontier p114-118
WHITMAN, WALT
Alden--Pioneer p253-255
Amer.Her.--New (11) p E406
Boardman--Civil p153
Carman--History (1) p543, 548-
550
Dulles--United p111-112
Harlow--Story p246
Hine--American p91, 94, 190, 320,
331, 339
Kraus--U.S. p372, 386-387, 434,
486
Life--New (5) p8, 10, 12, 62
Meredith--World p122
Morris--Ency. p568-569
Mott--Golden p109-112

Our literary p115
Randel--Centennial. See index
p475
, and Abraham Lincoln
Our literary p118-119
, and Herman Melville
Our literary p114-115
, as poet
Our literary p120-121
-Biography
Morris--Ency. p730
-"Democracy"; democratic
vistas
Commager--Heritage p828-
830
Trachtenberg--Demo. p351-
366
, Influence of
Mumford--Brown p31
-"Leaves of grass"
Our literary p116-119
-Letters on Civil war
Burner--America (1) p327-335
-"Mannahatta"
Cook--City p4-5
, on America
Larkin--Art p261
, on post-war society
Mumford--Brown p29-30
-Views of John Burroughs, 1863-
1871
Angle--American p428-429
WHITMAN FAMILY (Oregon)
Boardman--Jackson. p52-53
-Massacre, 1847
Hine--American p94
WHITNEY, ANNE
Warren--Pictorial p154, 157, 159
WHITNEY, ASA
Carman--History (2) p66
WHITNEY, CASPAR W.
-"Evolution of the country club"
Harris--Land p134-146
WHITNEY, ELI
See also COTTON GIN
Amer. Her. --New (5) p442-448,
E185
Boardman--Virginia p77-78
Boorstin--Americans p30-33
Commager--Heritage p445-446
Furnas--Americans p302-305
Life--Sweep (4) p12, 138
-Views of Nathan Miller
Miers--American p112-116
WHITNEY, HENRY M.
Portraits--Americans p86
WHITNEY, WILLIAM C.
-Navy reorganization, 1886

Morris--Ency. p258
WHITTIER, JOHN GREENLEAF
Amer. Her. --New (6) p E221-222
Boardman--Jackson. p149-150
Brooks--Flower. p396-403; see
also index p549
Harlow--Story p245
Hart--Popular p135
Morris--Ency. p569
Mott--Golden p109
Nye--Unembar. p103-104
Our literary p86-87
-Biography
Morris--Ency. p730-731
-Home (Amesbury, Mass.)
Vanderbilt--Living p16
WHITTLING. See WOOD CARVING
WHYMPER, FREDERICK
Watkins--Gold p144-145
WICHITA INDIANS
Brown--Westerners p82-83
"WICKLAND" (Home of Charles
Anderson Wickliffe; three gover-
nors) (Barstown, Ky.)
Vanderbilt--Living p120
"WIDE AWAKES" (Republican group)
Boardman--Civil p27
WIGGIN, KATE DOUGLAS
Adelman--Famous p269-270
WIGS AND WIGMAKERS
-Hairpieces, theatrical
Viewpoints p170
-"Perukers"
Wilson--Early p74
, Women's
Earle--Two cent. (2) p423-527
Ross--Taste p204
WILCOX, ELLA WHEELER
Adelman--Famous p259
Nye--Unembar. p123-124
WILCOX, HORACE C.
Bode--Anatomy p127-131
WILCOX, MARRION
-"North and south from the
Brooklyn Bridge," 1894
Cook--City p10
"WILD WEST SHOWS"
Boardman--Gilded p171
Marzio--Nation p425, 427
Nye--Unembar. p191-192
WILDE, OSCAR
-"The American man," 1887
Davie--Profile p383-384
WILDERNESS
See also FRONTIER
-Settlements
Commager--Heritage p273-
300

WILDERNESS BATTLE
Dannett--Noble p281, 283, 287,
302, 324
Life--Union (6) p16, 24-25, 59-
60, 84-85, 89, 105
WILDLIFE
See also types of wildlife
Furnas--Americans. See index
p1014
Hine--American p177-178, 185-
186, 331
WILEY, BELL IRVIN
, on Southern yeomen (Civil war)
Miers--American p197-201
WILKES, CHARLES
Amer. Her. --New (6) p E222
Boardman--Civil p66-67
Boardman--Jackson. p170
Morris--Ency. p233
-Biography
Morris--Ency. p731
-Expedition
Ross--Heroines p110-111
-"Suppression of the Americans"
Ridge--America's p470-472
WILKINSON, JAMES
Boardman--Virginia p28-31
WILLAMETTE RIVER AND VALLEY
See also OREGON
Bartlett--New p101-102, 322
Billington--Far p81, 84, 104,
114-115, 156-157
WILLARD, EMMA HART
Adelman--Famous p128-129
Boardman--Virginia p165-166
Furnas--Americans p741-742
Gurko--Ladies p62-63, 66
Harlow--Story p252
Heath--Women (4) p4
Life--Sweep (4) p61, 66
Macksey--Book p67
Neidle--America's p30
Reader's--Story p433
Tyler--Freedom's p251, 254,
429, 437
Warren--Pictorial p70-71, 137-
141
-Biography
Morris--Ency. p731
WILLARD, FRANCES ELIZABETH
Adelman--Famous p205-206
Boardman--Civil p190-191
Boardman--Gilded p156-157
Cable--American p298-299
Furnas--Americans. See
index p1014
Gurko--Ladies p261-263, 288
Heath--Women (4) p19
Macksey--Book p32, 276

Warren--Pictorial p137-139, 141
-Biography
Amer.Her.--New (11) p E406-07
Morris--Ency. p731
-Temperance crusade
Commager--Heritage p998-
1001
WILLARD, SOLOMON
Boorstin--Americans p17-18
WILLIAMS, WILLIAM (BILL)
Hine--American p54-55
Reader's--Story p164
Treasury Amer. p160-161
WILLIAMSBURG, VIRGINIA
, in Civil war
Dowdey--Experiment p9, 16,
178, 184
WILLIS, NATHANIEL PARKER
Nye--Unembar. p109-110
Our literary p21
WILLIS, SARA PAYSON ("FANNY
FERN")
Bode--Anatomy p214-216, 257
Hart--Popular p93-95
WILMINGTON, DELAWARE
, in Civil war
Dowdey--Experiment p145, 266,
268, 292, 327, 385, 391, 400
WILMOT, DAVID
Harlow--Story p283
Life--Sweep (4) p135, 139
-Biography
Amer.Her. --New (7) p E258
WILMOT PROVISO
Amer. Her. --New (7) p E258-259
Boardman--Jackson. p194-195
Carman--History (1) p599-601, 603
DeVoto--Year p208, 289-292
Harlow--Story p283, 286
Kraus--U.S. p433-434
Life--Sweep (4) p135-137, 139
Morris--Ency. p202
WILSON, BLUFORD
Randel--Centennial p205-206, 226
WILSON, FRANCIS
Blum--Stage Profile 28
WILSON, JAMES GRANT
, on Washington Irving, 1855
Angle--American p275-278
WILSON, SAMUEL. See "UNCLE
SAM"
WILSON-GORMAN ACT, 1894
Dulles--United p141
Harlow--Story p470-471
WILTSIE, CHARLES M.
, on Nullification
Miers--American p174-178
WIMAR, CARL
Amer. Her. --New (6) p E222

Hine--American p290-292
WINDMILLS
Bartlett--New p219-220
Marzio--Nation p156
Reader's--Story p114
Treasury Amer. p152-153
Wilson--Vanish. p60-61
-West
 Amer.Her. --New (9) p770
 Hine--American p157-158, 331
WINDOWS
Lynes--Domestic. See index p308
, Bay (oriels)
 Ross--Taste p147
-Screens
 Lynes--Domestic. p129-132
-Shades and blinds
 Dreppard--Pioneer p69
"WINDSHIP WAGONS"
Partridge--As p73
WINE
Marzio--Nation p597
-California, 1870's
 Johnson--Pictorial p166-167
-Italians in industry
 Marzio--Nation p362
"WINEMA" (Indian woman)
Ross--Westward p104-105
WINGFIELD, GEORGE
Watkins--Gold p169-171, 221
WINNEBAGO INDIANS
Andrews--Indian leaders p45, 76-77, 84
Boardman--Jackson. p71
WINSLOW, JOHN ANCRUM
Amer.Her. --New (8) p E296
"WINSOR CASTLE." See "PIPE SPRING NATIONAL MONUMENT"
WINSTON-SALEM, NORTH CAROLINA
-Historic houses
 Vanderbilt--Living p127
WINTER
-1886-1887
 Bartlett--New p233
 Ridge--America's p610-612
WINTER SPORTS
See also SPORTS AND GAMES; names of sports
Hilton--Way p98-100
"WINTERTHUR" (home of Henry Francis Dupont, Winterthur, Del.)
Vanderbilt--Living p76-79
WINTHROP, ROBERT
Life--New (5) p32-33

WIRELESS. See TELEGRAPH; WESTERN UNION
WIRT, WILLIAM
Amer.Her. --New (5) p E185
Boardman--Virginia p141
WIRZ, HENRY, CAPTAIN
Andrews--Women p218-220
Randel--Centennial p242-244
WISCONSIN
Carman--History (1) p374-377, 783
Handlin--This p204-212, 304, 365-366
Hine--American p100, 184, 190, 249-250, 257
-1876
 Randel--Centennial p107
-Green Bay
 Drury--Midwest p144-146
-Madison
 Handlin--This p211-213
-Prairie du Chien
 Drury--Midwest p147-148
WISCONSIN UNIVERSITY
Randel--Centennial p418-419
WISE, JOHN
Dreppard--Pioneer p99
Garrison--Lost p25-29
-"The West Point of the Confederacy"
 Jones--Shaping p179-189
WISLIZENUS, ADOLPH
, on "The Rendezvous," 1839
 Angle--American p223-226
WISTAR, ISAAC JONES
Commager--Heritage p511-516
WISTER, OWEN
Hine--American p138, 268, 270-272, 278, 280, 282, 294, 342
-Biography
 Amer.Her. --New (11) p E407
WITTENMYER, ANNIE TURNER
Dannett--Noble p311-312, 340, 342, 388-390, 393
Young--Women. See index p389
-Biography
 Young--Women p380-381
WITTKE, CARL
, on immigrants
 Miers--America p244-248
WIVES
See also OREGON--Missionaries; SEATTLE, WASHINGTON-- Brides
, Confederate
 Dowdey--Experiment p65-66, 69, 84
, in nursing

Dowdey--Experiment p88,
93, 241
"WOBBLIES." See I. W. W.
(INDUSTRIAL WORKERS OF THE
WORLD)
WOLCOTT, EDWARD OLIVER
Portraits--American p18
WOLFE, CATHERINE LORILLARD
Adelman--Famous p198
WOLFE, ELSIE DE
Ross--Taste p139-143
WOMACK, ROBERT ("CRAZY
BOB")
Watkins--Gold p98-100
WOMAN'S CHRISTIAN TEMPER-
ANCE UNION (W. C. T. U.)
Amer. Her. --New (11) p E407
Cable--American p298-299
Dannett--Noble p390
Furnas--Americans. See index
p1014
Life--Reaching (8) p39
Macksey--Book p32, 276
Sochen--Herstory p180-181
Walker--Every. p143-144
Warren--Pictorial p137-139
-Founding, by Frances Willard,
1874
Commager--Heritage p998
WOMAN'S STATE TEMPERANCE
SOCIETY OF NEW YORK
Gurko--Ladies p157-158, 163-164
WOMEN
See also GIRLS; "LADIES'
WAR"; names of organizations
Bartlett--New p149, 349-358
Boardman--Gilded p155-157
Boardman--Jackson. See index
p212
Boardman--Virginia p77, 121,
164-166, 183-184, 193
Carson--Polite p91-93
Furnas--Americans. See index
p1014
Harris--Land p191-214
Hunt--Life p73-84
Reader's--Story p429-434
Ross--Taste p255
Trollope--Domestic. See index
p. xviii
-1800
Boardman--Virginia p183-184
-1800-1880's
Ross--Taste p279-280
-1876
Hilton--Way p112-129; see
also index p216
Randel--Centennial. See

index p475
-1890's
Dulles--United p102-104
-19th century, late
Keller--Affairs p442-443
-Abolitionists. See ABOLITION-
ISTS--Women; AMERICAN ANTI-
SLAVERY SOCIETY, Women in;
ANTISLAVERY MOVEMENT--
Women
-Activities
Lynes--Domestic. See index
p308
Ross--Taste p295
, Increased freedom in
Life--Reading (8) p44, 51,
55-56
, and mining camps
See also GOLD MINES AND
MINING--Camps--Women,
Lack of
, and war
Sochen--Herstory p160-166
-Antislavery movement. See
ANTISLAVERY MOVEMENT--
Women
-Architectures--Greek revival.
See ARCHITECTURE--Greek
revival, and women
-Art. See ART--Women
, as citizens
-Views of Susan B. Anthony
Hurd--Treasury p101-102
-Astronomy and astronomers.
See ASTRONOMY AND ASTRON-
OMERS--Women
, Attitude toward
Handlin--This p306
-Authors. See AUTHORS--
Women; AUTHORS--Best
sellers--Women
-Baths and bathing, Beach. See
BATHS AND BATHING. Beach
--Women
-Bicycling. See BICYCLING--
Women
-Blacks. See NEGROES--Women
-Boarding houses. See BOARD-
ING HOUSES--Women
-Books and reading. See BOOKS
AND READING--Women
-"Boston Group." See "BOSTON
GROUP" (Women reformers)
-California, scarcity of
Life--Sweep (4) p137
-Childbearing. See CHILDBEAR-
ING
-Church. See CHURCHES--

Women, status of; RELIGION--
Women
-Cigarettes. See CIGARETTES
--Women
-Civil war. See also CIVIL
WAR--Women
, pre Civil war
    Young--Women p3-25
-Clothing and dress. See
CLOTHING AND DRESS--
Women
-Clubs. See CLUBS, Women's
-"Coldness"
    Cable--American p87
, College--first generation
    Sochen--Herstory p186
-Colleges and universities.
See COLLEGES AND UNIVER-
SITIES--Graduates; Students;
Women's--OBERLIN COLLEGE
-Columbian Exposition. See
COLUMBIAN EXPOSITION,
Women in
-Conversation
    Lynes--Domestic. p195
-Crafts and craftsmanship.
See CRAFTS AND CRAFTS-
MANSHIP--Women
-Crime and criminals. See
CRIME AND CRIMINALS--
Women
-Culture
    See also types of culture
    Handlin--This p390
    Wright--Culture p226-230
-"Declaration of Independence"
    Burner--America (1) p280-
    282
    Life--Sweep (4) p65
, Dominant
    Furnas--Americans p885-886
-Editors. See MAGAZINES
AND NEWSPAPERS--Women
editors
-Education. See COLLEGES
AND UNIVERSITIES, Women's;
EDUCATION--Women
-Employment. See LABOR--
Women; WOMEN--Occupations
-Entertainments
    Handlin--This p136
-Equal rights
    See also AMERICAN EQUAL
      RIGHTS ASSOCIATION;
      WOMEN--Suffrage; WOMEN'S
      RIGHTS CONVENTIONS; names
      of individuals
    Amer. Her. --New (6) p491

Boardman--Jackson. p127-130,
    188
Borden--Portrait (1) p191-194
Burner--America (1) p280-282
Carman--History (1) p523-525
Commager--Heritage p422-424
Davidson--Life (2) p376-377
Furnas--Americans p489-495,
    887-888
Handlin--This p199-200, 209,
    219-221
Harlow--Story p254-255
Life--Sweep (4) p64-66
Linton--Bicentennial. See
    index p448
Macksey--Book p21, 86-87
Reader's--Story p338, 431-435
Ross--Taste p296
Walker--Every. p54, 144-145,
    199-202
Warren--Pictorial p80
-1876
    Hilton--Way p123-128
, and Abigail Scott Duniway
    Ross--Heroines p166-171,
    173-178
-Early aspects
    Tyler--Freedom's p426-429
-"Observations on the real
    rights of women," by Hannah
    Mather Crocker
      Warren--Pictorial p69
-Views of Frederick Douglass
    Gurko--Ladies p102, 105,
    112, 231-232, 247, 280, 313
-Etiquette. See ETIQUETTE--
Women
-Explorers. See EXPLORERS--
Women
, Famous
    See also names of famous
      women
    Bonte--America p155
-Fashion. See FASHION--
Widows; --Women
-Femininity
    Carson--Polite p144-145, 150-
    151
    Gurko--Ladies p7-8, 10, 12-14,
    29, 37, 151, 220, 272-274, 304-
    305
-Feminists
    See also REFORM--Women;
      etc.
    Life--Sweep (4) p61, 64
, First white, to cross Rocky
Mts.
    Tunis--Frontier p114

, Frontier
    See also WOMEN--Pioneers;
    names of women
    Sochen--Herstory p112-115
-Gold mines and mining. See
    GOLD MINES AND MINING--
    Camps--Women, Lack of;
    GOLD RUSH--California,
    Women in; GOLD RUSH--
    Women in
-Hats. See HATS, Women's
-Health and dress
    Tyler--Freedom's p440-442
-Homemakers
    Hunt--Life p75-76
    Macksey--Book p15-16
-Hospital ships. See
    HOSPITALS--Ships--Civil
    war, Women in
-Hotels. See HOTELS, Women
    in
-Household labor. See
    HOUSEWORK--Women
    Walker--Every. p26-29, 34,
    81, 224-225, 229-230
-Ice skating. See ICE SKATING,
    1976--Women
, Ideal of
    Nye--Cultural p142-143
-Immigrants
    Handlin--This p107, 253, 256
, in communistic and religious
    groups
    Tyler--Freedom's p442-443
, in domestic service
    Reader's--Story p430-431
, in factories
    See also LABOR--Women;
    WOMEN--Millworkers
    Amer. Her. --New (2) p427-
    429
    Cable--American p94
    Reader's--Story p429-430
, in "genteel" era
    Carson--Polite p142-162
, in slave states
    Hunt--Life p44
, in trade
    Macksey--Book p164-166
, in war
    See also WOMEN, and war
    Macksey--Book p55
-Indian relations. See INDIANS
    --Crusade for, by women;
    INDIANS--Women; , Captives by
-Intelligence
    Gurko--Ladies p7, 11-14, 18,
    29, 69, 78, 106, 109, 127, 199,

303-304
    Hilton--Way p113-114, 125
-Inventors. See INVENTORS--
    Women
-Jews. See JEWS--Women
-Journalists. See JOURNAL-
    ISTS--Women
-Kentucky
    Wright--Culture p77
-Labor. See LABOR--Women;
    WOMEN, under types of labor
-Labor unions. See LABOR
    UNIONS--Women
-Law and lawyers. See LAW
    AND LAWYERS--Women
-Legal status
    See also MARRIED WOMEN'S
    PROPERTY ACT OF NEW
    YORK
    Gurko--Ladies. See index
    (under Legal and economic
    handicaps of women)
    -Married women
    Keller--Affairs p468-470
    -Unfair laws
    Hilton--Way p126-128
-Leisure and prestige
    Furnas--Americans p486-487
-Liberals' support
    Tyler--Freedom's p450-452
-Limitations
    Cable--American p107
    -Views of John Todd, 1867
    Adelman--Famous p189-191
-Magazines. See MAGAZINES--
    Women editors; Women's
-Manufacturing. See MANU-
    FACTURING--Women
-Marriage. See MARRIAGE,
    Women, Legal position; WOMEN
    --Legal status; MARRIED WOM-
    EN'S PROPERTY RIGHTS
-Mayors. See MAYORS--Women
-Medicine. See MEDICINE--
    Books for women; --Women;
    MIDWIVES
-Middle class. See MIDDLE
    CLASS--Women
-Millworkers
    See also LOWELL TEXTILE
    MILLS--Women employees
    Furnas--Americans p476-480
    Harlow--Story p209-210
-Missionaries
    See also MISSIONARIES--
    Oregon--Wives
-Morality
    -Moral power, 1800-1860

Sochen--Herstory p119-151
-Mormons. See MORMONS--
Women
-Motion pictures. See MOTION
PICTURES--Women
-Mountaineering. See
MOUNTAINS--Climbers--Women
-Musicians. See MUSICIANS--
Women
-Negroes. See NEGROES--
Women
-Northwest. See NORTHWEST
--Women
-Novelists. See NOVELISTS--
Women
-Nudity. See NUDITY, of
women
-Occupations
See also CRAFTS AND
CRAFTSMANSHIP--Women;
WOMEN, Professional;
names of occupations
Boardman--Gilded p155
Furnas--Americans. See
index p1014
Life--Reaching (8) p38-39, 43
, on Oregon trail
Davie--Profile p149-150
-Painters and paintings. See
PAINTERS AND PAINTINGS,
Portrait--Women
-Physicians. See PHYSICIANS
--Women
-Picnics, 1876
Hilton--Way p51-52
-Pioneers
See also PIONEERS--Women
--West
Heath--Women (4) p3
Ross--Westward p172-195
-Life
Lynes--Domestic. p29-31
, Work of
Van Wagenen--Golden p63-
64
-Poets and poetry. See POETS
AND POETRY--"The women of
the South"
-Politics and statecraft
Hunt--Life p74
Macksey--Book p32-33
-Populism appeal
Keller--Affairs p573
, Post Civil war
Keller--Affairs p158-161
Sochen--Herstory p181-183
-Prairie life
Lynes--Domestic. p33-34

-Presidential candidates
Butterfield--Amer. p217
Warren--Pictorial p131-133
, Professional
Reader's--Story p436-437
Sochen--Herstory p101-106
Tyler--Freedom's p429-435
-Prudery. See PRUDERY--
Women
-Public speakers
Furnas--Americans p479-480,
491
Gurko--Ladies. See index
(under Public speaking) p325
-Recreation, early 1800's
See also WOMEN--Amusements;
--Sports and games
Dulles--History p95-98, 151
-Reform. See "BOSTON GROUP"
(women reformers); REFORM
AND REFORMERS--Women
-Religion. See RELIGION--
Women
-Resorts. See RESORTS--Women
-Rights. See WOMEN--Equal
rights; --Legal status
, Role of
Handlin--This p119, 181, 194,
236-239, 273-275, 304-305, 380
, Self-made
Furnas--Americans p893
, Self-support of
Carson--Polite p192
-Silliness, freedom from
Lynes--Domestic. p60-61
-Singers. See SINGERS--Women
-Social status
Gurko--Ladies p4, 6-9, 26, 87-
88, 97, 174, 178, 276, 303, 305,
309
-Social work
Life--Reaching (8) p39
-South. See SOUTH--Women
, Sporting. See IDAHO--Sporting
women
-Sports and games. See SPORTS
AND GAMES--Women
-Stockbrokers. See STOCKBROK-
ERS--Women
-Suffrage
See also names of suffrage
organizations; names of
leaders
Butterfield--Amer. p216-217
Cable--American p264-265
Dannett--Noble p389-390
Furnas--Americans p887
Gurko--Ladies. See index p327

Hilton--Way p126-127
Life--Reaching (8) p42, 56
Life--Sweep (4) p65
Macksey--Book p86-87
200 Years (2) p88-89
Warren--Pictorial p114-122;
see also index p228
-1876
  Hilton--Way p126-127
-Kansas amendment
  Warren--Pictorial p114-
  115
-Split in movement
  Gurko--Ladies p120, 193,
  223-229, 231-237
-State laws, 1869-1896
  Warren--Pictorial p142
-Suffragettes
  Life--Steel (7) p16, 77
-Utah
  Bartlett--New p358
-Views of Susan B. Anthony,
1873
  Davie--Profile p121-123
-West
  Dulles--United p104
  Hine--American p174-175,
  328
-Wyoming
  Bartlett--New p357-360
  Warren--Pictorial p120-121
-Teachers. See TEACHERS--
Women; --Wages--Women
-Technology, Role in
  Reader's--Story p430
-Temperance movement
  See also WOMEN'S CHRIS-
  TIAN TEMPERANCE UNION
  Furnas--Americans p495, 636-
  641, 737
  Tyler--Freedom's p448-450
-Theater
  Dulles--History p104
  Furnas--Americans p564-565,
  567-568, 757-758
-Trade and traders. See
TRADE AND TRADERS--
Negroes--Women
-Travel and travelers
  See also names of women
  Carson--Polite p92-93
, Unfortunate
  Wilson--Early p183-184
-U.S. Treasury Dept.
  -Civil war
    -Women clerks
      Partridge--As p58-59
-Vicksburg. See VICKSBURG

(MISS.) BATTLE
-Views of
  See also CROCKER, HANNAH
  MATHER--"Observations on
  the real rights of women";
  CROCKETT, DAVY, on
  Lowell's women employees,
  1834
-Views of Chauncey M. Depew
(Toast to women)
  Hurd--Treasury p103-105
-Views of Frederick Marryat
  Burner--America (1) p196-200
-Washington (state). See WASH-
INGTON (state)--Women
-Wax--Modeling. See WAX--
MODELING, Women in
-Wealth. See WEALTH--Women
-West
  Hine--American. See index
  p371
  Young--Women p139-156
WOMEN'S CENTRAL ASSOCIATION
OF RELIEF, N.Y. City
  Dannett--Noble. See index p418
-Organization, 1861
  Young--Women p76
WOMEN'S CRUSADE
  Furnas--Americans p637-641, 737
WOMEN'S RIGHTS CONVENTIONS
  See also SENECA FALLS CON-
  VENTION
  Gurko--Ladies. See index p328
  Tyler--Freedom's p454
WOOD, FERNANDO
  Amer.Her.--New (8) p E296
  Butterfield--Amer. p174
WOOD, JETHRO
  Boardman--Virginia p79
  Harlow--Story p215
WOOD, JOHN TAYLOR
  Dowdey--Experiment p162, 187-
  189, 205, 324, 365, 412-413, 424,
  427-428
WOOD, LEONARD
-Biography
  Amer.Her.--New (12) p E443
WOOD, SALLY S.B.K.
  Warren--Pictorial p70
WOOD
  See also LUMBER AND LUM-
  BERING
  Bartlett--New p237-238
-1876
  Hilton--Way p160
, as fuel
  Van Wagenen--Golden p157-
  158

, Cord
Van Wagenen--Golden p159-
160
-Handicrafts in
Van Wagenen--Golden p141-
160
, in building
Boardman--Virginia p158
, Pine
Van Wagenen--Golden p113-
114, 124, 154-155, 159
-Woodpiles
Wilson--Vanish. p74
WOOD CARVING
Boardman--Virginia p156
Larkin--Art p103
McClinton--Antiques p255-256,
259-260
WOOD ENGRAVINGS
Larkin--Art p253-255
-Woodcuts
, First in "Penny papers"
Butterfield--Amer. p126
WOODBRIDGE, WILLIAM C.
Furnas--Americans p587-588
WOODBURY, ISAAC BAKER
Chase--America's p162-163
Howard--Our p148-149
WOODCOCK, THOMAS S.
-Eric Canal ride, 1836
Angle--American p195
WOODENWARE
Dreppard--Pioneer p270, 275,
277-278
WOODFORD, STEWART LYNDON
-Biography
Amer.Her.--New (12) p E443-
444
WOODHULL, VICTORIAL CLAFLIN
Butterfield--Amer. p217
Furnas--Americans p643-646
Gurko--Ladies p230, 243-249, 287
Jones--Age p10, 120-121
Lynes--Domestic. p177-178
Macksey--Book p163
Sochen--Herstory p177-178
Warren--Pictorial p131-132
"WOODLAWN" (Black House,
Ellsworth, Me.)
Vanderbilt--Living p19
WOODS, DANIEL B.
, on gold mines; life in diggings,
1849
Davie--Profile p156-157
WOODSMEN. See FRONTIERSMEN
WOODWARD, C. VANN
Furnas--Americans p754, 847-
848

WOODWARD, CHARLOTTE
Gurko--Ladies p99-100, 102
WOODWORTH, SAMUEL
Boardman--Jackson. p158-159
-Favorite songs
Grimsted--Notions p25-37
WOODWORTH, SELIM
DeVoto--Year p115, 412-413, 417,
419, 422-426, 428-429
WOOL, JOHN ELLIS
-Biography
Amer.Her.--New (7) p E259
WOOL
See also SHEEP; SPINNING AND
SPINNING WHEELS
Handlin--This p125-126, 147, 166-
167, 316
Langdon--Everyday (2) p250-255
Van Wagenen--Golden. See index
p280
-Carding
Van Wagenen--Golden p261-
263, 265
Wilson--Vanish. p56
WOOLSEY, ABBY HOWLAND
Dannett--Noble p29, 31, 122, 130,
196, 263, 278, 280, 355, 373, 391, 393
WOOLSEY, CAROLINE C.
Dannett--Noble p124, 130, 192-193,
264, 277, 304, 358-360, 363-364,
373
WOOLSEY, CHARLES WILLIAM,
JR.
Dannett--Noble p30-31, 43, 75, 77,
126-130, 133, 167-168, 259, 355,
365
WOOLSEY, GEORGEANNA M.
("GEORGY")
Dannett--Noble. See index p419
Young--Women p179, 184-185, 289-
291, 307
WOOLSEY, HARRIET ROOSEVELT
("HATTY")
Dannett--Noble p126, 131, 192, 265,
279, 305, 358-360, 375
WOOLSEY, JANE NEWTON STUART
Dannett--Noble p30-31, 120, 126,
133, 247, 264, 277, 354, 360, 365,
373, 385
WOOLSEY FAMILY
-Biography
Young--Women p381-382
WOOLSON, CONSTANCE FENIMORE
Adelman--Famous p197
Our literary p138
WOOLWORTH, FRANK W.
Nostalgia p36-39
Portraits--Americans p47-48

"WOOLWORTH'S"
-Building, New York city
Furnas--Americans p769
-First stores
Portraits--Americans p47
WOOSTER COLLEGE (Wooster, O.)
Boorstin--Americans p157
WORCESTER, NOAH
Tyler--Freedom's p401-402
WORCESTER, SAMUEL AUSTIN
Amer.Her.--New (5) p E185
WORCESTER VS. GEORGIA
Amer.Her.--New (5) p397-398;
E185
WORDSWORTH, WILLIAM
Brooks--Flower. See index
p550
WORK, HENRY CLAY
Chase--America's p180
Howard--Our p266-268
WORK. See LABOR
WORKINGMEN'S PARTY (1828-
1830)
See also LABOR--Women
Boardman--Jackson. p85-86
Butterfield--Amer. p95
Morris--Ency. p168
WORKMAN, FANNY
Macksey--Book p238-239
WORKMAN'S COMPENSATION
Keller--Affairs p401-404
WORLD ANTI-SLAVERY CON-
VENTION (London, 1840)
Gurko--Ladies p2-3, 48-51, 55,
68, 83-85, 92, 117, 158
-Women delegates
Warren--Pictorial p88-89
WORLD SERIES. See BASEBALL
WORLD'S COLUMBIAN EXPOSI-
TION (Chicago, Ill.), 1893
Bartlett--New p443-445, 448
Boardman--Gilded p179-180
Collins--Story p273
Life--Reaching (8) p83, 94-101
Reader's--Story p251
WORLD'S INDUSTRIAL AND COT-
TON CENTENNIAL EXPOSITION
(New Orleans, La., 1884-1885)
Reader's--Story p251
WORMELEY, KATHARINE
PRESCOTT
Adelman--Famous p237
Dannett--Noble p148, 152, 159-
160, 162, 187, 194, 196, 283,
392-393
Young--Women p177-178, 180-
184, 187-188, 290, 308, 311, 322
-Biography

Young--Women p382-383
WOUNDED KNEE CREEK MASSA-
CRE, 1890
Andrews--Indian leaders p164
Andrews--Indians p32-35
Boardman--Gilded p96
Tunis--Frontier p144
"WOVOKA" (INDIAN) (JACK WIL-
SON)
Andrews--Indian leaders p164
Boardman--Gilded p96
Hine--American p202
WRESTLING
Dulles--History p73, 171
WRIGHT, ELIZUR
Boardman--Civil p134-135
Portraits--Americans p69-70
WRIGHT, FRANCES ("FANNY")
Boardman--Jackson. p86
Boardman--Virginia p193
Furnas--Americans p489-491
Gurko--Ladies p32-33, 35, 44
Life--Sweep (4) p61
Neidle--America's p30, 33-37
Sochen--Herstory p149
Tyler--Freedom's. See index
p608
Warren--Pictorial p80-81
Wright--Every. p69
, and "Nashoba"
Tyler--Freedom's p206-211
, on Subtreasury (1838)
Walker--Reform p77-80
-Views of Frances Trollope
Trollope--Domestic. See
index p. xix
WRIGHT, FRANK LLOYD
Mumford--Brown p166-174
WRIGHT, GEORGE
Walker--Every. p155-156
WRIGHT, JOHN S.
, on Chicago, Ill.
Cook--City p44-45
WRIGHT, JONATHAN JASPER
Butterfield--Amer. p222
WRIGHT, MARTHA
Gurko--Ladies. See index p328
Life--Sweep (4) p64
WRIGHT, ORVILLE AND WILBUR
(WRIGHT BROTHERS)
-Early years
Wilson--American p344
-First biplane kite
Garrison--Lost p74
WRIGHT, PAULINA. See DAVIS,
PAULINA WRIGHT
"WRIGHTS" (Craftsmen)
Wilson--Early p74

WRITING. See PENMANSHIP
WYCKOFF, WALTER A.
-"The workers"
  Harris--Land p100-117
WYETH, JOHN
  Chase--America's p188-189
  , and "repository of sacred
  music"
    Lowens--Music p133-134,
    140, 142-155
WYETH, NATHANIEL JARVIS
  Billington--Far p58-59, 61-63,
  65, 72-73, 80
  Boardman--Jackson. p52
  Boorstin--Americans p13-14
  Gilbert--Trail p130-131, 134
  Portraits--Americans p122-123
  -"Failure of the first invad-
  ers," 1847
    Ridge--America's p445-447
  -"The first American invaders,
  1832"
    Ridge--America's p444-445
WYOMING
  Bartlett--New p114, 151, 243,
  338, 357-360
  Hine--American p113, 135, 174,
  270, 279, 328
  Life--Steel (7) p51-52, 55-56, 59
  -1876
    Randel--Centennial p141-142
  -Johnson county war (Powder
  River war)
    Hine--American p308
  -Pacific City
    Bartlett--New p359-360
  -Woman Suffrage amendment
    Warren--Pictorial p120-121

                    X

XENOPHOBIA (Denying foreigners'
  rights)
  Furnas--Americans. See index
  p1015

                    Y

Y. M. C. A. See YOUNG MEN'S
  CHRISTIAN ASSOCIATION
Y. W. C. A. See YOUNG WOMEN'S
  CHRISTIAN ASSOCIATION
YACHTS AND YACHTING
  Cable--American p277
  Davidson--Life (2) p70-71
  Dulles--History p142-143, 148,
  239-240
  Life--Reaching (8) p26-27, 46-47
  Reader's--Story p184
  Ross--Taste p96-97
"YAHA HATO" (Seminole Indian)
  Andrews--Indian leaders p72
YALE, CAROLINE
  Macksey--Book p73
YALE UNIVERSITY
  Tyler--Freedom's p255
  Wright--Culture. See index p275
  -Religion vs. radicalism
    Tyler--Freedom's p29-30
  -Views of Charles W. Eliot
    Hurd--Treasury p106-109
YANCEY, WILLIAM L.
  Life--New (5) p50-51, 89-91, 94,
  132
  -Biography
    Amer. Her. --New (7) p E259
"YANKEE CLIPPERS"
  Furnas--Americans p359-360
"YANKEES"
  Bartlett--New p118, 120-121, 123
  Mussey--Old p81-125
  -Use of word
    Marzio--Nation p142
"YARBS." See HERBS
YARROS, RACHEL SLOBODENSKY
  Neidle--America's p204-205
YAZOO LAND COMPANIES
  Carman--History (1) p326-327, 395
  Kraus--U. S. p310-311
  Morris--Ency. p138-139
"YELLOW BIRD" (Indian)
  Hine--American p371
YELLOW FEVER
  Boardman--Gilded p178
  Boardman--Virginia p179-180
  Hilton--Way p85-87
  Holzman--Stormy p18, 101-103, 135
  Hunt--Life p208-211
  Randel--Centennial p326-327
"YELLOW JOURNALISM"
  See also names of individuals,
  newspapers
  Furnas--Americans p857-863
  Harlow--Story p429-430
  Jones--Age p108-109
  Life--Reaching (8) p36-38, 40-41,
  130
  Walker--Every. p191-195
"YELLOWSTONE" (steamboat)
  Tunis--Frontier p111-112
YELLOWSTONE ACT, 1872
  America 200 p73-74
YELLOWSTONE NATIONAL PARK
  Gilbert--Trail. p55, 60, 190, 192-196

Hine--American p50, 179-181,
187-188, 285, 294
YELLOWSTONE RIVER
Boardman--Virginia p99-100
"YOHOLO MICCO" (Creek Indian)
Andrews--Indian leaders p64-65
YORKTOWN (VIRGINIA) BATTLE
Life--Union (6) p23, 27, 53-54, 70
YOSEMITE VALLEY
Gilbert--Trail. p108-110
Hine--American p184-188, 293
Viewpoints p110-111
-Discovery and naming
-Views of L. H. Bunnell
Davie--Profile p158-159
YOUNG, ANN ELIZA (ANN
ELIZA WEBB)
Brown--Westerners p142, 216-
224, 229
Hine--American p231, 341
YOUNG, BRIGHAM
See also "BEE HIVE HOUSE";
MORMONS
Amer. Her. --New (6) p E222
America's Hist. p370-372
Billington--Far. See index
p323-324
Boardman--Jackson. p126
Brown--Westerners p118, 128,
137-142
Carman--History (1) p508-509
Handlin--This p307-312
Harlow--Story p272-273
Hine--American p81, 142, 229,
231-233
Maurois--Illus. p137, 139
Tunis--Frontier p122-123
Wright--Every. p212, 214
, and exodus
DeVoto--Year p437-439, 444-
445, 449
, from Nauvoo
DeVoto--Year p74-98,
439-440
, and Mormon Battalion
DeVoto--Year p235-242, 301,
312-318, 370-375, 404
, at winter quarters
DeVoto--Year p432-439
-Biography
Morris--Ency. p734
-Caravan organizations
DeVoto--Year p149
-"The cooperative experiment:
the economy, 1847"
Ridge--America's p515-517
-Desert
DeVoto--Year p450-454, 463-

464, 475, 480, 483-487, 504-
505, 507
-The Mormon trek to Utah, 1846
Davie--Profile p112-113
-Views of Jules Rémy
Commager--Heritage p542-546
YOUNG, EWING
Case--Empire p73-83
"YOUNG AMERICA" MOVEMENT,
1840-1852
Morris--Ency. p215-216
YOUNG MEN'S CHRISTIAN ASSOCI-
ATION
Handlin--This p359, 386
YOUNG WOMEN'S CHRISTIAN
ASSOCIATION
Handlin--This p359
YUMAN INDIANS
Amer. Her. --Indians p304, 323,
384

Z

ZAKRZEWSKA, MARIE E. ("DR.
ZAK")
Neidle--America's p191, 193, 197,
200-202
ZERRAHN, CARL
Howard--Our p215
ZEUNER, CHARLES
Howard--Our p146-147
ZOAR (SEPARATIST SETTLEMENT)
(Zoar, Ohio)
Tyler--Freedom's p128-130
Vanderbilt--Living p150
ZOOLOGY AND ZOOLOGISTS
Morris--Ency. p529-530
Nye--Cultural p89-90
ZOOS
, First, 1876
Hilton--Way p183-184
ZUÑY INDIANS
DeVoto--Year p379-380
Gilbert--Trail. p208-209
-Pottery
Marzio--Nation p171-172

A
Abbott, Emma
Abell, Mrs. L. G.
Adams, Abigail
Adams, Louisa
Adams, Maude
Addams, Jane
Agassiz, Elizabeth Cabot
Albine, Sister
Alcott, Louisa May
Allen, Samantha (Marietta Holley)
Aloysia, Sister
Alston, Theodosia Burr. See
  Burr, Theodosia
Ames, Mary C.
Andrews, Eliza Frances
Angeline, Princess (Indian)
Anthony, Susan Brownell
Antin, Mary
Arthur, Ellen
Astor, Caroline Schermerhorn
  (Mrs. William Backhouse, Jr.)

B
Bagley, Lucy
Bagley, Sarah
Bankhead, Minerva
Barlow, Arabella
Barnard, Charlotte Alington
Barnes, Jane
Barr, Amelia Edith
Barrows, Katherine Isabel
Barry, Mrs. William J.
Bartlett, Amy. See Warner,
  Anna Bartlett
Barton, Clara
Bateman, Kate
Bayard, Tryphena Cady
Bayer, Adele Parmentier
Beach, Amy Marcy
Beaver, Mrs. Herbert
Beecher, Catherine Esther
Behan, Ada
"Bellona." See Eaton, Margaret

O'Neale Timberlake
Benton, Jessie. See Fremont,
  Jessie Benton
Bernhardt, Sarah
Bethune, Louise Blanchard
Bickerdyke, Mary Ann ("Mother")
Bigelow, Ellen
"Bird Woman." See Sacajawea
  (Indian woman)
Blackenstoe, Virginia. See Reed,
  Virginia
Blackwell, Antoinette Brown
Blackwell, Elizabeth, Dr.
Blackwell, Emily
Blackwell, Mrs. Henry. See
  Stone, Lucy
Blake, Lillie Devereaux
Blatt, Josephine
Blavatsky, Helena Petrovna
Bloomer, Amelia Jenks
Bly, Nellie, pseud. (Cochrane,
  Elizabeth)
Bolton, Sarah T.
Bond, Carrie Jacobs
Booth, Evangeline
Booth, Mary Louise
Borden, Gail
Borden, Lizzie Andrew
Botta, Anne Charlotte Lynch
Botume, Elizabeth Hyde
Boyle, Belle
Bradwell, Myra
Branch, Mrs. John
Bremer, Fredrika
Brown, Antoinette. See Blackwell,
  Antoinette Brown
Brown, Maria D. ("Grandmother")
Brown, Tabitha
Brownell, Kathy
Brunel, Mary Blackmar, Dr.
Burk, Martha Cannary. See
  "Calamity Jane"
Burlend, Rebecca
Burnett, Frances Eliza Hogdson

Burr, Theodosia (Alston, Theodosia
  Burr)
Butler, Sarah Hildreth

C
Cabrini, Francesca (Mother)
Cady, Elizabeth. See Stanton,
  Elizabeth Cady
"Calamity Jane" (Mary or Martha
  Jane Cannary)
Calhoun, Mrs. John C.
Call, Mary Kirkman
Carey sisters. See Cary
Carroll, Anne Ella
Carse, Matilda Bradley
Carter, Carolina Louise Dudley
  (Mrs. Leslie Carter)
Cary, Alice
Cary, Annie Louise
Cary, Constance
Cary, Hettie (Hetty)
Cary, Jennie
Cary, Mary Ann Shadd
Cary, Phoebe
Cassatt, Mary Dudley
Catherine, Sister
Caton sisters
Catt, Carrie L. Chapman
Chase, Kate. See Sprague, Kate
  Chase
Chestnut, Mary Boykin Miller
Chew, Miss. See Mason, Mrs.
  Jane
Child, Lydia Maria
Chopin, Kate O'Flaherty
Churchill, Jeannette (Jennie
  Jerome, Lady Randolph)
Claflin, Tennessee. See Cook,
  Tennessee Claflin
Clappe, Louise Amelia Knapp
  Smith (Dame Shirley)
Cleather, Alice Leighton
Cleveland, Frances Folsom
Cochrane, Elizabeth. See Bly,
  Nelly
Cook, Tennessee Claflin ("Tennis
  C.")
Coolidge, Clarissa Baldwin
Coppin, Fanny Marion Jackson
Cornelia, Sister
Cornell, Kate Lyon
Crabtree, Charlotte
Crandall, Prudence
Crocker, Hannah Mather
Croly, Jane Cunningham
Crosby, Frances Jane ("Fanny")
Curzon, Lady. See Leiter, Mary
  Victoria, Lady Curzon

Cushman, Charlotte Saunders
Cushman, Pauline
Custer, Elizabeth Bacon
Cutts, Adele

D
Darling, Flora
Davenport, Fanny
Davis, Paulina Wright
Davis, Rebecca Harding
Davis, Varina Howell
Dawson, Sarah Morgan
DeMorest, Ellen L. C.
DeWolfe, Elsie, Lady Mendl
Dickinson, Anna Elizabeth
Dickinson, Emily Elizabeth
Dimock, Susan
Divers, Bridget
Dix, Dorothea Lynde
Dodd, Anna Bowman
Dodge, Grace
Dodge, Mary Elizabeth Mapes
Donelson, Emily Donelson
Doremus, Sarah Platt Haines
"Dorion woman" (Indian)
Dow, Joy Wheeler
Dow, Peggy
Dressler, Marie
Drew, Louisa Lane (Mrs. John)
Duchesne, Rose Phillipine
Duckett, Elizabeth Waring
Dudzik, Josephine
Duncan, Isadora
Duniway, Abigail Scott
DuPont, Eleuthere Irenee

E
Eames, Emma
Earle, Alice Morse
Eaton, Margaret O'Neale Timber-
  lake (later Buchignani)
Eddy, Mary Baker Glover
"E.D.E.N.," Mrs. See Southworth,
  Emily
Edmonds, Sarah Emma (Franklin
  Thompson, pseud.)
Eggleston, Sarah Dabney
Elssler, Fanny
Esterhazy, Countess. See Griffin,
  Mrs. Charles
Etheridge, Anna
Evans, Augusta Jane
Evans, Manda Evanich
Everitt, Susan

F
Farnham, Eliza W.
Farrar, Mrs. John

Fay, Amy
Fedde, Elizabeth
Felton, Rebecca
Fern, Fanny. See Willis, Sara
    Payson
Fisher, Dorothy Canfield
Fiske, Mary Augusta Davey
Fiske, Minnie Maddern
Fitzgerald, Emily (Mrs. Jenkins)
Fleming, Wilhelmina Patten
Fletcher, Alice C.
Flynn, Elizabeth Gurley
Folsom, Frances
Formad, Marie K., Dr.
Forten, Charlotte
Foster, Abigail Kelley
Fowle, Elida Rumsey
Fowler, Lydia Folger
Fox, Margaret & Katherine
Freeman, Alice Elvira
Freeman, Mary Eleanor Wilkins
Fremont, Jessie Benton
Fremstad, Olive
Frietchie (Fritchie), Barbara
Fuller, Loie
Fuller (Sarah) Margaret
    (Marchioness Ossoli)

G
Gage, Matilda
Gardner, Isabella Stewart ("Belle")
Garfield, Lucretia
Gay, Mary Ann Harris
Geer, Elizabeth
Gibbons, Abigail
Giesler-Anneke, Mathilde
    Franziska
Gilbert, Anne Hartley
Gilman, Charlotte Perkins
Gilson, Helen Louise
Gougar, Helen
Grant, Ellen ("Nellie") (Ellen
    Grant Sartoris)
Grant, Julia
Gratz, Rebecca
Graves, Mary
Green, Henrietta ("Hetty")
Greenaway, Kate
Greenhow, Rose O'Neal
Griffin, Mrs. Charles
Griffin, Mrs. William P.
Grimké, Angelina
Grimké, Sarah Moore

H
Hadley, Piety Lucretia
Hale, Sarah Josepha
Hall, Anne

Hamilton, Elizabeth Schuyler
Hancock, Cornelia
Hancock, Winifred Scott
Harland, Marion, pseud. (Mrs.
    Edward Payson Terhune)
Harper, Ellen Watkins
Harris, Eliza
Harrison, Anna
Harrison, Carolina
Hawley, Harriet Foote
Hawthorne, Sophia Peabody
Hayes, Lucy
Hazeltine, Nellie
Hearst, Phoebe Apperson
Heinemann, Barbara
Held, Anna
Helm, Emilie Todd
Hemans, Felicia
Hemmingway, Eliza R.
Hentz, Caroline Lee
Heron, Matilda
Hewitt, Sophia Henriette
Hobbs, Lucy
Hoge, Jane (Mrs. A.H.)
Holbrook, Agnes Sinclair
Holley, Marietta. See Allen,
    Samantha
Holmes, Mary Jane
Holstein, Anna
Hopkins, Mary Sherwood
Hosmer, Harriet
Howe, Julia Ward
Howland, Eliza Woolsey
Howland, Mary Woolsey
Hoxie, Vinnie Ream
Hunt, Harriet K.
Hurd-Mead, Kate
Huxley, Nellie

I
Ingelow, Jean
Ingham, Mrs. Samuel
Irwin, Harriet
Irwin, May

J
Jackson, Dorothy Quincy
Jackson, Helen Hunt ("H.H.,"
    pseud.)
Jackson, Rachel Donelson
Jacobi, Mary Putnam
"Jane" (Indian woman) (Mrs. Peter
    Skene)
Jeanes, Anna T.
Jemison, Mary
Jewett, Sarah Orne
Johnson, Eliza
Johnson, Ellen

Jones, Annie
Jones, Mary Cadwalader
Jones, Mary Harris ("Mother
    Jones")
"Julia" (Indian woman)
Junel, Eliza Bowen

K
Keene, Laura
Kelley, Florence
Kellogg, Clara Louise
Kelly, Myra
Kemble, Frances Anne ("Fanny")
Kilgore, Carrie Burnham
Kimball, Martha Gertrude
Knight, Margaret
Koren, Else Elizabeth

L
Lamb, Martha Joanna Reade
Lane, Harriet
Laney, Lucy
Larcom, Lucy
Lazarus, Emma
Lease, Mary Ellen
Leavitt, Mary
Lee, Ann ("Mother")
Lee, Henrietta
Lee, Mrs. Robert Edward
LeGrand, Julia
Leiter, Mary Victoria, Lady
    Curzon
Leslie, Mrs. Frank
Lewis, Estelle Anne Blanche
Lewis, Idawalley
Lhevinne, Rosina, Mme.
Liliuokalani, Queen of Hawaii
Lincoln, Mary Todd
Lincoln, Nancy Hanks
Lind, Jenny
Livermore, Mary Ashton
Livingston, Cora
Lockwood, Belva Ann
Logan, Olive Ann
Longmire, Mrs.
Lothrop, Amy (pseud.)
Loughborough, Mary Ann
Lovejoy, Julia
Low, Juliette Gordon
Low, Lydia
Lowell, Josephine Shaw
Loyola, Mary, Sister
Lozier, Clemence Sophia
Lucas, Lena Brooke
Lukens, Rebecca
Lyon, Mary

M
McClintock, Mary Ann

McDowell, Mary E.
McGuire, Judith Brockenbrough
McKay, Charlotte E.
McKinley, Ida
MacLean, Annie M.
McLure, Margaret A. E.
McPeek, Mrs. Allie
Madison, Dorothy Payne Todd
    ("Dolley")
Magoffin, Susan Shelby
Mahoney, Mary E.
Mannes, Clara Damrosch
Mansfield, Arabella
Maria Christina, Queen of Spain
Marlowe, Julia
Martineau, Harriet
Mason, Mrs. James ("Miss Chew")
Mendl, Lady. See De Wolfe, Elsie,
    Lady Mendl
Menken, Adah Bertha (Adah Isaacs)
Mergler, Maria Josepha
Meyer, Annie
Meynell, Alice
Miller, Elizabeth Smith
Mitchell, Margaret Julia ("Maggie")
Mitchell, Maria
Modjeska, Helena
"Molly B'Damn"
Monroe, Elizabeth
Montez, Lola
Moore, Julia A.
Morgan, Sarah Fowler
Morris, Clara
Morris, Esther Hobart
"Mother Jones." See Jones, Mary
    Harris
Mott, Lucretia Coffin
Mowatt, Anna Cora
Murfree, Mary
Murphy, Virginia Reed
Mussey, Ellen

N
Nation, Carrie Amelia Moore
Nichols, Clarina Howard
Nichols, Mary Grove
Nightingale, Florence
Noel, Mary
Norbertine, Sister
Nordica, Lillian
Northend, Mary Harold
Noyes, Joan Humphrey

O
Oakley, Annie
Oatman, Olive
O'Connell, Anthony, Sister
Olnhausen, Mary Phinney von
O'Neale, Peggy. See Eaton,

Margaret O'Neale Timberlake
Ord, Mrs.
Osborne, Susan M.
Ossoli, Marchioness. See
    Fuller, (Sarah) Margaret
Otis, Emily Marshall
Ottendorfer, Anna Uhr
Ould, Mattie
Owen, Marie
Owens, Bethenia
Owens, Mary S.

P
Painter, Hettie K.
Palmer, Alice Freeman
Palmer, Amelia
Palmer, Bertha Honoré
Palmer, Mrs. Potter
Parker, Cynthia Ann
Parloa, Maria
Parrish, Lydia G.
Parton, Sara Payson ("Fanny
    Fern")
Patterson, Elizabeth (Elizabeth
    Bonaparte)
Patti, Adelina
Peabody, Elizabeth Palmer
Peale, Raphaelle
Pearsall, Rachel
Peck, Annie
"Peg-leg Annie"
Perry, Nora
Pettigrew, Susan
Phelps, Elizabeth Stuart
Pierce, Jane
Pinkham, Lydia E.
Poppenheim, Mrs. C.C.
Porter, Jane
Preston, Ann
Pryor, Mrs. Roger
Putnam, Mary Traill Spence
Putnam-Jacobi, Mary C.

R
Rabinowitch-Kempner, Lydia, Dr.
Randolph, Emily
Reed, Amy L.
Reed, Margaret Keyes
Reed, Virgnia (Blackenstoe,
    Virginia)
Reynolds, Belle
Richards, Ellen Henrietta Swallow
Richards, Laura
Richards, Linda
Ricketts, Fanny
Rogers, Agnes
Rogers, Harriet
Rogers, Louisa Kendall
Roosevelt, Edith

Rose, Ernestine
Royall, Anne
Royce, Sarah
Ruffin, Josephine
Ruffin, Viola Knapp
Rumsey, Elida. See Fowle, Elida
    Rumsey
Russell, Lillian
Russell, Tillie
Rutledge, Ann

S
"Sacajawea" ("Bird Woman") (Indian
    woman)
Safford, Mary J.
Sage, Mrs. Russell
Sager, Catherine
Sanger, Margaret
Sansom, Emma
Sartoris, Ellen Grant. See Grant,
    Ellen ("Nellie")
Schaumberj, (Schaumburg), Emilie
Schumann-Heink, Ernestine
Scott, Abigail. See Duniway, Abi-
    gail Scott
Scott, Mrs. Taylor
Sedgwick, Catherine Maria
Sembrich, Marcella
Semmes, Raphael
Seton, Elizabeth (Mother)
Severance, Caroline
Shaw, Anna Howard
Shaw, Pauline Agassiz
Sherwood, Mary Elizabeth
"Shirley, Dame," pseud. See
    Clappe, Louise Amelia ...
Sholes, Lillian
Sigourney, Lydia Huntley
Skene, Mrs. Peter. See "JULIA"
    (Indian woman)
Smedes, Susan Dabney
Smith, Adelaide W.
Smith, Elizabeth
Smith, Ermine Adelle
Smith, Margaret Bayard
Smith, Mrs. Samuel Harrison
Smith, Seba
Smith, Sophia
Snow, Eliza
Souder, Emily Bliss
Southworth, Emily (Mrs. E.D.E.N.)
Spalding, Eliza Hart
Spencer, Lily
Sprague, Kate Chase
Stanford, Jane Lathrop
Stanton, Elizabeth Cady
Starr, Belle
Starr, Ellen
Stephens, Ann

Stevenson, Sara Yorke
Stewart, Maria W.
Stone, Cornelia Branch
Stone, Lucy
Stowe, Harriet Elizabeth Beecher
Sullivan, Mrs. Algernon Sydney
Sullivan, Anne
Surratt, Mary
Swissheim, Jane Grey

T
Tarbell, Ida Minerva
Taylor, Fanny
Taylor, Lucy Hobbs
Taylor, Margaret
Templeton, Fay
Terhune, Mrs. Edward Payson.
  See Harland, Marion, pseud.
Terrell, Mary Church
Thaxter, Celia
Thomas, Edith Matilda
Thomas, Julia
Thompson, Franklin. See
  Edmonds, Sarah Emma
Tilden, Harriet
Tilton, Elizabeth
Timberlake, Margaret
Timberlake, Virginia
Todd, Mary. See Lincoln, Mary
  Todd
Tompkins, Sally, Captain
Trader, Ella K.
Trollope, Frances ("Fanny")
Truth, Sojourner
Tubman, Harriet Ross
Tyler, Adeline, Sister
Tyler, Julia
Tyler, Letitia

V
Van Buren, Hannah
Van Es, Elizabeth
Van Lew, Elizabeth
Van Ness, Marcia Burns
Van Vries, Margaret Hardenbroek
Victoria, Queen
Von Olnhausen, Mary Phinney. See
  Olnhausen, Mary Phinney von

W
Wald, Lillian D.
Walker, Mary E., Dr.

Walker, Mary Richardson
Walker, Sarah
Ward, Sallie
Ward, Mrs. Samuel
Warner, Anna Bartlett (Amy
  Bartlett, pseud.)
Warner, Susan (Elizabeth Wetherell)
Warren, Mercy Otis
Webb, Ann Eliza. See Young, Ann
  Eliza
Wells, Ida B.
Wetherell, Elizabeth. See Warner,
  Susan
Wharton, Edith Newbold Jones
Wheeler, Candace
White, Ellen G. H.
Whitman, Alice Clarissa
Whitman, Narcissa Prentiss
Whitney, Anne
Wiggin, Kate Douglas
Wilcox, Ella Wheeler
Willard, Emma Hart
Willard, Frances Elizabeth
Willis, Sara Payson ("Fanny Fern")
"Winema" (Indian woman)
Wittenmyer, Annie Turner
Wolfe, Catherine Lorillard
Wolfe, Elsie de
Wood, Sally S. B. K.
Woodhull, Victoria Claflin
Woodward, Charlotte
Woolsey, Abby Howland
Woolsey, Caroline C.
Woolsey, Georgeanna M. ("Georgy")
Woolsey, Harriet Roosevelt ("Hatty")
Woolsey, Jane Newton Stuart
Woolson, Constance Fenimore
Workman, Fanny
Wormeley, Katharine Prescott
Wright, Frances ("Fanny")
Wright, Martha
Wright, Paulina. See Davis,
  Paulina Wright

Y
Yale, Caroline
Yarros, Rachel Slobodensky
Young, Ann Eliza (Ann Eliza
  Webb)

Z
Zakrzewska, Marie E. ("Dr. Zak")

WITHDRAWAL